Windows Performance Secrets

Mark L. Van Name
Bill Catchings
Richard Butner

201 West 103rd Street
Indianapolis, IN 46290

Windows Performance Secrets

Copyright © 1998 by Mark L. Van Name, Bill Catchings, and Richard Butner

International Standard Book Number: 0-7897-1752-2

Library of Congress Catalog Card Number: 98-85723

Printed in the United States of America

First Printing: September, 1998

00 99 98   4   3   2   1

Trademarks

Warning and Disclaimer

Executive Editor
Brad Koch

Managing Editor
Sarah Kearns

Editor
Tom Dinse

Production
Laurie Casey
Kim Cofer
Cheryl Lynch
Daniela Raderstorf

Overview

Contents

About the Authors

Mark. L. Van Name, Author

Mark L. Van Name is Vice President, Product Testing, for Ziff-Davis Inc. In that role, he manages ZD's central product-testing groups, including ZD Labs and the Ziff-Davis Benchmark Operation (ZDBOp). He was the co-founder and Co-Director of ZDBOp for Ziff-Davis, and was also the Editorial Director of Ziff-Davis' *Windows Sources*. With Bill Catchings, he is the author of over a thousand computer-related articles that have appeared in most major computer publications. They write a column, "Looking Forward," that appears each week in *PC Week*, where they have been columnists since 1990.

Mark's background is in software development and consulting; he worked in that field for 17 years before joining Ziff-Davis in 1992. He has both an M.S. and a B.S. in Computer Science.

He also writes science fiction and has had stories published in publications such as *Isaac Asimov's Science Fiction Magazine, Full Spectrum 3, The Year's Best Science Fiction, Ninth Annual Edition, When The Music's Over*, and *Intersections: The Sycamore Hill Anthology* (which he co-edited with John Kessel and Richard Butner).

Bill Catchings, Author

Bill Catchings is the Director of ZDBOp, a group he co-founded with Mark L. Van Name. As Director, Bill has played a key role in the development of all of the benchmarks used in this book. With Mark, Bill has written over a thousand articles and columns on computers, technology, and related topics. These articles have appeared in dozens of computer publications over the last fifteen years. Their column, "Looking Forward," continues to appear every week in *PC Week*.

Bill's background is in software development, with close to 20 years of experience. During that time he developed a wide variety of software products, including the original versions of the Kermit file transfer protocol. He has both an M.S. and B.S. in Computer Science from Columbia University.

Richard Butner, Author

Richard Butner is a freelance writer and computer consultant. He was the Chief Researcher at ZDBOp for the first five years of ZDBOp's existence. His computer-related articles appear in such magazines as *Yahoo! Internet Life* and *Windows Sources*.

Richard's background is in hardware and software engineering. He holds an M.S. in Computer Engineering and English and a B.S. in Electrical Engineering.

He also writes fiction and has had stories published in anthologies such as *When The Music's Over* and *Intersections: The Sycamore Hill Anthology* (which he co-edited with John Kessel and Mark L. Van Name).

Dedication

For all the people who have worked at ZDBOp. We're honored to have worked with you.

Acknowledgments

Many people helped make this book possible, and it would not have been possible without their help.

We obviously could not have produced the book without the benchmarks, which are the products of the Ziff-Davis Benchmark Operation. We'd like to thank all the people who have worked at ZDBOp to create these testing tools, the world's best benchmarks. We're also grateful to Ziff-Davis for being both a great place to work and the only media company in the world to fund and nurture a benchmark development group.

The equipment on which we ran the benchmarks came from many companies that were gracious enough to lend us their hardware. We'd like to extend our thanks to Compaq Computer Corp. for all the test systems it loaned us, and particularly to Compaq's Ed Woodward, who worked with us to make those loans possible. We'd also like to thank ATI Technologies, Inc; Creative Labs, Inc; Diamond Multimedia Systems, Inc.; Evergreen Technologies, Inc.; IBM Corp.; Intel Corp.; Microsoft Corp.; Nexar Technologies, Inc.; Quantum Corp.; Trinity Works, Inc.; and V Communications, Inc. for graciously loaning us hardware upgrades and software for our testbed. Our thanks also go to Aaron Allsbrook for doing some of the initial testing work.

The good folks at Que were very tolerant of the huge amount of time it took us to prepare this book. We owe a special debt to Brad Koch, Executive Editor, who initiated the project, always believed in it, and made it happen. We'd also like to thank Tom Dinse, our Development Editor, who led the book's passage from manuscript to print.

Finally, we'd each like to thank all our families and friends for putting up with us on what had to seem like an interminable journey.

Specifically, Mark would like to thank his family—Rana, Sarah, and Scott Van Name—and his extended family—(in alphabetical order) Anna Bess Brown, Adrea Castater, Joshua Castater, David Drake, Jo Drake, Jennie Faries, Eric Hale, Randy Long, Gina Massel-Castater, Penny Ray, and Allyn Vogel—for their tolerance.

Bill offers his thanks to his family—Susie, Becky, Nate, and Davey. Now you finally can have the basement back.

Richard would like to thank Molly and Lucy.

Tell Us What You Think!

As the reader of this book, *you* are our most important critic and commentator. We value your opinion and want to know what we're doing right, what we could do better, what areas you'd like to see us publish in, and any other words of wisdom you're willing to pass our way.

As the Executive Editor for the Operating Systems team at Macmillan Computer Publishing, I welcome your comments. You can fax, email, or write me directly to let me know what you did or didn't like about this book—as well as what we can do to make our books stronger.

Please note that I cannot help you with technical problems related to the topic of this book, and that due to the high volume of mail I receive, I might not be able to reply to every message.

When you write, please be sure to include this book's title and authors' names as well as your name and phone or fax number. I will carefully review your comments and share them with the author and editors who worked on the book.

Fax: 317-581-4663
Email: opsys@mcp.com
Mail: Executive Editor
           Operating Systems
           Macmillan Computer Publishing
           201 West 103rd Street
           Indianapolis, IN 46290 USA

Introduction

The headlines are enticing. A new generation of ever more powerful processors, lightning-fast graphics adapters, speedy CD-ROM drives: We live in a never-ending spiral of increasing performance. PCs are getting faster all the time.

But how much faster? And, which of the many choices available are going to give you the biggest performance boost for your dollar? Getting objective, reliable information about how all these hot new technologies relate to *your* PC has been an almost impossible task. Let's face it: Windows gives up its performance secrets grudgingly, when it gives them up at all.

Until now.

With this book and a little work, you can stop guessing and start knowing exactly what kind of performance these new technologies will deliver to *you*. Whether you're aiming to boost the performance of your current PC, shopping for a whole new system, or buying upgrades or whole PCs in quantity for your company, this book can help.

In these pages, you'll find three kinds of help.

The first is understanding. We're not talking about just knowing what the latest buzzwords mean, though we will explain them. We're talking about in-depth information on the factors that determine your PC's performance. When the other folks talking PCs at a party start slinging megahertz and megabytes, you can respond (and, yes, show off) with a more accurate and useful comment. You for example, might reply "Megahertz may matter to the uninitiated, but what really matters is creating a balanced system."

If that's all we offered, though, you'd be stuck at the theoretical level, where most books on this subject leave you. In this book, we go beyond theory and provide hard facts about performance. We ran hundreds and hundreds of tests just so you could see exactly how much performance boost each type of PC technology can deliver. We ran these tests on a wide variety of systems, under all three current versions of Windows: Windows 98, Windows 95, and Windows NT 4.0. You can easily find the results for the PC type and operating system closest to what you're running.

With these test results, in only a few minutes of reading you can have more accurate information about PC performance than was ever before available. Don't wonder whether fiddling with operating system parameters is worth your time, or if upgrading your processor or buying more RAM is worth your money. Instead, check out our test results for hard data on exactly how much of a win such changes would be.

And we didn't just make up the tests we ran: We used the world standards for PC performance, Ziff-Davis's Winstone and WinBench benchmarks.

We could have stopped there, but we didn't. We knew that we could not possibly test every system type you might own—and we sure couldn't test your system. But you can, because we've also included in this book not only the complete, latest versions of Winstone and

WinBench, but also instructions for using those benchmarks. If you want to know exactly how your system is performing today, you can use those benchmarks to run as many of the same tests we ran as are useful to you. If you want to know how much boost a software or hardware change will deliver, run the benchmarks before and after you make that change. You can even take the benchmarks with you as you evaluate new PCs. If you're buying in quantity for your company, you can apply all these same guidelines and tests to those groups of machines.

With the combination of the understanding you can gain here, the hundreds of test results we provide, and the benchmarks themselves, you'll have all the performance-analysis tools you need. You'll be ready to measure and know exactly how much benefit you can realize from both today's PC technologies and each new technology that comes down the pike.

So, if you care about the performance of your PC or those of others, read on and learn the secrets of Windows performance.

How to Use This Book

We know that each time you open this book, you might be reading it for a different reason. We want to make it as easy as possible for you to get the maximum benefit each time you consult this book, whatever the reason you turned to it. Whether your goal is to learn about PC performance, upgrade your system, buy a new PC, or manage the upgrading and purchasing of multiple PCs, we've arranged the book so you can quickly find the information you want.

You're welcome, of course, to simply read this book from cover to cover. If you have the time, that would indeed be the best way to truly understand performance and your PC, because we've crammed each chapter with lots of interesting and useful data, data you're likely to miss in a quick skim.

We realize, though, that your time is precious, and we want to make sure you get the most value for the least effort from this book. So, let's look at some of the paths you might take into these pages.

If your goal is to understand PC performance—and to know when a vendor or anyone else is telling the truth about performance—start with the four chapters in Part I. They're fairly short and will give you a great deal of useful and important basic information. Then, turn to the "Cocktail Party Tips" sections in each of the chapters in Parts II, III, and IV. These tips will give you some of the key results and conclusions of each chapter. With this combination of introductory chapters and tips under your belt, you'll both understand the basics of performance and know where to turn in this book when you're facing a performance-related decision, such as how to upgrade your current PC or which new PC to buy.

If instead you are considering upgrading your current PC, take a different route through this book. The path begins in almost the same way: Read the first three chapters in Part I so you can better understand both your upgrade options and how to take maximum advantage of this book. Then, use that information to decide what areas of performance optimization are of interest to you. The chapters in Parts II, III, and IV cover each major performance area, so go to the chapters that address the areas you find of interest. In each of those chapters, read the introductory material. Then, find the system we tested that most closely corresponds to your current system. Start by picking the operating system you're running; we supply results for Windows 98, Windows 95, and Windows NT 4.0. Then go to the section on the processor we tested that's closest to the one in your PC, and you'll either find something similar to your current system or at least see results for a system that's close enough. Once you've chosen the appropriate test system here, simply check out the results of our performance tests to see how much each type of upgrade will do for you. Those results will give you the facts you need to decide how much RAM to buy, which software tuning options to employ, and so on.

Follow a different path through the book if you're considering buying a new PC. In that case, this book can help you sort through the myriad of options you'll encounter and make sure you get the maximum performance from your purchase. Begin, as in the other cases, with the first two chapters in Part I, but then go to Chapter 4, "Benchmarks and Buying New Systems." Your next stops should be the chapters in Parts III and IV that address the areas in which you face the most decisions. You'll certainly have to choose the processor and the amount of RAM for your system; Chapters 8, "Optimizing Your System's Processor," and 9, "Optimizing Your System's RAM," respectively, cover those topics. You may also want to delve into the areas, such as graphics performance, in some of the other chapters. In each of these chapters, read first the general material, then the test results for the operating system you will be running and the processor type closest to those you are considering.

We have to warn that you will definitely be choosing from a group of PCs that use processors that did not exist when we did the tests that produced most of the results in this book. Don't worry, though; you can still use the test results for the processor most like the ones in the PCs you're considering. In addition, you can use the benchmarks to gather your own test results, then compare those results to the results in Ziff-Davis magazines and on Ziff-Davis' Web site, www.zdnet.com. (Because every Ziff-Davis media enterprise worldwide uses these same benchmarks, you can easily find results for most of the latest systems.) You can even take the benchmark CDs to your favorite store, a practice we encourage, and demand the salespeople let you put their systems to the test.

If you do plan to run your own benchmark tests, be sure to check out Appendixes A and B. These appendixes show you how to install and use the benchmarks. When you're done with the benchmarks and want to remove them from your system, read Appendix C for step-by-step instructions on the uninstallation process.

If you're responsible for upgrading or buying multiple machines for an organization, then understanding PC performance and optimization is really part of your job. In that case, you should consider reading the bulk of the book. Some chapters, such as Chapter 14, "Optimizing for Games," and maybe Chapter 12, "Optimizing Your CD-ROM Subsystem," may not help you much, but all the others could.

If you're responsible for multiple PCs, you may also stand to profit significantly from running your own tests. After all, even a cheap RAM upgrade can become a costly exercise if you're doing it for a hundred PCs, so you should do everything you can to make sure the upgrade will yield benefits. In this case, for example, you would certainly profit from studying our RAM results in Chapter 9, and you should seriously consider running your own RAM experiments. Similarly, before buying 50 or a 100 new PCs, you may want to run the benchmarks on a representative machine from each of two or three vendors and then compare the results. You may even be able to demand that the vendors supply you with results; another advantage of using industry-standard benchmarks is that just about every PC vendor is also using them. As above, Appendixes A and B are the right places to turn for instructions on how to run the benchmarks on the CDs we've included with this book. Appendix C explains how to uninstall them.

How This Book Is Organized

We've organized *Windows Performance Secrets* to make it as easy as possible for you to understand the performance of PCs running any of these three varieties of Windows. We've set up the book so you can use it both to make your PC perform at its best and to choose the best performing PC when you're buying a new one. We've divided the book into five parts, with a total of fourteen chapters and three appendixes. The rest of this section describes the contents of those chapters and appendixes.

Part I: Achieving Maximum Performance

Chapter 1, "Performance Basics," reviews the basics of PC performance, in the process explaining both what performance is and why it matters. After reading this chapter, you should have a good overview of how the different subsystems of your PC determine its performance. You will also understand what bottlenecks are and how they can prevent your PC from realizing its full performance potential.

Chapter 2, "Benchmarks and You," describes the fundamentals of how benchmarks work and what the different kinds of benchmarks are. You will learn from this chapter some key, fundamental information about Winstone and WinBench, the benchmarks we used to produce the test results in this book.

Chapter 3, "Benchmarks and Your Current PC," shows how you can use this book and the benchmarks it includes to get the best possible performance from your PC. It explains the complementary processes of measuring performance and detecting bottlenecks. This chapter also gives you some general tips on what are generally the best places to spend your money when you're upgrading your PC.

Chapter 4, "Benchmarks and Buying New Systems," explains how you can use performance results and benchmarks to make an informed buying decision the next time you set out to get a new PC. You will learn how to use the benchmarks this book includes and the benchmark results in Ziff-Davis publications, Web sites, and other media enterprises to compare systems from different vendors. With these tools, you'll be able to make the best choice for both your budget and your performance needs.

Part II: Software Optimization

Chapter 5, "Windows 98 Software Tuning," shows you how to use the software tuning options in this newest version of Windows to boost a PC's performance. In this chapter we discuss the tuning options Windows 98 provides. Using the information here, you will be able to make software changes—changes that will cost you little or no money—that will increase the performance of your Windows 98 PC.

Chapter 6, "Windows 95 Software Tuning," examines the role of software tuning in a Windows 95 PC's performance and walks you through the types of software tuning options Windows 95 provides. Using the information in this chapter, you will be able to make software changes—changes that will cost you little or no money—to your Windows 95 PC to increase its performance.

Chapter 7, "Windows NT Software Tuning," explores the software tuning options and tools available under Windows NT 4.0. You will learn what you can change in your NT system and how to use NT's built-in performance monitoring tools to help you tune your system's performance.

Part III: Hardware Optimization

Chapter 8, "Optimizing Your System's Processor," looks at the processor, or CPU, in your PC and how it affects the system's overall performance. This chapter discusses why the measure processor vendors most quote, megahertz (MHz), is in reality a poor metric of performance, and it explains what you should use instead. Our many test results will show you how to pick the right processor upgrade for your existing PC and how to choose the appropriate processor for any new system you might purchase.

Chapter 9, "Optimizing Your System's RAM," deals with the role of RAM in system performance and the types of RAM upgrade options available. You will learn about the most common RAM technologies and the different techniques PC vendors use to maximize a system's RAM performance. The test results in this chapter will also help you choose the right amount of RAM for your PC.

Chapter 10, "Optimizing Your Graphics Subsystem," examines the PC's graphics subsystem and its role in overall system performance. You will see the types of graphics subsystem optimization options that are available and will be able to pick the right graphics adapter for your current or future PC. Hard test results will help you understand exactly how much gain, both in raw graphics speed and in overall system performance, different graphics options will deliver.

Chapter 11, "Optimizing Your Disk Subsystem," delves into the hard disk subsystem and explains the factors that play a role in maximizing its performance. You will see that factors other than the hard disk itself can have a big effect on the disk performance you experience. You'll also learn what you can do to optimize your hard disk subsystem's performance.

Chapter 12, "Optimizing Your CD-ROM Subsystem," shows the elements of your PC that can affect the performance of its CD-ROM subsystem. You'll learn why you should not rely on simplistic vendor claims of 8X, 16X, or 32X CD-ROM drive performance. You'll instead see how to measure CD-ROM performance and how to pick the CD-ROM drive that delivers the speed you need.

Part IV: Special Situations

Chapter 13, "Power Saving and Portables," looks at the special performance issues that can arise when you're using a notebook or laptop PC. You will learn how the way you set a notebook's power-management options can affect its performance and how you can decide what tradeoffs to make between battery life and performance. This chapter concentrates on Windows 98 and Windows 95, because the vast majority of notebook users currently are not running Windows NT on their notebooks.

Chapter 14, "Optimizing for Games," examines the special performance challenges that many games present to PCs. Games often have performance requirements that are quite different from those of typical PC applications, and this chapter takes you on a quick tour of those differences. It also explains some of the best things you can do to make your PC run well with typical games.

Part V: Appendixes

Appendix A, "Using Winstone 98," explains what you need to know to install and use the latest version of Winstone, which is on one of the CDs included with this book. After reading this chapter, you should be able to generate your own set of Winstone performance numbers similar to those in the many tests whose results appear in this book.

Appendix B, "Using WinBench 98," describes what you need to know to install and use the latest version of WinBench, which is on the other CD included with this book. When you're done with this chapter, you should be able to run your own WinBench tests and generate results similar to those we've presented throughout this book.

Appendix C, "Uninstalling the Benchmarks," tells you how to remove Winstone 98 and WinBench 98 from your PC when you're done with them. If you do install either or both benchmarks, be sure to read this appendix, because to completely remove them you need to follow this procedure.

What's on the CD-ROMs

As you have no doubt gathered by now, this book is all about performance, and the Ziff-Davis benchmarks are the best tools for measuring PC performance. Much of what is in this book is the result of almost two years of extensive use of two Ziff-Davis PC benchmarks, Winstone and WinBench. So you can run the benchmarks yourself, this book includes on two CD-ROMs the latest versions of those benchmarks, Winstone 98 and WinBench 98.

> **NOTE**   Check out the years on the benchmarks we've mentioned, and you
> may feel a little confused. We conducted the Windows 98 research in
> this book using Winstone 98 and WinBench 98, but we performed the Windows 95
> and Windows NT 4.0 studies using Winstone 97 and WinBench 97. The CD-ROMs
> that come with this book contain Winstone 98 and WinBench 98. What's up?
>
> The answer is simple: The benchmark release cycle is such that we had to use the prior
> (97) versions of these two benchmarks to complete our Windows 95 and Windows NT
> tests. For our Windows 98 tests, though, we needed to use the latest and greatest
> benchmark releases on this newest member of the Windows family. We also wanted you
> to have those latest and greatest benchmarks, so they're what we included on the book's
> CD-ROMs.
>
> Thus, though the descriptions in the appendixes and in the Windows 98 sections of this
> book describe the versions on the CD-ROMs, the results we discuss in the book's
> Windows 95 and Windows NT sections come from the earlier versions. The two
> versions are similar in operation and function, and the results they produce are similar,
> but those results are not comparable. (Should you need any comparison results for the
> newer versions of the benchmarks, just turn to any PC review in a Ziff-Davis media
> enterprise.)

Each benchmark is large enough to require its own CD-ROM. These benchmarks are
complete products you can use for a wide range of performance testing. As such, the
CD-ROM for each includes an Autorun installation procedure, documentation, and,
of course, the benchmark itself.

The Ziff-Davis Benchmark Operation (ZDBOp), a division of Ziff-Davis, develops these
benchmarks for use by Ziff-Davis media properties worldwide. These properties include
the *PC Magazine*, *PC Week*, *Computer Shopper*, and *PC/Computing* publications, as well as
the ZDNet Web site (www.zdnet.com) and ZDTV: Your Computer Channel. Ziff-Davis
also makes these benchmarks available to the public, so they have become worldwide
purchasing standards on which everyone, from vendors to large organizations to individual
users, depends.

For more information on using the CD-ROMs and the benchmarks on them, see Appendix A, "Using Winstone 98" and Appendix B, "Using WinBench 98." You can also consult
the extensive documentation on the CD-ROMs. For the latest information about Ziff-
Davis's benchmarks, check out ZDBOp's Web page at www.zdbop.com.

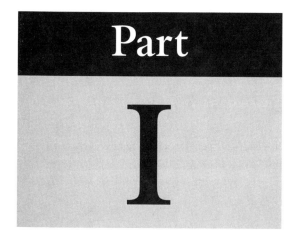

Part

I

Achieving Maximum Performance

Chapter

1

Performance Basics

To understand the secrets of performance and to get the most performance possible from a PC, you have to do more than just buy new parts or change software settings. You have to understand the basics workings of a PC and the factors that determine its performance. The first step in gaining that understandinthe to realize that performance analysis is a discipline in its own right, a discipline with its own technical and intellectual underpinnings. Learning those basics will take you a long way toward being able to boost PC performance.

In this chapter we explain those basics. Our goal here is to give you the background you need to make the most of the material in the chapters that follow.

We readily admit that you can get plenty of the value of this book by skipping this information and jumping right into the test results. You can, for example, skip to Chapter 9, "Optimizing Your System's RAM," locate our RAM recommendation for your system, and you and your PC will be fine. Doing so, though, would limit your ability to know how to react as the operating system and applications you're running evolve and their RAM requirements change. If instead you take the time to learn the key elements of performance analysis, you'll be able to cope with such changes easily.

By understanding the factors in PC performance you'll be able to better extrapolate from this book to almost any performance-sensitive situation you may encounter.

To make sure you have the knowledge you need to face such situations, in this chapter you will learn:

- Why performance matters

- The ways most people think about PC performance, and review the factors that determine it

- The way your interactions with your PC help define what you perceive as its performance

- Why, despite so much advertising to the contrary, there's a lot more to your PC's performance than the megahertz (MHz) of its processor

- That the processor is certainly a major factor in how well a PC performs, but that the right supporting players can make a PC look dramatically better—and the wrong ones can cripple it

- The factors that contribute to the overall performance of your PC

- What bottlenecks are

- That perhaps the most important concept in performance analysis is the bottleneck, which can cause an otherwise good system to perform poorly

- Specifically how bottlenecks affect performance

- That no matter what you do, in the end, every system has bottlenecks: It's the nature of performance

- How one piece of a system can slow down the rest of that system, sometimes dramatically

- How to find the bottlenecks in a system

- Why it's important to use the right benchmark

- The differences between benchmarks that characterize the performance of the whole PC and those that gauge the speed of only one part of the PC

Performance Basics

1.1. Cocktail Party Tips

PC performance is much easier to discuss informally than it is to define precisely. In most conversations, if someone mentions PC performance, you know at an abstract level what they mean: How fast the PC goes.

More precisely, most folks intuitively understand that performance is a measure of how much work a PC can do in a given amount of time. The more work you can accomplish in a fixed amount of time, the better.

Most people also intuitively understand a corollary, that doing the same amount of work in less time is another way to express better performance. If your spreadsheet recalculates more quickly, your performance is better.

Pretty much everyone will also agree that more performance is better. Whether the work you're doing is spell checking, spreadsheet recalculation, or playing video clips, a PC that performs better will make your computing experience better.

That's about where the agreement ends, however. Dig deeper, and you're likely to find that what one person means by performance may be very different from your own conception. People who stay in the same application all day, for example, may not care at all about how long that application takes to load. They might even count on using that load time each morning to get their coffee. If, by contrast, you start and stop different applications all day, the time your PC takes to launch those applications might be the single thing that annoys you most about the system's performance.

Clearly, the critical part of the PC performance equation is the definition of the work the PC needs to do. That definition will vary from person to person, because each of us uses our PC differently. What each of us quite rightfully wants is a PC that is fast at doing the work we demand of it.

If all you ever do with your CD-ROM drive, for example, is install a new application every month or two, do you really care much about that drive's speed? Probably not. On the other hand, if you regularly run applications that access databases on CD-ROMs, the drive's speed may matter greatly. It could make the difference between your being able to work steadily on a project and your having to spend lots of wasted time watching the drive churn. Similarly, a hot 3D graphics card is of little use if all you run is Word and Excel, but it could be critical if you're a Quake II junkie.

The second most common PC party question we hear is how to maximize the performance of a PC. (The most common question is whether Bill Gates really is evil. We'll help you with the performance question, but you'll have to decide your own answer to the one about Gates.) The simple answer is, find the system's bottleneck, the part that is slowing the system the most, and fix it.

Because we all use our PCs differently, to get any more specific than that you have to understand what the questioner does with his or her PC. Don't let vendor claims or statistics tempt you into drawing quick conclusions. If you don't first gain an understanding of how the questioner is using his or her PC, any advice you give will be just a guess.

Don't believe the guy who instantly answers, "You need a faster hard disk." He may be right for some folks, but he'll be wrong for at least as many. The right answer is another question: "What do you do with your PC?"

The remaining chapters in Part I will give you some general information on how to use this book and the benchmarks it includes to take the answer to that question and propose useful performance improvements.

1.2. Does Performance Matter?

Every now and then, we run into people who claim PC performance really doesn't matter. "PCs are fast enough," they'll say, or, "At some point soon, PCs will be fast enough, and you won't care about performance anymore."

Those people must never upgrade their software.

Tomorrow's software almost always requires more computing horsepower than the programs you're running today. New software provides new capabilities, and those capabilities need hardware support. We could argue all day about whether this *should* be true, but almost no one would argue that it *isn't* true. If you're not convinced, compare the minimum requirements on some of your older software to those of your most recent applications.

None of this would matter, of course, if the newer software didn't attract users. If we were content to run the same programs forever, the performance requirements of new software wouldn't matter to us. Most folks, though, find enough value in new releases that regular software upgrades are a fact of computing life.

We all could, of course, choose to run the newer applications on older hardware and simply tolerate slower performance, but we rarely elect to do so. We want to spend as little time waiting on our computers as possible.

That's a sensible desire. Computers may be expensive, but people are even more expensive. Making people wait for their computers for as little as even 10 minutes a day adds up to almost 50 hours a year. At only $10 per hour, that's $500 of productivity lost. Move into common white-collar salary ranges, and the cost per year quickly approaches that of a new computer. Worse, we know we wait a lot more than 10 minutes a day on our computers. (And we try for a pay rate greater than $10 an hour!) We recently heard an analysis of how much time Americans wait annually for Windows to start. The total number of person-hours was greater than the number of hours all the people at Microsoft work in a year. Little things really can add up.

The potential time and money savings alone are reason enough to put a little effort in boosting PC performance. In addition, consider how much you have invested in your computer hardware and software. You've probably sunk from $1,000 to $3,000 or more into your PC. If, by investing a few hundred dollars more, or some of your valuable time, you can make that purchase work better and potentially last longer, that's a good deal. By optimizing your PC's performance you can get both more for your money and put off an expensive new PC purchase a little longer.

To be fair, for some people their current computer is fast enough. (We have a friend happily running Word for DOS 5.0 on a 486, and we're glad for folks like him.) If you're content with your PC and the applications it runs, and if you don't plan to change those applications, this book's biggest benefits for you will be theoretical.

However, we need and want to run the hottest and most interesting of the current and future applications. You can blame Microsoft and others for developing slow, bloated applications that require more hardware support, but we don't want to give up any of the cool features of those programs. If, like us, you always want more performance from your PC, you've definitely come to the right place.

1.3. Slices of the Performance Pie

As we noted above, the most important factor in PC performance is how well the entire system operates. Like a pie, though, your PC is composed of a number of different slices that combine to make up the whole. We usually refer to these slices as your PC's subsystems. Common subsystems that affect almost everyone are your hard disk, graphics, and processor/RAM. (We often lump together the processor and RAM because of how tightly related they are in a modern PC. We'll delve into this issue in later chapters.)

Subsystem is one of those computer-boy terms that can easily feel both intimidating and unnecessary. After all, most ads are for components: CPU chips, hard drives, graphics cards, and so on. So you might reasonably ask, why not just refer to those components and drop this extra term?

The reason is that components alone simply cannot tell the whole performance story. In a modern Windows PC, no hardware component ever acts entirely on its own. Instead, to do its job, each piece of hardware has to interact with other hardware components, firmware, device drivers, and other software.

Consider, for example, the hard drive in your PC. When you think about disk space, you think of that drive. And if you needed more space, you'd probably just go out and buy another drive. Yet that drive is really part of the hard disk subsystem, a subsystem that includes your hard disk controller, the RAM caches on both that controller and the drive itself, the Windows disk and controller device drivers, and the Windows disk-caching software. Each time you use your disk, all these pieces must cooperate to get the data you want or to store the data you're saving. All these pieces are interrelated, and the way they work together determines the "hard disk" performance you experience.

As you can see in Figure 1.1, not all of these pieces contribute equally to your PC's performance. In a typical system running typical business applications, the processor/RAM subsystem has the biggest influence on performance. The disk and graphics subsystems are roughly equal to each other, with disk being slightly more important to most users. These two combined are still less important than the processor/RAM subsystem.

Remember that Figure 1.1 is just a guideline. Not all users, of course, run typical business applications. Nor are all PCs configured to get maximum performance from each subsystem. Different applications also stress these subsystems in different combinations. Consequently, sometimes you'll care more about the performance of an individual subsystem, such as your graphics subsystem, than this breakdown would indicate. The bulk of Part III, of this book, "Hardware Optimization," deals with maximizing the performance of each these subsystems.

In addition to these three main subsystems, other subsystems contribute to the performance of some more specialized applications or functions. Your PC's CD-ROM, full-motion video, 3D, sound, power management, and networking subsystems can all affect performance in different applications. When you're running such an application, one of these subsystems may even be one of the most important performance factors in your system. Play a game that uses 3D graphics, for example, and 3D speed will be vital. (Your hard disk subsystem will also pretty much fall out of the performance pie during such games.) Parts of

Chapter 10, "Optimizing Your Graphics Subsystem," Chapter 12, "Optimizing Your CD-ROM Subsystem," and the chapters in Part IV, "Special Situations," deal with all of these subsystems except networking. We'll leave to another book the job of exploring networking issues.

Performance Basics

Figure 1.1.
Several subsystems contribute to overall PC performance. The three most important are processor/RAM, hard disk, and graphics. Here's a breakdown of the importance of each of those subsystems in typical PC performance.

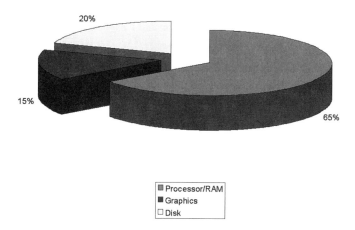

- ■ Processor/RAM
- ■ Graphics
- □ Disk

For most applications most of the time, however, these subsystems have little or no effect on performance.

One factor that plays an important role in almost all aspects of PC performance is the operating system you're running, whether it's Windows 98, Windows 95, or Windows NT 4.0. The operating system is effectively part of each of the subsystems, because it's the software that orchestrates all the work your PC does. Think of it as the crust that holds together both the whole pie and each of the slices. To maximize performance, you need to make sure you have correctly set up and tuned your operating system. We examine this part of the performance pie in Part II, "Software Optimization."

1.4. Passing the Bottleneck

Knowing the role of different subsystems in overall PC performance is vital, but that knowledge alone won't help you improve the way your PC performs. To do that, you have to get into finding and fixing bottlenecks.

A bottleneck is something that's slowing the overall system. Picture a bottle of water with a very narrow neck. The width of that neck determines how quickly you can pour water from the bottle. No matter how big you make the bottle or how much water you put into it, you still can't pour water from it any more quickly than the narrow neck will allow. Widen the neck, though, and you'll be able to pour more quickly. The neck places a limit on the bottle's pouring performance.

Similarly, when you're doing something on your PC, something is putting a limit on the speed your PC can perform that function. That thing is the bottleneck. Find it, conceptually widen it (that is, make it faster or replace it with something faster), and the whole PC will run faster.

A great and all-too-familiar example of the bottleneck phenomenon occurs regularly during Web browsing. You can have a fast PC communicating with a fast server, and yet the Web pages flow down your screen like molasses. You know your PC can display images a lot more quickly than that, because you've seen it do so on many occasions with many different applications. The problem is that your PC is not the bottleneck; the modem is. No matter what processor you put in your computer, or what graphics card, or how much RAM you give the system, the modem will still make most pages appear as if drawing each pixel is a monumental task. Plug the same computer into a T1 connection, and browsing the same Web pages will almost certainly be a rather different experience.

If you haven't already figured it out, once you have a faster connection, the bottleneck in Web browsing may well then become the Web itself. In that case, adding more connection speed or a faster computer would not yield much improvement in your browsing experience, because you'd be optimizing the wrong parts of the performance equation.

Consider the example in Figure 1.2. The bars represent the time it takes a PC to do a particular task. For ease of explanation, we've set the time to be 100 seconds. The individual parts of each bar show the time the PC spends in each subsystem as it's doing that work. The original configuration reflects a typical PC subsystem balance, much like the one we described earlier.

When you look at this example, it's clear that the PC is spending about two-thirds of its time in the processor/RAM subsystem, so that subsystem is the main bottleneck. If you did not know that fact, however, you might elect to focus on the wrong subsystem. You could, for example, buy a hot new graphics adapter and quintuple the performance of the graphics subsystem. Though that faster graphics adapter would certainly boost your performance, the overall performance improvement would be only eight percent.

Clearly, knowing what to optimize is vital.

It's also important to have realistic expectations about the level of performance improvement a change will deliver. To continue this example, let's say you've read an ad for a new graphics card that will "quintuple your graphics performance." You'd like faster graphics and this level of improvement sounds good, so you buy the card. You take it home, install it in your PC…and the PC feels barely different.

Did the graphics card vendor lie to you? No. As Figure 1.2 shows, the time in the graphics subsystem really did shrink by a factor of five, so the card is in fact five times faster than the previous adapter.

Figure 1.2.

Optimizing a subsystem that's not the main bottleneck yields little overall benefit. Here, a typically balanced PC sees only an 8% improvement from quintupling the performance of its graphics subsystem.

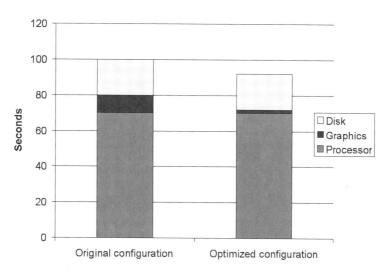

Performance Basics

You may, however, have been deceived, and you certainly allowed yourself to have unrealistic expectations.

This example shows why you have to identify the biggest bottleneck and concentrate your optimization efforts there if you want the biggest possible performance gain. Here, even if your graphics card was infinitely fast and took no time to do any of its operations, the most you could speed up the overall system *on this type of work* would be 10%. Change the type of work, of course, and the balance of the time the PC spends in each subsystem might also change.

Let's now look at a hypothetical unbalanced system, one with an obvious bottleneck. Figure 1.3 shows a PC with a clear graphics bottleneck, the kind of system that might result from sticking an outdated graphics adapter into an otherwise modern PC. In this example the PC is spending so much of its time in the graphics subsystem that this graphics bottleneck is masking the performance potential of the rest of the system. Quintuple the performance of this graphics subsystem, as we did in the optimized configuration in this chart, and you get a very large overall performance boost (about 40%). Before the optimization, the rest of the system was basically twiddling its thumbs waiting for the graphics adapter to do its thing.

Any major subsystem in your PC could be a bottleneck that's inhibiting its overall performance. We have encountered systems in which the bottleneck was the processor, the amount of RAM, the hard disk, the graphics adapter, and even the operating system. In special situations, even other subsystems—CD-ROM, 3D graphics, network—can be the bottleneck.

In later chapters, we will look at how you can test a system to determine which subsystem is most likely to be the bottleneck. However, you can often make a pretty good, educated guess about which part of your PC is your major performance problem: It's usually the oldest part. To pick an easy example, if you've already upgraded your processor, added RAM, and put in a new graphics adapter, it's a pretty good bet that your hard disk is the bottleneck.

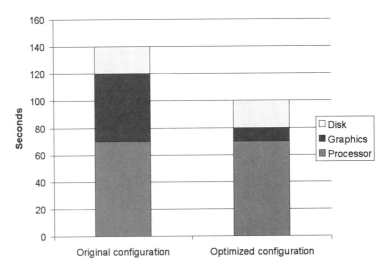

The bottleneck might also be something far more fundamental in your system: The motherboard, and the bus on that board. If you've done a lot of PC upgrades, you may well have already seen this happen. At some point, you have to replace the motherboard. A new motherboard will typically let you run faster processors, work with faster RAM, and move data along a faster bus than was possible on your previous system. Even if you replace nothing else, the PC is likely to perform better.

A new motherboard will naturally make something else the bottleneck, and you'll have to find out what it is. That's why we calling it chasing bottlenecks.

1.5. From Here...

This chapter explained both the importance of PC performance and the concepts you need to find and eliminate performance bottlenecks. The next step is to understand how you can use benchmarks to measure and improve PC performance.

The following chapters provide more information on how you can use benchmarks both to understand the value of upgrade options for your current PC and to evaluate different systems when you're considering buying a new PC.

■ Chapter 2, "Benchmarks and You," explains how benchmarks work and how you can use and understand them to your advantage.

■ Chapter 3, "Benchmarks and Your Current PC," discusses how to use benchmarks to increase the performance of the system you already have.

■ Chapter 4, "Benchmarks and Buying New Systems," shows you how to use benchmarks to buy the new PC that performs best for your needs.

Performance Basics

Chapter 2

Benchmarks and You

Benchmarks lie at the heart of this book. To prepare for the book, we spent hundreds of hours running tests using benchmarks. In this chapter and throughout this book, we invest a great deal of time discussing not only the results of those tests but also the benchmarks themselves.

For any of this to make sense, we obviously need to explain just what benchmarks are—and why they matter to you.

The word "benchmark" has a wide variety of meanings, each of which makes sense within a particular context. Benchmark crude oil, for example, is a common term in some contexts, but we don't use it here. In this book, we focus only on computer benchmarks. At the highest level, a computer benchmark is a tool for measuring how fast some part, or even all, of a computer operates. In this sense, a benchmark produces one or more results that indicate the speed of the thing it's measuring.

For a benchmark to be useful, it must possess many traits. It must, for example, measure something you care about. It must do so in a way that is repeatable, so you get the same result each time you run it. It must produce results that you can understand and use to make comparisons with the results from other tests. This chapter examines these traits and the other key issues benchmarks must address.

In this chapter, you will learn:

- Specifically what a benchmark is and how one should work

- A little about some important benchmarks from days gone by (hey, a little history never hurt anyone)

- Some background on what benchmarks used to be and why those used for this book are state-of-the-art

- How to know what a benchmark is measuring

- How to interpret the numeric results that benchmarks typically produce

- How to understand the techniques benchmarks use to measure performance

- The advantages and disadvantages of each benchmark technique, which can help you interpret benchmark results

- The key concepts underlying the benchmarks we use in this book

- How Ziff-Davis's Winstone and WinBench benchmarks (the industry standards for PC performance) work and what their results mean

2.1. Cocktail Party Tips

If you're standing around at a party and you happen to mention that you bought this book, people may well look at you funny. After all, most people have no clue what a computer benchmark is, much less why you would spend any money on a book about them. If they ask what the book is about, or if you just feel like enlightening them, you can say that benchmarks are basically tools for measuring the performance of an entire computer system or some aspect of that system. Benchmarks thus give you a way to differentiate computer systems and the individual pieces that make up such systems. If you use benchmarks correctly, the results they produce can help you decide what changes to make to speed up your existing system or what new system to buy.

To get such information, you have to follow two rules that are easier to state than to follow:

1. Use the right benchmarks.

2. Use them correctly.

The right benchmarks are those that test your PC with work that is similar to the work you perform. That work should also involve all the same aspects of the PC as your work. To pick an overly simple example, if you never use your PC's CD-ROM drive, you certainly wouldn't care about a benchmark whose sole function was to measure CD-ROM performance.

The right benchmarks for you should also produce results that you can both understand and use. Ideally, these results would tell you not only how fast your PC is, but also why it performs the way it does.

Using benchmarks correctly is often harder than it sounds. Most good benchmarks come with strict rules about how you should use them. Unfortunately, in our experience most people who use benchmarks try to cut corners and skip (or take a shortcut around) some of those rules. The results are usually unsatisfactory.

Winstone and WinBench, the benchmarks we used in this book, are the industry standards for PC performance. They have earned this status by providing objective, repeatable results that accurately reflect real-world performance. The two benchmarks function as a team. Together, they produce both realistic, overall PC performance measurements and more specific results that you can use to understand the reasons for the overall results. Winstone gauges overall PC performance; WinBench measures the performance of all the major PC subsystems.

We've included the latest versions of those benchmarks, Winstone 98 and WinBench 98, on the CD-ROMs that come with this book. These benchmarks, which the Ziff-Davis Benchmark Operation (ZDBOp) developed, are the current state of the art in PC benchmark technology. When someone asks you what PC

Benchmarks and You

benchmarks they should be using, you can point them to Winstone and WinBench.

You can also use the benchmarks yourself to test the performance of your PC. In many cases, you can also save yourself a lot of work and simply use the results in this book to understand PC performance.

2.2. The Real Scoop on Benchmarks

Let's start with two basic definitions. For the purposes of this book, a benchmark is a tool for measuring the performance of computers. Performance is a measure of the work a system does divided by the time the system took to do that work.

Consequently, to calculate performance a benchmark can take one of two approaches:

1. See how much work a system can get done in a fixed period of time, or

2. See how long it takes a system to perform a fixed amount of work.

In theory, either approach can work, and different benchmarks take different approaches.

In principle, a benchmark doesn't have to be a piece of software. It could be a human procedure, something as simple as using a stopwatch to time how long Microsoft Word takes to save a document. Early PC benchmarks were often such stopwatch-based tests.

Using a stopwatch, however, is both tedious and, if you're not careful, error-prone. To be fair, we have to note that with practice you can become very good at using stopwatches for such measurements. Years ago, we did a lot of this kind of benchmarking, and we were able to produce very repeatable results. In general, on multiple instances of the same test our results were within two hundredths of a second of each other. We never did find a cure for the tedium, though.

Because of the problems inherent in using stopwatches and other external timing devices, benchmarks are usually software programs. These programs typically include the timing mechanisms they need. The timer itself can be a challenge for benchmark designers, because it must be both accurate enough for the benchmark's purposes and not too difficult to implement.

Timing, though, is not the major problem in benchmarking. That honor goes to defining the workload, the work the benchmark's tests perform. The definition of the workload determines in large part both how the benchmark will work and what its results will mean.

The ideal benchmark for each of us would have a workload that is exactly the same work we do with our PCs. We have long said that the best benchmark for each person would do all the functions that person does in a day and time how quickly a system can complete those functions. The problem with this approach is obvious: Each of us would need our own benchmark. Most folks don't have the time, money, or inclination to create such a beast.

Companies, however, sometimes do. If a project is expensive enough, the cost of designing and implementing such a benchmark is lower than the cost of making the wrong purchase choice. The ever-shorter development schedules most companies must now meet have, however, made such projects increasingly rare.

Odds are that you, like the rest of us, will have to make do without such customized and extensive benchmark efforts. Instead, we'll have to rely on benchmarks that other people have created. The key is to find those benchmarks that are sufficiently close to what we do that their results apply well to our work.

2.3. A Very Short, Very Abridged History of Benchmarks

Over the years, many people, companies, and groups have created benchmarks. The reasons they did so are as varied as their creators. Some were vendors that wanted to show the superiority of their products. Others were university researchers studying performance. Still others were individuals or even whole groups dedicated to developing these tools.

For all these groups, the process of creating a benchmark has followed the same basic path: You write some code that causes the computer system to do the kind of work that matters to you. If, for example, you wanted to test how fast a system could execute floating-point operations, you would write some code that performed a lot of floating point operations and see how fast the system could execute that code.

One of the earliest benchmarks of note was Whetstone. Its goal was to test the speed with which a computer system could perform integer operations. It's notable both because it was, in its day, quite influential, and because it used the word "stone" in its name. The practice of using "stone" to indicate a benchmark continues to this day. An early benchmark for measuring floating-point speed, for example, was named Dhrystone, and one of the benchmarks on the CD-ROMs this book includes is Winstone.

Some of the most common sources of benchmarks are vendor consortia, such as the Transaction Processing Performance Council and the Standard Performance Evaluation Corporation (SPEC). In these consortia, multiple vendors band together to develop benchmarks in areas of mutual interest. SPEC, for example, has developed several benchmarks, the best known of which is probably SPECint. As its name implies, SPECint is an integer performance benchmark. SPEC designs its benchmarks to run on many different types of platforms and typically achieves that portability in part by providing the source code to its benchmarks. Benchmarks such as SPEC's often reflect a great deal of work and thought, but they are typically aimed at performance-analysis professionals. Few other users are likely to run them.

Most early benchmarks came either from the UNIX and academic communities or from such vendor consortia. The phenomenal success of the personal computer in the 1980s brought computing to a much wider audience than ever before, and it also made performance issues a concern for large segments of that audience. After all, with new generations of PCs appearing every 18 months or even faster, buyers needed some objective way to sort the hype of vendor performance claims from the reality of how shipping PCs actually performed. Predictably, a new group of benchmarks appeared.

The early PC benchmarks came from a variety of sources, notably *PC Magazine* and other PC-oriented publications. These benchmarks, like the PC market itself, were fledgling efforts that provided some useful measures of PC speed but which tended to be simplistic. One popular—and for a while useful—PC benchmark from *PC Magazine* tested the clock speed of the PC's processor by seeing how fast that chip could execute noop (no operation) instructions. Though these instructions by definition did no work, the time the processor took to execute them provided an indication of the fastest speed at which the chip could do anything.

Though our opinions no doubt reflect our involvement in benchmarks (see the disclosure note below), we truly believe the last several years have brought a major improvement in PC benchmarks. The improvement has been so great that PC benchmarks are arguably the best in all of the computer industry. The current generation of PC benchmarks, and notably those we've included in this book, can, when you use them properly, provide an extremely accurate view of pretty much every significant aspect of a PC's performance.

| WARNING | **Disclosure:** We're biased in favor of these benchmarks. We believe our bias accurately reflects the quality of these products, but we want to make clear our involvement with them. Mark and Bill were the founders and Co-Directors, and Richard was the Chief Researcher, of ZDBOp, the group that produces Winstone, WinBench, and Ziff-Davis' other industry-standard benchmarks. Bill continues to this day as the Director of that group, and Mark is Vice President of Product Testing for Ziff-Davis, in which capacity ZDBOp reports to him. Richard left the group a while ago to become a freelance writer and also devote most of his work time to this book. (We told you it took a lot of testing!) With over 15 million copies of its benchmarks distributed to date, we think Ziff-Davis has a right to claim them as industry standards, but we wanted to make sure you knew our involvement. |

2.4. The Whole or the Parts?

One of the most important characteristics of any benchmark is what it's trying to measure. Many benchmarks, for example, attempt to give an overall measure of a complete system's performance. We call these products "system-level" benchmarks. Other benchmarks, by contrast, try to gauge the performance of a particular part of a system, such as a PC's disk subsystem. We call these tools "subsystem-level benchmarks." We use the term "subsystem" rather than "component" because in a modern PC each part of the system—graphics, disk, or whatever—invariably involves a variety of hardware and software components.

Some benchmarks do actually try to focus exactly on a particular piece of hardware in a system and avoid the effects of all the other system components that would normally be involved when a user works with the system. For example, a benchmark from a disk-drive vendor might aim to measure only the speed with which a drive can transfer bytes when running at its peak rate. We call these products, "component-level" benchmarks.

Each of these types of benchmarks has different typical traits and uses.

2.4.1. System-level Benchmarks

System-level benchmarks provide a measure of overall system performance. Most produce a single overall score for each system. Some, such as Winstone 98, can produce multiple scores, each of which reflects the system's performance when running a particular workload.

The great beauty of system-level benchmarks is that their scores are typically easy to understand. With them, you can make statements like, "My computer is only a 37, and the new one in the store is a 75," and be both accurate and reasonably sure that the person to whom you're speaking understands that the new system is twice as fast as yours. (Assuming linear scores, like those Winstone 98 produces, what you're really saying, of course, is that the new system is twice as fast as yours *on the benchmark test's workload*.)

The one big drawback of system-level benchmarks is that they don't help you much if your goal is to figure out *why* your system performed as it did. In the above example, what exactly makes the new PC score twice as fast as your system? Does the newer unit have a faster processor? A great graphics card? A screaming hard disk? Or, some combination of all of these? Though you can theorize, and often theorize accurately, with a system-level benchmark you cannot know for sure what is causing the performance difference.

What you can do, however, is use system-level benchmarks to compare subsystems by using one of the basic techniques of science: Change one variable, and hold everything else constant. To see, for example, how much effect different graphics adapters would have on overall performance, you could conduct the following experiment. Measure your PC's performance with any one adapter. Replace that adapter with a different one, and measure the PC's performance again. Repeat until you've tried out all the adapters. Each time, be sure to follow proper test procedure (we outline that procedure for Winstone 98 and WinBench 98 in Appendixes A and B). When you finish, you'll have an accurate gauge of the different levels of overall system performance the different graphics adapters can produce.

As we noted earlier, the one problem of such studies is that sometimes the overall performance effects they will show will be fairly small, because not all subsystems contribute equally to overall performance. Still, these studies are often great ways to see just how much return a particular investment, such as a new disk, will deliver. We conducted hundreds of these studies during the preparation of this book.

2.4.2. Subsystem-level Benchmarks

As the term implies, subsystem-level benchmarks concentrate on measuring the performance of one or more subsystems. As we noted earlier, by subsystem we mean not a single piece of hardware, but rather all the hardware and software components that are active in any one performance area. When you read or write to a PC's hard disk, for example, you're actually involving not just the hard disk but also the hard disk controller, the disk device drivers, and the hard disk caching software that comes with Windows. Collectively, these hardware and software pieces are the hard disk subsystem.

Other common and important PC subsystems include graphics, processor, and CD-ROM. We discuss the performance of each of these, as well as of the disk subsystem, in later chapters in this book.

Subsystem-level benchmarks are particularly good at two tasks: Focusing on the differences in performance of two implementations of a given subsystem, and helping you understand why one system performs better than another. The first ability makes these benchmarks great tools for seeing just how much disk performance, for example, two different disk subsystems could deliver on the same PC. The second ability helps you dig into why two PCs produced different scores on a subsystem-level benchmark.

The subsystem-level focus of benchmarks of this type is also the source of their one limitation: Knowing that one subsystem is twice as fast as another will not necessarily help you know how much overall system performance improvement the faster subsystem will deliver. If the graphics subsystem, for example, is only 10% of the overall performance of a system, doubling that subsystem's performance will not give more than a 5% improvement in the system's overall speed.

Because of this limitation, you have to interpret subsystem-level benchmark results with care. Otherwise, you might interpret a completely accurate statement that subsystem implementation A was twice as fast as B as saying that you can expect a doubling in overall performance. We see this kind of misinterpretation happen all the time, and it's a shame, because the reaction of many people is to blame the benchmark. The benchmark is doing its job; it's the listener who is failing.

We've used WinBench to conduct hundreds of subsystem-level tests in this book, and the results of those tests can help you make smart purchase choices. We just have to keep them in the proper context, something we try to do throughout the book.

2.4.3. Component-level Benchmarks

Component-level benchmarks look at the performance of specific system components. Rather than trying to measure disk subsystem speed, for example, a component benchmark might try to gauge just the performance of the disk itself. The scores such benchmarks produce tend to be very specific to the component they're testing. In the case of a disk, these numbers might be the disk's peak transfer rate and average access time.

Because these tests attempt to isolate a particular component, they often have to avoid doing the kind of work real users perform, because that work almost always unavoidably involves at least entire subsystems, if not the whole system. Instead, their tests must focus on very particular aspects of the component they're measuring. A disk test might measure access time by timing how long a disk head takes to travel one-third of the distance across the disk platter. Does such a number matter to you? Unless you make disk drives or know how frequently your work causes a disk head to move one-third of the way across the disk, probably not.

Component-level tests tend to produce lots of numbers and to be difficult to understand. Engineers and developers of hardware components as hard disks tend to use and understand these benchmarks, but they are not very useful to most of us. Most folks have no clue how important such particular technical characteristics are in their daily work. Nor do we! That's why we stick to subsystem-level benchmarks and do not use any of component-level benchmarks in this book.

2.5. A Benchmark Taxonomy

The level at which benchmarks try to measure performance is only one way to categorize them. Another important characteristic of each benchmark is the type of workload it uses and the way it delivers that workload. We see benchmarks as falling into four main categories that reflect different workloads and workload-execution styles:

1. Application-based benchmarks

2. Playback benchmarks

3. Synthetic/profiled benchmarks

4. Inspection tests

Each of these approaches has its own advantages, natural uses, and limitations.

2.5.1. Application-based Benchmarks

Application-based benchmarks, as their name implies, try to gauge system performance by executing real applications. To be precise, these benchmarks use some sort of application scripting tools to cause the applications to perform a variety of tasks. Application-based benchmarks are the most intuitively appealing and generally sensible to most folks. They feel more real in large part because they're running some of the same applications that people use. Because they tend to perform quite a bit of work, these benchmarks also are generally less subject to the effects of the oddities of a particular system or subsystem implementation.

The mere fact that a benchmark is application-based, however, is not enough to guarantee that it is good or useful for your purposes.

One key issue is application selection: Does the benchmark run the right set of applications for you? If the benchmark's developer chose to have it run nothing but esoteric CAD applications, for example, and all you run all day is Word, Excel, and a Web browser, the benchmark's results will be of little value to you.

Another vital consideration is the work the benchmark's test scripts make the applications perform. If a benchmark runs Word, for example, but all it does is run the grammar checker repeatedly, its results will probably not reflect the way you use Word.

The final key aspect of such benchmarks is the quality with which their developers implemented them. Scripting tools unavoidably impose some overhead, so developers of application-based benchmarks must use those tools to script application work without unduly perturbing the results. Mess up in this area, and a benchmark might easily be spending a significant amount of its time in its overhead portions—essentially running the scripts and not doing anything resembling the work real users perform.

The right way to build an application-based benchmark is to use applications that represent the interests of the benchmark's users, to have those applications perform work that is as close as possible to the work those users perform, and to execute that work with as little overhead as possible. Winstone follows this exact formula, and the result has been that it has become the industry's leading application-based benchmark.

The results that Winstone and other application-based benchmarks produce are typically rather easy to understand. If system A scores a 15 and system B a 30, for example, we know that for the benchmark's types of applications and work, B is twice as fast as A.

When we finish talking about application-based benchmarks to user groups and other audiences, we almost always get the same question: "Why would you use any other kind of benchmarks?" We've previously cited one such reason: It's somewhere between very difficult and impossible to use application-based benchmarks to isolate the performance of individual subsystems. Other types of benchmarks can often do a better job in this area. The other main reason is that creating representative, low-overhead, reliable application-based benchmarks is a very difficult job.

2.5.2. **Playback Benchmarks**

If you want to measure the performance of an individual subsystem, something we noted application-based benchmarks do not handle well, one of the most advanced techniques is Ziff-Davis' proprietary *playback*. Playback, as its name implies, is a technology for replaying an application's interactions with a particular subsystem—without having to run the actual applications! By playing back all of the application's interactions with a particular subsystem, playback technology ensures that a test is doing the same work—in that subsystem—as the application. By playing back only the interactions with that subsystem, playback technology ensures you measure just that subsystem. The result is an accurate and focused subsystem performance measure that mirrors how real applications use the subsystem.

WinBench uses playback technology to gauge the performance of several different subsystems. Different WinBench playback tests let you focus on a PC's disk, graphics, and CD-ROM subsystems. The first two tests reflect the disk and graphics work, respectively, that the applications in Winstone perform. By using the Winstone application scripts as their bases, these tests make WinBench a natural teammate to Winstone. WinBench's CD-ROM playback tests reflect the CD-ROM activity of several leading CD-ROM–based applications.

Playback technology is conceptually fairly easy to understand. Think of it like a VCR that can replay graphics or disk or CD-ROM or other subsystem work tapes, and you've pretty much got it.

That analogy, of course, begs a key question: Who made those subsystem tapes?

The answer, of course, is the developers at ZDBOp. To see how they do it, let's take WinBench's graphics playback tests as an example. The WinBench team developed graphics subsystem activity recorders, known around ZDBOp as *graphics loggers*, that they can run while the Winstone tests are running. The graphics loggers capture every graphics call to the Windows graphics application programming interface (API) that the applications in Winstone make. The loggers capture those calls and all of their parameters, compress the information, and save the compressed data to disk. (The compression is vital, because the graphics log for an individual application script can run to gigabytes in size.) This compressed data file is the *graphics log*.

When you run the resulting WinBench graphics playback test, it reads in the log from disk, decompresses it, and sends the exact same calls to the Windows graphics API. The result looks exactly the same as if the Winstone applications were running. Unlike Winstone's tests, however, these tests are not running any activity other than graphics, so WinBench can time and report the speed of just these graphics operations. WinBench uses similar tools and techniques to play back the disk and CD-ROM activity of applications.

Results from playback benchmarks are fairly simple to understand when your only goal is to compare them to one another. If one score is twice that of another, the higher-scoring subsystem in question is working basically at twice the speed of the lower.

Where you can easily go astray with subsystem-based benchmarks such as WinBench is if you try to write a formula that uses the results of different subsystems to produce an overall performance measure. Though such formulas are tempting—and we know many folks who've spent days and days trying to perfect them—they invariably don't work well. The reason is that, because playback benchmarks isolate one subsystem at a time, they don't measure how well different subsystems work together. Those interactions are vital to overall system performance. Our position in this area is simple: Don't waste time trying to concoct such formulas. Instead, use Winstone and WinBench as a team, Winstone as your tool for measuring overall system performance, and WinBench as the way to dig into the performance of individual subsystems.

At this point in any benchmark discussion, we invariably hear another question: "Okay, if you have application-based benchmarks and playback-benchmarks that reflect the subsystem work of the applications, why do you need any other types of benchmarks?" Indeed, in this book we focus primarily on the results from application-based and playback benchmark tests. So, why do you need anything else?

2.5.3. Synthetic/profiled Benchmarks

The answer, as you might expect, is that not all areas of system performance lend themselves to playback technology. Processor performance is one such example. In theory, you could simply log every processor instruction an application executed and play it back. Putting this theory into practice, however, is incredibly difficult. For one thing, modern processors perform instructions at such rapid rates that any instruction logs would be huge. Plus, you need special probes to capture the instructions as the processor is executing them. Processor companies such as Intel often have tools for doing some of this work, but even with their best tools the task is difficult—and few have access to those tools.

Consequently, most benchmarks measure the speed of processor subsystems though specially coded *synthetic* benchmark tests.

The history of benchmarking is full of synthetic processor tests, such as Whetstone and the Sieve of Erastothenes. The challenge such tests face is how to accurately reflect the way real applications interact with a system's processor. Historically, most synthetic benchmarks have done a bad job in this area. Consider, for example, one of the curses of synthetic processor benchmarks: Code size. Synthetic tests such as the two we just mentioned are typically so small that their code fits in the processor's internal (Level 1, or L1) cache. Real applications, however, often do not even fit within the much larger external (Level 2, or L2) cache that most modern processors have. This size difference can lead to hugely different performance characteristics, and thus to inaccurate measurements.

The way to deal with this problem is pretty much what you'd expect: Examine what real applications do, then make the synthetic test mimic their behavior. The process of examining real applications to learn how they interact with a given subsystem is known as *profiling*. Even when you can't log every action an application takes with a particular subsystem, you can often build a profile of its overall activity with that subsystem. The processor test in WinBench (CPUmark$_{32}$) represents a great deal of development time, time the developers spent making its activity profile match those of the applications in Winstone.

Synthetic benchmark results are rarely as easy to understand as the results of application-based or playback benchmarks. Synthetic benchmarks often have units, such as millions of operations per second, that reflect the workings of the subsystem they're measuring. These results are often difficult to relate to real-world performance. The easiest way to get value from them is to compare several of them: that is, to see the number of operations per second that four or five different PCs can perform. This approach at least will let you get some sense of the relative speed of the items you're comparing. We won't use synthetic benchmark results a great deal in this book, but there are times when they're the best tools available.

2.5.4. Benchmark Inspection Tests

One last type of benchmark test remains. Sometimes, you want to look at some aspect of performance that it is impossible or highly difficult to measure with any of the previous types of benchmarks. Maybe you're trying to gauge the speed of a subsystem whose activity you cannot yet profile, or one that few applications currently use.

In such cases, the answer is to turn to *inspection tests*. These tests are ones that are not using applications, not playing back application work, and not reflecting much application profiling; if they did any of those things, they'd be in a different category. Consequently, they tend to be tools that developers created to focus more on isolating performance differences than on doing what users do. For example, you might want to measure the access time of a hard disk or the line-drawing speed of a graphics adapter, just to get a handle on the performance level of those basic capabilities.

Okay, we admit it: Few of us would actually get much value from those measurements. If your job is building disk drives or graphics adapters, however, or if you work regularly with such products, you would probably feel differently. Thus, as you might expect, subsystem and component vendors often love these benchmarks and the kinds of results they create. Those results, however, are very difficult to relate to real-world performance, and we won't use them much in this book. (If you're really into such techie measurements, however, we haven't forgotten you; you will find a wealth of such tests in WinBench.)

2.6. Types of Results

As we've mentioned earlier, different benchmarks can produce several different types of results. Understanding the different types and their meanings is vital if you want to interpret them correctly.

The simplest benchmark result is the amount of time the thing you're measuring takes to perform the work you're asking it to do. If PC A does a job in a minute and PC B performs the same work in 30 seconds, B is clearly faster at that work than A. The problem with reporting elapsed times is that bigger numbers are worse than smaller numbers, a relationship that's counter-intuitive for most folks. Put the above two results in a graph; if your eyes just flit over the graph you'll tend to assume the bigger one is better.

A careful reading will reveal the truth, of course, but most benchmarks don't take any chances. Instead of going with elapsed times, most benchmarks produce results in which bigger numbers are better.

One way to do that is to report throughput or rate-based scores. These results tend to be the number of something that the thing you're testing could perform per unit time. Metrics of this type have descriptions such as thousands of bytes per second or millions of pixels per second. The good news about these numbers is that they are quite technically accurate; the bad news is that they are often very hard to relate to anything. Most of us don't know, for example, whether a result of 10 million pixels-per-second is fast or slow.

The most common way to get around this drawback is to use a technique known as *normalization*. To normalize a result, you state it in terms of how fast some base comparison device can do the same work. To compute such results, you take the elapsed time or rate results of your test and divide them by the corresponding results of a base device. If, for example, you are comparing the overall performance of PCs A and B and you made A the base, you would report simply that B is twice as fast as A. To make such results presentable, most benchmarks set the base machine's score to some number—1, 10, and 100 are common—and then compare other things to it. This technique is known as *scaling* the scores to 1, 10, or whatever.

Normalized scores are typically unitless (that is, they measure no specific rate and make sense only when you use them comparison with other such scores). So, while you can't find any obvious meaning to a score of 30 sitting on a page or screen all by itself, you get a pretty good picture if you know that the base machine has a score of 10.

2.7. Winstone and WinBench

In this book we measure performance by using two benchmarks, Winstone and WinBench. Because the testing in this book spanned two years, and because we needed the very latest benchmarks to accurately gauge the performance of Windows 98, we actually ended up using two versions of each benchmark: Winstone 97 and Winstone 98, plus WinBench 97 and WinBench 98. This usage is no problem as long as you only compare scores from the same versions, and we of course stick to that rule in this book. (Don't ever compare the results of two different versions of the same benchmark, because the tests have generally changed so much that such comparisons are meaningless.) We've enclosed the latest version of each benchmark, Winstone 98 and WinBench 98, on the CDs this book includes, so you can also do your own tests.

Appendix A and Appendix B outline how to use those benchmarks. Before you even begin, or before you start using the results we've generated, it's helpful to understand the range of tests the benchmarks offer and how those tests fit into the various categories we've described.

Because the two versions of each benchmark share similar basic concepts, we will use their names without the year designator to cover both versions. Thus, when we say "Winstone" we'll be referring to both versions. For facts particular to a either version, we'll be sure to include the year.

2.7.1. Winstone

Using our earlier taxonomy, Winstone is a system-level, application-based benchmark that produces normalized, scaled scores. It measures 32-bit PC performance by running actual 32-bit applications under Windows. Winstone 97 uses 14 applications to test performance; Winstone 98 uses 16. Both versions group those application-based tests into Business tests and more targeted High-End tests.

All of Winstone 97's tests would run on either Windows 95 or Windows NT. Winstone 98's Business tests will also run on both those Windows versions and Windows 98, but its High-End tests will run only on Windows NT. We used Winstone 98 for all our Windows 98–based tests.

As you might imagine from a benchmark that involves so many applications, Winstone is big. It contains about 150MB of data, so it is available only on CD-ROMs like the one this book includes. On-line and diskette distributions are not really options. Winstone 97, by the way, is no longer available, because Winstone 98 has replaced it.

Winstone executes applications by using scripts that ZDBOp developers based on a large survey of the way users interact with their applications, plus input from the application vendors on how people use their applications. Winstone scripts thus perform such common functions as opening a document, recalculating a spreadsheet, searching, and spell-checking. When possible, the developers used documents and presentations from real users to make the scripts even more reflective of actual usage. Figure 2.1, for example, shows a Winstone 97 Microsoft Word script doing things much like what most folks do in Word.

Figure 2.1.

Winstone 97 runs Microsoft Word through its paces much as a user does.

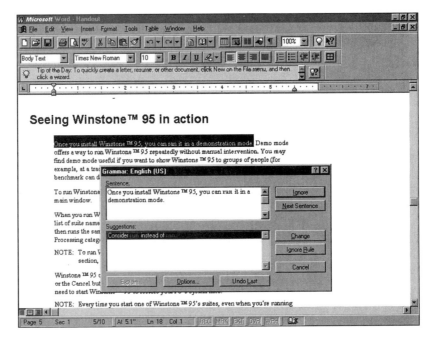

To run an application script, Winstone must first install that application. To make sure it doesn't mess up your PC, Winstone must leave your hard disk in the same state after its tests as before you ran them. To meet these two goals, Winstone installs each application onto your hard disk before it runs the test script for that application. When the application's script completes, Winstone deletes the application from your disk.

> **WARNING** To run the copy of Winstone 98 on the CD this book includes, you must agree to the benchmark's license agreement. Part of that agreement is a stipulation that you will not pirate the applications the benchmark includes. ZDBOp has taken a number of steps to make such actions both more difficult (including encrypting the application files on the CD) and less desirable (including throwing out all the application files its tests do not use), but the onus is on you not to attempt such a theft. Software piracy is a bad thing, so don't do it either by trying to hack Winstone or by any other approach.

For each application script it runs, Winstone computes the score in the same basic way. It first times how long the PC you're testing took to complete the script. It then normalizes that time to the time a base machine took to complete the same script. The two versions of Winstone used different base machines.

Winstone 97 actually employed two different base machines for the two application groups because of the different performance demands of the Business and High-End applications it contained. The base machine for its Business scores was a Gateway PC with a 66-MHz Intel 486 processor, 1024 by 768 graphics resolution, and 16MB of RAM. For the High-End scores, the base machine was a Dell XPS P100c with a 100-MHz Intel Pentium CPU, 1024 by 768 graphics resolution, and 32MB of RAM. Also, the two portions of Winstone 97 had different minimum system requirements: To run the Business tests, a system needed only 16MB of RAM, but to run the High-End tests the minimum was 32MB.

Winstone 98 used a more powerful base machine and thus was able to use the same system for both its Business and High-End tests. That system was a Dell Dimension PC with a 133-MHz Intel Pentium processor, 1024 by 768 graphics resolution with 16-bit color, and 32MB of RAM. Because the benchmark's High-End tests run only on Windows NT, the base machine was running NT.

Once Winstone has normalized a test run's time to the time of the base machine, it then uses harmonic means of these normalized scores and the weights of each application and category to compute the overall and category scores. The weights of the applications reflect their market share; more on that below. Winstone then scales its overall Business and High-End scores to the corresponding scores of the base machine, which by definition the developers set to 10.0. Winstone scales the category scores and the individual High-End application scores (we list the

Benchmarks and You

applications in the High-End Winstone section below) to a score of 1.0 on the same base machine. The different scaling factors make it generally easy to tell category scores from overall scores.

As you can probably already tell, Winstone can produce quite a few different scores. Those scores differ slightly between the two versions of Winstone, so let's take them one at a time.

Winstone 97 can produce the following scores, many of which we use in this book:

- An overall Business Winstone score

- Publishing, Database, and Word Processing/Spreadsheet business category scores

- An overall High-End Winstone score

- Application Development, CAD/3-D, and Image Editing High-End category scores

- Individual scores for each of the six High-End applications

The scores Winstone 98 can yield are similar, but there are a few differences:

- An overall Business Winstone score

- Publishing, Database, and Word Processing/Spreadsheet business category scores

- An overall High-End Winstone score

- Individual scores for each of the seven High-End applications

- A task-switching score

The reason both Winstone versions produce so many different scores is to make it as easy as possible for you to find the results that most represent the kind of work you do on your PC.

A few paragraphs ago, we promised more information on the weights of the Winstone applications. To understand those, we need to look at how ZDBOp chose the applications in Winstone.

Business Winstone

ZDBOp wanted to include in the Business Winstone tests those business applications with the largest market shares. To determine those applications, ZDBOp consulted with ZD Market Intelligence (ZDMI), a leading market-research firm (and, yes, another part of Ziff-Davis). They determined which applications had the largest unit market shares by averaging actual application sales for the current year with special ZDMI projections for the coming year. The applications in both Winstone versions reflected the result.

This process led Winstone 97 to use the eight leading applications, in three categories, in Table 2.1.

Table 2.1. Applications and categories in Business Winstone 97.

Publishing	Database	Word Processing/ Spreadsheet
Adobe PageMaker 6.0	Borland International Paradox 7.0	
Corel Systems CorelDRAW! 6.0 Paradox 7.0	Microsoft Access 7.0	Lotus Development Corp. WordPro 96
Microsoft PowerPoint 7.0	Microsoft Excel 7.0	Microsoft Word 7.0

For Winstone 98, this process led to the nine applications in four categories in Table 2.2:

Table 2.2. Applications and categories in Business Winstone 98.

Publishing	Browser	Database/ Spreadsheet	Word Processing
Corel Systems CorelDRAW! 7.0	Netscape Navigator 3.01	Corel Quattro Pro 7.0	Corel WordPerfect 7.0
Microsoft PowerPoint 97		Lotus 1-2-3 97	Microsoft Word 97
		Microsoft Access 97	Microsoft Excel 97

A few things obviously changed between the two versions of Winstone. In addition to newer applications that reflected what people were currently using, Winstone 98 also merged spreadsheets into the database category and added a Web browser category. This addition reflects the incredible widespread usage of browsers.

Benchmarks and You

The applications in both Winstone versions are so well known that you could probably have guessed most or even all of them. The odds are also pretty high that you're using at least some version of several of them.

How does all this affect the weight each application has in the Business Winstone scores? Simple: The market share of each application serves as that application's weight in the calculation of the Business Winstone scores. Thus, the more widespread the usage of an application, the more it affects the Business Winstone scores.

We should note there is one exception to this rule: The weight of the Browser category score in the overall Business Winstone 98 result. Because browsers are both incredibly widely used and yet free, the normal rules didn't seem to apply well to them. ZDBOp and a group of Ziff-Davis editors consequently decided to give the Browser category a weight of ten percent.

High-End Winstone

ZDBOp and that same group of editors—editors from such Ziff-Davis publications as *PC Magazine*, *Computer Shopper*, *PC Week*, and *PC/Computing*—collectively chose the applications in the High-End Winstone tests. The goal they sought, and which we believe they achieved, was to represent a diverse group of performance-sensitive user communities.

For Winstone 97, they chose the six high-end applications shown in Table 2.3. As that table shows, they divided these applications into three categories. Due to the very different user communities these application categories address, all six applications have equal weight in Winstone 97's overall High-End score.

Table 2.3. Applications and categories in High-End Winstone 97.

Application Development	*CAD/3-D*	*Image Editing*
Microsoft Visual C++ 4.1	Advanced Visual Systems Application Visualization System (AVS) 3.0	Adobe Photoshop 3.0.5
	Visual Numerics PV-WAVE 6.0	Micrografx Picture Publisher 6.0
	Bentley Systems' MicroStation 95	

This group followed a similar process in choosing the High-End applications in Winstone 98. As the following list shows, the result this time was seven applications—but no categories. Having worked with Winstone 97 and listened to user and industry feedback, the group felt that the categories added little value to High-End Winstone. For the same reason as in Winstone 97, the seven applications have equal weight in Winstone 98's overall High-End score:

Adobe Premiere
Adobe Photoshop 4.01
Advanced Visual Systems Application Visualization
    System(AVS)/Express 3.1
Bentley Systems' MicroStation 95
Microsoft FrontPage 97
Microsoft Visual C++ 5.0
Visual Numerics PV-WAVE 6.1

2.7.2 WinBench

As we discussed earlier, WinBench works naturally as part of a team with Winstone. WinBench lets you single out individual PC subsystems and see how the Winstone tests exercised those subsystems.

WinBench is, however, much more difficult to categorize than Winstone, in large part because it contains so very many tests—over 200! WinBench is definitely a subsystem-level benchmark, but no one of our benchmark test types applies to all of its tests. Some of those tests, including the best-known and most commonly used ones, are playback tests. Others are profiled synthetic tests, and still others are inspection tests.

WinBench does not just contain tests that reflect the work of the applications in Winstone. It also provides tests that let you measure the performance of a wide variety of other subsystems, such as the CD-ROM and full-motion video subsystems, that do not play a role in the work the Winstone tests perform. WinBench also offers tests of the performance of a PC's processor/RAM and DirectDraw subsystems.

The key areas in which WinBench does measure the subsystem work of the Winstone tests are in its graphics and disk tests. Because there are both Business and High-End Winstone tests, WinBench naturally contains Business and High-End versions of its disk and graphics tests. These tests are playback tests that replay the graphics and disk activities, respectively, of the Winstone Business and High-End applications.

The following list gives a quick overview of the many tests in WinBench 97:

Business Graphics WinMark 97
High-End Graphics WinMark 97

Benchmarks and You

Over 70 graphics inspection tests
Business Disk WinMark 97
High-End Disk WinMark 97
Disk Read, CPU Utilization
Disk Write, CPU Utilization
16 additional disk inspection tests
CD-ROM WinMark 97
CD-ROM CPU Utilization
CD-ROM Access Time
15 additional CD-ROM inspection tests
CPUmark$_{16}$
CPUmark$_{32}$
Over 30 DirectDraw inspection tests
Over 50 full-motion video tests

The CPUmark pair, whose members are the processor/RAM tests, deserve a quick explanation. CPUmark$_{16}$ measures how well the processor/RAM subsystem handles 16-bit applications, and CPUmark$_{32}$ gauges how well that subsystem executes 32-bit applications.

WinBench 98 has a similar set of tests, though some, such as the 16-bit processor/RAM test are gone, some are new, and many reflect ZDBOp's continuing development efforts. Following is a quick overview of those many tests:

Business Graphics WinMark 98
High-End Graphics WinMark 98
Over 70 graphics inspection tests
Business Disk WinMark 98
High-End Disk WinMark 98
Disk Read Access Time
Disk Read CPU Utilization
Disk Read Transfer Rate
16 additional disk inspection tests
CD-ROM WinMark 98
CD-ROM Access Time
CD-ROM CPU Utilization
CD-ROM Transfer Rate
CPUmark$_{32}$
FPU WinMark 98
Over 30 DirectDraw inspection tests
Over 20 full-motion video tests

As we noted above, these tests span all the test types we discussed earlier.

Graphics WinMark

The most famous WinBench test is the Graphics WinMark. It's a playback test that actually plays back all the graphics activities the Winstone application tests perform. WinBench has both Business and High-End Graphics WinMark tests, because Winstone has both Business and High-End application tests. As you can see in Figure 2.2, the WinBench playback tests (here, a WinBench 97 test) look almost exactly like their Winstone counterparts.

Figure 2.2.
Here, WinBench 97 plays back the graphics portion of the Microsoft Word script from Winstone 97.

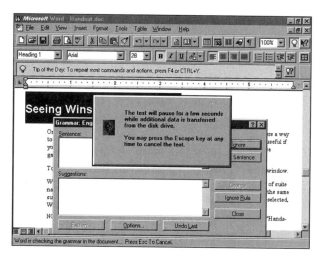

We say "almost exactly" because you will see one difference. Periodically during any Graphics WinMark test, a small box will appear in the middle of the screen and inform you that WinBench 97 is getting additional data that it needs to continue the test. This box appears whenever WinBench must fetch from disk (or CD-ROM, if you're running the benchmark from the CD) the next portion of its playback log. This periodic fetch process is necessary because, as we noted in our discussion of playback benchmarks, the graphics logs are very large. Even in their highly compressed form, they consume tens of megabytes of space. (By the way, WinBench turns off its timer whenever it must fetch this data, so it times only true graphics activity.)

Each version of WinBench can produce Graphics scores that correspond to all the scores the same-year Winstone version can produce. WinBench also normalizes all these scores to those of the appropriate Winstone base machine.

The Graphics WinMark scores are by no means the same as any of Winstone's scores, however. WinBench produces the Graphics WinMark by running a series of practically non-stop graphics stress tests; that's how it focuses on the graphics subsystem. The application tests in Winstone, by contrast, intentionally intersperse graphics, disk, and processor work, just as real user application work does.

Benchmarks and You

Disk WinMark

The Disk WinMark tests, like their Graphics WinMark cousins, come in both Business and High-End versions. As you'd expect, these WinBench Disk WinMark tests play back all the timed application disk activity of the Winstone application tests. In the course of these operations, these disk tests use many directories, hundreds of files, and a lot of disk space. WinBench 97's tests use roughly 90MB for the Business tests and 370MB for the High-End tests. WinBench 98's tests use about 170MB for the Business tests and 160MB for the High-End tests.

These tests give you the option of receiving the amount of the PC's processing power, or *processor utilization*, the system is using during that test. The lower the processor utilization, the better, because more processing power is then available for other types of work.

The Disk WinMark tests are among the dullest of WinBench's tests, because they naturally take a while to do all that disk work, and yet they give you no real visible feedback. About the only thing you can see is the flashing of the disk light—a good sign the tests are doing what they're supposed to do.

CD-ROM WinMark

The CD-ROM WinMark test in each WinBench version uses the same disk playback technology as the Disk WinMark tests, but it naturally uses that technology to read from the CD-ROM instead. These tests do not, however, reflect the work of any Winstone tests, because the Winstone applications, once installed, generally do not interact with the CD-ROM subsystem. The CD-ROM tests instead play back the CD-ROM operations of six leading CD-ROM applications in three areas: Business/Productivity, Games and Entertainment, and Reference and Education. As with the Disk WinMark tests, there's not a lot for you to watch while the tests are running, but you will probably be able to hear your CD-ROM drive working hard!

To run any of the CD-ROM WinMark tests (or any of the other CD-ROM tests), you must have the CD that contained WinBench in your CD-ROM drive. That CD uses a special file layout that the CD-ROM WinMark tests require. This layout reflects the way the files were laid out on the CDs of the applications whose CD-ROM activity ZDBOp logged to produce these tests. By using this accurate layout and ZD's playback technology, the CD-ROM WinMark tests provide a good indication of the actual performance you will see with a CD-ROM drive. This performance is often rather different from the theoretical, but usually unachievable, maximum performance that 24X or 32X drives tout.

CPUmark$_{32}$

CPUmark$_{32}$ is a synthetic test that reflects profiling of the processor work the 32-bit applications in Winstone perform. The goal of CPUmark$_{32}$ is obviously to isolate and measure the performance of the processor subsystem. The processor subsystem includes not just the CPU, but also the L2 cache and the PC's memory as well. This test does not take into account the amount of RAM a system has, but the speed at which that RAM operates will definitely affect the test's result—as it should. Increasing the size of the L2 cache will also increase your CPUmark$_{32}$ score.

CPUmark$_{32}$ contains special C code whose processor-usage characteristics correlate highly with those of the profiled applications. That profiling revealed a great deal of information about the applications' processor usage, including such characteristics as L2 cache-hit rates, instruction frequency, and branch characteristics. The benchmark developers modified the instruction stream of this C code until its profile closely matched that of the profiled applications.

FPU WinMark 98

Like CPUmark$_{32}$, the FPU WinMark 98 test is a synthetic test that lets you isolate and measure the performance of the processor subsystem. The difference between the two tests is that CPUmark$_{32}$ does not exercise the floating-point capabilities of a PC's processor, while the FPU WinMark 98 test by design focuses on those floating-point capabilities. Thus, if you run floating-point intensive applications, you might well want to use this test.

The FPU WinMark 98 test is also like CPUmark$_{32}$ in that it does not take into account the amount of RAM a system has but does reflect the speed at which that RAM operates.

The special C code that composes the FPU WinMark 98 test uses five algorithms to stress a processor's floating-point capabilities. Those algorithms perform the following functions:

- A Poisson equation

- A Fast Fourier Transform

- A calculation of planetary orbitals

- A calculation of the areas of polygons

- A Gauss-Jordan elimination-of-coefficient matrix of linear equations

The algorithms have weights that represent how well they apply to typical real-world floating-point usage. The test uses these weights to compute a single FPU WinMark 98 score.

CPUmark$_{16}$

CPUmark$_{16}$ appears only in WinBench 97, and it is the only 16-bit test in either WinBench version. It is similar to CPUmark$_{32}$, but as its name implies, it operates as a 16-bit application. WinBench 97 includes this test because at the time of that benchmark's release, many 16-bit applications were still in common usage.

Like its 32-bit cousin, CPUmark$_{16}$ also measures the performance of the processor/RAM subsystem, though this time at running 16-bit applications. Also like that other version, it is indifferent to the amount of RAM in a system. This test is also special C code that reflects profiling, though in this case the profiling was of an earlier, 16-bit version of Winstone.

Inspection Tests

As Tables 2.5 and 2.6 showed, both WinBench versions include a broad array of inspection tests in addition to the tests we've just covered. The goal of these inspection tests is to give you tools you can use to isolate a particular area of PC performance, such as running a full-motion video, drawing lines, or executing DirectDraw screen BLTs. While most of these tests will be of interest to only a small group of people, that small group will find these tests very valuable. We will use only a few of these tests in this book, though not as a primary measure of performance.

Full-motion Video Tests

WinBench lets you test video playback performance by running video clips at a variety of data rates and frame rates, with different video coders/decoders (CODECS), and, in WinBench 98, either zoomed or unzoomed. Zoomed tests run at the current screen resolution, and WinBench scales them to fit that resolution. Unzoomed tests run at a specified resolution (several options are available) and appear centered on the screen when that resolution is smaller than the current display resolution (see Figure 2.3).

ZDBOp produced these clips to work at different transfer rates. You can run them from the CD-ROM or hard disk. These tests let you know how many frames your machine is dropping during the video clip, as well as what the maximum frame rate possible is for a particular clip. A crucial additional metric is the processor utilization. This number indicates how much of the processor the PC had to use to play the clip. Because you often want the processor to be free to do additional work while you're playing a video clip, you want this number to be as low as possible.

DirectDraw Tests

WinBench also includes a set of 3D DirectDraw inspection tests. DirectDraw is a Windows application programming interface that games and other graphical applications use to display images under Windows 98, Windows 95, or Windows NT. The DirectDraw tests perform a variety of operations, such as memory-to-screen bit transfers, that such applications also need to perform. Although these tests are synthetic tests that do not reflect application profiling, they can give you a good feel for a PC's DirectDraw performance.

Figure 2.3.
WinBench 97's full-motion video tests use a variety of video clips to measure video performance.

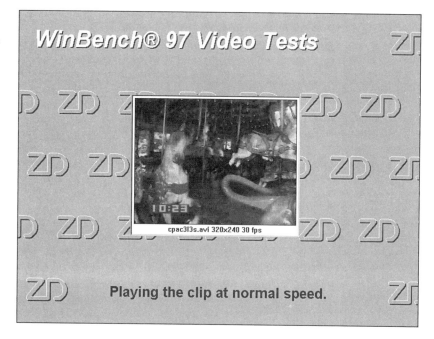

Graphics, Disk, and CD-ROM Inspection Tests

Finally, WinBench also includes a bunch of other inspection tests that you can use to delve deeply into graphics, disk, or CD-ROM performance. If, for example, you wanted to understand more about lower-level disk performance characteristics, you could use WinBench's assortment of additional disk tests.

2.8. From Here...

In this chapter we've taken you through a quick overview of the benchmarks we used in this book, two of which are available on the CD-ROMs this book includes. In the next two chapters, we fill in the details on how you can take full advantage of these programs. With these tools and the material in those chapters, plus the many test results in Chapters 5 through 14, you can optimize the performance of your existing PC or buy a new PC with the best possible combination of price and performance for your needs.

The following two chapters provide more information on how you can use the benchmarks to maximum advantage. The first two appendixes explain how to use and install the benchmarks.

- Chapter 3, "Benchmarks and Your Current PC," will explain how you can use Winstone 98 and WinBench 98 to increase the performance of your current PC.

- Chapter 4, "Benchmarks and Buying New Systems," will show you how Winstone 98 and WinBench 98 can help you buy the best performing new PC for your needs.

- Appendix A, "Using Winstone 98," will tell you how to install Winstone 98 and use it to produce performance results.

- Appendix B, "Using WinBench 98," will explain how you can install WinBench 98 and use it to produce performance results.

Chapter

3

Benchmarks and Your Current PC

One of the most important goals we have for this book is to help you maximize the performance of your current PC. We do want to help you understand all the ins and outs of your system's performance, and we've done a lot of work toward that end, but helping you make the best possible performance-enhancement decisions is even more important.

Decisions usually involve trade-offs, and these performance-related choices are no different. One of the most important trade-offs you'll have to evaluate is whether to spend time—but no money—simply tuning your PC's operating software or to plunge in and buy some hardware upgrades. This book contains material that will help you regardless of the option you pick, but because it involves spending money, the hardware upgrade path occupies the bulk of the book.

Following that path is fundamentally tricky, because a lot of vendors will offer to take your money. Each will promise performance improvements, of course, so you'll have to sort out through a lot of information, much of it conflicting. The key to coming out ahead is finding the investments that produce the greatest performance return on your investment. The tests we've done throughout this book will give you a solid sense of which areas generally yield the best returns. To make sure that data applies to you, you can use the benchmarks the book includes (and the information on using them that we've supplied) to precisely measure that return for your system.

This chapter examines the key trade-offs and decisions you will need to consider to get the most performance from your existing system—while keeping your wallet as intact as possible. In this chapter, you will learn:

- How changes to your existing PC affect its performance

- What kind of changes in performance you can expect—and what level of improvement is unrealistic—so that you will know when upgrading is wise and when it's time to consider buying a whole new PC

- What your best choices are for the most performance increases

- What types of system changes are most likely to yield the performance improvements you seek

- What your cheapest choices are for increasing performance

- Which changes you can do on the cheap and which to avoid if money is tight

- How benchmarks can help you decide how much of your PC to change

- How you can use the results and benchmarks in this book to make the right decisions about which subsystems to change and how much to change them

- What you should do if you are planning to upgrade multiple PCs

■ Why the buying power from upgrading multiple machines can often help you get potential vendors to aid you in evaluating the performance return each of your upgrade options will generate

3.1. Cocktail Party Tips

With a drink or two under their belts, most people at a party will claim expertise in almost anything. Looking for a new car? They'll know which one you should buy. Wondering how the world can ever bring peace to the Middle East? No problem; they'll have the answer. Almost no one, however, will claim to know how to get more from your PC. Say, "My computer is too slow. What can I do to make it faster?" and the group around you will fall silent.

Clearly, this knowledge gap is an opportunity for you to shine.

Looking good in this situation isn't easy. Part of the reason others fall silent is that the answer is not simple. Performance optimization is a complex question whose answer varies from situation to situation. Of course, bringing peace to the Middle East is even more complex, and people feel no reticence about telling you how to do that, so complexity is not the only reason for their silence. Most people just know so little about what goes on in their computers that they have no idea how to formulate even surface-level answers.

We can't give you cocktail-party tips that do much more than that, because the situation is indeed complex. We can, though, give you three useful guidelines.

First, you can tell the questioners there's almost no chance they're going to be able to make their current PCs as fast as the hottest new systems available. If that's their goal, they should just buy new PCs. Mind you, they could change enough in their systems to make them as fast as the performance leaders, but if their labor has any value at all, it's probably cheaper to buy a whole new system.

You also can let people know right up front that getting more performance from their computer will almost certainly mean spending money. You can gain some performance improvement by changing operating-system settings; for exactly how much you can gain, see the chapter in Part II, "Software Optimization," that applies to the Windows version you're running. You can also boost a portable's speed by fiddling with its battery-conservation settings; check out Chapter 13, "Power Saving and Portables". For the big gains, however, you have to buy hardware.

For those willing to plunk down some money for hardware upgrades, the best advice you can give is that if they have less than 32MB of RAM, they should buy more RAM. Even if they have 32MB of RAM, buying more RAM may well help. Up to a point—a point we explain in Chapter 9, "Optimizing Your System's Ram,"—buying more RAM is like eating chicken soup: It may not cure what ails

Benchmarks and Your Current PC

you, but it doesn't hurt and it's often soothing. While other hardware upgrades can be very useful, how much, if any, performance improvement they'll deliver will vary greatly from system to system.

3.2. All or Nothing at All

If you decide you really must have more PC speed, the first and biggest issue you have to address is a variant of the old "build or buy" question: Do you fix up your existing system, or just buy a new one? Buying a new system is almost always easier, but it's also almost always more expensive, so you need to consider this choice carefully.

To decide whether to upgrade your current PC, consider three key questions: Is the increase you want possible by upgrading your current PC? Is such an upgrade worth its dollar cost? And, is the upgrade worth the effort it will cost you?

You should always start with your upgrade goals, because there's no point in proceeding until you're sure you can get what you want. The most important factor in deciding whether you can reach your goal is what you currently have.

To pick an extreme example, suppose your goal is to run the latest and greatest games with all the zip you've seen from the newest systems. If you have a PC with a 133-MHz Pentium processor, you might be able to reach your goal. You'd have to install a processor upgrade, add a hot graphics card, and maybe even stick in some RAM, but the resulting system would let you run many, maybe even most, of the latest games. (Check out Chapter 8 for information on processor upgrades, Chapter 9 for the gains possible from RAM increases, and Chapter 10 for the scoop on graphics adapters.)

Now, suppose instead that your current system has a 386 CPU. You're basically hosed. Modern games require lots of processing power and specialized graphics cards. A 386-based motherboard will not be able to handle the level of processor you'll need, nor the PCI—let alone AGP—graphics adapter you'll require. Worse, the motherboard may not even be able to support more than 16MB of RAM. About all you'll be able to use from that system is its case and power supply.

Even if it is possible to upgrade your system to what you need, you have to decide whether the performance boost you can achieve is worth the money it will cost you. Our rule of thumb is that you should not spend more on upgrades than half or at most two-thirds of the cost of a new system. Our reasoning is that any system you upgrade will probably not be as fast as the latest new PCs, yet it is likely to last only half as long as those new systems. That factor—the upgraded PC's useful life span—is key to deciding if you should do an upgrade. If an upgrade won't make it useful for long, why bother? The other key is whether the upgrade will leave your system with any performance to spare, a factor we call "headroom." If you have no headroom, the next demanding application down the pike will leave you desperate to upgrade again. If you have a little headroom, the upgrade is likely to last longer.

The final factor you have to consider is whether an upgrade is worth your time and effort. All of the above analysis assumes your time is free, when in fact the most valuable commodity today is often your time. When you include the amount of your time you'll have to invest to do the upgrade, you'll have a more accurate estimate of the upgrade's cost. Of course, *this* analysis ignores one crucial intangible, whether you enjoy fixing up your system. Some people like to work on cars, others on houses. We've always preferred working on computers. We and many others feel a certain amount of satisfaction when we've done an upgrade. You have to decide for yourself if you're in this group with us. If so, you'll find a great deal of useful upgrade information in this book. If not, you can still make wiser purchase choices by using the book's studies and the benchmarks it includes.

3.3. Picking Your Changes

Once you've decided to upgrade your system, you have to figure out what approach to take. We see three main approaches. The key difference between them is the factor you value most: The best possible performance, money, or time. You need to choose which of these matter most to you, and then proceed accordingly. You can also obviously blend these approaches, say by wanting the most performance for the least time, but doing so almost inevitably involves compromises that you should make consciously. Don't, for example, expect to be able to achieve truly great performance from an upgrade without investing a lot of time and money.

3.3.1. Going for the Biggest Improvements

If, as Tom Cruise said in *Top Gun*, you "feel the need for speed," then the path of maximum performance is for you. Table 3.1 summarizes the level of performance boost different upgrades are likely to deliver. As with any such table, this one reflects typical results, in this case the level of performance increase we found while writing this book. Your mileage will definitely vary.

Buying additional RAM is one of the best ways to boost performance, particularly if you have only 8MB of RAM and a Pentium-class or better processor. Even if your processor is slower or you have 16MB of RAM, more RAM is still probably a good choice.

We rank a CD-ROM drive upgrade high if you have an old 1X, 2X, or 4X CD-ROM drive. While the current 16X, 24X, and 32X drives are not as much faster than your current drive as the "multiplier" in their names would indicate, they are noticeably faster if you run applications that use CD-ROMs extensively.

Benchmarks and Your Current PC

Whether to upgrade your graphics adapter is a hard call. If you don't run any 3D applications, you probably shouldn't bother unless your graphics adapter is at least two years old. If you do run 3D apps, particularly games, any 3D adapter more than a year old is a good upgrade candidate. PC 3D technology is improving so rapidly that every year brings two generations of improvement, and you will notice the improvements on the hottest new games.

You many be surprised that we rank processor upgrades as low as we do (we know Intel, AMD, IDT, and Cyrix/National Semiconductor will hate this). The reason is not that the processor isn't important to system performance; it clearly is one of the very most vital components in any system. The problem is that finding a processor upgrade that will work for your PC is often difficult. For example, you cannot currently buy any upgrades that will let a PC with a Pentium-class processor run a Pentium II. In addition, most processor upgrades simply cannot deliver the full rated speed of the processor they contain, because the motherboard and RAM in your system are probably tuned for the slower processor the system originally contained.

Adding a new hard disk or tuning your operating system can definitely yield worthwhile results, especially for people with disk-intensive applications. These choices, however, are the least likely of the options to give you a big performance boost. If maximizing performance is your goal, try these upgrades in this order:

> Buy more RAM if your PC has 8MB or less and a Pentium-class or faster processor
> Replace your CD-ROM drive if it is a 4X or slower drive and you use it a decent amount
> Replace your graphics adapter if it is more than two years old or if you need 3D capabilities
> Upgrade your processor if possible
> Add a new hard disk
> Buy Windows 98 or Windows 95 performance-boosting software
> Tune Windows 98 or Windows 95 (defragging the hard disk is the first step)
> Tune Windows NT

3.3.2. Going for the Cheapest Upgrades

If you're feeling a bit tight, you might decide to let your wallet guide your way. Table 3.2 summarizes the relative cost of performance upgrades, though costs will always vary somewhat and great bargains are often available to those willing to shop hard. (Yes, this is a plug for some services of our company, but we'd be remiss if we didn't make it: You'd be amazed at the bargains you can find in the pages of *Computer Shopper* or online at ZDNet's Netbuyer, www.netbuyer.com.)

A couple of the software options, such as defragging your hard disk under Windows 98 or Windows 95 are free, so it's hard to beat them. Most of the software utilities are also inexpensive; you can typically get them for under $50. A new CD-ROM drive will usually set you back less than $100, as will RAM, as long as you're not buying too much. Most new graphics adapters are in the $100 to $300 range, though if you add enough options—extra RAM, TV output, and so on—you can certainly run up the price. Processor upgrades range from about $150 on up to over $400. Hard disks are typically in the $150 to $500 range.

These prices are obviously subject to change, but with the exception of the cost of RAM, they have remained remarkably constant. What's changed is what you can get for the money. The cost of a megabyte of disk storage, for example, has fallen so much that a couple of gigabytes today costs less than 500MB not long ago. If minimizing expense is your goal, try these upgrades in this order:

> Tune Windows 98 or Windows 95
> Tune Windows NT
> Buy Windows 95 tuning software
> Replace your CD-ROM drive
> Add RAM
> Replace your graphics adapter
> Upgrade your processor
> Add a new hard disk

3.3.3. Going for the Easiest Upgrades

If time is your most precious commodity, then go for the upgrades that are the simplest and least time-consuming to perform. Table 3.3 ranks the possible upgrades in this order.

A couple of the software options, notably defragging your hard disk under Windows 98 or Windows 95, require almost no effort on your part. Installing additional RAM should not take too much time, provided, of course, that everything goes smoothly. Replacing a graphics adapter isn't bad, but then you have to worry about getting the adapter's driver working and getting Windows in order. You can spend an amazing amount of time on these issues. A processor upgrade should also be fairly straightforward, though in our experience the odds that everything will go well are lower than with RAM upgrades and about the same as with graphics-adapter upgrades. The physical issues with replacing a CD-ROM drive or hard disk are worse than with the other upgrades, though neither is all that hard if you simply proceed slowly and carefully. With a hard disk upgrade you typically do have to go through the process of formatting the drive and then loading it with whatever software and data you want on it. If minimizing effort is your goal, try these upgrades in this order:

> Tune Windows 98 or Windows 95
> Buy Windows 98 or Windows 95 tuning software
> Tune Windows NT

Buy more RAM
Replace your graphics adapter
Upgrade your processor
Replace your CD-ROM drive
Add a new hard disk

3.4. Using the Benchmarks to Decide How Much

Once you've decided you're going to do an upgrade and you know what you want to upgrade, you still have to figure out how far to go, how much performance to buy. Say you're sure you need a CD-ROM drive; should you get the fastest 32X CD-ROM drive? Or is the 24X model plenty? What processor upgrade should you buy? How much RAM is enough? These questions can drive you crazy.

The good news is that the chapters in Part III, "Hardware Optimization," of this book provide a way to quantify the answers to those questions. Between the hundreds of test results we provide and the ability to run the benchmarks yourself, you can decide just how much performance return different upgrade options will provide.

Suppose, for example, that your PC's processor is a fairly recent 200-MHz Pentium with MMX, and you're trying to decide how much RAM to buy. Turn to Chapter 9, "Optimizing Your System's RAM," find your version of Windows, and check on our studies for that processor (or the processor most like yours, if we haven't tested yours). Figure 3.1 shows a sample chart from Chapter 9 that looks at performance versus amount of RAM. This chart tells you that for such a machine running typical business applications, you should upgrade to at least 32MB of RAM. You could buy more, but the additional RAM probably won't be worth the additional expense.

3.5. Upgrading Multiple PCs

If you're trying to get the most performance from multiple systems, following these steps is even more important than with a single system. After all, the fact that you're dealing with many PCs magnifies everything: The money cost, the time cost, and the potential return. You consequently should spend more time evaluating just how much return each potential performance investment will deliver.

While we recommend that anyone considering an upgrade run the benchmarks on both their current system and the system as it would be after each prospective upgrade, we realize doing that is simply usually not possible. (Who wants to take back RAM once you've installed it?) We've structured much of this work so you can avoid that work. But, if you're considering upgrading multiple PCs, you should consider buying one example of each upgrade and measuring how much of a performance boost it produces. These measurements will take time, but they can save you the time—and cost—of doing useless or low-return upgrades on multiple PCs. You may, for example, want to spend some time measuring the speed boost you get from putting different amounts of RAM in a system.

Figure 3.1.

Business Winstone 97 performance versus RAM size for a PC with a 200MHz Pentium processor with MMX running Windows 95.

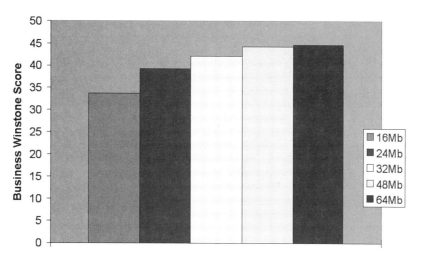

3.6. From Here...

In this chapter, we've given you some ideas of how you can use the information in this book and the benchmarks it includes to get the most performance from your current PC. In subsequent chapters we provide a great many test results and explain how you can use those results to get the most performance from your system. We also explain how to use the benchmarks to perform a more detailed performance analysis of your system.

Which of these chapters you go to from here depends a great deal on what you're trying to accomplish.

- Chapter 4, "Benchmarks and Buying New Systems," will show you how to use this book and the benchmarks if you're considering buying a new PC. This chapter will help you buy the best performing new system for your needs.

- The chapters in Part II, "Software Optimization," explain how to use the performance-optimization features of Windows 98, Windows 95, and Windows NT, respectively, to boost PC performance. These chapters are particularly helpful if you decide to try some software-based improvements.

Benchmarks and Your Current PC

■ The chapters in Parts III, "Hardware Optimization," and IV, "Special Situations," discuss the different PC subsystem and how much performance increase you can get by upgrading each of them. These chapters are chock full of test results that show real examples of the possible improvements you can achieve under Windows 98, Windows 95, and Windows NT.

■ Appendix A, "Using Winstone 98," will tell you how to install Winstone 98 and use it to gauge the overall speed of your PC.

■ Appendix B, "Using WinBench 98," will show you how to install WinBench 98 and use it to measure the performance of your PC's many subsystems.

Chapter

4

Benchmarks and Buying New Systems

A new PC is one of the more expensive purchases most people will make. Though PCs aren't in the same league as houses or cars, even cheap new ones cost as much as many high-end home-electronics components or pieces of furniture. A new PC is also something most of us hope we can keep for a while. Consequently, if you care at all about PC performance, you want the fastest system you can afford.

The trick is how you identify that system.

The marketplace isn't going to make this choice easy. Nowadays, it often seems like any store that can scare up a few spare feet of shelf space is going into the computer business. They're trying to compete with the already established direct mail- and Web-order vendors, such as Dell and Gateway, the screwdriver shops that assemble their own systems, the dedicated computer superstores, and on and on. Each store or vendor will offer you a wide variety of options at a broad range of prices. You can read spec sheets all day, but in the end you'll still have to make a lot of guesses.

Our goal in this chapter is to help you minimize the number of those guesses you have to make, and to help you make the smartest possible guesses when you do have to guess. In this chapter, you will learn:

- What to learn before you shop

- What are the technologies and issues you need to know before you shop, and where you can go to learn about them

- What steps to take before you shop

- What to do while you shop

- How to take charge of your shopping experience and not let sales pitches sway you

- A simple way to avoid some of the sales traps that await unsuspecting shoppers

- What to do if you are shopping for multiple PCs

- How to take advantage of the buying power you represent when purchasing multiple machines, and how you can get potential vendors to give you information and assistance they typically would not offer the buyer of a single PC

4.1. Cocktail Party Tips

No one's bashful when it comes to buying a new computer. Mention at a party that you're in the market for a new PC, and everyone will have an opinion about what you should do. Experience and expertise don't seem to be necessary; just about everyone who's ever touched a PC turns into a purchasing expert the moment the question arises.

This book will give you the expertise you need to make truly informed, accurate recommendations. Of course, to gain that expertise, you really have to read the whole book. Fortunately, we can get you started with some fact-based tidbits that will quickly make you more accurate than most of those who will offer their opinions.

Start by pointing out that there's no point to buying capabilities they don't need now and won't need for the life of the PC (probably two to five years). Unless they're playing a game of techie one-upmanship or simply must have every new technology, they shouldn't invest in anything they can't use now. Buying a PC DVD drive when they were first available, for example, would have left you with almost no software to play on a device that was likely to cause you problems and that would be outdated in months. (Remember, new technologies change faster than established ones.)

We're embarrassed to have to admit that we speak from experience on this example. We've already had to disable the DVD-playing capability of our first-on-the-block systems with DVD drives, because they caused the machines to crash frequently.

Instead, encourage people to be smarter than we were, and if they can at all manage to do so, wait a bit for newer technologies to settle out. You can almost always add such components later.

On the performance front, the best advice you can give most folks is to aim for the price/performance sweet spot. Tell them not to even try to get the fastest possible system, because they'll end up paying a hefty premium to get an extra five or ten percent more performance or capability. In practice, this rule usually means you should buy a PC that uses the second fastest processor available and that has plenty of RAM. The premium you have to pay to get the fastest available processor is rarely on par with the performance boost that chip will deliver.

A couple other useful specific tips that will apply to most folks: Don't go high-end for graphics, especially 3D graphics, adapters. A year from now today's hottest 3D card will feel old. Do buy a big disk, because you can never have enough disk space.

4.2. Be Informed

The best advice we can give about buying a new system is to be informed. Reading this book is a good start, but new technologies and issues are always appearing. To keep up on the current state of the PC art, our admittedly biased

Benchmarks and Buying New Systems

recommendation is that you read an issue or two of your favorite ZD publication. Such publications as *PC Magazine, Computer Shopper,* and *PC Computing* are treasure troves of product reviews and technology information. You can also find information from those publications and other sources on the Web at ZDNet, `www.zdnet.com`. Both these print and online sources provide reviews of the latest and greatest systems and components. And these sources get their performance results from the same benchmarks that we've included with this book! You'll thus be able not only to better understand their performance results, but also to run similar tests on your own.

Doing this reading before you begin shopping should give you a good handle on the latest performance and other PC issues. Though we cannot predict as we write this book exactly what those hot issues will be, you can be sure to find them in these sources.

4.3. Before You Shop

The next step you should take depends on whether you're buying your first PC.

If you are, check out the sources in the previous section and read some reviews of the latest and greatest PCs. Pay attention to their benchmark scores, and get an idea of the level of performance you can expect from the range of systems you can afford. You'll use that information in the next step, which we discuss in the following section.

If you're buying an additional or replacement PC, then you already have some experience with PC performance. After all, you use your current PC and have a sense of how well it performs, when it's too slow, and so on. You can use the benchmarks we've included with this book to quantify that sense. Run the benchmarks on your current system to see just how well it performs. Winstone 98 is the best choice for gauging your system's overall performance, so start with it. (See Appendix A, "Using Winstone 98," for details on using this benchmark.) Study the Winstone scores that most reflect the kind of work you do. If, for example, you primarily use common business applications such as WordPerfect and Excel, you can simply focus on the overall Business Winstone 98 score. If you instead have more specialized needs—perhaps you run Photoshop all day—use the closest applicable High-End Winstone score.

> **NOTE**   If your PC's processor is slower than a 66MHz 486, don't bother to benchmark your system. Much as we hate to be the ones to say it, your current system is slow and anything you buy will feel wonderfully fast.

By having these scores, you'll be able to see just how much faster a new PC is likely to be. As we mentioned in the last section, you can look through ZD's magazines and Web site and see how typical current PCs are scoring on the benchmarks. Compare those results to the scores of your PC, and you'll have a pretty good idea of how much faster a new system would be for the kind of work you do. PCs evolve so quickly that the odds are good that you'll find that a new system might easily double or triple your current overall performance.

4.4. Going to the Store

The final step is to start shopping. We'll refer to it as going to the store, but the same principles apply if you're buying from a direct vendor by calling an 800 number or filling in a form on a Web page. Your goal at this step is to get the most performance you can afford. The key to doing that is to determine *before* you buy a system just how well that system performs on the benchmarks. If you can get that information, you'll be able both to see how the new system's performance would compare to that of your current PC (if you have one) and how it compares to the speed of other systems you could buy.

Armed with this information, you can use the benchmarks themselves to make these comparisons. Both Winstone 98 and WinBench 98 let you compare test scores directly in a tabular form in their results viewer. You can also export results into an Excel spreadsheet; Figure 4.1 shows an example of some exported Winstone results. (See Appendix A for information on how you can export Winstone 98 results.) After you have the results in Excel, you can do whatever you want with the numbers. You can graph them or decide to divide the results by the price or make any other calculations that would help you make your decision.

The tricky part about all this, the part we've entirely avoided so far, is how you get the benchmark results for a system you haven't purchased yet.

The answer is to be demanding and show no fear.

If a store has some systems that interest you, take the Winstone 98 CD-ROM from the back of this book to the store and ask the people there to let you run the benchmark on their PCs. If they balk, point out that you can find PCs at a lot of other places just as easily. You can also sell them by offering to share your results; it'll probably be the first time they've ever really known how well their PCs perform. You can either bring a diskette of previous results with you to the store or just take home these results on an empty diskette. Once home, you can pore over them at your leisure.

This approach will obviously not make the salespeople love you. It will, however, save you from having to listen to a salesperson drone on about how fast this or that PC is. You will instead have hard facts on which to base your purchase decision. You can even do the salespeople a favor (plug alert!): If they ask about the benchmarks, send them to the ZDBOp Web site (`www.zdbop.com`) or tell them to buy this book, and they can have their own copies.

Figure 4.1.

Winstone 98 lets you compare in Excel the results from its tests on your PC to those of systems you are considering buying.

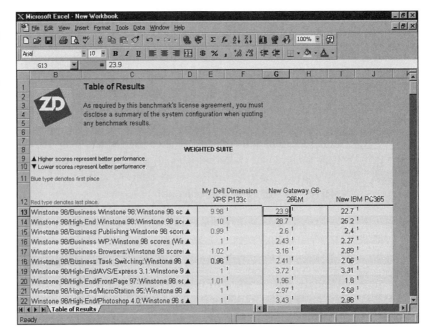

If you're considering buying a PC via the Web or mail order, you obviously can't benchmark that system yourself. You can, however, request benchmark results from the vendors whose products you're evaluating. You do need to be explicit and cite the settings under which they should generate the Winstone 98 results. The good news is that most vendors today already have Winstone results for all their leading configurations.

The reason specifying settings is important is that you should always make apples-to-apples comparisons when you're evaluating PC performance. To pick an extreme example, you wouldn't want to be unwittingly comparing the bench-mark results of a PC with 8MB of RAM with those of a PC with 64MB, even if the PCs had the same processor, because the comparison would make no sense. You would basically be measuring the performance difference RAM can cause rather than any intrinsic performance differences between the two machines.

That level of error is fairly easy to catch, but more subtle ones can still affect performance. If you're not careful, for example, you might find yourself compar-ing the performance of two systems running at different color depths. For accurate data, work hard to make sure the systems you compare have configura-tions that are as similar as possible.

4.5. Buying Multiple PCs

As useful and important as these steps are when you're buying one PC, they're even more valuable when you're preparing to purchase multiple systems. The money at stake is obviously higher, and so is the number of people your decision will affect. Put in the time to do a thorough job of performance evaluation, and you can save a lot of money—and avoid some upset users.

We obviously recommend that you run the benchmarks both on any existing systems you'll be replacing and on all your candidate new systems. You should also study the many results we present in this book for different PC configurations and even consider spending some time doing your own research. If you're not sure how much RAM to get for each system, for example, you might want to do a shorter version of the RAM experiments we discuss in Chapter 9.

You can also often get vendors to help you in these efforts. As a volume purchaser, you're more likely to command their attention than someone buying a single system. Where folks buying one PC will probably have to settle for whatever benchmark results the vendor already has on hand, you may well be able to demand that vendors provide results for the specific configurations you're considering. Many companies and government agencies regularly do exactly that. For a vendor to participate in their bidding processes, it must provide Winstone scores for its systems. This practice helps those groups—and can help you—make the best possible purchase decision.

4.6. From Here...

In this chapter, we've discussed some ways you can use the information in this book and the benchmarks it includes to buy the best-performing new PC you can afford. In subsequent chapters we cover every major PC subsystem and how you can measure its performance. We also explain how to use the benchmarks to analyze in depth the performance of any your system you're considering purchasing.

Which chapters you should read next depends on what you're trying to accomplish.

- The chapters in Parts III, "Hardware Optimization," and IV, "Special Situations," discuss the different PC subsystems and how you can measure their performance. With this information you can choose the best-performing components for every PC subsystem, as well as evaluate overall system performance.

- Appendix A, "Using Winstone 98," will tell you how to install Winstone 98 and use it to gauge the overall speed of any PC you're considering buying.

Benchmarks and Buying
New Systems

■ Appendix B, "WinBench 98," will show you how to install WinBench 98 and use it to measure the performance of the many subsystems of any PC you're considering purchasing.

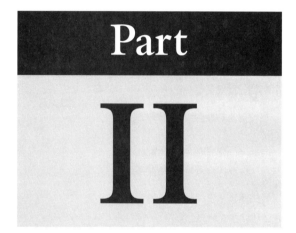

Part

II

Software Optimization

Chapter 5

Windows 98 Software Tuning

The transition to Windows 95 from Windows 3.1 was a software revolution. Windows 95 was the result of years of development and was very different, both externally and internally, from its predecessor.

The transition to Windows 98 from Windows 95, by contrast, is simple software evolution in action. The two versions of Windows are very similar operating systems that share a common code base. If you think of Windows 98 as Windows 95 plus a bunch of bug fixes and Internet Explorer, you won't be far wrong. (Yes, before Microsoft can sic its PR people on us, there's more to Windows 98 than that, but not tons more.)

Because Windows 98 and Windows 95 share the same basic internal architecture, they share many performance characteristics. It should come as no surprise, then, that many of the software-only tuning tips we'll give you in this chapter will also appear in Chapter 6, "Windows 95 Software Tuning," which focuses on ways you can improve the performance of a Windows 95 PC. Windows 98 does improve on Windows 95 by taking care of many of the software tuning tasks you used to have to do manually, but you can still tweak some tuning options to maximize your PC's performance.

To learn which options to tweak—and which aren't worth your time—read on. In this chapter, you will learn:

- How your PC's operating system plays a key role in its overall performance

   Windows 98 is more than just the interface between you and your computer. You'll learn how to work with the OS to get the most possible performance from your PC.

- How much of a performance boost you can realistically expect from your Windows 98 tuning efforts

   Windows 98 actually does a decent job of managing its own performance options. You certainly can tune it to maximize your PC's performance, and we encourage you to do so, but it's good to start those efforts with realistic expectations.

- What safe and easy tuning options are useful for everyone

   Some tuning options are so simple and so useful that everyone with a few minutes to spare should take advantage of them. You will learn about such options, including how defragmenting your hard disk and downloading the right graphics device drivers can speed up your system.

- What specialized options for tuning you may want to investigate

   Some software tuning options, such as those involving your PC's CD-ROM drive or its BIOS, won't help every PC equally. You'll learn what these are, whether they apply to your PC, and how to take advantage of them.

■ Some performance myths and the truths behind them

Some Windows 98 tuning ideas look good and get a lot of lip service by many users, but when we put them to the benchmark test, they just didn't pan out. You'll learn which ideas to avoid and thus save your time.

■ How some software utilities can help you keep your PC running well

Not all the Windows 98 software optimizations you can do come for free with the operating system. To get some of them, you have to use special utilities, utilities you must either buy or download from the Web. You will learn about some key utilities and how you can use them to boost your PC's speed.

5.1. Cocktail Party Tips

Everybody loves free stuff, and nowadays it seems like everybody loves the Web. The next time you're at a party and someone asks for performance tips, you can capitalize on both these trends by bringing up software optimization.

Start with disk optimization. Many people go months or years without defragmenting their disks, and disk fragmentation can slow a system. Your PC runs best when all the pieces of each of your file are in order on your disk. As you change files over time, however, pieces of those files can end up scattered, or fragmented, across the disk. Defragmenting the disk is the process of running a special piece of software—the defragmentation utility, or defragmenter—that puts those file pieces back together so your PC can read them from disk faster. Windows 98 comes with a free disk defragmenter, so all you have to do is tell it to run.

If you really want to show off, you can point out that the defragmenter in Windows 98 is actually better than the one in Windows 95, because this new one can re-order the files of your applications so those programs start faster.

Graphics device drivers should be your next target—and your chance to hook into the Web. You can often increase PC performance just by downloading a new graphics device driver, and those drivers are available free on the Web.

You can also point questioners to CD-ROM caching options and some performance-optimization utilities.

Do yourself and your friends a favor, however, and set their expectations correctly. For most folks, none of these changes is likely to yield a huge performance boost. Though exceptions do exist—a heavily fragmented and very full disk have a friend's PC crawling—most of these changes will yield only small improvement. If you or any of your friends want the best possible performance, though, you should definitely look into software tuning options.

5.2. The Role of the Operating System

An operating system (OS) is software that controls how your computer works. It provides to applications services like writing to the disk, displaying menus on the screen, and generally controlling the hardware that makes up your computer. There is a lot more to a modern operating system than the obvious software that controls the hardware. The OS really includes device drivers and even the BIOS. All of this software is between your application and the hardware and thus can have a noticeable impact on performance.

There are many operating systems, but the most popular ones for microcomputers are Windows and Mac OS. Versions of the UNIX operating system are also available for microcomputers. Differences between operating systems used to be more obvious: a DOS machine presented the old C:\ prompt, a UNIX machine presented an even more cryptic command prompt, while the Mac OS machine used a graphical interface. Nowadays, most popular operating systems have some type of graphical interface, and Windows (in all its forms) is easily the most popular operating system for microcomputers.

If most operating systems look similar now, with trashcans or recycle bins for deleted files, with desktops strewn with icons, are they all the same? No. The real differences between operating systems are hidden behind the scenes, in how the operating systems implement multitasking, security, and performance enhancements such as disk caching.

Because most things your applications do require the operating system to intervene, it can have a major role in performance. The OS can both speed things up such as by handling disk caching or slow things down by doing things inefficiently. In this chapter we'll be looking at the performance enhancements that Windows 98 implements, and we'll look at ways to tweak them to optimum levels.

5.3. What to Expect

We will admit up front that you should not expect big performance gains from software tuning. Windows 98 improves somewhat on the automatic tuning that Windows 95 performs, and Windows 95 does a decent job in most performance areas. Windows 98 also does not expose many options for you to work with.

Finally, software tuning tends to be more system specific so we cannot offer as much blanket advice as we can in other chapters of this book.

This last point means that we could not run the benchmarks as much in these software chapters as we did elsewhere. We picked some examples where we could and in other places we give you ideas that you can investigate yourself on your system. You will potentially have options on your system that are not available on other computers. If you want to get the full benefit of software tuning, you will have to do some experimentation for yourself. The good thing about the benchmarks included with this book is that you can know what impact any changes you might make are having.

5.4. What to Do First

The biggest piece of useful advice we can give is to be careful when making changes to your system. This is true whether you are trying performance experiments or just installing a new application. The first part of that is to back up your system before making any changes. This means not just your data, but your Registry settings and things you can't save electronically such as your BIOS settings. Those you need to write down and store in a safe (where you will remember) place.

We assume you already know how to back up your files, but you may not be aware of all of the important information stored in the Registry. The Registry is a part of Windows that keeps track of things for applications and Windows itself. These things can be everything from your current sound settings to application file locations to your Minesweeper top score. Some back up programs don't save this information and your system will not be the same without it. After all, it took you months to get your Minesweeper expert score under 60 seconds.

Particularly before you make changes to software settings on your system, make sure to back up critical system files and your Registry. If you accidentally change a Registry setting, you'll save yourself a lot of hair pulling and wasting time by having copies to fall back on.

You can back up your system with the Backup program that Windows 98 provides, or with one of the many popular backup programs available from third-party vendors—these backup programs typically support a wider variety of backup media. Whatever you do, make sure that your backup program saves all of you system files, including the Registry.

5.5. Optimizations for the Masses

Much of this chapter is about optimizations to avoid, and areas that might prove fruitful for some people. The tuning options in this section, however, apply to almost everyone. Not only that, but these are pretty safe and have few, if any, downsides. So feel free to read these and run right out and implement them.

5.5.1. Putting the Disk Pieces back Together

Whether you like it or not, your hard disk is suffering from disk fragmentation. Don't worry, disk fragmentation doesn't mean your hard drive is actually breaking into separate pieces. It's a state that naturally occurs on your computer as you read, write and delete files over time. On a pristine, unfragmented system, all files are stored in contiguous (in a row) areas on the disk. In other words, the bytes that make up a particular file are stored on the disk right next to each other. Contrast this to a fragmented hard disk, where the bytes that make up a file are scattered all over the hard disk. Windows 98 handles this condition as part of the file system, so it can find all the separate pieces and present them to, say, your word processing application as one file. But the fact that the hard disk subsystem has to search for and then retrieve the pieces of the file from all over the disk means a performance hit for you.

You can't stop fragmentation from occurring; it's going to happen due to the way the Windows 98 file system works. (Windows 98 is not unique in this failing; most operating systems suffer from disk fragmentation.) The Windows 98 file system is based on the FAT file system from DOS. Windows 98 actually can use one of two FAT file systems, either FAT16 or FAT32. We'll look at FAT32 later on in this chapter. In the FAT file system, files are stored in units on your disk known as clusters or allocation units. In turn, these clusters are made up of a certain number of sectors on your hard drive. The operating system looks at the hard drive in terms of clusters, while the hard drive itself (and its associated controller hardware) looks at the physical disks in terms of sectors.

The operating system divides a particular file that you want to save into clusters on your hard drive. Many times, these clusters are contiguous. The file is not fragmented as it's written to disk. However, that's not always the case. When you delete a file, the clusters it used to occupy become available. Let's say you just deleted a 30KB file and then you want to write a 50KB file. It's quite likely that the operating system will begin writing the 50KB file into the 30KB hole (and again, the hole will really be a multiple of the cluster size). After it has filled that hole, though, there'll still be about 20KB of the file left to write. It will then have to skip along on the hard disk until it finds more room to write the rest of the file. Thus, this file will be fragmented. Because you're constantly reading, writing, and deleting files, fragmentation is the natural result of the FAT16 and FAT32 file systems.

So, you can't stop fragmentation. You can, however, reverse its effects. Windows 98 provides a utility called Disk Defragmenter that can defragment all the files on your hard drive. In other words, it hunts for fragmented files and moves their data around until every file on your machine is contiguous and unfragmented. If you haven't paid attention to disk fragmentation, it might take quite a while to defragment your disk.

Windows 95 included Disk Defragmenter, but the Disk Defragmenter in Windows 98 is truly new and improved. Disk Defragmenter in Windows 98 also can increase your application-loading speed. Using technology licensed from Intel, the Windows 98 Disk Defragmenter monitors the way your programs start up: which files and DLL's load in what order. By tracking this information, Windows 98 can re-order the clusters on your disk so that clusters for a particular program load in sequence. Normally, blocks of code and data for a particular program don't load in the order in which they're stored on disk. The defragmentation technology built into Windows 98 improves this situation.

Of course, none of this is of any use unless you defragment your disk regularly. To defragment your disk, do the following:

1. Bring up the Start menu.

2. Choose the Programs option to bring up the Programs menu.

3. Choose the Accessories option to bring up the Accessories menu.

4. Now, instead of choosing Games like you normally do, choose the System Tools option.

5. Click on Disk Defragmenter. This starts the Disk Defragmenter program.

6. Disk Defragmenter will prompt you to specify which drive you'd like to defragment. This will likely be your C: drive. Click on the OK button. You can also choose All Hard Drives if you have more than one hard drive or partition.

After you've clicked OK, Disk Defragmenter will check the fragmentation of the drive you've selected. If the drive is significantly fragmented, defragmentation begins immediately. If the drive is only slightly fragmented, Disk Defragmenter suggests that you don't need to defragment the disk at this time. You can still click on the Start button to have the program completely defragment your disk. To see the details, click on the Show Details button (see Figure 5.1).

Because disk fragmentation affects performance, part of the standard testing procedure used for all of the studies in this book is to completely defragment the hard disk before every test run. We suggest that you make this a part of your standard testing procedure too. Even if you're not going to run benchmark tests on a particular machine, you should still ensure that the disk is defragmented on a regular basis. We defragment our hard disks weekly.

Because this is our standard procedure, we were hard pressed to find any machines that were fragmented. Our test machines are carefully set up and defragmented so often that we rarely see fragmentation of more than 1% or 2% at most. Consequently, we don't actually run tests on fragmented versus defragmented machines in this chapter. If you've had your PC for a long time and never defragmented it, you'll likely see a much higher level of fragmentation. We really can't give you a good figure for the value of defragmentation, but given that it is so easy to do, you would do well to follow that procedure.

Figure 5.1.

The Show Details option of the Windows 98 Disk Defragmenter shows the progress of your hard disk's defragmentation in graphical form.

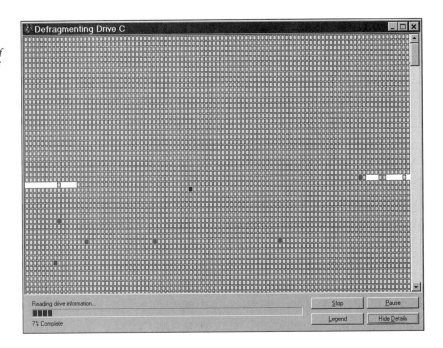

One way to ensure that your disk stays defragmented is to use the Task Scheduler included with Windows 98. The Task Scheduler is a scheduling program that runs in the background, starting up other tasks as necessary. In Windows 98, the Task Scheduler is one of the default icons in the system tray. You can set up the Task Scheduler by double-clicking its icon in the system tray.

5.5.2. Graphics Drivers

Another type of software that affects Windows 98 PC performance is the device driver. Though all device drivers can affect performance, graphics-adapter drivers can have such a big effect and change so often that they deserve special mention.

Device drivers are so important because they're the software pieces that serve as the interfaces between the operating system and the hardware on which it's running. By using device drivers, the OS doesn't have to contain special code for every possible hardware configuration. Instead, it can interface with drivers via standard application programming interfaces (API), and let the drivers directly handle all the vagaries of the hardware.

Windows 98 has the same device driver architecture as Windows 95. So, if you're upgrading your PC from Windows 95 to Windows 98, you probably already have all of the drivers your system needs.

If you're buying a new PC that already has Windows 98 installed, it will almost certainly come with drivers for all the hardware on it. Like most modern operating systems, Windows 98 includes drivers for a large range of hardware. By having these drivers built-in, Windows 98 lets most users avoid having to hunt for drivers for all the pieces of hardware in their systems.

The problem is that the drivers Windows 98 contains may well not give the best possible performance. No one is to blame for this situation. The fact is that graphics-adapter vendors are constantly changing their drivers, and the new drivers are typically—though not always—faster than the older ones. The drivers in Windows 98 were probably fairly current as of the date Microsoft released the operating system to manufacturing, but new drivers almost certainly have appeared since that date.

In Chapter 10, "Optimizing Your Graphics Subsystem," we'll discuss your PC's graphics subsystem in depth, but let's concentrate now on the graphics drivers. To change the graphics drivers on your PC, do the following:

1. Right-click on an empty portion of your Windows 98 desktop.

2. Click on the Properties selection of the pop-up menu.

3. The Display Properties sheet will appear. Click on the Settings tab.

4. Click the Advanced button. The properties sheet for your particular display adapter will appear. Click on the Adapter tab (see Figure 5.2).

5. To change the graphics driver, click the Change button.

6. The Update Device Driver Wizard will appear. If you simply follow its instructions and click the Next button when it tells you to do so, Windows 98 will search for a better driver for you.

7. If you want to install a new graphics driver that you've downloaded or have on floppy disk or CD-ROM, do the following. When that wizard appears, toggle the radio button labeled Display a list of all the drivers in a specific location, so you can select the driver you want, then click the Next button.

8. Now, click on the Have Disk button to install the drivers you want from a floppy disk or from a directory on your hard disk to which you downloaded the drivers.

Figure 5.2.

The Display properties sheet allows you to install a new graphics device driver.

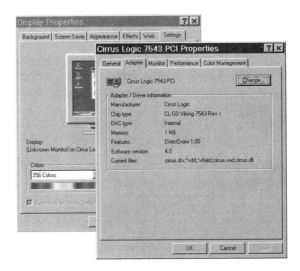

Now that you know how to install a new graphics driver, it's time to get one. The best place to acquire the driver for your PC's graphics adapter is from the Web site of the vendor that made the adapter. All major graphics-adapter vendors maintain both Web sites and ftp sites from which you can download their latest drivers. Here's a list of some of the more popular graphics board vendors and their Web sites:

ATI Technologies	www.atitech.ca
Diamond Multimedia Systems, Inc.	www.diamondmm.com
Genoa Systems Corporation	www.genoasys.com
Hercules Computer Technology, Inc.	www.hercules.com
Matrox Electronic Systems Ltd.	www.matrox.com
Number Nine Visual Technologies	www.nine.com
NVIDIA Corporation	www.nvidia.com
STB Systems, Inc.	www.stb.com

To show the effects of changing graphics drivers, we used a Windows 98 PC with a 166MHz Pentium processor, 32MB of RAM, and a Matrox MGA Millenium graphics board. We ran Business Winstone 98 to see if changing the drivers had a measurable effect on the performance of real-world applications. To check out how the performance of the graphics subsystem changed with different drivers, we also ran the Graphics WinMark tests from WinBench 98. We first ran tests using the drivers from the Matrox Web site. (The most recent version of these drivers were dated late 1997, so they weren't even that recent.) We then ran the same tests with the graphics drivers that Windows 98 provided for this adapter.

Consequently, the old or "before" drivers in this little study were the ones from the Matrox Web site, while the new or after drivers were those Windows 98 provided (see Figure 5.3).

Figure 5.3.

Business Winstone 98 results for the Pentium 166 machine, before and after updating to the graphics drivers bundled with Windows 98.

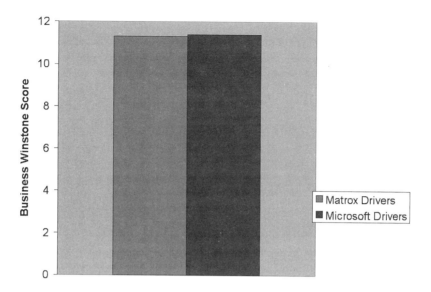

Windows 98 Software Tuning

The Business Winstone 98 results in Figure 5.3 show no improvement. The minuscule increase in the Winstone score is far below the normal level of variability for Winstone.

The individual Business Winstone 98 category scores in Figure 5.4 tell much the same story as the overall score. None of the application categories show a gain that's above the level of variability for Winstone. These results and the overall Business Winstone score suggest that typical business applications, such as those in Winstone 98, won't perform better with these new drivers.

Figure 5.4.

Business Winstone 98 category scores for the Pentium 166 machine, before and after updating to the graphics drivers bundled with Windows 98.

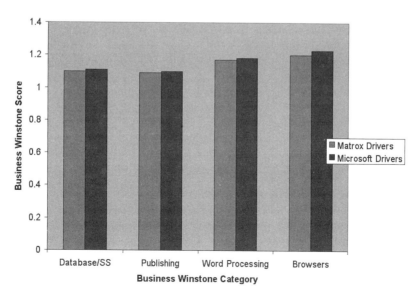

As we discussed in Chapter 2, "Benchmarks and You," however, overall performance isn't always the whole story. If you care a lot about graphics performance, you can often profit by looking at what's happening in the graphics subsystem alone. The right tool for that job is WinBench 98, specifically its Graphics WinMark tests. These tests play back the actual graphics operations from the Winstone applications but eliminate all of the other activity in Winstone. Their results, therefore, tell you how just the graphics subsystem is doing.

As we've mentioned previously, we did the Windows 98 testing in this book using Winstone 98 on a pre-release version of Windows 98. Because of this unavoidable setup—as we write this, Windows 98 has only recently gone gold and is not yet shipping—we were unable to get scores for the Task-Switching tests under Windows 98. This problem is the reason the graph in Figure 5.5 contains results for all of the Business Graphics WinMark categories except the Task Switching category. (This problem should not reflect poorly on Windows 98 or on Winstone and WinBench 98; problems like this happen when you test pre-release or freshly released software.)

Figure 5.5.

Graphics WinMark 98 results for the Pentium 166 machine, before and after updating to the graphics drivers bundled with Windows 98.

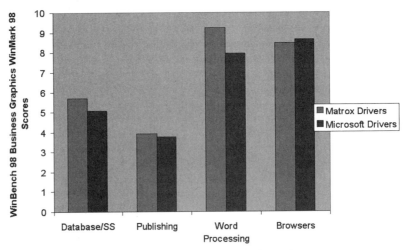

As you can see in Figure 5.5, the Business Graphics WinMark category scores tell a different story from the Winstone 98 scores. The Matrox drivers are clearly the better performers here, with only the Browser category showing no significant difference between the two graphics drivers. The Word Processing category gains a whopping 14% in performance with the Matrox drivers.

When you dig into the High-End Graphics WinMark scores in Figure 5.6, the overall improvement is not as large as it was with the Business Graphics category scores, but the Matrox drivers are still over 4% faster than the Microsoft drivers.

Looking at the individual application scores in the High-End Graphics WinMark 98 tests in Figure 5.7 gives you some of the reasons why.

Figure 5.6.

Graphics WinMark 98 results for the Pentium 166 machine, before and after updating to the graphics drivers bundled with Windows 98.

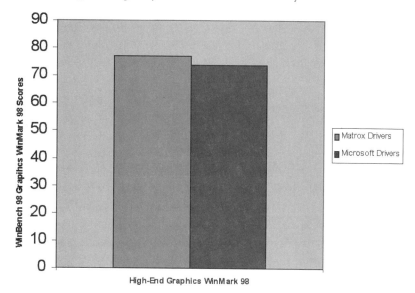

Figure 5.7.

Graphics WinMark 98 results for the Pentium 166 machine, before and after updating to the graphics drivers bundled with Windows 98.

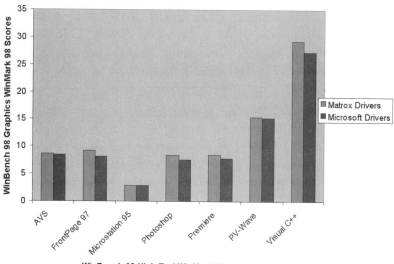

Some applications, like Microstation 95, are completely unperturbed by the driver change. FrontPage 97 and Photoshop show the greatest performance increase with the Matrox drivers. In none of the cases are the results with the Microsoft drivers better than those with the Matrox drivers.

We picked this particular example to illustrate two key points. First, don't expect the default graphics adapter drivers in Windows 98 to be particularly great.

Windows 98 Software Tuning

Though such drivers may have recent dates, they are often just first-cut attempts from vendors. As they did with Windows 95 drivers, vendors will start releasing updated, and typically faster, drivers for Windows 98 when the new operating system catches on with buyers. Consequently, you should watch the Web site of your graphics-adapter vendor for new, Windows 98–specific drivers, and try them out when they're available.

The second point is that you should base decisions on test results, not on such simple things as release dates. Newer drivers aren't always better, even though they usually are. To be sure, use the benchmarks we included with this book.

5.5.3. Windows 98 Graphics Performance Setting

There is another place to look for possible performance improvements to your graphics drivers. This setting is on the System Properties Performance tab. To get to this tab, do the following:

1. Choose Control Panel from the Settings section on your Start menu.

2. Double-click on the System Control Panel to open it.

3. Click on the Performance tab.

4. Click on the Graphics button in the Advanced settings section. This displays the Advanced Graphics Settings dialog box (see Figure 5.8).

Figure 5.8.

The Advanced Graphics Settings dialog box lets you turn your graphics performance to its maximum.

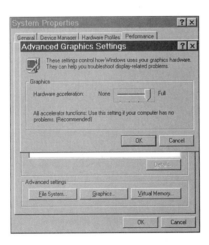

There's a single slider control on this dialog box that allows you to adjust graphics hardware acceleration from None to Full. Windows 98 defaults to leaving this setting on Full and that's where we recommend you leave it too. This setting is mainly useful for troubleshooting problems you might be having with your graphics subsystem. If you feel that you aren't getting the graphics performance you expect, though, you might want to check this setting to ensure that you or your system vendor did not accidentally leave it at something other than full acceleration.

5.5.4. Eliminate 16-bit Device Drivers

We've already stressed the importance of checking for and installing newer drivers for your graphics board. Keeping drivers up to date is a task that extends to all of the hardware in your system, though. The main thing you want to ensure is that all of the drivers in use are 32-bit drivers designed for use with Windows 98, *not* 16-bit drivers.

Windows 98 bundles 32-bit device drivers for a vast array of hardware: graphics adapters, multimedia devices, disk controllers, etc. However, there's still plenty of legacy hardware or cutting-edge hardware that requires drivers that don't come with Windows 98. If Windows 98 can't find a new device driver for a particular piece of hardware during installation, it will use the previous 16-bit device driver that you already have on your system. This driver will be slower and possibly lacking in advanced features.

5.6. Specialized Optimizations

Not all software optimizations are equally applicable to all people. The ones we will look at in this section are specialized because they will not be encountered all the time, such as software optimizations to speed up your CD-ROM access. Others are specialized because they vary from one system to another such as making any modifications to your system's BIOS. Even though these performance optimizations are less general-purpose than the ones in the previous section they are still worth looking into for most people.

5.6.1. The CD-ROM Cache

Windows 98 caches data for the CD-ROM drive in the same way that it caches data for the hard disk. Of course, it can only perform read-ahead caching in the case of the CD-ROM drive, because you can't write data to the CD-ROM drive. Your CD-ROM cache is separate from your hard disk cache. As a matter of fact, the cached CD-ROM data in RAM can be swapped out to the swap file on your hard disk. This would obviously be useless and redundant for cached hard disk data in RAM, but it still works for the CD-ROM drive because your hard disk is still significantly faster than your CD-ROM drive (and in turn, RAM is faster than your hard drive).

As with the hard disk cache, you have some control over the size of the read-ahead buffer used for the CD-ROM cache. In fact, adjusting the size of this cache is one of the software configuration tweaks that you can and should do to improve performance. CD-ROM drive speeds are typically given as 1X, 2X, 4X, 8X, and so on. This industry standard terminology can be somewhat confusing and misleading (as you'll learn in Chapter 12, "Optimizing Your CD-ROM Subsystem"). A single-speed (1X) CD-ROM drive can read a sequential stream of data at the same speed as your audio CD player—150KB per second (KB/s). A 2X CD-ROM drive can read data at twice this rate, or 300KB/s. This speed improvement is accomplished by spinning the disc at a higher speed. Obviously, the faster CD-ROM drives would need larger read-ahead buffers, because they can access more data per unit time.

You should double-check that the CD cache settings are set properly for your CD-ROM drive. You can change this setting to have Windows 98 optimize caching for single-speed, double-speed, triple-speed, and quadruple-speed or higher CD-ROM drives. To get at these settings, do the following:

1. Choose Control Panel from the Settings section on your Start menu.

2. Double-click on the System Control Panel to open it.

3. Click on the Performance tab.

4. Click on the File System button in the Advanced settings section. This displays the File System Properties dialog box.

5. Click on the CD-ROM tab (see Figure 5.9).

Figure 5.9.
The CD-ROM Performance dialog box allows you to set the size of your CD-ROM drive's read-ahead cache.

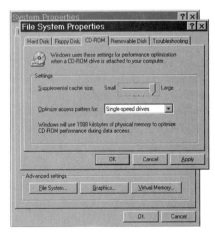

On this dialog box, you'll see two controls. One is a slider allowing you to adjust the Supplemental cache size from small to large, and the other is a drop-down box allowing you to specify the speed of the CD-ROM drive for which you want Windows 98 to optimize access. You should definitely adjust the Optimize access pattern for setting to match the speed of your CD-ROM drive. On most newer systems, that will simply be Quad-speed or higher. After you've told

Windows 98 what speed drive you have, you can then adjust the cache size from small to large. Both of these controls work in tandem to calculate the actual cache size that Windows 98 will use, from a minimum of 64KB to a maximum of 1238KB (if you set it for Quad-speed or higher and Large).

We set out to test the CD-ROM caching by running the CD-ROM WinMark 98 test from WinBench 98. The CD-ROM WinMark 98 test measures the performance of a PC's CD-ROM subsystem by playing back CD-ROM operations. These CD-ROM operations are the actual ones performed by six real-world applications.

We tested at two CD-ROM cache settings: the minimum setting, and the maximum cache size. The minimum setting corresponds to a Supplemental cache size of Small and Optimize access pattern for set to No read-ahead. This actually sets the CD-ROM cache size to 64KB. The maximum cache size corresponds to a Supplemental cache size of Large and Optimize access pattern for set to Quad-speed or higher. This sets the CD-ROM cache size to 1238KB. (Obviously, we did this because the CD-ROM drives in our testbed were 4X drives or faster.) We tested on several different machines to see if the speedup (if any) caused by a larger cache was also dependent on processor type. We tested the Pentium 75 and Pentium 100 machines at 16MB RAM and the other machines at 32MB RAM. In the case of the Pentium 75 and Pentium 100 machines, we wanted to make sure that increasing the CD-ROM cache size didn't adversely affect performance of machines with minimal amounts of RAM. (To find out why we think 16MB is a minimal amount of RAM, turn to Chapter 9, "Optimizing Your System's RAM.")

Figure 5.10 shows that across the board, the systems showed between 14% and 18% improvement. As you can see, all of these machines got approximately the same percentage boost by using the maximum CD-ROM cache size. In fact, the overall scores for the CD-ROM WinMark 98 test on the different machines are very similar. This would indicate that CD-ROM performance on these machines is not tied directly to CPU speed. Not surprisingly, the CD-ROM drives in all but the Pentium 200MMX system are the same Compaq model.

There are a few things to consider here with this data. First, this was for 4X drives. Faster drives may well not experience the same benefit since the difference between the CD-ROM drive's speed and that of the hard drive and RAM will be less. You also may see other differences based upon the model and manufacturer of the CD-ROM drive. This is definitely an experiment you should try yourself as it is easy and free to do.

If you don't feel like doing this experiment, or if your system is similar to those we tested, just fix the setting for your CD-ROM Performance tab. Adjust the Supplemental cache size to Large, and set the Optimize access pattern for to match the speed of the CD-ROM drive in your PC. Of course, you won't see this boost unless you're running applications that use the CD-ROM drive. But, the cost is free and we see little potential for problems arising from changing this setting.

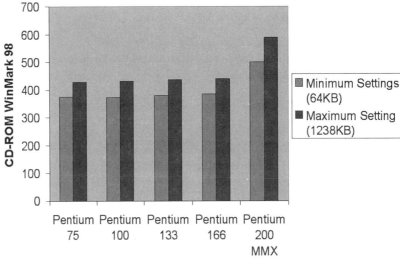

Figure 5.10.
CD-ROM WinMark 98 results for the different processor types at the minimum and maximum CD-ROM cache sizes

5.6.2. BIOS Settings

Every PC has a BIOS (Basic Input Output System). The BIOS is the code that runs when you first power on your computer, before the operating system takes control. It also acts as a basic, standardized interface to much of your PC's hardware. The BIOS is stored in some type of ROM (Read-Only Memory) device on your system motherboard.

Many different manufacturers, such as AMI, Award, and Phoenix produce BIOS software for use in motherboards. There is no one standard set of features offered by all BIOS's. Most folks ignore their BIOS completely, although most BIOS's offer a password option that some folks use. If you dig down deep into the BIOS, though, you're likely to find settings that affect hardware performance.

A word of warning here: you can really screw up your system if you change BIOS settings without knowing what you're doing. Even if you're confident about what you're doing, you should copy down all of your current BIOS setup on paper before you change anything. Although there are some potential benefits from investigating your BIOS settings, this section can be safely skipped by the faint of heart.

Going through a comprehensive list of all the possible BIOS settings you could change that affect performance is beyond the scope of this book. The best place for you to start is with your system manual or your motherboard manual if you have a separate motherboard manual. These manuals should explain the different BIOS options available in your PC. You might find that some are set for compatibility with older operating systems. After you've done that, a great place to find out more about BIOS issues is The BIOS Survival Guide, on the Web at `www.lemig.umontreal.ca/bios/bios_sg.htm`. So, while it's definitely possible to tweak the BIOS settings to your advantage only do so if you know what you are doing.

> **WARNING** Don't even think about changing your BIOS settings until you have studied your system manual or motherboard manual and until you have copied down all of your current BIOS settings on paper.

Here's a real-world example of how you can screw things up by monkeying with BIOS settings. We set out to test the performance gains possible on our Compaq Pentium 133 machine by only changing BIOS settings. One setting that caught our eye was PCI VGA SNOOP. This setting controlled whether or not the system snooped VGA palette writes on the PCI bus. Hey, it sounded like it might have some effect. So, we enabled this option and re-booted. Our display immediately went, in technical terms, kaflooey. The colors of the Windows startup screen were distorted, and after the startup screen vanished, our desktop did not appear. Luckily we've memorized the Windows keystrokes, so we were able to shut down the computer without benefit of the display. We quickly returned the PCI VGA SNOOP setting back to its original value.

A setting we did more serious investigation with had to do with the hard drive subsystem. It was Hard Drive DMA, and initially it was disabled. This is the default setting because it avoids incompatibilities with certain older disk caching software from the Windows 3.1 era. DMA stands for Direct Memory Access. DMA allows a certain peripheral device (say, the hard drive) to talk directly to system memory, without burdening the CPU chip with the transfer. It does this via a DMA controller chip or DMA circuitry. Because we were fairly confident that this setting would not interfere with our Windows 98 setup, we decided to investigate whether enabling hard drive DMA would improve real-world performance. It certainly sounded like it would.

We ran Business Winstone 98 on the Pentium 133 machine that had this BIOS option. We also ran the Disk WinMark tests from WinBench 98, to quantify the speed-up (if any) imparted to the disk subsystem by adjusting this setting.

The results shown in Figure 5.11 after we enabled hard drive DMA are not significantly different than those with the hard drive DMA disabled in the BIOS. To determine the real effects of this setting on the disk subsystem, we ran the Disk WinMark 98 tests from WinBench (see Figure 5.12). Remember, these tests play back the exact disk operations that the applications in Winstone perform, thus isolating disk subsystem performance.

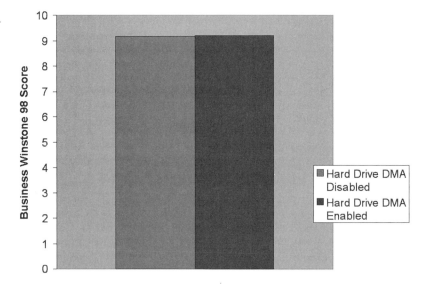

Figure 5.11.

Business Winstone 98 results for the Pentium 133 machine, before and after enabling hard drive DMA in the BIOS.

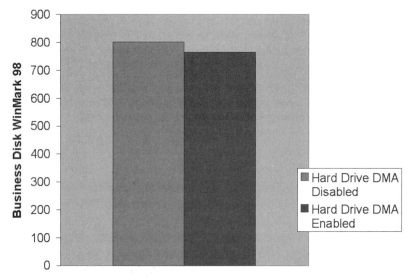

Figure 5.12.

Business Disk WinMark 98 results for the Pentium 133 machine, before and after enabling hard drive DMA in the BIOS.

Here we see a 5% drop in performance when we enable hard drive DMA. We'd get a performance decrease if we just enabled this setting without then doing benchmark testing! In this case of this particular machine, you should leave the hard drive DMA setting as it stands in the BIOS.

We've mentioned this previously, but we should emphasize it here again. The main conclusion that you should draw from these results is that it's important to do your own benchmark testing. While certain options and settings may sound tempting, don't just blindly adjust them without verifying that you're getting the performance boost you think you're getting.

We can't predict what settings will be available to you through your system's BIOS. We just want to let you know that it's possible to alter system performance by adjusting the BIOS settings, and if you really want to get all the performance out of your system, it's worth looking at the BIOS.

5.7. Debunking Some Myths

Not all the avenues we tried for this book produced performance benefits. Some of them turned out to be dead ends. Somewhat surprising to us was that some of the performance enhancements we thought might help or that we read about elsewhere turned out to not only not help, but in some cases, hurt performance. We share some of those with you here, not just to warn you away from them, but also to show you why it is important to investigate claims rather than just accept them blindly.

5.7.1. Disk Cache

Cache is one of the most important concepts to learn if you want to understand computer performance. (We'll talk about cache in the processor and RAM chapters as well.) In short, the concept of caching means storing the most needed information in a faster cache of data rather than a slower, larger area. Caching works because programs and operating systems don't access each byte of data on the hard disk in an equally probable manner. Certain pieces of information turn out to be the most important, and therefore the most popular. Caching takes the most popular data and puts it in a faster place—it avoids the performance bottleneck. In the case of disk cache, it moves the data from a hard disk to buffers in the system RAM.

There are two separate kinds of disk caching: read-ahead and write-behind. Windows 98 performs read-ahead caching in an attempt to predict the data you'll need from your hard drive. It loads this data into the disk cache (again, in RAM) and then if you do need the data that Windows 98 has predicted (*read-ahead*) then it'll be available in the faster disk cache. The other type of disk caching is write-behind, where data is buffered in the disk cache before actually being written out to the hard drive. The caching mechanism in Windows 98 then ensures that the correct data is actually written out to the hard drive in the background.

You have some control over both the read-ahead and write-behind caching that Windows 98 performs. To access the read-ahead caching settings, do the following:

1. Choose Control Panel from the Settings section on your Start menu.

2. Double-click on the System Control Panel to open it.

3. Click on the Performance tab.

4. Click on the File System button in the Advanced settings section. This displays the File System Properties dialog box (see Figure 5.13).

Figure 5.13.

The File System Properties dialog box allows you to set the read-ahead cache size.

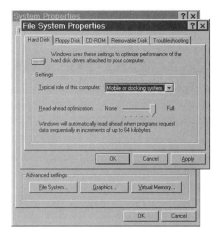

The two settings you can control are Typical role of this computer and the Read-ahead optimization. The choices for the role of the machine are Desktop computer, Mobile or docking system, and Network server. When you select one of these roles, Windows 98 will perform a normal, minimal, or maximum amount of caching respectively. Mobile systems are typically battery powered and so Windows 98 allows you to minimize caching on these systems to conserve power. Conversely, network servers usually spend most of their time doing hard disk access, so maximizing caching on these machines improves network performance.

The other setting on this dialog box is the Read-ahead optimization. This setting allows you to control how large a read-ahead buffer Windows 98 will use. Typically, this slider control is set all the way to the right, on Full, which means Windows 98 will read data into a 64KB buffer. You can also move this slider to the left to decrease the buffer size to 32KB, 16KB, 8KB, 4KB, and 0KB (in other words, no read-ahead caching).

The Read-ahead optimization setting controls the amount of memory Windows 98 will use when a program requests sequential data. In other words, how much further ahead of the program's request will be read into the disk cache, in anticipation. This setting can be adjust from 0KB (no read-ahead) to a maximum of 64KB. It is normally set to Full, which is the maximum setting.

Typical Role of this Computer

We've seen several magazine articles that claim you can improve performance even on your desktop machine by changing the Typical role of this computer setting to Network Server. We wanted to test this assertion out to see if it was worth doing. We ran Business Winstone 98 to see if these would prove correct or not. We ran with typical amounts of RAM, so that if shifting the percentage of disk cache versus application RAM space caused any performance differential, we'd be likely to spot it. (We did not use the corresponding Business Disk WinMark 98 because it does not vary if there is less RAM available for applications as that might confuse the results.)

The Typical role of this computer setting controls the overall size of the disk cache. On a desktop computer, the cache is set to a smaller size, to ensure that there's plenty of RAM left over for the applications you run on a typical desktop machine. When you set this to Network Server, Windows 98 uses more system RAM for the disk cache, leaving less RAM left over for use by applications. This makes sense for network servers because they are typically bottlenecked in the disk subsystem.

Figure 5.14 puts the lie to the assertion that you should change the role of your machine to server. These findings would make us reticent to recommend this change if you're running Windows 98. There appears to be little or no difference in performance, no matter what processor your machine is based around. As always, the bottom line to all of this is clear: Test on your own if you want to adjust a file system setting for optimal performance.

Figure 5.14.

Business Winstone 98 results for a variety of systems varying the Typical role of this computer setting.

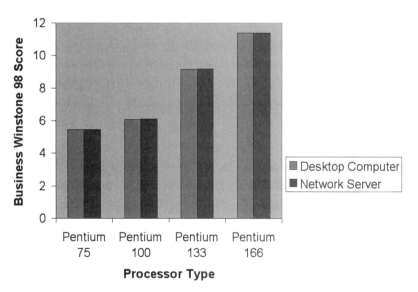

This conclusion brings us to one of the central conclusions of this chapter: always check out optimizations with real-world tests. Don't just do what some magazine or book tells you (OK, except for this book!) without benchmarking the before and after cases.

Read-ahead Caching

Another area that seems potentially ripe for optimization is that of read-ahead caching. We realize that on most systems, this setting is already set to the maximum, but we wanted to investigate the effects of read-ahead optimization on real-world, measurable performance. So, being the kind of guys we are, we ran Business Winstone 98 with the read-ahead optimization to 0KB (essentially turning it off) and to its normal maximum setting. We did this on a variety of systems with different processors.

As you can see in Figure 5.15, turning off the read-ahead optimization had no real impact on the Business Winstone 98 scores for any of the systems we tested. While it is possible that a different algorithm for reading ahead might lead to some performance differences, the options presented to us by Windows 98 leave little for us to hope for in the way of performance improvements in this area.

Figure 5.15.

Business Winstone 98 results for a variety of systems with read-ahead optimization on and off.

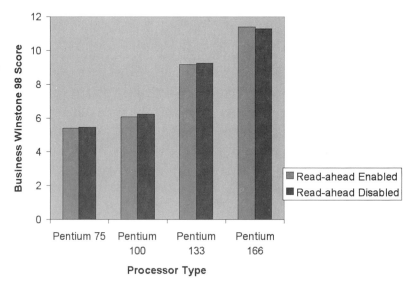

Write-behind Caching

Windows 98 does not allow you such finely grained control over write-behind caching. In fact, we don't recommend that you touch the write-behind setting unless you're troubleshooting a problem with your hard drive. You can access this control, however, by doing the following:

1. Choose Control Panel from the Settings section on your Start menu.

2. Double-click on the System Control Panel to open it.

3. Click on the Performance tab.

4. Click on the File System button in the Advanced settings section. This displays the File System Properties dialog box.

5. Click on the Troubleshooting tab (see Figure 5.16).

Figure 5.16.
*The File System
Properties
Troubleshooting
dialog box allows
you to disable
write-behind
caching, but we
do not recom-
mend you do so.*

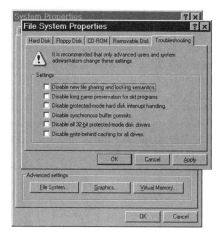

You'll now see six check boxes which allow you to disable certain features of the Windows 98 file system. One of these is Disable write-behind caching for all drives. If you check this box, Windows 98 will write data directly to the disk as opposed to buffering it in a RAM cache. We don't recommend disabling this option nor any of the other options on this tab—it is the aptly named Trouble-shooting tab, and we hope you never have to touch it.

5.7.2. The Swap File and Virtual Memory

Like most modern operating systems, Windows 98 implements virtual memory so that you can run programs that require more RAM than your PC contains. Windows 98 uses space on the hard disk to simulate additional RAM as needed by the applications you're using. This all goes on in the background, and as far as the application is concerned, it has the RAM it needs. Of course, it's not that simple or easy, because your hard disk is much slower than RAM. Windows 98 uses a swap file on your hard disk to simulate the virtual memory, and the transfer of data to or from the swap file is called *paging*. When Windows 98 decides to page, you'll know it—you'll wait while your hard drive buzzes along as your system seemingly does nothing. What's happening is that Windows 98 is moving data between RAM space and virtual memory space on your hard disk. The more RAM you have, the less paging Windows 98 has to do. To find out more about the amount of RAM you should have in your system, see Chapter 9.

Windows 98 uses a dynamic swap file, and the default setting is for Windows 98 to set up and use this file on its own. You can, however, change this default if you wish. If you attempt to do so, you'll see a dialog box advising you that these settings can adversely affect system performance and that they should be adjusted by advanced users and system administrators only. Unless you know what you're doing, you should heed this warning. Still, Windows 98 not only allows you to specify the minimum and maximum sizes for the swap file if you wish, it also allows you to disable virtual memory entirely. This is not recommended by Microsoft or by us, however. In fact, if you disable virtual memory entirely, it's likely that many of your applications, as well as the Windows operating system itself, will fail in mysterious and frustrating ways—when you're as obsessed with testing as we are, you learn things like this.

We've spotted magazines, books, and Web sites touting claims such as one that the default setting for Windows 98 Virtual Memory (Let Windows handle my virtual memory settings) does not yield the best performance. We decided to test out this suggestion to see if it's true. Here are the suggested actions that we heard about and followed:

1. Choose Control Panel from the Settings section on your Start menu.

2. Double-click on the System Control Panel to open it.

3. Click on the Performance tab.

4. Click on Virtual Memory (see Figure 5.17).

5. Choose Let me specify my own virtual memory settings.

6. Specify the same value for the minimum and maximum swap-file size. Calculate this value by multiplying the amount of real installed RAM by 2.5. In our case, we created a 40MB swap file on our 16MB machine.

7. Press OK, and then OK again, signifying that you want to restart your computer.

Figure 5.17.

The Virtual Memory Performance dialog box lets you tinker with your system's virtual memory settings.

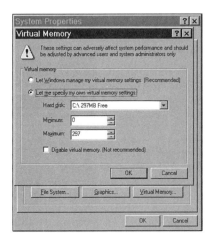

These actions were *supposed* to enhance system performance. We applied them to our Pentium 100 machine with 16MB RAM, and got the following results with Business Winstone 98, as shown in Figure 5.18.

Figure 5.18.

Business Winstone 98 results on the Pentium 100 machine, before and after the "recommended" swap-file setup changes.

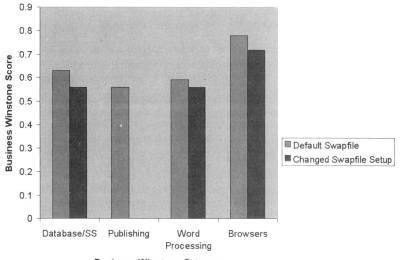

Wow! We're glad we didn't just follow these suggestions blindly. After we changed the swap-file setup, Business Winstone 98 failed because the Publishing category failed. Changing the swap-file setup caused some of the applications in Winstone to time out. While this doesn't necessarily mean that you'll have similar problems when you do day-to-day work with these same applications, it is not a good sign. Looking at the Winstone categories that did run to completion on both setups, we see that in all cases the default swap file performs better than the "recommended" swap-file setup. In the case of the Database/Spreadsheet category, performance dropped by eleven percent! We quickly returned our Pentium 100 machine back to its original state.

WARNING   Don't change your swap-file settings unless you're sure you know what you're doing. Changing swap-file settings can adversely affect system performance.

One situation where you might want to adjust the virtual memory settings is where you have more than one physical hard drive in your system. In this case, you may see some improvement by locating the swap file on a separate hard drive from the rest of your Windows files. We'll cover this situation in Chapter 11, "Optimizing Your Disk Subsystem." The short form of this section is just leave well enough alone. And, if you read a performance claim be skeptical and check it out like we did.

5.7.3. File system Issues

If you're upgrading to Windows 98 from Windows 95, you have a choice of file systems you can use. The file system is the scheme a particular operating system uses to organize the files on your hard disk. Different file systems offer different features; for instance, the file system in Windows NT allows you to set up security and permissions that are not available with the Windows 9x file systems. To learn more about file systems, check out Chapter 11.

The new file system available with Windows 98 is called FAT32. Microsoft designed FAT32 to improve on the existing Windows file system, known as FAT16. FAT16 organized your hard drive into clusters, and the cluster size varied with the size of the hard drive. Because even the tiniest file had to occupy at least one cluster, FAT16 was wasteful of disk space. FAT32 uses 4KB clusters no matter what the size of your hard disk is. This ends up saving hard disk space. Again, to learn more about clusters, see Chapter 11.

Windows 98 includes a FAT32 Conversion Tool that allows you to safely change the file system on your hard disk from FAT16 to FAT32. This change can definitely give you more hard disk space, because of the cluster size change. But does it give you any performance improvement? We used both Winstone 98 and the Disk Tests in WinBench 98 to find out (see Figure 5.19).

Figure 5.19.

Business Winstone 98 results for the Pentium 166 machine, before and after updating to the FAT32 file system.

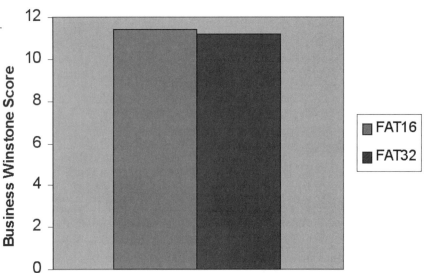

We see no performance improvement by upgrading to FAT32. The slight drop that's apparent on the graph is still below the level of variability for Winstone, so neither do we see a performance hit. Let's take a look at the Winstone category scores, shown in Figure 5.20, to see if there's any change there.

Figure 5.20.
Business Winstone 98 results for the Pentium 166 machine, before and after updating to the FAT32 file system.

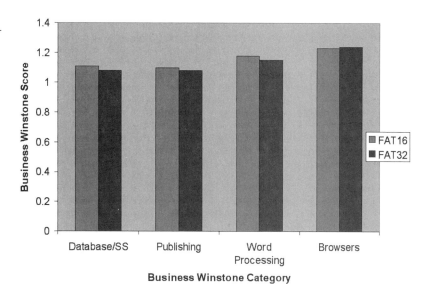

The variations are a little more apparent in the Winstone categories, but once again none of them are significantly greater than the level of variability for Winstone 98. We've seen plenty of cases where Winstone doesn't change, but the corresponding WinBench score does, though, so let's take a look at the WinBench Disk Tests (see Figure 5.21). It could be that any performance improvement caused by FAT32 is being masked by a bottleneck elsewhere in the system.

Figure 5.21.
WinBench 98 results for the Pentium 166 machine, before and after updating to the FAT32 file system.

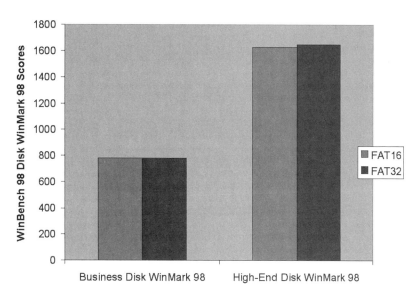

That turns out not to be the case here. The results for Disk WinMark 98 are almost exactly the same no matter what file system we use. For completeness sake, let's look at the business category and high-end application scores (see Figure 5.22).

Figure 5.22.

WinBench 98 results for the Pentium 166 machine, before and after updating to the FAT32 file system.

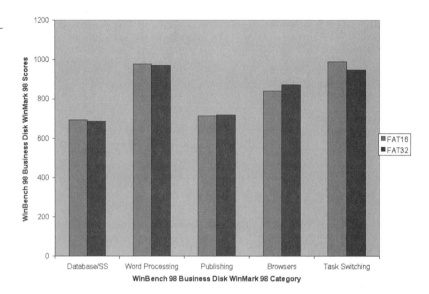

The category scores in the Business Disk WinMark tests show some slightly more interesting results. The Browsers category shows a 4% improvement after we move to FAT32. Unfortunately, the Task Switching category shows a 4% performance decrease when we switch to FAT32. Because we use Web browsers and we switch from task to task, these test results don't make us favor one file system over the other. Besides, a 4% boost isn't that much higher than the level of variability for Winstone, and might not be perceptible to the average user.

Finally, let's look at the High-End application scores from the Disk WinMark tests (see Figure 5.23). Here we see that most applications do not change when we upgrade to FAT32. Microstation 95 does show a 5% performance increase, so perhaps we should suggest FAT32 to all of you Microstation 95 users out there.

Actually, the final conclusion we draw is that performance just doesn't change much between FAT16 and FAT32. That's not a knock on FAT32, however, because FAT32 has desirable benefits other than performance. You can recover wasted disk space by upgrading to FAT32, so if you need more disk space (and who doesn't?) you should look at converting to FAT32.

Figure 5.23.
WinBench 98 results for the Pentium 166 machine, before and after updating to the FAT32 file system.

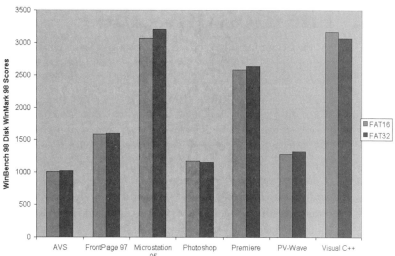

WinBench 98 High-End Disk WinMark 98 Application

5.8. Software that Can Help

By no means are all of the possible software improvements ones that are available just by knowing the right place to look in Windows 98. There are a number of products available that claim to help you enhance the performance of your system, such as Symantec's Norton Utilities. To review and evaluate these products is beyond the scope of this book. The products are typically under $100 and may be worth the money. We would recommend that you check publications such as *PC Magazine* for current reviews of these products before you run out and buy one. If nothing else, this chapter should have convinced you to be leery of performance enhancement claims.

If you really do want to continue investigating on the cheap you may want to look at some of the shareware and freeware products available. Again, we will not go into them in this book, but you have the tools with the benchmarks included with this book to do your own investigation. You can find these tools on the Web in places like ZDNet's Help Channel (`www.zdnet.com/zdhelp`) and the ZDNet Software Library (`www.hotfiles.com`).

The key to using any of these products is to try them out using the techniques we used in this chapter—save, install, test, and then decide. Admitting you were wrong and going back to the way things used to be is better than having to live with the mistake forever.

5.9. The Bottom Line

At the beginning of this chapter, we gave you some universal ways to get more performance out of your operating system software such as getting the latest device drivers and defragmenting your disk regularly. We also looked at some more specialized performance tuning you might want to do such as tuning your CD-ROM's use of cache. Throughout this chapter we have tried to not lead you to expect too much in the way of free, software-only performance enhancement. We emphasized the latter to diminish any unrealistic expectations. As we've seen through the varied testing, you can get performance improvements in the real-world through only software tweaking. You just have to know what you're doing, and you need to run your own benchmark tests to verify the performance improvement. Still, with a few exceptions, Windows 98 is likely to already be running in a pretty good state on your PC.

The other thing to take away from this chapter, though, is that it never hurts to learn more about how your operating system and your computer interact. This will only help you troubleshoot problems and make buying decisions further down the road. Knowledge is power!

And with power comes responsibility, so one last time we need to emphasize that when you're under the hood of your PC, you're working cautiously. As we've noted, you can really screw things up if you don't know what you're doing. You should be backing up all important files (including the Registry) on your system on a regular basis anyway.

5.10. Testing You Can Do

The best thing about the testing we did in this chapter is that you can duplicate it without any added hardware. You don't need to con a local computer dealer into letting you borrow this or that peripheral. The first thing to check, as always, is the real-world performance gains that Winstone 98 can show you. Pay attention to the category scores or application scores that correspond to programs or program types that you typically run. Some of these software tweaks help certain programs but hinder others. To really get under the hood, running the corresponding WinBench 98 that pertains to the subsystem you've tweaked: Disk WinMark 98, CD-ROM WinMark 98, Graphics WinMark 98, etc. Those test scores will give you a clearer picture of exactly how your software adjustments are affecting system performance.

As always, make sure to follow proper testing procedure too: defragment your hard disk completely and cold boot your machine before each test run. Make apples-to-apples comparisons by only changing one setting at a time. There's no point in testing your machine, making a bunch of changes, and then testing again.

You'll never know which adjustment (or set of adjustments) really changed performance.

> **NOTE** Complete directions for running the current versions of Winstone and WinBench can be found in Appendixes A, "Using Winstone 98," and B, "Using WinBench 98."

5.11. From Here...

We've tried to give you a taste of most of the free optimizations available to you in this chapter. If you'd like to learn more about the particular subsystems we covered, check out the following chapters. They go further in depth about the hardware and software working behind the scenes in your PC.

- Chapter 10, "Optimizing Your Graphics Subsystem," will show you how to optimize your graphics setup and how to choose the best combination of screen resolution and color depth.

- Chapter 11, "Optimizing Your Disk Subsystem," will show you how to upgrade or optimize your hard disk and how to really optimize your swap file.

- Chapter 12, "Optimizing Your CD-ROM Subsystem," will further explore CD-ROM drive speeds, comparing manufacturer's ratings with real-world measurements.

Chapter

6

Windows 95 Software Tuning

Microsoft designed Windows 95 from the ground up to be easier to use than its predecessor, Windows 3.1. Windows 95 has turned out to be a wildly popular operating system, and its ease of use was one of the factors that contributed to its popularity. Microsoft also designed Windows 95 to require less *tweaking*, or adjustment, of the various low-level settings that control the system hardware and software. Many users of Windows 3.1 had to constantly edit their SYSTEM.INI, WIN.INI, CONFIG.SYS, AUTOEXEC.BAT, and other system files every time they added new hardware or wanted to improve the performance of their system. Microsoft's goal with Windows 95 was obviously to have the operating system control these settings without any user intervention. To a large extent, they fulfilled this goal.

However, there are still some software-only (in other words, free except for your time) tuning tips for Windows 95—otherwise this chapter would be only one page long! Some things like defragmenting your hard disk on a regular basis and getting the latest device drivers are applicable for everyone. Other tuning options, such as those for your CD-ROM drive or BIOS, are less applicable to everyone, but can still have an important benefit. Still other tuning options are ones that you may hear claims about, but are best avoided.

If you want to learn about the software that works behind the scenes to make computers zip or crawl, read on. In this chapter, you will learn:

- How the operating system plays a key role in performance

  Windows 95 is more than just a pretty face on your computer. You will learn how it can help or hinder the performance of your computer.

- What you should realistically expect from tuning Windows 95

  While tuning Windows 95 can enhance your performance, Windows 95 does a pretty good job on its own. You will understand what is realistic to expect from your software tuning efforts.

- What safe and easy tuning options are useful for everyone

  You will learn about how defragmenting your hard disk and getting the latest graphics device drivers can speed up your system without much work on your part.

- What specialized options for tuning you may want to investigate

  Some software tuning options such as those involving the CD-ROM drive or the BIOS do not apply equally to everyone, but you may want to check into them for your system.

■ What performance tuning claims you should be aware of or avoid

Some ideas for tuning Windows 95 look good on the surface, but just don't pan out in practice. We tried some of the claims we have read about elsewhere and give you some ideas about what to avoid.

■ How some software utilities can help you keep your system running well

Not all the software optimizations you can do are included with Windows 95 or are free. Instead, some of them are from utilities available on the Web or as products in stores. You will learn how these utilities can help you with your system.

6.1. Cocktail Party Tips

Imagine that you're at a cocktail party, one also attended by one of your pals who is always bugging you with computer questions. This *friend*, who is not only annoying but cheap, asks you, "How can I get more performance from my computer without spending a dime?" Throw him a quick bon mot in the hopes he will go away. "What little you can accomplish would go faster if you defragmented your disk regularly." When he tries to find out if you really know what you are talking about explain that disk fragmentation occurs over time as pieces of a file get scattered over the hard disk. Defragmenting the disk moves those pieces together so that the computer can get them off the disk faster. Windows 95 has the ability to fix this up, you just have to tell it to do so.

If the party pariah presses you for more free ideas, explain that he would do well to get the latest graphics device drivers and might even consider doing something with his CD-ROM drive caching. And, if he can spring for a few dollars, there are some software products he can buy to help him in his quest for performance. Or, if he just can't part with a dollar, there are some products available for downloading from the Web.

Finally, explain to the gathering crowd of performance sycophants that they should not expect too much of a performance boost from just making software changes. However, for the initiated such as yourself, there are worthwhile things you can do if you can afford the time.

6.2. The Role of the Operating System

An operating system (OS) is software that controls how your computer works. It provides to applications services like writing to the disk, displaying menus on the screen, and generally controlling the hardware that makes up your computer.

Windows 95 Software Tuning

There is a lot more to a modern operating system than the obvious software that controls the hardware. The OS really includes device drivers and even the BIOS. All of this software is between your application and the hardware and thus can have a noticeable impact on performance.

There are many operating systems, but the most popular ones for microcomputers are Windows and Mac OS. Versions of the UNIX operating system are also available for microcomputers. Differences between operating systems used to be more obvious: a DOS machine presented the old C:\ prompt, a UNIX machine presented an even more cryptic command prompt, while the Mac OS machine used a graphical interface. Nowadays, most popular operating systems have some type of graphical interface, and Windows (in all its forms) is easily the most popular operating system for microcomputers.

If most operating systems look similar now, with trashcans or recycle bins for deleted files, with desktops strewn with icons, are they all the same? No. The real differences between operating systems are hidden behind the scenes, in how the operating systems implement multitasking, security, and performance enhancements such as disk caching.

Because most things your applications do require the operating system to intervene, it can have a major role in performance. The OS can both speed things up such as by handling disk caching or slow things down by doing things inefficiently. In this chapter we'll be looking at the performance enhancements that Windows 95 implements, and we'll look at ways to tweak them to optimum levels.

6.3. What to Expect

We will admit up front that you should not expect big performance gains from software tuning. Partially that is because Windows 95 does a decent job of automatically tuning your system in most performance areas. Windows 95 also does not expose many options for you to work with. Finally, software tuning tends to be more system specific so we cannot offer as much blanket advice as we can in other chapters of this book.

This last point means that we could not run the benchmarks as much in this chapter as we did elsewhere. We picked some examples where we could and in other places we give you ideas that you can investigate yourself on your system. You will potentially have options on your system that are not available on other computers. For example, there are multiple versions of Windows 95. A more recent version (often referred to as OSR2) that has been shipped with machines (you can't buy it except with a new system) since mid-'97 has some different options from the earlier Windows 95. Unfortunately, the computers we used in our testbed had the original, older version of Windows 95.

So, if you want to get the full benefit of software tuning, you will have to do some experimentation for yourself. The good thing about the benchmarks included with this book is that you can know what impact any changes you might make are having.

6.4. What to Do First

The biggest piece of useful advice we can give is to be careful when making changes to your system. This is true whether you are trying performance experiments or just installing a new application. The first part of that is to back up your system before making any changes. This means not just your data, but your Registry settings and things you can't save electronically such as your BIOS settings. Those you need to write down and store in a safe place, that you will remember.

We assume you already know how to back up your files, but you may not be aware of all of the important information stored in the Registry. The Registry is part of Windows that keeps track of things for applications and Windows itself. These things can be everything from your current sound settings to application file locations to your Minesweeper top score. Some back up programs don't save this information and your system will not be the same without it. After all, it took you months to get your Minesweeper expert score under 60 seconds.

Particularly before you make changes to software settings on your system, make sure to back up critical system files and your Registry. If you accidentally change a Registry setting, you'll save yourself a lot of hair pulling and wasting time by having copies to fall back on.

One way you can back up the Registry by simply copying the files that contain it, USER.DAT and SYSTEM.DAT, to a floppy. To do this, do the following:

1. Boot up into Safe Mode so that Windows 95 does not load the Registry. Do this by pressing F8 while restarting your computer, after you see the Starting Windows 95 message. This will bring up a menu of boot choices. Select Safe Mode Command Prompt from this menu.

2. Change to the Windows directory by typing cd \Windows (or whatever directory you've installed Windows into) at the command prompt.

3. Un-hide the Registry files with the attrib command. Type attrib `-h` `-s` `-r` `system.dat` and `attrib` `-h` `-s` `-r` `user.dat` at the command prompt.

4. Copy the files to floppy (assuming the a: drive is your floppy drive) by typing `copy` `system.dat` `a:` and `copy` `user.dat` `a:` at the command prompt.

5. Hide your Registry files again by typing `attrib` `+h` `+s` `+r` `system.dat` and `attrib` `+h` `+s` `+r` `user.dat` at the command prompt.

Windows 95 Software Tuning

If for some reason your Registry needs to be restored, boot your computer into Safe Mode as described above. Copy the two files from the floppy disk back to your \Windows directory.

You can also use the CfgBack program which comes with Windows 95 to back up your Registry. This handy utility lets you keep up to nine different backup copies of your Registry and lets you restore any of them as desired. However, CfgBack does not run from the Safe Mode command line, so if you've really trashed your setup (such that you can't boot into Windows 95), CfgBack won't be of any help. Always keep copies of USER.DAT and SYSTEM.DAT as described above, even if you also use CfgBack.

6.5. Optimizations for the Masses

Much of this chapter is about optimizations to avoid and areas that might prove fruitful for some people. The tuning options in this section, however, are applicable to almost everyone. Not only that, but these are pretty safe and have few, if any, downsides. So, feel free to read these and run right out and implement them.

6.5.1. Putting the Disk Pieces back Together

Whether you like it or not, your hard disk is suffering from disk fragmentation. Don't worry, disk fragmentation doesn't mean your hard drive is actually breaking into separate pieces. It's a state that naturally occurs on your computer as you read, write, and delete files over time. On a pristine, unfragmented system, all files are stored in contiguous (in a row) areas on the disk. In other words, the bytes that make up a particular file are stored on the disk that are right next to each other. Contrast this to a fragmented disk, where the bytes that make up a file are scattered all over the disk. Windows 95 handles this condition as part of the file system, so it can find all the separate pieces and present them to, say, your word processing application as one file. But the fact that the hard disk subsystem has to search for and then retrieve the pieces of the file from all over the means a performance hit for you.

You can't stop fragmentation from occurring; it's going to happen due to the way the Windows 95 file system works. (Windows 95 is not unique in this failing; most operating systems suffer from disk fragmentation.) The Windows 95 file system, known as VFAT (for virtual file allocation table), is based on the FAT file system from DOS. In this system, files are stored in units on your disk known as clusters or allocation units. In turn, these clusters are made up of a certain number of sectors on your hard drive. The operating system looks at the hard drive in terms of clusters, while the hard drive itself (and its associated controller hardware) looks at the physical disks in terms of sectors.

The operating system divides a particular file that you want to save into clusters on your hard drive. Many times, these clusters are contiguous. The file is not fragmented as it's written to disk. However, that's not always the case. When you delete a file, the clusters it used to occupy become available. Let's say you just deleted a 30KB file and then you want to write a 50KB file. It's quite likely that the operating system will begin writing the 50KB file into the 30KB hole (and again, the hole will really be a multiple of the cluster size). Once it has filled that hole, though, there'll still be about 20KB of the file left to write. It will then have to skip along on the hard disk until it finds more room to write the rest of the file. Thus, this file will be fragmented. Because you're constantly reading, writing, and deleting files, fragmentation is the natural result of the FAT and VFAT file systems.

So, you can't stop fragmentation. You can, however, reverse its effects. Windows 95 provides a utility called Disk Defragmenter that can defragment all the files on your hard drive. In other words, it hunts for fragmented files and moves their data around until every file on your machine is contiguous and unfragmented. If you haven't paid attention to disk fragmentation, it might take quite a while to defragment your disk.

Other utilities are available for disk defragmentation. Back in the old days, you had to buy third party software to defragment your disk—it wasn't provided by the OS. You can still buy other packages such as Norton Utilities (from Symantec) and Nuts & Bolts (from Helix) that promise to defragment your disk more quickly and efficiently than the built-in Disk Defragmenter in Windows 95. However, if you're like us and you're loathe to spend excess dollars, you can defragment your disk by doing the following:

1. Bring up the Start menu.

2. Choose the Programs option to bring up the Programs menu.

3. Choose the Accessories option to bring up the Accessories menu.

4. Now, instead of choosing Games like you normally do, choose the System Tools option.

5. Click on Disk Defragmenter. This starts the Disk Defragmenter program.

6. Disk Defragmenter will prompt you to specify which drive you'd like to defragment. This will likely be your C: drive. Click on the OK button. You can also choose All Hard Drives if you have more than one hard drive or partition.

After you've clicked OK, Disk Defragmenter will check the fragmentation of the drive you've selected. If the drive is significantly fragmented, defragmentation begins immediately. If the drive is only slightly fragmented, Disk Defragmenter suggests that you don't need to defragment the disk at this time. You can still click

Windows 95 Software Tuning

on the <u>S</u>tart button to have the program completely defragment your disk. To see the details, click on the Show <u>D</u>etails button (see Figure 6.1).

Figure 6.1.

The Show Details option of the Windows 95 Disk Defragmenter shows the progress of your hard disk's defragmentation in graphical form.

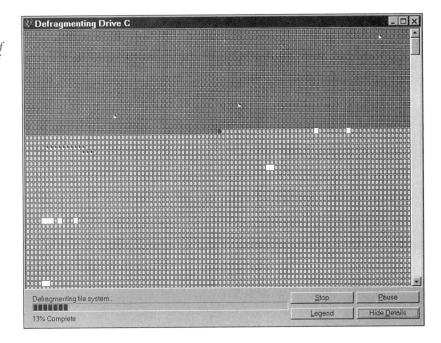

Because disk fragmentation affects performance, part of the standard testing procedure used for all of the studies in this book is to completely defragment the hard disk before every test run. We suggest that you make this a part of your standard testing procedure too. Even if you're not going to run benchmark tests on a particular machine, you should still ensure that the disk is defragmented on a regular basis. We personally defragment our hard disks weekly.

Because this is our standard procedure, we were hard pressed to find any machines that were fragmented. Our test machines are carefully set up and defragmented so often that we rarely see fragmentation of more than 1% or 2% at most. Consequently, we don't actually run tests on fragmented versus defragmented machines in this chapter. If you've had your PC for a long time and never defragmented it, you'll likely see a much higher level of fragmentation. We really can't give you a good figure for the value of defragmentation, but given that it is so easy to do, you would do well to follow that procedure.

One way to ensure that your disk stays defragmented is to use the System Agent, part of the Microsoft Plus! Pack for Windows 95. The System Agent is a scheduling program that runs in the background, starting up other tasks as necessary. In its default configuration, the System Agent runs Disk Defragmenter periodically as well as running ScanDisk and checking for low disk space.

6.5.2. Graphics Drivers

Another area that affects everyone's Windows 95 performance is your system's device drivers in general and specifically your graphics adapter device driver. A device driver is a piece of software that serves as an interface between the operating system and a particular piece of hardware. This allows the operating system to not worry about the vagaries of every piece of hardware as it can leave that knowledge to the device drivers.

Windows 95 supports a much larger range of hardware than Windows 3.1 did. This support means that the average user doesn't need to hunt for drivers for all of the peripherals installed in his or her system. So, Windows 95 includes support for a variety of graphics adapter boards. However, the drivers provided by Microsoft with Windows 95 might not necessarily give the best display performance. The art of writing graphics drivers is an arcane one, and graphics board vendors are constantly rewriting their display drivers to eliminate bugs and to improve performance. Graphics adapters no longer just drive the display (your monitor), they also accelerate the common graphics calls that Windows makes.

You'll learn more about setting up your graphics subsystem in Chapter 10, "Optimizing Your Graphics Subsystem." For now, though, let's take a look at how you can update the graphics drivers on your system. To do this, do the following:

1. Right-click on an empty portion of your Windows 95 desktop.

2. Click on the Properties selection of the pop-up menu.

3. This brings up the Display Properties sheet. Click on the Settings tab.

4. Click the Change Display Type button. The Change Display Type dialog box will appear.

5. In the Adapter Type area, click the Change button.

6. This brings up the Select Device dialog box. Windows 95 will by default show you only device drivers which it believes are compatible with your display hardware (see Figure 6.2).

7. If you want to install a new graphics driver that you've downloaded or have on floppy disk or CD-ROM, at this point you would click the Have Disk button.

Installing a new device driver may sound great, but it does beg the question of where do you get new graphics drivers? The best place to acquire them is from the home Web pages of the vendors themselves. All major graphics board vendors have Web presences, and all maintain ftp sites where you can download the latest drivers. Here's a list of some of the more popular graphics board vendors and their Web sites:

Windows 95 Software Tuning

ATI Technologies   www.atitech.ca
Diamond Multimedia Systems, Inc.   www.diamondmm.com
Genoa Systems Corporation   www.genoasys.com
Hercules Computer Technology, Inc.   www.hercules.com
Matrox Electronic Systems Ltd.   www.matrox.com
Number Nine Visual Technologies   www.nine.com
STB Systems, Inc.   www.stb.com

Figure 6.2.

The Select Device dialog box for the Display Control Panel allows you to install a new graphics device driver.

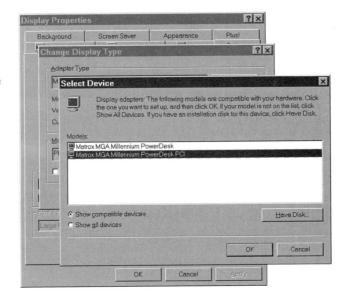

It's likely that the graphics driver versions you find at these Web sites will be much more recent than the release date of Windows 95. In many cases, the newer drivers will give you significantly better performance than the ones included with Windows 95. It's in the manufacturer's interest to optimize their graphics drivers for performance (and to fix bugs).

To show the effects of updating graphics drivers, we tested our Pentium 166 machine that contains a Matrox MGA Millenium graphics board. We tested the machine at 16MB RAM, a typical amount. (We actually recommend more RAM than this as a standard amount; to find out why, read Chapter 9, "Optimizing Your System's RAM.") We ran both Business Winstone 97 and High-End Winstone 97, to see if updating the drivers had a measurable effect on the performance of real-world applications. To check out how the drivers souped up the graphics sub-system, we also ran the Graphics WinMark tests from WinBench 97. First we ran tests using the drivers that Compaq had provided on this machine when they initially loaned it to us for testing. Then we re-ran the tests after updating the graphics drivers to the latest versions available from the Matrox Web site (www.matrox.com).

The Business Winstone 97 results in Figure 6.3 show a slight improvement with the newer drivers, about 3% overall. While this improvement may not seem like much, it is enough to matter and given the small amount of effort, worth pursuing.

Figure 6.3.

Business Winstone 97 results for the Pentium 166 machine, before and after updating to the latest Matrox Millenium graphics drivers.

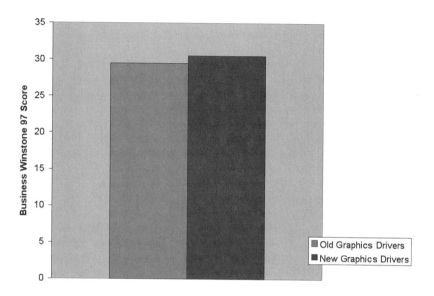

The individual Business Winstone 97 category scores shown in Figure 6.4 tell much the same story as the overall score. The Database and Desktop Publishing suites show a 4% gain, while the Word Processing/Spreadsheet applications show a 3% increase.

Figure 6.4.

Business Winstone 97 category scores for the Pentium 166 machine, before and after updating to the latest Matrox Millenium graphics drivers.

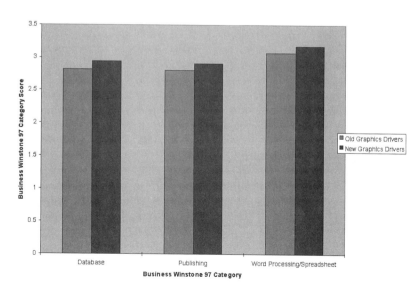

Windows 95 Software Tuning

We also looked at the performance changes from the graphics device drivers on High-End Winstone 97. For the High-End Winstone 97 tests, we increase RAM to 32MB. Because these applications are more graphically intensive than typical business applications, we thought we might see more of a boost.

As you can see from Figure 6.5, the results are around a 3% improvement, about the same as they were for Business Winstone. Again, this is not an earth-shattering improvement, but one worth pursuing.

Figure 6.5.

High-End Winstone 97 score for the Pentium 166 machine, before and after updating to the latest Matrox Millenium graphics drivers.

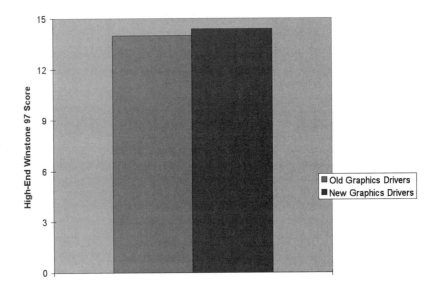

The story becomes more interesting, however, when we look at the individual application scores from High-End Winstone. Here, in Figure 6.6, we see differences as large as 8%.

For the individual applications the increase varies from 8% for MicroStation 95 to 1% for Photoshop. This increase probably means that the typical mix of graphical operations that MicroStation performs contains more optimizations. The Photoshop numbers, however, are probably brought down significantly because it is still bottlenecked by the amount of RAM in this system.

It's important to note that these increases are just at or above the level of variability of Winstone scores. This brings up an important point: repeatability testing. When Winstone and WinBench are developed, the developers perform extensive testing under controlled conditions to ensure that the results are repeatable within about 3%. In our testing, we found the numbers to be even more repeatable, so we consider even a few percent increase significant. So, while the increase we're seeing in Business Winstone 97 with the newer graphics drivers is at or barely above the margin of variability, we can be fairly confident what we are seeing is not just a testing artifact.

Figure 6.6.
High-End Winstone 97 individual application scores for the Pentium 166 machine, before and after updating to the latest Matrox Millenium graphics drivers.

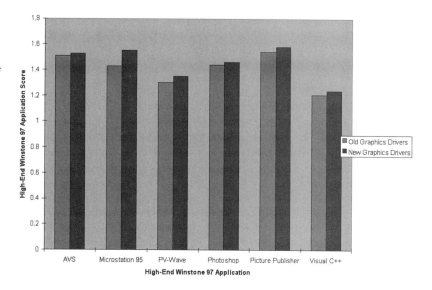

To confirm this assertion, let's look at the WinBench 97 results. WinBench 97's Graphics WinMark tests play back the actual graphics operations from the Winstone applications. Therefore, the Graphics WinMark 97 tests isolate the graphics subsystem, so the results aren't as dependent on bottlenecks such as hard disk or processor speed.

As we discussed in Chapter 1, "Performance Basics," graphics performance is about 15% of the overall system's performance. So, it should take an increase over 20% in graphics performance to yield a 3% overall improvement. In Figure 6.7, you can see the results we actually got.

The 27% increase in the Business Graphics WinMark 97 and the 20% increase in the High-End Graphics WinMark 97 bear out our hypothesis. This results show in practice how the effects of performance improvements in one of the smaller pieces of the performance pie described in Chapter 1 get muted in overall performance.

Figure 6.8 shows that the Business Graphics WinMark 97 category scores are similar to the overall just as the Business Winstone 97 category scores echoed that of the overall Business Winstone 97 score. Just as the most interesting Winstone 97 numbers in this section were the individual High-End Winstone 97 application scores, the same is true of their WinBench 97 counterparts, shown in Figure 6.9.

Figure 6.7.

Graphics WinMark 97 results for the Pentium 166 machine, before and after updating to the latest Matrox Millenium graphics drivers.

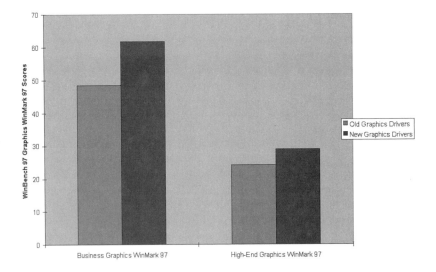

Figure 6.8.

Business Graphics WinMark 97 category results for the Pentium 166 machine, before and after updating to the latest Matrox Millenium graphics drivers.

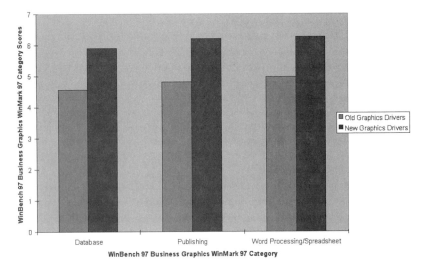

These results do not correspond quite as nicely to their Winstone 97 counterparts as the others have. That is due in large part to the nature of the individual applications. A score that covers a wide range of applications is more impervious to variability than one from a single application. Regardless, however, you can see a noticeable graphics benefit for all of the High-End Winstone 97 applications using the updated drivers.

These results should convince you to update your graphics drivers now. Be aware, though, that these values are simply the ones we discovered for this particular situation. There's no guarantee that updating your graphics drivers will give you any performance boost. In any case, the newer drivers clearly perform better than the older ones. There's no reason not to keep your drivers updated. It's a free and easy way to squeeze the last drops of performance out of your system. Besides, it's always good practice to update your drivers with the latest releases, if only to get the bug fixes.

Figure 6.9.

High-End Graphics WinMark 97 application results for the Pentium 166 machine, before and after updating to the latest Matrox Millenium graphics drivers.

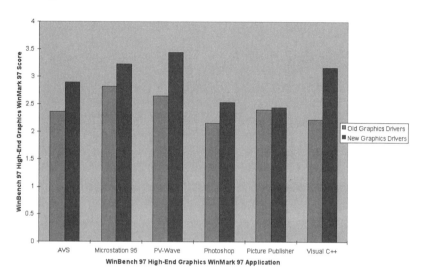

6.5.3. Windows 95 Graphics Performance Setting

There is another place to look for possible performance improvements to your graphics drivers. This setting is on the System Properties Performance tab. To get to this tab, do the following:

1. Choose Control Panel from the Settings section on your Start menu.

2. Double-click the System Control Panel to open it.

3. Click on the Performance tab.

4. Click the Graphics button in the Advanced settings section. This displays the Advanced Graphics Settings dialog box (see Figure 6.10).

There's a single slider control on this dialog box, which allows you to adjust graphics hardware acceleration from None to Full. Windows 95 defaults to leaving this setting on Full and that's where we recommend you leave it too. This setting is mainly useful for troubleshooting problems you might be having with your graphics subsystem. If you feel that you aren't getting the graphics performance you expect, though, you might want to check this setting to ensure that you or your system vendor did not accidentally leave it at something other than full acceleration.

Figure 6.10.

*The Advanced
Graphics Settings
dialog box lets
you turn your
graphics
performance to its
maximum.*

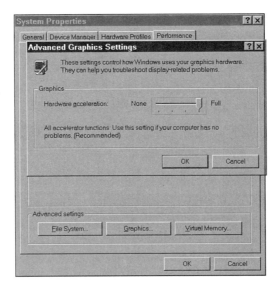

Figure 6.10.

*The Advanced
Graphics Settings
dialog box lets
you turn your
graphics
performance to its
maximum.*

6.5.4. Eliminate 16-bit Device Drivers

We've already stressed the importance of checking for and installing newer drivers for your graphics board. Keeping drivers up to date is a task that extends to all of the hardware in your system, though. The main thing you want to ensure is that all of the drivers in use are 32-bit drivers designed for use with Windows 95, not 16-bit drivers.

Windows 95 bundles 32-bit device drivers for a vast array of hardware: graphics adapters, multimedia devices, disk controllers, and so on. However, there's still plenty of legacy hardware or cutting-edge hardware that requires drivers that don't come with Windows 95. If Windows 95 can't find a new device driver for a particular piece of hardware during installation, it will use the previous 16-bit device driver that you already have on your system. This driver will be slower and possibly lacking in advanced features.

6.6. Specialized Optimizations

Not all software optimizations are equally applicable to all people. The ones we will look at in this section are specialized because they will not be encountered all the time, such as software optimizations to speed up your CD-ROM access. Others, such as making any modifications to your system's BIOS, are specialized because they vary from one system to another. Even though these performance optimizations are less general purpose than those in the previous section, they are still worth looking into for most people.

6.6.1. The CD-ROM Cache

Just as the Windows 95 file system that handles hard disk access was re-written in 32-bit code, so was the compact disk file system. In fact, that's what it's called: CDFS, for Compact Disk File System.

Windows 95 caches data for the CD-ROM drive in the same way that it caches data for the hard disk. Of course, it can only perform read-ahead caching in the case of the CD-ROM drive, because you can't write data to the CD-ROM drive. Your CD-ROM cache is separate from your hard disk cache. As a matter of fact, the cached CD-ROM data in RAM can be swapped out to the swapfile on your hard disk. This would obviously be useless and redundant for cached hard disk data in RAM, but it still works for the CD-ROM drive because your hard disk is still significantly faster than your CD-ROM drive (and in turn, RAM is faster than your hard drive).

As with the hard disk cache, you have some control over the size of the read-ahead buffer used for the CD-ROM cache. In fact, adjusting the size of this cache is one of the software configuration tweaks that you can and should do to improve performance. Windows 95 can't determine what speed CD-ROM drive you have. CD-ROM drive speeds are typically given as 1X, 2X, 4X, 8X, and so on. This industry standard terminology can be somewhat confusing and misleading (as you'll learn in Chapter 12, "Optimizing Your CD-ROM Subsystem"). A single-speed (1X) CD-ROM drive can read a sequential stream of data at the same speed as your audio CD player—150KB per second (KB/s). A 2X CD-ROM drive can read data at twice this rate, or 300KB/s. This speed improvement is accomplished by spinning the disc at a higher speed. Obviously, the faster CD-ROM drives would need larger read-ahead buffers, because they can access more data per unit time.

Because Windows 95 can't detect what speed CD-ROM drive you have, it leaves the CD cache settings at a default state that does *no* read-ahead caching. You can change this setting to have Windows 95 optimize caching for single-speed, double-speed, triple-speed, and quadruple-speed or higher CD-ROM drives. To get at these settings, do the following:

1. Choose Control Panel from the Settings section on your Start menu.

2. Double-click the System Control Panel to open it.

3. Click on the Performance tab.

4. Click the File System button in the Advanced settings section. This displays the File System Properties dialog box.

5. Click on the CD-ROM tab (see Figure 6.11).

On this dialog box, you'll see two controls. One is a slider allowing you to adjust the Supplemental cache size from small to large, and the other is a drop-down box allowing you to specify the speed of the CD-ROM drive for which you want Windows 95 to optimize access. You should definitely adjust the Optimize access pattern for setting to match the speed of your CD-ROM drive. On most newer systems, that will simply be Quad-speed or higher. Once you've told Windows 95 what speed drive you have, you can then adjust the cache size from small to large. Both of these controls work in tandem to calculate the actual cache size that Windows 95 will use, from a minimum of 64KB to a maximum of 1238KB (if you set it for Quad-speed or higher and Large).

Figure 6.11.

The CD-ROM Performance dialog box allows you to set the size of your CD-ROM drive's read-ahead cache.

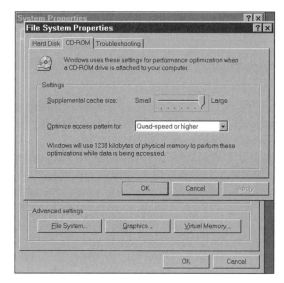

The CD-ROM settings allow you to exert some control over your system, as the Windows 95 default setting is probably wrong. Windows 95 can't detect what speed CD-ROM drive your system has. Because of this, it sets the CD-ROM cache size to the lowest common denominator. When you first open the CD-ROM dialog box, Optimize access pattern for: will be set to No read-ahead. (Obviously, this assumes that your system vendor has not changed this setting at the factory.) As explained previously in this chapter, you should adjust this setting to match your CD-ROM drive. In all probability, with newer systems you'll set this to Quad-speed or higher.

We set out to test the CD-ROM caching by running the CD-ROM WinMark 97 test from WinBench 97. The CD-ROM WinMark 97 test measures the performance of a PC's CD-ROM subsystem by playing back CD-ROM operations. These CD-ROM operations are the actual ones performed by six real-world applications.

We tested at two CD-ROM cache settings: the Windows 95 default, and the maximum cache size. The default setting corresponds to a Supplemental cache size of Small and Optimize access pattern for set to No read-ahead. This actually sets the CD-ROM cache size to 64KB. The maximum cache size corresponds to a <u>S</u>upplemental cache size of Large and <u>O</u>ptimize access pattern for set to Quad-speed or higher. This sets the CD-ROM cache size to 1238KB. (Obviously, we did this because the CD-ROM drives in our testbed were 4X drives or faster.) We tested on several different machines to see if the speedup (if any) caused by a larger cache was also dependent on processor type. We tested most machines at 16MB RAM, as this is a common RAM amount. Also, we wanted to make sure that increasing the CD-ROM cache size didn't adversely affect performance of machines with minimal amounts of RAM. (To find out why we think 16MB is a minimal amount of RAM, turn to Chapter 9.) We tested the Pentium 200 MMX system with 64MB of RAM to get an idea of what the boundaries of the benefits might be.

Figure 6.12 shows that across the board, the systems showed between 13% and 16% improvement. As you can see, all of these machines got approximately the same percentage boost by using the maximum CD-ROM cache size. In fact, the overall scores for the CD-ROM WinMark 97 test on these different machines are very similar. This would indicate that CD-ROM performance on these machines is not tied directly to CPU speed. Not surprisingly, the CD-ROM drives in all but the Pentium 200MMX system are the same Compaq model.

Figure 6.12.
CD-ROM WinMark 97 results for the different processor types at the default and maximum CD-ROM cache sizes.

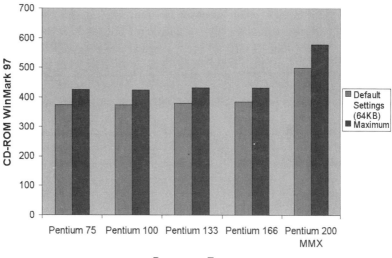

There are a few things to consider here with this data. First, this was for 4X drives. Faster drives may well not experience the same benefit since the difference between the CD-ROM drive's speed and that of the hard drive and RAM will be less. You also may see other differences based upon the model and manufacturer of the CD-ROM drive. This is definitely an experiment you should try yourself as it is easy and free to do.

If you don't feel like doing this experiment or your system is similar enough to the ones tested, you should fix the setting for your CD-ROM Performance tab. Adjust the Supplemental cache size to Large and set the Optimize access pattern for to match the speed of the CD-ROM drive you've got in your machine. Of course, you won't see this boost unless you're running applications that use the CD-ROM drive. But, the cost is free and we see little potential for problems arising from changing this setting.

6.6.2. BIOS Settings

Every PC has a BIOS (Basic Input Output System). The BIOS is the code that runs when you first power on your computer, before the operating system takes control. It also acts as a basic, standardized interface to much of your system hardware. The BIOS is stored in some type of ROM (Read-Only Memory) device on your system motherboard.

Many different manufacturers, such as AMI, Award, and Phoenix produces BIOS software for use in motherboards. There is no one standard set of features offered by all BIOS's. Most folks ignore their BIOS completely, although most BIOS's offer a password option that some folks use. If you dig down deep into the BIOS, though, you're likely to find settings that affect hardware performance.

A word of warning here: you can really screw up your system if you change BIOS settings without knowing what you're doing. Even if you're confident about what you're doing, you should copy down all of your current BIOS setup on paper before you change anything. Although there are some potential benefits from investigating your BIOS settings, this section can be safely skipped by the faint of heart.

> **WARNING**   Don't even think about changing your BIOS settings until you have studied your system manual or motherboard manual and until you have copied down all of your current BIOS settings on paper.

Going through a comprehensive list of all the possible BIOS settings you could change that affect performance is beyond the scope of this book. The best place for you to start is with your system manual or your motherboard manual if you have a separate motherboard manual. These manuals should explain the different BIOS options available in your PC. You might find that some are set for compatibility with older operating systems. After you've done that, a great place to find out more about BIOS issues is *The BIOS Survival Guide*, on the Web at `www.lemig.umontreal.ca/bios/bios_sg.htm`. So, while it's definitely possible to tweak the BIOS settings to your advantage, only do so if you know what you are doing.

Here's a real-world example of how you can screw things up by monkeying with BIOS settings. We set out to test the performance gains possible on our Compaq Pentium 133 machine by changing only BIOS settings. One setting that caught our eye was PCI VGA SNOOP. This setting controlled whether or not the system snooped VGA pallette writes on the PCI bus. Hey, it sounded like it might have some effect. So, we enabled this option and re-booted. Our display immediately went, in technical terms, kaflooey. The colors of the Windows 95 startup screen were distorted, and after the startup screen vanished, our desktop did not appear. Luckily we've memorized the Windows 95 keystrokes, so we were able to shut the computer down without benefit of the display. We quickly returned the PCI VGA SNOOP setting back to its original value.

A setting we did more serious investigation with had to do with the hard drive subsystem. It was Hard Drive DMA, and initially it was disabled. This is the default setting because it avoids incompatibilities with certain older disk caching software from the Windows 3.1 era. DMA stands for Direct Memory Access. DMA allows a certain peripheral device (say, the hard drive) to talk directly to system memory, without burdening the CPU chip with the transfer. It does this via a DMA controller chip or DMA circuitry. Because we were fairly confident that this setting would not interfere with our Windows 95 setup, we decided to investigate whether enabling hard drive DMA would improve real-world performance. It certainly sounded like it would.

We ran Business Winstone 97 on the Pentium 133 machine that had this BIOS option. We also ran the Disk WinMark tests from WinBench 97, to quantify the speed-up (if any) imparted to the disk subsystem by adjusting this setting.

While the results shown in Figure 6.13 after we enabled hard drive DMA are slightly higher (about 2%) they're still low enough to be almost insignificant. We dug further by running the Disk WinMark 97 tests from WinBench. Remember, these tests play back the exact disk operations that the applications in Winstone perform, thus isolating disk subsystem performance.

The Business Disk WinMark 97 showed a 5% improvement (see Figure 6.14). This is a minor improvement that might be worth implementing, but it is hard to know what the adverse consequences might be. Worse, we saw a minor decrease in performance on some of the applications in High-End Winstone.

We've mentioned this previously, but we should emphasize it here again. The main conclusion that you should draw from these results is that it's important to do your own benchmark testing. While certain options and settings may sound tempting, don't just blindly adjust them without verifying that you're getting the performance boost you think you're getting.

We can't predict what settings will be available to you through your system's BIOS. We just want to let you know that it's possible to alter system performance

Windows 95 Software Tuning

by adjusting the BIOS settings, and if you really want to get all the performance out of your system, it's worth looking at the BIOS.

Figure 6.13.

Business Winstone 97 results for the Pentium 133 machine, before and after enabling hard drive DMA in the BIOS.

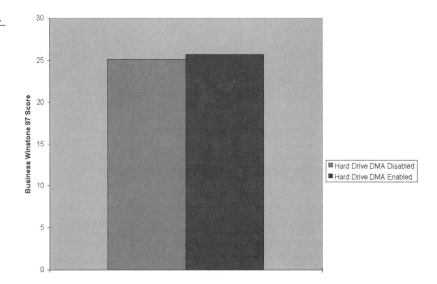

Figure 6.14.

Business Disk WinMark 97 results for the Pentium 133 machine, before and after enabling hard drive DMA in the BIOS.

6.7. Debunking Some Myths

Not all the avenues we tried for this book produced performance benefits. Some of them turned out to be dead ends. Somewhat surprising to us was that some of the performance enhancements we thought might help or read about elsewhere turned out to not only not help, but in some cases, hurt performance. We share some of those with you here, not just to warn you away from them, but also to show you why it is important to investigate claims rather than just accept them blindly.

6.7.1. Disk Cache

Cache is one of the most important concepts to learn if you want to understand computer performance. (We'll talk about cache in the processor and RAM chapters as well.) In short, the concept of caching means storing the most needed information in a faster cache of data rather than a slower, larger area. Caching works because programs and operating systems don't access each byte of data on the hard disk in an equally probable manner. Certain pieces of information turn out to be the most important, and therefore the most popular. Caching takes the most popular data and puts it in a faster place—it avoids the performance bottleneck. In the case of disk cache, it moves the data from a hard disk to buffers in the system RAM.

There are two separate kinds of disk caching: read-ahead and write-behind. Windows 95 performs read-ahead caching in an attempt to predict the data you'll need from your hard drive. It loads this data into the disk cache (again, in RAM) and then if you do need the data that Windows 95 has predicted (*read-ahead*) then it'll be available in the faster disk cache. The other type of disk caching is write-behind, where data is buffered in the disk cache before actually being written out to the hard drive. The caching mechanism in Windows 95 then ensures that the correct data is actually written out to the hard drive in the background.

You have some control over both the read-ahead and write-behind caching that Windows 95 performs. To access the read-ahead caching settings, do the following:

1. Choose Control Panel from the Settings section on your Start menu.

2. Double-click the System Control Panel to open it.

3. Click on the Performance tab.

4. Click the File System button in the Advanced settings section. This displays the File System Properties dialog box (see Figure 6.15).

The two settings you can control are Typical role of this machine and the Read-ahead optimization. The choices for the role of the machine are Desktop computer, Mobile or docking system, and Network server. When you select one of these roles, Windows 95 will perform a normal, minimal, or maximum amount of caching respectively. Mobile systems are typically battery powered and so Windows 95 allows you to minimize caching on these systems to conserve power. Conversely, network servers usually spend most of their time doing hard disk access, so maximizing caching on these machines improves network performance.

Windows 95 Software Tuning

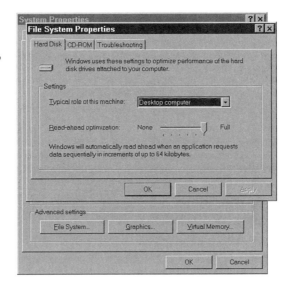

The other setting on this dialog box is the Read-ahead optimization. This setting allows you to control how large a read-ahead buffer Windows 95 will use. Typically, this slider control is set all the way to the right, on Full, which means Windows 95 will read data into a 64KB buffer. You can also move this slider to the left to decrease the buffer size to 32KB, 16KB, 8KB, 4KB, and 0KB (in other words, no read-ahead caching).

The Read-ahead optimization setting controls the amount of memory Windows 95 will use when a program requests sequential data. In other words, how much data ahead of the program's request will be read in anticipation into the disk cache. This setting can be adjusted from 0KB (no read-ahead) to a maximum of 64KB. It is normally set to Full, which is the maximum setting.

Typical Role of this Machine

We've seen several magazine articles that claim you can improve performance even on your desktop machine by changing the Typical role of this machine setting to Network Server. We wanted to test this assertion out to see if it was worth doing. We ran Business Winstone 97 to see if these would prove correct or not. We ran with typical amounts of RAM, so that if there was any performance differential caused by a shifting percentage of disk cache versus application RAM space, we'd be likely to spot it. (We did not use the corresponding Business Disk WinMark 97 because it does not vary if there is less RAM available for applications as that might confuse the results.)

The Typical role of this machine setting controls the overall size of the disk cache. On a desktop computer, the cache is set to a smaller size, to ensure that there's plenty of RAM left over for the applications you run on a typical desktop machine. When you set this to Network Server, Windows 95 uses more system RAM for the disk cache, leaving less RAM left over for use by applications. This makes sense for network servers because they are typically bottlenecked in the disk subsystem.

Figure 6.16 shows the results to be decidedly mixed. On the lower speed processors, changing the setting to Network Server actually significantly lowers performance as much as 12%. This is obviously not the outcome we were looking for. As the speed of the processor increases the benefit from using more cache with the Network Server setting begins to kick in. For the Pentium 133 and 166 systems, we see a 3% performance increase. These findings would make us reticent to recommend this change unless you first made sure these results bore themselves out on your computer.

Figure 6.16.

Business Winstone 97 results for a variety of systems varying the Typical role of this machine setting.

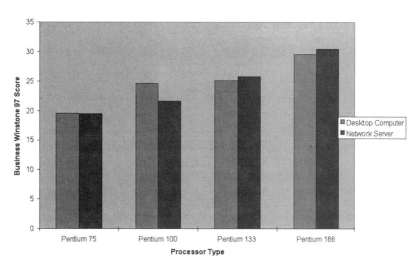

To see if we could get a bigger picture on this setting, we decided to try High-End Winstone 97. For this, we increased the system RAM to 32MB as required by this test.

In Figure 6.17 we see no real difference in the machine roles, indicating that the tradeoff between disk cache size and application RAM space doesn't affect the high-end performance in this configuration. Couple this lack of any significant change with the mixed results from the Business Winstone 97 tests and we have to conclude that this setting is not one that is likely to yield you any real benefit. The bottom line to this is that you'll need to do testing of your own if you want to adjust a file system setting to improve your performance.

This conclusion brings us to one of the central conclusions of this chapter: always check out optimizations with real-world tests. In the case of at least a couple of the systems we tested here, we would've experienced a performance drop if we had blindly followed someone's advice to edit the disk cache settings.

Windows 95 Software Tuning

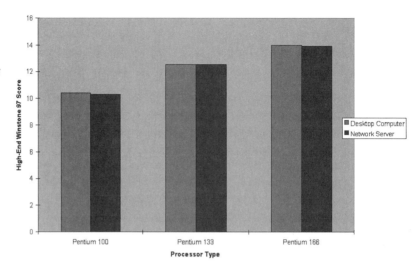

Figure 6.17.

High-End Winstone 97 results for a variety of systems varying the Typical role of this machine setting.

Read-ahead Caching

Another area that seems potentially ripe for optimization is that of read-ahead caching. We realize that on most systems, this setting is already set to the maximum, but we wanted to investigate the effects of read-ahead optimization on real-world, measurable performance. So, being the kind of guys we are, we ran Business Winstone 97 with the read-ahead optimization to 0KB (essentially turning it off) and to its normal maximum setting. We did this on a variety of systems with different processors and 16MB of RAM.

As you can see in Figure 6.18, turning off the read-ahead optimization had no real impact on the Business Winstone 97 scores for any of the systems we tested. While it is possible that a different algorithm for reading ahead might lead to some performance differences, the options presented to us by Windows 95 leave little for us to hope for in the way of performance improvements in this area.

Write-behind Caching

Windows 95 does not allow you such finely grained control over write-behind caching. In fact, we don't recommend that you touch the write-behind setting unless you're troubleshooting a problem with your hard drive. You can access this control, however, by doing the following:

1. Choose Control Panel from the Settings section on your Start menu.

2. Double-click the System Control Panel to open it.

3. Click on the Performance tab.

4. Click the File System button in the Advanced settings section. This displays the File System Properties dialog box.

5. Click on the Troubleshooting tab (See Figure 6.19).

Figure 6.18.
Business Winstone 97 results for a variety of systems with read-ahead optimization on and off.

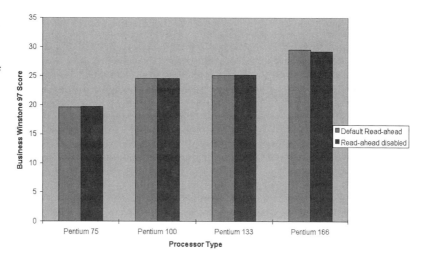

Figure 6.19.
The File System Properties Troubleshooting dialog box allows you to disable write-behind caching, but we do not recommend you do so.

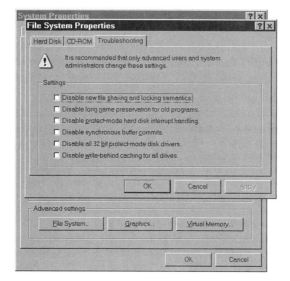

You'll now see six check boxes which allow you to disable certain features of the Windows 95 file system. One of these is Disable write-behind caching for all drives. If you check this box, Windows 95 will write data directly to the disk as opposed to buffering it in a RAM cache. We don't recommend disabling this option nor any of the other options on this tab—it is the aptly named Troubleshooting tab, and we hope you never have to touch it.

6.7.2. The Swap File and Virtual Memory

Like most modern operating systems, Windows 95 implements virtual memory so that you can run programs which require more RAM than you have installed in your machine. Windows 95 uses space on the hard disk to simulate additional RAM as needed by the applications you're using. This all goes on in the background, and as far as the application is concerned, it has the RAM it needs. Of course, it's not that simple or easy, because your hard disk is much slower than RAM. Windows 95 uses a swap file on your hard disk to simulate the virtual memory, and the transfer of data to or from the swap file is called *paging*. When Windows 95 decides to page, you'll know it—you'll wait while your hard drive buzzes along as your system seemingly does nothing. What's happening is that Windows 95 is moving data between RAM space and virtual memory space on your hard disk.

It's the swap file that allows you to run, as Microsoft states that you can, Windows 95 on a 4MB machine. We do not recommend doing this unless you have a lot of time on your hands, but it is possible. Your computer will spend most of the time paging to and from the swap file. The more RAM you have, the less paging Windows 95 has to do. To find out more about the amount of RAM you should have in your system, see Chapter 9.

Windows 95 uses a dynamic swap file, and the default setting is for Windows 95 to set up and use this file on its own. You can, however, change this default if you wish. If you attempt to do so, you'll see a dialog box advising you that these settings can adversely affect system performance and that they should be adjusted by advanced users and system administrators only. Unless you know what you're doing, you should heed this warning. Still, Windows 95 not only allows you to specify the minimum and maximum sizes for the swap file if you wish, it also allows you to disable virtual memory entirely. This is not recommended by Microsoft or by us, however.

We've spotted magazines, books, and Web sites touting claims such as one that the default setting for Windows 95 Virtual Memory (Let Windows handle virtual memory settings) does not yield the best performance. We decided to test this suggestion to see if it's true. Here are the suggested actions that we heard about and followed:

1. Choose Control Panel from the Settings section on your Start menu.

2. Double-click the System Control Panel to open it.

3. Click on the Performance tab.

4. Click on Virtual Memory (see Figure 6.20).

5. Choose Let me specify my own virtual memory settings.

6. Specify the same value for the minimum and maximum swapfile size. Calculate this value by multiplying the amount of real installed RAM by 2.5. In our case, we created a 40MB swapfile on our 16MB machine.

7. Press OK, and then OK again, signifying that you want to restart your computer.

8. After your computer restarts, open the SYSTEM.INI file for editing.

9. Add the following lines to the [vcache] section of the SYSTEM.INI file:

   MinFileCache=4096

   MaxFileCache=4096

Figure 6.20.

The Virtual Memory Performance dialog box lets you tinker with your system's virtual memory settings.

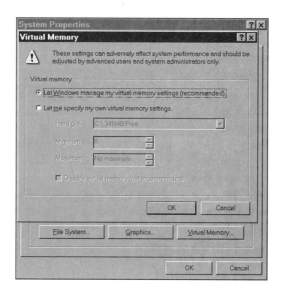

These actions were *supposed* to enhance system performance. We applied them to our Pentium 100 machine with 16MB RAM, and got the following results with Business Winstone 97 as shown in Figure 6.21.

Wow! We're glad we didn't just follow these suggestions blindly. As you can see, the overall Business Winstone 97 score drops off by 16%. We also saw that for Winstone 97's Desktop Publishing category, performance drops by an amazing 30%! We quickly returned our Pentium 100 machine back to its original state.

 WARNING Don't change your swapfile settings unless you're sure you know what you're doing. Changing swapfile settings can adversely affect system performance.

Figure 6.21.

Business Winstone 97 results on the Pentium 100 machine, before and after the recommended swapfile setup changes.

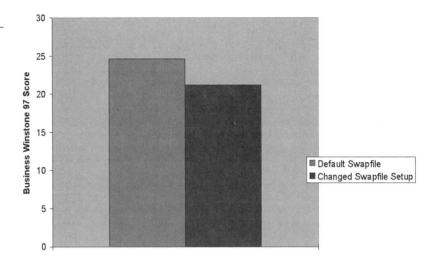

One situation where you might want to adjust the virtual memory settings is where you have more than one physical hard drive in your system. In this case, you may see some improvement by locating the swap file on a separate hard drive from the rest of your Windows files. We'll cover this situation in Chapter 11, "Optimizing Your Disk Subsystem." The short form of this section is just leave well enough alone. And, if you read a performance claim be skeptical and check it out like we did.

6.8. Software that Can Help

By no means are all of the possible software improvements available just by knowing the right place to look in Windows 95. There are a number of products available that claim to help you enhance the performance of your system, such as Symantec's Norton Utlities. To review and evaluate these products is beyond the scope of this book. The products are typically under $100 and may be worth the money. We would recommend that you check publications such as *PC Magazine* for current reviews of these products before you run out and buy one. If nothing else, this chapter should have convinced you to be leery of performance enhancement claims.

If you really do want to continue investigating on the cheap you may want to look at some of the shareware and freeware products available. Again, we will not go into them in this book, but you have the tools with the benchmarks included with this book to do your own investigation. You can find these tools on the Web in places like ZDNet's Help Channel (`www.zdnet.com/zdhelp`) and the ZDNet Software Library (`www.hotfiles.com`).

The key to using any of these products is to try them out using the techniques we used in this chapter—save, install, test, and then decide. Admitting you were wrong and going back to the way things used to be is better than having to live with the mistake forever.

6.9. The Bottom Line

At the beginning of this chapter, we gave you some universal ways to get more performance out of your operating system software, such as getting the latest device drivers and defragmenting your disk regularly. We also looked at some more specialized performance tuning you might want to do such as tuning your CD-ROM's use of cache. Throughout this chapter we have tried to not lead you to expect too much in the way of free, software-only performance enhancement. We emphasized the latter to diminish any unrealistic expectations. As we've seen through the varied testing, you can get performance improvements in the real-world through software tweaking alone. You just have to know what you're doing, and you need to run your own benchmark tests to verify the performance improvement. Still, with a few exceptions, Windows 95 is likely to already be running in a pretty good state on your PC.

The other thing to take away from this chapter, though, is that it never hurts to learn more about how your operating system and your computer interact. This will only help you troubleshoot problems and make buying decisions further down the road. Knowledge is power!

And with power comes responsibility, so one last time we need to emphasize that when you're under the hood of your PC, you're working cautiously. As we've noted, you can really screw things up if you don't know what you're doing. You should be backing up all important files (including the Registry) on your system on a regular basis anyway.

6.10. Testing You Can Do

The best thing about the testing we did in this chapter is that you can duplicate it without any added hardware. You don't need to con a local computer dealer into letting you borrow this or that peripheral. The first thing to check, as always, is the real-world performance gains that Winstone can show you. Pay attention to the category scores or application scores that correspond to programs or program types that you typically run. Some of these software tweaks help certain programs but hinder others. To really get under the hood, run the corresponding WinBench that pertains to the subsystem you've tweaked: Disk WinMark, CD-ROM WinMark, Graphics WinMark, and so on. Those test scores will give you a clearer picture of exactly how your software adjustments are affecting system performance.

Windows 95 Software Tuning

As always, make sure to follow proper testing procedure too: defragment your hard disk completely and cold boot your machine before each test run. Make apples-to-apples comparisons by changing only one setting at a time. There's no point in testing your machine, making a bunch of changes, and then testing again. You'll never know which adjustment (or set of adjustments) really changed performance.

> **NOTE** Complete directions for running the current versions of Winstone and WinBench can be found in Appendixes A, "Using Winstone 98," and B, "Using WinBench 98."

6.11. From Here...

We've tried to give you a taste of most of the free optimizations available to you in this chapter. If you'd like to learn more about the particular subsystems we covered, check out the following chapters. They go further in depth about the hardware and software working behind the scenes in your PC.

- Chapter 10, "Optimizing Your Graphics Subsystem," will show you how to optimize your graphics setup and how to choose the best combination of screen resolution and color depth.

- Chapter 11, "Optimizing Your Disk Subsystem," will show you how to upgrade or optimize your hard disk and how to really optimize your swapfile.

- Chapter 12, "Optimizing Your CD-ROM Subsystem," will further explore CD-ROM drive speeds, comparing manufacturer's ratings with real-world measurements.

Chapter

7

Windows NT Software Tuning

Windows NT 4.0 put a new face on NT, adding the Windows 95 GUI (graphical user interface) to the strong underlying operating system of Windows NT 3.51. The appearance changes in NT 4.0 are only the beginning, however. More than in earlier versions, NT 4.0 is designed so that it optimizes its software configuration. Because of this fact, there aren't too many software tweaks available to the average desktop user.

Most of this book is based on running the benchmark programs before and after performing hardware or software changes. The results then allow you to measure the performance difference of the changes. In this chapter, we'll run some performance studies with the benchmarks to examine parameters you can change. Because of the self-tuning capabilities of NT 4.0, however, there are not many things we can test. We think running the benchmarks is the best way to determine real-world performance, but it's not the only way to examine system performance. Windows NT 4.0 includes the very useful Performance Monitor (PerfMon) which allows you to analyze your system's resource usage. PerfMon, is a very powerful tool for understanding performance characteristics. In this chapter, you'll learn the basics of using NT's PerfMon. For those of you who may find PerfMon a bit daunting or may not wish to delve so deeply into Windows NT 4.0 system performance, we've included information on using a simpler tool that is part of the NT Task Manager.

If you want to get a handle on how the software configuration affects the performance of your NT machine, read on.

In this chapter, you will learn:

- How the Windows NT 4.0 operating system can affect performance

  The swapfile and disk cache work behind the scenes to make your computer work faster and more efficiently. In the following sections, you'll learn how these settings and other operating system components can affect performance.

- What you can change in the Windows NT 4.0 operating system to affect performance

  Windows NT 4.0 does its best to tune itself for performance. There are some things, such as your swapfile size, that you can change. You'll see what effect those changes can have and also other areas to explore on your own.

- How to use the Windows NT 4.0 Performance Monitor

  The Performance Monitor is a powerful tool when used in conjunction with the benchmark programs. We'll show you how to use it.

- How to use the Windows NT 4.0 Task Manager

For those of you not interested in learning all the intricacies of the Performance Monitor, the Task Manager offers a simpler tool, albeit one with fewer capabilities.

7.1. Cocktail Party Tips

The odds of getting asked about Windows NT 4.0 performance at a cocktail party are pretty slim, at least in the circles we travel in. On the off chance that you are asked, your best response is something like, "Optimizin' ain't what it used to be." Then, go on to reminisce about the old days when men were men and computers required experts. The reason for this answer is that Windows NT 4.0 was designed to tune itself, and we've found this generalization to be true on our NT 4.0 test machines. We found some software tuning tips of value in the previous chapters on Windows 98 and Windows 95, but there are fewer such tips for NT 4.0. On the other hand, NT 4.0 offers more opportunities for understanding how your system performs.

A natural question you may have is why should you bother reading the rest of this chapter? You should read on precisely because of NT 4.0's complexity. While the software tuning options for NT 4.0 are few, the potential for performance problems is still there. No operating system can magically overcome a performance bottleneck. In this chapter we'll be discussing a new tool in our arsenal: the Performance Monitor that comes with NT 4.0. This is not a replacement for WinBench and Winstone. This is a tool that measures how NT 4.0 uses resources on your computer such as memory and processor. You can use this tool in addition to the benchmark programs to learn more about how your PC operates and to determine where any performance bottlenecks exist.

Just be aware, though, that we're not going to unearth a magical performance switch buried deep in the Windows NT 4.0 control panels. Optimizin' ain't what it used to be.

Windows NT Software Tuning

7.2. NT Tuning Concepts

In a modern twist on an old saw, before tuning comes understanding. In the case of NT, there is a decent amount of understanding you should acquire. We will only skim the surface of Windows NT in this chapter, but our goal is to give you enough information to learn and explore more on your own.

If you have only recently become interested in system performance, you might not appreciate operating systems like Windows NT 4.0. Optimizing a DOS or a Windows 3.1 system involved intensive editing of the CONFIG.SYS, AUTOEXEC.BAT, WIN.INI, and SYSTEM.INI files. Determining what lines to add, what lines to remove, and what lines to edit involved checking and cross-checking the operating system manuals and all of the relevant hardware manuals. In some cases, software settings were not documented at all, but instead handed down as lore among performance wizards. Most performance enhancing software, such as disk caches, RAMdisks, and memory managers, had to be configured by hand. Every time that one system parameter changed, such as the amount of installed RAM, you had to go back and re-think and re-configure your disk caches and memory managers for optimal performance.

That era is mostly behind us now. Modern operating systems like Windows 98, Windows 95, and Windows NT 4.0 examine your system and set up the disk caches, swapfiles, and memory configurations accordingly. These constructs are still there, you just don't need to set them up yourself. However, to understand how your computer works, you've got to understand how this software affects performance.

7.2.1. Virtual Memory

Virtual memory comprises the physical RAM in your system plus the swapfile on your hard disk. Virtual memory works by moving less recently used program code and data onto your hard disk and then moving it back into physical RAM as needed. The total amount of memory available is the sum of your physical RAM and the swapfile on your hard disk. Windows NT 4.0, like all modern operating systems, supports virtual memory. Unfortunately, virtual memory is not a panacea for a memory shortage in your computer. If the required data or code is not in physical RAM when its needed, Windows NT 4.0 has to resort to reading it from the much slower hard disk.

Virtual memory uses units of memory called pages. In Windows NT 4.0, the page size is 4KB. The process of moving pages of code or data between the hard disk and physical RAM is called paging. When a program needs a particular page of code or data, and that page is not in physical RAM, a page fault occurs. Each page in memory is stored in a page frame. When Windows NT 4.0 moves a page from the swapfile to physical RAM, it must first find an empty page frame. If all the page frames are full, then a page frame must be written out to the swapfile before it can be emptied and used.

The swapfile in Windows NT 4.0 is a file called pagefile.sys. With the default settings, pagefile.sys is dynamically allocated. When your computer *pages,* it writes out data from RAM to the swapfile, or reads in data from the disk to RAM. The virtual memory subsystem built into the operating system keeps track of what information is where.

Paging to and from the swapfile is what makes virtual memory work, but paging is also a noticeable cause of delays on your computer. For example, when you minimize an application and switch to another application, the first application gets paged out to the hard disk as the second application needs more RAM. When you switch back to the first application, everything grinds to a halt and your hard disk light starts flashing furiously. The operating system is paging the application in from the virtual memory on the hard disk to the physical RAM in your system.

The more RAM you have, the less your computer will need to page. Of course, the amount of paging your computer does depends on the number of applications you have open at any given time, and the size of all the data files that you have open with those various applications. In general, though, the more RAM you have, the better, and if you could somehow have enough RAM such that your system never needed to page, that would be ideal. You can learn more about the importance of the amount of RAM in your system in Chapter 9, "Optimizing Your System's RAM."

7.2.2. Disk Caching

The concept of caching is an important one in computing performance, and we cover different aspects of it in several chapters of this book. Caching is storing the most important information in a faster cache to speed up access. Caching works because certain pieces of information on your computer are more popular, or more often used, than other pieces. Caching ensures that the popular data is located in a faster place.

Let's look at the example of disk caching. Your hard disk is much slower than your system RAM. Hard disk access times are measured in milliseconds. Dynamic RAM access time, for standard SIMMs and DIMMs, is measured in nanoseconds. The disk cache is an area of physical RAM where recently used data from the hard disk is stored. When a program needs to read from or write to the hard disk, the cache management software attempts to find the data in the cache or to write the data to the cache. Because the cache is in physical RAM, it's significantly faster than the hard disk.

When you read data from the hard disk, the caching component of Windows NT 4.0 puts a copy of that data into the disk cache in RAM. The next time an application goes to read the data it gets it from RAM in a fraction of the time it would have taken to read it in from the hard disk.

In a further wrinkle on disk caching called read-ahead caching, Windows NT 4.0 reads ahead on the disk from where you just requested data and places a copy of that next block of data from your hard disk into the disk cache in RAM as well. In other words, it predicts that the next time your system reads from the disk, it'll be from the area on the hard drive that it has just copied into the disk cache. If this happens, the disk read operation happens much more quickly, because the data is being read out of RAM and not directly from the hard disk.

Ideally, your cache would always contain the data that a particular program needs to read in. When that data is in the cache, we call it a cache hit. A cache miss occurs when the requested data is not in the cache, and the disk must be accessed. The hit rate of the cache is a percentage of how often a cache hit occurs. At some point, you'll have to read in data from the disk, so your hit rate will never be 100%. However, hit rates in the nineties are quite common.

Hard disk cache management also requires that the hard disk get updated when the cache is written to. Windows NT 4.0 implements this through a technique called write-back caching. Write-back or write-behind caching is the mirror of read-ahead caching. When your system needs to write to the hard disk, Windows NT 4.0 may buffer that write into the disk cache in RAM first. Your application proceeds along more quickly, and Windows NT 4.0 ensures that the correct data is written out to the physical hard disk in the background. Generally, the operating system waits until a number of disk changes have accumulated or the disk is not busy, then it writes them to the disk simultaneously. The other type of write caching is write-through caching. In the case of write-through caching, the disk is updated immediately after the cache is written to.

The cache size in Windows NT 4.0 is dynamic; it changes based on how much physical RAM your system has and by how programs use memory. You can't adjust the cache size in Windows NT 4.0 the way you can in other operating systems. You can, however, add more physical RAM to your system. This will, in turn, increase the size of the disk cache. You can learn more about system RAM requirements in Chapter 9.

7.3. NT Software Tuning Options

Now that we've spent a little time exploring some key performance-related aspects of the Windows NT 4.0 operating system, let's see what we can tune. Windows NT 4.0 does not offer as many software tuning options as Windows 95 or other earlier Windows versions. Windows NT 4.0 is designed to adapt on-the-fly so that it's always running with optimal disk and memory settings. There are, however, some things you can do to help Windows NT 4.0 do its job of optimizing performance.

7.3.1. Virtual Memory and the Swapfile

As we discussed earlier, the swapfile, or paging file, is the heart of the virtual memory system that most modern operating systems implement. Virtual memory allows you to run programs which require more RAM than you have physically installed in your system. Virtual memory works by using space on your hard disk to simulate the additional RAM applications need while you're running them. It is obvious that paging in things from disk is slow, but that is better than not being able to run things that need more RAM than you have. On the other hand, there is a cost to managing the virtual memory and the swapfile. If you have more than you need, it may affect performance, so let's experiment with the size of the swapfile and see what the effect on performance is.

When you install Windows NT 4.0, the operating system sets up pagefile.sys on your hard disk. This swapfile is dynamically allocated, but NT 4.0 sets a minimum and maximum size for the file. Windows NT 4.0 sets these sizes based on how much physical RAM you have in your system and how much space is available on your hard disk. Unlike most other software settings in Windows NT 4.0, you can alter the maximum and minimum sizes of the swapfile. To do this:

1. Choose Control Panel from the Settings section on your Start menu.

2. Double-click the System Control Panel to open it.

3. Click the Performance tab.

4. Click the Change button in the Virtual Memory section. This displays the Virtual Memory dialog box (see Figure 7.1).

5. The Virtual Memory dialog box displays a list of your hard disks and the minimum and maximum swapfile size (for each drive, if applicable).

6. Choose Initial Size under the Paging File Size for Selected Drive section. Edit this field to the value you wish.

7. Choose Maximum Size in this same section. Edit this field to the value you wish.

8. Click the Set button to set these new sizes.

9. Click the OK button twice to close the Virtual Memory dialog box and then System Properties box. Windows will prompt you to reboot your machine.

10. When your machine has finished rebooting, the swapfile will be using the new settings you've selected.

How We Tested

We wanted to investigate how system performance was affected by reducing the swapfile size from the default values that Windows NT 4.0 set up. In the case of our Windows NT 4.0 systems, we ran tests with the default values, then we decreased the swapfile size by at least half until the systems failed to run all of the Winstone tests. We did not increase the size of the swapfile as it is rather large by default and (as the results show) the performance was unlikely to get any better with the applications that are in Winstone 97. You would generally want to increase the size only if your applications need more virtual memory than NT provides by default.

Figure 7.1.

Change the swapfile size with the Virtual Memory settings.

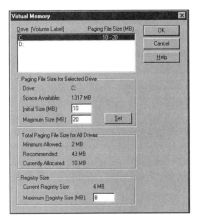

Our basic findings show that different processor speeds and different applications are affected differently by the swapfile change. We saw improvements of over 5% and, in one case, degradation of 15%. Generally, we saw modest improvements from decreasing the size of the swapfile. We also saw that while the slower Pentium systems showed a modest improvement by decreasing the swapfile size, the faster systems showed both decreases and increases in performance with a smaller swapfile, depending on the application.

While you might find some performance boost by fiddling with swapfile size, in general, at some point while you're decreasing swapfile size, your applications will fail. Because you can't necessarily predict how your system will be loaded down by different applications, using a decreased swapfile size to enhance performance is not a simple matter. The following sections may give you some clues about how your system and applications would respond. Find the section following that most closely resembles the processor in your system. As always, the best results will be those actually produced on your system.

Pentium 133

The 133MHz Pentium is the slowest system we use in our NT testing. We set out to investigate changes in the swapfile size on this machine, starting with the defaults as set by the operating system. Windows NT 4.0 initially set the minimum size of the swapfile to 43MB and the maximum to 93MB. We ran the Business Winstone 97 and High-End Winstone 97 tests on this configuration. We then revised the swapfile settings to a minimum of 20MB and a maximum of 40MB and re-ran the tests. Finally, we ran with a minimum swapfile size of 10MB and a maximum of 20MB.

In Figure 7.2, the overall Business Winstone 97 score increases by a modest 3.5% when we halve the size of the swapfile. Halving the size again caused failure. You can see how managing a larger swapfile can cause a small degradation in performance. Reducing the swapfile too far, however, makes it impossible for the applications in Business Winstone 97 to operate correctly. In fact, reducing the swapfile to a minimum of 10MB and a maximum of 20MB caused the applications to fail for all of the tests on this system. Keep that in mind before you go changing the swapfile size on your system. The performance increase of 3.5% in the overall Business Winstone 97 score is not monumental, but it is worth exploring further. As you will see, what you use your computer to do will affect these results. Let's look at the category scores to see the effect on different types of business applications.

Figure 7.2.

Business Winstone 97 performance versus swapfile size for a Pentium 133 PC.

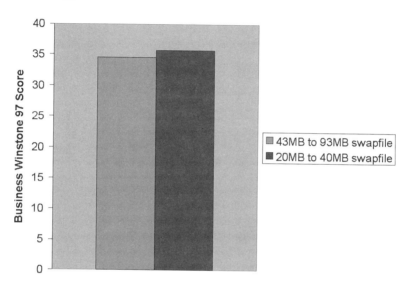

As you can see in Figure 7.3, the category results show the Database and Publishing categories improving by around 5% from reducing the swapfile. The Word Processing/Spreadsheet applications show only about a 2% increase. Changing the swapfile size obviously affects different applications rather differently. One possible reason is that some applications are more in need of virtual memory while others are helped more by additional disk bandwidth. The size of the swapfile affects the ratio of these two competing needs. While that theory makes lots of sense, we don't claim to be able to predict which applications will be helped from reducing the swapfile. This area is one in which you really do need to do your own testing. While a 2% increase may not be worth the trouble, 5% certainly is.

The High-End Winstone 97 results shown in Figure 7.4 reveal another part of the story. The overall improvement is less than 1%—an elusive if not illusory one. Thus, if you're interested in tweaking swapfile size for added performance, you need to pay attention to the applications you're running. Let's examine the High-End category and individual applications scores to see where, if anywhere, improvements may be lurking.

Figure 7.3.

*Category scores
from Business
Winstone 97
tests versus
swapfile size for
a Pentium 133
PC.*

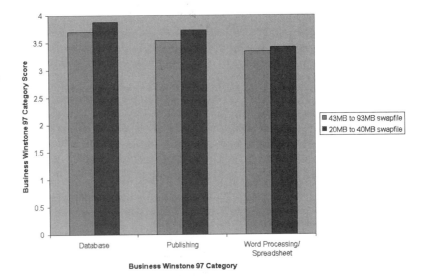

Figure 7.4.

*Overall High-
End Winstone
97 performance
versus swapfile
size for a
Pentium 133
PC.*

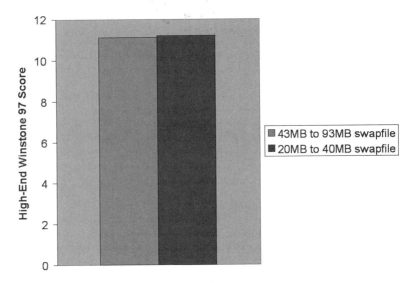

The High-End Winstone 97 category results in Figure 7.5 show the Application Development and CAD/3-D categories as improving under 1% like the overall High-End Winstone 97 score. Such and improvement is hardly worth pursuing. The over 2% increase in the Image Editing category, however, looks more promising. Again, let's look deeper into the individual applications to see what application is getting the benefit from reducing the size of the swapfile.

When we look at Figure 7.6 to see the individual results for the applications that High-End Winstone 97 comprises, we see that the one application that shows some improvement with our first decrease in swapfile size is Picture Publisher, with a respectable 4.5% improvement. For all of the other high-end applications, these tests show it's not worth your time attempting to tweak the swapfile size on a Pentium 133-class processor. The big caution, however, as we've seen on all the tests on the Pentium 133 machine, is that a swapfile that's too small will cause your applications to fail.

Figure 7.5.

Category scores from High-End Winstone 97 tests versus swapfile size for a Pentium 133 PC.

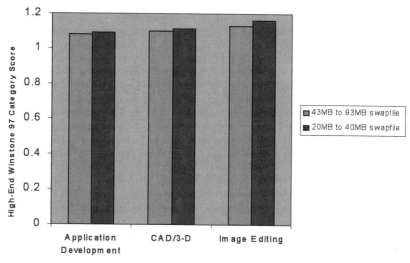

Pentium 166

Windows NT 4.0 on the 166MHz Pentium used the same default swapfile sizes as the 133MHz Pentium. Windows NT 4.0 initially set the minimum size of the swapfile to 43MB and the maximum to 93MB. We ran the Business Winstone 97 and High-End Winstone 97 tests on this configuration. We then revised the swapfile settings to a minimum of 20MB and a maximum of 40MB and re-ran the tests. Finally, we ran with a minimum swapfile size of 10MB and a maximum of 20MB.

As with the Pentium 133, Winstone was unable to complete its tests with the final swapfile size. With this system, however, we were unable to even complete all of Business Winstone 97 with the intermediary swapfile size. Specifically, the Publishing category failed to complete successfully. Consequently, we were unable to get an overall Business Winstone 97 score, but we did get results for the Database and Word Processing/Spreadsheet categories. We need to reiterate here that you will have to be careful to make sure your applications run if you decide to lower your swapfile size. Fortunately, as the procedure we outlined earlier showed, the process of changing the swapfile size is not too difficult. If an application fails, you just have to push the size up.

Windows NT Software Tuning

In Figure 7.7, the successful Business Winstone 97 category results 3% and 2% respectively. The applications in the Publishing category were unable to complete at all. Changing the swapfile size obviously affects different applications rather differently. Each application has a different balance of virtual memory and disk bandwidth requirements. The size of the swapfile affects the ratio of these two competing needs. We readily concede that the Windows NT 4.0 defaults are probably just fine. On the other hand, we are speed freaks and we are always looking for a little more performance. If you are like us, this area is one in which you really do need to do your own testing. The 2% to 3% increase on this machine may not be worth the trouble, but the 5% we saw earlier certainly is.

Figure 7.6.

Individual application scores from High-End Winstone 97 tests versus swapfile size for a Pentium 133 PC.

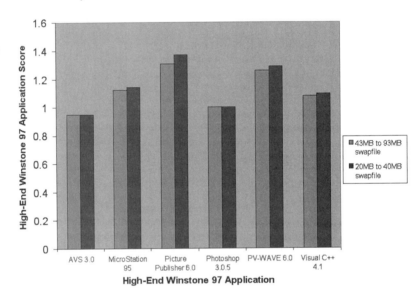

The High-End Winstone 97 results shown in Figure 7.8 show more promise than those for Business Winstone 97. The overall improvement is more than 3%. Three percent is generally what we consider significant for performance differences, so this is enough of an improvement that we need to look further. The big question we have is why there is a noticeable improvement on the Pentium 166 when there was not one on the Pentium 133. Sadly, the answer is not one we can be sure about. All of the results in this section indicate improvements due to swapfile changes are very sensitive to the particular configuration. As with the other systems, the improvements due to swapfile changes also tend to vary from application to application. Let's examine the High-End category and individual applications scores to see what caused this performance increase.

The High-End Winstone 97 category results in Figure 7.9 show the Application Development and CAD/3-D categories improving under 2%. This result is similar to that of High-End Winstone 97 on the Pentium 133. Such an improvement is hardly worth pursuing. The 6% in the Image Editing category, however, looks even more promising than what we saw on the Pentium 133. Again, let's look deeper into the individual applications to see which applications are getting the benefit from reducing the size of the swapfile.

Figure 7.7.

Category scores from Business Winstone 97 tests versus swapfile size for a Pentium 166 PC.

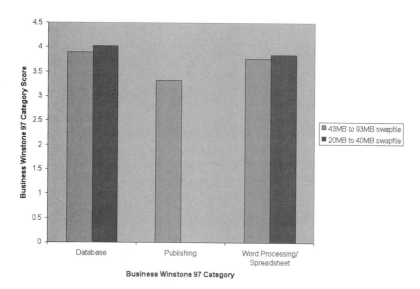

Figure 7.8.

Overall High-End Winstone 97 performance versus swapfile size for a Pentium 166 PC.

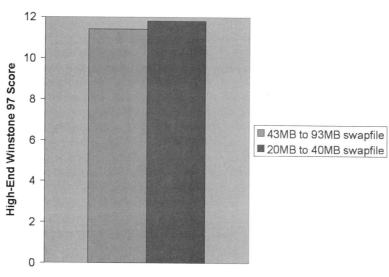

Windows NT Software Tuning

Let's look at Figure 7.10 to see the individual results for the applications that make up the High-End Winstone 97 categories. In these results we see that AVS and PV-Wave show improvements of two or three percent. More interesting are the improvements of over 4% and 8% for Picture Publisher and Photoshop, respectively. Our testing of the Pentium 166 with the High-End Winstone 97 applications shows there are gains to be had. This whole section, however, is really about different systems and different applications producing different results, so you would be best off doing your own testing to see what benefits you might get. The big caution, however, as we've seen on all the tests on the Pentium 166 machine, is that a swapfile that's too small will cause your applications to fail.

Figure 7.9.

Category scores from High-End Winstone 97 tests versus swapfile size for a Pentium 166 PC.

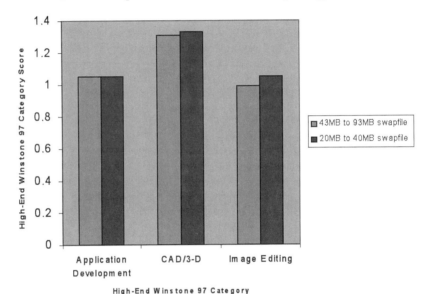

Figure 7.10.

Individual application scores from High-End Winstone 97 tests versus swapfile size for a Pentium 166 PC.

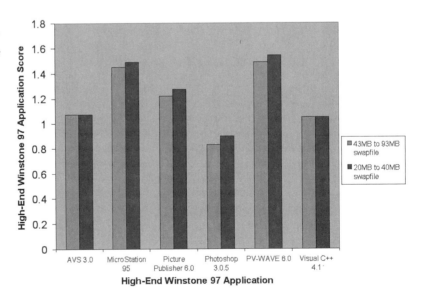

Pentium 200 MMX

As with the other systems, we started our investigation into the effects of changes in the swapfile size on the Pentium 200 MMX system by using the default size set by the operating system. Windows NT 4.0 initially set the minimum size of the swapfile to 75MB and the maximum to 125MB. We ran the Business Winstone 97 and High-End Winstone 97 tests on this configuration. We then revised the swapfile settings to a minimum of 20MB and a maximum of 40MB (consistent with our tests on the other systems) and re-ran the tests. Finally, we ran with a minimum swapfile size of 10MB and a maximum of 20MB. The results for this system were bad enough that if we had tested it first we might never have looked at any other systems.

In Figure 7.11, the overall Business Winstone 97 score decreases by almost 2% when we reduce the size of the swapfile. As with the other systems, lowering the size again caused the applications to fail. If these scores are not enough to warn you away, keep that in mind before you go changing the swapfile size on your system. Let's look at the category scores to see the effect on different types of business applications.

Windows NT Software Tuning

Figure 7.11.
Business Winstone 97 performance versus swapfile size for a Pentium 200 MMX PC.

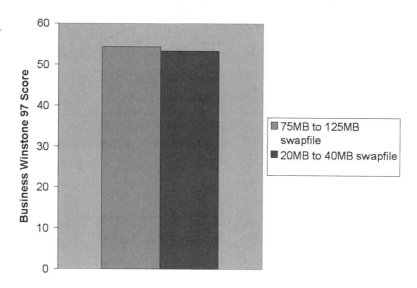

The Business Winstone 97 category results in Figure 7.12 show that the Database category is the big reason for the overall performance drop. Its drop of almost 7% swamps the less than 2% improvement of the Publishing and Word Processing/ Spreadsheet categories. We again see that changing the swapfile size obviously affects different applications rather differently. Sadly, we don't know how to predict which applications will benefit from reducing the swapfile. This area is one in which you really do need to do your own testing. And in the case of a system like our Pentium 200 MMX, you should not decrease the swapfile size.

Figure 7.12.

Category scores from Business Winstone 97 tests versus swapfile size for a Pentium 200 MMX PC.

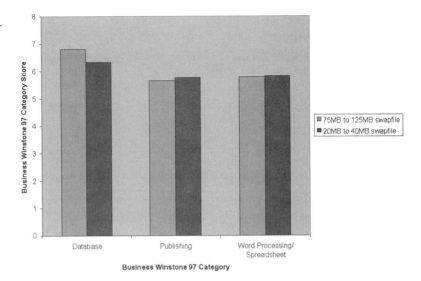

The High-End Winstone 97 results shown in Figure 7.13 show an even more dramatic performance decrease. The overall decrease is almost 7%. While this figure is enough to convince us to not make the change for this system, we were still very curious to see which categories and applications contributed most to the performance drop. Let's examine the High-End category and individual applications scores to see from where the decrease comes.

Figure 7.13.

Overall High-End Winstone 97 performance versus swapfile size for a Pentium 200 MMX PC.

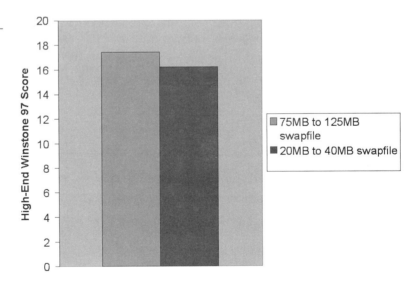

The High-End Winstone 97 category results in Figure 7.14 show the Application Development and CAD/3-D categories as only slightly affected by lowering the swapfile size (a 1% increase and a 1% decrease, respectively). Such improvement is hardly worth pursuing. It is the Image Editing category that accounts for the big performance loss, at over 15%! Given that the previous two systems increased their performance most in this category, the applications are obviously very sensitive to the swapfile size. Let's look deeper into the individual applications to see what applications are getting hit the most by reducing the size of the swapfile.

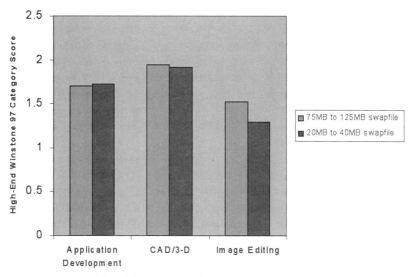

Figure 7.14.

Category scores from High-End Winstone 97 tests versus swapfile size for a Pentium 200 MMX PC.

When we look Figure 7.15 for the individual results for the applications that High-End Winstone 97 comprises, we see that most of the applications change by only 1% or 2%, hardly worth worrying about. Two of the applications, Microstation and Visual C++, actually managed to complete in the even smaller swapfile size that failed pretty much everywhere else on all of the systems we tested. The performance was not noticeably lower. Photoshop, however, drops over 20% on the intermediate swapfile size! This change is so large that we have to assume that Photoshop is really having problems running on this particular system with a reduced swapfile size. The bottom line for this system and others like it is to leave the swapfile size alone.

Pentium Pro 200

Like the other systems, we tested the Pentium Pro 200 system by starting with the swapfile size set to the defaults Windows NT 4.0 selected. Windows NT 4.0 initially set the minimum size of the swapfile to 75MB and the maximum to 125MB. We ran the Business Winstone 97 and High-End Winstone 97 tests on this configuration. We then revised the swapfile settings to a minimum of 20MB and a maximum of 40MB (consistent with our testing on the other systems) and re-ran the tests. Finally, we ran with a minimum swapfile size of 10MB and a maximum of 20MB.

Figure 7.15.

Individual application scores from High-End Winstone 97 tests versus swapfile size for a Pentium 200 MMX PC.

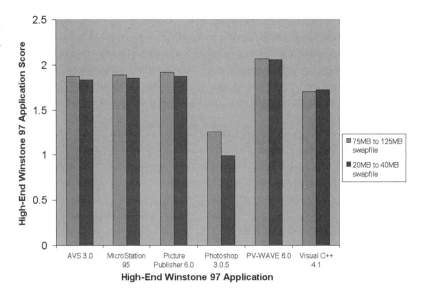

In Figure 7.16, the overall Business Winstone 97 score changes by less than 1% when we lower the size of the swapfile. This is not a significant change. As on the other systems, lowering the size again caused the applications to fail. Possibly out of morbid curiosity, let's look at the category scores to see the effect on different types of business applications.

Figure 7.16.

Business Winstone 97 performance versus swapfile size for a Pentium Pro 200 PC.

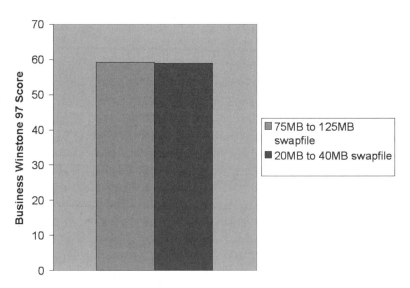

The category results in Figure 7.17, show a mild improvement in the Database category and an even milder decrease in Word Processing/Spreadsheet performance. The Publishing category, however, tanks with a decrease of over 6%.

Changing the swapfile size obviously affects different applications rather differently, but in this case it is not worth making the change for any of the application categories. We still need to look at the High-End Winstone 97 results to see if they are like those of the Pentium 200 MMX system (bad) or like those on the Pentium 166 (good).

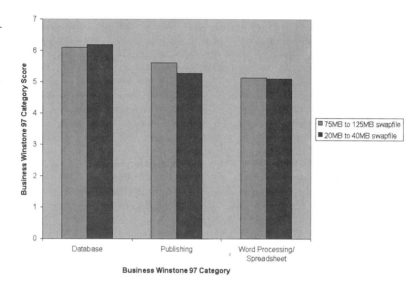

As luck would have it, the High-End Winstone 97 results in Figure 7.18 show something in between. The overall improvement is less than one percent—an elusive if not illusory one. Thus, if you're interested in tweaking swapfile size for added performance, you need to pay attention to the applications you're running. Let's examine the High-End category and individual applications scores to see where, if anywhere, improvements may be found.

The High-End Winstone 97 category results in Figure 7.19 show the CAD/3-D category decreasing by under 1%. In contrast, Application Development and Image Editing increase by over 3.5% and 2.5% respectively. Such improvement is worth at least looking into further. Let's look deeper into the individual applications to see what applications are getting benefit from reducing the size of the swapfile.

When we look at Figure 7.20, the individual applications results from High-End Winstone 97, we see results all over the map. Microstation and PV-WAVE are basically unchanged. AVS drops by over 3%. Photoshop increases by 3% and Picture Publisher by 2.5%. Obviously, you will need to investigate this for yourself given the range of results the High-End Winstone 97 applications reveal.

Windows NT Software Tuning

Figure 7.18.

*Overall High-
End Winstone
97 performance
versus swapfile
size for a
Pentium Pro 200
PC.*

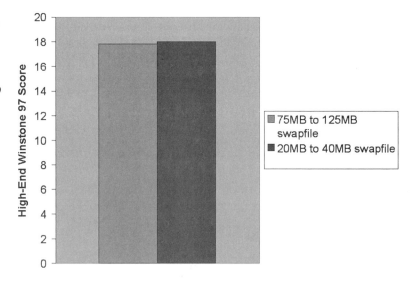

Figure 7.18.

*Overall High-
End Winstone
97 performance
versus swapfile
size for a
Pentium Pro 200
PC.*

Figure 7.19.

*Category scores
from High-End
Winstone 97
tests versus
swapfile size for
a Pentium Pro
200 PC.*

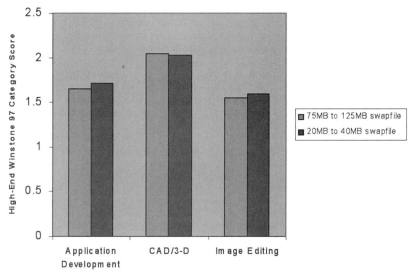

7.3.2. The Filesystem and Performance

When you run Windows 95, you have no control over the type of filesystem you use. The filesystem is the logical structure of files as stored on a hard disk. Starting with DOS, the filesystem on most PC's was referred to as the FAT, or File Allocation Table. Windows 95 updated this to VFAT and later to FAT32.

Figure 7.20.
Individual application scores from High-End Winstone 97 tests versus swapfile size for a Pentium Pro 200 PC.

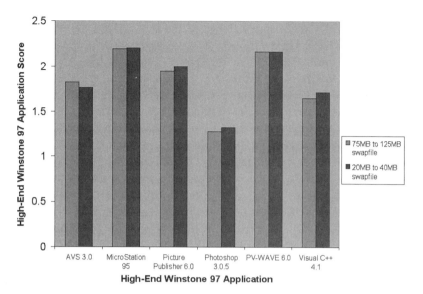

Windows NT 4.0 supports the FAT filesystem but it also supports NTFS, the NT File System. This is the filesystem that Microsoft designed exclusively for Windows NT 4.0. FAT and its variants are understood (in other words, can be read from and written to) by a number of operating systems, but only Windows NT 4.0 can use NTFS partitions.

NTFS is a more powerful filesystem than FAT; it offers extensive security and access control features that FAT does not. Unlike Windows 95, you must log in to a Windows NT 4.0 machine, whether it's a workstation or a server. You can use the file access controls on NTFS partitions to strictly control which users or groups can use directories or files on both workstations and servers.

NTFS also allows for selective compression of files or directories, a feature not found in VFAT. All of these features come with a performance price, though, as you'd expect. If you don't need these added features, you might try using FAT on your Windows NT 4.0 system for a performance boost. If you'd like to learn more about the performance difference between NTFS and FAT, read Chapter 11, "Optimizing Your Disk Subsystem."

7.3.4. Disk Fragmentation

Disk fragmentation is a natural process that occurs as you write and delete files on your hard disk. When your system is fully defragmented, all files are stored in contiguous areas on the disk (in order). The smallest unit that a file takes up on the hard disk is a cluster. In the completely defragmented state, the data that make up a particular file are stored in clusters on the disk that are right next to each other. On a fragmented hard disk the data that make up files are not contiguous. Clusters that make up a particular file can be scattered all over the hard disk. The operating system takes care of hunting all these clusters down; that's built into the filesystem code. Your applications don't care whether a particular file is fragmented or not, because the operating system transparently pieces the file together from all of its clusters. *You* should care, though, because the more a file is fragmented, the more your hard disk drive has to search for all of the pieces that make up the file. That takes time and that means a performance hit for you.

You can't stop fragmentation from happening. Files are stored in units on your disk known as clusters or allocation units. In turn, these clusters are made up of a certain number of sectors on your hard drive. The operating system looks at the hard drive in terms of clusters, while the hard drive itself (and its associated controller hardware) looks at the physical disks in terms of sectors. Windows splits the file that you want to save into clusters on your hard drive. Many times, these clusters are contiguous, so the file is not fragmented. When the clusters are not contiguous, the file is fragmented. How does fragmentation happen? When you delete a file, the clusters it used to occupy become available. Let's say you just deleted a 30KB file and then you want to write a 50KB file. It's quite likely that the operating system will begin writing the 50KB file into the 30KB hole (and again, the hole will really be a multiple of the cluster size). After it's filled that hole, though, there'll still be about 20KB of the file left to write. It will then have to skip along on the hard disk until it finds more room to write the rest of the file. Thus, this file will be fragmented. Because you're constantly reading, writing, and deleting files, fragmentation occurs.

Windows NT 4.0 does not include a bundled disk defragmentation tool as Windows 95 does. This situation may change in future versions of Windows NT 4.0. Currently, the most popular tool to defragment Windows NT 4.0 partitions is Diskeeper from Executive Software. If you want to squeeze all of the performance out of your Windows NT 4.0 disk subsystem, consider getting a copy of Diskeeper and running it on your system.

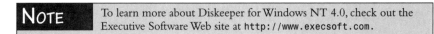

NOTE To learn more about Diskeeper for Windows NT 4.0, check out the Executive Software Web site at `http://www.execsoft.com`.

7.3.5. Graphics Driver Settings

Graphics drivers are an example of a piece of software that affects system performance. No matter what kind of graphics board you have installed in your system, it's possible to change overall system performance with the graphics driver software.

The graphics driver is the software that talks to the hardware of your graphics board, translating the instructions from Windows into the hardware-specific routines that your particular graphics board understands. Graphics board manufacturers constantly update their graphics drivers to fix bugs and to improve performance. So, one way to ensure that your graphics subsystem is performing as quickly as it can is to update your graphics board drivers frequently.

Other graphics driver settings that affect performance are resolution and color depth. Resolution is how large your display is, expressed as the height and width in pixels. A pixel is a picture element, one of the tiny dots on your monitor that makes up the overall display. Common resolutions are 640×480, 800×600, and 1024×768. The first number is how wide the display is in pixels and the second is how high the display is in pixels. Each pixel on the screen corresponds to data stored in your graphics board's memory. The higher the resolution, the more data your graphics subsystem has to deal with every time it updates the screen. The time it takes to scroll down a page screen may be slower, but at the same time the page contains more data, so it is hard to really figure out the performance change.

Color depth affects performance more noticeably. Color depth is the size of the palette of colors that your graphics subsystem can display, expressed in a number of bits. A color depth of 16 bits indicates that your graphics subsystem is set to display 65,536 distinct colors, because two to the sixteenth power is 65,536. Each pixel on the screen would then be represented by a 16-bit value, indicating its color at any given moment. Because the amount of data that your graphics subsystem has to manipulate increases as you increase color depth, graphics performance usually decreases as you increase color depth.

We won't be covering NT-specific information about graphics driver settings in this chapter. If you want to learn more about how your graphics driver settings affect system performance, read Chapter 10, "Optimizing Your Graphics Subsystem."

7.4. NT Performance Tools

Even though Windows NT 4.0 is a desktop PC operating system, you can tell it either thinks it is, or at least wants to be, a big computer operating system. Direct evidence of this desire can be seen in the Windows NT 4.0 Performance Monitor. PerfMon, as it is often called, is based on performance tools common on minicomputers and mainframes. It adds to these solid technical underpinnings a graphical user interface and is consequently a lot more approachable than its larger computer counterparts. Microsoft considered performance important enough to spend lots of time on making Windows NT 4.0 self-tuning, and they even threw in a second performance monitoring tool within the Task Manager for the user only casually interested in performance analysis. We'll look at both of these tools in the following sections.

7.4.1. Performance Monitor

Performance Monitor does just what its name implies: It allows you to monitor the performance of Windows NT 4.0 systems. PerfMon can track a large number of parameters, such as cache hit rate, page fault count, and processor utilization. It tracks this data in real time, but it also logs this data and can generate charts and

Windows NT Software Tuning

reports. In addition, you can set PerfMon to warn you when a particular parameter exceeds a preset threshold.

You must be logged in as the supervisor or supervisor equivalent to run PerfMon. To start the Performance Monitor, choose Administrative Tools from the Programs section on your Start menu. Performance Monitor should be listed as one of the administrative tools. By default, PerfMon starts up in the Chart view, with no counters displayed. In other words, you get a big empty graph.

In PerfMon lingo, you need to add counters to your view before you can see anything happening. Counters are measurements such as page faults per second, or processor utilization, or available bytes. Each counter is associated with a particular object. The objects that PerfMon can count as it runs include physical RAM, the hard disk, the swapfile, the disk cache, processes (programs), and threads. When you run PerfMon, you customize the view to observe the counters that pertain to the objects you're interested in. After you've got a particular view set up, you can save the settings for that view into a file, so that you can easily recall the view the next time you run PerfMon. You've got a choice of four different view types in PerfMon: Chart, Report, Alert, or Log. Let's take a look first at how to add some counters to the Chart view:

1. From the menu bar, choose Edit and then Add to Chart. This brings up the Add to Chart dialog box (see Figure 7.21).

Figure 7.21.

Add counters to the Performance Monitor chart with the Add to Chart dialog box.

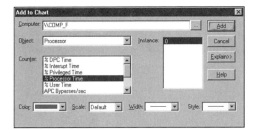

2. You can run PerfMon over a network; this explains the Computer field. Running PerfMon over the network is beyond the scope of this book.

3. First, choose the Object you're interested in, such as Processor, Memory, Cache, or Paging File. This choice affects which counters show up in the Counters field. For this example, choose the Memory object.

4. Now, choose which Counter you want to observe. For example, you can now choose Page Faults/sec.

5. You can also, if you wish, control the formatting of the line that you're adding to the graph with the Color, Scale, Width, and Style controls.

6. If you don't know what a particular counter is, click on the Explain>> button for a definition (see Figure 7.22).

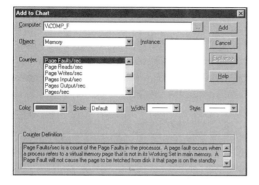

Figure 7.22.

*Use the Explain
button to get
definitions for
counters.*

7. Finally, click the <u>A</u>dd button to add the new counter to your graph. PerfMon will automatically choose a new color for the next counter you add to your graph. When you're finished, click the <u>D</u>one button.

8. PerfMon now graphs the counters you've selected (see Figure 7.23). In this case, we're measuring Page Faults/sec.

Figure 7.23.

*Observe changes
in counters over
time with the
main Chart
windows in
Performance
Monitor.*

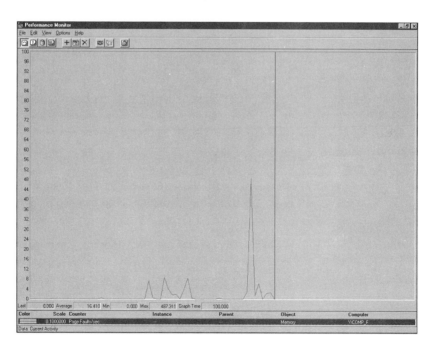

Windows NT Software Tuning

You can set up the object counters and options for each of the four types of views (Chart, Alert, Log, and Report). You can then save these settings into different settings files designed for different monitoring tasks.

By default, PerfMon updates the information you're viewing once per second. This is probably fine for most basic uses of PerfMon. If PerfMon isn't updating the view quickly enough for you, you can adjust the update interval. PerfMon is not a magical program that doesn't load your system down, though. Like Heisenberg's Uncertainty Principle in quantum mechanics, using PerfMon to observe system behavior can actually change system behavior. If you set the performance interval to a very short interval, you can load your system down as it does nothing but update the PerfMon view. Conversely, if you set the update interval too long, the data returned by PerfMon will be imprecise, and you might miss some interesting peaks or valleys. To set the update interval in PerfMon in the Chart view:

1. From the menu bar, choose Options and then choose Chart. This brings up the Chart Options dialog box.

2. The Chart Options dialog allows you to add the legend, value bar, vertical grid, horizontal gird, and vertical labels to your chart. You can also switch between graph and histogram formats, and set the maximum vertical value. To set the update interval, choose Interval (seconds) and adjust the value accordingly.

3. Click OK to save your changes.

Even though PerfMon offers different types of views, including Log files, you might want to do more sophisticated manipulation of the data that PerfMon gathers. PerfMon allows you to export the data you're measuring to a tab delimited (*.tsv) or comma delimited (*.csv) text file. You can then import this file into most popular spreadsheet and database programs. To export data to another format:

1. On the File menu, click Export Chart. The Performance Monitor – Export As dialog box appears.

2. In Save as type, click either Export TSV Files (*.tsv) or Export CSV Files (*.csv). Check the documentation of the program you'll import this data into to see whether TSV or CSV files would work best.

3. Enter a File name for the file that you want to export, and click Save.

You can use the Alerts view to have PerfMon track events and then notify you when a counter exceeds a specified value. The Alert view records the time and date when any of the counters you've specified exceeds the given value. You can also set up PerfMon to run a specified program when an alert condition occurs. To use the Alert view:

1. On the View menu, click Alert. Performance Monitor switches to Alert view.

2. On the Edit menu, click Add to Alert. This brings up the Add to Alert dialog (see Figure 7.24). As you did on the Chart view, choose Objects

and Counters as you desire. If you need a definition for a particular counter, highlight it and then click Explain>>.

Figure 7.24.

Add counters to the Alerts view with the Add to Alert dialog box.

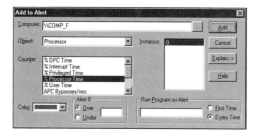

3. Set the Alert If Over or Alert If Under value. You can also set Run Program On Alert for either the First Time or Every Time.

4. After you've added all the counters you wish, click Done. You will now see the Alerts view with the counters you've set up. PerfMon generates an entry in this view each time the alert level is exceeded (see Figure 7.25).

Figure 7.25.

Monitor when counters exceed preset values with the Alerts view of Performance Monitor.

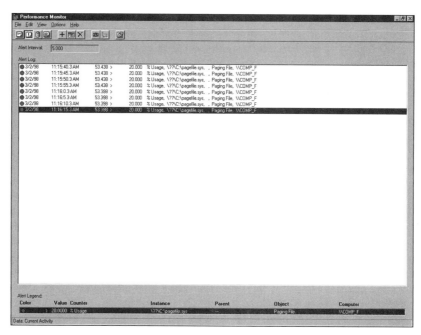

Reports let you display the constantly changing data values for selected counters in a columnar, report form. Unlike charts, reports do not give you a visual trail of data over time. Reports are useful if you want to print out snapshots of counter values for a particular moment in time. To use the Report view:

1. On the View menu, click Report. PerfMon switches to Report view.

2. On the Edit menu, click Add to Report. This brings up the Add to Report dialog (see Figure 7.26). As you did on the Chart view, choose Object and Counters as you desire. If you need a definition for a particular counter, highlight it and then click Explain>>.

Figure 7.26.

Add counters to the Reports view with the Add to Report dialog.

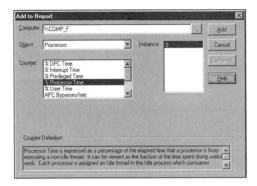

3. After you've added all the counters you wish using the Add button, click Done. You will now see the Report view with the counters you've set up. PerfMon updates this report every update interval (see Figure 7.27).

Figure 7.27.

Monitor counters in tabular form using the Report view of Performance Monitor.

You can use the Logs view in PerfMon to collected data which you can view later. Log files are useful if you want to look at a large amount of data collected over a long time, to perform detailed trend analysis. To use the Log view:

1. On the View menu, click Log. PerfMon switches to Log view.

2. On the Edit menu, click Add to Log. This brings up the Add To Log dialog (see Figure 7.28). You can only choose Objects, not Counters, to add to the log view.

Figure 7.28.

Add counters to the Log view with the Add to Log dialog.

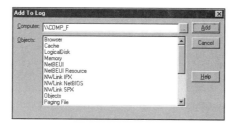

3. You must also set up the log file to use the log view. On the Options menu, choose Log. This brings up the Log Options dialog (see Figure 7.29). Enter the name of the log file and the update interval here. You can also use the Log Options dialog to start and stop logging.

Figure 7.29.

Set up the log file with the Log Options dialog.

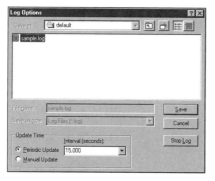

The best way to learn to use PerfMon is to just open it up and play around with it. Try adding counters and objects to the four different views and then observe the data collected. If you are uncertain what a particular counter measures, use the Explain feature. While PerfMon is running, start up some other applications you use and do some sample work, toggling back to the PerfMon screen to see how your work affects the counters you're observing.

After you've collected some data, export it to a spreadsheet or database program and manipulate it there. Take a look at log files that you've collected over a few days' time. After you get your hands a little dirty, you'll see what a powerful tool PerfMon is.

Windows NT Software Tuning

After you've determined which views are most useful to you and which counters you're interested in, make sure to save your settings so that you won't need to set up a view again every time you start PerfMon. To save settings for a particular view:

1. On the File menu, click Save Settings. You can either Save Settings In Current Settings File or Save Settings As a settings file. (After you've saved settings, you can then re-use them with the File, Open command.)

2. To save settings for all four views at once, on the File menu, click Save Workspace.

Why do we recommend using PerfMon when we're such cheerleaders for the Winstone and WinBench programs? PerfMon can be useful because the benchmark programs run only one application at a time, or play back operations from one particular application at a time. That strategy makes sense for a number of reasons. Many users are only running one application at a time: a word processor, an e-mail program, or a Web browser. For repeatability and therefore validity of results, the benchmark programs only run one application at a time. However, if you want to investigate how your system runs a number of different tasks simultaneously, you can use PerfMon. This is especially helpful if you usually use specialized applications that are not typified by the applications in Winstone. That's why we can recommend PerfMon as an additional investigative tool on Windows NT 4.0 systems.

As we've discussed, there are not many software settings that you can tweak in Windows NT 4.0. If you suspect that you have a memory problem, or bottleneck, the cheapest solution is to add more RAM. You can, however, adjust the swapfile size, if your system is continually running low on virtual memory. Windows NT 4.0 will advise you with a dialog box when virtual memory is running low.

If you think you have a shortage in your virtual memory system, the most important counter to monitor is Page Faults/sec. This tells you how often data is not found in the physical RAM. If requested data is not in physical RAM, slower disk I/O is required. If you have a high amount of page faults per second, you don't have enough memory.

You should also monitor Pages Input/sec. Pages Input/sec measures hard page faults. Hard page faults occur when the requested data is not located in the physical RAM, including the disk cache. In other words, a hard page fault means that the system had to use the slower hard disk. A soft page fault occurs when the requested data is not in the virtual memory, but rather in the disk cache. Any page fault requires extra system processor time to handle it, but hard page faults are the ones that really slow your system down.

Monitor these counters as you use your computer under a normal workload. If you experience a high sustained rate of Page Faults per second, and a significant percentage of that value is Pages Input per second, you probably have a memory shortage.

You can attempt to cure your memory shortage by increasing the size of the swapfile, but this will not lower the number of hard page faults in your system. Only adding more RAM will lower the number of hard page faults. To look at how much total memory (physical and virtual) you have, monitor Available Bytes. If you increase the swapfile size or add more physical RAM, you should see a change here.

7.4.2. Task Manager

If Performance Monitor is too daunting an application for you, you should try the Task Manager. Many folks use Task Manager to start and stop programs, but the Task Manager in Windows NT 4.0 also can monitor performance. It is much less sophisticated than PerfMon, but it also doesn't require the setup that PerfMon does. For instance, you can't log data with Task Manager. If you want to monitor the typical variables of interest in your system, though, Task Manager is a simple, user-friendly solution. To use Task Manager:

1. Press the Control, Alt, and Delete keys simultaneously (Ctrl-Alt-Del) to bring up the Windows NT 4.0 Security dialog box.

2. Click the Task Manager button. This brings up the Task Manager application. Task Manager uses three tabs: Applications, Processes, and Performance.

3. Click on the Performance tab. This gives you a dynamic view of system performance, including graphs and numeric displays of processor and memory usage (see Figure 7.30).

The main readouts are the CPU Usage bar, the CPU Usage History chart, the MEM usage bar, and the memory usage history chart. There are also numeric readouts for the number of total handles, total threads, total processes, physical memory, commit charge (virtual memory), and kernel memory.

Task Manager also adds a miniature CPU usage gauge to your system tray while it's running. This gauge mirrors the gauge on the main Task Manager windows. When you touch it with the mouse cursor, it displays the percentage of processor use in text format. Another useful feature is the setting Always On Top on the Options menu. When checked, this keeps the Task Manager window in view as you switch between other applications.

If Performance Monitor is too much to tackle, try leaving the Task Manager running while you do your daily work. Check its CPU and memory usage graphs periodically, and you'll be surprised at how much you can learn about what's going on behind-the-scenes in your system.

Windows NT Software Tuning

Figure 7.30.
Use Task Manager as a simple way to monitor system resource usage.

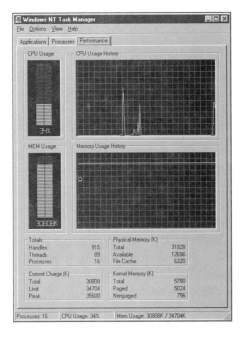

7.5. The Bottom Line

Our conclusion in this chapter is a simple one: in terms of software configuration, Windows NT 4.0 optimizes itself well enough that you don't have to do anything. If you really want to get the last little bit of performance out of your NT system by only changing software, you can try changing the swapfile size and getting the latest drivers. If you are willing to spend some money and change some hardware, you should read the chapters on RAM and the other subsystems such as processor, graphics and disk, to determine whether or not hardware upgrades are in order.

If you have more time on your hands, though, you will learn more about how your system operates and how the various subsystems depend on each other by running PerfMon.

7.6. Testing You Can Do

The main lesson of this chapter was learning to use Performance Monitor. As we've noted, though, there simply aren't many things you can do to further optimize the software settings in NT 4.0. As always, if you make any system changes, such as the swapfile changes that we experimented with, you should measure them with Winstone and the relevant subsystem tests in WinBench. If you are a typical business user, run Business Winstone. If you are a typical high-end user running graphics, 3-D/CAD, or software development applications, run High-End Winstone. In the case of our swapfile experiment, it's unlikely that WinBench tests would be of use. After a certain minimum amount of RAM is reached, WinBench is RAM-insensitive. If you're performance nuts like we are, though, you might want to run All Tests with both benchmarks, just for the heck of it. You never know what you might find.

When you do run the benchmarks, make sure you follow proper testing procedures. Those procedures include defragmenting the disk before each run and restarting your computer before each test run. For maximum repeatability of results, run in automated batch mode from your Startup group. This ensures that your PC is in the same state at the start of each test. Finally, run each test several times in each configuration to make sure your results are repeatable.

> **NOTE** Complete directions for running Winstone and WinBench can be found in Appendixes A, "Using Winstone 98," and B, "Using WinBench 98."

7.7. From Here...

Because Windows NT 4.0 is designed to be self-tuning, this chapter is unlike any of the other testing chapters. The software optimizations you can perform on Windows NT 4.0 are rather limited. You can still get a much better feel for what's going on under the hood in your NT machine by running the PerfMon or Task Manager as we've shown in this chapter. You can, however, explore other optimizations that are free or inexpensive software changes such as graphics driver settings and updates.

The following chapters will provide more information on these optimizations and others related to the Windows NT 4.0 tuning we've discussed in this chapter.

- Chapter 9, "Optimizing Your System's RAM," will show you how to optimize your RAM amount, the easiest and cheapest way to boost overall system performance through hardware changes.

- Chapter 10, "Optimizing Your Graphics Subsystem," will show you how to optimize your graphics setup and how to choose the best combination of screen resolution and color depth.

- Chapter 11, "Optimizing Your Disk Subsystem," will show you how to upgrade or optimize your hard drive.

Windows NT Software Tuning

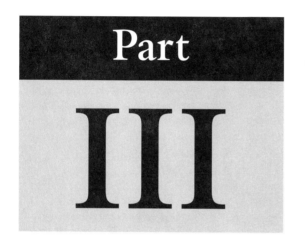

Part

III

Hardware Optimization

Chapter

8

Optimizing Your System's Processor

The processor, or CPU chip, is the brain of your system. When you ask someone what kind of PC they have, they'll likely respond, "it's an ancient 486-33 box" or a "screaming new Pentium II 400." Most PC model numbers are an encoded version of the CPU type and speed. In the old days, there weren't nearly as many types and speeds of processors as there are now, and (in general) you weren't able to upgrade your processor. This has changed drastically in recent years. Now there's a wide array of processors available in new systems and upgrades for existing systems.

The PC processor marketplace used to be the sole province of Intel, makers of the 80x86 family of chips. The original CPU chip in the first IBM PC was an 8088 running at 4.77MHz. Compare this clock speed to some of the newer 450MHz Pentium II systems: it's over ninety times slower! These days, it's pointless to have anything less powerful than a 486 processor if you want to run a current version of Windows (and realistically, you're better off with a Pentium). To run the Internet Explorer 4.0 that comes with Windows 98, Microsoft recommends at least a Pentium processor. One advantage to the fact that Microsoft and Intel have dominated the PC hardware and software space is that most applications are backward compatible with some set of CPU chips. While newer chips have added functionality and new instruction sets and features, they can still run programs written for DOS.

Even though the CPU chip is the first thing that comes to mind when you think of a particular PC, you might be surprised to find that it's not necessarily the most important determinant of performance. If you upgrade your existing system with a processor that's running at twice the frequency, you won't get anywhere near twice the performance out of your machine. Even if you buy a brand new system with a processor that runs at twice the clock speed of the processor in your current system, real-world performance probably won't double. If it does, it's probably because of a faster disk, more RAM, or a faster graphics board as much as it is because of a faster CPU. Still, many folks find processor upgrades to be worth the money, and everyone needs to know when it's advantageous to buy a brand-new system with a faster processor. If you want to learn more about your processor subsystem, how the type and speed of your CPU chip affect performance, and about what you should expect from a processor upgrade, read on.

In this chapter, you will learn:

■ Why your CPU matters

There are several different CPU manufacturers and many different CPU chips available. In the following sections you'll learn about the history and current state of PC-compatible processors. Technology marches on though, and that's definitely true in the processor market. By the time this book hits the stands, we're sure there'll be even newer, faster processors out there.

- Why your CPU doesn't matter

  While increasing speeds (measured in megahertz) sound nice, processor speed alone isn't a reliable indicator of how your system will perform.

- What is the processor subsystem?

  The CPU chip is really part of the processor subsystem in your PC, which consists of the CPU chip, associated levels of cache memory, main memory (RAM), and the busses that tie all these components together.

- How to pick the right processor for your OS

  Windows 98, Windows 95, and Windows NT use your CPU in slightly different ways. You'll learn how to decide on a processor or upgrade depending on which OS you're running.

- How to pick the right processor for your applications

  You also need to carefully choose a processor based on what applications you plan to run. High-end, graphically intensive applications can often take advantage of (or require) more advanced CPU's than normal business applications.

- Implications of MMX technology

  One of the new topics on the processor scene is MMX. You'll learn what this technology means for you and whether you should be concerned.

8.1. Cocktail Party Tips

When your computer buddy at the cocktail party asks you which processor you're running in your PC, and at what speed, answer the question politely and truthfully, then add, "But, as we all know, megahertz are meaningless." Your buddy will probably be flabbergasted, but on reflection it's easy to see why this is true. A 200MHz Pentium system is not going to be twice as fast as the same system running a Pentium at 100MHz. There are too many other variables at work.

Once your friend recovers, you can expand on your response a bit. Megahertz are meaningless compared to more accurate performance tests based on real-world applications. Dropping a faster chip into a system that's bottlenecked elsewhere isn't going to give you blazing performance. Also, you've got to examine the benefit you're getting from a processor upgrade versus its cost to justify purchasing it instead of waiting around until the time when you can buy a whole new system. So, to help you flesh out your cocktail party conversation, we've tested several processor upgrades in this chapter, as well as testing out other aspects of system design that affect performance. Keep in mind, though, that we were limited to testing upgrades that were available when we performed our tests.

Optimizing Your System's Processor

Many of these upgrades won't be on the market when you purchase this book. You can still glean valuable information from this chapter by gaining a better understanding of how your CPU affects performance, and also by learning there's more to processor subsystem performance than just clock speed. Factors like L1 and L2 cache and system bus speed all play a very significant role in processor subsystem and, more importantly, overall system performance.

In general, a processor upgrade isn't going to perform as well as a new system based on a processor of similar speed. The cost differential might make the upgrade worthwhile, though (see Figure 8.1). These results are for older systems, but the general principle still applies to systems available today.

Figure 8.1.

Upgrading the processor in a 486-66 system gets a little more than half the performance of buying a new Pentium 75 system, but at about one-fifth the cost.

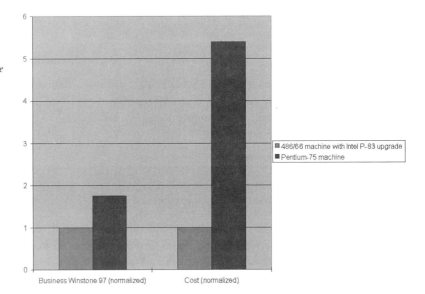

We've normalized the scores in this chart to show you the bang you get for your buck. While this is a pretty impressive bang-for-the-buck ratio, you still might be better off buying more RAM or a faster hard disk if you've got a limited budget. Processor upgrades aren't meant to bring you to the cutting edge of technology. They're really more of a way to extend the useful life cycle of older machines. While most operating systems and programs have iron-clad requirements regarding the amount of RAM and hard disk space required, the minimum requirement for processor is often just a 386 or 486.

Some applications though, especially games or high-end graphics applications that perform a lot of floating point operations, do have more stringent processor requirements. Newer applications will take advantage of MMX technology—if you want to run such an application, you'll have to at least get an MMX upgrade for your PC. Our studies show, though, that you'll never get the performance out of an upgrade that you'd get by buying a brand new system.

Here's another example of how megahertz are meaningless. If you look at the Business Winstone 97 scores for a number of machines in our testbed, you'll see that there's no simple pattern, even if all the machines have the same amount of RAM and the same operating system, Windows 95 (see Figure 8.2). Sure, you see increasing performance with increasing processor speed, but not strictly by the change in megahertz. That's because there are so many other factors that influence system performance: bus width and speed, memory speed, and cache size, as well as graphics and disk subsystem performance.

So, tell your friend at the cocktail party that "megahertz are meaningless, but if you're too broke to buy a new system, a processor upgrade can keep your aging machine current a bit longer."

Figure 8.2.

Business Winstone 97 performance across systems based on different processors.

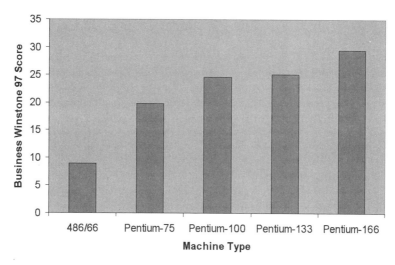

8.2. Why Your CPU Matters

The CPU chip is easily the most complicated and most expensive chip in any PC. PC's have always used chips from the Intel x86 family as their CPU's, in contrast to Mac OS computers which have used Motorola 680x0 and PowerPC CPU chips. There are several key features of a particular CPU chip that will have some effect on system performance. As we've noted, the clock frequency rating, measured in megahertz, is one such feature. Other features include the size (width) of the address and data busses. A processor with more address lines can use more memory than a processor with fewer address lines. Similarly, a processor with more data lines can read or write data more quickly than a processor with fewer data lines (because it can access a larger amount of data per clock cycle). CPU chips use special holding places, called registers, and the size of these registers is also important. Modern CPU chips also contain some amount of processor cache. The amount and type of this cache is yet another feature that affects performance.

Optimizing Your System's Processor

8.3. Processor Subsystem versus CPU Chip

We're making a distinction in this book between the CPU chip and system RAM, even though these two components are really part of the processor subsystem. When measuring performance, it's often more useful to think of the main subsystems in your computer rather than the individual components. For instance, you can buy the most screaming new graphics board for your PC, but if you run the Microsoft VGA drivers, you're not going to get the performance you'd get if you ran drivers specifically written for that board. The driver software, as well as the graphics board, are part of the graphics subsystem in your PC. The processor subsystem consists of the CPU chip and its on-board cache (L1 cache), secondary processor cache (L2 cache), main memory (RAM), and the busses which tie these components together.

The concept of cache is an important and potentially confusing one that crops up in many different places when you talk about PC performance. In this chapter we'll be talking about processor cache. Processor cache is an area of very fast memory that holds some of the current instructions and data that the CPU chip will likely execute or access. This memory runs as fast as the CPU itself does, which is not the case for main memory. The cache is filled by cache controller hardware, which reads in instructions and data from main memory that the CPU is likely to execute or access next. In this way, the cache allows your system to run without waiting on the slower system RAM, as long as the instructions or data that the CPU needs are in the cache. There are various levels of cache in a system. Cache that's built into the CPU chip itself is called level 1 (L1) cache. L1 cache became a standard feature of the CPU starting with the 486 family of processors. (See Table 8.1.) Cache that is separate from the CPU chip but also distinct from main system RAM, is called level 2 (L2) cache. Level 2 cache was originally found on the system motherboard, but now processors like the Pentium II come in a large package that contains both a CPU chip and some amount of L2 cache. Keep in mind that processor cache is completely different from disk cache: the disk cache is an area in main memory used to cache data on your hard disk. You'll learn more about cache in Chapter 9, "Optimizing Your System's Ram."

Table 8.1. Clock frequency and internal cache size of popular Intel-compatible processors.

Processor	MHz	L1 cache size
8088	4.77	0
80286	6 – 20	0
80386	16 – 33	0

Processor	MHz	L1 cache size
80486	16 – 100	8-16KB
Pentium	60 – 200	8KB + 8KB
Pentium Pro	150 – 200	8KB + 8KB
Pentium MMX	166 – 266	16KB + 16KB
Pentium II	233 – 400	16KB + 16KB
AMD K6	166 – 233	32KB + 32KB
Cyrix 6x86MX	150 – 188	64KB

We've divided the processor subsystem into separate CPU and RAM chapters for this book, because those two components are the ones you can add or upgrade in your system easily. Once you've bought a particular motherboard, you're stuck with a particular system bus design, and even in some cases with a certain amount of L2 cache (more on this later). Now let's take a look at the evolution of the Intel x86-compatible line of processors.

8.4. Ancient History

The original IBM PC was designed around the Intel 8088 processor. This chip ran at 4.77 MHz, or 4.77 million cycles per second. The clock frequency of a CPU chip is it's *heartbeat*, but it's not necessarily the amount of time it takes to execute a single instruction. Only the most basic of instructions can execute in one CPU clock cycle. This chip had no L1 cache and it could only address one megabyte (1MB) of RAM. While its internal registers were 16 bits wide, its data bus was only 8 bits wide.

The next interesting processor to come along was the 80286. It was eventually available in a variety of clock speeds from 6MHz to 20MHz. The 286 (as these chips are commonly known) was the heart of IBM's PC-AT model. It could address what seemed like a whopping amount of memory at the time: all of 16MB. The data bus was 16 bits wide. In the mid-'80's, Intel released the 80386 chip, and PC-compatible manufacturers, starting with Compaq (who beat IBM to the punch) released systems based on the 386. The 386 was a 32-bit processor, able to access 4GB of memory. This 32-bit address bus is still big enough for any desktop PC of today. Other features popped up in various models of the 386 chip—there were power-saving versions (the SL series) and economical versions with a narrower data bus (the SX series). This was the beginning of the time when you had to choose processors on criteria other than just clock speed.

8.5. The 486 Family

The 80486 ushered in the era of widespread acceptance of Windows—it's power and new features allowed users to run a graphical user interface at an acceptable speed. The 486 introduced L1 cache (8KB or 16KB) as well as other new features including a built-in math coprocessor, or floating point unit (FPU). Previous CPU chips required an additional, external chip to perform floating point math operations. As with the 386, the 486 eventually came in a wide variety of flavors (including versions without a built-in FPU). The most important innovation that eventually showed up in the 486 family was the concept of clock doubling. These chips, known as 486DX2 models, ran internally at twice the clock speed of the system. So, for instance, while the motherboard clock might run at 25MHz, a 486DX2/50 can be plugged into this system and it will run internally at 50MHz—twice the speed of the motherboard. The speed doubling only occurs inside the CPU chip, so external components are not affected nor do they have to be replaced to handle the increased speed. After the DX2, there's the inappropriately named DX4. It doesn't quadruple the system clock speed, as you'd expect, it triples it. So a DX4/100 chip fits into a motherboard running at 33MHz and then the internal processor speed is 100MHz.

8.6. Sidebar: Troubleshooting CPU Problems

CPU problems are fairly easy to spot. If you power on your system and the power LED comes on but nothing else happens at all—nothing appears on the monitor—then you might have had a CPU chip or motherboard failure. This assumes, of course, that you've checked the obvious things such as good cable connections between all your system components.

CPU failures are rare compared to hard disk or controller card failures, but it's certainly possible to zap the CPU chip with static electricity while you're working inside your computer, and power surges or lightning strikes can also fry system components like the CPU chip. The main enemy of the CPU chip is heat. Generally, the faster a processor is, the more power it consumes and correspondingly the more heat it gives off. If you open your system up, the CPU chip should be easy to spot because it will likely be crowned by either a heat sink or a small fan. A heat sink is a finned aluminum structure that conducts heat away from the CPU and dissipates it more efficiently. Some processors, especially processor upgrades, dispense with the heat sink and instead attach a small fan to the top of the CPU chip (in addition to the system cooling fan located on the case of your PC). If this fan fails, or if the heat sink becomes disconnected from the processor, the CPU chip can overheat and sustain permanent damage.

Heat can be a problem especially if you overclock your CPU. Overclocking your CPU means running it at a clock speed that is greater than that specified on the chip. This is possible because chip makers rate the maximum speed of CPU chips fairly conservatively. Hobbyists who want to squeeze every possible drop of performance out of their system without paying extra overclock, but we don't recommend it. While it can work for some people with no problems, it's not worth the risk, and it can cause untraceable problems. Systems that run fine at their rated speeds will often exhibit inexplicable problems when overclocked— GPF's and other unrecoverable application errors.

8.7. The Pentium Family

In 1992, Intel introduced the Pentium processor and also launched a massive "Intel Inside" campaign. By this time, a few companies such as AMD and Cyrix had reverse engineered Intel's chip designs and were producing Intel-compatible CPU chips. The Pentium was so named because Intel could not trademark the numbers "586." As with the 486, along with faster clock speeds and larger bus widths, the Pentium introduced some architectural improvements.

8.7.1. Pentium MMX

The Pentium with MMX technology was introduced in 1996. MMX technology introduces new instructions and new registers that are designed to speed up multimedia code.

8.7.2. Pentium Pro

Intel released the Pentium Pro before the Pentium with MMX technology, but it's still a generation ahead. It's also known as the P6 (but oddly enough, not the Sexium).

8.7.3. Pentium II

As we were writing this book, Intel introduced a whole new generation of processor, the Pentium II. This processor essentially combines the best aspects of the Pentium MMX and Pentium Pro chips into a new package which combines the CPU chip itself with L2 cache.

8.8. Cyrix Processors

Cyrix developed processors that are comparable to Intel's 386, 486, and Pentium designs. The Cyrix processor known as the 6x86 is positioned as a cheaper alternative to the Pentium. Cyrix labels their processors according to performance rating, not according to clock frequency.

Optimizing Your System's Processor

8.9. AMD Processors

Like Cyrix, AMD manufactures chips designed to compete with Intel's. In general, they are comparable to Intel chips but cheaper. However, with the wide variety of types of CPU chips available these days, the best way to determine whether a particular chip is comparable with any other chip, no matter who the manufacturer is, is to run real-world performance tests.

8.10. Processor Upgrades

You used to be stuck with the CPU chip that came in your computer. Now, though, most computer manufacturers install their CPU chips in a ZIF (zero insertion force) socket to allow you to easily install a processor upgrade. When you install a processor upgrade, you typically remove your existing CPU chip and replace it with a new CPU chip or with a circuit board that includes a new CPU chip as well as other parts. On some systems, you may have to adjust jumpers on the motherboard to increase the system bus speed and to adjust the multiplier value that determines how much faster than the system bus the CPU chip runs.

The most obvious performance improvement stems from the fact that a processor upgrade is typically running faster than the CPU chip it replaced: the internal clock frequency is higher. For instance, you can replace your Pentium 75 processor with a Pentium MMX upgrade processor which will be able to run at 150MHz internally. But the benefit of this increased internal clock speed is only one part of how the processor upgrade works. Upgrade designers often choose CPU chips that have larger L1 caches than the chips they are replacing. The larger L1 cache compensates for the slower system RAM that these CPU chips have to work with.

No matter what the upgrade designers do, though, an older system with a processor upgrade is never going to equal the performance of a new system based around the same processor. Even though folks classify their system initially based on the CPU, one Pentium 75 box is not equivalent to all other Pentium 75 boxes. This is especially true in the case of upgraded units. In terms of processor subsystem performance alone, the system bus (controlled by the motherboard), processor cache, and main RAM will determine performance, and these system components are typically slower or smaller on older systems. You should never expect to equal the performance of current systems simply by upgrading to a current CPU chip, or you will be disappointed. Unfortunately, even reputable computer magazines have been susceptible to the marketing hype of processor upgrade manufacturers. When you read that you can "achieve Pentium 150 performance with your Pentium 75 machine" with a particular upgrade you should skip on to the next column and allow yourself to feel superior to the computer journalist in question.

Upgrading your CPU also allows you to take advantage of new features inherent in the newer chips. The buzzword recently has been MMX technology. Intel invented this but other manufacturers such as AMD and Cyrix are already selling chips with the MMX-compatible instruction set and registers. When we did the testing for this chapter, Intel offered a Pentium OverDrive upgrade with MMX technology for Pentium 75, Pentium 90, and Pentium 100 based existing systems. MMX upgrades for faster systems are now on the market. If you have a relatively new system that doesn't support MMX, but you'd like to take advantage of MMX-aware applications and games, keep an eye out for these upgrades. In some cases, you'll be able to upgrade your computer simply by replacing the CPU chip itself.

8.11. Sidebar: Brain Surgery—How to Upgrade Your CPU

How exactly do you go about installing your processor upgrade? Two words: Very carefully. Even folks who feel comfortable opening their PC and installing new adapters or new RAM should take extra care when dealing with the CPU chip. The CPU chip is the most susceptible to damage caused by electrostatic discharge (in other words, getting zapped).

The first thing you should do when you want to install your processor upgrade is read the manual. While we tend to skip this step for many upgrades we install or programs we run, we've found that it's necessary in this case. Besides, the manuals for processor upgrades are usually pretty thin and painless. The upgrade manual will probably refer you to your system (or system motherboard) manual, so make sure you have that handy. If you're the kind of person who tosses out the documentation that comes with hardware and software, you're asking for trouble down the road when you want to fix a problem with your system or when you want to upgrade it.

The second step for many processor upgrades involves running software supplied by the processor upgrade manufacturer. This software can check your system for compatibility (because not all processor upgrades are compatible with all systems) or it can upgrade the BIOS of your system to handle the upgrade. Note that these programs are not completely bug-free. When we were installing the Intel Pentium OverDrive with MMX Technology upgrade, the program supplied by Intel determined that our Compaq systems were compatible with the upgrade. This turned out not to be the case. After some troubleshooting with Intel, we tried upgrading the system BIOS to the latest version from Compaq. This change did the trick, and we were then able to install the upgrade. You might want to take this step too, no matter what the compatibility checking software determines, of updating your system BIOS to the latest version available from your system or motherboard manufacturer.

Your processor upgrade kit will contain the CPU upgrade unit itself, manuals, software, and usually a chip-extraction tool. It will probably not contain an anti-static wrist strap. If you spend a lot of time inside the guts of your system, you'll find that this device is well worth the few bucks you'll spend on it. We know. During testing for this chapter, we foolishly replaced a CPU chip without wearing a grounding strap, assuming that we had discharged ourselves by touching the metal case of the system we were upgrading. Unfortunately, we built up more static charge (probably due to the carpeting in our testing area) and zapped the chip when we touched its pins to the socket inside the system—the audible pop let us know what to expect, and sure enough, the system was dead as a doornail when we powered it up. Lucky for us, upgrade manufacturers send us multiple evaluation units. You will not probably be so lucky, so that's why we advise that you buy and use an anti-static grounding strap.

So, you've got your system opened up and you're grounded to it with your wrist strap. Your system will probably contain one of three types of sockets into which you'll install the upgrade unit: an empty non-ZIF socket, a non-ZIF socket with the existing processor, or (if you're lucky) a ZIF socket with the existing processor. You can spot the ZIF socket because of the tiny lever attached to one side. Lifting this lever is what causes the socket to release its grip on the pins of the processor chip. If you've got a single non-ZIF socket, you'll have to use the chip extraction tool provided with your upgrade kit to remove the old processor. You do this by sliding the edge of the tool underneath the chip and gently prying up all four sides of the chip until it's free of the socket. Take care when you do this, because you'll want to preserve your old CPU chip in case there are problems you need to troubleshoot with your new upgrade. A bent or broken pin on a CPU chip can render it completely useless.

If you've got a ZIF-socketed processor, just lift the lever and remove the chip. You may also have to remove a restraining clip on the heat sink to get the processor out. Once you're staring at an empty socket, you're ready to install the upgrade. If your upgrade chip comes with an attached fan, make sure that it's installed properly (some of these fans require than you attach them to the CPU chip and then attach their power leads to jumpers on the upgrade unit or on the motherboard). Orient the pins on the upgrade chip with the holes in the socket by matching up pin 1. Pin 1 is always designated by a diagonal line in the corner of the socket or by the corner of the chip that has a diagonal chunk missing.

For a ZIF socket, all you need to do is push the lever back down into position, making sure that the processor upgrade it fully seated down onto the socket. Non-ZIF sockets require that you carefully press down on the upgrade unit until it's firmly inserted into the socket. Take great care to make sure that the pins on all four sides of the chip are properly aligned before you do this, or you're asking for a bent pin and a permanently damaged upgrade chip. Do make sure, though, that you firmly position the upgrade in place. We've made the mistake of putting the system back together without checking this. The system was dead when we rebooted, and we thought the worst (blown chip). In fact, when we disassembled the system for troubleshooting, it turned out that the CPU upgrade wasn't pushed all the way into the socket.

Once you've got the upgrade inserted and your system put back together, power on your system. If nothing comes up on your monitor, double check that you've reconnected your monitor properly as well as your keyboard and mouse. If those connections check out, open up your system and check that the processor upgrade is seated properly in the socket, and that any cooling fan is properly installed. If all of this checks out, you might have to contact your processor upgrade manufacturer for technical support (because your system might be incompatible, or you might've blown your processor upgrade with static discharge).

Once you've got your processor upgrade working, you might want to run some benchmarks on it to see just how much of a performance improvement you got for you money. In the following sections, we'll discuss some benchmark results from testing we performed on Windows 98, Windows 95, and Windows NT with various processor upgrades and with various changes to the processor subsystem. (See Table 8.2 for some recommended processor/operating system combinations.) Keep in mind that the processors and processor upgrades that were available when we did this testing might not be on the market when you're reading this book. The concepts revealed, however, will be the same.

Table 8.2. Minimum recommended processors for various operating systems and software.

Software	Processor Requirement
Windows 3.1 real mode	8088
Windows 3.1 standard mode	80286
Windows 3.1 enhanced mode	80386
Windows 95	80386DX
Windows NT 4.0	80486-25
Quake	Pentium 90
Microsoft's PC 97 standard	Pentium 166

Optimizing Your System's Processor

8.12. Windows 98 and Your CPU

As far as the processor subsystem is concerned, Windows 98 is very similar to Windows 95. The march of technological progress during the three years between Windows 95 and Windows 98 hasn't slowed, though. Windows 98 includes Internet Explorer 4.0, and Microsoft recommends at least a Pentium processor to run that program. Yes, you can still run Windows 98 on a 486, but you will probably find that annoying, unless it's loaded with RAM and a fast hard disk.

8.12.1. How and Why We Tested

We ran both Business Winstone 98 and WinBench 98 Processor Tests for this section. We chose RAM amounts for our test systems based on typical RAM amounts in existing systems (and not necessarily what we'd consider the optimal RAM amounts; for those, skip on to the next chapter). We tested the processor upgrade available for our Pentium 75 and Pentium 100 based systems. To demonstrate the effects of system bus speed and clock multiplication, we ran studies on our Pentium 133 and Pentium 166 based systems altering only those settings.

Our default graphics setup was 1024×768×256 for these machines. This represents the most common resolution and color depth settings that users currently run. If you'd like more information on resolution and color depth and how they affect performance, see Chapter 10, "Optimizing Your Graphics Subsystem."

We also defragmented the hard drives of each machine before we ran each test. It's always good testing practice to fully defragment a hard drive and then reboot your machine before starting a test.

8.12.2. Pentium 75

The upgrade for our Pentium 75 machine was the Intel OverDrive Processor with MMX Technology. This replaces the existing Pentium 75 chip with a Pentium MMX chip running internally at 2.5 times the bus speed of the computer. In this case, the Pentium 75's bus speed is 50MHz, so the OverDrive runs internally at 125MHz.

The upgrade increases CPU speed by 67%, but we wanted to see how this translated into real-world performance. We ran a Business Winstone 98 test and got about a 29% increase in the speed of the machine running standard business applications (see Figure 8.3). This is a very significant increase in speed, but it is less than half of the speed-up in the CPU chip itself. This will be the first illustration of many that should show you that doubling CPU speed does not double overall performance.

Figure 8.3.

Business Winstone 98 Scores on the DeskPro 575 running Windows 98, before and after upgrading the CPU.

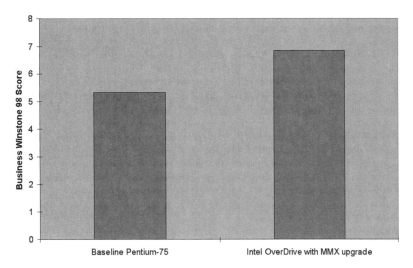

The category scores do not all see the same benefit from the CPU upgrade (see Figure. 8.4). The big winner is the Browsers category, which shows a 50% improvement with the CPU upgrade. Word processing applications show about a 31% improvement, while the publishing applications show a 27% improvement. The database and spreadsheet applications show only a 23% improvement. This should still be quite noticeable to anyone using this particular machine. Let's see how the processor subsystem is operating before and after the upgrade by looking at the pertinent WinBench results.

Figure 8.4.

Business Winstone 98 category scores on the DeskPro 575 running Windows 98, before and after upgrading the CPU.

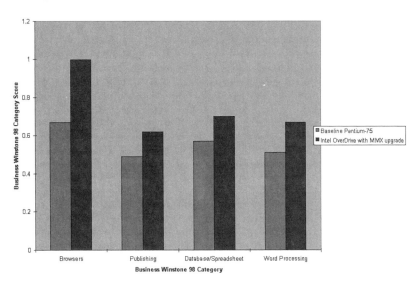

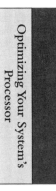

Optimizing Your System's Processor

The WinBench 98 Processor Tests, CPUmark$_{32}$ and FPUmark, show a more dramatic change in the processor subsystem caused by the upgrade (see Figure 8.5). Remember, CPUmark$_{32}$ measures overall processor subsystem speed, while FPUmark measures the floating-point performance of the processor subsystem. The MMX upgrade gives up a 53% increase in the CPUmark$_{32}$ score and a whopping 69% increase in the FPUmark score. Thus, in this case the processor subsystem really does speed up approximately as much as the internal CPU speed. The real-world performance doesn't approach this value, but it is still hard to ignore speed-up in the 20% and 30% range, and the 50% speed-up we saw in the Browsers category.

Figure 8.5.
WinBench 98 Processor Test scores on the DeskPro 575 running Windows 98, before and after upgrading the CPU.

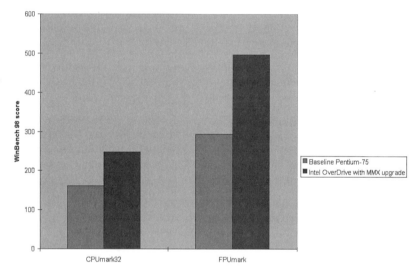

8.12.3. Pentium 100

Our Pentium 100 system had similar upgrade options as our Pentium 75 system: we could use the Intel OverDrive Processor with MMX Technology. This upgrade was supposed to boost our CPU to a 166MHz Pentium with MMX Technology, but this turned out not to be the case. Let's take a look at the numbers and try to figure out what happened.

The Business Winstone 98 score goes up by 16% after the upgrade (see Figure 8.6). Looking back at the results of the upgraded Pentium 75 machine, we see that the scores after the upgrade on both models are essentially the same. Shouldn't we expect that the Pentium 100 machine would get more of a performance boost?

Figure 8.6.

Business Winstone 98 scores on the DeskPro 5100 running Windows 98, before and after upgrading the CPU.

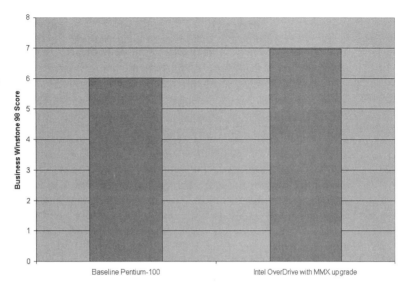

The category scores from the Business Winstone 98 tests are equally less dramatic (see Figure 8.7). The big winner is once again the Browsers category, with a 32% speedup. All of the other categories show speed-up in the 10% to 17% range. The raw scores are fairly close to the raw scores from the upgraded Pentium 75.

Figure 8.7.

Business Winstone 98 category scores on the DeskPro 5100 running Windows 98, before and after upgrading the CPU.

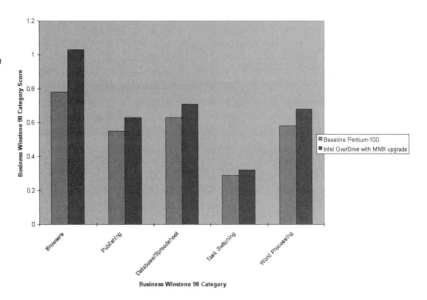

Optimizing Your System's Processor

These matching scores are the clues that allowed us to figure out what was going on. The MMX OverDrive upgrade is supposed to take a Pentium 100 machine to a 166MHz MMX CPU. However, this assumes that the Pentium 100 machine is a newer model that uses a 66MHz system bus. The upgrade chip then multiplies this clock by 2.5 to get the internal frequency of 166MHz. However, our Pentium 100 machine is an older model that uses a clock doubled 50MHz system bus. Unfortunately, there are no jumper settings on this particular motherboard to set it to faster operation. We're stuck with this frequency, which the upgrade then multiplies by 2.5 to get an internal clock frequency of 125MHz—the same internal frequency at which the upgrade in our Pentium 75 system was running. This explains why the scores from the upgraded Pentium 100 and the upgraded Pentium 75 match.

The point of all of this is not that there's anything wrong with this particular upgrade. You just need to be sure that your system really can handle the specific processor upgrade you've chosen.

The Processor Test scores reflect our diminished expectations (see Figure 8.8). CPUmark$_{32}$ and FPUmark increase by about 28% each. Remember, the WinBench 98 Processor Tests only test your PC's processor subsystem. While 28% faster sounds good on paper, it's only meaningful if you can get that same performance gain out of a real-world application. That's why it's important to use WinBench 98 in tandem with Winstone 98. Winstone can tell you how fast your system is relative to another system, however it's configured or upgraded. WinBench can help you isolate subsystem performance and track down system bottlenecks.

Figure 8.8.

WinBench 98 Processor Test scores on the DeskPro 5100 running Windows 98, before and after upgrading the CPU.

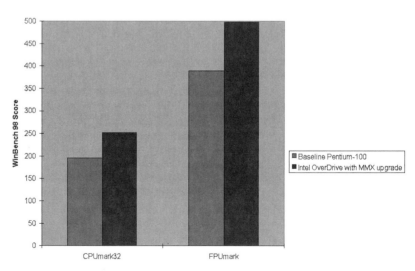

In attempting to upgrade our Pentium 100, we learned that you've got to be very careful to make sure that your existing system can take full advantage of the CPU upgrade. Still, even with our older Pentium 100 machine, we saw some dramatic performance gains, especially with browser applications.

8.12.4. Pentium 133

We decided to take a different tack with our Pentium 133. We decided to use it for some testing that shows the effects of system bus speed and of system clock multiplication on performance.

Let's recap what we've discovered about the system bus and the CPU speed. The system bus, or motherboard speed, of a Pentium system is either 50, 60, or 66MHz. (As we were finishing up this book, systems with 100MHz system busses had just become available.) This system bus speed is multiplied by 1, 1.5, 2, 2.5, or 3 to get a range of frequencies from 60 to 200MHz for the standard (classic) Pentium chips. This multiplication factor is technically known as the Core-to-Bus freqency ratio, the core meaning the guts of the CPU chip itself. This ratio is controlled (again, on classic Pentium chips) by voltages applied to pins on the CPU chip. You can control these voltages via jumpers or switches on the motherboard, and in some systems you can also control the system bus frequency.

Switches on our Compaq Deskpro 5133 allowed us to test six different bus speed/core speed combinations: 66/133, 60/120, 66/100, 50/100, 60/90, and 50/75. That would make the Core-to-Bus frequency ratios 2, 2, 1.5, 2, 1.5, and 1.5 in that order. That range of settings is determined by the motherboard manufacturer.

Wait a minute—why would anyone want to decrease the speed at which their processor or system bus was running? Where are the processor upgrade tests for this machine? Well, no one would want to decrease their processor or bus speed, obviously. When we performed the original tests for this chapter, our testbed did not include any CPU upgrades for our Pentium 133 machine. Still, there are valuable lessons to be learned from examining our processor/bus speed studies on this machine. These tests illustrate how these components combine to affect overall system performance, and to further illuminate our original point that megahertz is meaningless.

We ran our Deskpro 5133 through the Business Winstone 98 paces at all possible bus speed/core speed combinations (see Figure. 8.9). If megahertz is meaningless were not true, you'd expect performance scores to drop off linearly with decreasing CPU frequency. This isn't the case, though. Take a look at the two scores for the CPU running at 100MHz. One is with a 66MHz system bus multiplied by 1.5; the other is with a 50MHz bus doubled. The latter configuration scores about four percent less on the overall Business Winstone 98 even though the CPU chip is running at the same internal speed. Every time any operation that the CPU performs can't be done completely internally (that is, without accessing the L2 cache or the main system RAM), the system with the faster bus is at an advantage. Also, look at the difference between the score of the 100MHz speed (doubling the 50MHz bus) and the 90MHz speed (multiplying the 60MHz bus by 1.5); it's a mere 1% difference. The higher core CPU speed of the 100MHz case is offset by the higher bus speed in the 90MHz case.

Figure 8.9.

Business Winstone 98 scores on the DeskPro 5133 running Windows 98, varying the CPU and bus speeds.

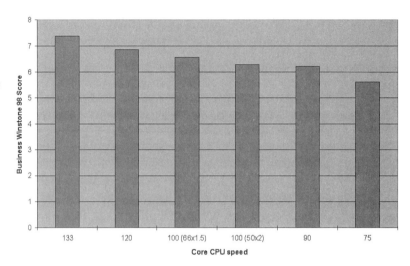

The category scores of Business Winstone 98 (for this same set of speed combinations) mirror the overall curve (see Figure 8.10). In the case of the database and spreadsheet applications, the 90MHz setting is actually faster than the 100MHz setting with the 50MHz system bus. The other interesting feature of this graph is the range of the Browser category scores—browser performance is more affected by CPU speed than the other application categories.

Figure 8.10.

Business Winstone 98 category scores on the DeskPro 5133 running Windows 98, varying the CPU and bus speeds.

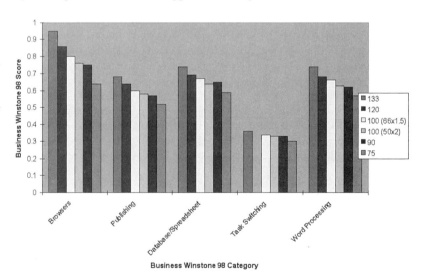

In the case of WinBench 98 Processor Test scores, we see a slightly different pattern to the CPUmark$_{32}$ and FPUmark curves (see Figure 8.11). While the FPUmark score barely changes between the two 100MHz settings, the CPUmark$_{32}$ shows the least change between the 90MHz and initial 100MHz setting. Overall, the FPUmark score changes more with dropping CPU speed than does the CPUmark$_{32}$ score. This reflects the different way in which typical floating-point operations break out of L1 and L2 cache, thus stressing the system bus differently than the operations in CPUmark$_{32}$.

Figure 8.11.
WinBench 98 Processor Test scores on the DeskPro 5133 running Windows 98, varying the CPU and bus speeds.

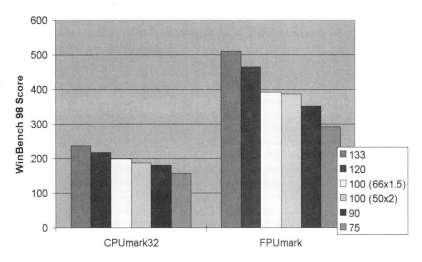

What does all this mean for you, the user, if you're never going to handicap your system by slowing down the CPU? It means that you should pay attention to more than just the raw CPU speed, especially if you're just running business applications. The system bus speed—the speed at which the CPU accesses L2 cache, and the upper bound on RAM access—also affects system performance.

These factors affect performance whether you're buying a new system or a CPU upgrade for your existing system. In the end, you'll want to see how a new system or a CPU upgrade will improve real-world performance. One of the best ways to do this is, in our admittedly biased opinion, is to check reviews in magazines like *PC Magazine* or *Computer Shopper*. These magazines use the ZDBOp industry-standard benchmarks in their reviews, so you can be assured of meaningful results to help you when you shop.

8.12.5. Pentium 166

We repeated our bus speed/core speed combination tests for the Pentium 166 machine in our testbed. This machine allows for a different range of settings than the Pentium 133 model. In this case, you can adjust switches on the motherboard to get the following bus speed/core speed combinations: 66/166, 60/150, 66/133, 60/120, 66/100, and 50/75. The corresponding Core-to-Bus frequency ratios are 2.5, 2.5, 2, 2, 1.5, and 1.5.

The Business Winstone 98 results (see Figure 8.12) would be even more puzzling to someone who doesn't understand the megahertz are meaningless concept. The exact same system scored less on the 60/150 setting than on the 66/133 setting! How could this be?

Figure 8.12.

Business Winstone 98 scores on the DeskPro 5166 running Windows 98, varying the CPU and bus speeds.

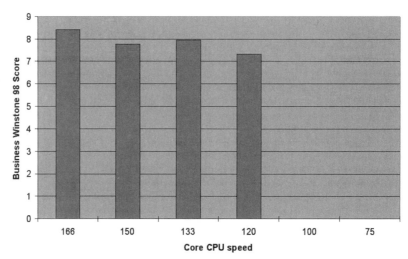

The 150MHz setting is running on a 60MHz system bus. That means that every time the processor can't complete an operation without accessing the L2 cache or system RAM, it's operating on a slower bus than that of the 66/133 settings. Of course, the other feature of interest on this graph is that Winstone failed completely on the two lowest speed settings.

The curves for the category scores (see Figure 8.13) mirror the overall curve. We've eliminated the 100MHz and 75MHz settings from the chart because we were not able to get any category scores at those settings (instead, we got the infamous Blue Screen of Death). In all cases, the 133MHz setting is faster than the 150MHz setting. Even though the core speed of the processor dropped, the system bus speed went up. The mix of low-level operations, and the hit rate of the L1 cache determine how much these two factors will influence performance.

The WinBench 98 Processor Test curves (see Figure 8.14) are surprising, given what we've seen with Winstone. The 150MHz setting outscores the 133MHz setting on both CPUmark$_{32}$ and FPUmark. Once again, the machine is so handicapped at the 100 and 75MHz settings that it can't complete the tests. From this graph we'd conclude that the operations in CPUmark$_{32}$ and FPUmark don't correlate as well with system bus speed as does Winstone.

Figure 8.13.
Business Winstone 98 category scores on the DeskPro 5166 running Windows 98, varying the CPU and bus speeds.

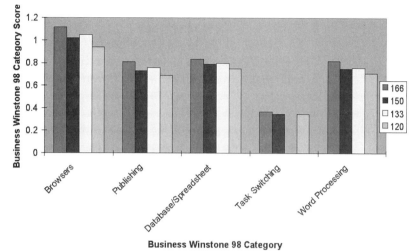

Figure 8.14.
WinBench 98 Processor Test scores on the DeskPro 5166 running Windows 98, varying the CPU and bus speeds.

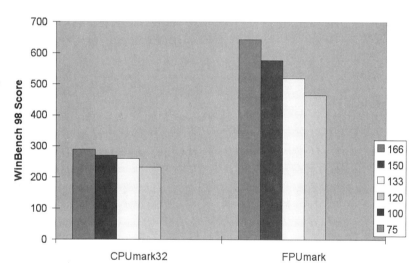

Our conclusions for our Windows 98 bus speed/core speed study on the Pentium 166 machine are the same as those we discovered on the Pentium 133 machine. Pay attention to system bus speed, especially if you're only running business applications. That doesn't mean you have to upgrade every time a new processor rolls out with a faster system bus, but it does mean you should take into account factors other than the core CPU speed when picking your processor.

8.12.6. CPU Summary: Windows 98

Let's take a quick look back at the Winstone 98 scores we've seen running on Windows 98.

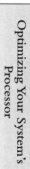

Optimizing Your System's Processor

We ran all of these machines with 16MB RAM. This chart shows (see Figure 8.15) that our upgraded Pentium 75 easily bests the Pentium 100, but still doesn't attain the performance of our Pentium 133 machine. This makes sense, because the core speed of the upgrade is 125MHz. However, it's easy to see from this graph that overall performance as measured by Business Winstone 98 is not linearly correlated with internal CPU speed. This is a mantra we'll repeat in the sections on Windows 95 and Windows NT: don't just focus on core CPU speed when you think about processor performance. Other factors you need to take into account include system bus speed and L2 cache amount.

Figure 8.15.

Business Winstone 98 scores across various processor types on machines running Windows 98.

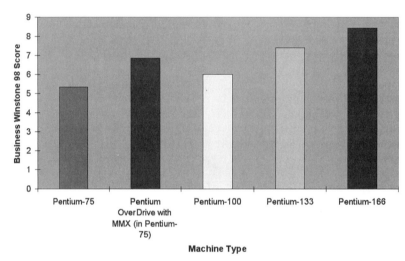

8.13. Windows 95 and Your CPU

Microsoft introduced Windows 95 as a 32-bit operating system, requiring a 32-bit processor. In fact, there's still some 16-bit code lurking at the core of Windows 95. Because of this, processors that are optimized mainly for 32-bit code (like the Pentium Pro) don't perform as well on Windows 95 benchmark tests, all other factors held equal. One of the design goals of the new Pentium II chip was to take advantage of the architectural improvements in the Pentium Pro while improving the performance on both 16-bit and 32-bit code. Unless you're a programmer, you shouldn't worry too much about these deep inner workings of Windows 95, because there is no easy upgrade path from a classic Pentium system to these newer chips.

The minimum required processor to run Windows 95, as stated by Microsoft, is a 386DX. Unless you're just using your PC to play Solitaire, you should completely ignore this requirement. Yes, it's true that you can run Windows 95 on a 386DX machine with only 4MB RAM, although only the most masochistic of us would want to do this. Minimum requirements are usually stated to entice users of low-end systems to upgrade, and not as actual working configurations. We've found that a 486DX2/66 with at least 8MB RAM is the slowest machine that still makes using Windows 95 anywhere near tolerable.

8.13.1. Sidebar: Show me the cache

Once you've installed a particular processor in your system, you're stuck with a certain amount of Level 1 (L1) cache. That's the processor cache that's included in the CPU chip itself. Intel introduced L1 cache in the 486 line of processors, and the amount and type of L1 cache has been increasing and improving ever since. The latest MMX technology chips from Intel, AMD, and Cyrix all increase this amount. The Pentium with MMX technology chips from Intel have dual 16KB caches for instructions and data. The AMD K6 chips have dual 32KB caches, and the new Cyrix 6x86MX (M2) chip contains a unified 64KB cache.

Depending on the type of motherboard you have, you may be able to add or upgrade your Level 2 (L2) cache. Many systems use a DIMM (dual in-line memory module) style connector for the L2 cache, as opposed to just soldering it directly to the motherboard. Level 2 cache is located off of the CPU chip but on the processor bus, so it runs at the same speed as the processor bus (in contrast to main system RAM). In the case of new processors like the Pentium II, L2 cache is included in the processor package itself. Some vendors sell systems without L2 cache to hit a particular price point, but we don't recommend such configurations in desktop systems. The performance improvements caused by the addition of L2 cache are too significant to ignore.

L2 cache size matters because it allows the processor and the cache controller hardware to keep more of the working set of the programs you're running in the faster cache memory. The most intelligent caching controller won't be of any use if it doesn't have enough cache memory to work with. However, give a system enough L2 cache and performance increases significantly. Let's take a look at some concrete results (see Figure 8.16).

We ran these L2 cache tests on a Nexar PC in our testbed. The Nexar PC is modular and designed specifically to allow you to upgrade the individual compo-nents (CPU chip, L2 cache, RAM, hard disk). To show the relative importance of L2 cache versus system RAM, we ran tests at what we consider the low-end amount of RAM, 16MB, and a RAM amount that only a power user would use, 80MB. We ran with no L2 cache and with 512KB of L2 cache, giving us four RAM/L2 combinations.

As you can see, the Business Winstone 97 results show the importance of L2 cache. The overall score for the machine with only 16MB RAM but with L2 cache installed is greater than the score for the 80MB configuration with no L2 cache. No amount of RAM is going to make up for a complete lack of L2 cache, because main RAM will always be slower than cache memory. Even holding either of the RAM amounts steady, there's about a 30% increase in real-world performance by adding L2 cache. This alone should make you wary of purchasing systems with no L2 cache, but let's take a deeper look.

Figure 8.16.

Business Winstone 97 scores with and without L2 cache, for two different levels of RAM.

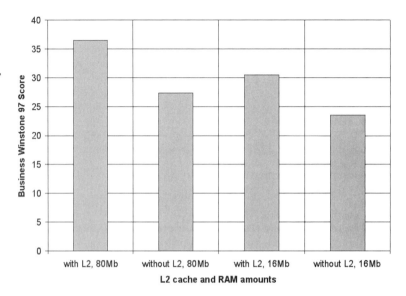

The WinBench 97 Processor Tests stress the processor subsystem, and the results for our L2 cache study (see Figure 8.17) bear this out. Once you've satisfied the minimum RAM requirement to run WinBench 97, adding more RAM does not affect the scores significantly—WinBench 97 is a fairly RAM-insensitive test. However, it's easy to see the effect that the presence of L2 cache has on the WinBench 97 Processor Test scores. That's because L2 cache is an integral part of the processor subsystem.

Figure 8.17.

WinBench 97 Processor Test scores with and without L2 cache, for two different levels of RAM.

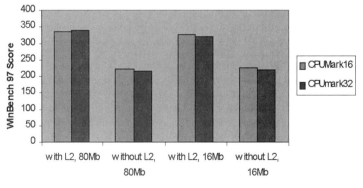

If you need any more convincing, take a look at the High-End Winstone 97 scores for our power user configuration (see Figure 8.18). We didn't run High-End Winstone 97 on the 16MB configuration because it does not meet the minimum requirement of 32MB RAM. As with Business Winstone 97, we get around a 30% increase in performance by adding L2 cache.

Figure 8.18.

High-End Winstone 97 scores with and without L2 cache.

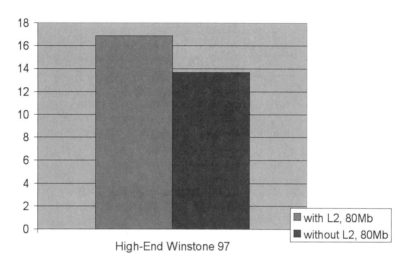

High-End Winstone 97

It's up to you to determine where the bottlenecks in your system are, and to upgrade those components. Should you worry about upgrading L2 cache in an existing system? If you've got a system with no L2 cache, then we believe you should (given that your system isn't RAM starved or seriously deficient in some other way). Of course, you'll have to have a system that allows you to install L2 cache. If you've got an empty DIMM slot for this purpose, we recommend that you fill it. You will definitely notice the results.

8.13.2. How We Tested, Why We Tested

We ran our complete suite of tests for the studies in this section: Business Winstone 97, High-End Winstone 97, and WinBench 97 Processor Tests. We chose RAM amounts for our test systems based on typical RAM amounts in existing systems (and not necessarily what we'd consider the optimal RAM amounts; for those, skip on to the next chapter). That means that we ran the Business Winstone 97 tests on systems with 16MB RAM. When we ran High-End Winstone 97 tests, we took the system RAM to 32MB (the minimum required to run High-End Winstone 97). As for the processor upgrades themselves, we picked representative ones that were available at the time of testing. There will always be new processor upgrades on the market. In some cases, there were no upgrades yet available for our test machines. To demonstrate the effects

Optimizing Your System's Processor

of system bus speed and clock multiplication, we ran studies on these machines altering only those settings.

Our default testing setup was at 640×480×256 for the 486DX-2/66 machine, and 1024×768×256 for the other machines. These represent the most common resolution and color depth settings that users currently run. If you'd like more information on resolution and color depth and how they affect performance, see Chapter 10, "Optimizing Your Graphics Subsystem."

We also defragmented the hard drives of each machine before we ran each test. While disk fragmentation tends to be low on systems that run the Windows 95 System Agent defragmentation utility regularly, it's still good testing practice to fully defragment a hard drive and then reboot your machine before starting a test.

8.13.3. The Low End—486/66

Our low-end machine, the 486DX2/66, had the most upgrade options at the time we tested. Our Compaq DeskPro model was packaged in a slimline case and did not come with a separate OverDrive socket. So, we had to carefully remove the 486DX2/66 chip from its non-ZIF sockets to accomplish all of our upgrades. We tested three separate upgrades in this system: the Intel Pentium OverDrive 83MHz, the Evergreen 586, and the Trinity Works PowerStacker 5x86 133. The Intel design obviously upgrades the CPU to a faster Intel Pentium chip. The Evergreen and Trinity Works upgrades are based around the AMD 5x86 133MHz chip.

We were unable to get the AMD-based upgrade chips for our 486 machine to run Business Winstone 97 to completion, which is somewhat worrisome; however, all of the upgrades for our 486 could run the individual Business Winstone 97 suites. If you want an absolutely ironclad guarantee of compatibility with all the software currently running on your Intel-based system, you might want to focus on the Intel upgrades. The old saw in computer buying used to be that no one ever got fired for buying an IBM computer. This is still true of Intel and CPU chips.

The packages that all of our upgrades came in were festooned with graphs showing dramatic performance increases after the upgrade is installed. Our testing showed a little less drama in the results. We got about a 27% increase in the Business Winstone 97 score after upgrading the 486 machine with the Intel Pentium 83 upgrade kit (see Figure 8.19). This is a very significant performance increase, but it does not approach the 50% to 100% increase figures on the box.

How does the upgrade work and achieve this performance jump? As we've seen, the system clock in a 486DX2/66 machine is running at 33MHz, doubled to get the 66MHz internal speed of the CPU chip. Instead of doubling the system clock, the Pentium 83 upgrade multiplies the system clock by 2.5 to get the 83MHz internal speed. Also, the Pentium 83 upgrade differs from a standard Pentium chip in that its L1 cache contains 16KB for instructions and 16KB for data, while the standard Pentium chip has dual 8KB caches. The extra L1 cache helps to make up for the slower system bus (and therefore, L2 cache and memory access speed) in the older machine.

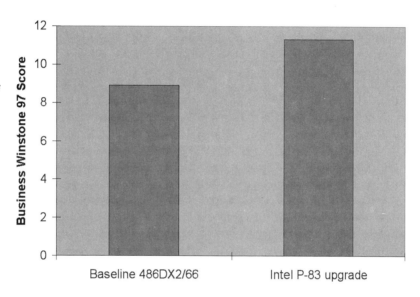

Figure 8.19.
*Business
Winstone 97
Scores on the
DeskPro 4/66i
running Windows
95, before and
after upgrading
the CPU.*

The upgrade kit also includes a voltage regulator that converts the 5 Volt system supply (standard for 486 and earlier motherboards) to the 3.3 Volts needed by the Pentium chip. Finally, the upgrade includes a fan to dissipate the heat generated by the faster and hotter Pentium. The original 486DX2/66 chip only used a passive heat sink for this purpose.

Let's split out the Business Winstone results by category so we can compare to the AMD-based upgrades from Evergreen and Trinity Works (see Figure 8.20). The AMD-based upgrades are newer but, as you can see, not necessarily faster than the Intel Pentium 83 upgrade. Indeed, all of the scores after we performed any of the three upgrades are essentially the same (given the margin of variability that Winstone 97 scores can show). These upgrades use the AMD 5x86 chip running at 133MHz internally. That's quadrupling the existing 33MHz system clock. The AMD 5x86 only has a single 16KB L1 cache for both instructions and data, compared to the dual 16KB caches in the Pentium 83 upgrade. This alone can account for the fact that the performance gains caused by all of the upgrades are about the same even though the processors are running at different speeds internally. Indeed, the marketing literature for the Evergreen 586 states that you should expect Pentium 75 level performance from this upgrade.

Optimizing Your System's Processor

Figure 8.20.

Business Winstone 97 category scores on the DeskPro 4/ 66i running Windows 95, before and after upgrading the CPU.

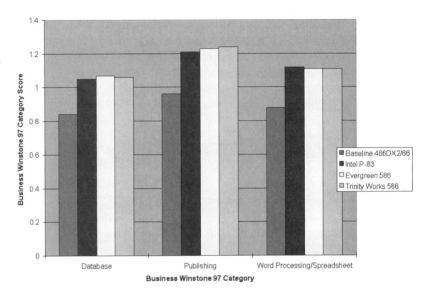

Looking at the WinBench 97 Processor Test results, we once again see that the scores after upgrade, no matter which upgrade we used, are in line (see Figure 8.21). The CPUmark$_{32}$ score on the AMD-based upgrades is somewhat (about 3%) greater than the score obtained by the Intel upgrade. This differential is so small that you might be wise to take other factors into account when purchasing your processor upgrade.

Figure 8.21.

WinBench 97 Processor Test scores on the DeskPro 4/66i running Windows 95, before and after upgrading the CPU.

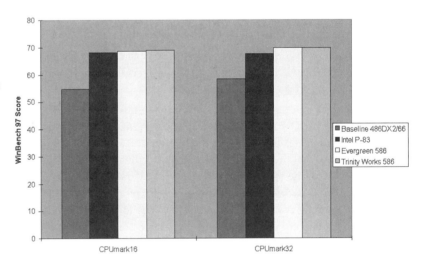

While the Trinity Works and Evergreen upgrades are based around the same CPU chip and they give similar performance boosts, they're not necessarily created equal. The Trinity Works kit came with a video tape demonstrating how to install the upgrade, as well as a heavy-duty German-made chip lifter tool, and a CD of free Internet-related software. If extra freebies like this are important to you, they might be more important to your buying decision than a percentage point of performance here or there. Of course, holding performance equal, you'll probably be best off buying the cheapest upgrade.

To get the maximum performance out of your aging 486 system, consider any of these upgrades. The AMD-based ones will likely give you the best bang-for-buck ratio. If you want an ironclad guarantee of compatibility, you might want to get the Intel OverDrive chip instead.

8.13.4. Pentium 75

We had two upgrade options for our Pentium 75 machine: the Intel OverDrive Processor with MMX Technology and the Evergreen PR166 Pentium Upgrade. Our Pentium 75 unit sported a ZIF (zero insertion force) processor socket, so actually swapping in the upgrade chip was much easier than in the 486DX2/66 machine. Unfortunately, we were only able to successfully use the Intel OverDrive with MMX upgrade in this machine. The Evergreen upgrade was not compatible with all Pentium-based systems at the time we tested; in fact, the compatibility list on the box only listed a few brand names. That's because the upgrade requires a BIOS update. At the time of our testing, the Evergreen PR166 upgrade was not compatible with our Compaq Deskpro 575 and Deskpro 5100. The engineers at Evergreen are constantly working on the BIOS update code to support more machines, though. You can get a current compatibility listing at Evergreen's Web site at www.evertech.com.

The Intel upgrade didn't come with a list of compatible or incompatible machines. Instead, Intel provides a diagnostics diskette that includes the diag.exe program, which is supposed to check your machine's BIOS to determine whether you need a BIOS update before installing the upgrade. Unlike Evergreen, Intel does not provide the BIOS update code. The Intel diagnostic program checks your machine and then tells you whether you need to get a BIOS update from your system or motherboard manufacturer.

What is the BIOS, anyway? BIOS stands for Basic Input/Output System. The BIOS controls the system when it starts up, before your operating system loads up from the hard disk. It also acts as a basic, standardized interface to your system hardware. The BIOS is stored in some type of ROM (Read-Only Memory) device on your system motherboard. In years past, if you wanted to upgrade your BIOS, you had to buy a newer ROM and swap it into the BIOS socket. Most systems now use flash ROM or electrically eraseable ROM, which can be reprogrammed in the host system. To upgrade the BIOS on a modern system, you'll typically download the new BIOS code from the manufacturer's Web site, use it to create a boot diskette, boot your machine from this diskette, and run the provided program to actually update your system BIOS.

Optimizing Your System's Processor

We ran into a slight problem when performing the Intel upgrade. We ran the diagnostic program diag.exe and it stated that our system was compatible with the upgrade and did not need a BIOS update, so we continued with the upgrade process. We powered down the computer, opened the case, and grounded ourselves. The processor in our Pentium 75 dissipates heat via a passive heat sink that's held on with a restraining clip. We removed this heat sink and then the processor itself by opening the socket handle. We carefully installed the OverDrive upgrade, making sure to align the processor so that the pin 1 notch lined up. We lowered the socket handle to lock the chip in place and we closed the system case and powered on the system.

Nothing happened. The screen was dead. First things first: we checked the monitor, keyboard, and mouse cables. We opened up the system to make sure the processor upgrade was seated firmly in the socket. We even (gulp) read the manual to see if there were any caveats we missed. To make sure that we hadn't blown the upgrade with static discharge, we removed it and tried installing it in the Compaq Deskpro 5100. We followed the same procedure and got the same results—no response at all after the upgrade, but the systems worked fine with their original processor. At this point we were worried that we had indeed fried the upgrade chip. We contacted Intel tech support, and after explaining our problem in detail, they asked us for the specific model numbers of the machines we were upgrading. They checked their records and recommended getting BIOS updates from Compaq, even though the diagnostic program stated that our machines didn't need BIOS updates.

We downloaded the latest BIOS software from the Compaq Web site and installed it on the Deskpro 575 and 5100. Voilà! We reinstalled the upgrade and it worked fine. All of this work just goes to show that software isn't foolproof. While there's usually very little reason to worry about keeping your BIOS software up-to-date (unless there's a specific bug you need to work around), you might want to check it before you perform any major upgrade like a CPU upgrade. It certainly can't hurt to get a newer BIOS from your system or motherboard manufacturer.

So, after a lot of hard work, we got the Intel Pentium OverDrive with MMX Technology installed. This upgrade replaced our Pentium 75 chip, running at 1.5 times the system bus speed of 50MHz, with a Pentium MMX chip running internally at 2.5 times the system bus speed, or 125MHz. That's a 67% increase in internal CPU speed, but as we've seen you should expect anywhere near this amount of speed-up in real-world performance. We ran a Business Winstone 97 test and got about a 30% increase in the speed of the machine running standard business applications (see Figure 8.22). This is a very significant increase in speed, but before you go out an plunk down your money for a processor upgrade, read on. If you've only got a limited budget, you might better spend your money by buying more RAM or a larger hard disk for your machine (see Chapters 9,

"Optimizing Your System's RAM," and 11, "Optimizing Your Disk Subsystem").
If you need MMX for a specific program, or if you've got the dollars to spare, this
upgrade will extend the usable lifetime of your existing Pentium machines.

Figure 8.22.

*Business
Winstone 97
Scores on the
DeskPro 575
running Windows
95, before and
after upgrading
the CPU.*

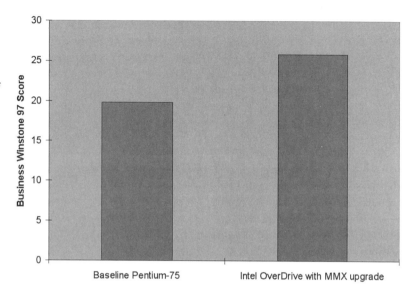

Interestingly, the 30% speed-up we saw in the overall Business Winstone 97 score
was not consistent in the three category scores (see Figure 8.23). The word
processing and spreadsheet programs showed the most improvement, over 34%.
The publishing programs showed less than a 25% increase in performance. What
does this mean for you? If you're running desktop publishing applications like
PageMaker, we encourage you to make sure your other subsystems are up to snuff
before looking into a CPU upgrade.

The WinBench 97 Processor Tests show the dramatic change in the processor
subsystem caused by the upgrade. We saw increases in these scores in the 70% to
90% range (see Figure 8.24). How is this possible, when the internal CPU speed
only increased by 67%? Again, it's most likely due to the larger L1 cache on the
OverDrive with MMX upgrade. The Pentium with MMX Technology has dual
16KB L1 caches, while the standard Pentium has dual 8KB L1 caches.

Many buyers purchased Pentium 75 based machines, avoiding the first round of
the Pentium 60 and Pentium 66 models. You'll avoid being a beta tester for the
latest generation of new processors by following this cautious buying strategy. If
you've got a Pentium 75 machine, or an office full of them, you could see
significant performance gains by installing a faster MMX upgrade. This is especially true for basic word processing and spreadsheet applications. We recommend
ensuring that the RAM and disk in the machine in question are adequate before
buying the relatively pricy processor upgrade, though.

Optimizing Your System's Processor

Figure 8.23.

Business Winstone 97 category scores on the DeskPro 575 running Windows 95, before and after upgrading the CPU.

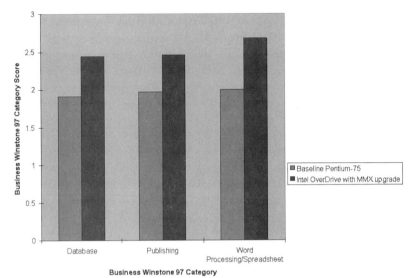

Figure 8.24.

WinBench 97 Processor Test scores on the DeskPro 575 running Windows 95, before and after upgrading the CPU.

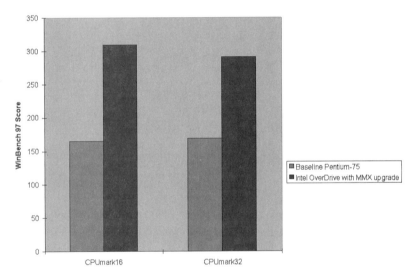

8.13.5. Sidebar: Another Pentium 75

Because the Compaq DeskPro system in our main testbed was not yet compatible with the Evergreen PR166 upgrade, we did some additional testing on a Gateway P5-75 to determine the performance increase users should expect. The Evergreen PR166 is called a Pentium Upgrade but in reality it's based around the IBM 6x86L PR166+ chip. The chip designation is a P-rating, and not the actual internal clock speed of the chip. The chip only runs at 133MHz internally. While the box touts 166MHz performance, you should be more skeptical. We were, and so we ran some Winstone 97 and WinBench 97 tests.

First we had to install the upgrade chip. The Evergreen PR166 upgrade requires a BIOS update, but the update is provided by Evergreen (as opposed to the Intel upgrade). We booted from the provided Evergreen floppy disk and upgraded the flash BIOS on the Gateway system. We also had to adjust the motherboard jumpers on the Gateway system before installing the upgrade. That's because we had to adjust the system motherboard speed. A normal Pentium 75 motherboard is running at 50MHz, which the CPU multiplies by 1.5 to get its internal speed of 75MHz. For the IBM 6x86L chip to run at its top speed, you have to adjust the system bus speed to 66MHz. The CPU then doubles this to get the internal speed of 133MHz. Of course, to accomplish this, you've got to have a system based on a motherboard that supports 66MHz operation. If you have an older system, the jumpers or switches that control the system motherboard frequency may not allow you to set the system to 66MHz operation. You should check this before spending money on an upgrade that you won't be able to use at its top speed. If your system bus can only be adjusted to 60MHz, then the upgrade will only run internally at 120MHz, not at 133MHz. You can always run a chip at a slower frequency than its rating, but you won't get the performance you could be getting. We'll talk more about bus speed and internal CPU speed later in this chapter.

In the case of this Gateway system, we ran our tests with 32MB RAM. Because of this, be aware that the results with the Evergreen PR166 on the Gateway P5-75 system are not directly comparable to the results with the Intel MMX OverDrive upgrade on our Compaq Deskpro 575. They do serve to illustrate the importance of RAM on performance. The performance increases we saw with 32MB RAM in the system were greater on the Winstone tests but smaller on the WinBench tests. This would indicate that our Deskpro 575 was still bottlenecked by its RAM amount. Let's take a look.

We got a whopping 40% speed-up in the overall Business Winstone 97 score (see Figure 8.25). Compare this to the 30% speedup we saw in our Compaq system.

The individual category scores also show more consistency in the performance increase (see Figure 8.26). Again, we're looking at the performance increase, and not the raw numbers. While the bars for the publishing score indicate higher scores than for the other two categories, the performance increase caused by the upgrade (the difference in the two scores divided by the original score) is about the same.

Optimizing Your System's Processor

Figure 8.25.

Business Winstone 97 scores on the Gateway P5-75 running Windows 95, before and after upgrading the CPU.

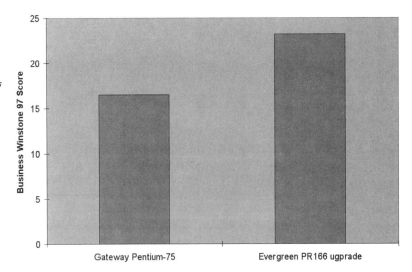

Figure 8.26.

Business Winstone 97 category scores on the Gateway P5-75 running Windows 95, before and after upgrading the CPU.

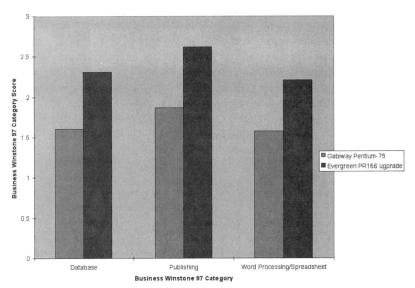

The gains on the WinBench 97 Processor Tests are not as dramatic as the gains we saw with the Intel MMX OverDrive upgrade. In this case, they're in the 50% to 60% range (see Figure 8.27). Remember, the WinBench 97 tests are largely RAM-independent, once you've got a certain minimum amount of RAM in your system. In this case, the addition of the IBM 6X86L upgrade didn't change the L1 cache dramatically. The IBM 6x86L has a combined 16KB L1 cache, as opposed to the dual 8KB L1 cache in the standard Pentium chip. So we should expect less of an impact on the processor subsystem than with the Intel MMX OverDrive, which doubled the total size of the L1 cache.

Figure 8.27.

WinBench 97 Processor Test scores on the Gateway P5-75 running Windows 95, before and after upgrading the CPU.

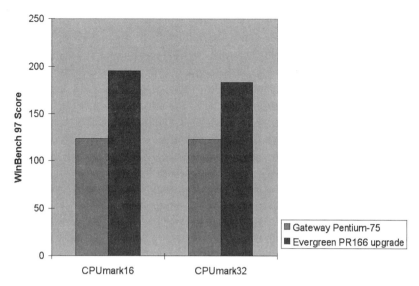

8.13.6. Pentium 100

Our Pentium 100 system had similar upgrade options as our Pentium 75 system. We could use the Intel OverDrive Processor with MMX Technology. We could not use the Evergreen PR166 upgrade, because as we related above, the BIOS update provided with the upgrade did not yet work with our Compaq systems. The Intel upgrade was supposed to boost our CPU to a 166MHz Pentium with MMX Technology, but this turned out not to be the case. Let's take a look at the numbers and try to figure out what happened.

The Business Winstone 97 score only goes up by about 4% after the upgrade (see Figure 8.28). Looking back at the results of the upgraded Pentium 75 machine, we see that the scores after the upgrade on both models are essentially the same. Shouldn't we expect that the Pentium 100 machine would get more of a performance boost?

The category scores from the Business Winstone 97 tests are equally puzzling. In the case of the publishing tests, performance actually dropped after the upgrade! (See Figure 8.29.) Once again, the category scores of the upgraded Pentium 100 and the category scores of the upgraded Pentium 75 match almost exactly.

These matching scores are the clues that allowed us to figure out what was going on. The MMX OverDrive upgrade is supposed to take a Pentium 100 machine to a 166MHz MMX CPU. However, this assumes that the Pentium 100 machine is a newer model that uses a 66MHz system bus. The upgrade chip then multiplies this clock by 2.5 to get the internal frequency of 166MHz. However, our Pentium 100 machine is an older model that uses a clock doubled 50MHz system bus. Unfortunately, there are no jumper settings on this particular motherboard to

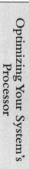

set it to faster operation. We're stuck with this frequency, which the upgrade then multiplies by 2.5 to get an internal clock frequency of 125MHz—the same internal frequency at which the upgrade in our Pentium 75 system was running. This explains why the scores from the upgraded Pentium 100 and the upgraded Pentium 75 match.

Figure 8.28.

Business Winstone 97 scores on the DeskPro 5100 running Windows 95, before and after upgrading the CPU.

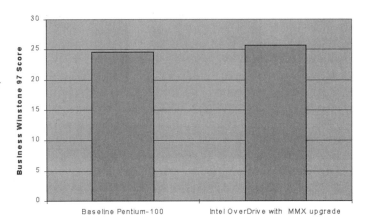

Figure 8.29.

Business Winstone 97 category scores on the DeskPro 5100 running Windows 95, before and after upgrading the CPU.

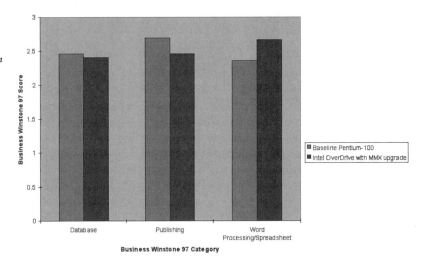

The point of all of this is not that there's anything wrong with this particular upgrade. You just need to be sure that your system really can handle the specific processor upgrade you've chosen.

We also ran some High-End Winstone 97 tests on the upgraded Pentium 100. We got a boost of about 33% overall after the upgrade (see Figure 8.30).

Figure 8.30.
High-End Winstone 97 scores on the DeskPro 5100 running Windows 95, before and after upgrading the CPU.

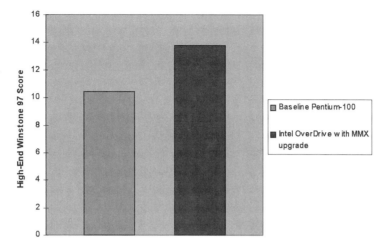

The individual category scores show you which high-end applications are more dependent on processor power (see Figure 8.31). The CAD and 3-D applications get a 46% boost in performance, while the image editing and application development programs benefit only in the 20% to 25% range. This makes sense because of the nature of the typical operations that CAD and 3-D programs use: floating point operations and other algorithms that are processor-bound. While image editing programs also use similar operations, they are typically bottlenecked more in RAM or disk due to the large files they use.

Figure 8.31.
High-End Winstone 97 category scores on the DeskPro 5100, Windows 95, before and after upgrading the CPU.

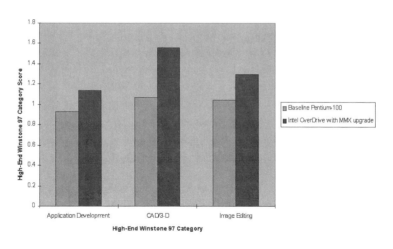

The Processor Test scores increase by about 40% for the 16-bit tests and by about 50% for the 32-bit tests (see Figure 8.32). Remember, the WinBench 97 Processor Tests only test your PC's processor subsystem. While 50% faster sounds good on paper, it's only meaningful if you can get that same performance gain out of a real-world application. That's why it's important to use WinBench 97 in tandem with Winstone 97. Winstone can tell you how fast your system, however it's configured or upgraded, is relative to another system. WinBench can help you isolate subsystem performance and track down system bottlenecks.

Figure 8.32.
WinBench 97 Processor Test scores on the DeskPro 5100 running Windows 95, before and after upgrading the CPU.

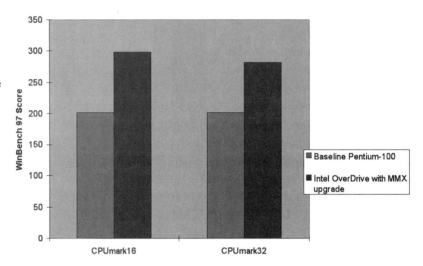

In attempting to upgrade our Pentium 100, we learned that you've got to be very careful to make sure that your existing system can take full advantage of the CPU upgrade. Still, even with our older Pentium 100 machine, we saw some dramatic performance gains, especially with CAD and 3-D applications. These are the exact applications that will probably take advantage of the MMX instruction set in the future. If you do CAD or 3-D modeling work and you've already spent money upgrading your Pentium 100 system with RAM, a fast hard disk, and a speedy graphics board with lots of graphics memory, you might want to look at getting an MMX upgrade for your machine.

8.13.6. Pentium 133

When we did the testing for this section of the chapter, Intel and third-party manufacturers had not yet released upgrade kits for machines based on chips faster than the Pentium 100. We didn't want our Pentium 133 and Pentium 166 machines to feel left out, though, so we decided to use them for some testing that shows the effects of system bus speed and of system clock multiplication on performance.

Let's recap what we've discovered about the system bus and the CPU speed. The system bus, or motherboard speed, of a Pentium system is either 50, 60, or 66MHz. This system bus speed is multiplied by 1, 1.5, 2, 2.5, or 3 to get a range of frequencies from 60 to 200MHz for the standard (classic) Pentium chips. This multiplication factor is technically known as the Core-to-Bus freqency ratio, the core meaning the guts of the CPU chip itself. This ratio is controlled (again, on classic Pentium chips) by voltages applied to pins on the CPU chip. You can control these voltages via jumpers or switches on the motherboard, and in some systems you can also control the system bus frequency.

Switches on our Compaq Deskpro 5133 allowed us to test six different bus speed/core speed combinations: 66/133, 60/120, 66/100, 50/100, 60/90, and 50/75. That would make the Core-to-Bus frequency ratios 2, 2, 1.5, 2, 1.5, and 1.5 in that order. That range of settings is determined by the motherboard manufacturer.

Wait a minute—why would anyone want to decrease the speed at which their processor or system bus was running? Well, no one would. We're doing it here to illustrate how these components combine to affect overall system performance, and to further illuminate our original point that megahertz is meaningless.

We ran our Deskpro 5133 through the Business Winstone 97 paces at all possible bus speed/core speed combinations (see Figure 8.33). If megahertz is meaningless weren't true, you'd expect performance scores to drop off linearly with decreasing CPU frequency. This isn't quite the case, though, because other factors are involved. Take a look at the two scores for the CPU running at 100MHz. One is with a 66MHz system bus multiplied by 1.5; the other is with a 50MHz bus doubled. The latter configuration scores about 5% less on the overall Business Winstone 97 even though the CPU chip is running at the same internal speed. Every time any operation that the CPU performs can't be done completely internally (that is, without accessing the L2 cache or the main system RAM), the system with the faster bus is at an advantage.

Figure 8.33.

Business Winstone 97 scores on the DeskPro 5133 running Windows 95, varying the CPU and bus speeds.

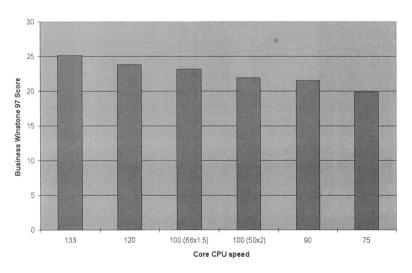

Optimizing Your System's Processor

The category scores of Business Winstone 97 (for this same set of speed combinations, see Figure 8.34) mirror the overall curve. As we saw with the previous upgrade sections, the word processing and spreadsheet programs seem to be more affected by processor speed. The graph bears this out because the decreasing performance curve is steepest for the word processing and spreadsheet category.

Figure 8.34.

Business Winstone 97 category scores on the DeskPro 5133 running Windows 95, varying the CPU and bus speeds.

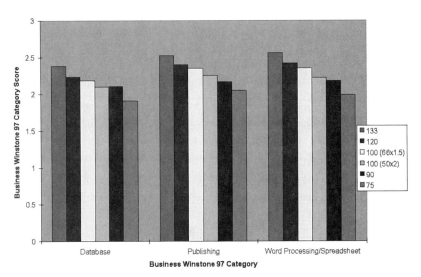

The graph for the overall High-End Winstone 97 scores (see Figure 8.35) shares some features with the Business Winstone 97 graph—the largest performance drop is going from the 90MHz to the 75MHz setting. However, in general the curve is flatter and more consistent in this case. That's probably due to the fact that some of the applications High-End Winstone comprises are more processor-bound than the applications in Business Winstone. Hence, the core speed of the CPU is more directly related to performance because there's a larger percentage of time spent executing instructions which don't need to access the L2 cache or system RAM. From our prior experience that showed that the CAD and 3-D applications in High-End Winstone are the most sensitive to processor speed, we would guess that this particular curve would be the steepest.

Our testing bears this out (see Figure 8.36). All of the application categories show a more linear roll-off with decreasing CPU speed than did the applications in Business Winstone 97.

In the case of WinBench 97 Processor Test scores, we see a dramatic drop-off moving from 133MHz to 120MHz as well as the 90MHz to 75MHz drop we saw with Winstone scores (see Figure 8.37).

What does all this mean for you, the user, if you're never going to handicap your system by slowing down the CPU? It means that you should pay attention to more than just the raw CPU speed, especially if you're just running business applications. The system bus speed—the speed at which the CPU accesses L2 cache, and the upper bound on RAM access—also affects system performance. If you run high-end applications, especially 3-D and CAD applications, you might want to keep your eyes peeled for future processor upgrades for your system. These applications take better advantage of faster processors.

Figure 8.35.
High-End Winstone 97 scores on the DeskPro 5133 running Windows 95, varying the CPU and bus speeds.

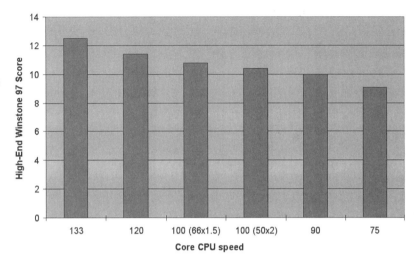

Figure 8.36.
High-End Winstone 97 category and application scores on the DeskPro 5133 running Windows 95, varying the CPU and bus speeds.

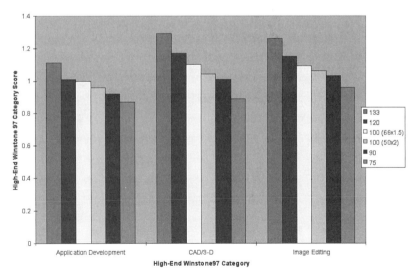

8.13.8. Pentium 166

We repeated our bus speed/core speed combination tests for the Pentium 166 machine in our testbed. This machine allows for a different range of settings than the Pentium 133 model. In this case, you can adjust switches on the motherboard to get the following bus speed/core speed combinations: 66/166, 60/150, 66/133,

60/120, 66/100, and 50/75. The corresponding Core-to-Bus frequency ratios are 2.5, 2.5, 2, 2, 1.5, and 1.5.

Figure 8.37.

WinBench 97 Processor Test scores on the DeskPro 5133 running Windows 95, varying the CPU and bus speeds.

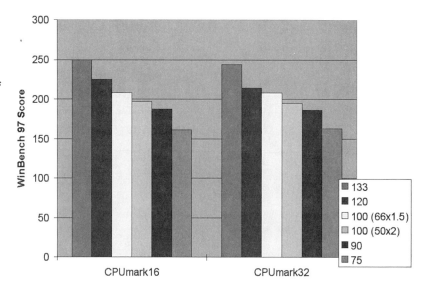

The Business Winstone 97 results (see Figure 8.38) would be even more puzzling to someone who doesn't understand the megahertz are meaningless concept. The exact same system scored less on the 60/150 setting than on the 66/133 setting! How could this be?

Figure 8.38.

Business Winstone 97 scores on the DeskPro 5166 running Windows 95, varying the CPU and bus speeds.

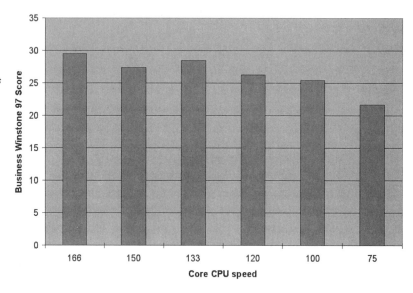

The 150MHz setting is running on a 60MHz system bus. That means that every time the processor can't complete an operation without accessing the L2 cache or system RAM, it's operating on a slower bus than that of the 66/133 settings. We've seen that the Business Winstone 97 applications aren't as processor-bound as the High-End applications, so these results, which look wrong at first blush, actually make sense. That's why some folks who bought 150MHz Pentium machines weren't necessarily getting a bargain compared to those who stuck with 133MHz Pentiums.

The curves for the category scores (see Figure 8.39) mirror the overall curve. Other data points similar to the seemingly odd 150MHz to 133MHz comparison show up. The database scores for the 60/120 and 66/100 combinations are exactly the same. Again, even though the core speed of the processor dropped, the system bus speed went up. The mix of low-level operations, and the hit rate of the L1 cache determine how much these two factors will influence performance.

Figure 8.39.

Business Winstone 97 category scores on the DeskPro 5166 running Windows 95, varying the CPU and bus speeds.

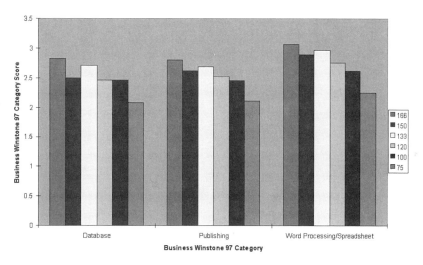

The High-End scores, as with the Pentium 133, don't exhibit a counterintuitive turn—they fall off with decreasing core processor speed (see Figure 8.40). Note, however, that the 60/150 and 66/133 scores are still very close to each other, within the limits of variability of the Winstone test.

The category scores also remind us of the curves from the Pentium 133 (see Figure 8.41). It appears that our theory about the High-End applications, especially the CAD/3-D programs, holds true. They are more processor-bound and more likely to correlate directly to the core-speed of the CPU than business applications. Only the applications development category (the Visual C++ application) shows the peculiar dip at 150MHz that we saw with all of the business programs.

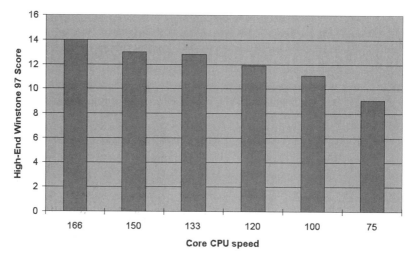

The WinBench 97 Processor Test curves (see Figure 8.42) don't present any surprises. The largest performance drop occurs when the system bus downshifts from 66 to 50MHz. There is no dip at the 150MHz point, although the 32-bit test scores for the 60/150MHz combination are only about 3% higher than those of the 66/133MHz combination.

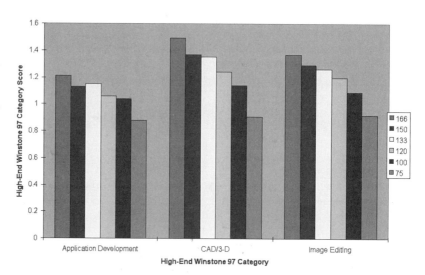

Our conclusions for our Windows 95 bus speed/core speed study on the Pentium 166 machine are the same as those we discovered on the Pentium 133 machine. Pay attention to system bus speed, especially if you're only running business applications. If you're running high-end applications, especially CAD and 3-D, stay on the lookout for future processor upgrades, but only after you've ensured that your system has plenty of RAM and a fast hard disk and graphics card.

Figure 8.42.

WinBench 97 Processor Test scores on the DeskPro 5166 running Windows 95, varying the CPU and bus speeds.

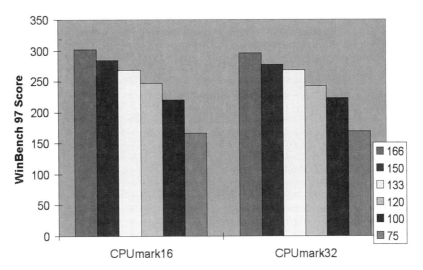

8.13.9. CPU Summary: Windows 95

Let's take a quick look back at the Winstone 97 scores we've seen. First, the business results.

This chart shows how the Pentium 83 upgrade in the 486DX2/66 machine still doesn't attain the base performance of our Pentium 75 unit (see Figure 8.43). Conversely, when we upgraded our Pentium 75 machine with the OverDrive with MMX Technology upgrade, it got higher Business Winstone 97 scores than both the Pentium 100 and the Pentium 133 baselines, even though it was only running internally at 125MHz. We attribute this to the increased amount of L1 cache on the upgrade chip.

The High-End Winstone scores show a similar boost that pounds home our point that megahertz are meaningless. The upgraded Pentium 100 machine bested the High-End Winstone 97 score of the Pentium 133 machine, and came close to matching the High-End Winstone 97 score of the Pentium 166 (see Figure 8.44). Note that High-End Winstone 97 requires at least 32MB of RAM to run, so these systems were not bottlenecked in the RAM department.

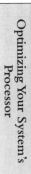

Optimizing Your System's Processor

Figure 8.43.

Business Winstone 97 scores across various processor types on machines running Windows 95.

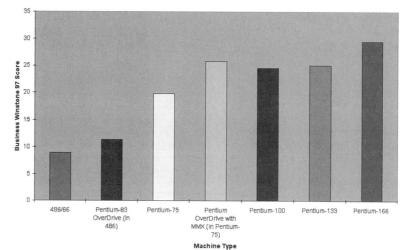

Figure 8.44.

High-End Winstone 97 scores across processor types on machines running Windows 95.

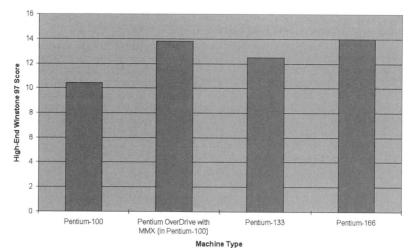

8.14. Windows NT and Your CPU

In terms of CPU, the most obvious difference between Windows NT and Windows 95 is the minimum requirement. Windows 95 claims that it will run with a 386DX processor, while Windows NT 4.0 requires a 486/25 processor at a minimum. As with other specifications such as minimum RAM amount, NT requires more of this resource because NT is a more powerful operating system with a more sophisticated kernel architecture.

8.14.1. How We Tested

As under Windows 95, we ran Business Winstone 97, High-End Winstone 97, and WinBench 97 Processor Tests (CPUmark$_{16}$ and CPUmark$_{32}$). We ran the same set of bus speed/core speed tests that we ran during the Windows 95 testing, as no processor upgrades were yet available for our NT-based machines at the time we tested. For the Pentium 133, we tested Business Winstone 97 and WinBench 97 Processor Tests at 16MB RAM and High-End Winstone 97 at 32MB RAM. For the Pentium 166, we ran all tests at 32MB RAM.

8.14.2. Pentium 133

We didn't know whether to expect that the bus speed testing curves would look similar to those we found under Windows 95. Let's take a look at the Business Winstone 97 overall scores. To recap from the Windows 95 section, we tested by varying the bus speed and core CPU speed through all the supported combinations on our Compaq Deskpro 5133.

Bingo! We've already discovered different behavior under Windows NT. The overall score dips pronouncedly at the 60/120MHz setting before increasing again at the 66/100MHz setting (see Figure 8.45). The scores then drop off with decreasing CPU speed. This is different from the results under Windows 95, which simply steadily decreased. The CPU stays busier under Windows NT, and therefore it breaks out of L1 cache more often to access the L2 cache or main memory. These accesses are limited by the speed of the system bus, so it's possible to get situations as the one above where the faster system bus beats out the faster core speed.

Figure 8.45.

Business Winstone 97 scores on the DeskPro 5133 running Windows NT, varying the CPU and bus speeds.

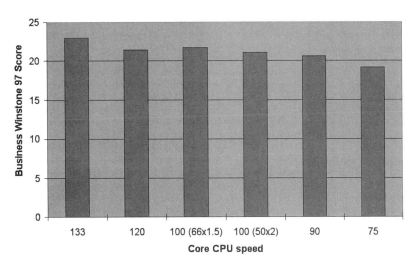

Optimizing Your System's Processor

The category results for Business Winstone 97 show that this dip at the 60/ 120MHz setting is most pronounced in the publishing applications, while it doesn't occur at all in the database applications (see Figure 8.46). As under Windows 95, the steepest curve (meaning the application type most sensitive to CPU speed) belongs to the word processing and spreadsheet applications.

Figure 8.46.

Business Winstone 97 category scores on the DeskPro 5133 running Windows NT, varying the CPU and bus speeds.

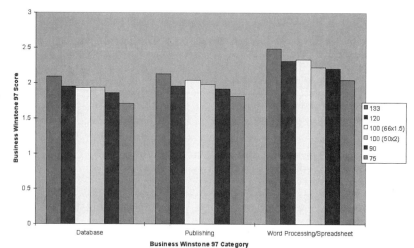

The results for High-End Winstone return to the steadily decreasing curve (see Figure 8.47). We attribute this to the fact that the applications in High-End Winstone are processor-bound and therefore more sensitive to core speed rather than system bus speed.

Figure 8.47.

High-End Winstone 97 scores on the DeskPro 5133 running Windows NT, varying the CPU and bus speeds.

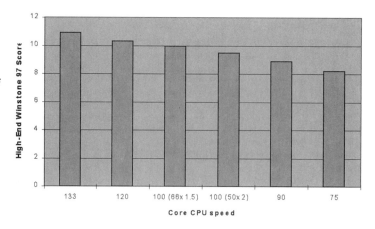

The High-End Winstone 97 category scores should look familiar (see Figure 8.48). Once again, the category that changes the least with changing CPU speed is Application Development. CAD and 3-D applications change the most with changing CPU speed, with the Image Editing applications somewhere in the middle.

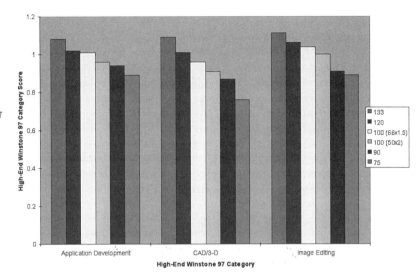

The WinBench 97 Processor Test results aren't very surprising. The scores drop off steadily as the bus speed/core speed combination drops (see Figure 8.49). It is interesting to note that the 50/100MHz combination scores only marginally better than the 60/90MHz combination—once again, system bus speed proves to be important as well as core CPU speed.

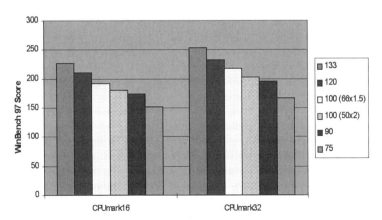

Optimizing Your System's Processor

The curves are slightly different under Windows NT, but our basic recommendations remain the same as for Windows 95. If you run business applications, pay as much or more attention to system bus speed as you do to core processor speed. If you run high-end applications, you may want to look at future CPU upgrades, but only if you're sure your RAM, graphics, and hard disk subsystems are up to snuff.

8.14.3. Pentium 166

Holding RAM at a constant 32MB (a reasonable assumption for a Pentium 166 machine running Windows NT) we ran the same set of bus speed/core speed tests at the combinations available on our Compaq Deskpro 5166: 66/166, 60/150, 66/133, 60/120, 66/100, and 50/75. The corresponding Core-to-Bus frequency ratios are 2.5, 2.5, 2, 2, 1.5, and 1.5.

This curve should be very familiar to you by now if you've read the rest of this chapter. Once again, there's a significant dip at the 60/150MHz setting which is bested by the 66/133MHz setting (see Figure 8.50).

Figure 8.50.

Business Winstone 97 scores on the DeskPro 5166 running Windows NT, varying the CPU and bus speeds.

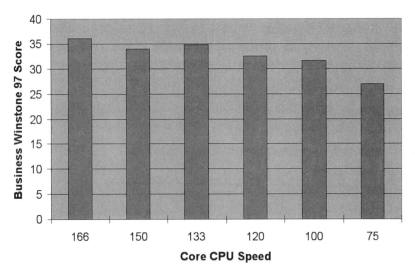

In the case of our Pentium 166 with more RAM, all of the category curves reflect this dip (see Figure 8.51). In fact, the percent change in each of the category scores as bus/core speed changes is about the same across categories. This only strengthens our argument that system bus speed, something that's rarely mentioned in an advertisement, should be one of the factors you consider when purchasing a new system.

The High-End Winstone 97 results do not dip, but the 60/150 and 66/133 scores are exactly the same (see Figure 8.52). System bus speed still matters, even with the CPU-intensive applications that make up High-End Winstone 97.

Figure 8.51.

Business Winstone 97 category scores on the DeskPro 5166 running Windows NT, varying the CPU and bus speeds.

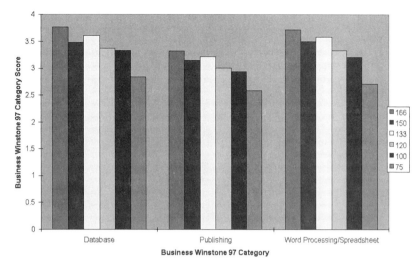

Figure 8.52.

High-End Winstone 97 scores on the DeskPro 5166 running Windows NT, varying the CPU and bus speeds.

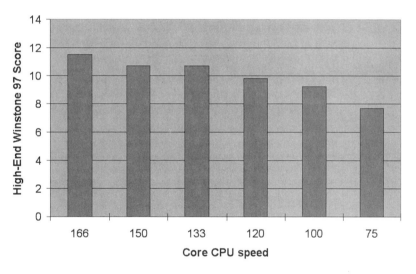

At first glance, the category results for High-End Winstone 97 on this machine may be confusing (see Figure 8.53). However, the same basic shape, the curve with a dip, holds. As we've seen several times before, the CAD and 3-D applications are the most sensitive to core processor speed. In the case of this Pentium-166, the Application Development (Visual C++) scores aren't affected nearly as much by changing processor speed, indicating that performance of this program is bottlenecked elsewhere.

Even the 16-bit Processor Test scores show us the curve with the dip (see Figure 8.54), while the 32-bit Processor Test scores still decrease steadily (although the difference between the 60/150 score and the 66/133 score is very small). Why should this be? The answer is in the names of the tests themselves. The 16-bit

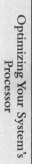

Processor Test is based on 16-bit program code, instructions which operate on data in 16-bit chunks. It sounds silly to hobble a processor with a 64-bit data bus with such operations, but you must remember that before Windows 95 and Windows NT, program code written for PC's was 16-bit. Parts of the Windows 95 kernel still are 16-bit code. So, if a processor is running this code, it's going to access the system bus more often, because it's dealing with data only in 16-bit chunks. It makes sense that we see the pronounced dip on the 16-bit test before we see it on the 32-bit test.

Figure 8.53.

High-End Winstone 97 category and application scores on the DeskPro 5166 running Windows NT, varying the CPU and bus speeds.

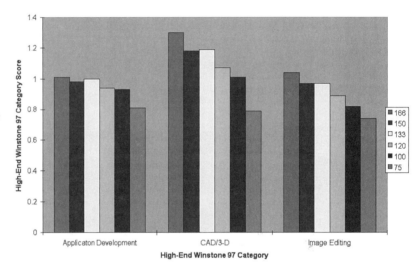

Figure 8.54.

WinBench 97 Processor Test scores on the DeskPro 5166 running Windows NT, varying the CPU and bus speeds.

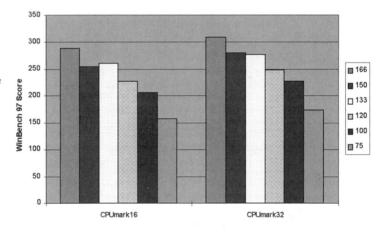

8.14.4. CPU Summary: Windows NT

If you don't believe us now, you never will: megahertz (meaning raw CPU speed) are meaningless. The results for Windows NT, while differing slightly from our Windows 95 results, bear this out. In general we've seen that Windows NT requires more processor subsystem power, and therefore factors other than core CPU speed play an even more important role under Windows NT. If you're running Windows NT and want to buy a new system or upgrade your existing processor, pay attention to things like system bus speed and amount of L2 cache as well as core CPU speed.

8.15. MMX and CPU Performance

The latest buzzword when folks talk about CPU chips is MMX. Intel released the Pentium with MMX Technology chips, and AMD and Cyrix have followed suit with their K6 and 6x86MX chips respectively. MMX Technology basically means that the CPU chip supports new instructions which speed up multimedia operations, as well as a new set of registers especially designed to work with these instructions. It's very difficult to buy a new Windows-based machine without getting some form of MMX CPU chip. If your current CPU is not an MMX chip, don't worry. So far, the applications that take advantage of the MMX instruction set are limited to a few games and to specific high-end applications, like certain Photoshop operations. However, MMX-aware applications for standard business productivity aren't far off.

Just how much more performance will you get from an MMX-based PC? We don't know. That's because software developers have made it difficult to get direct access to the MMX functionality of a particular piece of software. To follow our apples-to-apples rule of testing, we would ideally test an MMX machine (such as the Deskpro 6000 in our testbed) running an MMX-aware application, then we would disable the MMX instructions and re-run the tests. Unfortunately, this functionality was not available at the time we ran our tests.

Maybe it's all for the better. If you're buying a brand-new system, you'll probably get some type of MMX processor, whether it's from Intel or one of their competitors. Unless you have a specific MMX-only application you need to run, it's probably not worth it to get an MMX upgrade chip solely for performance benefits. Your money would be better spent on RAM, as you'll find out in the next chapter.

8.16. The Bottom Line

We must admit, we had a hidden agenda in this chapter, but we're not sure how hidden we kept it. Megahertz is meaningless, we chanted, and we feel that's true.

Optimizing Your System's Processor

If you take only one thing away from this chapter, we think it should be this: read the next chapter about RAM!

We've covered a lot more ground than that, though, so let's recap. If you're trying to decide what CPU you need for a new system, make sure you take into account other factors than just the core CPU speed. As we've seen, system bus speed can be as much or more important in determining system performance. If you're interested in upgrading the CPU in your current system, make sure that your other subsystems are up to snuff. Don't expect a CPU upgrade alone to magically make your system run as fast as a brand new system based around the same processor. As we saw with our 486DX2/66 system, adding an AMD 5x86 processor running at 133MHz did not magically transform that system into the equivalent of a Pentium 133 machine.

If your machine doesn't match up directly with one of the machines in this chapter, don't worry. Just remember the basic concepts that you've learned. Pay attention to specs other than the CPU core speed. Look at L1 cache size and system bus speed. Don't be swayed by a single megahertz rating. Besides, there'll be newer processor upgrades available to you that we didn't get to test. When in doubt, check reviews and benchmark results in fine magazines such as *PC Magazine* and *Computer Shopper* (we must again disclose here our Ziff-Davis biases).

8.17. Testing You Can Do

If you can con your local computer dealer into letting you borrow a CPU upgrade, or into selling you one contingent on the fact that it satisfies your testing, you can try some CPU testing on your own. The most important thing to remember is that the bottom line is how the CPU upgrade affects real-world performance. That's why Winstone tests should be the first thing you run. WinBench Processor Tests can also be helpful, but they won't give you the whole story on how much real performance to expect from your CPU upgrade. Do us a favor and don't bother with some of the other, smaller processor tests that are out there.

That's really all there is to it. Make sure to follow the tips in this chapter when installing your upgrade, and follow proper testing procedure too: defragment your hard disk completely and cold boot your machine before each test run.

> **NOTE** Complete directions for running Winstone and WinBench can be found in Appendixes A, "Using Winstone 98," and B, "Using WinBench 98," respectively.

8.18. From Here...

If you read no other chapter in this book, please take our advice and read the next chapter on RAM. We feel that many systems in users hands in the real world are RAM-starved, and adding RAM to a system gives you the most bang for your buck. However, because the CPU chip and system RAM are really both part of the processor subsystem, they both affect performance. All the elements of performance are inter-related.

The following chapters will provide more about CPU-related topics.

- Chapter 9, "Optimizing Your System's RAM," will show you how to optimize your RAM amount for a particular CPU.

- Chapter 10, "Optimizing Your Graphics Subsystem," will show you how to optimize your graphics setup for a given CPU chip you have.

Optimizing Your System's Processor

Chapter 9

9

Optimizing Your System's RAM

When most people talk about the speed of a PC, the first thing they mention is its processor. And, as we discussed in Chapter 8, "Optimizing Your System's Processor," processor speed is definitely a huge factor in system performance.

No processor, though, can reach its full potential without the right type and amount of RAM (Random Access Memory) support.

In our experience the single most common PC performance bottleneck is main memory. The main problem is not usually the type of RAM technology the system uses, though as we'll discuss in this chapter different RAM technologies do perform differently and you should try to pick the best one when you're deciding which new PC to buy. Once you've purchased a PC, though, you're stuck with whatever RAM technologies its motherboard supports.

No, the source of this common problem is much simpler: Most PCs don't have enough main memory. This is actually good news, because it means there's a good chance that the biggest limiter of your PC's performance is one you can control—the amount of RAM it contains. And, RAM is one of the cheaper hardware upgrades you can buy; as we write this, 16MB of RAM runs right around fifty bucks. RAM prices have been dropping over the last few years, and we expect that downward price trend to continue.

Of course, you can't just run out, buy a bunch of RAM, install it, and expect your performance to instantly improve. Nothing in life, or at least nothing with computers, is ever that simple. For any given system, there's a RAM *sweet spot*, the amount of RAM that gives you maximum performance for the smallest possible cost. Add RAM beyond this sweet spot, and you'll get little to no return on your RAM investment. Add too much RAM, and in some systems you can actually lower performance; we'll explain that later in this chapter. The version of the Windows operating system you're running, the applications you're using, and the processor in your PC all play a role in determining this sweet spot. Even different applications running on the same operating system have different sweet spots.

In this chapter, we'll show you how to use Winstone to find that sweet spot for your operating system, applications, and processor.

The importance of RAM, by the way, is nothing new. Not only has RAM always been an important part of system performance, the amount you need for optimum performance has continually risen. To put RAM in its historical PC perspective, consider this: In the original PC architecture, the maximum amount of RAM you could have was 640K bytes.

The Intel 808x processor family that powered the first PC could address only a total of 1MB of RAM, and the original PC designers held back some RAM in part for system uses and in part because they felt 640KB would be enough. After all, the memory footprint of the DOS operating system, the amount of RAM DOS consumed, was a mere fraction of this 640KB. Today, both DOS and this memory limit appear somewhere between quaint and downright silly.

Operating systems have grown a great deal in size and complexity since that first version of DOS, and their RAM footprints have increased accordingly. The advent of Windows and its ability to use system RAM as a hard-disk cache raised the RAM bar considerably. PCs with less than 4MB of RAM quickly became almost useless for Windows apps and found themselves consigned to boat-anchor duty. Windows 95 set its absolute minimum amount of RAM to 8MB, and Windows 98's and Windows NT's minimum configurations were 16MB. More importantly, these minimum RAM amounts were just that—minimums—and anyone seeking maximum performance should expect to need more.

The trend of increasing memory requirements shows no signs of abating. The operating systems continue to want more RAM, and so, too, do the applications, which are also growing bigger all the time and which share system memory with the operating system.

System memory is not, of course, the only place RAM appears in a modern PC. Most PCs today also have at least two levels of processor cache plus RAM dedicated to their graphics adapter memory, and other PC components sometimes have their own RAM. We'll briefly review each of these RAM types in this chapter.

In this chapter, you will learn:

- What's RAM got to do with it?

  RAM comes in many different types and plays several different roles in a modern PC. Say "RAM" to most PC users, and they'll typically think of main system memory, but RAM doesn't stop there. Typically, your processor subsystem will have two levels of RAM cache, and your graphics accelerator, hard disk controller, and, if you have one, network interface card will contain their own RAM. In the sections in this part of the chapter you'll learn just why RAM is so important, how different RAM technologies work, and the different roles RAM plays.

- How to pick the right amount of RAM for your processor

  As a general rule, the faster the processor in your PC, the better it can utilize additional RAM. No single rule, though, can tell you the right amount of RAM for a particular processor. Fortunately, you don't have to depend on over-generalized rules; you have the benchmarks. We'll show you how to use Winstone to find the RAM sweet spot for your PC—the RAM amount that delivers maximum performance for the minimum investment. In case you don't feel like running your own RAM tests, we'll also analyze a ton of results from dozens of our own experiments on a range of processor types.

■ How to pick the right amount of RAM for your operating system

Your processor is, of course, only one factor to consider when you're trying to pick the optimal amount of RAM for your PC. The operating system you run will also play a big role in your choice, because Windows 98, Windows 95, and Windows NT have different RAM demands. We'll analyze test results from all three operating systems.

■ How to pick the right amount of RAM for your applications

The final determinant of the right amount of RAM for your PC is what you do with the PC, the kinds of applications you run. High-end graphically intensive applications, for example, often require more RAM than standard business-oriented applications. Winstone contains tests that use a broad selection of both business and high-end applications, and we'll analyze a large set of test results for both groups.

9.1. Cocktail Party Tips

If people ask you what they should do to improve their PC's performance, blithely respond, "Buy more RAM." The odds are very good that your advice will be sound. Indeed, our research shows that for your money, adding more RAM is likely to yield more benefit per dollar than any other system upgrade that you might make.

The party talk gets a lot more complicated if anyone asks the next logical question: How much RAM should my system have? As this chapter shows, there's no simple answer to that question. You'll just have to tell the crowd, which by now has surely gathered around, that their mileage will vary depending on a few key factors: The type of processor in their systems, the operating system they're running, and the applications they use.

If they press the issue, here's a quick tip for each of these areas:

In general, the faster your processor, the greater the benefit you'll get from more RAM (see Figure 9.1).

Figure 9.1.

Sample results for Windows 95 and Windows NT show how much different processors gained in Business Winstone performance from the presence of additional RAM.

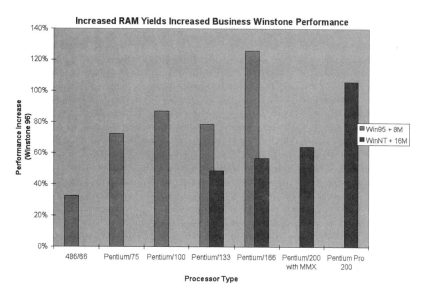

On the operating system front, Windows 98 and Windows 95 generally need less RAM than Windows NT. You can actually run Windows 95 with 8MB, though we sure don't recommend it. You really want at least 16MB, and typically more, for both it and Windows 98. Windows NT basically ups the ante on both fronts: Don't even try it in less than 16MB, and expect to need at least 32MB for anything resembling reasonable performance.

When it comes to applications, the best rule of thumb is that standard business apps, such as Microsoft Word and Excel, typically need less RAM than such high-end applications as Photoshop. For example, our research shows that, in general, on Windows 98 and Windows 95 24MB is a tolerable amount of RAM for business apps, but for high-end applications 48MB is more appropriate. As you'd expect from the operating system information above, both these numbers are somewhat higher for Windows NT. You should also plan on adding more RAM if your work involves multitasking (running multiple applications at the same time).

9.2. The Role of RAM

Memory plays a vital and central role in modern PCs. After the processor, RAM is the most essential component of a system. Its primary function is to act as the fast storage in which a processor keeps its data and instructions. Without RAM, the processor can do very little.

Many other parts of a typical modern PC also use a variety of RAM in a variety of ways. A RAM cache can let a system speed up components such as a hard disk that run at much slower speeds than the processor. RAM is also essential for graphics adapters, because it's where they hold the images and image data they're drawing on the screen.

Let's look at some of the many ways your PC uses RAM.

9.2.1. Main Memory

When a PC advertisement or product review quotes a RAM amount, it's usually referring to main memory. The operating system loads its own executable portions into this RAM from your hard disk, and it also has to load into RAM all the applications you run. These programs comprise instructions and data that the processor can execute and manipulate.

Your system's main memory does more, though, than just act as the place from which the processor executes programs. It also serves as a *cache* for data your PC is reading from its hard disk(s).

If you've been a PC owner or user for a while, you probably remember when Microsoft introduced SmartDrive, its first disk-caching software. (Other companies had already been selling add-on disk-cache software.) With SmartDrive, your PC set aside an amount of system RAM for use as a disk cache. SmartDrive, or any other disk-caching software, uses that memory to hold copies of the most popular or most recently read bits of data on your hard disk. Then, when the processor asks the hard drive again for that data, the disk-caching software intercepts the request and hands back the data from the cache. Because the system can get to data in RAM dramatically faster than it can read hard-disk data, the whole process speeds up greatly. As long as caching software does its job and keeps the RAM cache and the hard drive in synch, your overall performance increases.

How dramatic is the difference in performance between a typical hard disk and the typical PC's main memory? A hard disk typically takes tens of milliseconds to access a chunk of data, while system RAM takes tens of nanoseconds to access data. The potential performance improvements are clearly huge.

The concept of caching is a very important one that pops up in many different personal computer subsystems. Caching works because programs—both applications and operating systems—don't access each byte of data they're using, whether that data is on a hard disk or in main memory or just about anywhere else, equally often. Certain pieces of information turn out to be the most important, and therefore the ones the software uses most often, at certain times. Caching takes the most popular data and puts it in a faster place, the cache, and thus avoids the performance bottleneck of the original, slower source.

9.2.2. Sidebar: Troubleshooting RAM Problems

The good news is that RAM rarely goes bad. The bad news is that when it does, you're going to have a tough time. RAM problems can be very difficult, if not impossible, to troubleshoot. Because RAM is an integral part of the processor subsystem, the computer's brain, a RAM failure rarely produces any obvious or even understandable error message. Instead, something very bad will frequently happen.

If your PC's motherboard uses parity RAM and any of that RAM goes bad, you might be lucky enough to see a parity error message screen.

More likely, though, is that if any of your RAM goes bad you'll see one of the most common ways a RAM error will manifest itself in Windows: A Fatal Exception Error, the infamous blue screen of death. If you've never seen a blue screen, let us know; we may need to nominate your PC for sainthood. Blue screens pop up for many more reasons than RAM errors, however, so don't assume your RAM is bad just because you see one.

If your PC produces blue-screen errors frequently, or if you get a memory-parity error, RAM should be one of the things you check. If you've recently upgraded your RAM or added RAM to your system, you should be particularly suspicious that bad RAM is the culprit. RAM chips are sensitive to static discharge, so you might've damaged your RAM while installing it. (Later in this chapter we give some tips for buying and adding RAM so you can avoid this and other common RAM-related pitfalls.)

The best way for most of us to check for bad RAM is to run some sort of diagnostic program. Many general-purpose diagnostic packages, such as the popular Norton Utilities, will test your PC's RAM. You can also buy more specialized programs, such as RAMexam from Qualitas, whose sole goal is to thoroughly test your RAM. If you don't want to invest in yet another program, you can often search on-line and find a freeware or shareware program that tests RAM.

All these programs test RAM in the same basic way: By reading from and writing to every location in your PC's main memory and checking for errors each time.

We've found that the ZD benchmark programs are actually quite useful for system tests. Even though their goal is to measure performance, not to diagnose system problems, the benchmarks do exercise your PC more strenuously in a shorter period of time than you would normally. Many folks uncover problems with their PCs simply by running All Tests in Winstone and WinBench.

9.2.3. L1 and L2 Cache

Most PCs today have one or more processor caches. Don't confuse these with disk caches: Disk caches boost disk performance by caching in RAM frequently used disk data, while processor caches speed up main memory itself by using smaller caches of much faster RAM. The caching concept is the same in both cases, though: Use a fast container to hold the most popular data. Processors have become so fast that RAM by comparison runs much slower. The RAM in processor caches is very special, very fast, and very expensive memory known as static RAM, or more commonly, SRAM. Just as the goal of a disk cache is to minimize the number of times the system has to wait while it's reading data from disk, the goal of processor caches is to minimize the number of times the processor has to read from the slower main memory.

Processors typically use two caches. The first, Level 1 or simply L1, is actually on the processor itself. All 486, Pentium, Pentium Pro, and Pentium II-class processors contain some amount of L1 cache. L1 cache is the fastest cache a processor can use, because it is actually on the processor and runs at the processor's speed. The Pentium has 16KB of L1 cache, which it splits 8KB for instructions and 8KB for data. Cyrix's 6x86 has a 16KB unified L1 cache, which means the cache can hold both instructions and data, and it also has a 256-byte instruction-line cache. AMD's 5K86 CPU has a split cache, with 16KB for instructions and 8KB for data. The Pentium MMX chip doubles the original Pentium L1 caches to 16KB each for data and instructions.

Most of the time when people mention cache, they are referring to Level 2 (L2) cache, or external processor cache. This cache is typically not on the processor chip itself, though it's often in the same overall complex or module as the processor. The Pentium Pro CPU module, for example, does include an L2 cache, which is available in several sizes and runs at the processor's speed.

DRAM technology is getting faster, and SRAM for caches is expensive, so some vendors are offering cacheless systems aimed at lower price points. Such systems simply can't, however, wring the same performance from their processor as well-designed similar systems with L2 caches.

9.2.4. Sidebar: RAM and Virtual Memory

Let's say you're sitting at a PC with only 16MB of RAM and you want to work on a set of five very large photographic image files. You open the first, a 4MB file, in PaintShop Pro. One by one, you open the remaining files. When you're done, you have over 20MB of files open—which means they're in memory, right? You've used 20MB of RAM just for the image files themselves, and that doesn't even count the RAM the operating system and PaintShop Pro need. But the PC only has 16MB of RAM. How is it possible that the system can do this?

Two words: *virtual memory*.

Modern operating systems, such as Windows 98, Windows 95, and Windows NT (as well as OS/2 and the Mac OS and the many UNIX variants) implement virtual memory, a setup in which applications that require more memory than the amount physically installed in the PC can still run. In a virtual memory setup the operating system, behind the scenes and unbeknownst to the applications, uses space on the hard disk to simulate more RAM. It moves, or swaps, data and program code back and forth between the disk and main memory as it needs to do so to keep the applications running. From the application's perspective, the system appears to have a huge amount of memory available.

Though the application doesn't know any better, you will, because virtual memory will always be a great deal slower than real RAM; after all, hard disks are dramatically slower than RAM. If you've ever been working along and then had to wait because your system's hard drive started buzzing frantically, you were running up against the swapping your system had to do to move the data it needed between RAM and the virtual memory space on your hard disk.

If you think much about overall PC system design, you can't help but wonder at the odd ways systems use RAM and hard disks. The system employs a software cache in main RAM to speed up the hard disk, then turns right around and uses hard disk space to simulate more RAM when they need it. This seemingly odd pairing of features works because the disk cache (which is RAM) and the virtual memory (which is disk) are both managed by the operating system, which coordinates what's essentially an endless game of musical chairs.

As far as the operating system is concerned, it wants to cache as much data going to and from the hard disk as possible in RAM. It also wants to swap the contents of RAM to the hard disk as little as possible. Running this dance is a key function of the OS. It determines when the RAM available is getting low, and then writes the least-recently-used RAM pages to disk. This low on RAM condition occurs much less frequently than do the disk reads and writes that happen all the time, and which the OS caches in its RAM disk cache if possible.

The interconnectedness of these subsystems is something you must keep in mind if you want to optimize your system's performance. Until you can buy a computer with gigabytes of non-volatile RAM—something you're not likely to see anytime soon at anything resembling reasonable prices—if you want peak performance you're going to have to consider both disk performance and RAM performance.

9.2.5. Video RAM

Just as the CPU is not the only processor in your PC, the system's main memory is not the only RAM in it. The other processors in your system need RAM to hold data and from which to execute instructions. Almost all PCs today have processors in their graphics and disk subsystems. These chips are typically specialized processors, not general purpose ones like your main system CPU, but they still need RAM.

Video or graphics adapters use their RAM to store a representation of what's on the display at any given moment. That's why the amount of RAM on your graphics adapter limits the resolution and color depth of the images you can display. The graphics adapter uses this RAM, which is typically Video RAM, or VRAM, to update the display. (For more information on graphics and VRAM, see Chapter 10, "Optimizing Your Graphics Subsystem," which covers your PC's graphics subsystem.)

9.2.6. Other RAM

RAM also typically shows up in most other key PC subsystems, including your PC's hard disk controller, CD-ROM controller, and network interface board. In most cases, the device that runs the subsystem uses this RAM for some form of caching.

Hard-disk controllers originally used RAM simply as buffers to hold the contents of tracks they were reading ahead. Some controllers, though, ended up using RAM as a full-blown hardware cache. CD-ROM controllers have similar RAM caches.

Any network interface boards you might have installed in your computer use their RAM to buffer frames from the network. Frames make up the packets of information that your network interface board uses to communicate with a server or servers.

In their constant efforts to drive down prices and thus reach more potential buyers, some PC vendors periodically try to do away with as many of these different sources of RAM as possible and instead move all system RAM into one main pool. The common industry term for this design is the Unified Memory Architecture (UMA). In its simplest form, a UMA design means that main memory and graphics memory share the same physical RAM. While UMA promises performance gains over traditional no-cache systems, there were no widely available UMA-based machines at the time of this writing.

Intel's recent Advanced Graphics Port (AGP), which is available primarily on Pentium II systems, is another way for a system to use main memory in place of graphics memory.

9.2.7. Windows 98 and 95 versus Windows NT

Windows 98 and Windows 95 share the same basic code base and so behave internally rather similarly. Both of them thus handle memory in the same basic way. That way is so different from the way Windows NT treats memory that we'd have to write another whole book just to cover the topic. These differences start with the fact that Windows NT requires more RAM to simply load itself and go on from there. These differences are why we ran separate experiments on each operating system.

These differences are likely to slowly disappear over time as Windows 98 grows closer to Windows NT, because one day Microsoft would like to have a single desktop OS. (Windows 95 doesn't figure into these plans, because Microsoft's goal is for everyone who uses it to upgrade to either Windows 98 or Windows NT.) In the meantime, the one thing of which we can be certain is that these operating systems will continue to grow in size—so their memory requirements are also likely to continue to increase.

This trend is nothing new. At a conference a while ago, we saw an entertaining presentation from Nathan Myhrvold of Microsoft. He noted that just as processor subsystem speed had for some years grown at an annualized rate of about 44%, so too had the number of lines of code in Windows NT—and the value of Microsoft stock!

9.3. RAM Technologies

The biggest RAM-related problem system designers face is how to keep the processor running at full speed. Whenever the processor needs something from RAM and the RAM subsystem is unable to deliver that data the moment the processor needs it, the processor sits idle. Each cycle the processor sits idle is called a wait state. More wait states means slower overall performance, because the processor isn't reaching its full potential.

The most obvious solution to this problem is simply to build PCs with RAM that is fast enough to keep up with their processors. Unfortunately, doing so isn't really possible. Processor clock speeds have increased dramatically in the lifetime of the PC. RAM speeds, or cycle times, have also improved, but nowhere near as much.

For instance, since the introduction of the first IBM PC, processor clock speeds have gone from the 4.77MHz of the 8088 in that PC to the 400MHz and faster speeds of the Pentium II chips, and Pentium II processors as fast as 450MHz are likely in late 1998. Those gains represent an over eighty-fold increase in just raw clock speed—and that doesn't count the many improvements in the speed with which processors execute instructions internally. In the same timeframe, typical DRAM chip speeds have only doubled, from a common access time of 120 nanoseconds to 60 nanoseconds.

Another RAM-related issue also affects performance. DRAM in its simplest form requires the system to refresh any location the processor accesses, because the act of reading a bit of data basically destroys it. This refreshing takes time, and during that time the processor cannot read that bit of RAM.

One common member of the current generation of dynamic RAM is fast page-mode DRAM, or FDRAM. The best way to understand this and other RAM technologies is to think of memory as an array. Each piece of data you want has a location, or address, in that array. The address is a row number and a column number. With Page Mode memory, when the system goes to read the data at some address, it begins by activating the appropriate row in the DRAM array, and then it activates the first column of data in that row to find the memory it needs.

FDRAM memory subsystems are faster than older DRAM subsystems, because as they are refreshing one particular column of data—a time during which the processor would have to wait if it wanted more data from memory—they are activating the next column of data. The idea is that the next piece of data the processor will need is likely to be the one in the memory location adjacent to the previous piece. Of course, this activation of the next row works well only with sequential reads from memory, because once the FDRAM subsystem has set up the initial read it can activate successive columns of data more quickly, but the good news is that such reads are fairly common. When the processor wants sequential memory locations, this technique basically can give it a burst of data from RAM.

Two other RAM types, EDO DRAM (sometimes called Hyper-Page mode) and Burst EDO DRAM (BEDO), are also varieties of page-mode RAM.

EDO RAM works in the same basic way as FDRAM, but it uses an additional trick to minimize the amount of time the processor spends waiting for memory. (The tricks RAM designers have created to improve system speed are often esoteric and not really what this book is about, so we'll give you just the short form here.) EDO RAM leaves its output data buffer on after the system has found the particular piece of information it needed, so the processor can immediately read from that buffer if it so desires. The buffer stays on until the next column access or next read cycle begins. This approach lets burst transfers happen more quickly, which shortens the overall time to read from memory and thus improves the system's overall performance.

This technology turns out to require little change to existing memory designs, is relatively easy for memory makers to implement, and costs little more than fast-page-mode RAM. Consequently, many system makers use it, and if you can get this faster technology memory, you generally should.

Many newer systems support another type of RAM technology, Synchronous DRAM (or SDRAM). SDRAM comes on a 168-pin DIMM (dual inline memory module) package. A key feature of SDRAM is that it synchronizes all of its operations to the processor clock signal. This design makes it popular with vendors, because the interfaces that control it are easier to design and build, its parts are simpler to manufacture, and the time it takes to access any particular row is lower. The memory bus to which current SDRAM DIMMs connect typically runs at 66MHz in most PCs, so the system can transfer data between it and the processor faster than typical transfers to and from EDO RAM. The newer, high-end Pentium II-based systems increase this bus speed to an even faster 100MHz.

SDRAM modules have one drawback of note: They are not generically compatible the same way many SIMMs are, due to the tighter timing requirements and the manufacturer-specific interfaces they tend to use. Consequently, plenty of new systems still use EDO SIMMs.

One key point to always remember when you're considering RAM upgrades is that you can only use the types of RAM your motherboard supports. Buy RAM that your system can't use, and you'll only have wasted your money. See the sidebar on how to buy the right SIMMs for more information if you're considering a RAM upgrade.

9.3.1. Sidebar: How to Buy the Right SIMMs

If you decide you need more RAM, you'll need to do a little research to make sure you buy the right memory modules (SIMMs or DIMMs). A SIMM is a Single In-line Memory Module, a tiny rectangular circuit board to which a manufacturer has directly soldered RAM chips. A SIMM fits into a special connector on your system's motherboard. A DIMM, as we noted earlier, is another way to package RAM, a Dual Inline Memory Module.

The first step in buying RAM is to determine the speed of the RAM your system requires. Vendors express RAM speed in access time, which they cite in nanoseconds (ns): 80ns, 70ns, 60ns, and so on. Your system manual should tell you what speed of RAM your system requires. If it doesn't, or if you've lost the manual, try looking at the existing SIMMs or DIMMs on your motherboard. The RAM chips on these modules typically sport a manufacturer's code that includes the access time. For instance, a SIMM loaded with Mitsubishi chips on whose backs the string "M5M44100AJ 304SM06-7" appear is a 70ns part; the -7 at the end of the part code is the key indicator here.

In addition to the speed of your RAM, you also need to know how the system has divided it into banks. Banks are groups of system RAM that systems use to further boost performance slightly. When you upgrade RAM, you have to add an entire bank. This information is also typically available from your system's manual. (If it's not already clear, try never to lose your system manual. We make a point of keeping all of the manuals that come with our hardware shelved near the machine.) If you no longer have your system manual, you can make some quick guesses about the banks in your system and thus about how many SIMMs you will need. At the time of this writing, most Pentium and Pentium Pro-based systems use banks of two 72-pin SIMMs. Older systems may require banks of two, four, or even eight older 30-pin SIMMs. You can tell these SIMMs from the newer ones by their smaller size and larger contacts, the shiny legs that go into the memory module.

An obvious factor that is nonetheless easy to overlook is the number of open RAM slots on your motherboard. Don't buy more SIMMs or DIMMs than you have open slots. If you have no open RAM slots, make sure you buy higher capacity SIMMs or DIMMs than those already in your system, because you'll have to take out and replace those existing modules.

The final piece of information you need is whether your system uses parity or non-parity SIMMs. Parity RAM contains an extra bit for each eight bits of memory. The memory control circuitry on the motherboard generates the contents of this parity bit so that each 9-bit byte always contains an odd number of binary 1's. When the system reads from memory, special parity-checking circuitry takes a look at each 9-bit byte and generates a parity error if this *odd-parity* condition is not true. This approach obviously costs more bits of RAM, but it is a quick way to verify that a byte's contents are probably okay. Many system manufacturers ship their systems with non-parity RAM or with parity checking disabled on the motherboard.

The overall concept that leads to each of these rules is the same: Buy RAM that matches the existing RAM in your system. If, for example, you have a bank of two, non-parity, 70ns EDO RAM SIMMs, when you upgrade buy two more SIMMs of non-parity, 70ns EDO RAM. Many systems will let you get away with mixing RAM with slightly different characteristics, but we don't recommend it. Your best is to buy SIMMs (or DIMMs) that exactly match, in all but manufacturer name, the ones already in your system.

9.4. Cache Technologies

Cache RAM, like DRAM, comes in different flavors. (We're discussing here the L2 cache, the SRAM the CPU uses to speed up main memory accesses.) The simplest form of SRAM uses an asynchronous design in which the cache memory and the CPU are not working in lock step. In such designs, the CPU sends an address to the cache, the cache looks up the address, and then it returns to the CPU the data at that address. This approach consumes an extra cycle at the beginning of each access while the cache looks up the tag of the data the CPU wants.

Some caches use a synchronous design, in which the cache buffers the incoming addresses to spread the address-lookup routine over two or more clock cycles. The SRAM stores the requested address in a register during the first clock cycle. During the second, it retrieves the data at that address and delivers it to the CPU. Because the cache has already stored the next address the CPU wants, it can fetch the data at that address at the same time that the CPU is reading the data from the previous request. The synchronous SRAM can then, when appropriate, transmit a burst of subsequent data elements without having to receive any additional addresses from the CPU. When the CPU wants this burst of data, the cache is effectively able to respond much faster and thus speed up the system.

Pipeline burst SRAM is another form of synchronous SRAM. Pipelining is a process in which the cache spreads the process of fetching its data over three clock cycles. Though this approach causes the cache to delay its fulfillment of the first request, it can service a subsequent one every clock cycle. Pipelining essentially adds an output stage that buffers data the cache has read from memory locations so that subsequent memory reads don't have to spend the time to go all the way to main memory to get the data they need. (That work has already happened, when necessary, while the cache was servicing other requests.) As with all of these burst-oriented techniques, pipelining works most effectively when the CPU wants the data in a sequential sequence of memory addresses.

9.5. When More RAM is Bad

Conventional wisdom holds that too much of just about anything can be bad for you, and that rule certainly can be true of RAM. We've talked to folks with too much money on their hands who loaded up their systems with 128MB of RAM and then were startled to find that their PC performance actually dropped—that's right, dropped. The reason for this seemingly unlikely behavior lies in the way many processor L2 caches operate.

As we discussed earlier in this chapter, the L2 cache on the system motherboard (or in a slot on the system motherboard or in the processor complex) holds the most frequently used main memory data in a small amount of expensive, high-speed SRAM. The processor can get to that data far more quickly than it could retrieve the information from main memory, so the system runs faster. Though it's easy to think of the L2 cache as just a bunch of SRAM, the cache actually consists of that SRAM and some controlling circuitry, the cache controller logic. The cache memory itself is also not a monolithic set of bytes: It contains both RAM that holds data and what's known as tag RAM. The tag RAM stores the address of the real memory locations whose contents match the data that's in the data RAM cache. Because the amount of tag RAM in any given cache is limited, the range of main memory addresses the tag RAM can hold is limited. This limitation amounts to an upper limit on the amount of real memory the system can cache. On many motherboards, this limit is 64MB, which means the tag RAM can hold addresses only for the first 64MB of main memory.

This limit has a profound effect: The system cannot cache any memory above this limit. Any programs or data located in that memory are effectively running on a system without an L2 cache, and, as we saw in Chapter 8, that means a huge performance hit.

This limit still might not seem like a problem, because you might reasonably note that few, if any, of your applications will need more than the cacheable 64MB of RAM. Unfortunately, that fact doesn't count in this situation, because much of the operating system loads into main memory from the top down—right into that uncached RAM!

So, if you have a motherboard that can't cache all of the RAM you've put on it, you could well see a drop in performance. We've never seen a modern motherboard that couldn't cache at least 64MB of RAM, but if you want to go beyond that amount, you should definitely check your system or motherboard manual to make sure your L2 cache can handle the extra RAM. If you don't check first, don't blame us when your performance drops.

9.5.1. Sidebar: How to Install RAM

When you've bought some RAM and are ready to install it, open your PC and locate the open SIMM (or DIMM; we'll assume SIMM here) slots on its motherboard. If you don't have any open SIMM slots, you'll first have to remove the existing modules you're planning to replace.

In most current machines, you should install SIMMs in pairs. We'll summarize the key points of RAM installation here, but always check your owner's manual for special instructions.

Put on your grounding strap or whatever you use to make sure you're not going to zap your system with static electricity. If you're not using anything to ground yourself, you're taking your system's life in your hands. Many SIMM kits come with an inexpensive grounding strap, but if yours did not you can usually get such a strap at any local computer shop or electronics store. By wearing a grounding strap, you ensure that you won't build up a large static charge.

Don't open the conductive bag that almost certainly holds your SIMMs until you're ready to install them. SIMMs come with a central slot that lets them fit into SIMM slots only when you have oriented them properly, so the next step is to orient them so that they will fit. Insert the SIMM at a slight angle, then rotate it until it's perpendicular to the motherboard. You may need to pull back the restraining tabs on either side of the SIMM to do this. Once you've positioned the SIMM properly, the restraining tabs should lock into place on either side of it.

Once you've got your RAM installed, you can prevent problems with it—and with your other system components—by making sure to plug your PC into a surge-suppressing power strip. If you use a modem, you'll want to get a surge-suppresser for your phone line also. Many power strip manufacturers produce models that include both power outlets and phone-line surge suppression connections. If you really want to prevent future problems, get an uninterruptible power supply (UPS). You'll avoid the problems and potential data loss that surges, brownouts, and blackouts can cause.

People often ask us if they really need to worry about all this surge suppression hoo-hah. The answer is a definite yes. We've learned this lesson more than once the hard way (which does beg the question of how well we've learned it, but, hey, everybody makes mistakes). While we were writing this book, for example, one of our computers died because a lightning strike to the phone lines—not the power lines, the phone lines—fried its motherboard. We had to swap an entirely new motherboard into the PC, an operation that is a genuine pain, to get it working again. We quickly purchased a new surge suppresser that protected both the power and the phone lines for that PC.

> ### NOTE Where's WinBench?
>
> We've noted in a few spots in the book the fact that Winstone and WinBench are a natural testing pair. In many other chapters of the book we do extensive testing with both WinBench and Winstone. But not here.
>
> Why?
>
> The answer is that WinBench doesn't run real applications and so doesn't have the same RAM requirements as those applications. WinBench's goal is to test your PC's individual subsystems, not your overall system; Winstone is the right tool for testing overall system performance. Because of this difference in focus, WinBench's tests don't demonstrate the true effects you'll see by adding RAM to your PC. In fact, once WinBench has the minimum amount of RAM it needs to run its tests, adding additional RAM beyond that amount won't significantly change the results of its tests.

9.6. Windows 98 and RAM

As we explained in the introduction, bringing a PC up to its RAM sweet spot is one of the most cost-effective ways to boost its overall performance. The obvious trick is figuring out how much RAM you should get for your PC. As we also said, that amount depends on the processor, the operating system, and the applications you're running. We spent a great deal of time experimenting with lots of combinations of these factors so you can quickly and easily locate the sweet spot for your PC. In this part of the chapter we'll show you a broad range of results, and the accompanying sweet spots, for a variety of PCs running Windows 98. Later this chapter, we have the same types of results and analysis for Windows 95 and Windows NT. Feel free to jump to the section that best matches the system or systems you want to optimize.

9.6.1 How We Tested

For the studies in this section of the chapter we ran the Business Winstone 98 tests on a range of typical processors. That way, you can look at the results from the system with the same CPU as yours, or at those for a system with a processor that's similar to the one in your PC. We ran Business Winstone 98 studies on a variety of processors with RAM amounts varying, with one exception, from 16MB to 64MB. That exception is the system with a 75MHz Pentium processor, a unit that most likely Windows 98 user now consider sufficiently low-end that we capped its RAM configurations at 32MB.

Because we used Winstone 98 for our Windows 98 tests, and because High-End Winstone 98 requires Windows NT, we were not able to produce High-End Winstone results for Windows 98. Don't worry, though; you can still get a good sense of the right amount of RAM for applications like those in the High-End Winstone tests by using the High-End Winstone results in the Windows 95 section below. Though the two operating system are obviously different, the Windows 95 High-End test results will serve as a decent guide to the amount of RAM Windows 98 is likely to require to run the same applications well.

Our default testing setup used the graphics resolution and color-depth settings that we think are most common for PCs likely to run Windows 98: a resolution of 1024×768 and a bit-depth of 256 colors. For more information on resolution and color depth and how they can affect performance, see Chapter 10, which discusses your PC's graphics subsystem.

We defragmented the hard drive of each PC before we ran each Winstone test. Even though the level of disk fragmentation tends to be low on systems that run Disk Defragmenter regularly, we recommend you follow ZDBOp's standard testing practices and fully defragment a hard drive and then reboot your machine before you start each test. This practice lets you be sure the disk is in the same state each time you run a test.

As of when we ran our tests, the Task Switching tests in Business Winstone 98 and the (supposedly gold) build of Windows 98 on which we were testing did not get along. We consequently could not get Task-Switching test scores, which is why you won't see those scores in the graphs in this section.

9.6.2. Pentium 75

The first machine in our Windows 98 line-up is the Compaq DeskPro with a 75MHz Pentium processor. As we noted earlier, because most likely Windows 98 users now consider such systems fairly low-end, we tested it with only 16MB, 24MB, and 32MB of RAM.

Figure 9.2 shows the type of overall Business Winstone 98 score improvement we were able to achieve with different amounts of RAM. This chart is the first of many that should convince you to add enough RAM to your system to take it past its RAM bottleneck.

When we upgraded this Pentium 75-based PC from 16MB to 24MB of RAM, we achieved an overall increase in the Business Winstone 98 score of almost 20%. Taking the machine to 32MB of RAM, however, gave us only a boost of 5% beyond the 24MB score. A 5% improvement is significant and worth doing if you care a great deal about performance, but it pales beside the initial 20% boost (see Figure 9.3).

Figure 9.2.

Business Winstone 98 performance versus RAM size for a Pentium 75 PC running Windows 98.

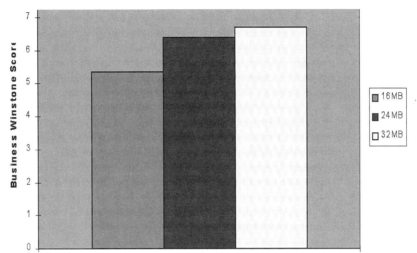

Figure 9.3.

Category scores from Business Winstone 98 tests versus RAM size for a Pentium 75 PC running Windows 98.

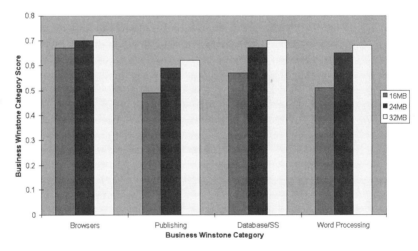

When we look at the application category scores, we see that the level of performance improvement you'll achieve by RAM varies greatly with the type of application you run. The application type that benefited most from additional RAM was Word Processing: Going from 16MB to 24MB of RAM produced a 28% boost in performance.

The Publishing applications and the Database/Spreadsheet applications also gained a significant increase of 20% and 18% respectively from the same RAM addition. The Browsers scores increased by only about 5%, however. This fact suggests that for browsers the performance bottleneck is not this RAM amount.

Instead, some other factor in the system is limiting their performance.

When we take this system from 24MB to 32MB, the performance gains are much less impressive. With the exception of the Browser category, all of the gains are in the 5% range. This increase is enough to make the total boost in the Word Processing category, from moving from 16MB to 32MB, a whopping 33%. Clearly, if you plan to run Word Processing applications on a similar PC under Windows PC and the system has less than 32MB of RAM, it's time to get more RAM.

For a Pentium 75-based PC, or for such similar systems as the earlier Pentium 60 and Pentium 66 PCs, we recommend getting 32MB of RAM for normal Business applications if your current system has 16MB or less of RAM. If your system has 24MB of RAM, you will see some performance gain, but not a lot, by moving to 32MB RAM.

9.6.3. Pentium 100

Starting with this machine and continuing for the rest of the Windows 98 test systems, we ran Winstone's tests at a wider variety of RAM amounts: 16MB, 24MB, 32MB, 48MB, and 64MB. It's possible to set up a machine with other RAM amounts, such as 40MB, but configurations other than the ones we tested are not common. (Some PCs certainly do contain much more than 64MB of RAM, but they're such a minority that we won't focus on them in this book.)

The RAM sweet spot for this machine under Windows 98 is obvious: 32MB. By taking this machine to 32MB, we were able to boost its performance significantly. Adding more RAM produced very small improvements (see Figure 9.4).

Figure 9.4.

Business Winstone 98 performance versus RAM size for a Pentium 100 PC running Windows 98.

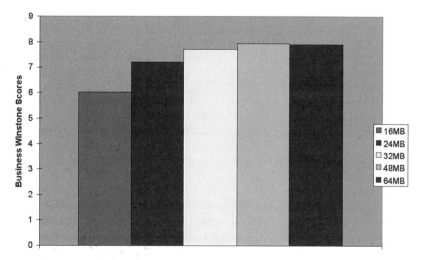

If you look closely, you'll notice that the Business Winstone 98 score with 64MB of RAM is actually a tad lower than the score with 48MB. This difference is not an anomaly; rather, it is small enough that it is just a fluctuation that's below the limit of variability for Winstone. As we've mentioned before, the tests in Winstone and WinBench produce highly repeatable results, but those results do vary slightly from run to run. If you see a variability of more than a few percent on a Winstone test, you probably are not using proper testing procedure. This minor result variance, however, is within that few-percent threshold.

The category results for this PC are similar to the ones we saw with the Pentium 75 system. Of note is the fact that, as with that other system, the Browser category does not show the performance improvement that the other categories show. The Word Processing category benefits most from added RAM, though even that gain is not big. (Moving from 32MB to 48MB of RAM yielded a four percent boost in the performance of the Publishing and Word Processing applications.) Going beyond the 48MB RAM level did not yield a significant increase in performance in any of the application categories (see Figure 9.5).

Figure 9.5.
Category scores from Business Winstone 98 tests versus RAM size for a Pentium 100 PC running Windows 98.

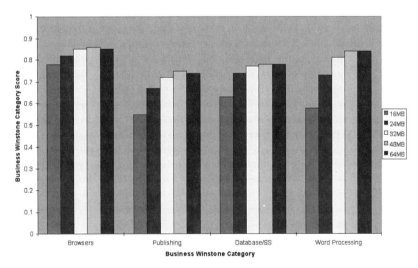

To find the optimal amount of RAM for your Pentium 100 based PC, as with most PCs, determine the most RAM-hungry application you'll be running. Our estimate is that 32MB of RAM should be your choice. You should certainly stay away from anything less.

9.6.4. Pentium 133

As you might expect, the trend we've seen with less powerful systems of diminishing returns as you add RAM continues with this system. We tested this PC with the same RAM configurations as the Pentium 100 unit in the previous section.

The graph of Business application performance versus RAM amount shown in Figure 9.6 is very similar to the graph we saw for the Pentium 100. The 32MB RAM amount is once again the sweet spot. This RAM amount is common in new machines at the time of this writing, but on older systems you might find 8MB, 16MB, or even 24MB of RAM. As these results show, any Windows 98 system in this class will benefit from having at least 32MB of RAM.

Figure 9.6.

Business Winstone 98 performance versus RAM size for a Pentium 133 PC running Windows 98.

The category scores for Business Winstone 98 are also similar to those we saw on the Pentium 100 system. The Word Processing applications benefit most from the presence of additional RAM. The Publishing applications also perform better with more RAM, while the Database/Spreadsheet and Browser applications just don't perform much better with more RAM (see Figure 9.7).

Figure 9.7.

Category scores from Business Winstone 98 tests versus RAM size for a Pentium 133 PC running Windows 98.

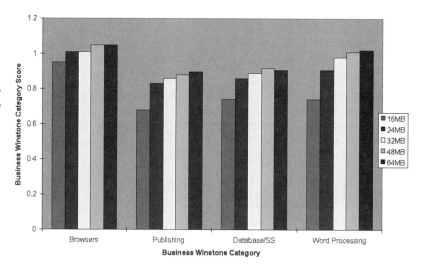

The bottom line if you have a Pentium 133 PC is clear: Get at least 32MB of RAM, and don't bother with more if you're only going to be running business applications.

9.6.5. Pentium 166

The Pentium 166 PC we tested is a representative of a class of systems that sold very well and were quite popular. It's also the first machine to show a real, albeit small, gain in Business Winstone performance by going to 48MB of RAM.

As Figure 9.8 shows, and as is the case with most PCs, you get your biggest performance boost by moving from 16MB to 24MB of RAM. Taking the RAM up to 32MB from 24MB buys you an additional 4% performance increase, as does going from 32MB to 48MB. That's a total boost of 34% that you can achieve by going from 16MB to 48MB of RAM. If you bought this system with 16MB of RAM and you can afford another 16MB or 32MB, buy it now.

Figure 9.8.

Business Winstone 98 performance versus RAM size for a Pentium 166 PC running Windows 98.

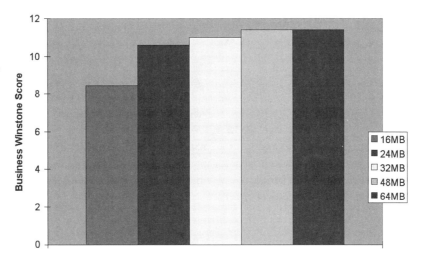

The Business category scores show that your performance gains really top out at 48MB of RAM (see Figure 9.9). The Word Processing applications are an exception to this rule, because their performance is slightly better with 64MB, but overall there's very little reason to move from 48MB to 64MB of RAM. If you want to wring the last few drops of performance out of your machine, though, you should consider upgrading to 48MB if you run publishing or word processing applications.

Figure 9.9.

Category scores from Business Winstone 98 tests versus RAM size for a Pentium 166 PC running Windows 98.

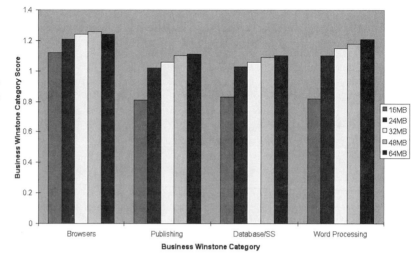

9.6.6. Pentium 200 MMX

Though we tested a Pentium 200 MMX system in all of our standard RAM sizes, few standard configurations of this system included only 16MB of RAM. In case you have such a system, however, we wanted you to know just how much of a performance boost a little more RAM could bring you.

As Figure 9.10 shows, business application performance on this system tops out when you have 48MB of RAM. The slight jump in the overall Business Winstone score that you see in the move from 48MB to 64MB of RAM is still within the benchmark's range of acceptable results variation. The biggest performance boost for this system comes, as it did all our Windows 98 test units, when we go from 16MB to 24MB of RAM.

Figure 9.10.

Business Winstone 98 performance versus RAM size for a Pentium 200 MMX PC running Windows 98.

The Business Winstone category scores in Figure 9.11 show that the sweet spot depends on the type of application you're running. The Browser category performance levels off at 24MB of RAM, while the Database/Spreadsheet category doesn't top out until 32MB, and the Word Processing and Publishing categories hit their peaks at 48MB of RAM. Going from 48MB of RAM to 64MB, even on this system, is overkill for business applications.

Figure 9.11.

Category scores from Business 98 tests versus RAM size for a Pentium 200 MMX PC running Windows 98.

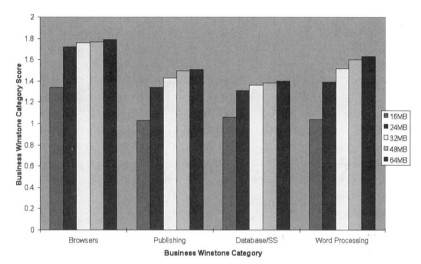

We recommend a minimum of 32MB RAM for machines of this caliber or higher. If you run most major business applications, you won't, however, see much of a performance boost by going beyond 48MB of RAM.

9.6.7. RAM Summary: Windows 98

Figure 9.12 brings together all the overall Business Winstone results for the different Windows 98 systems we tested.

In all cases, you clearly should have at least 24MB of RAM. You will also see a performance boost on most business applications when you move to 32MB of RAM. The faster your PC's processor, the greater that performance boost will be. Take 32MB of RAM as a practical minimum for Windows 98 systems. Go to 48MB if your system's processor is as fast or faster than a 200MHz Pentium and you want the best possible performance when you're running Word Processing or Publishing applications.

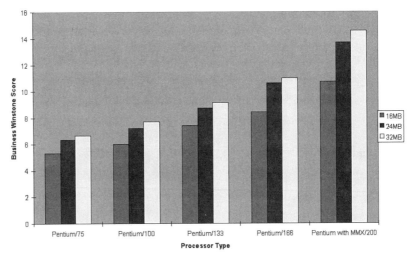

9.7. Windows 95 and RAM

As we did with Windows 98 above, we spent a great deal of time working with Windows 95, trying lots of combinations of different RAM amounts and processor types, so you can quickly and easily locate the RAM sweet spot for your PC. In this part of the chapter, we'll show you a broad range of results, and the accompanying sweet spots, for a variety of PCs running Windows 95. Later in this chapter, we have the same types of results for Windows NT. Feel free to jump to the section that best matches the system or systems you want to optimize.

9.7.1. The Bare Minimum

Plenty of PCs still in use today have only 8MB of RAM. Some started life under Windows 3.x, when 8MB was enough for many applications. Others were early Windows 95 systems. Regardless of how they ended up with only 8MB, these PCs are a special case: If you own one and are running Windows 95 (or are considering upgrading directly to Windows 98), move to at least 16MB of RAM as soon as you can.

The reason we give such an unqualified recommendation is that in the last few years nearly all standard business applications have grown to require, or at least to recommend, a system with 16MB of RAM. Winstone won't even run in less than 16MB.

Just so you don't have to take our word for it, however, we ran some experiments to show the dramatic performance increase you will realize by moving from 8MB to 16MB. To do so, we had to run an older version of Winstone, Winstone 96. We ran these tests, by the way, only for Windows 95. We expect the results would be similar for Windows 98, and Microsoft did not intend Windows NT 4.0 to run in 8MB at all, so neither of those experiments seemed worthwhile.

Figure 9.13 tells the story. As you can plainly see, the performance increase you can realize by moving from 8MB to 16MB on Windows 95 PCs is huge. Even on the slowest PC we tested, an older 486DX/66 system, the Winstone 96 score was almost twice as high when we doubled the RAM to 16MB. On systems with faster processors, the performance increase is more than double.

Figure 9.13.

Performance improvement from moving from 8MB of RAM to 16MB on Windows 95 using Winstone 96.

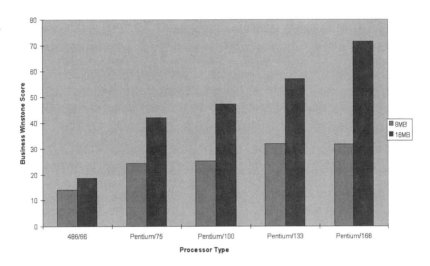

Consequently, we recommend a minimum of 16MB of RAM on *any* system you have or plan to purchase. Almost all system vendors clearly agree, as 16MB is even less than the minimum amount of RAM most system vendors offer on nearly all products. Should you run into any vendors selling 8MB base systems, as can happen in the low-end or used notebook market, plan to add RAM immediately. (To learn more about the special performance characteristics of notebook computers, check out Chapter 13, "Power Saving and Portables," in which we discuss how power-saving options on portable PCs can affect their performance.)

The only bad news is that the level of performance increase you'll get by going above 16MB of RAM is rarely as dramatic as the boost you gain by moving from 8MB to 16MB. In fact, as the experiments in this chapter show, the performance increase from additional RAM decreases until at some point, additional RAM has a small positive, zero, or even a negative effect on performance (see the earlier section, "When More RAM is Bad," for more information on this particular phenomenon).

9.7.2. How We Tested

For the studies in this chapter we ran both the Business Winstone 97 and the High-End Winstone 97 tests on a range of typical processors.

We felt both benchmarks were necessary, because RAM requirements for typical business applications and for high-end applications are often different. As we noted above, we also ran Winstone 96 on machines with 8MB and 16MB of RAM to show the huge increase in performance you can realize from that particular change.

We used a range of representative processors so you could easily find either a system with the same CPU as yours or one that's reasonably close. (As fast as new processors appear, we could never test every one available—we'd be writing an increasingly huge book forever!)

In our Business Winstone 97 studies, we ran tests with RAM amounts from 16MB to 64MB. We did not, however, choose exactly the same RAM amounts for each machine, because we did not want to test configurations you'd be unlikely to want to buy. We didn't, for example, try out our 486/66 system with 64MB of RAM, because it's unlikely that most folks would make such an upgrade. (You'd probably be better off with less RAM and a processor upgrade for about the same money.)

For our High-End Winstone 97 studies, we tested system configurations with 32MB, 48MB, and 64MB of RAM. While you could manage to create systems with other RAM amounts through creative RAM purchases (40MB, for instance, is possible), RAM prices are so low that we don't recommend buying SIMMs any smaller than 8MB for Pentium-level or faster systems.

Our default testing setup used the graphics resolution and color-depth settings that are most common for each machine class. Thus, for the 486DX-2/66 PC, we tested with a resolution of 640×480 and 256 colors, while on the other machines we set the resolution to be 1024×768 and used 256 colors. For more information on resolution and color depth and how they can affect performance, see Chapter 10, in which we discuss your PC's graphics subsystem.

We also defragmented the hard drive of each PC before we ran each Winstone test. Even though the level of disk fragmentation tends to be low on systems that run the Windows 95 System Agent defragmentation utility regularly, it's still good testing practice to fully defragment a hard drive and then reboot your machine before starting a test. This practice lets you be sure the disk is in the same state each time you run a test.

9.7.3. 486DX-2/66

Let's take a quick look at what RAM can do for our 486DX-2/66 PC. Not too many years ago, this machine was a state-of-the-art powerhouse, and now it has the sad distinction of being the lowest machine on our testing totem pole. Such is the nature of processor evolution. Intel introduced the DX-2 line of processors in 1992, and these days it's not reasonable to expect much more than five years of usable lifetime from a CPU chip architecture if you plan to run the most current applications and operating systems. (If you're willing to keep running the applications you bought at the same time as the PC, of course, you can probably get a great deal more use from the machine.)

As old in computer time as this architecture may be, plenty of 486DX-2/66-based machines are still out there and doing good work. If you have one of these systems or are just interested in what RAM can do for them, the test results below tell the story. As with all of the machines in our standard testbed, the PC we used was a Compaq DeskPro.

We tested this machine at two RAM amounts that represent common upgrades for such systems: 16MB and 24MB. As we noted at the start of our discussion of RAM test results, we don't recommend RAM sizes below 16MB. So, if you have a 486-based PC with less than 16MB of RAM, upgrading to 16MB is the first upgrade you should perform. The performance increase will be so obvious you won't need to run a benchmark program to detect it.

Once your 486 system contains 16MB of RAM, the big question is whether you would benefit from adding even more. Our testing shows only a 4% increase in the overall Winstone 97 score when we added eight more megabytes of RAM and took this system to a total of 24MB (see Figure 9.14). Winstone results can vary from test to test by as much as about 3%, so this performance difference is close to negligible. Consequently, unless you're dying to wring every possible drop of performance out of this machine configuration, for overall normal business use we'd recommend sticking with 16MB of RAM.

Figure 9.14.

Business Winstone 97 performance versus RAM size for a 486DX/66 PC running Windows 95.

As Figure 9.15 shows, a closer look at the detailed results for each type of application reveals that some application types will benefit more from this RAM upgrade than others.

When you break down the Business Winstone scores by application type into database, word processing/spreadsheet, and publishing packages, the results are similar graphs to those of the main graph of the overall Winstone score.

The word processing/spreadsheet score, however, increases noticeably—over 7%—from when the system goes from 16MB to 24MB of RAM. If you have a 486-based machine that you're primarily using for word-processing or spreadsheet programs, you can thus get a small but potentially noticeable boost by adding an 8MB SIMM (if your PC will let you add a single SIMM) to that system.

Figure 9.15.

Category scores from Business Winstone 97 tests versus RAM size for a 486DX/66 PC running Windows 95.

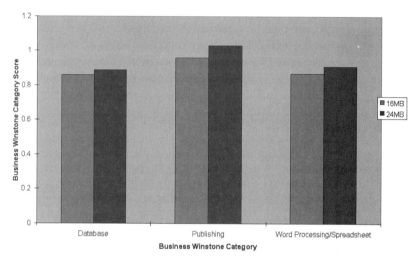

So, once your 486 machine has 16MB of RAM, we don't advise you to add any more RAM unless that system is an office workhorse or a home machine on which you run Word, Excel, or WordPro. If you do have such a PC and you want the absolute best performance possible, take the system to 24MB of RAM.

Adding any more RAM than will not, in general, produce any significant performance gains on these low-end PCs.

9.7.4. Pentium 75

The next machine in our line-up is the Pentium 75-based Compaq DeskPro. You may well find this system a more realistic low-end machine, because the boom in home-computer buying coincided in large part with the introduction of the second wave of Pentium processors, a wave that included the Pentium 75 CPU. We still, though, don't think many serious Photoshop users are running on a Pentium 75-based PC, so we limited our RAM studies on this system to the Business Winstone 97 tests (see Figure 9.16).

This trend is no real surprise, in part because many steps up in processor power also include less obvious improvements in other areas that affect performance.

Consider the jump from our 486/66 PC to one with a Pentium processor. In addition to the higher clock rate and faster internal instruction-execution capabilities you gain from the Pentium CPU, you also get faster data movement: The 486 machine has a 32-bit system bus, while Pentium and Pentium Pro machines have twice that, a 64-bit system bus. You can learn more about the system bus and how it affects performance in Chapter 8, in which we cover your PC's processor subsystem.

Figure 9.16.

Business Winstone 97 performance versus RAM size for a Pentium 75 PC running Windows 95.

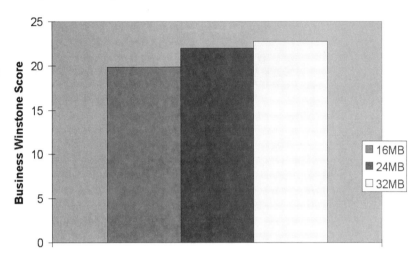

To get to specifics, check out Figure 9.17. When we upgraded this Pentium 75-based PC from 16MB to 24MB of RAM, we achieved an overall increase in the Business Winstone 97 score of about 11%. Taking the machine to 32MB of RAM, however, gave us only a boost of 3.6% beyond the 24MB score. Because this improvement is barely above the margin of variability of Winstone scores, we consider this increase negligible.

Figure 9.17 shows that the application category scores vary depending on the application type. Once again, the types of application that benefit most from increased RAM are word-processing and spreadsheet programs, and for them the boost is considerable: Going from 16MB to 24MB of RAM produces over a 20% jump in performance!

Database applications also show a significant increase of about 13% from the same RAM addition. The publishing scores do not increase at anywhere near the same rate, however, which means that for such applications the performance bottleneck is not this RAM amount. Some other factor in the system is limiting their performance.

The story is much more consistent when you take the system from 24MB to 32MB of RAM: None of the application types gain a significant performance boost. Performance does goes up, but not enough to matter much.

Figure 9.17.

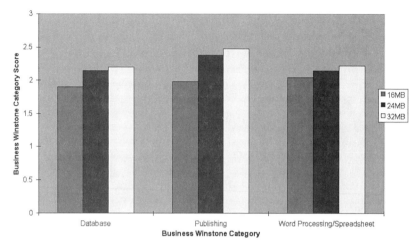

Figure 9.17.

Category scores from Business Winstone 97 tests versus RAM size for a Pentium 75 PC running Windows 95.

For a Pentium 75-based PC, or for such similar systems as the earlier Pentium 60 and Pentium 66 PCs, we recommend getting 24MB of RAM for normal Business applications. Just about any Business application that you run will be able to take advantage of this additional RAM and run significantly better with the extra memory. If you only run desktop publishing or business graphics applications, however, you should first consider getting a faster processor rather than more RAM.

9.7.5. Pentium 100

The Pentium 100-based PC is the first system on which we ran the High-End Winstone 97 tests while varying the RAM amounts. While you might try to run Photoshop or over high-end applications on a less capable PC, we don't recommend it. Starting with this processor, we also ran tests at a wider variety of RAM amounts.

As Figure 9.18 shows, this system has the same Business application sweet spot as its Pentium 75-based cousin: 24MB of RAM. We achieved a significant overall Business Winstone score increase of more than 11% by going from 16MB to 24MB of RAM. When we tried additional amounts all the way up to 64MB, the performance increases were pretty insignificant, in all cases being below the margin of variability for Winstone 97. These results show that the typical operations a business user is performing on such a system won't take advantage of RAM beyond 24MB. The operating system (including the RAM cache for the hard disk), the application in use, and the data the application is manipulating all fit neatly into a 24MB memory space.

Once again, when we inspect the category scores for Business Winstone 97, we conclude that 24MB of RAM is the sweet spot. The results for the Pentium 100 PC, however, are different from the ones we saw with the Pentium 75. On this system, the application type that benefits most from the jump from 16MB to 24MB is the publishing category. The most likely source of this difference is the increased processor power of the Pentium 100 chip, a factor that can help the sometimes demanding DTP and graphics apps. Moving RAM beyond the 24MB amount did not yield a significant increase in performance in any of the application categories (see Figure 9.19).

Figure 9.18.

Business Winstone 97 performance versus RAM size for a Pentium 100 PC running Windows 95.

Figure 9.19.

Category scores from Business Winstone 97 tests versus RAM size for a Pentium 100 PC running Windows 95.

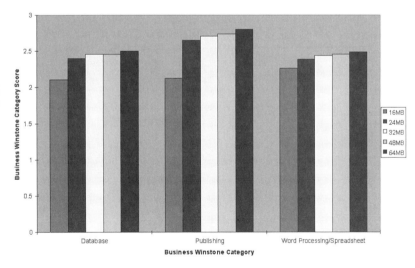

High-End Winstone 97 requires at least 32MB of RAM to run, so we ran tests using it with three RAM amounts: 32MB, 48MB, and 64MB of RAM. Once you've shelled out the cash for a machine on which you plan to run such applications as Photoshop, you'll also probably be buying RAM in larger amounts. While High-End Winstone 97, and therefore the applications it comprises, requires more RAM, a sweet spot similar to the one with Business Winstone shows up in Figure 9.20 when you plot performance versus RAM amount. In the case of this Pentium 100-based PC, you can gain a significant jump in performance by going from 32MB to 48MB of RAM. When you move from 48MB to 64MB of RAM, however, the performance improvement is negligible.

Figure 9.20.

Overall High-End Winstone 97 performance versus RAM size for a Pentium 100 PC running Windows 95.

Business Winstone 97 reports only an overall score and application category scores, so those are the results we've analyzed so far. High-End Winstone 97, however, gives you an overall result, category scores, and individual application scores. With all these results, you can dig deeper into this data if you're really interested in running a particular high-end application.

Let's look first at the High-End category scores in Figure 9.21. The main conclusion we can draw from this study is the category for which you *don't* need to add RAM: 3D/CAD applications. These products showed no significant performance increase with RAM amounts higher than 32MB.

The application-development and image-editing categories, by contrast, showed very large jumps in performance when we took the system from 32MB to 48MB of RAM. You can even see modest increases moving from 48MB to 64MB of RAM.

Looking at the individual application scores for High-End Winstone 97 shown in Figure 9.22, we see that the most dramatic increases occur with Adobe Photoshop. Photoshop shows a greater percentage increase in performance than any other high-end application when you take this Pentium 100-based PC from 48MB to 64MB of RAM. The other applications vary in their ability to take advantage of this extra RAM, so the sweet spot for all those apps is still 48MB.

To find the optimal amount of RAM for your Pentium 100-based PC, determine the most RAM-hungry application you'll be running. If you're a Photoshop user, go directly to 64MB of RAM, as you will see real benefits from having that much RAM. If you use high-end graphics applications that aren't intensive image-editing programs, you can probably get away with 48MB of RAM. If you run only Business applications, 24MB of RAM should be your choice. Stay away from the 16MB configuration for Business applications and from the 32MB configuration for high-end applications.

Figure 9.21.

Category scores from High-End Winstone 97 tests versus RAM size for a Pentium 100 PC running Windows 95.

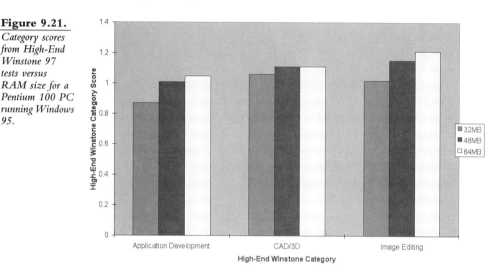

Figure 9.22.

Individual application scores from High-End Winstone 97 tests versus RAM size for a Pentium 100 PC running Windows 95.

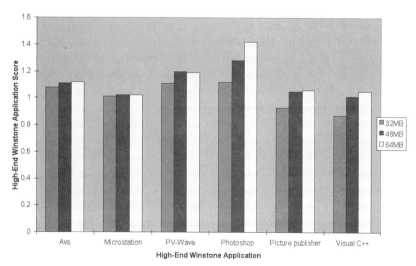

9.7.6. Pentium 133

The Pentium 133 configurations we've tested are near and dear to our hearts, because one of the PCs on which we composed this book is a Pentium 133-based machine.

The graph of Business application performance versus RAM amount shown in Figure 9.23 shows that once again, 24MB of RAM is the sweet spot; adding more RAM gains you very little performance boost.

Figure 9.23.

Business Winstone 97 performance versus RAM size for a Pentium 133 PC running Windows 95.

Finding these sweet spots at less common RAM amounts, by the way, might seem odd, but it can save you money, especially if you're specifying RAM upgrades not for one machine but for tens or hundreds of machines. At the time of this writing, the price of RAM SIMMs increases a little worse than linearly with the capacity of the SIMMs. Thus, a 16MB SIMM costs a bit more than twice what an 8MB SIMM will run you. This price difference means you can save a meaningful amount of money on your 16MB machines, for example, by upgrading with two 4MB SIMMs to 24MB total instead of using two 8MB SIMMs to go to 32MB of RAM.

The category scores for Business Winstone 97 basically mirror the overall Winstone curve for this machine. The significant feature these scores show in Figure 9.24 is that the category that exhibits the greatest performance increase is the publishing one, which improves quite a bit when the PC moves from 16MB to 24MB of RAM. So, if you're running PageMaker or a similar application, you're hog-tying your PC unless it has at least 24MB of RAM.

Once again, the Pentium 133 PC we tested shows the same basic performance characteristics as the Pentium 100 PC. For overall high-end application usage, the sweet spot remains at 48MB of RAM. Because this overall graph combines the results of all the individual application scores, we can often gain information by digging into category and individual application scores (see Figure 9.25).

As Figure 9.26 shows, the 3D/CAD category remains impervious to additional RAM, while the image editing category benefits a fair amount from additional RAM. The application development category is somewhere in the middle, because it shows a big boost when we moved the PC to 48MB of RAM but a much smaller one when we went from 48MB to 64MB.

Figure 9.24.

Category scores from Business Winstone 97 tests versus RAM size for a Pentium 133 PC running Windows 95.

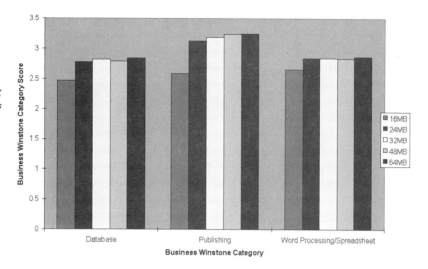

Figure 9.25.

High-End Winstone 97 performance versus RAM size for a Pentium 133 PC running Windows 95.

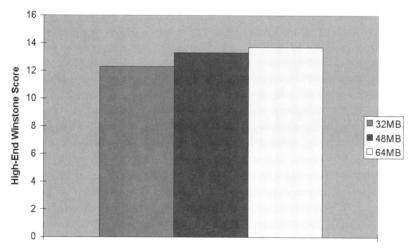

Diving into the individual High-End application results in Figure 9.27 shows that the real sources of these category performance gains are Photoshop and Visual C++, both of which show big boosts when we took the PC from 32MB to 48MB. Photoshop performance continued to improve greatly when we took the PC to 64MB, but the Visual C++ speed increase was much smaller.

For this Pentium 133 PC we can draw the same conclusions as we did with the Pentium 100 PC: If you're going to run only high-end applications similar to the ones in the 3D/CAD portion of Winstone 97, buying more than 32MB of RAM is a waste. If you're a Photoshop user, go directly to 64MB of RAM. For other high-end applications, get at least 48MB of RAM. For Business applications, the sweet spot is 24MB.

Figure 9.26.

Category scores from High-End Winstone 97 versus RAM size for a Pentium 133 running Windows 95.

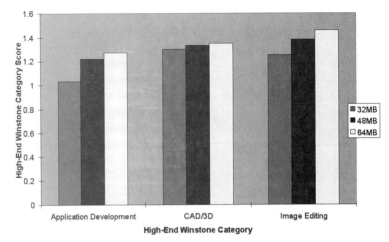

Figure 9.27.

Individual scores from High-End Winstone 97 versus RAM size for a Pentium 133 running Windows 95.

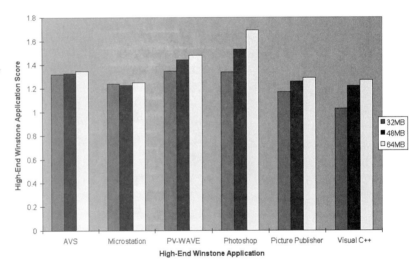

By the way, when you're looking at these graphs, you may notice that occasionally a score drops by 0.1 or 0.2 when we increase the amount of RAM in the PC. While the earlier section, When more RAM is bad, explained how increasing RAM can indeed hurt performance in certain cases, these scores are not examples of such behavior. Instead, these minor drops are normal variances in results that are well below the margin of variability for Winstone 97. While we follow proper testing procedure to obtain our Winstone results (including defragmenting the disk and restarting the machine before each test run) sometimes scores will still vary slightly. Unless these variances are more than a few percent, they are insignificant and mean only that, thanks to the intricacies of modern operating systems, no PC can be in exactly the same state twice.

9.7.7. Pentium 166

One of the more popular recent Business PC configurations was a Pentium 166 PC with 32MB of RAM. Let's find out if this RAM amount is the optimal one. (If you've been reading along from the beginning of the chapter, you might be able to guess what our answer will be.) Let's start with the overall Business Winstone 97 results in Figure 9.28.

Figure 9.28.

Business Winstone 97 performance versus RAM size for a Pentium 166 PC running Windows 95.

If you're running a PC with a Pentium 166 processor, the performance increase you can achieve by going to 32MB of RAM for Business applications may be attractive. Still, the greatest increase is the 16% jump in performance you get when you increase from 16MB to 24MB of RAM. Taking the RAM up to 32MB from 24MB buys you only an additional 4%, and going from 32MB to 48MB delivers only an extra 2% boost, an amount within the margin of variability of Winstone. So, while you could look at the graph and see that the increase in performance from 16MB to 48MB of RAM is 22%, that isn't as attractive as choosing the 24MB point, which delivers the most increase for the least investment.

Perhaps the most striking fact you can glean from the Business category scores in Figure 9.29 is that there's no point, from a performance perspective, in moving from 48MB to 64MB of RAM; the two RAM amounts yield virtually the same performance for business applications. If you need to wring the last drops of performance out of your machine, though, you might want to consider the 48MB configuration for desktop-publishing or word-processing applications. Going beyond 32MB won't do anything for the basic business database applications.

Figure 9.29.

Category scores from Business Winstone 97 tests versus RAM size for a Pentium 166 PC running Windows 95.

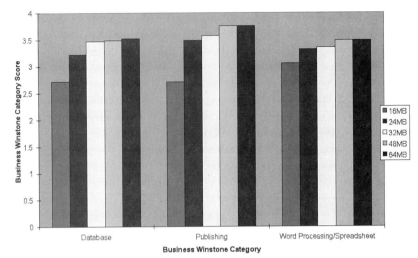

If you've been reading straight through this chapter, the shape of the graph of overall High-End Winstone 97 scores shown in Figure 9.30 should be very familiar. The 12% performance jump from 32MB to 48MB of RAM is hard to ignore, but going from 48MB to 64MB of RAM will deliver almost no overall high-end performance gain.

Figure 9.30.

High-End Winstone 97 performance versus RAM size for a Pentium 166 PC running Windows 95.

If you check out the high-end category test results (see Figure 9.31) and the individual application scores (see Figure 9.32), you might notice what appears to be another anomaly: The score for Visual C++ is lower at 64MB than at 48MB. This difference, though, is not really an anomaly, because it's still within the normal margin of variability for Winstone 97. Once again, with the exception of

Photoshop, performance maxes out at 48MB. Photoshop still does best with 64MB.

Figure 9.31.
Category scores from High-End Winstone 97 tests versus RAM size for a Pentium 166 PC running Windows 95.

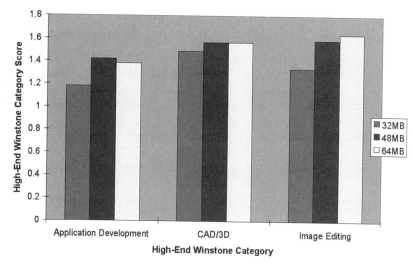

Figure 9.32.
Individual scores from High-End Winstone 97 tests versus RAM size for a Pentium 166 PC running Windows 95.

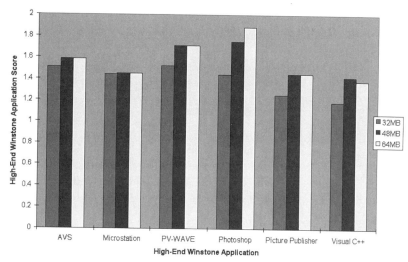

For PCs with the Pentium 166 processor, the RAM sweet spot for Business applications moves up to 32MB. If you're running high-end applications, you should get at least 48MB, and go all the way to 64MB if Photoshop is the app you use the most.

9.7.8. Pentium 200 MMX

The latest and most widely promoted change Intel has made to the x86 processor architecture is the addition of MMX instructions (see the earlier sidebar on

MMX technology). One of the first chips to incorporate MMX was the Pentium 200 with MMX CPU. We tested a Pentium 200 MMX system with our standard RAM sizes, even though you'd be hard pressed to buy a system that pairs one with less than 32MB of RAM, so we could see if the presence of MMX technology would change the performance curves we've seen so far.

Our test PC with the Pentium 200 with MMX CPU, unlike the systems with the other high-end processors (the Pentium 166 and the Pentium Pro 200), had significant performance gains on the overall Business Winstone 97 score all the way up to 48MB of RAM. As Figure 9.33 shows, the greatest jump still came from going from 16MB to 24MB of RAM.

Figure 9.33.

Business Winstone 97 performance versus RAM size for a Pentium 200 MMX PC running Windows 95.

Looking at the Business Winstone category scores in Figure 9.34, we also see less of a tendency for this system to flatten out as we add more RAM. Every category had a gain from each RAM increase up to 48MB, though the biggest winner from the 32MB to 48MB increase was the Publishing category.

The High-End Winstone 97 scores in Figure 9.35 also show the Pentium 200 MMX processor to have a greater ability than the others we tested to take advantage of higher RAM amounts. Even the performance increase from moving from 48MB to 64MB, a change that with other processors has produced little to no overall High-End Winstone score increase, here boosted that score by more than 7%.

Digging a little deeper into the High-End Winstone results with the category scores in Figure 9.36, we can see that the Image Editing applications were the biggest winners from the increase from 48MB to 64MB of RAM. The application development category showed the least increase in moving from 32MB to 48MB to 64MB.

Figure 9.34.

Category scores from Business 97 tests versus RAM size for a Pentium 200 MMX PC running Windows 95.

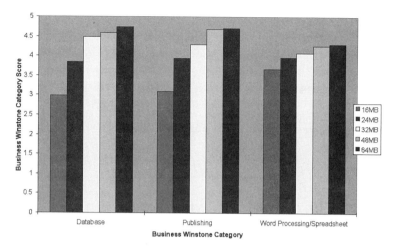

Figure 9.35.

High-End Winstone 97 performance versus RAM size for a Pentium 200 MMX PC running Windows 95.

Optimizing Your System's RAM

Photoshop, as Figure 9.37 shows, once again benefits the most from going all the way to 64MB of RAM.

The results for this system show that for PCs with a 200MHz (or faster) processor, RAM is a particularly good investment. You certainly should not even consider less than 32MB of RAM for such a system, and we recommend at least 48MB for just about any application you want to run. If high-end image-processing applications are important to you, step up to 64MB. The combination of MMX technology and this much RAM will yield a noticeable performance boost.

9.7.9. Pentium Pro 200

Until the Pentium 200 with MMX and the subsequent faster Pentium II family chips, the Pentium Pro 200 was Intel's powerhouse. Systems that used this processor consequently often had 32MB or more of RAM, and if you could still find any for sale today (an unlikely event as most vendors have moved exclusively to the Pentium II), they would almost certainly have at least 32MB of RAM. Even so, some earlier systems paired this processor with only 16MB of RAM, so we ran a full set of Business Winstone 97 tests at that amount to see if the performance curves for this machine matched up with the earlier generation of Pentium processors.

Figure 9.36.

Category scores from High-End Winstone 97 tests versus RAM size for a Pentium 200 MMX PC running Windows 95.

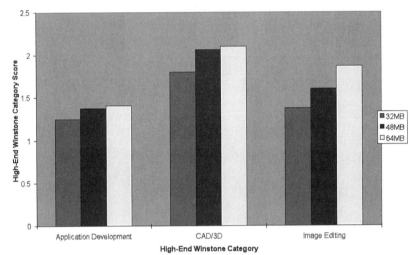

Figure 9.37.

Individual scores from High-End Winstone 97 tests versus RAM size for a Pentium 200 MMX PC running Windows 95.

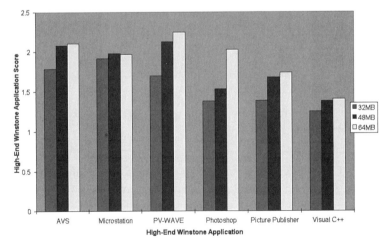

As we expected and as Figure 9.38 shows, the speed gain in overall Business Winstone performance from going from 16MB to 32MB of RAM is significant, about 15% Beyond that, however, business Winstone performance doesn't increase significantly as you add more RAM.

Figure 9.38.
Business 97 performance versus RAM size for a Pentium Pro 200 PC running Windows 95.

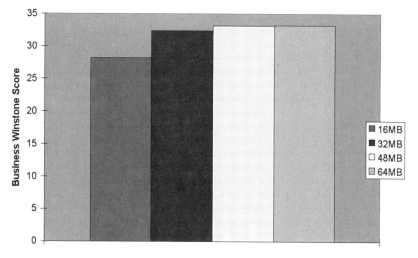

Digging deeper with the business category scores in Figure 9.39, we see that 32MB is indeed the sweet spot for all application categories, with the possible exception of the publishing category. If your PC is similar to the Compaq DeskPro in our testbed, for the apps in that category you'll still get over a 5% performance gain if you increase RAM to 48MB. For typical business applications, stick with 32MB.

Figure 9.39.
Category scores from Business 97 tests versus RAM size for a Pentium Pro 200 PC running Windows 95.

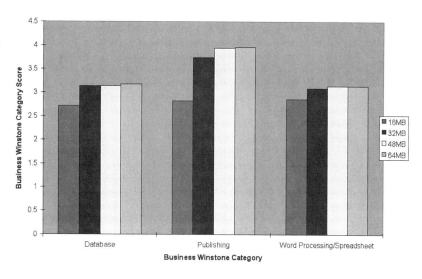

The graph of the overall High-End Winstone 97 results shown in Figure 9.40 should also look familiar. The sweet spot moves up to 48MB of RAM, but adding RAM beyond that amount yields no significant performance boost.

Figure 9.40.

High-End Winstone 97 performance versus RAM size for a Pentium Pro 200 PC running Windows 95.

The high-end category score results (see Figure 9.41) and individual high-end application results (see Figure 9.42) for the Pentium Pro 200 PC look very similar to those for the Pentium 200 MMX system. Image-editing applications are the only ones to show an increase from going to 64MB of RAM, with Photoshop in particular gaining quite a bit from this change. For all the other apps in High-End Winstone, the RAM sweet spot remains at 48MB.

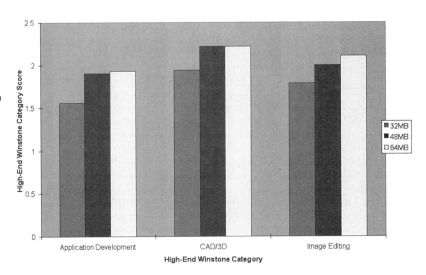

Figure 9.41.

Category scores from High-End Winstone 97 tests versus RAM size for a Pentium Pro 200 PC running Windows 95.

Our recommendations if you have a Pentium Pro 200-based machine are basically the same as our recommendations for folks with Pentium 166 PCs: Get a minimum of 32MB of RAM even if you're running only business applications. Move to 48MB of RAM for high-end applications, and pay the tab for 64MB if you use image-editing applications such as Photoshop.

Figure 9.42.

Individual scores from High-End Winstone 97 tests versus RAM size for a Pentium Pro 200 PC running Windows 95.

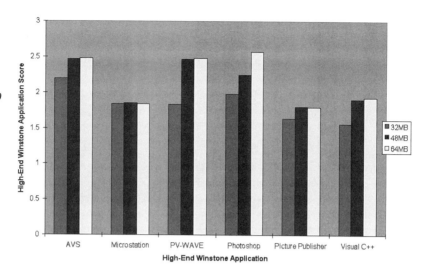

9.7.10. RAM Summary: Windows 95

Figure 9.43 brings together all the overall Business Winstone results for the different processors and RAM amounts we tested.

Figure 9.43

Summary of overall Business Winstone 97 performance versus RAM size for Windows 95.

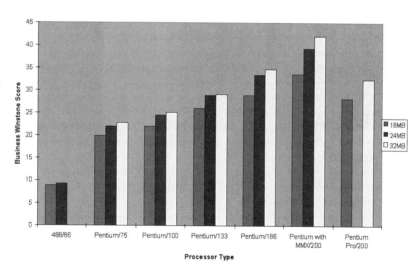

With the exception of the 486/66-based PC, we find the sweet spot for business applications is a minimum of 24MB of RAM. For machines with faster processors (those with a Pentium 166 or better), you should probably go to 32MB of RAM because you are likely to gain noticeable performance increases from this change.

If you'll be using your PC to run high-end applications like those in High-End Winstone 97, Figure 9.44 shows that the overall sweet spot is 48MB of RAM. Exceptions abound, however. For example, you might want to stick with just

32MB of RAM for processors less powerful than the Pentium 166, and as the previous individual application result charts have shown, 64MB remains your minimum ideal if Photoshop performance is important to you.

Figure 9.44.

Summary of overall High-End Winstone 97 performance versus RAM size for Windows 95.

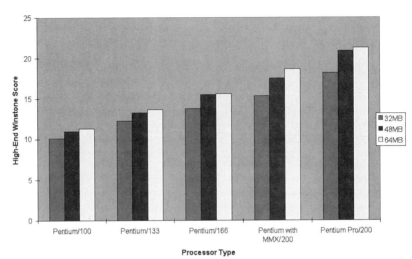

You may also have noticed that the ideal amount of RAM for most PCs often isn't the amount with which they came from the vendor. Those to whom cost is no object might want to say the heck with our studies and just load up their RAM slots as an easy path to maximum performance, but they'd be wrong; check out the earlier section, "When More RAM is Bad," for the reason why.

9.8. Windows NT and RAM

As we did with Windows 98 and Windows 95, we experimented with a variety of Windows NT systems and applications to help you easily locate the sweet spot for your Windows NT PC.

Windows NT 4.0 is a very different beast from Windows 95. When it comes to RAM, the simplest way to view this difference is that NT requires more RAM. The absolute minimum for NT 4.0 is 12MB of RAM—an amount we do not recommend you try. But, there's more to NT than an increased RAM footprint. The NT kernel, the central code that makes up the operating system, is very different from the Windows 98 and Windows 95 kernels, because it must support the enhanced security and crash protection features that are part of Windows NT. While Microsoft made Windows NT 4.0 *look* like Windows 95, and while Windows 98 and Windows 95 appear largely similar (particularly if you install Microsoft's Internet Explorer on Windows 95), NT's inner workings are still much more complicated than Windows 98's or Windows 95's. In the following studies we'll show you how the amount of RAM in your NT system affects its application performance and thus how you can find the sweet spot for your particular processor and application combination.

9.8.1. How We Tested

Because the absolutely lowest amount of RAM anyone should even consider for a Windows NT system is 16MB, we skipped the 8MB Winstone 96 testing that we did on Windows 95. (If you also read the Windows 98 section, you'll recall we skipped that low-end amount in our Windows 98 tests as well.) The minimum RAM amount we used in our Business Winstone 97 tests was 16MB, and then we increased the amounts to 64MB, although as you'll see the amounts we picked for each machine vary. For our High-End Winstone 97 experiments, we tested at 32MB, 48MB, and 64MB of RAM.

We kept the same graphics resolution and color depth setups with these Windows NT tests as we used with our Windows 98 and Windows 95 tests: A resolution of 1024×768 with 256 colors.

9.8.2. Pentium 133

Let's start with the Pentium 133-based PC. Though you certainly could run Windows NT 4.0 on a machine with a slower processor, we don't recommend it and consequently did not test NT performance on any slower machines.

If you followed our Windows 98 and Windows 95 RAM studies earlier in this chapter, you'll immediately see in Figure 9.45 a big difference between the way Windows NT 4.0 and Windows 98 or Windows 95 use RAM. Because NT has a larger memory footprint, the minimum RAM it needs to really cook is much higher. Check out the almost 50% increase in speed when we took this system from 16MB to 32MB; clearly, you wouldn't want to skimp on that second 16MB. This level of performance improvement is very much like the one we saw when we went from 8MB to 16MB of RAM on our low-end Windows 95 systems. For this reason, we recommend 32MB of RAM as the minimum for any Windows NT 4.0 PC on which you're going to run anything more complicated than Solitaire.

When we took the system's RAM beyond 32MB, however, the overall Business Winstone performance increase was insignificant.

The business category scores in Figure 9.46 further support our 32MB minimum recommendation for Windows NT PCs: Every Business Winstone category shows a great leap in performance when we move from 16MB to 32MB.

The overall High-End Winstone results in Figure 9.47 somewhat surprised us by looking remarkably like those for the same tests under Windows 98 or Windows 95. In particular, we had expected that moving to 64MB of RAM would yield a boost over 48MB. We were wrong. Boosting 48MB of RAM to 64MB yielded no noticeable improvement in the overall High-End Winstone score. Whatever the added footprint of the Windows NT operating system, 48MB of RAM is enough to handle both it and the application workspace on systems with this class of processor.

Figure 9.45.

Business 97 performance versus RAM size for a Pentium 133 PC running Windows NT.

Figure 9.46.

Category scores from Business 97 tests versus RAM size for a Pentium 133 PC running Windows NT.

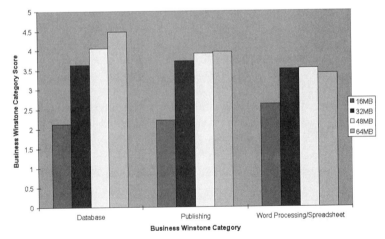

Having seen those results, though, the High-End Winstone category scores in Figure 9.48 came as no surprise. As with the overall score, the High-End category scores are very similar to the Windows 98 and Windows 95 cases here. If you're running 3D/CAD applications, you might be able to get away with 32MB of RAM. Otherwise, get at least 48MB of RAM. Figure 9.49 clearly shows that you should also strongly consider getting 64MB of RAM if you use Photoshop or another RAM-intensive image-processing application.

Figure 9.47.

High-End Winstone 97 performance versus RAM size for a Pentium 133 PC running Windows NT.

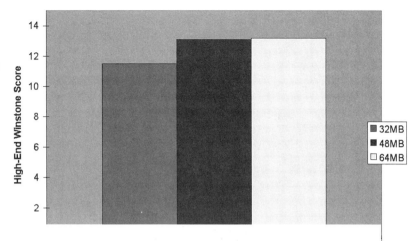

Figure 9.48.

Category scores from High-End Winstone 97 tests versus RAM size for a Pentium 133 PC running Windows NT.

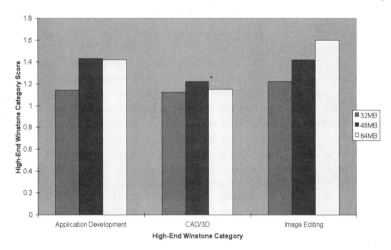

By the way, remember not to get bogged down in the numerical results when you're studying the performance results in the graphs in this book. Having the actual results is important, of course, and that's why we provide both them and the benchmarks you can use to get your own results. More important, however, are the trends and similarities among different charts and experiments, so look for those trends in the system(s) most like yours. With this Pentium 133-based PC running Windows NT, for example, though the exact result numbers are different from those of the Pentium 166-based PC running Windows 98 or Windows 95, the overall curve shape is similar to the results of that system under those other Windows versions.

Figure 9.49.

Individual scores from High-End Winstone 97 tests versus RAM size for a Pentium 133 PC running Windows NT.

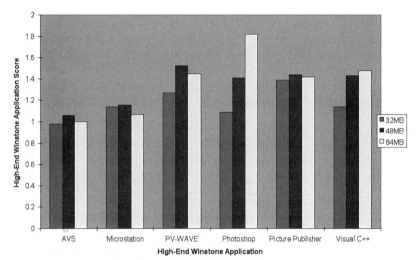

What all the charts for this system make clear is that no matter what, it should have a minimum of 32MB of RAM. For high-end applications, take it to 48MB, and get 64MB for applications such as Photoshop.

9.8.3. Pentium 166

In our Windows 98 and Windows 95 RAM studies, the PC with the Pentium 166 CPU was the first one that we might reasonably call high-powered. It, the PC with the Pentium 200 MMX processor, and the machine with the Pentium Pro 200 CPU all behaved similarly in their RAM usage in most of those tests with the other versions of Windows. Let's see if this trend holds true for those same systems when they're running Windows NT 4.0.

As Figure 9.50 shows, the result is another turn of our broken record: You're cheating yourself unless you run Windows NT 4.0 in at least 32MB of RAM. Though the overall Business Winstone results for this Pentium 166 system are like those for the Pentium 133 PC in this regard, the two diverge in their behavior when you take them to 48MB of RAM: The Pentium 166 PC's overall business performance increases about 10% from this move. Let's take a look at the Business Winstone category scores in Figure 9.51 to see why that's happening with this system when it did not occur with the Pentium 133-based PC.

As this chart shows, though the Word Processing/Spreadsheet scores stay basically flat above 32MB, both the publishing and database scores continued to increase when we took the PC's RAM beyond 32MB. So our sweet spot for lots of folks who run only Word and Excel on Windows NT remains at the familiar 32MB. For those who run database or publishing business apps, however, the boost you can get by going to 48MB of RAM is worth the cost.

Figure 9.50.

Business 97 performance versus RAM size for a Pentium 166 PC running Windows NT.

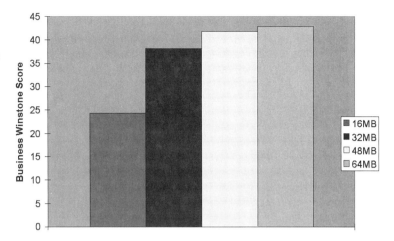

Figure 9.51.

Category scores from Business 97 tests versus RAM size for a Pentium 166 PC running Windows NT.

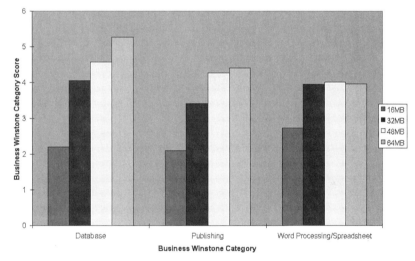

Figure 9.52 shows that for this system, as for the Pentium 133 machine, the sweet spot for high-end applications appears to be at the 48MB mark. With this system, however, the overall high-end app performance boost you can get by moving from 48MB to 64MB of RAM is seven percent. That number is big enough to be interesting but not large enough to be compelling.

The High-End Winstone category scores in Figure 9.53 provide more data. They show that the image-editing and application-development apps definitely benefit from having 64MB in the system, while the CAD/3D apps improved very little above 48MB.

So the big decision you have to make with this system is whether moving to 64MB of RAM is worth the cost. The most reasonable answer is that this move is probably worth making, particularly if you're at all looking to keep this system for a while. First, because the RAM requirements of operating systems and applications constantly increase, if you expect to upgrade either or both of those during the life of this PC, taking the system to 64MB is reasonable. In addition, if you want to move your PC to a 48MB configuration, you're going to have to use 8MB SIMMs. These SIMMs are still available, of course, but if you're working in an environment in which you might later upgrade your motherboard and scavenge parts from your current PC, you'll probably be better off buying RAM that will have a longer useful life.

Figure 9.52.

High-End Winstone 97 performance versus RAM size for a Pentium 166 PC running Windows NT.

Figure 9.53.

Category scores from High-End Winstone 97 tests versus RAM size for a Pentium 166 PC running Windows NT.

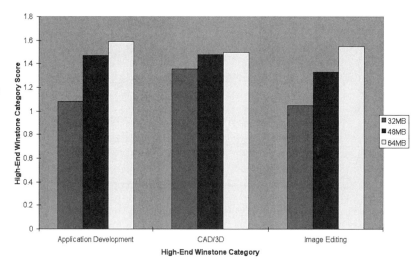

We can also learn more by digging into results for the individual high-end applications on our Pentium 166 running Windows NT (see Figure 9.54).

48MB of RAM still emerges as the overall sweet spot, and it remains the minimum we'd recommend for these applications. As you can see, however, Photoshop and, to a lesser degree, Visual C++ can realize useful performance gains when you take the system up to the 64MB mark.

Figure 9.54.
Individual scores from High-End Winstone 97 tests versus RAM size for a Pentium 166 PC running Windows NT.

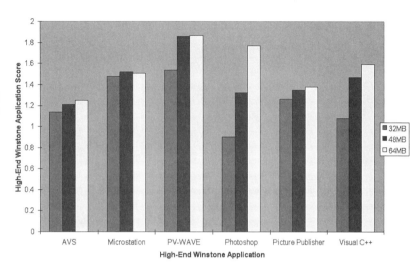

For this Pentium 166-based PC, if you run only word-processing and spreadsheet applications, once you have the minimum 32MB of RAM we recommend for NT 4.0, you might be set. If you run more than just these apps, however, the 48MB configuration can deliver a noticeable speed improvement. This configuration will also work well for many high-end applications, but if you're running sophisticated Photoshop or other image-editing programs, or if you're an application developer who wants the very best performance, 64MB would be a better choice.

9.8.4. Pentium 200 MMX

In our RAM tests with the other versions of Windows, the Pentium 200 MMX-based PC won the prize for being best able to take advantage of additional RAM. Let's see if it can also claim that crown when running Windows NT.

As with all our NT tests, the overall Business Winstone results (see Figure 9.55) clearly demonstrate the importance of having a minimum of 32MB of RAM on your NT PC. Anything less than this amount is almost certain to act as a serious bottleneck on the horsepower of the Pentium 200 MMX chip. Beyond that amount, however, the performance gains quickly trail off. The overall Business Winstone score increases about 6% when the system goes from 32MB to 48MB, and you gain almost no improvement by moving from 48MB to 64MB of RAM.

Figure 9.55.

*Business 97
performance
versus RAM size
for a Pentium
200 MMX PC
running Windows
NT.*

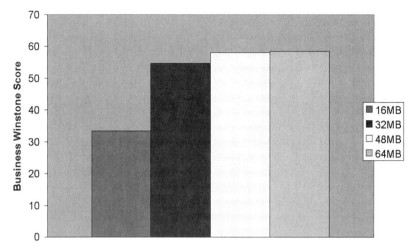

The Business Winstone category scores in Figure 9.56 show that this Pentium 200 MMX system is much like the Pentium 166 PC. If you take the system's RAM to 48MB, database users and desktop publishers will see some performance advantages, but folks who run only word-processing and spreadsheet programs will not. None of the business apps show any benefit from moving the system to 64MB.

Figure 9.56.

*Category scores
from Business 97
tests versus
RAM size for a
Pentium 200
MMX PC
running Windows
NT.*

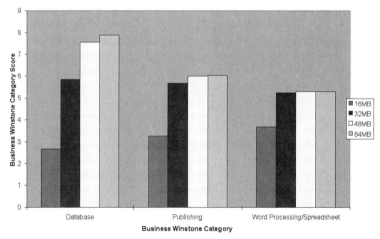

When you examine the overall High-End Winstone results in Figure 9.57, the performance increase when you take the system from 32MB of RAM to 48MB of RAM is a very hard-to-ignore 20%. This improvement is the NT cousin of a phenomenon we also saw with Windows 98 and Windows 95: When you add RAM, the performance curves of the higher-powered processors don't flatten out as quickly as those of the slower processors. This observation is clearly true in the case of high-end applications on this system, where there's still a 6% performance gain when you go from 48MB to 64MB.

Figure 9.57.

High-End Winstone 97 performance versus RAM size for a Pentium 200 MMX PC running Windows NT.

When you drill down into the High-End Winstone category (see Figure 9.58) and individual (see Figure 9.59) scores for this system, perhaps the most interesting feature to note is that the curve for 3D/CAD applications is no longer flat. In fact, those applications realize a 10% increase in speed moving from the 32MB to the 48MB configuration. The curves otherwise appear similar to those of our NT tests on the Pentium 166 PC, with Photoshop, as always, taking the title of the most RAM-hungry program in the group.

Figure 9.58.

Category scores from High-End Winstone 97 tests versus RAM size for a Pentium 200 MMX PC running Windows NT.

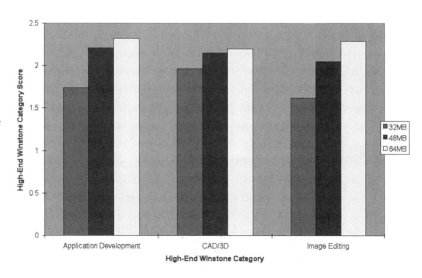

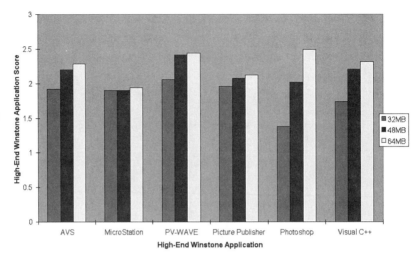

Figure 9.59.
Individual scores from High-End Winstone 97 tests versus RAM size for a Pentium 200 MMX PC running Windows NT.

Our test results for this Pentium 200 with MMX PC make a clear point: If you have a high-powered processor, do yourself a favor and feed it with plenty of RAM. You should, of course, not even consider going below 32MB of RAM on this system, and 48MB will be a more realistic minimum for many users. For high-end applications, go ahead and spring for 64MB; you'll be glad you did.

9.8.5. Pentium Pro 200

Our final NT test system is a configuration that has been very popular with software developers: The Pentium Pro 200 running Windows NT 4.0. In fact, the developers at ZDBOp built two iterations of Winstone and WinBench on this class of system.

On the overall Business Winstone tests (see Figure 9.60), this machine behaves much like the Pentium 200 MMX PC. The jump from 16MB to 32MB is huge, but you can also still get an appreciable performance gain of about 9% by going from the 32MB to the 48MB configuration. Adding RAM beyond 48MB is unnecessary for typical business application usage.

When you look at the individual Business Winstone category scores in Figure 9.61, you can easily spot some differences between this machine and the Pentium 200 MMX PC. In particular, though the results for the database category flatten out quickly after 32MB, the scores for the publishing category continue to increase significantly as you move to 48MB. The opposite is true of the Pentium 200 MMX results. So, if you're running applications such as PageMaker on a Pentium Pro PC, you should definitely consider taking your system up to 48MB of RAM. Database, word-processing, and spreadsheet users will probably be able to get away with just 32MB of RAM.

Figure 9.60.

Business 97 performance versus RAM size for a Pentium Pro 200 PC running Windows NT.

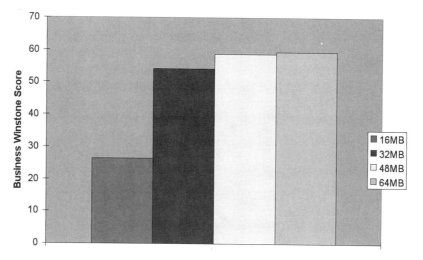

Figure 9.61.

Category scores from Business 97 tests versus RAM size for a Pentium Pro 200 PC running Windows NT.

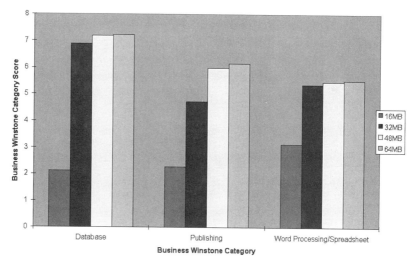

Looking at the overall high-end scores in Figure 9.62, we can see that the boost the Pentium Pro 200 PC gets from increased RAM is slightly higher when you move from 48MB to 64MB of RAM than the increase we observed when we made the same change on the Pentium 200 MMX system. Perhaps more importantly, with an 18% increase going from 32MB to 48MB of RAM, there's no reason you shouldn't pop for at least that added 16MB.

The high-end category (see Figure 9.63) and individual application (see Figure 9.64) performance curves should be very familiar to you if you've read this whole chapter. While most of the categories and applications level off at 48MB of RAM, Photoshop blasts into outer space with 64MB of RAM. If you're a software developer, you might want to note that you could also gain a significant performance increase (about 9%) by going from the 48MB to the 64MB configuration.

Figure 9.62.

High-End Winstone 97 performance versus RAM size for a Pentium Pro 200 PC running Windows NT.

Figure 9.63.

Category scores from High-End Winstone 97 tests versus RAM size for a Pentium Pro 200 PC running Windows NT.

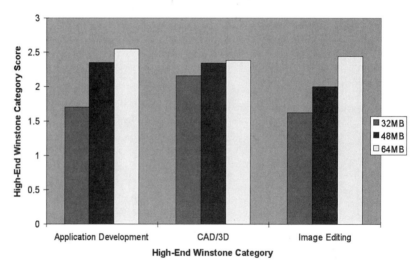

To sum up what we recommend for the Pentium Pro 200 PC running Windows NT, if all you're going to do is run normal business applications, you'll probably be fine sticking with 32MB of RAM. If you run high-end applications or desktop publishing programs, take your system to 48MB. Graphic designers and software developers should definitely spring for at least 64MB of RAM.

Figure 9.64.

Individual scores from High-End Winstone 97 tests versus RAM size for a Pentium Pro 200 PC running Windows NT.

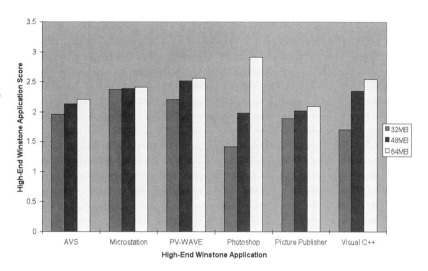

9.8.6. RAM Summary: Windows NT

Let's recap the results of our tests on the Windows NT machines. In general the sweet spots for NT PCs are about 16MB more than those for Windows 98 or Windows 95 systems, though some exceptions do, of course, exist.

As Figure 9.65 shows, our low-end NT machine, the Pentium 133, hits the sweet spot for business applications at 32MB of RAM. All the other systems really hit their business strides when you move all the way to 48MB of RAM.

Figure 9.65.

Summary of overall Business Winstone performance versus RAM size for Windows NT 4.0.

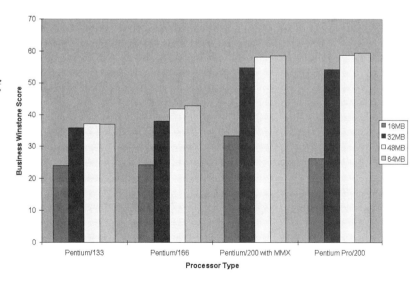

The story for high-end applications, as you can see in Figure 9.66, is similar. Here, our low-end machine maxes out at 48MB of RAM, while the other PCs can benefit from having additional RAM. As always, Photoshop users should get as much memory as they can, with 64MB a practical minimum on NT systems.

Figure 9.66.
Summary of overall High-End Winstone performance versus RAM size for Windows NT 4.0.

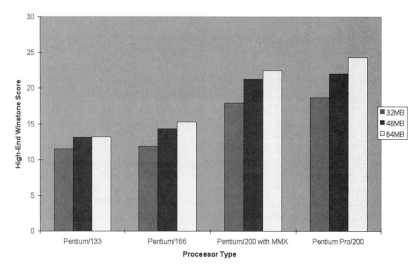

9.9. The Bottom Line

We've shown the results of many experiments in this chapter, and we've shown you the RAM sweet spots for a variety of processors and applications running under Windows 98, Windows 95, and Windows NT 4.0. If your system matches any of the configurations we tested, you should now have all the information you need to choose the most cost-effective RAM configuration.

But what if your PC doesn't directly match one of our test systems? Many PCs certainly won't. Then how do all of these conclusions apply to you?

The best way to determine this is by studying all of the graphs, to see the patterns that form because of certain basic principles. For example, Windows NT requires more RAM than Windows 98 or Windows 95, and more powerful processors can take better advantage of additional RAM than less powerful chips. You can also take advantage of the set of experiments for the PC we tested that most closely matches your system. Our 486DX-2/66 results, for example, should be similar (again, in shape, not in exact value) to those for any machine using a 486 or 486-compatible CPU. If you have a PC with a Pentium or Pentium II–class processor, look at the suggestions for the Pentium or Pentium with MMX chip in this chapter that has the closest clock frequency to the one in your PC.

When you're trying to determine the optimal RAM size for your PC, you should also consider a few other factors in addition to raw performance on individual applications. For example, though all of the testing we've done in this book involved running one application at a time, if you spend a lot of time multitasking (running more than one program at once), your RAM needs will be higher than what we've recommended here. Also, if you've already tweaked your system's RAM usage, for instance, to increase the size of its disk cache, you will need to adjust our RAM estimates accordingly.

That said, you're unlikely to go too far wrong if you use the studies in this chapter as a guide. To make that easy, Table 9.1 provides a simple chart that covers the most common situations we've discussed in this chapter:

Table 9.1. A quick guide to the RAM sizes we recommend for some common PC configurations.

If you have this kind of system	Get this much RAM
486-based PC, running Windows 95	16MB
Pentium class PC, running Windows 98 or 95 business applications	32MB
Pentium class PC, running Windows 98 or 95 high-end applications	48MB
Any PC running Photoshop	64MB
Pentium class PC, running Windows NT business applications	48MB
Pentium class PC, running Windows NT high-end applications	64MB

9.10. Testing You Can Do

Maybe your system doesn't contain one of the processors on which we conducted this chapter's tests. Maybe it does, but you're not satisfied by simply matching your PC with one from our testbed. Maybe you just want to do your own tests to be sure.

Whatever the reason, if you're interested in finding the optimal amount of RAM for your PC, you've come to the right place. The copy of Winstone 98 that comes with this book is one tool you need for such tests; the other is a set of SIMMs of varying sizes. (Hey, we didn't say these tests were cheap.) If you're testing for your company because you're going to purchase a large number of PCs, buying these SIMMs might be a good investment. If you're just testing your own PC, you'll either have to plunk down your own money or beg and borrow the SIMMs you need.

The setup of the memory banks in your PC will determine the set of SIMMs you should have on hand for a complete RAM study. Basically, you want enough SIMMs to try every RAM configuration you might reasonably choose. If, for example, you have a 16MB Pentium machine that uses 72-pin SIMMs, you'll need two 4MB SIMMs, two 8MB SIMMs, and two 16MB SIMMs just to test all the reasonable RAM configurations from 16MB to 48MB.

Once you have the SIMMs you need, the next step is to determine what applications you'll be running on the PC you want to test, and then run the closest corresponding Winstone tests. If you're only going to run Excel, for example, there's no point in worrying about your High-End Winstone score. On the other hand, if you, like us, are completeness freaks, you'll want to run all possible tests on all the RAM configurations you're considering. When you do, make sure you follow proper testing procedures each time you run any Winstone test. That procedure includes defragmenting the disk before each test run and restarting your computer before each run. If you're really persnickety about results, you'll run Winstone in automated batch mode from your Startup group so you can be absolutely sure the PC is in the same state at the start of each test. You'll also run each test several times in each configuration to make sure your results are repeatable. We did.

NOTE	You can find complete directions for running Winstone 98 in Appendix A, "Using Winstone 98."

When you have all the Winstone results you want, you can graph them in Winstone itself or examine them in Excel or any other spreadsheet program you choose. Be sure to take a look not only at the raw scores but also at the percentage increase that occurs in those results as you upgrade the PC from one RAM configuration to the next. Compare your results to the results in this chapter, but focus on the shapes of the performance-improvement curves, not on the scores themselves. Once you've done this, you should be able to find the sweet spot for your PC and applications, and then you'll know how much RAM is right for your PC.

9.11. From Here...

As we've said many times, all the elements of performance are interrelated. RAM affects other parts of the PC, such as its processor, disk, and graphics subsystems. If you want peak performance, you should not only consider upgrading your RAM, but also look into optimizing those subsystems.

The following chapters contain sections that provide more information
on other topics related to RAM.

- Chapter 5, "Windows 98 Software Tuning," shows you how to take
  advantage of the software optimization options built into Windows 98 to
  improve your PC's performance.

- Chapter 6, "Windows 95 Software Tuning," shows you how to optimize
  your PC's performance by, among other things, using RAM as a disk
  cache under Windows 95.

- Chapter 7, "Windows NT Software Tuning," shows you how to use
  Windows NT's performance-optimization features to improve your PC's
  performance.

- Chapter 8, "Optimizing Your System's Processor," examines every key
  aspect of processor performance, including how the L2 cache RAM
  affects your PC's overall performance.

- Chapter 10, "Optimizing Your Graphics Subsystem," explains how you can
  achieve the best possible graphics performance and discusses the right
  amount of RAM for your PC's graphics adapter.

- Chapter 11, "Optimizing Your Disk Subsystem," discusses how you can set
  up RAM as a disk cache and use other techniques to speed up your disk
  subsystem.

Chapter

10

Optimizing Your Graphics Subsystem

Windows is both an operating system and a Graphical User Interface (GUI). The key word here is *graphical*. When you think of the operating system, you don't think of the virtual memory manager, the disk access routines, or the thread scheduler, instead you think of the windows and icons on your desktop. And, when you think of your computer, you probably don't think of the circuit boards and wires inside the case, you think of the displayed user interface. The display, or monitor, is the final link in the chain of the graphics subsystem. The heart of the graphics subsystem is the graphics board, sometimes called a video board, but the graphics subsystem also includes the monitor, the system bus, and the device drivers and other software that allow applications to display information on that hardware.

Graphics boards are probably the most hyped piece of hardware in terms of how they're advertised. "Screaming," "Turbo," "Wicked," "Souped Up" and a host of other terms from the hot-rod world appear in ads for graphics boards, terms you'd rarely see in, say, an advertisement for RAM. Buying a new graphics board can pay off in performance as well as enhanced features and greater capabilities. Even if you don't want to buy a new graphics board, though, you can still optimize your current graphics subsystem by ensuring you're running at the optimum resolution and color depth with the proper graphics drivers. So even if you don't have the cash to buy the latest Ultra-Mega-Overkill graphics board, read on to find out how to wring every drop of performance from your current hardware.

In this chapter, you also will learn:

- What your graphics subsystem is

  The graphics subsystem includes more than just the graphics board; it includes other components like the monitor, system bus, and device drivers. In the following sections, you'll learn how these components interact to generate the graphical interface that is Windows.

- How your operating system affects graphics performance

  Windows 98, Windows 95, and Windows NT handle graphics differently. You'll learn how to determine your graphics subsystem needs based on which operating system you're running.

- How to determine whether you need a new graphics board

  There is a dazzling array of graphics boards available, with new ones released every month. You'll learn how to determine if you need a new graphics board, and how to quantify the benefits of a new board.

- How to optimize the performance of your existing graphics board

  If you can't afford a new graphics board, you can still improve the performance of your existing setup. You'll learn how screen resolution and color depth affect graphics and video performance. You'll also learn the importance of keeping the software drivers for your graphics board up-to-date.

10.1. Cocktail Party Tips

We've got a couple tips for you from this chapter for when your smarty party pal asks you about graphics performance. The two tips are "update, update, update" and "smaller is better." Your friend will scratch his head when you reel these tips off, giving you a chance to expound further.

When we say, "update, update, update" we are referring to your graphics device driver. Graphics device driver programmers are some of the busiest in the business. If you look at the version number of the graphics driver for your board, it's more likely to be something like 4.03.00.3110 than it is to be 1.0. Graphics board manufacturers are constantly fixing bugs, updating features, and supporting new enhancements in their driver software. Importantly for this book, they are constantly optimizing their graphics drivers for performance. You can often speed up your graphics subsystem simply by getting the latest driver available for your board straight from the manufacturer's Web or FTP site.

"Smaller is better" sounds counterintuitive. "Bigger is better" is what we've all been taught, whether the subject in question is bank accounts or sumo wrestlers. When we say "smaller is better," we're referring to the screen resolution and color depth of your graphics setup. Screen resolution is a measure of how much you can fit on your display: how many pixels wide and how many pixels high. A pixel is a picture element—one of the tiny dots that together create the picture on your monitor. Resolution is usually expressed as 640×480, 800×600, or 1024×768 where the first numbers refer to horizontal by vertical pixel counts. Those are three of the most popular screen resolutions for Windows PC's. The first resolution, 640×480, is VGA resolution, the lowest common denominator of PCs over the last few years.

Color depth is a way of quantifying the size of the palette of colors your graphics subsystem can display. Color depth is expressed in number of bits. For instance, a color depth of 8 bits indicates that the display can render 256 distinct colors, because 2 to the eighth power is 256. Common color depth settings for Windows PC's are 8 bit, 16 bit, 24 bit, and 32 bit. The old VGA standard of sixteen colors equates to a 4-bit color depth.

It's tempting to run at the highest possible resolution and color depth that your graphics board supports. You've paid for the board, why not run with over 16 million colors (24 bit color depth) at a resolution of 1280×1024 (over four times the screen real estate of the old VGA standard)? The answer is "smaller is better," or at least faster. To get the best performance out of your graphics subsystem, you

Optimizing Your Graphics Subsystem

should usually run at the lowest color depth and resolution that you and your applications can tolerate. With lower the resolution or color depth, there's less information for your graphics subsystem to deal with each time it updates the display. Less information means less processing time, and that means a faster display. There is, of course, a tradeoff of performance versus productivity and quality of your computing usage.

So, the longer versions of our tips are update your graphics drivers as often as you can, and when it comes to screen resolution and color depth, smaller is faster.

10.2. What's a Graphics Subsystem?

We use the phrase *graphics subsystem* instead of graphics board because it's the entire subsystem that affects performance, no matter what the graphics board vendors would like you to believe. If you install a brand-new Ultra-Mega-Overkill 9000 in your 386 based PC, you will not see the performance increase that someone installing that same graphics board in a Pentium II will see. You might not see any performance increase at all! That's due to our old friend the bottleneck. If there's a bottleneck in your graphics subsystem at some point other than the graphics board itself, that bottleneck will limit the optimum graphics performance of your machine.

So, what is the graphics subsystem? The graphics subsystem of a Windows PC includes the monitor, graphics adapter, graphics driver, and the bus used to carry information to and from the processor subsystem—thus, the CPU itself is in some sense a piece of the graphics subsystem. When you buy an entire PC, you'll pick the monitor and possibly the graphics board as the graphics options, but in reality the system bus (or local graphics bus), CPU chip, and related software will also affect graphics performance.

Many don't remember the pre-Windows days when PC's had text-only displays. Old-timers remember the days of the monochrome display adapter (MDA), the Hercules Graphics Adapter (HGA), the Color Graphics Adapter (CGA), the Enhanced Graphics Adapter (EGA). It's hard to find anything below the Video Graphics Adapter (VGA) specification now, and even basic VGA boards have been superseded by third party boards sporting 2 to 4MB of Video RAM in new PCs. If you have less than a VGA board, you won't be able to run Windows 98, Windows 95, or Windows NT 4.0.

Most of these boards are lumped under the term SVGA, for Super VGA, but this isn't a strict definition as the term VGA is. VGA was the high-end graphics adapter for IBM's PS/2 line of computers, available built-in to certain models or as an add-in graphics board. Third party manufacturers quickly built boards that conformed to the VGA specification, and thus VGA became the base-level adapter for Windows 3.1, Windows 95, Windows NT, and Windows 98. Microsoft included a graphics driver that supported the VGA display with all of these versions of Windows.

SVGA boards add more memory and different graphics accelerator chips to achieve greater color depth and resolution than is possible with a VGA board. Basically, any board that provides more capabilities than a VGA board can be considered an SVGA board. Thus the term is somewhat meaningless: one SVGA board might support resolutions up to 1024×768 pixels while another might support resolutions up to 1280×1024 pixels. Instead of the generic Microsoft VGA driver, SVGA boards require specific driver software from their manufacturers to take advantage of the higher modes of operation. Windows 98, Windows 95, and Windows NT 4.0 come with Microsoft-written graphics drivers that support a variety of graphics boards, but in general you're better off getting a driver from your board's manufacturer, as they've probably spent more time writing faster, bug-free driver software.

The more data that is displayed, the more has to get down the pipe from the application in question (or the OS) and through the graphics subsystem out to the monitor. This means that the higher resolution and higher color depth you choose, the more work the graphics subsystem has to do to refresh the screen. If you need to repaint a VGA screen (640×480 pixels at 258 colors) you need to transmit the color value for each pixel to the display. 640×480 gives you 307,200 pixels. Each pixel requires 8 bits of color information to determine which of 256 colors to display (one byte) so that's over 300,000 bytes of data moving to the screen. Compare this to the amount of data that someone running at a resolution of 1024×768 in TrueColor (24-bit) mode has to move: 1024×768 gives you 786,432 pixels. Multiply that by three to get the total number of bytes of data (24-bit color would mean three bytes of data for each pixel) and you get 2,359,296 bytes! That is almost eight times as much data.

Fortunately, these huge amounts of data aren't merely being copied from somewhere in system RAM to the display. If that were the case, you'd never get anything done. The graphics accelerator is what gets you around this potential bottleneck. Just about any graphics board you buy now is really a graphics accelerator: a board designed around a graphics chipset that accelerates common graphical operations in Windows. These boards are faster because the chipsets are designed to specifically accelerate Windows graphics calls, because they use special memory architectures that are faster than system RAM for displaying data on the screen and because they use wider data buses than the typical system bus.

The advent of graphics accelerators went hand in hand with the advent of local buses. Local buses are special system buses that are directly connected to the CPU. The first common one was the VL-bus, but in newer PC's the PCI bus is the current standard, and AGP is now very popular. The original SVGA adapters plugged straight into the older, slower, ISA bus slots.

Optimizing Your Graphics
Subsystem

There are several different kinds of specialized RAM that various graphics accelerators use, although they can commonly be referred to as VRAM (Video RAM). VRAM is different from system DRAM in that it is dual-ported: it can be read from and written to at the same time. Thus, the circuitry that actually drives the monitor can be reading data from the VRAM while the graphics accelerator chip is writing data to the VRAM. There is a seemingly endless array of graphics memory like Window RAM, SGRAM, and so on. All of these embody different techniques to allow fast access to the graphics card RAM by both the display and the graphics accelerator hardware.

After you've bought your graphics board, make sure you keep the drivers up-to-date. Not only will you get any bug fixes, but you will likely get performance enhancements and support for new operating system features. Graphics board manufacturers are constantly working to wring more performance out of their driver software.

10.3. Changing for Performance

The graphics subsystem offers a variety of options for improving performance. None of these are too expensive and most of them are ones you can do safely and easily. We will explore four different things you can do in this chapter. The one you definitely should do is to get the latest graphics device drivers for your system. Not only can this improve performance, but it can also fix other problems in your system that you never realized were caused by your graphics subsystem. We also look at how you can adjust your graphics resolution and number of colors to balance performance versus appearance. Finally, we will look at what kinds of improvements you can get by purchasing a new graphics adapter.

10.3.1. Getting New Drivers

One of the cheapest and easiest things you can do to improve your graphics performance is to update your graphics device drivers. In addition, you can also take advantage of any bug fixes that vendors have added to the drivers as well. (We have often been surprised at the things a new graphics driver can fix. We won't bore you with the details, but once upon a time we fixed a malfunctioning color printer by getting the latest graphics drivers.)

Most if not all of the major graphics board vendors make the latest versions of their graphics drivers available for free via the Web or FTP. Here's a list of the Web sites of some of these vendors.

ATI Technologies	www.atitech.com
Diamond Multimedia Systems, Inc.	www.diamondmm.com
Genoa Systems Corporation	www.genoasys.com
Hercules Computer Technology, Inc.	www.hercules.com

Intergraph Computer Systems   www.intergraph.com
Matrox Electronic Systems Ltd.   www.matrox.com
Number Nine Visual Technologies   www.nine.com
STB Systems, Inc.   www.stb.com

You may also want to check out the Web site of the vendor of your system if your graphics card came with the system. They often do not have the latest and greatest driver, but they usually have tested the drivers with your particular configuration. Implicit in that statement is the concern that newer is not always better. It is always possible that new software can break something that used to work. As is true for any of the enhancements in this book, please back up your system before you change anything.

To give you a quick idea what kind of performance improvements you may see by upgrading your graphics device drivers, here is some testing we did with a Pentium 75 system under Windows 95. We tested this machine by using older and newer versions of the graphics drivers for the Matrox Millenium board, to see how upgrading the driver would help our performance.

The Winstone 97 results in Figure 10.1 are relatively unperturbed by upgrading to a newer version of the Matrox Millenium driver software. If you just look at this graph, the benefits of keeping your graphics drivers up-to-date are not evident: the overall improvement is only half a percent. But we're interested in graphics subsystem performance, so let's take a look at WinBench 97's Graphics WinMark 97.

Figure 10.1.

Business Winstone 97 results for the Pentium 75 machine, upgrading the Millenium drivers from the version shipped with the board to the latest version available from Matrox.

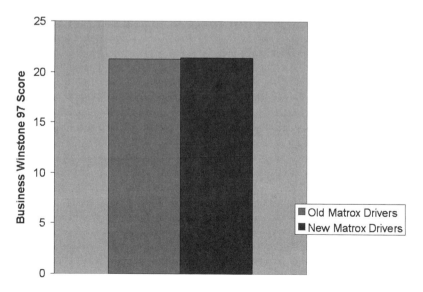

The WinBench 97 results in Figure 10.2 show the drastic improvement in the graphics subsystem we get from updating the drivers. This improvement is likely masked in the Winstone score due to a bottleneck elsewhere in the amount of RAM, or in the disk or processor subsystem. In other words, improvements that actually speed up the graphics subsystem aren't visible to users of general applications, but the potential is there to get better graphics performance. With an overall speed-up of over 30%, we have to recommend that you pay close attention to the age of your graphics drivers. We look at the performance improvement from changing graphics drivers under Windows 95 in more depth as part of the software enhancements in Chapter 6, "Windows 95 Software Tuning."

Figure 10.2.

WinBench 97 Business Graphics WinMark 97 results for the Pentium 75 machine, upgrading the Millenium drivers from the version shipped with the board to the latest version available from Matrox.

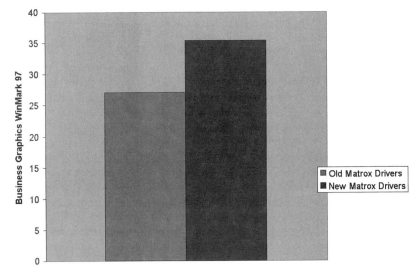

For those of you who are using Windows 98, you probably will have to wait a while for vendors to ship improved graphics drivers. This will be especially true if you upgraded to Windows 98 on a system with an older graphics adapter. You can see in Chapter 5, "Windows 98 Software Tuning," some of the mixed results we had with finding newer graphics drivers for Windows 98.

10.3.2. Adjusting Resolution and Color Depth

How you choose to display information on your screen has a direct influence on both performance and on your viewing pleasure. Unfortunately, the relationship is an inverse one—the higher the resolution and the higher the number of colors (which help define viewing pleasure), the lower the performance of your graphics subsystem. The higher the resolution or color depth is, the more information that has to be processed to display the full screen. The increased real estate you get at higher resolutions is a greater burden on the graphics subsystem in many cases. Sometimes you will want or need to bear that burden. Certain applications require you to run at a minimum specified resolution that's greater than VGA, or at a higher color depth. If you're editing digital photos on your PC, there's no point in reducing the color depth to 256 colors in an attempt to get better performance. Also, you might simply prefer to have higher resolution to keep track of several different programs running in different windows. You'll have to use your own judgment to determine the best tradeoff between your user interface needs and your performance needs.

In some cases you might find that real-world performance goes up when moving from a lower to a higher resolution. This is counter-intuitive, but possible. Graphics board manufacturers often spend more time optimizing their drivers for the most popular resolution modes.

To change your resolution or color depth, the procedure is basically the same in Windows 98, Windows 95, or Windows NT 4.0:

1. Right-click on your desktop background. (You may need to minimize application windows you have open to do this.) This displays the context menu for your desktop.

2. Select the Properties option by clicking on it. This displays the Display Properties dialog box.

3. Choose the Settings tab by clicking on it. If you've installed proprietary graphics drivers, you may have different tabs. For instance, if you are using a Matrox MGA-based board and the corresponding drivers, you might have a tab labelled MGA Settings.

4. Use your mouse pointer to grab the sliding control under the title Desktop Area. Move this control to the desired resolution.

5. Click on the Color palette drop-down box and choose the number of colors you'd like your display to use.

6. Click on the OK button to save your settings.

In the following sections we will look at a number of different combinations of processors, operating systems, resolutions, and bit depths to see the effect on performance. You should find the operating system you are using and then find the combinations that most resemble your own system and curiosity. As we say often, for the results most applicable to your particular situation, run some experiments on your own system. Find what balance of performance and viewing pleasure works best for you.

10.3.3. Getting a New Graphics Card

In this chapter, we will look at one final thing you can do to increase the performance of your graphics subsystem—buy a new graphics card. This is the one solution we will examine in this chapter that will cost you money. The current prices of graphics adapters, however, are not that prohibitive. Typical prices run from under $100 on up to $300. The higher priced cards are usually for special needs with 3D being a particular one of note. (We will not deal with 3D in this chapter, but we do discuss some of the issues in Chapter 14, "Optimizing for Games.") Performance of 3D graphics is largely a concern only to gamers. The performance, however, has improved dramatically over the last year or two and it will continue to do so for another year or two. If 3D performance is important to you, you really do need to get a new graphics adapter.

In the following sections we will look at some examples of the gains you can expect from replacing a graphics adapter. This area is one in which your mileage really will vary, but sadly it will be hard for you to find out by how much. As a simple rule of thumb, you should consider any graphics adapter that is over two years old a candidate for replacement. If you have already replaced other parts of your system, especially the processor, you should seriously consider replacing your graphics adapter. While its impact on overall performance is not that large, it can become a significant bottleneck for all that you do.

10.3.4. How Much Graphics Memory?

Whether you are buying a new adapter or considering upgrading your current one, you need to think about how much RAM you want on the card. One answer is, of course, as much as you can get. A possibly better way of approaching the problem is to remember that the amount of memory on your graphics accelerator board limits your maximum color depth and screen resolution. While we generally recommend keeping your resolution and color depth moderate to low for better performance, it's important to understand how much graphics memory you'll need to run at a particular color depth/resolution combination. We'll call the graphics memory on your graphics card VRAM, even though there are several different kinds of RAM used on graphics boards: VRAM, DRAM, WRAM, and so on. You can learn more about different kinds of RAM in Chapter 9, "Optimizing Your System's RAM."

To calculate how much VRAM you'll need for a particular resolution and color depth, multiply the height and width values of the resolution together to find out the number of pixels (picture elements) on the screen. Then multiply this value by the color depth expressed in bits. Divide this value by eight to convert from bits to bytes, and the result tells you the minimum VRAM you need. Here's an example. If you want to run at 640×480 resolution, but with 24-bit color, you would need

640×480×24 = 7,372,800 bits = 921,600 bytes

This is 900KB, which means you'd need a graphics board with at least 1MB VRAM to run this display. Graphics boards typically now come with VRAM in multiples of a megabyte. With the current price of RAM so low, we would not consider buying a graphics adapter with less than 4MB of RAM.

10.4. Windows 98 and the Graphics Subsystem

The heart of the Windows graphics subsystem is the Graphics Device Interface or GDI. The GDI was present in earlier versions of Windows, and became even more powerful in Windows 95 and then Windows 98. When an application wants to draw a line or a shape, it makes a GDI call. In Windows 95, the GDI performance was beefed up by moving much of it to more efficient 32-bit code. This is all buried deep under the hood, and you have no control over the GDI.

Windows 98 comes bundled with drivers for many popular graphics accelerator boards, so you can be up and running immediately no matter what hardware you're using. You should still install the driver software that the board manufacturer wrote for your hardware. In general, you'll find that this software gives you better performance than the bundled mini-drivers, as well as more features.

As we've discussed, you can adjust the resolution and color depth with all Windows 98 graphics drivers. With specific ones installed for your graphics board, you might also gain control over color temperature, gamma correction, virtual desktops, and specific performance settings. If you're a typical business user, you might not be interested in these settings, but if you're a high-end hotshot, they could come in handy. For all of these reasons, we recommend that you keep your graphics drivers up-to-date.

Windows 98 also adds support for multiple monitors and TV tuners to the existing Windows 95 graphics capabilities, but basically it is very similar to Windows 95 in its treatment of graphics features.

10.4.1. How We Tested

We ran Business Winstone 98 for the Windows 98 section. Also, we ran the graphics tests in WinBench 98. These are also known as the GDI Playback Tests, a term that more accurately describes these tests, because they play back the GDI (Graphics Device Interface) calls from the Winstone 98 tests, without any of the other calls (such as disk accesses). Because of this, the graphics tests in WinBench 98 measure the performance of only the graphics subsystem.

Unless we were specifically interested in testing changes in screen resolution or color depth, we tested at a resolution of 1024×768 and an 8-bit color depth (256 colors), as these are fairly typical settings.

Optimizing Your Graphics Subsystem

As always, we completely defragmented the hard drives of each machine before we ran each test, even though we were testing graphics performance. This is always a good testing procedure to follow. We also ran each test immediately after a cold reboot.

10.4.2. Pentium 75

The first machine we tested on was our Pentium 75. Many home users will have a machine similar to this one sitting in the corner of the living room. Many of those folks will wonder if the promise of increased performance will really come true should they buy a new graphics board for their PC. We tested our Pentium 75 with its original graphics board, the built-in Compaq QVision PCI, and then we upgraded it with a Matrox Millenium board. In both cases the machine contained 16MB RAM.

In Figure 10.3, we see only a 3% increase in performance by upgrading the graphics board. The category scores showed a slightly better result for the Publishing and Word Processing categories, but the results is still not that large. This is a significant amount, particularly when you consider the relatively small percentage of overall system performance is attributable to the graphics subsystem. This number, however, is probably a lot less than you'd expect if your only knowledge about graphics boards was from vendor claims or advertisements.

Figure 10.3.

Business Winstone 98 results for the Pentium 75 machine, upgrading the graphics board from the Compaq QVision PCI to the Matrox Millenium.

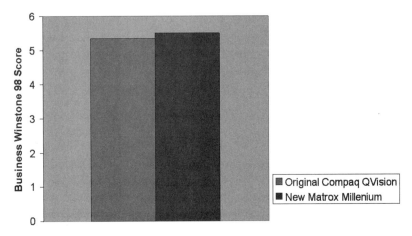

To look more closely at the graphics performance of this change we need to turn to WinBench 98's Graphics WinMark 98. The WinBench results tell a very different story. While Winstone measures overall performance (and is therefore limited by any system bottlenecks, whether in the graphics subsystem, or the disk or the processor), WinBench Graphics Tests measure only graphics subsystem performance. The graphics board upgrade from the QVision PCI to the Matrox Millenium, shown in Figure 10.4, gives us a 27% increase in the speed of the graphics subsystem. The category scores (not shown here) vary from 15% to nearly 30%. For graphics intensive applications, this upgrade does show some real improvement.

Figure 10.4.
WinBench 98 Business Graphics results for the Pentium 75 machine, upgrading the graphics board from the Compaq QVision PCI to the Matrox Millenium.

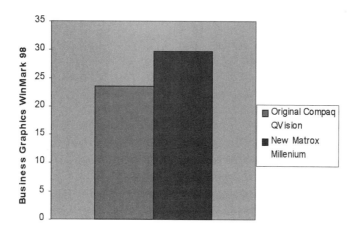

10.4.3. Pentium 100

We stuck with the Business Winstone 98 tests and their corresponding Graphics Tests in WinBench 98 for our Pentium 100 machine. We wanted to see if the same hardware upgrade—moving from the built-in Compaq QVision PCI to a Matrox Millenium—acted differently on a slightly faster machine than our Pentium 75, albeit with the same amount of RAM (16MB).

A more capable system than our Pentium 75, the Pentium 100 shows more improvement when we upgrade from the QVision PCI to the Matrox Millenium. The results in Figure 10.5 show the overall Business Winstone 98 score goes up by 4% instead of 3%. Remember, this is Winstone—this is actual overall performance improvement you'd see when running typical business applications. 4% might not sound like a lot, but it is a meaningful performance increase. This result also shows how the faster the processor is, the more it can be bottlenecked by a slow subsystem like the graphics one in this example.

The WinBench 98 Graphics WinMark scores improve immensely with our graphics upgrade, even better than they did on the Pentium 75 (see Figure 10.6). Thus, we see a rule emerging: for any given graphics upgrade, the effects of the upgrade will be more prominent on more capable systems, with more capable in this case meaning systems with faster processors or more RAM. Here we get a 32% overall performance boost in the graphics subsystem. We see the same pattern we've seen before: significant gains on the Publishing, Database/Spreadsheet, and Word Processing categories, while the Browser and Task Switching categories show smaller improvement—smaller

Figure 10.5.

Business Winstone 98 results for the Pentium 100 machine, upgrading the graphics board from the Compaq QVision PCI to the Matrox Millenium.

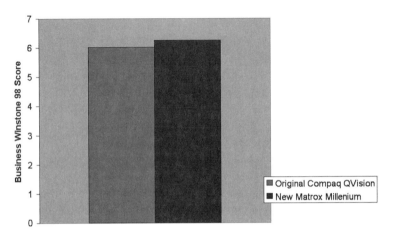

Figure 10.6.

WinBench 98 Business Graphics results for the Pentium 100 machine, upgrading the graphics board from the Compaq QVision PCI to the Matrox Millenium.

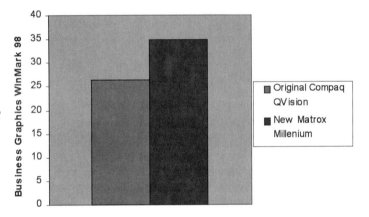

10.4.4. Pentium 133

The Pentium 133 machine is a more capable Windows 98 system. In this and the following sections we'll look at some other aspects of graphics subsystem performance: the effects of changing the color depth and screen resolution.

Color depth is expressed in bits. It's the number of bits the graphics board uses to represent the color of each pixel (picture element) on your monitor. So, the old VGA standard of 16 possible colors means that the color depth is 4 bits, or two to the fourth power, which is sixteen. An 8-bit depth gives you 256 possible colors, and 16-bit depth gives you 65,536 colors to choose from. Many folks never change the display settings from their factory defaults, and often the manufacturer will ship with the color depth and screen resolution set to their maximum. If you've never twiddled these settings, you don't know what performance benefits you're missing.

It's easy to see why color depth affects graphics performance. Every time your PC updates the display, it's moving data from the CPU across the system bus (or graphics bus) to the graphics board, which then performs necessary calculations and refreshes the display. So you would guess that less data moving would mean higher performance. Updating a screen composed of pixels associated with a high bit depth should be more time consuming than updating a screen composed of pixels with (in the case of a monochrome display) a bit depth of one. Let's see if this guess is borne out on our Pentium 133 machine, first by running our main workhorse, the Business Winstone 98 tests.

We tested at 16-, 8-, and 4-bit depths, but our first graph shows an immediate problem: Winstone 98 would not run to completion on this machine using a 16-bit color depth. This is probably due to a complicated interaction between Winstone 98, the graphics drivers, and the pre-release version of Windows 98 we were testing on. Don't interpret this result as a poor reflection on any of those pieces of software, though. It's a typical situation you'll find when you test on beta and pre-release software, especially pre-release operating systems. In Figure 10.7, we included the Business Winstone 98 category scores so you could see the effect on performance.

Figure 10.7.

Business Winstone 98 category scores for the Pentium 133 machine, varying the color depth from 65,536 colors (16-bit) to 8 colors (4-bit).

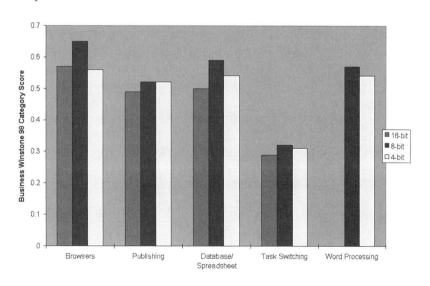

The category scores for the 16-bit, 8-bit, and 4-bit depths, though, show the 8-bit setting as the clear winner. We get a 6% boost in overall business performance by using 256 colors instead of 16. There could be several reasons for this result. Probably the most obvious one is that the graphics board manufacturer, recognizing that fewer and fewer folks run with 16 colors nowadays, might not have optimized the code that handles that color depth as the code that handles higher color depths. Another part of the explanation is that all current RAM technologies address data 8 bits at a time. Writing 4-bit pixels to the screen probably requires multiple writes of the same byte of RAM. Such access will violate most of the assumptions about memory access (sequentially) that cards make for maximum performance.

As usual, we'll turn to WinBench 98 to look at the performance under closer scrutiny.

As we expected, Figure 10.8 shows the peak performance at 8 bits in an even more pronounced fashion when measured with the Business Graphics tests in WinBench 98. When we compare it to the 16-bit setting here with WinBench 98, it's 70% faster! Most of the application category tests mirror the shape of the overall Winstone curve: 8-bit wins, 4-bits comes in second, and 16-bits a close third. If you're running at a higher bit depth simply because that's how the PC was set up when you bought it, you might not be getting all the performance you can out of your graphics subsystem. Of course, you may well choose to live with lower performance in return for higher visual quality.

Figure 10.8.
WinBench 98 Business Graphics results for the Pentium 133 machine, varying the color depth from 65,536 colors (16-bit) to 8 colors (4-bit).

The other display setting that you can change is the screen resolution. Screen resolution is expressed as the number of pixels making up the width and the number of pixels making up the height of your screen. In other words, the standard VGA display of 640×480 is 640 pixels wide and 480 pixels tall, giving you a total of 640×480 = 307,200 pixels making up the VGA display. The higher the resolution, the more pixels, and the more data and calculations required of the graphics subsystem. We would guess that a lower resolution would result in better performance, since the graphics subsystem would have to manipulate less data. As with color depth, many manufacturers ship their systems with the resolution maxed out. Let's take a look at the relative performance when we adjust this setting on our Pentium 133 machine.

We tested at two popular resolutions: 1024×768 and 800×600. Due to the minimum requirements of Business Winstone 98, we cannot test at 640×480. While all of the overall and category results are better for the 800×600 case, Figure 10.9 shows there are no big benefits from lower screen resolution. The improvement is only a couple of percent. Part of the reason here is that while higher resolution means more pixels per screen, it also means it takes fewer screens to display a document. If you have a choice between lowering color depth or resolution, our results have shown that you'll reap more performance by lowering color depth to 8 bits.

Figure 10.9.

Business Winstone 98 results for the Pentium 133 machine, varying the screen resolution from 1024×768 to 800×600.

The WinBench results in Figure 10.10 are equally undramatic, and back up our conclusion that the performance benefits gained by lowering color depth are far greater than those gained by lowering screen resolution.

Let's also take a look at how color depth affects full-motion video playback. We can't measure this with Winstone 98, but we can use the Video Tests in WinBench 98. We'll copy the video test files to the hard disk before running the tests, thus removing the CD-ROM drive from the performance equation. Because WinBench 98 includes a large number of video test clips, we've chosen one of the action clips, one encoded with Cinepak and recorded at a resolution of 640×480 and transfer rate of 900KB per second, as our test sample.

Figure 10.10.

WinBench 98 Business Graphics WinMark 98 results for the Pentium 133 machine, varying the screen resolution from 1024×768 to 800×600.

First, let's take a look at the frame rate results. For every WinBench 98 Video Test clip, you can obtain up to five different results: maximum frame rate, temporal quality, visual quality, audio quality, and CPU utilization. The maximum frame rate measures the number of frames per second the PC was able to display while attempting to play back every frame of the clip as fast as possible, without sound.

Figure 10.11 show that the Cinepak clip essentially fails completely to run with 4-bit color, turning in a measly two frames per second *maximum* rate. This is likely due to a driver problem, since few people would anticipate running full-motion video clips with a sixteen color palette. The maximum frame rate with 8-bit color is over 30fps, but the maximum frame rate with 16-bit color is only twenty-seven frames per second. That means that this PC can't play back the clip at its normal speed, which isn't satisfactory.

Figure 10.11.

WinBench 98 Video Test frame rate results (for selected action clips) for the Pentium 133 machine, varying the color depth from 65,536 colors (16-bit) to 8 colors (4-bit).

These results back up what we discovered with Winstone 98 and the Graphics Tests in WinBench 98: the graphics subsystem is more efficient when running with 8-bit color as opposed to 16-bit color. Let's take a look at other Video Test results.

The next Video Test result we'll look at is visual quality. Visual quality shows the PC's ability to keep up while playing the test clip, and is measured in number of frames dropped. The ideal result for this test is zero frames dropped. As we can see in Figure 10.12, none of the three color depth settings allowed the PC to play back the clip without dropping frames, but the 8-bit setting caused the least dropped frames. Because there are only 450 frames in the video, you can see that the 4-bit setting dropped almost all of them! Our basic conclusion is that this machine wouldn't be our first choice to play back real-time video clips. Our other conclusion is that once again the 8-bit setting wins.

Figure 10.12.

WinBench 98 Video Test visual quality results (for selected action clips) for the Pentium 133 machine, varying the color depth from 65,536 colors (16-bit) to 8 colors (4-bit).

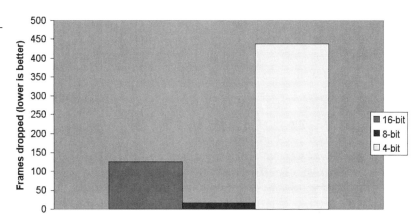

The final Video Test result we'll look at is CPU Utilization. This is a measure of how much work it takes for the CPU to play back the video clip. Ideally, this will be as low a number as possible—a video subsystem isn't much good if it burdens your CPU down completely to play back a video clip. In Figure 10.13 we see that in all three cases, the CPU is heavily burdened by playing this clip back. In the 4-bit and 16-bit cases, almost all of the CPU's available work is taken up by playing back the video clip. Once again, the 8-bit setting wins.

The color depth of your display can significantly affect performance, and we recommend you set it to 8-bit color (256 colors) unless you absolutely have to set it higher for a particular application or for your own aesthetic sense.

10.4.5. Pentium 166

Starting with the Pentium 166 machine, we changed our graphics board testbed a bit. First off, we ran all tests at 32MB RAM, a typical amount for machines of this

Optimizing Your Graphics Subsystem

caliber. The Compaq Deskpro 5166 in our testbed came with a Matrox Millenium graphics board, so we needed a different graphics board for the upgrade. The newer board we decided to test with was the ATI 3D Pro Turbo PC2TV; the particular model in our testbed came with 8MB of VRAM. As the name suggests, this board also comes with a TV tuner. Is newer better? Is more VRAM better? These were questions we wanted to answer.

Figure 10.13.

WinBench 98 Video Test visual quality results (for selected action clips) for the Pentium 133 machine, varying the color depth from 65,536 colors (16-bit) to 8 colors (4-bit).

The ATI board bests the Matrox board in Figure 10.14 by a modest 2.7%. We saw a similar few percentage points of improvement for each category. Overall, though, our performance did not "scream" or "burn" or "rip" simply by dropping in a new graphics board. The real moral here is that just because an adapter is new, does not necessarily mean it is better. You should make sure you either test a new card yourself or get results from a trusted publication. Failing that, vendors will often have WinBench or Winstone results available for comparison. Be aware, of course, they tend to only show these when they think they will win.

Figure 10.14.

Business Winstone 98 results for the Pentium 166 machine, upgrading the graphics board from the Matrox Millenium to the ATI 3D Pro Turbo PC2TV.

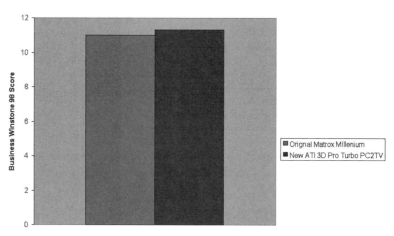

The WinBench 98 Business Graphics WinMark 98 tests results in Figure 10.15 show that the ATI board is boosting performance of the graphics subsystem by about 5%. The applications that show the most improvement are word processing and database/spreadsheet. In the case of browsers, though, performance falls off by 5%.

Figure 10.15.
WinBench 98 Business Graphics WinMark 98 results for the Pentium 166 machine, upgrading the graphics board from the Matrox Millenium to the ATI 3D Pro Turbo PC2TV.

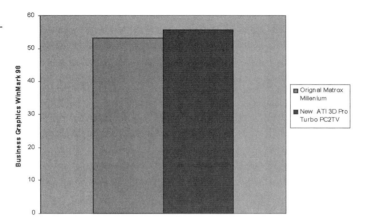

The lesson to learn here is to be skeptical of the *newer and bigger.* The additional VRAM on the ATI board is doing nothing to boost performance—all it can do is allow you to run at higher screen resolutions or color depths. On the other hand, you do get higher resolutions, more colors, 3D acceleration, and the ability to display TV signals on your PC. Performance is not enough reason for this upgrade, but the other improvements may well be.

10.4.6. Pentium 200 MMX

Let's use the Pentium 200 MMX machine and once again take a look at the performance tweaks you can perform for free, by adjusting the color depth and screen resolution. This machine in our testbed also came outfitted with a Matrox Millenium board, but with more VRAM installed. We have a broader range of possible color depth and resolution settings with this machine, so we decided to test as many of those as we could, with our trusty Winstone 98 and WinBench 98.

Once again, we had some testing failures, so in Figure 10.16 we show the category scores, but not an overall score. The Database/Spreadsheet category of Winstone 98 would only run to completion on the 8-bit color depth setting. Thus, we can't compare overall Winstone 98 scores. We see two distinct kinds of curves with the categories that did run to completion: Word Processing gets faster as we decrease color depth. The Browser and Publishing categories peak at 16-bit color depth. Our general rule that lower color depth means faster performance is still true in most cases, but when in doubt you should do your own testing.

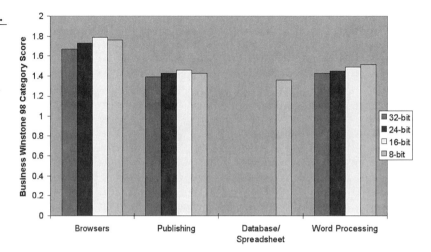

Figure 10.16.

Business Winstone 98 results for the Pentium 200 MMX machine, varying the color depth from 4 billion colors (32-bit) to 256 colors (8-bit).

The WinBench 98 tests show a similar but more pronounced picture (see Figures 10.17). Once again, we had some testing failures in the Database/Spreadsheet category. Here we see that the Word Processing and Browser categories get faster as we decrease color depth. The Publishing applications still peak with the 16-bit setting. In general, though, it takes more graphics power to pump more colors onto the screen. The graphics subsystem really has a lot less work to do if you don't overburden it with a huge color palette.

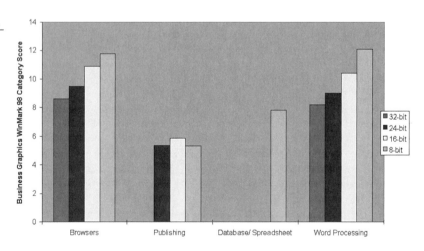

Figure 10.17.

WinBench 98 Business Graphics results for the Pentium 200 MMX machine, varying the color depth from 4 billion colors (32-bit) to 256 colors (8-bit).

Let's now take a look at some resolution tests we performed on our Pentium 200 MMX machine.

As we saw on the Pentium 133, the performance change with lowered screen resolution is quite small. In Figure 10.18, the difference in the overall Business Winstone 98 score is under 1%. Once again, we can attribute this to the more complex interaction between the actual work done in the benchmark and the performance. More on the screen means more work to put them there, but it also means that the system has to display fewer screens to show the same information. Regardless of the reasons, it is clear that color depth has a greater effect on performance than does resolution.

Figure 10.18.

Business Winstone 98 results for the Pentium 200 MMX machine, varying the screen resolution from 1024×768 to 800×600.

As we would expect, the WinBench 98 scores show a little more improvement than the Winstone 98 scores in the previous chart. The 2% in Figure 10.19 for the WinBench 98 Business Graphics WinMark 98 is not much to write home about. The category scores show similar less than spectacular results.

Figure 10.19.

WinBench 98 Business Graphics results for the Pentium 200 MMX machine, varying the screen resolution from 1024×768 to 800×600.

We've seen how graphics board upgrades are not necessarily as dreamy as they seem, because of bottlenecks elsewhere. We've also seen the importance of keeping your graphics drivers up-to-date. In terms of free performance improvements, nothing beats lowering your color depth setting to 16-bits or 8-bits. When in doubt, test it out!

10.5. Windows 95 and the Graphics Subsystem

The heart of the Windows graphics subsystem is the Graphics Device Interface, or GDI. The GDI was present in earlier versions of Windows, and became even more powerful in Windows 95. When an application wants to draw a line or a shape, it makes a GDI call. In Windows 95, the GDI performance was beefed up by moving much of it to more efficient 32-bit code. This is all buried deep under the hood, and you have no control over the GDI.

A difference from Windows 3.1 that you *can* control is the driver software that directly controls the graphics board you're using (under instruction from the Windows OS). Windows 95 comes bundled with mini-drivers for many popular graphics accelerator boards, so you can be up and running immediately no matter what hardware you're using. You should still install the driver software that the board manufacturer wrote for your hardware. In general, you'll find that this software gives you better performance than the bundled mini-drivers, as well as more features.

As we've discussed, you can adjust the resolution and color depth with all Windows 95 graphics drivers. With specific ones installed for your graphics board, you might also gain control over color temperature, gamma correction, virtual desktops, and specific performance settings. If you're a typical business user, you might not be interested in these settings, but if you're a high-end hotshot, they could come in handy. For all of these reasons, we recommend that you keep your graphics drivers up-to-date.

10.5.1. How We Tested

We ran both of our Winstone 97 test suites, Business and High-End, for this chapter. Also, we ran the Graphics Tests in WinBench 97. These are also known as the GDI Playback Tests, a term that more accurately describes these tests, because they play back the GDI (Graphics Device Interface) calls from the Winstone 97 tests, without any of the other calls (such as disk accesses). Because of this, the Graphics Tests in WinBench 97 measure the performance of only the graphics subsystem.

Unless we were specifically interested in testing changes in screen resolution or color depth, we tested at a resolution of 1024×768 and an 8-bit color depth (256 colors), as these are fairly typical settings.

As always, we completely defragmented the hard drives of each machine before we ran each test, even though we were testing graphics performance. This is always a good testing procedure to follow. We also ran each test immediately after a cold reboot.

10.5.2. 486/66

Our testbed's 486 computer, a Compaq DeskPro 486/66, is a slim-line computer with an ISA bus on a riser board. Because most graphics boards are now built for the PCI bus, we were unable to install any of our test graphics boards in this machine. The lesson to learn here is that you need to know whether or not your machine is truly upgradable before you run out and buy an upgrade component. You should also ensure that any machines you buy will be upgradable for the near future. Of course, you can't foresee everything. The new AGP (Advanced Graphics Port) graphics boards require an AGP-compatible motherboard.

10.5.3. Pentium 75

The first machine we could really test was our Pentium 75. Many home users will have a machine similar to this one sitting in the corner of the living room. Many of those folks will wonder if the promise of increased performance will really come true should they buy a new graphics board for their PC. We tested our Pentium 75 with its original graphics board, the built-in Compaq QVision PCI, and then we upgraded it with a Matrox Millenium board. In both cases the machine contained 16MB RAM.

Overall, in Figure 10.20, we see almost an 8% increase in performance by upgrading the graphics board. This is about the same increase we get in the Database category, while the Word Processing and Spreadsheet categories show a full 10% speed-up. On the other hand, the Publishing category only shows about a 5% performance increase. These improvements are rather significant for Winstone improvements. Our rule of thuMB is that graphics performance is about 15% of the overall performance pie. An 8% overall improvement in Winstone 97 shows that in this system, the graphics subsystem is the performance bottleneck.

Winstone 97 measures overall performance (and is therefore limited by any system bottlenecks, whether in the graphics subsystem, or the disk or the processor), WinBench Graphics Tests measure only graphics subsystem performance. As you can see from Figure 10.21, the Business Graphics WinMark 97 confirms the higher level of performance improvement when we look solely at the graphics subsystem. The graphics board upgrade, from the QVision PCI to the Matrox Millenium, gives us about a 22% increase in the speed of the graphics subsystem. The Publishing category again shows considerably less improvement than the other two categories, at about 15%. The other categories show a speed-up of about 25%. Both the Winstone 97 and WinBench 97 indicate that for this system, the performance improvements from replacing the graphics adapter are worth the effort and expense.

Figure 10.20.

Business Winstone 97 results for the Pentium 75 machine, upgrading the graphics board from the Compaq QVision PCI to the Matrox Millenium.

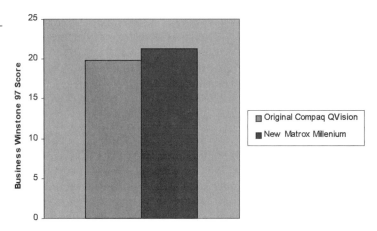

Figure 10.21.

WinBench 97 Business Graphics results for the Pentium 75 machine, upgrading the graphics board from the Compaq QVision PCI to the Matrox Millenium.

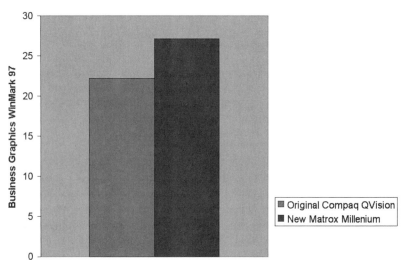

10.5.4. Pentium 100

We stuck with the Business Winstone 97 tests and their corresponding Graphics Tests in WinBench 97 for our Pentium 100 machine. We wanted to see if the same hardware upgrade—moving from the built-in Compaq QVision PCI to a Matrox Millenium—acted differently on a slightly faster machine than our Pentium 75, albeit with the same amount of RAM (16MB).

A more capable system than our Pentium 75, the Pentium 100 shows slightly more improvement when we upgrade from the QVision PCI to the Matrox Millenium. In Figure 10.22, we see an overall speed-up of 8%. The Database scores go up a full 12%! Remember, this is Winstone—this is actual overall performance improvement you'd see when running typical applications. The Publishing category lag as they did on the Pentium 75; they only improve 3%. As with the Pentium 75, these improvements are very significant, especially when they come from the graphics subsystem. Removing the graphics subsystem bottleneck can have a large improvement. Your mileage will, of course, vary, but it is obviously an area to experiment with on your system.

Figure 10.22.

Business Winstone 97 results for the Pentium 100 machine, upgrading the graphics board from the Compaq QVision PCI to the Matrox Millenium.

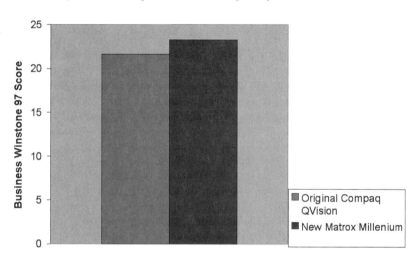

The WinBench 97 scores improve immensely with our graphics upgrade, even better than they did on the Pentium 75. Thus, we see a rule emerging: for any given graphics upgrade, the effects of the upgrade will be more prominent on more capable systems, with more capable in this case meaning systems with faster processors or more RAM. Here we get a one-third overall performance boost in the graphics subsystem, and once again the same pattern we've seen before: only an 18% boost for the publishing applications, while the other applications show improvements in the 30% to 40% range (see Figure 10.23).

We will say it again many times before this chapter is over and before this book is over—find the bottleneck. Or rather, be aware of it. In the case of a graphics upgrade, the more capable your system is in non-graphics areas (RAM and hard disk) the more improvement you'll see from a graphics upgrade, given that the graphics upgrade really does improve the graphics subsystem performance.

Optimizing Your Graphics Subsystem

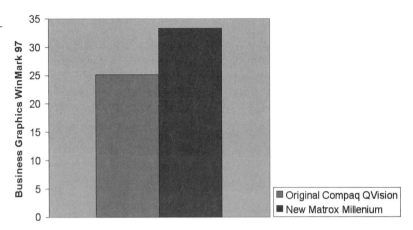

Figure 10.23.
WinBench 97 Business Graphics results for the Pentium 100 machine, upgrading the graphics board from the Compaq QVision PCI to the Matrox Millenium.

10.5.5. Pentium 133

The Pentium 133 machine is the first one on which we ran High-End Winstone 97 tests and High-End Graphics Tests from WinBench 97. Running the High-End tests required us to use 32MB RAM in this machine for these tests (for the resolution and color depth tests we downshifted to 16MB RAM). We wanted to see if our hardware upgrade, still going from the built-in QVision PCI to a Matrox Millenium board, showed even more improvement on the Pentium 133, or if the performance differential had leveled off. We also wanted to see how a board upgrade affected the high-end applications, and we wanted to take a look at how color depth and screen resolution affect graphics performance. Finally, we wanted to look at how color depth affected playback of full-motion video clips.

If you've read the previous sections on our Pentium 75 and Pentium 100 machines, the pattern should now be very familiar to you. By upgrading from the existing on-board Compaq QVision PCI graphics adapter to the Matrox Millenium, we see in Figure 10.24 an overall improvement in real-world business applications of about 8%. This is very similar to the results on the Pentium 75 and Pentium 100 systems. The Business Winstone categories show similar, though more varied, improvements. The Publishing category lags behind at a mere 3% (probably because RAM is the bottleneck for it rather than the graphics subsystem), while the other two categories, Database and Word Processing/Spreadsheet, show improvements of around 10%. As with the previous systems, this level of improvement is pretty substantial and certainly would cause us to upgrade our graphics adapters. Our best understanding of why the numbers are so high is that the graphics subsystem is the main bottleneck on these systems.

In Figure 10.25 we see a much greater performance improvement than we did previously, on the Pentium 100 with 16MB RAM, even though the graphics board upgrade is the same—going from the Compaq QVision PCI to the Matrox Millenium board. There's more potential graphics performance to wring from this system, even though as we saw with the Winstone results this will not necessarily mean similar gains in overall performance. We get about a 39% increase in the Business WinMark 97 score. In terms of the category scores, the greatest increase comes in the Word Processing and Spreadsheet categories, with over an 45% increase. The Database category shows slightly less improvement at about 34%, while the Publishing category shows the least improvement (as we've seen all along) at a still remarkable 26%.

Figure 10.24.

Business Winstone 97 results for the Pentium 133 machine, upgrading the graphics board from the Compaq QVision PCI to the Matrox Millenium.

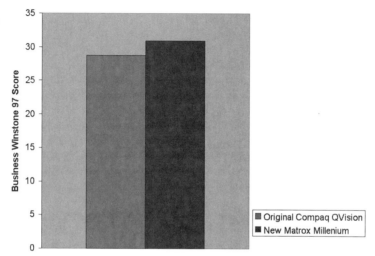

Figure 10.25.

WinBench 97 Business Graphics results for the Pentium 133 machine, upgrading the graphics board from the Compaq QVision PCI to the Matrox Millenium.

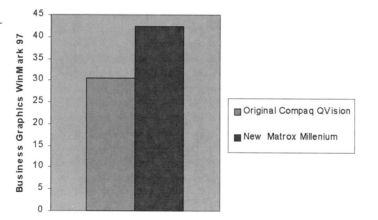

Optimizing Your Graphics Subsystem

Remember, though, this performance increase is only the graphics subsystem performance; that's what the graphics tests in WinBench 97 measure. You should think of Winstone 97 scores as measuring the true real-world performance you're getting from a particular upgrade, while WinBench scores allow you to dig deeper, to find *potential* sources of performance enhancement. This would be especially borne out if your work was more graphics intensive than that of the Winstone 97 benchmark.

Now that we're working on a Pentium 133, let's take a look at the results of High-End Winstone 97. You might expect that this graphics upgrade would show more improvement for high-end applications than it would for typical business applications. You would be wrong. Looking at Figure 10.26, we see that there's very little improvement in any of the High-End Winstone 97 application scores, with only a few exceptions. Overall, performance increases by less than 1%. Our guess that the graphics speed-up would help graphically intensive applications is borne out by the fact that the Image Editing category shows a 3% boost, with most of this coming from the 8% speed-up shown in Picture Publisher. The other applications are pretty boring. The Visual C++ score actually decreases slightly! In the case of Visual C++, this decrease is well below the margin of variability for Winstone 97, and so we can rightfully ignore it. What's going on, though?

Figure 10.26.

High-End Winstone 97 results for the Pentium 133 machine, upgrading the graphics board from the Compaq QVision PCI to the Matrox Millenium.

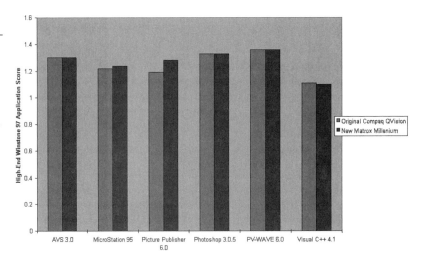

What's going on is that these high-end applications are not just graphically intensive, they're CPU-intensive, RAM-intensive, and disk-intensive too. They're high stress applications. Because of this, they tax a whole lot more than just your graphics board. Once again, we sound the chorus of "find the bottleneck!" It's likely that here in our test case, with a Pentium 133 with 32MB RAM, the bottleneck for high-end applications is at some point other than in the graphics subsystem. The WinBench 97 scores should bear this out, by showing a more noticeable improvement in the graphics subsystem itself.

Turning to the High-End Graphics WinMark 97 tests in WinBench 97, we again see more dramatic improvements than those in the High-End Winstone 97 (which do not isolate the graphics subsystem). In fact, the WinBench results do not really parallel the Winstone results in a linear fashion. This is probably because the high-end applications are bottlenecked on other subsystems. Since WinBench 97 looks at one subsystem at a time, those bottlenecks do not come into play. Here, as shown in Figure 10.27, counter to what we saw with Winstone 97, the greatest improvement is shown in the Visual C++ application! With the exception of the 3-D/CAD applications, all the other applications show a significant improvement.

Figure 10.27.
WinBench 97 High-End Graphics results for the Pentium 133 machine, upgrading the graphics board from the Compaq QVision PCI to the Matrox Millenium.

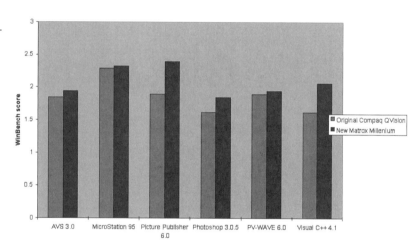

Our conclusion here is the same as it was for the business applications, only more so: dramatic improvements in the performance of the graphics subsystem do not necessarily lead to dramatic improvements in overall performance. While there is potential performance to be had from a graphics board upgrade, you should first pay attention to the RAM and hard disk subsystems to ensure that your scream-ing new graphics board is not held back by a pokey disk or a dearth of memory.

Now let's take a look at some tests that don't require buying a new graphics board. They don't even require you to download new drivers! We want to look at performance as it relates to two display parameters, color depth and screen resolution.

Remember, color depth is expressed in bits. It's the number of bits the graphics board uses to represent the color of each pixel (picture element) on your monitor. So, the old VGA standard of 16 possible colors means that the color depth is 4 bits, or two to the fourth power, which is sixteen. A bit depth of 8 gives you 256 possible colors, and a bit depth of 16 gives you 65,536 colors to choose from.

Many folks never change the display settings from their factory defaults, and often the manufacturer will ship with the color depth and screen resolution set to their maximum. This is fine for some users but not for us performance freaks!

It's easy to see why color depth affects graphics performance. Every time your PC updates the display, it's moving data from the CPU across the system bus (or graphics bus) to the graphics board, which then performs necessary calculations and refreshes the display. So you would guess that less data moving would mean higher performance. Updating a screen composed of pixels associated with a high bit depth should be more time consuming than updating a screen composed of pixels with (in the case of a monochrome display) a bit depth of one. Let's see if this guess is borne out on our Pentium 133 machine, first by running our main workhorse, the Business Winstone 97 tests.

We tested at bit depths of 16, 8, and 4 bits, but the results are not exactly what we (simplistically) predicted. As you can see in Figure 10.28, the 8-bit setting achieved the best performance, not the 4-bit setting. Now, the driver software itself didn't change (in other words, we did not use Microsoft's standard driver for the 4-bit setting and then proprietary drivers for the higher bit depths), so that's not the cause of the behavior we're seeing. However, within the driver software itself, different code paths may be running depending on the color depth selected. In other words, the graphics board manufacturer, recognizing that fewer and fewer folks run with 16 colors nowadays, might not have optimized the code that handles that color depth as the code that handles higher color depths. Another part of the explanation is that all current RAM technologies address data 8 bits at a time. Writing 4-bit pixels to the screen probably requires multiple writes of the same byte of RAM. Such access will violate most of the assumptions about memory access (sequentially) that cards make for maximum performance.

Figure 10.28.

Business Winstone 97 results for the Pentium 133 machine, varying the color depth from 65,536 colors (16-bit) to 8 colors (4-bit).

Remember, this is Winstone: this is real-world performance that we're measuring. Without spending a dime, on this system you could reap a 28% performance gain simply by lowering the color depth from 16 bits to 8 bits. Let's take a look at the WinBench 97 results to see how they show graphics subsystem performance in isolation.

The peak performance at 8 bits is even more pronounced when measured with the Business Graphics tests in WinBench 97, showing in Figure 10.29 a whopping 77% gain in performance going from a 16-bit color depth to an 8-bit color depth. The graphs for the application suites mirror this shape. Moving to 4 bits, however, causes a drop in performance. There is an important lesson here: you should always back up your conceptual knowledge with real-world testing. Our initial guess that fewer bits equal more performance turned out to be slightly flawed. If you're running at a higher bit depth, simply because that's how the PC was set up when you bought it, you might not be getting all the performance you can out of your graphics subsystem. Conversely, if you're running with just 16 colors, thinking that you're maximizing your graphics performance, you could be dead wrong.

Figure 10.29.

WinBench 97 Business Graphics results for the Pentium 133 machine, varying the color depth from 65,536 colors (16-bit) to 8 colors (4-bit).

In the absence of your own graphics studies, though, we recommend that you stick with an 8-bit color depth for best performance. We also realize, however, that you may well choose to instead maximize the appearance of your display. At least one of the three of us has opted for improved visual quality over performance. They key here, however, is we make that choice knowingly rather than by default.

The other display setting that you can change is the screen resolution. Screen resolution is expressed as the number of pixels making up the width and the number of pixels making up the height of your screen. In other words, the standard VGA display of 640×480 is 640 pixels wide and 480 pixels tall, giving you a total of 640×480 = 307,200 pixels making up the VGA display. The higher the resolution, the more pixels, and the more data and calculations required of the graphics subsystem. We would guess that a lower resolution would result in better performance, since the graphics subsystem would have to manipulate less data. As with color depth, many manufacturers ship their systems with the resolution as high as it will go. Let's take a look at the relative performance when we adjust this setting on our Pentium 133 machine.

We tested at three popular resolutions: 1024×768, 800×600, and 640×480. Unlike with color depth, these results do not yield a surprising shape. Instead, we see performance steadily increasing as we decrease the screen resolution. Figure 10.30 shows the overall Business Winstone 97 score at 640×480 is about 9% better than the score at 1024×768. This is not the massive gain we saw when lowering the color depth, but it is still quite significant. Part of the reason here is that while a higher resolution means more pixels per screen, it also means it takes fewer screens to display a document.

Figure 10.30.

Business Winstone 97 results for the Pentium 133 machine, varying the screen resolution from 1024×768 to 640×480.

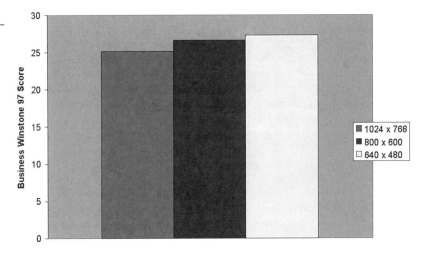

Many folks, however, will be limited by factors other than performance when adjusting these values. If you have specific applications that require a certain color depth or resolution, then those applications will limit how low you can adjust these settings. You also have to weigh the aesthetics and productivity of the resolution you choose. Here as well, more is not necessarily better. We seldom choose the highest resolution possible—not just to increase performance, but to prevent eyestrain as well. If you have to choice between lowering color depth or resolution, our results have shown that you'll reap more performance by lowering color depth.

The WinBench 97 Business Graphics WinMark 97 results in Figure 10.31 show a similar curve, although WinBench shows no benefit in lowering resolution from 800×600 to 640×480. This is due to the way WinBench 97 operates. To create the Graphics WinMark, developers at ZDBOp profile Winstone 97. For a variety of reasons including the lack of space, they record the Winstone 97 graphics at a few fixed resolutions. When WinBench 97 plays back one the logged graphics calls it picks the log recorded at a resolution that is equal or lower than the one on the system under test. At 800×640, WinBench 97 uses the same logs as at 640×480. Therefore, we would expect these results to be very similar. In any case, the performance benefits gained by lowering color depth are far greater than those gained by lowering screen resolution.

Figure 10.31.

WinBench 97 Business Graphics results for the Pentium 133 machine, varying the screen resolution from 1024×768 to 640×480.

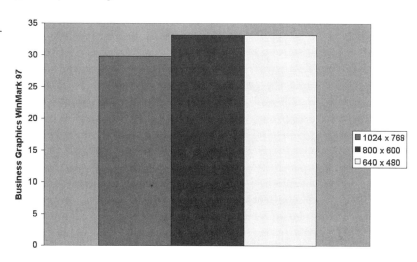

Let's also take a look at how color depth affects full-motion video playback. We can't measure this with Winstone 97, but we can use the Video Tests in WinBench 97. We'll copy the video test files to the hard disk before running the tests, thus removing the CD-ROM drive from the performance equation. Because WinBench 97 includes a large number of video test clips, we've chosen two of the action clips, one encoded with Cinepak, the other with Indeo. The Cinepak clip was recorded at a much higher resolution and data rate (640×480 and 900KB/sec) than the Indeo clip (160×120 at 300KB/sec).

First, let's take a look at the frame rate results. For every WinBench 97 Video Test clip, you can obtain up to five different results: maximum frame rate, temporal quality, visual quality, audio quality, and CPU utilization. The maximum frame rate measures the number of frames per second the PC was able to display while attempting to play back every frame of the clip as fast as possible, without sound.

As you can see in Figure 10.32, the lower-bandwidth Indeo clip plays back with approximately the same maximum frame rate, no matter what we set the color depth to. The Cinepak clip is a different story. With its increased resolution and data rate, it can clog up the graphics subsystem pipe when running at 16-bit color. Also, it essentially fails completely to run with 4-bit color, turning in a measly 2 frames per second *maximum* rate. Fortunately, few people would want to antici- pate running full-motion video clips with a 16-color palette.

Figure 10.32.

WinBench 97 Video Test frame rate results (for selected action clips) for the Pentium 133 machine, varying the color depth from 65,536 colors (16-bit) to 8 colors (4-bit).

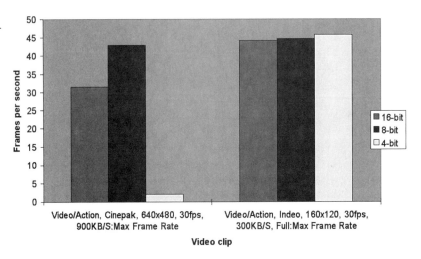

These results back up what we discovered with Winstone 97 and the Graphics Tests in WinBench 97: the graphics subsystem is much more efficient when running with 8-bit color as opposed to 16-bit color.

Another Video Test result we looked at was visual quality. Visual quality shows the PC's ability to keep up while playing the test clip, and is measured in number of frames dropped. The ideal result for this test is zero frames dropped. There were no real surprises here and the results were mostly independent of color depth. The exception is the Cinepak clip run at 4-bit color, reported dropping a whopping 442 frames. No other testing combinations reported dropped frames at all.

We've seen that upgrading the graphics board in our Pentium 133 provides us with some real-world gains, especially for business applications. The high-end applications would benefit more from more RAM or a speedier hard disk. In general, real-world comparison testing is the only sure determinant of the performance benefits you'll see by upgrading the graphics board. While the ads can be tempting, you might be better off ensuring your system isn't RAM-starved before upgrading the graphics board.

There still are some graphics tweaks you can perform to improve overall perfor- mance, though. The color depth of your display can significantly affect perfor- mance, and we recommend you set it to 8-bit color (256 colors) unless you absolutely have to set it higher for a particular application. Also, lowering your screen resolution can provide an additional performance boost, though not one as dramatic as lowering color depth.

10.5.6. Pentium 166

Starting with the Pentium 166 machine, we changed our graphics board testbed a bit. First off, we ran all tests at 32MB RAM, a typical amount for machines of this caliber. The Compaq Deskpro 5166 in our testbed came with a Matrox Millenium graphics board, so we needed a different graphics board for the upgrade. The newer board we decided to test with was the ATI 3D Pro Turbo PC2TV; the particular model in our testbed came with 8MB of VRAM. As the name suggests, this board also comes with a TV tuner. Is newer better? Is more VRAM better? These were questions we wanted to answer.

As you can see in Figure 10.33, newer isn't necessarily better, nor is more VRAM necessarily a performance boost. The Business Winstone 97 scores for the Pentium 166 did not change significantly whether we ran the Matrox Millenium board or the ATI 3D Pro Turbo PC2TV. There is a slight margin of variability when running Winstone, so a difference (a decrease in this case) of 1% or 2% between results isn't necessarily meaningful. A very real possibility is that there are other bottlenecks in the system preventing the new graphics card from having much effect on overall performance. Let's turn to WinBench 97 to look around any other potential bottlenecks.

Figure 10.33.

Business Winstone 97 results for the Pentium 166 machine, upgrading the graphics board from the Matrox Millenium to the ATI 3D Pro Turbo PC2TV.

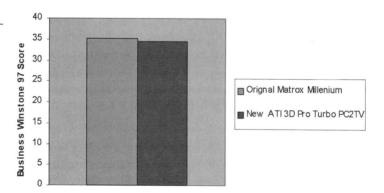

Ah ha! The WinBench 97 Business Graphics WinMark 97 results in Figure 10.34 show that the ATI board *is* pumping up the performance of the graphics subsystem as we expected it would. We see an overall performance increase of about 9% on the graphics portion of typical business applications. As with the Pentium 133, the applications that show the most improvement are word processing and spreadsheet. Those that show the least improvement are the publishing applications. In any case, this performance increase is being masked by other factors (as always, we'd guess a RAM or disk bottleneck) which is why the Winstone scores don't show this increase.

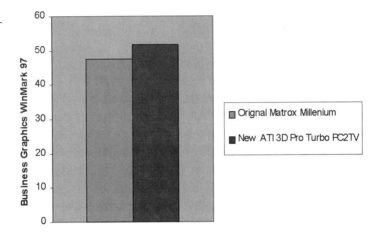

Figure 10.34.

WinBench 97 Business Graphics results for the Pentium 166 machine, upgrading the graphics board from the Matrox Millenium to the ATI 3D Pro Turbo PC2TV.

Let's check the High-End Winstone 97 results, to see if they shed any more light on the situation.

We see in Figure 10.35 that for High-End Winstone 97 applications, there's not much difference in the performance of these two graphics boards in this particular system. The only interesting data point is that the Picture Publisher result for the ATI board is almost 5% higher than that for the Matrox board. While this might be significant, it's probably no reason to run out and upgrade your graphics boards, even if Picture Publisher is the only application you run. Even more so than with Business Winstone 97, the applications in High-End Winstone 97 are likely to be bottlenecked by some subsystem other than graphics. So, to look at the graphics subsystem in isolation, we turn now once again to WinBench 97.

Figure 10.36 shows that like with the Business Graphics WinMark 97, the High-End Graphics WinMark 97 tests show the improvement the ATI upgrade provides. Overall, we get a 7% performance increase in high-end applications, close to the 8% we saw with business applications. The improvement shown by individual applications varies widely, with the CAD/3-D applications showing the least.

As with the Pentium 133, we conclude that the bottleneck in these systems is not in the graphics subsystem for the High-End Winstone 97 applications. While the newer graphics board does boost graphics performance, other factors prevent the real-world performance from mirroring this increase. Let's jump up to our

Pentium 200 MMX machine and take a look at the performance tweaks you can perform for free, by adjusting the color depth and screen resolution.

Figure 10.35.
High-End Winstone 97 results for the Pentium 166 machine, upgrading the graphics board from the Matrox Millenium to the ATI 3D Pro Turbo PC2TV.

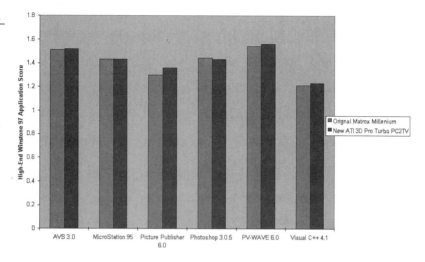

Figure 10.36.
WinBench 97 High-End Graphics results for the Pentium 166 machine, upgrading the graphics board from the Matrox Millenium to the ATI 3D Pro Turbo PC2TV.

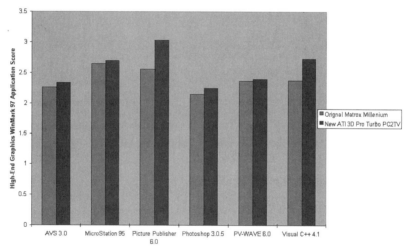

10.5.7. Pentium 200 MMX

This machine in our testbed also came outfitted with a Matrox Millenium board, but with more VRAM installed. Consequently, we have a broader range of possible color depth and resolution settings with this machine, so we decided to test as many of those as we could, with both Winstone 97 and WinBench 97.

In this set of tests, we left out 4-bit setting since we determined it to be impractical in testing our Pentium 133 machine. The results in Figure 10.37 are almost linear. Performance increases as we decrease the color depth. The most dramatic change is the 17% performance increase in the overall Business Winstone 97 score we see moving from 32-bit color depth to 8-bit color depth. In general, though, just dropping the color depth down one notch yields a significant performance boost.

Figure 10.37.

Business Winstone 97 results for the Pentium 200 MMX machine, varying the color depth from 4 billion colors (32-bit) to 256 colors (8-bit).

As we've seen before, Figure 10.38 shows how the Business Graphics WinMark 97 test results pull back the veil and reveal the innards of the graphics subsystem at work. Isolating this subsystem, we see that performance improves dramatically as we decrease color depth from 32 bits down to 24, 16, and finally 8 bits. While the overall Winstone score improved by about 17%, the overall Business Graphics score in WinBench improves over 180%! The graphics subsystem really has a lot less work to do if you don't overburden it with a huge color palette.

The trend continues with the applications in High-End Winstone 97 shown in Figure 10.39. The missing bars on the graph for the 32-bit depth setting indicate that the AVS test failed. Given what we've seen in years of testing, this is not unusual behavior nor should it be taken to show a problem with the hardware. The number one cause of Winstone test failures is buggy graphics drivers. This probably indicates a minor problem in the 32-bit color code in the particular driver we were running at the time of the test. As we mentioned before, it's important to keep your graphics drivers up-to-date. In general, we see that less colors means better performance. Even dropping down from 24-bit color to 16-bit color yields better performance. The lesson here is that you should be aware of what your color depth is set to, and you should set it as low as possible, given how you want to use your computer. Obviously, if you're doing serious image editing, you probably want to run with more than 256 colors. This tradeoff of performance versus viewing quality is one everyone needs to weigh carefully.

Figure 10.38.

WinBench 97 Business Graphics results for the Pentium 200 MMX machine, varying the color depth from 4 billion colors (32-bit) to 256 colors (8-bit).

Figure 10.39.

High-End Winstone 97 results for the Pentium 200 MMX machine, varying the color depth from 4 billion colors (32-bit) to 256 colors (8-bit).

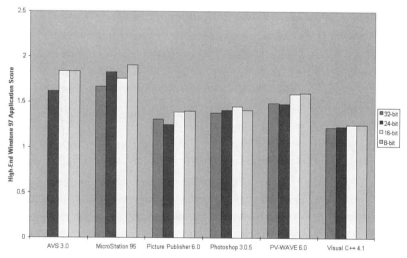

We also see the familiar stairstep results in Figure 10.40 with the High-End Graphics WinMark 97 playback. As color depth goes down, performance goes up. If we haven't convinced you to take a look at your Display Settings by now, we give up.

With the Pentium 133, we saw that screen resolution also affects performance, although not to the degree that color depth does. Let's take a look at some resolution tests we performed on our Pentium 200 MMX machine.

The performance change here in Figure 10.41 due to changing the resolution is quite small, small enough to be negligible given the variability of Winstone results. From this graph alone, it's tempting to posit that we can crank up the resolution to any value we wish, as long as we keep the color depth down.

Figure 10.40.

WinMark 97 High-End Graphics results for the Pentium 200 MMX machine, varying the color depth from 4 billion colors (32-bit) to 256 colors (8-bit).

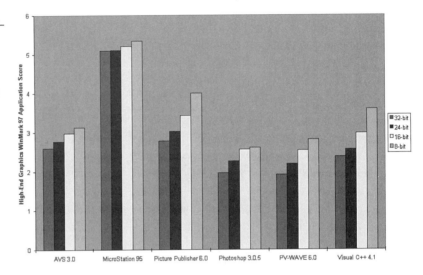

Figure 10.41.

Business Winstone 97 results for the Pentium 200 MMX machine, varying the screen resolution from 1024×768 to 640×480.

The Business Graphics WinMark 97 scores in Figure 10.42 show more improvement than the Winstone scores, but they are still not as impressive as what we saw when varying color depth. The most dramatic increase is in the overall score: we get a 7% improvement by downshifting from 1024×768 to 640×480. This improvement is significant, but is nothing compared to the 180% values we achieved by altering the color depth.

Figure 10.42.

WinBench 97 Business Graphics results for the Pentium 200 MMX machine, varying the screen resolution from 1024×768 to 640×480.

We can't run the High-End Winstone 97 tests at 640×480, but once again we see very little change when decreasing the resolution from 1024×768 to 800×600. We see in Figure 10.43 that AVS gets a real noticeable 20% boost, but the rest of the applications are pretty flat. The overall score improves by a little more than 3%. Again, these numbers are worth considering a change in resolution, but are nothing compared to the performance gains we got from decreasing the color depth.

Figure 10.43.

High-End Winstone 97 results for the Pentium 200 MMX machine, varying the screen resolution from 1024×768 to 800×600.

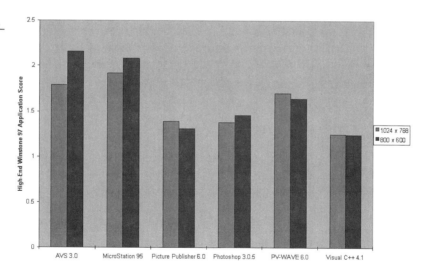

We've seen how graphics board upgrades are not necessarily as dreamy as they seem, because of bottlenecks elsewhere. We've also seen the importance of keeping your graphics drivers up-to-date. In terms of free performance improvements, nothing beats lowering your color depth setting to 16 bits or even 8 bits. Screen resolution, however, affects graphics performance to a much lesser degree.

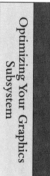

Optimizing Your Graphics Subsystem

10.6. Windows NT and the Graphics Subsystem

The changes to the graphics subsystem in Windows NT 4.0 are easy to see on the surface: the GUI (graphical user interface) looks very similar to that of Windows 95. Underneath the hood, though, NT 4.0 and Windows 95 (or Windows 98) are distinct operating systems. In general, NT trades security and reliability for performance. This is a generalization but you can easily see why it's true: every OS event in NT is more closely monitored than a similar type of event in Windows 95 or Windows 98.

That doesn't mean that Windows NT 4.0 hasn't been heavily optimized, compared to previous versions. In NT 4.0, the GDI (Graphics Device Interface) has been moved into the OS kernel itself. The kernel is the core of the operating system, and functions implemented in the kernel tend to run faster than those implemented elsewhere.

The software you can control, as with other versions of Windows, is the graphics driver that directly controls the graphics board you're using. As before, we recommend that you install the driver software that the board manufacturer wrote for your hardware, for better performance and more features.

Because the GUI of NT 4.0 is very similar to the Windows 95 and Windows 98 GUIs, editing the display driver settings is the same. You can control the resolution and color depth of your display with the Display Control Panel, accessible by right-clicking your desktop.

10.6.1. How We Tested

Because we were interested in seeing if upgrades under Windows 95 acted similarly to upgrades under NT 4.0, our testing strategy did not change for NT 4.0. We did test, however, all of the NT 4.0 systems with 32MB RAM, to reflect NT's greater appetite for RAM.

We ran both of our Winstone 97 test suites, Business and High-End. Also, we ran the Graphics Tests in WinBench 97. These are also known as the GDI Playback Tests, a term that more accurately describes these tests, because they play back the GDI (Graphics Device Interface) calls from the Winstone 97 tests, without any of the other calls (such as disk accesses). Because of this, the Graphics Tests in WinBench 97 measure the performance of only the graphics subsystem.

Unless we were specifically interested in testing changes in screen resolution or color depth, we tested at a resolution of 1024×768 and an 8-bit color depth (256 colors), as these are fairly typical settings.

As always, we completely defragmented the hard drives of each machine before we ran each test, even though we were testing graphics performance. This is always a good testing procedure to follow. We also ran each test immediately after a cold reboot.

10.6.2. Pentium 133

The Pentium 133 is the slowest machine in our testbed that we'll run NT 4.0 on. You can run on a machine with a slower processor, but we don't recommend it. We performed the same hardware upgrade that we did under Windows 95 to see if the performance differential changed under Windows NT 4.0.

We tested the Pentium 133 by upgrading its QVision PCI graphics board to a Matrox Millenium. You can see in Figure 10.44 that there is a significant performance improvement from the upgrade. The overall Business Winstone 97 score, that is, the measure of how well this machine runs typical business applications, improves by about 10%. The individual Business Winstone 97 categories show similar results varying from 4% to 12%.

Figure 10.44.

Business Winstone 97 results for the Pentium 133 machine, upgrading the graphics board from the Compaq QVision PCI to the Matrox Millenium.

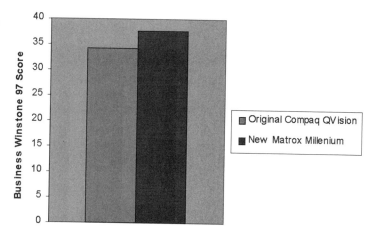

The Business Graphics WinMark 97 results in Figure 10.45 are, as we would expect, like the Business Winstone 97 results, only more so. Overall, we see a performance boost in the graphics subsystem of 32%. The Word Processing and Spreadsheet categories show the most improvement, while the database applications show the least. The word processing and spreadsheet applications (again, this is only the playback of the graphical operations of these programs) shows a whopping 42% increase. Even the database applications show a 14% speed-up in the graphics department.

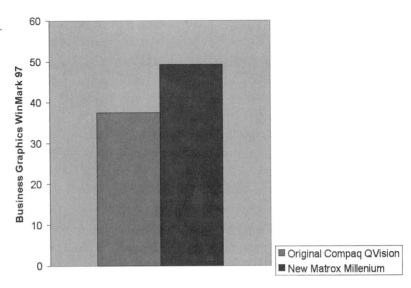

Figure 10.45.

WinBench 97 Business Graphics results for the Pentium 133 machine, upgrading the graphics board from the Compaq QVision PCI to the Matrox Millenium.

Unlike the results we saw under Windows 95, the High-End Winstone 97 results significantly improve with this graphics board upgrade. The overall score, the measure of how well this machine runs typical high-end applications, increases almost 5%—a small but meaningful amount. We can see in Figure 10.46 that the big winner is the PV-Wave application, whose score increases by over 10%. Let's take a look under the hood at the WinBench 97 graphics test scores.

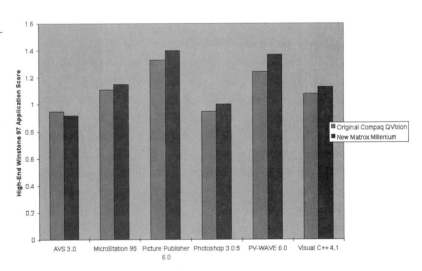

Figure 10.46.

High-End Winstone 97 results for the Pentium 133 machine, upgrading the graphics board from the Compaq QVision PCI to the Matrox Millenium.

The High-End Graphics WinMark 97 tests in Figure 10.47 tell a similar story. By focussing solely on the graphics subsystem, we can see that the Matrox board is significantly faster than the QVision PCI board, all else being held equal.

Individual applications see improvements of between 2% and 35% with PV-Wave the big winner. We get an overall speed-up in the High-End Graphics WinMark 97 of 19%. It would seem that NT is more capable of taking advantage of this particular graphics board upgrade than Windows 95 is. (It's impossible to compare the speed-up under NT 4.0 against the speed-up under Windows 98, because we ran tests on Windows 98 with newer versions of the benchmarks.) Let's see if this is also true of the Pentium 166.

Figure 10.47.
WinBench 97 High-End Graphics results for the Pentium 133 machine, upgrading the graphics board from the Compaq QVision PCI to the Matrox Millenium.

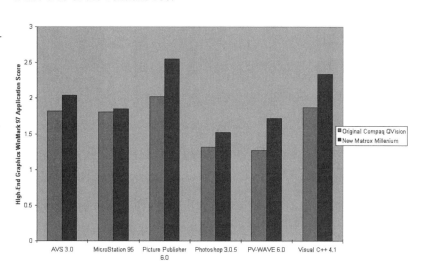

10.6.3. Pentium 166

We've seen that a hardware upgrade to a snazzier (for some definition of "snazzier") board didn't necessarily net us more real-world performance on our Pentium 166. We wanted to check and see if this was also true under NT 4.0. We also wanted to run some color depth and screen resolution studies under NT 4.0 to see if those curves looked similar to the ones we saw under Windows 95 and Windows 98. Finally, we wanted to check the effects of color depth on full-motion video performance. First, the hardware upgrade...

In Figure 10.48, the Pentium 166 shows no marked improvement when upgraded from the Matrox Millenium it shipped with the newer ATI 3D Pro Turbo PC2TV. Overall, we see about a 1% increase in the Business Winstone 97 result. That's below the margin of variability for Winstone 97 results, similar to the relatively flat curves we saw when we performed this same upgrade on this machine running Windows 95. The only real improvement is shown by the Publishing category; performance increases by about 5% with the hardware upgrade.

We have established with Winstone 97 that, for different applications, this board upgrade might or might not improve performance. In many cases, performance goes down. The Business Graphics WinMark 97 results in Figure 10.49 support this notion. Overall, the Business Graphics WinMark 97 is 5% lower after the hardware upgrade. As we saw with Business Winstone 97, though, the Publishing category shows some improvement.

Figure 10.48.

Business Winstone 97 results for the Pentium 166 machine, upgrading the graphics board from the Matrox Millenium to the ATI 3D Pro Turbo PC2TV.

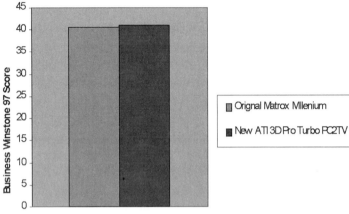

Figure 10.49.

WinBench 97 Business Graphics results for the Pentium 166 machine, upgrading the graphics board from the Matrox Millenium to the ATI 3D Pro Turbo PC2TV.

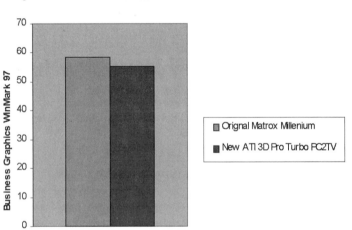

Overall, this board upgrade nets us no increase in the overall High-End Winstone 97 score. The individual application scores in Figure 10.50 show a more complicated story. Some scores went *down* for some applications after the upgrade. The big improvement is in Photoshop, which was almost 6% faster after the upgrade. Unless you know exactly which applications you'll be running and can pick accordingly, this graph shows you that choosing a graphics board isn't always as cut-and-dried as "Board A is faster than Board B."

Figure 10.50.
High-End Winstone 97 results for the Pentium 166 machine, upgrading the graphics board from the Matrox Millenium to the ATI 3D Pro Turbo PC2TV.

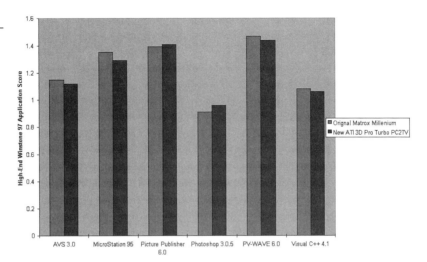

The High-End Graphics WinMark 97 results in Figure 10.51 are also a mixed bag. We see an overall improvement of about 6% (as opposed to the flat line we saw in High-End Winstone 97) but the individual applications show varying degrees of improvement or decline. All of the applications except Photoshop show better results with the original Matrox board. Photoshop outweighs them by showing a 48% improvement in performance with the ATI adapter. This graph should convince you to do your own testing if you're interested in only running one or two specific applications. We do have to note, however, that other advantages of the ATI 3D Pro Turbo PC2TV adapter, like its ability to display TV and higher resolutions and bit depths may make it a good choice any way.

Speaking of resolutions and bit depths, let's move on to testing their influence on performance under NT 4.0. Color depth isn't limited only by the amount of VRAM on the graphics board: it's also limited by the graphics driver itself. Because of differences between the NT graphics driver and the Windows 95 and Windows 98 graphics drivers, we tested at a slightly different set of color depths and resolutions under NT. The bottom line, as always, is that you can always do your own benchmarking to verify our conclusions for your specific situation.

This difference in the graphics driver structure should be apparent in the first graph in this section. We ran Business Winstone 97 on our Pentium 166 machine at three different color depths: 16 bits, 15 bits (32,768 colors), and 8 bits. (The use of 15 bits is because that allows for 5 bits each of red, green, and blue, unlike 16 bits.) We see very little change in the performance between the 16-bit and 15-bit color depths. The most significant data point in Figure 10.52 is that performance

Optimizing Your Graphics Subsystem

increases by about 9% on the overall score when we *decrease* the color depth to eight bits. This is similar to what we saw under Windows 95, although not quite as impressive. Our guess as to what's happening is this: the Windows NT graphics drivers are better optimized for higher color depths, as it's more likely that a typical NT user will be using a higher color depth.

Figure 10.51.

WinBench 97 High-End Graphics results for the Pentium 166 machine, upgrading the graphics board from the Matrox Millenium to the ATI 3D Pro Turbo PC2TV.

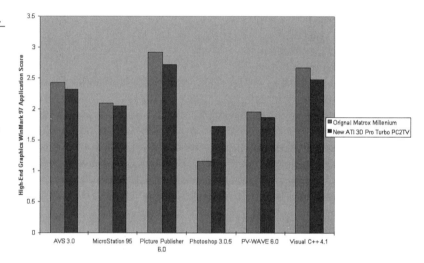

Figure 10.52.

Business Winstone 97 results for the Pentium 166 machine, varying the color depth from 65,536 colors (16-bit) to 256 colors (8-bit).

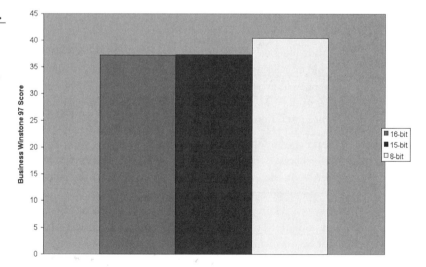

As we've seen countless times before, the Business Graphics WinMark 97 results back up the Winstone results. In this case, performance increases steadily as we drop from 16-bit to 8-bit resolution. The results in Figure 10.53 show the total increase to be almost 28%. If you don't mind the decreased number of colors for the work you do, you should seriously consider lowering your color depth.

Figure 10.53.

WinBench 97 Business Graphics results for the Pentium 166 machine, varying the color depth from 65,536 colors (16-bit) to 256 colors (8-bit).

We see more mixed behavior on the High-End Winstone 97 tests in Figure 10.54. For most of the tests, the change in performance isn't significantly above the level of variability we expect from Winstone 97 results. We see improvements as high as 10%, but on balance the overall improvement is only about 1%. Still, the best overall performance is that at the 8-bit color depth.

Figure 10.54.

High-End Winstone 97 results for the Pentium 166 machine, varying the color depth from 65,536 colors (16-bit) to 256 colors (8-bit).

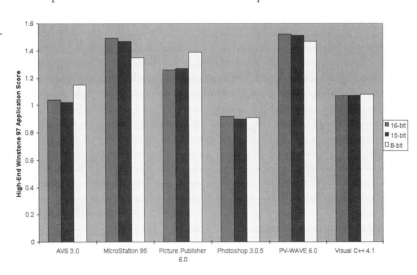

In Figure 10.55, the High-End Graphics WinMark 97 results show similarly mixed results as did the High-End Winstone 97 tests. Overall, there's no clear winner in the bit-depth department, one that scores best for every application. Still, the performance differentials are quite low, most below the variability limit for WinBench. If you are a heavy user of the applications in High-End Winstone 97, changing bit depth on a system like ours is not likely to yield you much in the way of performance improvements.

Figure 10.55.

WinBench 97 High-End Graphics results for the Pentium 166 machine, varying the color depth from 65,536 colors (16-bit) to 256 colors (8-bit).

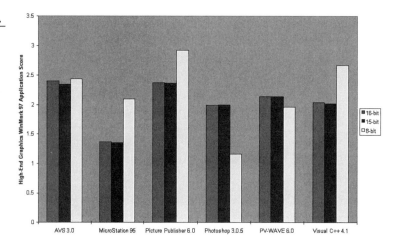

We have a much larger range of possible resolutions available to us, so let's see how screen resolution affects system performance.

The Business Winstone 97 results in Figure 10.56 exhibit the familiar resolution stair steps. The most drastic change is in the overall score, moving from the highest to the lowest resolution (1280×1024 to 640×480) we get a 14% performance boost. In general, just moving the resolution down a notch gives some kind of performance advantage, although the difference between the 1024×768 setting and the 1152×882 setting was quite small. You can look at this from the opposite direction: if you're currently running at 1024×768, but need a bit more screen real estate, moving up to 1152×882 (if your graphics card and driver support that) won't hurt your performance significantly. As always, your mileage may vary— different graphics adapters may exhibit different performance points due to different architectures. Run this experiment on your system and judge for yourself.

Our Business Graphics WinMark 97 tests from Figure 10.57 support what we saw with Winstone. An interesting data point here is the performance increase you get from dropping from 1024×768 to 800×600: a 10% boost! Remember, though, that's only how much the graphics subsystem speeds up. Overall, WinBench shows a 14% speed-up in the graphics subsystem when moving from 1280×1024 to 640×480 resolution. As we have noted elsewhere you need to balance the improved performance from lower resolution versus the potentially increased productivity you may experience from higher resolutions.

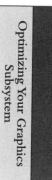

Figure 10.56.

Business Winstone 97 results for the Pentium 166 machine, varying the screen resolution from 1280×1024 to 640×480.

Figure 10.57.

WinBench 97 Business Graphics results for the Pentium 166 machine, varying the screen resolution from 1280×1024 to 640×480.

In Figure 10.58, the High-End Winstone 97 results show the increasing performance from decreasing resolution more dramatically. Remember to tailor your conclusions to the applications you run. Overall, the chart tells us that performance at 1024×768 is about 18% faster than performance at 1280×1024, for high-end applications. However, if you're a programmer, and you're only running development applications like Visual C++, you can see that there's almost no performance difference in running at any of the three resolutions we tested. Programmers notoriously need more screen real estate, and in this case we'd recommend the 1280×1024 setting.

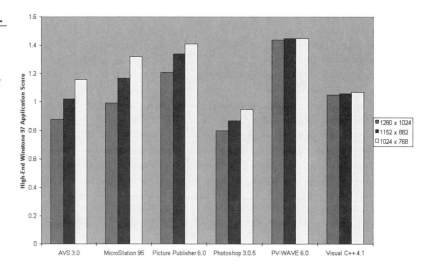

Figure 10.58.

High-End Winstone 97 results for the Pentium 166 machine, varying the screen resolution from 1280×1024 to 1024×768.

The High-End Graphics WinMark 97 results from Figure 10.59 support what we saw with High-End Winstone 97, although the lowest scoring resolution overall is the middle one, 1152×882, not the highest one, 1280×1024. Once again, we attribute this to driver optimization. The resolution of 1152×822 is not a popular resolution, and so the graphics driver code is probably not optimized as much for this resolution as for other resolutions.

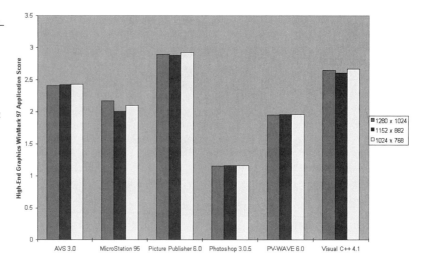

Figure 10.59.

WinBench 97 High-End Graphics results for the Pentium 166 machine, varying the screen resolution from 1280×1024 to 1024×768.

Finally, let's run some video tests under Windows NT to see another aspect of the influence of bit depth on performance.

The frame rate results in Figure 10.60 show an interesting picture. What you want to look at is which color depths produced maximum frame rates that are unacceptable. In the case of these 30 frames per second clips, we're looking for values significantly lower than 30. That points to the 24-bit color depth for the Cinepak clip, and the 32-bit and 8-bit color depths for the Indeo clip. Remember, these are two clips we chose out of many available in the WinBench Video Tests. The process of elimination tells us that the best performance is from the 16-bit or 15-bit color depth settings. Let's investigate further to see if other results from the Video Tests back this up.

Figure 10.60.

WinBench 97 Video Test frame rate results (for selected action clips) for the Pentium 166 machine, varying the color depth from 4 billion colors (32-bit) to 256 colors (8-bit)

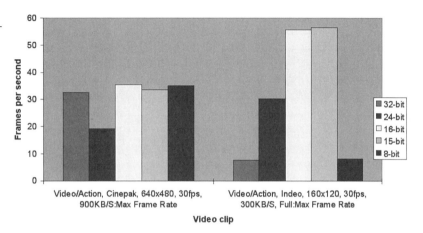

Visual quality measures the number of frames dropped; lower numbers are better. This graphs in Figure 10.61 show that the best performance is achieved at the 16-bit or 15-bit color depths. For the Indeo clip, these two settings were the only tested ones where no frames were dropped. For the higher bandwidth Cinepak clip, the PC dropped frames on all settings, but dropped the least on the 16-bit, 15-bit, and 8-bit settings. Once again, the process of elimination leads us to favor the 16-bit setting, which gives the same performance as 15-bit but with twice as many colors.

Figure 10.61.

WinBench 97 Video Test visual quality results (for selected action clips) for the Pentium 166 machine, varying the color depth from 4 billion colors (32-bit) to 256 colors (8-bit).

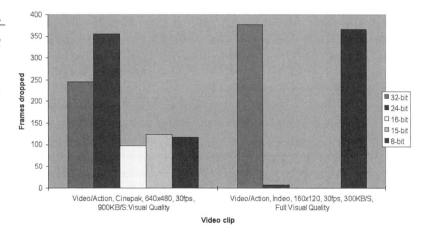

Finally, let's look at CPU Utilization. This is a measure of how much work the CPU has to expend to play a particular clip. Lower numbers are better because that means the CPU has more time to devote to other processes. In other words, playing the video does not bog down the rest of the computer. Figure 10.62 shows the 16-bit and 15-bit settings are once again the clear winners on the Indeo clip, turning in the lowest CPU utilization. We got mixed results on the Cinepak clip, where the results are not as differentiated.

Figure 10.62.

WinBench 97 Video Test CPU utilization results (for selected action clips) for the Pentium 166 machine, varying the color depth from 4 billion colors (32-bit) to 256 colors (8-bit).

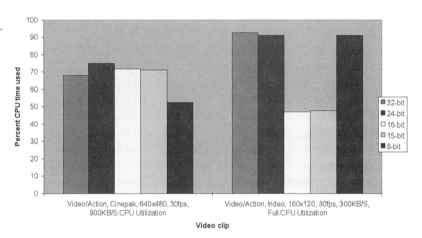

In conclusion, we'd stick with a 16-bit color depth on our NT machine if we were running lots of full-motion video clips.

10.7. The Bottom Line

At the cocktail party at the beginning of this chapter, our advice was to keep you graphics drivers up-to-date and to consider minimizing your screen resolution and color depth. The tests we've run show that these generalizations are true, and following them can yield real-world performance improvements. If you're in the market for a new graphics board, the upgrade tests in this chapter should give you more realistic expectations than you'd get from reading the average advertisement for a graphics accelerator. There are definitely performance benefits to be gained from a graphics upgrade, but we'd recommend you make sure your RAM and hard disk systems are in order first, to get the most out of the graphics upgrade.

We did not look at 3D graphics performance in this chapter. We discuss some of these issues in Chapter 14, "Optimizing for Games." The most important points about 3D graphics performance are that it is used largely for games and that it has improved dramatically (and it will continue to do so for another year or two). If you want 3D performance you really do need to get a new graphics adapter.

The other thing to take away from this chapter is that it's easy to experiment with your graphics subsystem. Even if you don't want to swap out hardware, changing color depth or resolution is so simple that you can try out a several different settings in a matter of minutes, deciding which combination works best for you. We just recommend that you take a few *more* minutes and run your own performance tests too.

10.8. Testing You Can Do

You'll have to con a computer dealer (or a friend) into loaning you a graphics board to duplicate some of the testing we performed in this chapter. Keep in mind that you can't just look at a Graphics WinMark score that a particular board achieved on another PC and compare it to your current graphics board in your PC. That violates the "apples-to-apple" comparison rule that we're always harping on. If you can get a hold of another graphics board, or several, you'll first want to run Winstone to find out if real-world performance improves or degrades as a result of swapping out graphics boards. Make sure to run the test suites that most closely resemble the applications that you typically run: either the Business Winstone tests or the High-End Winstone tests.

To get under the hood you should also run WinBench's Graphics Tests. Looking at WinBench results can help you determine how the graphics subsystem performance changes. If your graphics performance increases, but real-world performance does not, it's time to start hunting for bottlenecks elsewhere in your system.

Even if you can't get new graphics hardware to test, you can duplicate the testing we did with color depth and screen resolution. Just make sure that your PC is in the same state every time you test. As always, we recommend that you run tests immediately after defragging and then cold booting your machine.

NOTE	Complete directions for running Winstone and WinBench can be found in Appendices A and B.

10.9. From Here...

Graphics performance is the most obvious aspect of system performance, because Windows is a graphical user interface. In this chapter we've learned that you can improve graphics performance in more ways than just by buying a new graphics board. If you've tweaked your graphics subsystem, you might want to tune up other aspects of your system software configuration. If you really want to get the most out of your graphics subsystem, you should also pay attention to your processor subsystem and your CD-ROM subsystem (if you run full-motion video applications from CD).

Optimizing Your Graphics Subsystem

The following chapters will provide more information on the optimizations related to the graphics tips we've discussed in this chapter.

- Chapter 5, "Windows 98 Software Tuning," will show you other "free" (software-only) tuning tips for Windows 98 in addition to the graphics-related ones in this chapter.

- Chapter 6, "Windows 95 Software Tuning," will show you other "free" (software-only) tuning tips for Windows 95 in addition to the graphics-related ones in this chapter.

- Chapter 7, "Windows NT Software Tuning," will show you other "free" (software-only) tuning tips for Windows NT in addition to the graphics-related ones in this chapter.

- Chapter 12, "Optimizing Your CD-ROM Subsystem," will show you how to speed up your CD-ROM subsystem, thereby speeding up any CD-based full-motion video applications you're running.

Chapter

11

Optimizing Your Disk Subsystem

Space is something none of us ever have enough of, whether it's space in our garage or space on our hard drive. It's hard to believe that the original IBM PCs (and many other early personal computers) did not come with hard disks, but it's true. The operating system and applications ran from floppy disks, and that's where the computer stored all the data, too! This hassle ended with the advent of (relatively) cheap hard disk drives, also known at the time as Winchester drives or fixed disks. Today, only a masochist would dream of running a PC with no hard drive. (You'd only be able to use an older version of DOS if you wanted to do this).

The average user doesn't think much about the hard drive beyond its size when buying a new PC. It's hard to find a new PC with a hard drive smaller than 2GB these days. But hard drives are never as big as you need in the long run. Programs and data, like the junk in your garage, will grow to fill all available space. The file cache for your Internet browser and your swapfile chew up plenty of disk space, too. Eventually you're going to run out of room on your hard disk and you'll want to upgrade to a larger disk, or add a disk to your existing setup. If you want to find out how this can affect the overall performance of your PC, read on.

In this chapter, you will also learn:

- What your disk subsystem is

  The disk subsystem includes more than just the hard disk itself; it includes other components such as the disk controller, disk device drivers, hardware and software disk caches, and the system bus. In the following sections, you'll learn about the inner workings of this subsystem.

- How your operating system affects disk performance

  Windows NT, Windows 98 and Windows 95 can use the hard disk differently. You'll learn how to make decisions about your hard disk based on which operating system you're running.

- How to interpret common disk speed measurements

  The technical specification sheets for a particular hard disk can be confusing. You'll learn how to interpret the most common hard disk measurements. You'll also find out why these measurements aren't necessarily indicative of real-world performance.

- What techniques you can use to get the most out of multiple hard drives on your system

  Many times when you upgrade you add a second disk. How you use that second disk can have an influence on your system's performance. You'll learn the best way to set up a multiple hard drive system.

11.1. Cocktail Party Tips

If you're reading this book sequentially, you've spent some time at our "cocktail parties." Our trite tip for this chapter is "Space and speed, not specs!" Blurt this out at the cocktail party, and you're sure to get a puzzled look, even if your friend knows you're talking about PC hard drives.

What do we mean by "Space and speed, not specs"? The "space" part refers to disk space, that stuff you never have enough of. "Specs" are the endless technical specifications numbers manufacturers quote such as Average Seek Time, Average Rotational Latency, Rotational Speed, and Data Transfer Rate. "Speed" is the performance you really get in your applications. You should pay more attention to the space and the real performance rather than to one or the other of several engineering specifications the vendors tout on the box and in their literature.

As we'll see once we start digging into the performance data we obtained with WinBench and Winstone, it is hard to predict real-world performance simply by looking at the spec sheet for a particular hard drive. If you currently have a drive with a rotational speed of 2600 RPM (revolutions per minute), then will a drive with a rotational speed of 5400 RPM be twice as fast? If you've read other parts of this book, you'll probably be able to guess that the answer is "no." Just because a particular drive has specs that are significantly larger than your existing drive does not mean that it will be significantly faster.

To understand the reasoning behind this, you could either go to engineering school and learn about the mechanical and electrical theories behind the operation of a hard disk drive, or you could get a basic overview of hard drive operation and then perform real-world benchmark tests. We're going to do the latter.

In any case, given how much space the current popular software packages require, it's likely that you'll run out of space on your hard drive at some point. There are not many popular office suites we can point to which have decreased in size over the years! So, even if you're not concerned with performance, you're likely to want to upgrade your hard disk at some point. It's for this reason that we suggest that you pay more attention to how much disk space you require, rather than what the specifications of the latest drives to hit the market are.

11.2. What's a Disk Subsystem?

We'll use the phrase *disk subsystem* in this chapter along with hard disk or hard drive. Understanding this distinction is the key to understanding whether or not a hard drive upgrade will affect the performance of your machine. "Find the bottleneck!" will always be our mantra. If you install a new Ultra-SCSI disk drive in your machine without the corresponding Ultra-SCSI controller, you won't see the performance increase that the disk manufacturers hype in their ads.

Optimizing Your Disk Subsystem

The disk subsystem of a Windows PC includes the hard drive, disk controller, disk device drivers, hardware and software disk caches (if any), and the system bus which carries data from the disk controller to and from the processor subsystem. All of these factors combine to influence disk subsystem performance; you can't look at your hard disk mechanism in a vacuum and expect it to completely determine disk subsystem performance.

11.2.1. Disk Basics

The good news about hard drives is that they constantly get bigger and cheaper. They also get faster, and their physical dimensions decrease too. The bad news is that, as you might've noticed, your files expand to fill the available space. Nowadays it's hard to find a new system for sale with less than a 2GB hard drive. That's 400 hundred times the size of the 5MB hard drives that folks installed in the original PC-XT models. We don't even want to remember the personal computers we had that didn't have a hard drive at all! Strangely, those 5MB hard drives seemed big when we got them, but quickly ran out of room. Sound familiar?

Your two basic choices in hard drives are SCSI and IDE, but these terms really describe two different families of drive types. SCSI stands for Small Computer System Interface, while IDE stands for Integrated Drive Electronics. Simply put, SCSI drives are more suitable for servers or for very-high-end power users, while IDE is for the rest of us. SCSI typically is larger and sometimes faster than IDE, but also more expensive. If you're upgrading, this decision is already made for you, and that's fine. On-board controllers are built into IDE drives (also called ATA or Fast ATA) which in turn connect to your system motherboard; you don't need a separate controller card as with SCSI.

SCSI and IDE differ in terms of transfer rates. Transfer rates can be given as either burst or sustained. These differ for all the sub-flavors of IDE and SCSI. If you're concerned about these rates, sustained is the more meaningful one. Another number you'll see bandied about is spin rate or rotational speed, expressed in rpm (revolutions per minute). While you can expect a 10,000-RPM drive to be faster than a 3,000-RPM drive, don't use these values as meaningful performance comparisons. That's what the benchmarks Winstone and WinBench are for!

Other than performance and space, another thing to keep in mind when buying a drive is the size of the available drive bay in your machine. If you've got a free 5.25" bay, you'll probably need to buy a mounting kit to install a 3.5" drive there. The mounting kit is simply a bracket that screws on to the hard drive. The drive/ bracket combo then fits into the 5.25" bay with more screws. If you've only got 3.5" drive bays free, don't buy an old 5.25" drive!

The IDE Family

As we mentioned, drive terminology is an alphabet soup of confusion. Different manufacturers use different terms to describe similar drives that generally fall under the IDE umbrella. IDE, Enhanced IDE (EIDE), ATA, Fast ATA, Fast ATA-2, Ultra DMA, Ultra ATA, Ultra DMA/33, Fast ATA-3. Wow! The good news is that all of these specifications are backward compatible. If you plug a Fast ATA-3 drive into your existing IDE connection, it will work, but only at the old speed. The current standard seems to be moving to Ultra DMA.

Another acronym you'll see is PIO. Programmed Input/Output mode is the data-transfer technique. PIO Mode 0 was the original ATA spec, 3.33MB/sec maximum. Fast ATA supports PIO Mode 3, 11.1MB/sec maximum. Fast ATA-2 goes to PIO Mode 4, 16.6MB/sec. Now Ultra DMA (or Ultra ATA) supports various new modes up to 33.3MB/sec.

In the end, as long as you match up the highest/fastest mode your drive supports with your motherboard settings, this is all moot. What really matters is real-world performance. Use your BIOS to check that your motherboard is set to use the PIO mode that your hard disk supports. You can also determine whether you've got IDE support or EIDE support by looking at your BIOS. IDE supports two drives; EIDE four, and your BIOS should show either two or four "slots" for hard drives.

The size of IDE family drives is constantly increasing, but if you need a really huge drive, you've got to go SCSI.

The SCSI Family

SCSI is best at handling simultaneous requests and supports more drives: up to seven on one controller (assuming a single channel controller). SCSI also comes in a variety of flavors: SCSI (5MB/sec burst rate), Fast SCSI-2 (10MB/sec burst rate), Wide SCSI-2 (widened the bus to 16-bits from 8), and Fast/Wide SCSI-2 (combines the two to approach 20MB/sec burst rate). SCSI-3 comes in Ultra SCSI or Ultra Wide SCSI, which goes to 40MB/sec. This doubling is likely to continue.

Beyond hard drives, SCSI can support a wide variety of devices: tape drives, CD-ROM drives, removable media, and so forth.

Other Specifications

Other numbers (other than burst and sustained transfer rates) are used to describe drives. We recommend real-world testing! But let's define these terms so you can make some sense of them. Average access time is measured in milliseconds and tells you how long it takes the drive head to reach a spot on the disk on average. Faster is better, as the drive will find specific data that much faster. Rotation (spin) rate tells you how fast the disk spins underneath the drive head. Faster is better, because that much more data spins by underneath the head per unit time. However, you can't just compare spin rates, because data density on the disk itself affects the real transfer rate. Additionally, access time is determined by two factors: seek time and latency. Seek time has to do with how quickly the drive head can reach a particular track. Latency has to do with how quickly the disk spins to the right spot on that track.

Another touted number is the amount of cache memory on the drive. We've described cache a number of times and places in this book. Quite simply this cache allows the drive to get data it thinks you will need and store it in RAM for faster access later if you do need it. All of these specifications matter, and have some effect on performance, but you shouldn't use them to predict how much of a real performance boost you'll get from a particular drive. As always, that's what WinBench and Winstone are for.

11.3. Back it up!

Everyone, from the corporate user to the home aficionado, should back up their disks daily. No, really. We mean it! Backing up your disk, like scanning for viruses, is one of those chores that everyone thinks they can get by without doing.

Having a backup copy of your work is especially important when you're tinkering with the hard drives. If you add a second hard drive to your machine and then accidentally format your old disk instead of your new one, you will lose all of your data! And you know you will never be able to reproduce that high score in your favorite game (or your 1995 tax return!)

If your floppy drive is the only suitable backup device, you're in for a lengthy if not impossible backup process if you want to back up your entire hard drive. While hard disks have gotten a lot higher in capacity, floppies have not. Swapping in all those floppy disks can be a real strain on the elbow. If that's your only option, though, we still recommend that you back up to floppy disks. You can ease the strain by only backing up your data files: things like your Word and Excel documents, which you should be keeping in directories separate from the applications themselves. That way, if your hard disk does fail or crash in some way, you can reinstall Windows and your applications from the CDs they came on and then restore all of your documents. Of course, you'll lose all of the customizations and tweaks you've made to your OS this way. If you've got the money, it's worth investing in a tape drive or in one of the popular forms of removable media such as the Iomega Zip Drive or the SyQuest Syjet.

11.4. To Partition Or Not?

If you're adding a new hard drive to your system, it's tempting just to slap it in and, if it's preformatted for Windows, accept the manufacturer's idea of how it should be partitioned. We recommend that you take some time to think about how you'd like your hard drives partitioned. If you do it before you've actually placed data on the drive, you'll save yourself a lot of hassles later.

Partitions are separate areas on your hard disk. If you're only running one operating system on your machine, these separate areas just seem like different hard disks instead of one large hard disk. For instance, you could partition your 4GB hard drive into a 2GB C: partition, a 1GB D: partition, and a 1GB E: partition. Even though there's only one real hard drive, Windows Explorer shows you C:, D:, and E: drives. Partitioning is useful because you can use the different partitions to store data and programs that "belong" together. For instance, you could store the Windows OS on the C: partition, programs on the D: partition, and data on the E: partition. That way, you'd only need to back up your E: partition (given that you've got CD copies of your OS and applications).

The bottom line is: Take some time to think about how you want to partition your new disk, especially if you've bought a very large disk.

You can also use partitions to run more than one operating system on your PC, but that's beyond the scope of this book.

11.5. Disk Performance Options

We will look at a few different performance characteristics in the following testing sections. We will examine what the performance differences are between different hard disks. Our goal here is not to tell you what disk to buy. At the rate disk drives change, none of these are likely to still be on the shelves when you read this book. Instead, we want to show you the kinds of performance differences that typical hard disks will exhibit.

Many people decide to add a second hard disk rather than replace their original one. This tends to be easier since you don't have to move all of your old stuff around and gives you the advantage of having the storage capacity of both drives. A potential performance enhancement strategy is to move the Windows swapfile to the newer disk. Why would you want to do this? Many folks recommend this configuration to optimize performance. As you might remember from Chapter 9, the swapfile is the area on your hard disk which Windows uses to "swap" pages to and from system RAM when applications require more physical RAM than your system has. Depending on how much RAM you have and what applications you're running, swapping can be frequent or infrequent. The idea behind moving the swapfile to a second disk is that Windows can be reading and writing the

Optimizing Your Disk
Subsystem

swapfile at the same time that it's reading and writing data to your main hard disk. We wanted to test this theory. Another advantage is that the newer disk is probably the faster one and swap performance is something that we all want to maximize.

To make a second drive the Windows swap device do the following:

1. Right-click on "My Computer" on your desktop. (You may need to minimize application windows you have open to do this.) This displays the context menu for "My Computer" (or whatever you've named your machine).

2. Select the Properties option by clicking on it. This displays the System Properties dialog box.

3. Choose the Performance tab by clicking on it.

4. Under Advanced Settings, click on the Virtual Memory button. This brings up the Virtual Memory dialog box.

5. Click on the radio button entitled "Let me specify my own virtual memory settings."

6. Click on the drop down box entitled Hard disk and choose the second disk you've installed in your system, for instance, D:.

7. Click on the OK button twice to close the dialog boxes. When Windows prompts you to restart your system, click on OK again.

Look in the Windows 95 and Windows NT sections for details on how this technique fared in terms of performance in our tests. We also examine in the Windows NT section the performance differences between Windows NT's different types of filesystems.

The variety of systems we used in the testing we did for this chapter is not as broad as for of the other chapters. Testing on all the machines in our testbed would've produced a book-sized compilation of graphs on disk performance alone! While we limited the number of systems we tested on, the basic conclusions reached on the machines below should apply to your machine, whether yours is a slower or faster model.

11.6. Windows 98 and the Disk Subsystem

As we've mentioned throughout this book, Windows 98 and Windows 95 act very similarly, performance-wise. The big change between Windows 95 and Windows 98 as far as the disk subsystem goes is a change in the filesystem.

Windows 98 supports a new version of the VFAT filesystem, called FAT32. The version of VFAT in the original release of Windows 95 was known as FAT16. The layout of bytes on a FAT32 drive is very different from the layout on a FAT16 drive. FAT32 was designed especially for Windows 98; if you run multiple operating systems on your computer, the other operating systems will not be able to use any FAT32 partitions, unlike FAT16 which is understood by many operating systems. Of course, if you upgrade your existing PC to Windows 98, the filesystem will remain FAT16 until you use the FAT32 conversion utility. We looked at the performance difference between FAT16 and FAT32 in Chapter 5, "Windows 98 Software Tuning."

11.6.1. How We Tested

We attempted to run both Winstone 98 and the Disk WinMark tests from WinBench 98. The Disk WinMark tests play back the exact disk operations that the corresponding applications in Winstone 98 perform. So, for each Winstone overall, suite, or application score, there is a corresponding Disk Test score from WinBench 98. Because the Disk Tests only play back disk operations, they isolate and report on the performance of the disk subsystem.

As always, we completely defragmented the hard drives before we ran each test. This was especially important because we were measuring disk performance. Comparing a heavily fragmented hard disk to a new one with no fragmentation would not be valid. We also ran each test immediately after a cold reboot. We attempted to run tests on our Pentium 200 MMX machine, but as you'll see we ran into some problems.

11.6.2. Pentium 200 MMX

The Pentium 200 MMX uses SCSI disks, not EIDE disks. The unit came with a Seagate Barracuda 4LP disk, while our "upgrade disk" was a SCSI version of the Quantum Fireball ST. The specs on the installed Barracuda were, in general, better than those of the Fireball ST. For instance, the Barracuda is a 7200 rpm drive while the Fireball ST is a 5400 rpm drive. We wanted to see if this difference in specs translated into a difference in real-world performance. We have to point out that these results are not meant to knock this particular model of Quantum disk, as it is less expensive than the Seagate disk. You may have a similar disappointment in buying a new drive if you are not careful, however. Both disks used the Ultra-SCSI interface, which was supported by this machine.

Here's where we would normally look at the Winstone results for these two disk drives. Unfortunately, we can't make that comparison. When we ran Winstone on this system with the Seagate Barracuda drive installed, it ran to completion except for the Task Switching tests. This is fairly common, as you may see throughout the rest of this book. In many cases, the Task Switching portion of Winstone 98 does not run to completion on a Windows 98 system. This is not a big problem because it is not an essential part of Windows 98. When we attempted to run Winstone 98 on this system with the Quantum Fireball ST installed, we met with complete failure. Winstone timed out and was then unable to clean up the system without a re-boot, thereby losing all of the results from all of the tests. This is a very rare problem, and is not a poor reflection on the Quantum drive, Winstone 98, or Windows 98. It's something you'll run into when you're out on the bleeding edge of benchmarking. We'll have to settle for just WinBench 98 Disk WinMark 98 results for these two drives.

In Figure 11.1 we see that the Barracuda is indeed faster than the Fireball ST, as we'd suspect from the specifications. The disk subsystem performance is about 23% faster with the Barracuda drive. Note that this is still less than the 33% increase in rotational speed between the two disks. You should never assume that technical specifications translate directly into real-world performance gains. Normally, we would also have Winstone results here which would show an even smaller overall system performance difference between the two drives.

Figure 11.1.

Business Disk WinMark 98 results for the Pentium 200 MMX machine, varying the hard disk from the Seagate Barracuda 4LP to the Quantum Fireball ST.

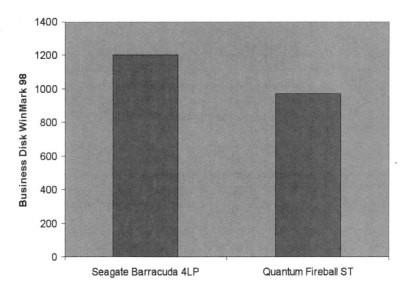

In Figure 11.2, the Barracuda is uniformly faster than the Fireball ST on the Business Disk WinMark 98 category tests, too. What's interesting here is that the%age speed-up (or slow-down, depending on which direction you read the graph) is very close for all of the different categories—always in the range of 20% to 26%. This is a different situation than we've seen with other subsystems like CPU or graphics, where different application types benefit drastically different amounts from an upgrade. Let's take a look at the High-End Disk WinMark 98 results and see if those reveal additional data about the performance differences of these two disk drives.

Figure 11.2.

Business Disk WinMark 98 category scores for the Pentium 200 MMX machine, varying the hard disk from the Seagate Barracuda 4LP to the Quantum Fireball ST.

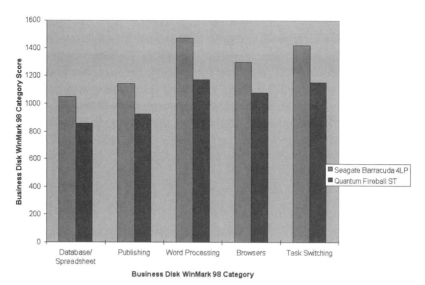

The High-End Disk WinMark 98 score in Figure 11.3 shows an even bigger drop than did the Business score. It drops by about 27% as we move from the Barracuda to the Fireball ST. All of the performance differentials we've seen so far have been in the 20% to 27% range, but this is the largest. Thus, we can conclude that the high-end applications take better advantage of the faster disk subsystem than do normal business applications.

Figure 11.3.

High-End Disk WinMark 98 results for the Pentium 200 MMX machine, varying the hard disk from the Seagate Barracuda 4LP to the Quantum Fireball ST.

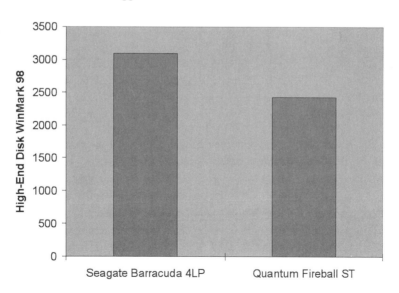

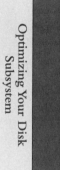

Optimizing Your Disk Subsystem

Looking at the individual application scores in Figure 11.4, we see even more drastic differences for certain applications. AVS and Visual C++ show the most benefit from using the Barracuda as opposed to the Fireball ST: about a 36% boost in disk subsystem performance for those applications. FrontPage 97 shows the least change, only about 14%. From the other testing on Windows 95 and Windows NT in this book, we have to note that you would see a smaller difference in overall system performance due to this configuration change. WinBench by design highlights a particular system and Winstone by its nature mutes the effect of any one subsystem because it mashes them all together.

Figure 11.4.

High-End Disk WinMark 98 application scores for the Pentium 200 MMX machine, varying the hard disk from the Seagate Barracuda 4LP to the Quantum Fireball ST.

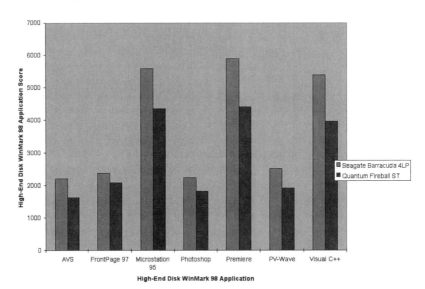

While we were thwarted from doing as much disk testing on Windows 98 as we'd have liked, our overall conclusion—don't trust specs, trust good benchmarks—still holds true, as we've shown. In general, the more sophisticated the application you're running, the more you can take advantage of a faster disk subsystem on Windows 98. You may want to look at the more extensive testing we were able to do on Windows 95 in the next section. Given the many similarities between the two operating systems, the conclusions in that section are very likely to hold true for Windows 98 as well.

11.7. Windows 95 and the Disk Subsystem

When folks migrated from Windows 3.1 to Windows 95, the most obvious change was in the user interface. One of the new features of the user interface was long filenames. No longer were you limited to the old 8.3 naming convention that had been around since IBM and Microsoft first released DOS. Long filenames are just one obvious feature that's available now because of underlying changes to how Windows handles hard disks.

Under the hood, what's changed is the filesystem code. The filesystem is the logical structure of files as stored on a hard disk. During the DOS/Windows 3.1 era, this filesystem was known as FAT, File Allocation Table. With the advent of Windows 95, the filesystem code was re-written as 32-bit protected mode software, and this new filesystem is known as VFAT, or Virtual FAT. Unlike the old FAT filesystem, VFAT allows directory entries for files to contain filenames of up to 255 characters.

Long filenames aren't the only new feature of the VFAT filesystem. Because VFAT is written in 32-bit protected mode code, it's faster than the older FAT filesystem.

In this section we're going to look at the effects of upgrading an existing hard disk and at moving the Windows 95 swapfile to a second hard disk. If you'd like to learn more about Windows 95 tweaks you can perform on the hard disk subsystem, such as defragmentation, check out Chapter 6, "Windows 95 Software Tuning."

11.7.1. How We Tested

We ran both Winstone 97 suites, Business and High-End, for the testing in this section. In the end, Winstone will always tell us what the real-world performance boost (or drop) is for a given upgrade or system tweak. We also ran the Disk Tests in WinBench 97. These tests play back the exact disk operations that the corresponding applications in Winstone 97 perform. So, for each Winstone overall, suite, or application score, there is a corresponding score from WinBench 97. Because the disk tests only play back disk operations without other bottlenecks coming into play, these tests report on the performance of the disk subsystem in isolation. They do not take into account, however, swapping activity. This limitation makes the correlation of Winstone and WinBench results more difficult than in the graphics subsystem.

As always, we completely defragmented the hard drives of each machine before we ran each test. This was especially important because we were measuring disk performance. Comparing a heavily fragmented hard disk to a new one with no fragmentation would not be valid. We also ran each test immediately after a cold reboot.

11.7.2. Pentium 133

Our Pentium 133 from Compaq came with a 1GB disk drive, a Quantum Fireball 1080A. The specifications for this drive state that it has an average seek time of 12 milliseconds, and uses the ATA-2 or Fast-ATA interface, which means it can theoretically burst out 16.6MB of data per second. Quantum loaned us a newer hard drive, a Fireball ST 4.3. At 4GB, this drive quadrupled our disk space, but of course we were more interested in how it would affect performance. The average seek time was rated at less than 10 milliseconds, but this drive supports the Ultra-ATA interface, which means that the buffer-to-host data rate can be as high as 33.3MB per second. This sounds very impressive, and if you'll pardon us for a moment, we're going to play dumb and pretend that we really expected this drive to be twice as fast as our existing drive, because 33.3MB/second is twice as much as 16.6MB/second. Now, let's take a look at our trusty Business Winstone 97 score and see if performance really doubles.

Nope, it doesn't! You probably knew it wouldn't, either, but this illustrates an important lesson: Don't let specs blind you to real-world performance measurements. Overall, we see in Figure 11.5 over a 4% increase in performance by installing the new disk. Before we figure out why this is happening, let's look at some other test results.

Figure 11.5.

Business Winstone 97 results for the Pentium 133 machine, upgrading the hard disk from the Quantum Fireball 1080A to the Quantum Fireball ST.

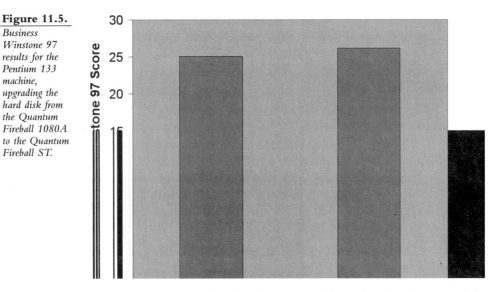

The category scores for Business Winstone 97 shown in Figure 11.6 reveal that the Publishing category applications benefit most from this disk upgrade; the score increases by about 6%. The other two categories, Database and Word Processing/Spreadsheet, increase by about 4%. This increase is above the margin of variability for Winstone 97, but it is still rather small.

The High-End Winstone 97 chart in Figure 11.7 looks even less impressive (given our initial assumptions that performance would double). Swapping to the newer disk gives us little more than a 2% increase in the High-End Winstone 97 score. Let's take a look at the individual High-End applications and see what applications get the biggest benefit from the upgrade.

Figure 11.6.

Business Winstone 97 category results for the Pentium 133 machine, upgrading the hard disk from the Quantum Fireball 1080A to the Quantum Fireball ST.

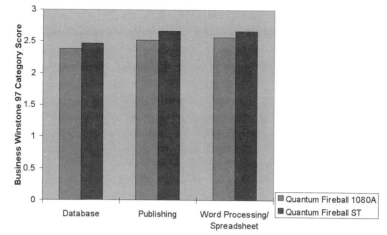

Figure 11.7.

High-End Winstone 97 results for the Pentium 133 machine, upgrading the hard disk from the Quantum Fireball 1080A to the Quantum Fireball ST.

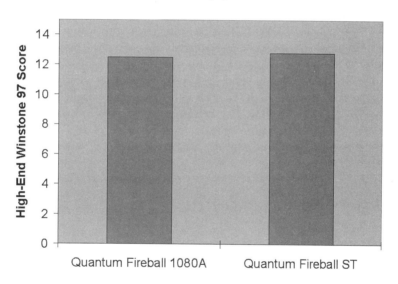

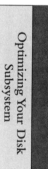

Optimizing Your Disk Subsystem

All of the applications in Figure 11.8 show at least some small improvement, but the standouts are Picture Publisher and Photoshop, improving 5% and 3% respectively. If you're reading this book in sequence, you might try predicting what we'll see with the WinBench results. As we've seen with other subsystems, often the Winstone score does not improve while the pertinent WinBench score does. This is a sign that the performance bottleneck in the system lies elsewhere. If this were the case with this disk upgrade (because the system was RAM-starved, say), we'd expect that the WinBench scores would show dramatic improvement, even though the gains we've seen with Winstone are not outstanding.

Figure 11.8.

*High-End
Winstone 97
individual
application
results for the
Pentium 133
machine,
upgrading the
hard disk from
the Quantum
Fireball 1080A
to the Quantum
Fireball ST.*

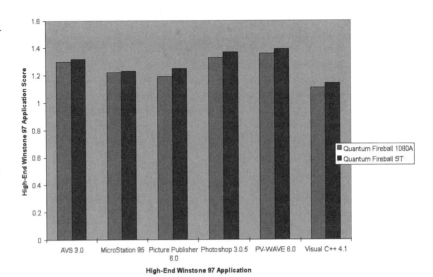

Figure 11.9 shows our assumption was a bad one. The performance differential measured by the Business Disk WinMark 97 mirrors that of Business Winstone 97, about 4%. Part of the reason that the score is not higher as we surmised is probably due to the fact that some of the performance increase is due to swapping activity which is not measured by WinBench. Swapping performance does contribute, however, to the performance in Winstone, as is does with most applications.

Figure 11.9.

*Business Disk
WinMark 97
results for the
Pentium 133
machine,
upgrading the
hard disk from
the Quantum
Fireball 1080A
to the Quantum
Fireball ST.*

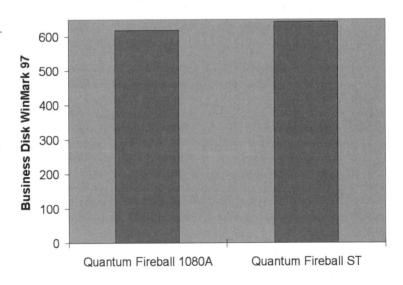

The category scores for the Business Disk WinMark 97 tests in WinBench 97 also mirror what we saw with the Business Winstone 97 categories. Figure 11.10

indicates that the applications in the Publishing category show the most improvement: about 5.5%. The Database and Word Processing/Spreadsheet categories trail that improvement by about a percent or so. This performance improvement confirms that the one we saw in Business Winstone 97 was a real one. And while the size of the improvement is not too great, it is a good reason to make sure the hard disk you buy is a good one.

Figure 11.10.

Business Disk WinMark 97 category scores for the Pentium 133 machine, upgrading the hard disk from the Quantum Fireball 1080A to the Quantum Fireball ST.

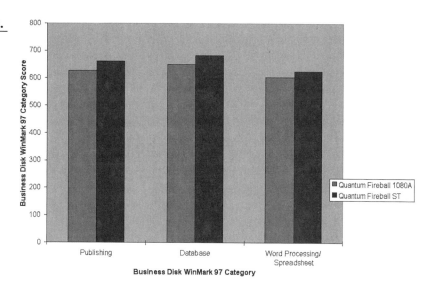

As we turn to the High-End Disk WinMark 97 score shown in Figure 11.11 we see that it barely changed at all! The High-End Disk WinMark 97 tests in WinBench 97 play back the exact same disk operations, in sequence, as their corresponding High-End Winstone 97 tests. With High-End Winstone 97, we saw an increase in the score that was barely above the margin of variability for Winstone. This is true with WinBench also.

We see some differences between the WinBench results here in Figure 11.12 and the earlier corresponding Winstone ones in Figure 11.8. With WinBench 97, Picture Publisher is the loser with a decrease of over 2%. Visual C++ in contrast comes out ahead with the upgrade by nearly 7%. The influence of swapping on Winstone 97 and its lack of influence on WinBench 97 is the most likely culprit. The most important things to take away from these numbers is that the improvement is minor and varies from application to application.

The summary of all of these results is that there is a real improvement, but hardly a big one. So what's going on? Where's our big increase the new drive's specs seemed to promise? The answer is two-fold. First, there was never a big increase to be had in the first place. Concentrating on a single specification (in this case, data rate from buffer-to-host) instead of looking at real-world benchmark results is wrongheaded. We could just as easily have concluded that performance wouldn't change because both disks have the same rotational speed (5400 rpm). Or, we could have predicted that performance would increase about 20%, because average seek time went from 12 milliseconds with the Fireball 1080A to less than ten milliseconds with the Fireball ST 4.3. Even in the absence of real-world results (a position we never like to be in) you shouldn't concentrate on one particular technical specification to the exclusion of all others.

Figure 11.11.

High-End Disk WinMark 97 results for the Pentium 133 machine, upgrading the hard disk from the Quantum Fireball 1080A to the Quantum Fireball ST.

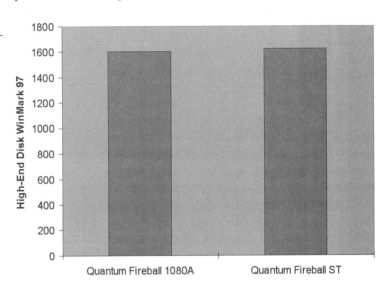

Figure 11.12.

High-End Disk WinMark 97 application scores for the Pentium 133 machine, upgrading the hard disk from the Quantum Fireball 1080A to the Quantum Fireball ST.

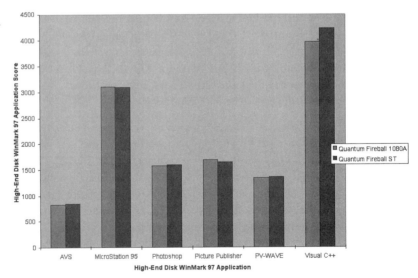

The second part of the answer as to what's going on is this: We're not getting the most out of this upgrade. Our Pentium 133 machine does not support the Ultra-ATA interface that the new disk supports. We're not *getting* any of the performance gains provided by Ultra-ATA, because the disk controller doesn't support that standard. This might be obvious to the more technically inclined reader, but it's a very important point. If you're going to upgrade a particular component in your system, you've got to make sure the rest of your system can take advantage of the capabilities of that new component. In this case, the motherboard on this Pentium 133 (where the disk controller is located) simply won't support Ultra-ATA capabilities. We're getting a slight performance boost out of the new disk, but mainly we're getting a lot more disk space.

Let's instead look at leaving both disks in the system and moving the swapfile to the second disk (the new one). This change will let application and data access go to the first drive and swapping go to the new drive.

The gain we see in Figure 11.13 with Business Winstone 97 with our new swapfile configuration is about the same as we saw simply by exchanging the old disk for the newer disk, about 4%. While this isn't enough to make us run out and buy second disks just to relocate the swapfile, it is above the margin of variability for Winstone 97 and therefore it's of interest if you want to get every possible bit of performance out of your system. These results also show the importance of swapping to performance. The applications are still on the old, slower drive, but they are operating 4% faster because of the new swap drive. This improvement is probably attributable to both the faster speed of the swap drive and the inherent advantage of being able to use two drives.

Figure 11.13.

Business Winstone 97 results for the Pentium 133 machine, varying the swapfile location from the same disk to a second disk.

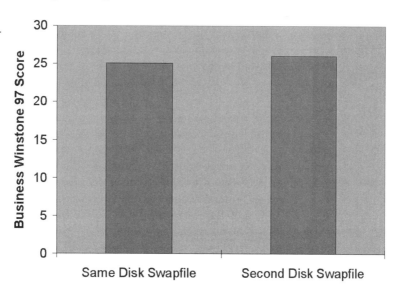

Splitting Business Winstone 97 out into its category scores, we see in Figure 11.14 that the Publishing and the Database applications get a 5% to 6% increase in performance with this new configuration, while the Word Processing/Spreadsheet applications eke out only a 2% increase. This is probably due to the greater stress the Publishing and Database applications place upon virtual memory (swapping).

Figure 11.14.

Business Winstone 97 category results for the Pentium 133 machine, varying the swapfile location from the same disk to a second disk.

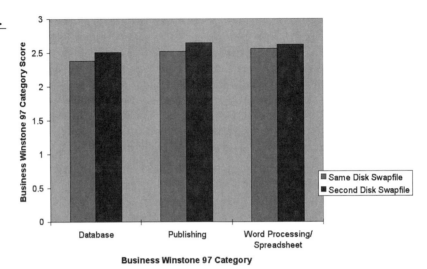

We can't compare the overall High-End Winstone 97 results, because this system was unable to complete the High-End Winstone 97 tests successfully in the 2-disk configuration. This isn't necessarily due to a hardware problem. It's probably due to a complex interaction going on between Windows 95 and the applications in Winstone 97. Just as there are obscure bugs in real applications, so will there be in Winstone 97. The bottom line is, if you do move your swapfile to a second disk, you should keep an eye out for potential bugs or incompatibilities.

We can look at some of the individual scores of Winstone 97, however (see Figure 11.15).

Looking at the individual applications that make up High-End Winstone 97, we see that the application that failed was Photoshop. As many graphic designers can tell you, Photoshop (while being a wonderful application) can be difficult to configure at times. Visual C++ shows a very dramatic improvement of 16%. If you do a lot of application development in Visual C++, this is performance you can take advantage of. Picture Publisher also shows a large improvement of about 10%, suggesting that other image editing applications would benefit from this new configuration. The other application scores are less impressive, but still of some note. Regardless of your application, using a faster disk for your swapfile, whether by replacing your existing drive or adding a new one, is definitely something you should consider.

If you are expecting WinBench 97 scores next, sorry. WinBench 97 is a relatively small application and does not make much if any use of swapping, so it is not an appropriate test tool for this set of experiments.

Figure 11.15.
High-End Winstone 97 individual application results for the Pentium 133 machine, varying the swapfile location from the same disk to a second disk.

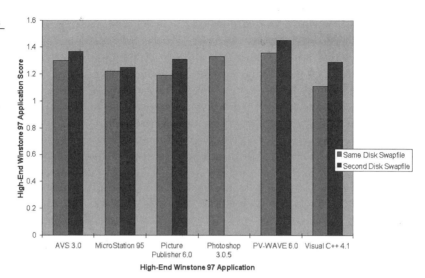

11.7.3. Pentium 166

We ran similar tests on our Pentium 166, which shipped from Compaq with a Seagate Medalist 2140 hard disk. We were still using our Quantum Fireball ST 4.3 as the upgrade drive. The Medalist's specs were similar to the original disk in our Pentium 133 (5400 rpm rotational speed, Fast ATA-2 interface) but the specified average access time was 10.5 milliseconds. By looking at just these specs, you'd expect even less of an improvement by upgrading to the Fireball ST, but then again the average latency of the Medalist was not as good as the average latency of the original Fireball in our Pentium 133. You can look at spec sheets all day; we'll let the benchmarks do the talking.

Indeed, the overall improvement shown in Figure 11.16 by Business Winstone 97 is about 8%, better than we saw with the upgrade on the Pentium 133. Because the new disk in this test is the same as the new disk in our Pentium 133 tests, you'd be tempted to draw a conclusion about the relative merits of their respective disks. You need to be careful in doing so—it is very possible that the slower processor was more of a bottleneck on the Pentium 133. As even elementary school science teachers tell you, change only one variable at a time. Putting aside comparisons with our previous section, we see here a good improvement in overall system performance by getting a newer disk drive.

As we look deeper into the upgrade, we see in Figure 11.17 the category scores from Business Winstone 97. They show that the Database applications benefited the most from a new disk, improving by more than 10%. Given the usual disk-bound nature of database applications, this makes sense. The Publishing applications improved by about 9%, while the Word Processing/Spreadsheet applications only improved 6%. This spread of performance improvements is more or less as you would expect. Let's turn to the High-End Winstone 97 applications where their greater diversity may reveal some surprises.

Figure 11.16.

Business Winstone 97 results for the Pentium 166 machine, upgrading the hard disk from the Seagate Medalist 2140 to the Quantum Fireball ST.

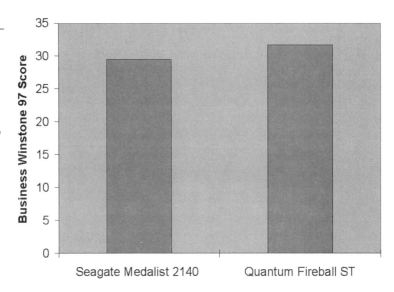

Figure 11.17.

Business Winstone 97 category results for the Pentium 166 machine, upgrading the hard disk from the Seagate Medalist 2140 to the Quantum Fireball ST.

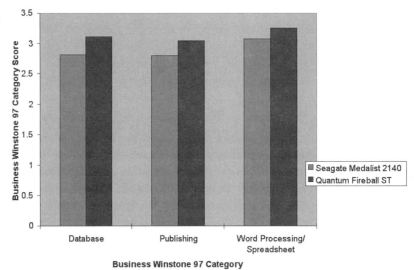

As with the business applications, the High-End Winstone 97 score shown in Figure 11.18 reveals more improvement for this upgrade than we saw with the Pentium 133. The High-End Winstone 97 score increases by about 6%, less than for the business applications. The most likely reason is that the more taxing High-End applications are bottlenecked more by the processor, RAM, and graphics subsystems. There is only so much the disk subsystem can do to improve overall system performance in the face of other bottlenecks.

Figure 11.18.

High-End Winstone 97 results for the Pentium 166 machine, upgrading the hard disk from the Seagate Medalist 2140 to the Quantum Fireball ST.

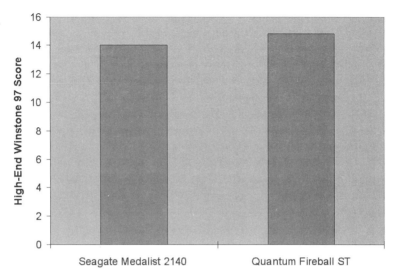

The standout result for the individual applications in High-End Winstone 97 is once again Picture Publisher. Figure 11.19 shows it improving by almost 15% with the new disk. Photoshop also shows a dramatic improvement. Compare this with MicroStation 95, which shows no improvement at all. Some of the applications may well have other bottlenecks than the disk or may just use the disk or virtual memory less. The key is to realize that different applications place very different demands on the subsystems that make up a system. On balance, however, this disk upgrade seems not to hurt any applications and really helps some of them.

Figure 11.19.

High-End Winstone 97 individual application results for the Pentium 166 machine, upgrading the hard disk from the Seagate Medalist 2140 to the Quantum Fireball ST.

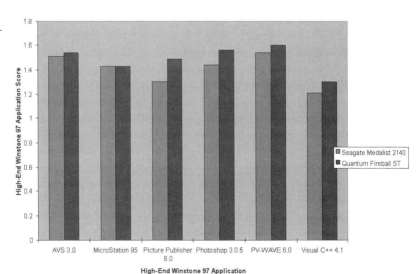

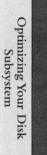

Optimizing Your Disk Subsystem

In Figure 11.20 we see that WinBench 97 does its job of isolating the performance of an individual subsystem. The results reflect those we saw earlier with Business Winstone 97; the Business Disk WinMark 97 increases by 14% when we swap in the new disk.

Figure 11.20.

Business Disk WinMark 97 results for the Pentium 166 machine, upgrading the hard disk from the Seagate Medalist 2140 to the Quantum Fireball ST.

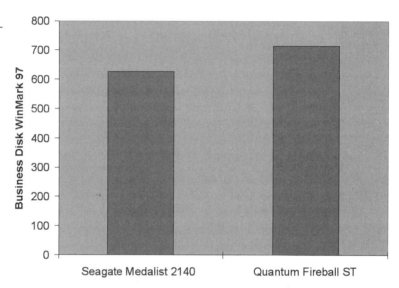

The Business Disk WinMark 97 category results in Figure 11.21 show the Database applications garner the most improvement at 17%. The Word Processing/Spreadsheet applications show about a 16% improvement. The disk playback of the Publishing applications only improves about 8% with the newer disk.

Figure 11.21.

Business Disk WinMark 97 category scores for the Pentium 166 machine, upgrading the hard disk from the Seagate Medalist 2140 to the Quantum Fireball ST.

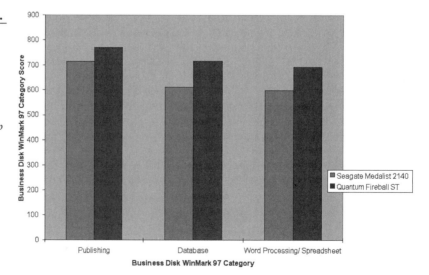

In Figure 11.22, the High-End Disk WinMark 97 score shows an overall improvement on how well the disk subsystem handles high-end applications of over 16%. This is as we would expect from WinBench—it generally shows results akin to Winstone's but of a higher magnitude.

Figure 11.22.

High-End Disk WinMark 97 results for the Pentium 166 machine, upgrading the hard disk from the Seagate Medalist 2140 to the Quantum Fireball ST.

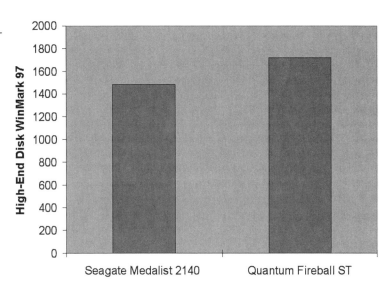

Finally, let's look at the individual application results from the High-End Disk Playback tests. As with Winstone, the MicroStation 95 results barely budge. All of the other applications show dramatic improvement except for PV-WAVE, which falls off by 14%! (See Figure 11.23.) We have to admit that we're not exactly sure what is happening there. The conclusion, however, is that we see real benefit from this disk upgrade. But, as we've said before, you can't rely solely on technical specifications to predict real-world performance. Also, you can't expect all applications to benefit equally from a particular upgrade. Nothing beats real-world testing.

Let's try our swapfile relocation experiments on this machine, using the existing Medalist as the main disk and adding the Fireball ST as a second disk where we'll locate the swapfile. Please note: the second disk isn't solely for the swapfile. That would be an absurd waste of disk space. Still, there should be plenty of room wherever you've located the swapfile, and you should defrag that disk regularly (as you should defrag all of your disks).

As we saw with the previous simple upgrade, our swapfile relocation trick shows more improvement on our Pentium 166 than it did on our Pentium 133. The gain we see in Figure 11.24 with Business Winstone 97 with our new swapfile configuration is a bit lower than we saw simply by exchanging the old disk for the newer disk, about 6%. An improvement of 6% is almost enough to make us

Optimizing Your Disk Subsystem

run out and buy second disks just to relocate the swapfile. These results also confirm the importance of swapping to performance. The applications are still on the old, slower drive, but they are operating 6% faster because of the new swap drive. This improvement is probably attributable to both the faster speed of the swap drive and the inherent advantage of being able to use two drives.

Figure 11.23.

High-End WinMark 97 application scores for the Pentium 166 machine, upgrading the hard disk from the Seagate Medalist 2140 to the Quantum Fireball ST.

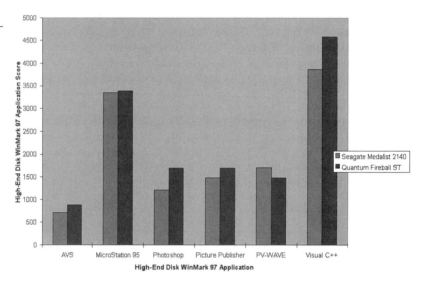

Figure 11.24.

Business Winstone 97 results for the Pentium 166 machine, varying the swapfile location from the same disk to a second disk.

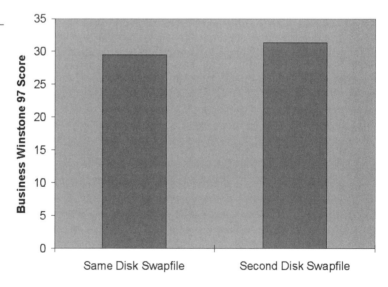

The individual category scores from Business Winstone 97 from Figure 11.25 show a familiar pattern: The Database category applications are best able to take advantage of improvements in the disk subsystem with about a 10% improvement. They are followed by the Publishing applications at 7%, with the Word

Processing/Spreadsheet applications taking up the rear at about 5%. This spread is probably due to the greater stress the Publishing and Database applications place upon virtual memory (swapping).

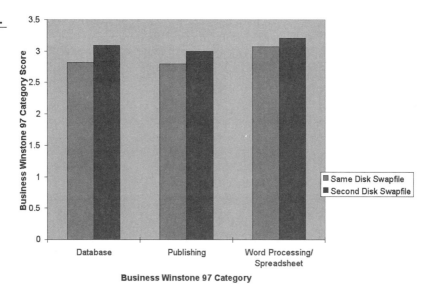

Figure 11.25.

Business Winstone 97 category results for the Pentium 166 machine, varying the swapfile location from the same disk to a second disk.

The High-End Winstone 97 results in Figure 11.26 do not show as much improvement as the Business Winstone ones. Nonetheless an approximately 4% overall gain is noteworthy. As before, this is largely due to swapping activity since the applications are still running on the older, slower disk. Let's look at the individual applications that make up High-End Winstone 97 to see from where the benefit arises.

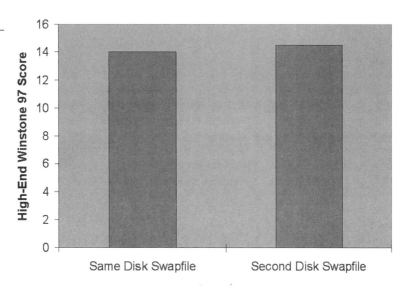

Figure 11.26.

High-End Winstone 97 results for the Pentium 166 machine, varying the swapfile location from the same disk to a second disk.

Optimizing Your Disk Subsystem

The chart in Figure 11.27 isn't as spectacular as the ones for the business applications. Performance goes up anywhere from 2% to 8%, depending on the application. Picture Publisher shows a large improvement of about 7% and Photoshop gets 8%. Visual C++ shows a solid improvement of 4%. If you do a lot of image editing or application development, this is performance you can take advantage of. The other application scores are less impressive, but still of some note. Regardless of your application, using a faster disk for your swapfile, whether by replacing your existing drive or adding a new one, is definitely something you should consider.

Figure 11.27.
High-End Winstone 97 individual application results for the Pentium 166 machine, varying the swapfile location from the same disk to a second disk.

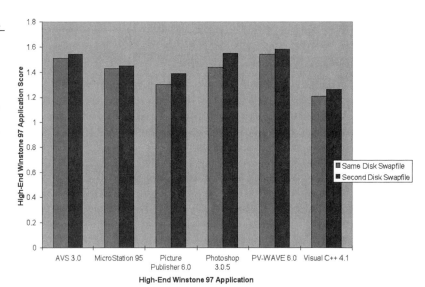

As with the Pentium 133 section, if you are expecting WinBench 97 scores next, sorry. WinBench 97 is a relatively small application and does not make much if any use of swapping, so it is not an appropriate test tool for this set of experiments.

11.8. Windows NT and the Disk Subsystem

Windows NT supports the VFAT filesystem that we discussed in the Windows 95 section. Windows NT also supports NTFS (NT File System). As you can guess, this is a filesystem designed exclusively for Windows NT. In fact, if you run multiple operating systems on your computer, the other OSs will not be able to use any NTFS partitions, unlike FAT and VFAT, which are understood by many operating systems.

Why would you want to use NTFS? The main reason for users is you must use NTFS to get the powerful security and access control features that NT offers. You must log in to a Windows NT machine, whether it's a workstation or a server. You can use the file access controls on NTFS partitions to strictly control which users or groups can use directories or files. NTFS also supports long filenames, and allows for selective compression of files or directories. VFAT only allows you to compress entire disks.

Still, if you are running NT 4.0 on your standalone PC, and you're not concerned about access control or other advanced features, you can use the VFAT filesystem. We added tests in this section to compare the performance of the FAT filesystem against NTFS.

11.8.1. How We Tested

We ran both Winstone 97 suites, Business and High-End, for the testing in this section. In the end, Winstone will always tell us what the real-world performance boost (or drop) is for a given system change. We also ran the Disk Tests in WinBench 97 where appropriate. These tests play back the exact disk operations that the corresponding applications in Winstone 97 perform. Because the WinBench disk tests only play back disk operations without other bottlenecks coming into play, these tests report on the performance of the disk subsystem in isolation. They do not take into account, however, swapping activity. This limitation makes the correlation of Winstone and WinBench results more difficult than in the graphics subsystem.

As always, we completely defragmented the hard drives of each machine before we ran each test. This was especially important because we were measuring disk performance. Comparing a heavily fragmented hard disk to a new one with no fragmentation would not be valid. We also ran each test immediately after a cold reboot.

We ran all of our tests on the Pentium 200 MMX machine and we kept the amount of RAM constant at 32MB. This reflects the higher memory requirements of Windows NT 4.0. Using this machine also allows us to highlight how "newer" isn't necessarily better.

11.8.2. Pentium 200 MMX

As we mentioned in the Windows 98 section, the Pentium 200 MMX uses SCSI disks, not EIDE disks. The unit came with a Seagate Barracuda 4LP disk, while our "upgrade disk" was a SCSI version of the Quantum Fireball ST. The specs on the installed Barracuda were, in general, better than those of the Fireball ST, so we wanted to see if our benchmark tests backed the specs up. For instance, the Barracuda is a 7200 rpm drive while the Fireball ST is a 5400 rpm drive. We must reiterate, these results are not meant to knock this particular model of Quantum disk, as it is less expensive than the Seagate disk. Both disks used the Ultra-SCSI interface, which was supported by this machine.

Figure 11.28 shows a surprising result—the score increases slightly, although by not enough to be very significant. Still, we would have expected to see the performance decrease rather than stay basically the same. We need to look at the category scores to see what is going on here.

Figure 11.28.

Business Winstone 97 results for the Pentium 200 MMX machine, varying the hard disk from the Seagate Barracuda 4LP to the Quantum Fireball ST.

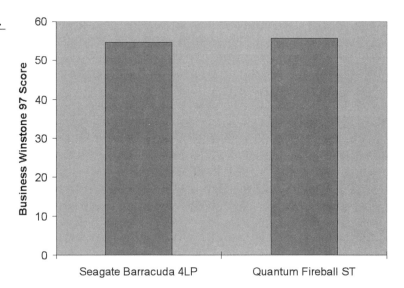

Figure 11.29 shows the Database category getting almost all of the improvement. The other scores are within a percent or so. In other tests, we have seen that the Database category is the most sensitive to swapping differences, so maybe that plays a role here.

Obviously, more data here would be a good thing. Unfortunately, we can't get a High-End Winstone 97 score. AVS failed repeatedly with the Fireball ST despite all our standard troubleshooting attempts. We think it's caused by a complex interaction between NT, the disk and the disk controller. Some days, you just can't win. We do have, however, the individual application scores and they are the ones that should give us the most information.

Indeed, the results in Figure 11.30 show a similar correlation with swapping. Picture Publisher and Photoshop stress swapping the most of the High-End applications and they see the most improvement. The best hypothesis we can offer is that Windows NT's swapping mechanisms map very well onto the Fireball ST. Probably the most important thing to take away from this chapter is that performance is a very complex critter and that it does not always act the way even experts expect it to. We now turn to WinBench 97 to see if it can help us understand a little bit better. Remember, it does not take swapping into account, so if swapping is what is causing the better performance of the supposedly lesser drive, WinBench should not see the same improvements as Winstone.

Figure 11.29.

Business Winstone 97 category results for the Pentium 200 MMX machine, varying the hard disk from the Seagate Barracuda 4LP to the Quantum Fireball ST.

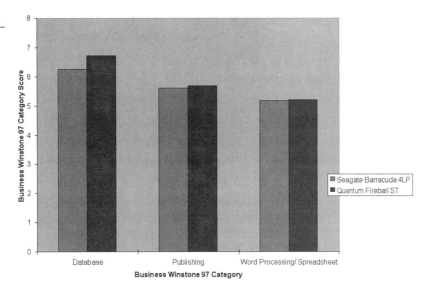

Figure 11.30.

High-End Winstone 97 individual application results for the Pentium 200 MMX machine, varying the hard disk from the Seagate Barracuda 4LP to the Quantum Fireball ST.

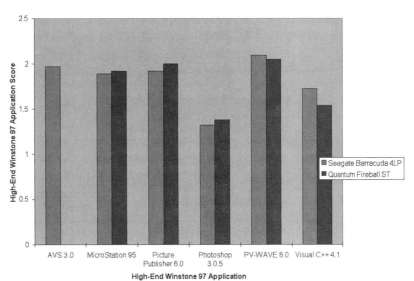

Optimizing Your Disk Subsystem

Wow! The WinBench 97 results in Figure 11.31 really show the Fireball ST in a less flattering light. The results reflect more of what we'd expect. Disk subsystem performance goes down when we swap in the Fireball ST; in this case Business Disk WinMark 97 decreases by 17%.

Figure 11.31.

Business Disk WinMark 97 results for the Pentium 200 MMX machine, varying the hard disk from the Seagate Barracuda 4LP to the Quantum Fireball ST.

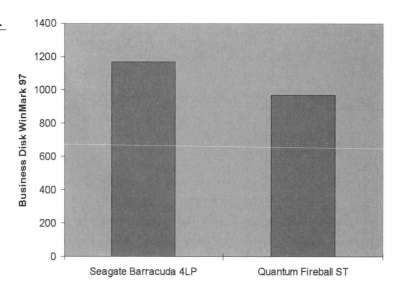

The category scores for the Business Disk WinMark 97 all drop rather substantially (see Figure 11.32). You can see from all of the WinBench 97 results here that simplistic answers are not always the best ones. Isolating the disk performance more or less bears out the specs. The real performance the end user will experience, however, as seen in the Winstone 97 results may be rather different.

Figure 11.32.

Business Disk WinMark 97 category scores for the Pentium 200 MMX machine, varying the hard disk from the Seagate Barracuda 4LP to the Quantum Fireball ST.

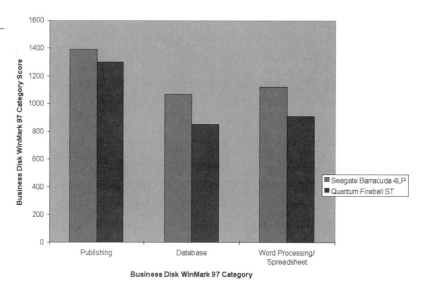

The High-End Disk WinMark 97 score in Figure 11.33 drops by about 16%. This result is about the same as for the Business Disk WinMark 97.

Figure 11.33.

High-End Disk WinMark 97 results for the Pentium 200 MMX machine, varying the hard disk from the Seagate Barracuda 4LP to the Quantum Fireball ST.

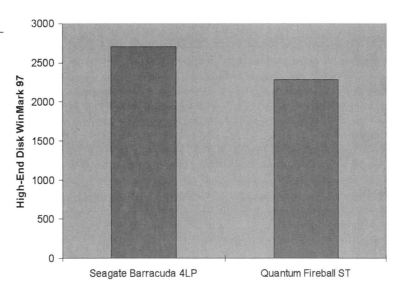

All the individual application scores from the High-End Disk WinMark 97, drop off significantly except for the Picture Publisher score. You can see in Figure 11.34 decreases as large as 22%. The bottom line here is that for pure disk activity, this "new" disk would be a bad choice. Some combination of luck and good drivers, however, make the slower drive a decent selection for swap activity. The important thing to note is that whatever is going on here, it is far more complex than trying to figure things out from reading the specs on a box.

Figure 11.34.

High-End Disk WinMark 97 application scores for the Pentium 200 MMX machine, varying the hard disk from the Seagate Barracuda 4LP to the Quantum Fireball ST.

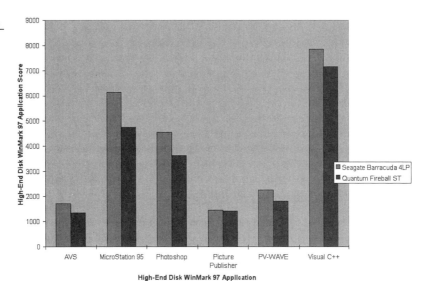

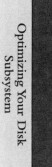

Optimizing Your Disk Subsystem

We tried out a swapfile relocation trick under Windows NT, to see if it would give us the same results as under Windows 95. One of the questions we had in this case was what would happen when we made the "upgrade" drive, the slower one in this case, our swap device. Generally this would be a bad idea. This drive, however, is the one that swapped under NT better than we expected in our previous test, so we were really curious what would happen. The Business Winstone 97 results in Figure 11.35 show no improvement by relocating the swapfile. To our minds, this result confirms that this particular drive works pretty well as a swapping device, despite its otherwise poorer characteristics.

Figure 11.35.

Business Winstone 97 results for the Pentium 200 MMX machine, varying the swapfile location from the same disk to a second disk.

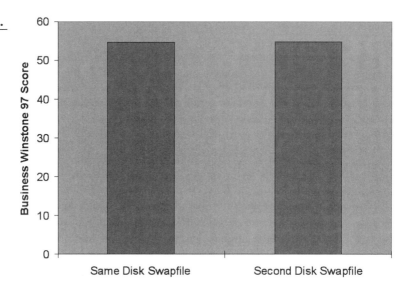

The Business Winstone 97 category scores in Figure 11.36 are what we would have guessed. There is a slight increase in the Database category score, the one we have come to associate with swapping improvements. The other categories bear out that we're not going to see any substantial performance increase with this situation.

In Figure 11.37, we can see that the overall High-End Winstone 97 score drops slightly when we move the swapfile. The drop of around 2% is not a big one, but it does indicate that this drive is not helping as much as we would expect from a faster drive in this situation.

Finally, as we look at the individual application scores in High-End Winstone 97, we see that AVS is the main application that takes a performance hit with our swapfile change, falling off by about 7%. Figure 11.38 also shows the rest of the applications dropping off a little bit or remaining the same. Again, the idea of using a second drive as the swap device is a good one, but you really want that drive to be a very good one. The situation with this particular drive where it outperforms its specs for swapping also serves as a warning that performance and upgrading is complicated and won't always go exactly according to plan.

Figure 11.36.

Business Winstone 97 category results for the Pentium 200 MMX machine, varying the swapfile location from the same disk to a second disk.

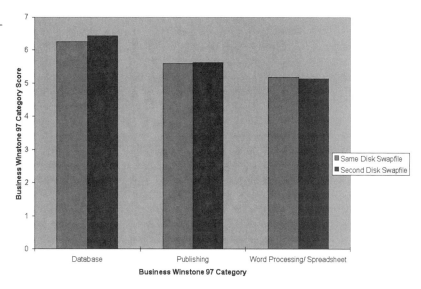

Figure 11.37.

High-End Winstone 97 results for the Pentium 200 MMX machine, varying the swapfile location from the same disk to a second disk.

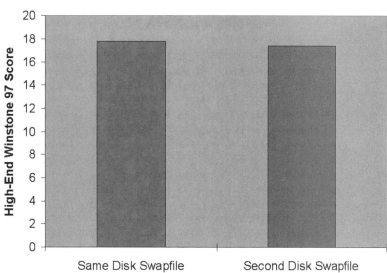

Optimizing Your Disk Subsystem

Another disk subsystem feature that's available to us under Windows NT is filesystem type. For some people, this is not a choice. If you want to take advantage of all of the security and sharing options that NT provides, you must use NTFS. However, for those of you with a choice, we looked at the performance of the FAT filesystem versus the performance of the NTFS filesystem.

Figure 11.38.

High-End Winstone 97 individual application results for the Pentium 200 MMX machine, varying the swapfile location from the same disk to a second disk.

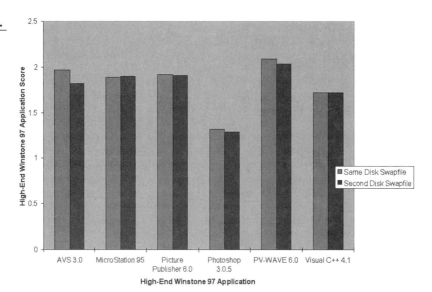

Figure 11.38.

High-End Winstone 97 individual application results for the Pentium 200 MMX machine, varying the swapfile location from the same disk to a second disk.

The overall Business Winstone 97 score in Figure 11.39 drops off by over 7% when we convert from the FAT format to the NTFS format. While we understand that the added features offered by NTFS mean more overhead, this decrease is more than we expected. Again, note that this drop is with Winstone. That means that the disk subsystem is slowing things down enough to slow down the whole system by 7%. We should look further into the results, but if this holds up, we would have to seriously consider not using NTFS for performance-sensitive situations.

Figure 11.39.

Business Winstone 97 results for the Pentium 200 MMX machine, varying the filesystem format from FAT to NTFS.

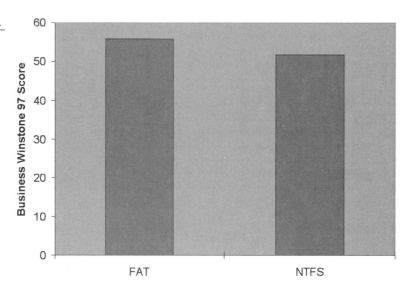

The Database applications in Figure 11.40 take the greatest hit, a whopping 20%, when we convert from FAT to NTFS. As we've seen before, this may be attributable to swapping. Publishing performance drops off by 7%, while Word Processing/Spreadsheet performance drops by 4%. There's no easy answer to which filesystem you should use, because you can't base your decision solely on performance. However, this might convince you to stick with NTFS if you're only using the system for light word processing applications, for instance.

Figure 11.40.

Business Winstone 97 category results for the Pentium 200 MMX machine, varying the filesystem format from FAT to NTFS.

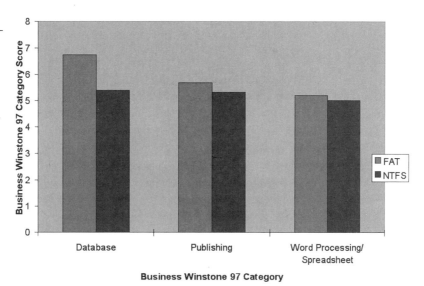

Once again we run into difficulty getting High-End Winstone 97 to run to completion. AVS failed consistently and so we weren't able to get an overall score.

Looking at the individual High-End Winstone 97 applications in Figure 11.41, the most spectacular drop is in Photoshop, one of 21%. Visual C++ also falls off by 14%. If you're running these applications on a single machine, with no need for the advanced features of NTFS, you should seriously consider not using NTFS.

Finally, let's wrap up by seeing if WinBench 97 shows a similar performance hit when moving from FAT to NTFS. Keep in mind that it should show the disk performance of the applications in isolation from the other subsystems and without the influence of swapping.

Indeed in Figure 11.42 the Business Disk WinMark 97 score falls by 17%. This greater decrease than we saw with the corresponding Winstone results is the consequence of isolating application disk performance. Let's see which kind of application is causing the drop.

Optimizing Your Disk Subsystem

Figure 11.41.

High-End Winstone 97 individual application results for the Pentium 200 MMX machine, varying the filesystem format from FAT to NTFS.

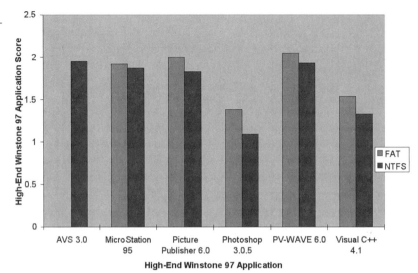

Figure 11.42.

Business Disk WinMark 97 results for the Pentium 200 MMX machine, varying the filesystem format from FAT to NTFS.

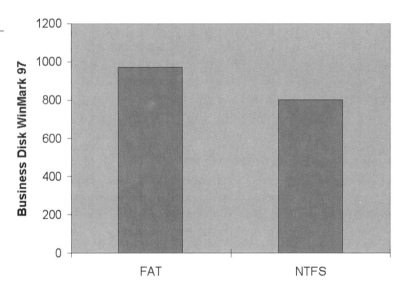

All of the Business Disk WinMark 97 categories in Figure 11.43 show a major performance hit. The results are the opposite of Winstone 97's categories, however. This is because they are not being penalized by the degradation of swap performance. Database is much more heavily depressed in the Winstone runs, because of its reliance on swapping.

If you aren't convinced yet about the performance penalty from NTFS, Figures 11.44 and 11.45 will convince you. The High-End Disk WinMark 97 score falls off by 23% when we move from FAT to NTFS!

Figure 11.43.

Business Disk WinMark 97 category scores for the Pentium 200 MMX machine, varying the filesystem format from FAT to NTFS.

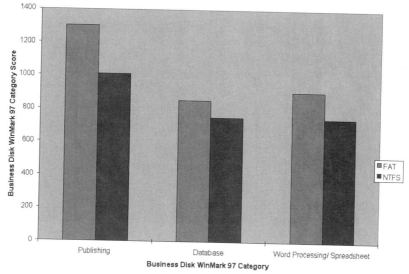

Figure 11.44.

High-End Disk WinMark 97 results for the Pentium 200 MMX machine, varying the filesystem format from FAT to NTFS.

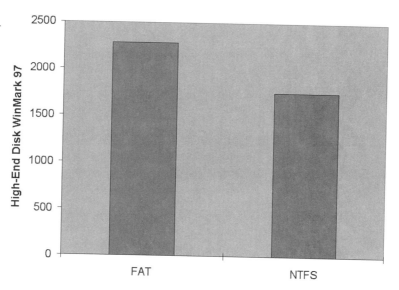

The individual High-End Disk WinMark 97 applications all fall off a great deal, except for PV-WAVE, which shows no change. Picture Publisher suffers the worst degradation at 35%. If you don't need what NTFS offers and performance matters to you, think twice before using it. One thing that some people do is use multiple partitions with one being NTFS. In that way you may be able to have the best of both worlds.

Optimizing Your Disk Subsystem

Figure 11.45.
High-End Disk WinMark 97 application scores for the Pentium 200 MMX machine, varying the filesystem format from FAT to NTFS.

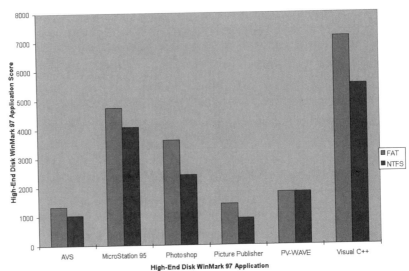

11.9. The Bottom Line

If you've read other chapters in this book, you know that we're performance mavens, ready to wring the last drop of oomph out of any PC. However, with the disk subsystem, we've discovered that jacking up the performance isn't as simple as just swapping in a brand new hard disk. Sure, you'll see performance gains (given the caveats we've discussed) but you'll probably want a new hard disk for reasons other than performance. With the growing space requirements of operating systems, office suites, Web browser caches, and other applications, it's easy to fill up several gigabytes of disk space on a single PC these days. A few years ago, only high-powered network servers contained gigabyte-sized disks!

The other thing you should take away from this chapter is a healthy skepticism when it comes to hard disk specs. We're not saying that technical specifications are meaningless, we're just saying you shouldn't use them as the sole predictor of performance. A disk rotating two times faster than your current disk will not double your Windows performance! In the end, real-world benchmark testing with Winstone and WinBench will show you the true performance of potential upgrades.

11.10. Testing You Can Do

As with all the other hardware based chapters, to do the testing we've done in this chapter, you'll need to get a loaner hard drive from a friendly computer dealer or just a friend. If you're an NT 4.0 user, you can duplicate the FAT versus NTFS tests we did, but be aware that once you've converted a FAT partition to NTFS, there's no easy way to convert it back without reformatting it.

Remember that you've got to hold all variables except for the one you're interested in constant while testing. This is our "apples to apples" rule. You can't compare Drive A in your PC to Drive B in your buddy's PC, because other factors (RAM, processor, and so on) come into play.

Once you've got some hard drives to tinker with, you'll to want first run Winstone. This will tell you the real-world performance benefit (or loss) from a particular upgrade. Make sure to run the tests within Winstone that most closely resemble your daily workload. If you're the average business user, you'll want to look at the Business Winstone score. If you *only* run Photoshop, though, you'll want to pay close attention to the Photoshop application score in High-End Winstone.

Once you've run Winstone tests, get down to the nitty-gritty with WinBench. This will help you determine if a particular disk upgrade really revs up the disk subsystem. If WinBench shows a performance increase but Winstone does not, it's time to play our favorite game, Find The Bottleneck. In the case of the disk subsystem, we'd first suggest checking that you have enough RAM in your machine.

NOTE	Complete directions for running Winstone and WinBench can be found in Appendixes A and B.

11.11. From Here...

Disk performance isn't flashy; it's all behind the scenes safely inside your system case. In this chapter we've learned that you can improve your disk performance, although you've got to pay attention to your entire disk subsystem. You can learn about other tricks involving the swapfile and the Windows filesystem in the chapters on software tuning. If you really want to get the most out of your disk subsystem, you should make sure that your system has plenty of RAM, because more RAM means a larger disk cache and also means less swapping.

The following chapters will provide more information on the optimizations related to the disk tips we've discussed in this chapter.

- Chapter 5, "Windows 98 Software Tuning," will show you software tuning tips for Windows 98, including tweaks for your swapfile and other filesystem parameters.

- Chapter 6, "Windows 95 Software Tuning," will show you software tuning tips for Windows 95, including tweaks for your swapfile and other filesystem parameters.

Optimizing Your Disk Subsystem

■ Chapter 7, "Windows NT Software Tuning," will show you software tuning tips for Windows NT, including tweaks for your swapfile and other filesystem parameters.

■ Chapter 9, "Optimizing Your System's RAM," will show you how to optimize the amount of RAM in your system which in turn affects how your system uses the hard disk.

Chapter 12

12

Optimizing Your CD-ROM Subsystem

The CD-ROM drive is a relative newcomer to the PC hardware scene. Personal computers have always had RAM, processors, disk drives, and graphics boards. The CD-ROM drive didn't appear in the typical personal computer until the early 90's. Nowadays it's hard to buy a PC that doesn't have a CD-ROM drive or some similar form of mass storage.

The importance of the CD-ROM drive varies for many users. Some folks will never use a CD-ROM drive. Some will use it only to play audio CD's while they work at their PC. Most of us will use it from time to time to install new applications or operating system software. Others will use CD-ROM based applications such as reference works and games. You'll have to look at how you use your CD-ROM drive to determine how much time and effort you'll want to put into analyzing its performance. If you use your CD-ROM drive on a regular basis or just want to get a better understanding of your CD-ROM subsystem, then read on.

In this chapter, you will also learn:

- What your CD-ROM subsystem is

  The CD-ROM subsystem includes more than just the CD-ROM drive itself; it includes other components like the CD-ROM controller, software and hardware caches, and the system bus. In the following sections, you'll learn about the inner workings of this subsystem.

- How your operating system affects CD-ROM performance

  Windows NT, Windows 98 and Windows 95 can use the CD-ROM drive differently. You'll learn how to make decisions about your CD-ROM drive based on which operating system you're running.

- How to interpret common CD-ROM speed measurements

  The common multiplier method of specifying CD-ROM drive speed can be hard to understand and misleading. You'll learn how to interpret this and other CD-ROM drive specifications. You'll also find out why these specs aren't necessarily indicative of real-world performance.

12.1. Cocktail Party Tips

Unlike RAM or CPU, it's unlikely that the lowly CD-ROM drive will inspire much debate at our fictional cocktail party. When you think of the CD-ROM drive in your system, you typically just think of what *speed* it is. In other words, single-speed, double-speed, 6X, 8X, 12X, and so on. The speed of a CD-ROM drive is supposed to be a measure of the data transfer rate. A single-speed CD-ROM has a transfer rate of 150KB/second. A double-speed CD-ROM has a transfer rate of 300KB/second, and so on. So, a CD-ROM drive that's advertised as "24X" should give us a transfer rate of 3600KB/second.

This linear increase in speed isn't mirrored by real-world testing, so our party tip for this chapter is "X ratings are a no-no." We're not talking about the motion picture rating system here. We're talking about the speed ratings that are plastered on the CD-ROM drives, the boxes they come in, and the ads they're advertised in. CD-ROM drive performance can't be summed up by a speed rating. In some cases, this speed rating can be deceiving.

As we'll see when we run WinBench tests, CD-ROM drive performance isn't merely a matter of the speed rating. A 16X drive isn't necessarily four times faster than a 4X drive. There are several reasons for this. One is that the manufacturers often use the maximum transfer rate, not the average transfer rate, when determining the "X factor." Another more complicated reason has to do with how the CD-ROM drive reads the data from the CD. The first CD-ROM drives used Constant Linear Velocity (CLV) technology. Newer drives use what's known as Constant Angular Velocity (CAV) technology. We'll learn more about these technologies later in this chapter. For now, what's important to us is that, in some cases, a CAV 10X drive could perform less well than a CLV 8X drive. In other words, you can't expect the speed rating alone to tell you all you need to know about a particular CD-ROM drive.

We still need to stress, though, that for many of you, CD-ROM drive performance will not be an issue. If you don't run CD-based applications and if you don't install a lot of software, you probably won't be too concerned with the performance of your CD-ROM drive.

12.2. CD-ROM Subsystem Basics

As we've done throughout the book, we use the term *subsystem* quite a bit. While the CD-ROM subsystem is typically not as complicated as the hard drive subsystem, it has similar components. Along with the CD-ROM drive itself, the CD-ROM controller, hardware and software caches, and system bus are included in the CD-ROM subsystem. For all practical purposes, though, the system bus doesn't figure heavily into CD-ROM performance. That's because CD-ROM data transfer rates are still so much slower than hard disk transfer rates; it would be hard to bog down the system bus with data streaming from the CD-ROM drive.

The original CD-ROM drive controllers were sound boards. Typically you'd buy a CD-ROM drive and it would come with an adapter that combined the CD-ROM controller with a 16-bit sound card. Nowadays, most CD-ROM drives are ATAPI compliant. As we learned in Chapter 11, "Optimizing Your Disk Subsystem," ATAPI and IDE mean essentially the same thing (at least for the purposes of this discussion). If you buy an ATAPI CD-ROM drive for your existing system, make sure you've got a secondary IDE port on your PC's motherboard. Don't connect your CD-ROM drive to the spare connector on the primary IDE connection, the one your hard drive is connected to. While it might work, many users report problems due to interference between signals for the CD-ROM drive and for the hard drive.

If you don't have a secondary IDE connection, you'll need to buy a new IDE interface board to connect your CD-ROM drive to. You can determine whether you have a secondary IDE connection in several ways: ask your system vendor or read the manual. These are the easiest ways, but ways most folks don't want to use for some reason. Alternately, you can open your machine and examine the motherboard for an empty ribbon cable connector labeled "secondary IDE" or something similar. If you're lucky, your secondary IDE connector might already be hooked to an (unterminated) ribbon cable.

If your motherboard only provides a primary IDE connector, you might want to get an interface card like Promise Technology's EIDEMax. This will allow you to keep your hard drives and other peripherals (like CD-ROM drives or tape drives) segregated between the primary and secondary IDE channels.

The CD-ROM drive itself, and to a lesser extent the CD-ROM drive controller, are the pieces of the CD equation that you can control. The hardware cache will be located on the CD-ROM drive itself, in most cases, so once you've picked a particular CD-ROM drive, you're stuck with the hardware cache. If you're interested in tweaking the software cache which Windows uses for the CD-ROM drive, check out the appropriate chapter from Part II, "Software Opimization," that matches your operating system.

Make sure to get all the hardware you need when you purchase a CD-ROM drive. Along with the drive itself, you'll also need a ribbon cable to connect to the secondary IDE connection, and possibly an audio cable to connect the CD-ROM drive to your existing sound board.

If you don't have a sound board, or if your sound board is quite old, you might want to check out what are called *multimedia upgrade kits*. These typically include a CD-ROM drive, a sound board, external speakers, and all the necessary hardware and cables. These kits make it easy to upgrade your old PC in one fell swoop so that you can take advantage of CD-ROM's and sound.

12.3. More on CD-ROM Drive Speeds

As we mentioned earlier, the industry-standard method of naming a particular CD-ROM drive's speed is somewhat problematic. If you've been reading this book in sequence, you know that we've debunked some of the common misconceptions about PC performance. Let's take a closer look at CD-ROM speed ratings and we'll see that they don't necessarily determine performance.

Data on computer a CD is stored in a standard fashion. Starting at the center of the disc, data is arranged in 2KB sectors. Early CD-ROM drives read this data with Constant Linear Velocity (CLV). As the circumference increases when you move from the center of the CD to the outer edge, so does the amount of data increase. In other words, there are more sectors of data at the outer edge of the CD than there are at the center. To transfer data at a constant rate, the CD-ROM drive rotates at varying speeds. The linear speed (the speed at which a unit of data is read) remains constant. When the drive reads data from the center of the disc, it rotates more slowly than it does when it reads data from the outer edge of the disc. Because the drive is designed to read data at a constant rate, the X rating can be a fairly accurate measure of drive speed.

The newer CD-ROM drives read data with Constant Angular Velocity (CAV). This means that the drive spins at a constant rotational speed, while it reads data at a varying rate. Because the amount of data read per unit time can vary depending on whether the drive is reading close to the center or close to the outer edge, there's no easy way to give a CAV CD-ROM drive a single speed designation. A particular CAV CD-ROM drive might read the center tracks at 8X speed while it reads the outer tracks at 16X speed. The manufacturer might then give this drive an average speed rating of 12X, based on the average transfer rate of a full CD. A full CD would contain 650MB of data, starting at the center and proceeding towards the outer edge. This assumption is what makes the speed ratings of CAV CD-ROM drives misleading. Most CD's are not full, and because the data starts at the center (where are CAV drive reads the slowest) the transfer rate will probably be lower than the manufacturer's stated average.

This is not to knock CAV drives. Most of the faster CD-ROM drives use CAV technology. The constant rotational speed requires less power, which is advantageous in a notebook computer. You just need to be skeptical when looking at CD-ROM drive speed ratings. A 12X CAV CD-ROM drive isn't necessarily going to perform better than a 10X CLV CD-ROM drive.

12.4. Other CD-ROM Drive Concerns

As we mentioned before, once you choose a particular CD-ROM drive, you're stuck with the amount of on-board cache it comes with. This on-board cache is RAM on the CD-ROM drive itself. This RAM is used to buffer the data read from the CD-ROM before its sent to the CPU. You can learn more about RAM and caching in Chapter 9, "Optimizing Your System's RAM."

Optimizing Your CD-ROM Subsystem

In general, the amount of cache RAM on a CD-ROM drive is designed to match up with the drive's transfer rate. Drives with higher transfer rates will require more buffer RAM. The main thing to look for is that the drive has some amount of RAM cache. You should be very skeptical of a CD-ROM drive with no on-board buffers. In general, look for at least 256KB of on-board cache.

A final concern with the CD-ROM subsystem is processor utilization. Processor utilization is a measure of how much work the CPU has to perform on a certain operation (in this case, reading data from the CD-ROM drive). If the CD-ROM processor utilization is 40%, then that means the processor spends 40% of its time reading data from the CD-ROM drive, leaving the remaining 60% of time to perform other operations with that data (for instance, to display the data on the monitor). Thus, for a given PC and CD-ROM test, a lower processor utilization value is better, because this means the processor has more time to perform other functions. Of course, a very slow CD-ROM drive can give you a very low processor utilization score, because it can't supply data to the CPU quickly enough. So don't get hung up on low CPU utilization scores without looking at the other results. As a particular CD-ROM drives transfers data at a higher rate, you should expect the processor utilization to go up, because the processor has to deal with more data per unit of time. In this chapter we'll be examining processor utilization for a variety of CD-ROM drives and tests.

12.5. Windows 98 and the CD-ROM Subsystem

Windows 98 adds native support for many new devices that have rolled out since the advent of Windows 95, including DVD drives. In other words, drivers for these new devices come bundled with Windows 98. These are still 32-bit protected mode drivers which obsolete the older 16-bit drivers you might've used with Windows 3.1 or DOS. With the exception of added device support, Windows 98 is very similar to Windows 95 when it comes to the CD-ROM subsystem.

12.5.1. How We Tested

We ran only WinBench tests in this chapter. Because Winstone runs from the hard drive (where you run most of your business applications) it is not appropriate to use for testing CD-ROM drives. The main test we used is the CD-ROM WinMark 98. This test, like many other WinBench tests, is a *playback* test. WinBench plays back actual CD-ROM operations profiled from a wide variety of popular CD-ROM applications. These applications fall into three general categories: Business and Productivity, Games and Entertainment, and Reference and Education. WinBench uses profiles from two applications out of each of these three categories to get an overall picture of the real-world performance of the CD-ROM subsystem. WinBench times how long a PC takes to play back the profiled CD-ROM operations, then calculates an overall score via a weighted harmonic mean. As we've discussed previously in this book, the weighted harmonic mean gives us an overall score based on the market share of the individual applications.

In addition to the CD-ROM WinMark 98 test, we've also run some full-motion video tests in this chapter. Because CD-ROMs are a common delivery system for full-motion video clips (and similar data), we wanted to test how well our various systems and CD-ROM drives played back full-motion video clips from CD. WinBench 98 provides a huge number of video clips, so we selected certain specific tests which we feel demonstrate important points about CD-ROM drive performance. You should note that we've omitted the Temporal Quality results from this section. The Temporal Quality results we got on our machines running a pre-release version of Windows 98 looked anomalous, and not pertinent to our discussion of CD-ROM subsystem performance.

Even though we were measuring CD-ROM drive performance, we still completely defragmented the hard drives of each machine before we ran each test. We also ran each test immediately after a cold reboot. This is good testing procedure which we always follow, no matter what you're measuring.

12.5.2. Pentium 75

Our Pentium 75 (a Compaq Deskpro 575) came outfitted with a 4X CD-ROM drive, as did most of the other systems in our testbed. This particular drive is a Sony CDU76E-Q. With this lower-end system, we decided just to see how performance changed when we upgraded to an 8X CD-ROM drive. In other words, would CD-ROM performance double across the board? The drive we chose as an upgrade was the Mitsumi FX810T. Let's take a look at our WinBench scores and see if performance really doubles (see Figure 12.1).

We see that performance does not double with our upgrade. Instead of a 100% increase in performance, we get about a 70% increase. We've quickly proven our basic assumption, that the industry standard CD-ROM drive speed rating isn't necessarily a completely accurate indicator of performance. In the case of these two drives, even though the speed rating doubles, the real-world performance does not. The Sony CDU76E has an average access time of 250ms, while the Mitsumi has an average access time of 150ms, so perhaps this accounts for the performance we're seeing: even though the maximum transfer rate doubles with the Mitsumi, the average access time does not halve. Both drives contains 256KB of cache.

Optimizing Your CD-ROM Subsystem

Figure 12.1.

CD-ROM WinMark 98 results for the Pentium 75 machine, changing the CD-ROM drive from the Sony CDU76E-Q to the Mitsumi FX810T.

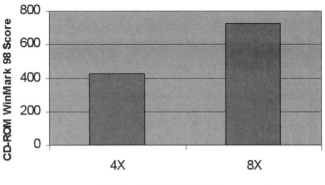

We also want to run some Video Tests on these two drives, to determine how they perform and to explore some concepts salient to full-motion video. We're going to run four similar test clips of an action sequence (a carousel) compressed with the Indeo codec. The clips are at resolutions of 320×240 and 640×480, and run in a window or are *zoomed* to fill the entire screen. Each of these clips should run at thirty frames per second. For each Video Test in WinBench, there are several results. The first result we're going to look at is Visual Quality, which is measured in the number of frames dropped (see Fiugre 12.2). This test result tells you how well the PC can keep up with the video clip. The ideal result for this test is zero, for that means that the PC dropped no frames during playback.

Figure 12.2.

WinBench 97 Video test Visual Quality results for the Pentium 75 machine, changing the CD-ROM drive from the Sony CDU76E-Q to the Mitsumi FX810T.

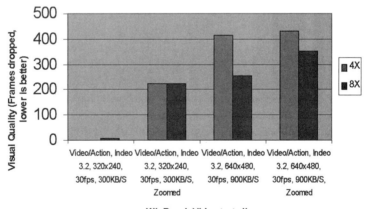

The amount of work that the CD-ROM subsystem has to do increases as we look at the clips in order. The normal, unzoomed, 320×240 clip has a data rate of 300KB/second. When we zoom this to fill the screen, the full-motion video subsystem has to do more work. The 640×480 clip has a data rate of 900KB/second, and then when we zoom that to fill the screen the video subsystem has to do even more work to attempt to display this video clip.

Looking at the Visual Quality results, we see that the number of frames dropped increases as the workload we just discussed increases. Because the 4X CD-ROM should only be capable of a 600KB/second data rate, we expect it to fail to display the 900KB/second clip properly. As you can see, it drops most of the frames in that 450 frame clip. What's interesting here is that the 8X CD-ROM drive, which should be capable of a 1200KB/second data rate, also drops a significant number of frames (over half) on the 640×480 clip. That's not something we'd expect to see if we simplemindedly believed in the 8X rating alone, or for that matter if we isolated the CD-ROM drive from all the other pieces of the video subsystem. Let's look at some other results from this same video test.

The Maximum Frame Rate result shows the number of frames per second that the PC can display of the chosen clip when WinBench plays the clip back as fast as possible, without sound. While you're never going to want to play back video clips as fast as possible, without sound, the Maximum Frame Rate test can give you an idea of the overall horsepower of your system when it comes to playing back video. The more frames per second your PC can display, the more time it will have to perform other tasks simultaneously. Figure 12.3 shows us that there's more to full-motion video performance than just the CD-ROM drive. Both the 4X and 8X drives max out at about 60 frames/second on the 300KB/second unzoomed clip. On all of the other clips, the maximum frame rate is considerably less than the nominal frame rate of the clip, which is unacceptable. Because both drives fail to play three of the four clips acceptably, we'd guess that there is a bottleneck elsewhere in the system, perhaps even in the graphics drivers themselves.

The CPU Utilization score is another one where higher values are usually worse, because CPU Utilization measures how much work the CPU had to do to play back a particular video clip. The more work the CPU has to do to play back a video clip, the less time it has to do other work while it's reading from the CD-ROM drive. When we look at the CPU Utilization graph for these same Video tests, we see that CPU Utilization approaches 100% for several of the clip/drive combinations we tested (see Figure 12.4). This means that there would be little time left over for the CPU to do anything other than play back those video clips.

By looking at the CPU Utilization, we can make a better guess at where the bottleneck is when we play back these clips. The 4X drive can't keep up with the 900KB/second clip, so it can't possibly swamp the CPU with data. You can see that utilization is about 40% for the two 900KB/second clips with that drive. The 8X drive, on the other hand, can supply data fast enough, but this swamps the CPU with data. We can see that both of these drives give unacceptable results for the 900KB/second clip *in this particular machine*, because the 4X drive can't keep up with the video clip, and the 8X drive loads down the rest of the video subsystem with data. Unless you don't want to do any other work while videos play, a CPU Utilization that approaches 100% is not good.

Figure 12.3.

WinBench 98 Video test Maximum Frame Rate results for the Pentium 75 machine, changing the CD-ROM drive from the Sony CDU76E-Q to the Mitsumi FX810T.

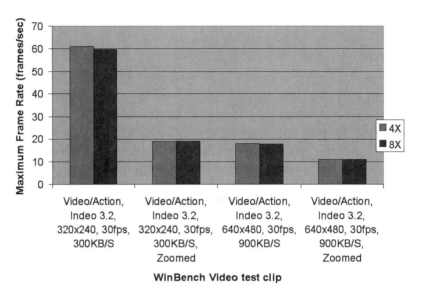

Figure 12.4.

WinBench 98 Video test CPU Utilization results for the Pentium 75 machine, changing the CD-ROM drive from the Sony CDU76E-Q to the Mitsumi FX810T.

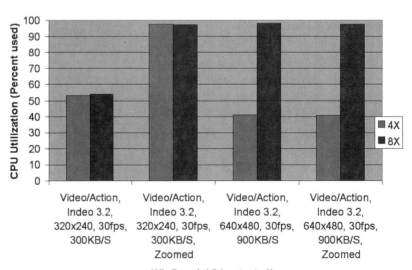

So we've learned that the common speed ratings of CD-ROM drives don't necessarily tell the whole story about true performance. Let's perform this same upgrade in a more capable machine and see if the choice of CPU changes the performance characteristics of this CD-ROM drive swap.

12.5.3. Pentium 100

Our Compaq DeskPro 5100 also came with a Sony CDU76E-Q CD-ROM drive. We tested with this drive and also with out Mitsumi FX810T, to see if the extra CPU horsepower of the Pentium 100 would change the results. First, the CD-ROM WinMark 98.

Our basic conclusion is still true: performance does not double from the 4X drive to the 8X drive. The graph in Figure 12.5 is not significantly different from the Pentium 75 graph, so we conclude that the added CPU power is probably not going to change the behavior of the CD-ROM subsystem or video subsystem very much. Let's take a look at our Video Tests with this new machine and see if this is true.

Figure 12.5.
CD-ROM WinMark 98 results for the Pentium 100 machine, changing the CD-ROM drive from the Sony CDU76E-Q to the Mitsumi FX810T.

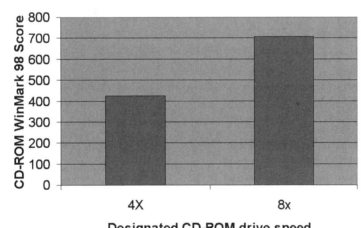

The test results for Visual Quality on the Pentium 100 do not show much difference from those on the Pentium 75. As we saw before, the situation is slightly more complicated than the simplistic drive speed ratings predict. As we increase the work that the CD-ROM subsystem has to perform, more and more frames drop out (see Figure 12.6).

The shape of the graph for the Maximum Frame Rate tests also does not change significantly. The raw scores are not terribly different from the scores we achieved with the Pentium 75 machine. The only acceptable results for the Maximum

Frame Rate are on the unzoomed, 300KB/second clip (see Figure 12.7). Let's see if the CPU Utilization has changed any from what we saw on the Pentium 75.

Figure 12.6.

WinBench 98 Video test Visual Quality results for the Pentium 100 machine, changing the CD-ROM drive from the Sony CDU76E-Q to the Mitsumi FX810T.

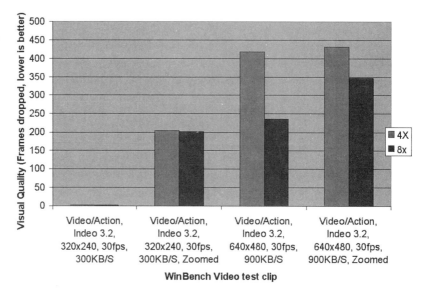

Figure 12.7.

WinBench 98 Video test Maximum Frame Rate results for the Pentium 75 machine, changing the CD-ROM drive from the Sony CDU76E-Q to the Mitsumi FX810T.

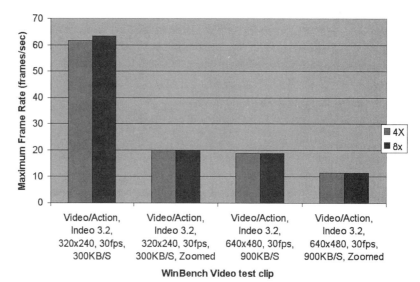

Once again, the results are very similar to what we saw with the Pentium 75. The only case that we deem to be acceptable playback is the unzoomed 300KB/second clip (see Figure 12.8). Remember, though, that these test values are for these particular video clips only. We've chosen them to illustrate the differences and similarities between these two CD-ROM drives. Systems less capable than our Pentium 75 have been playing back video clips throughout the 1990's. It's important to remember that these tests are directly pertinent only if you're going to be playing back videos from your CD-ROM drive. However, examining the results from these tests will give you a better understanding of the CD-ROM and video subsystems.

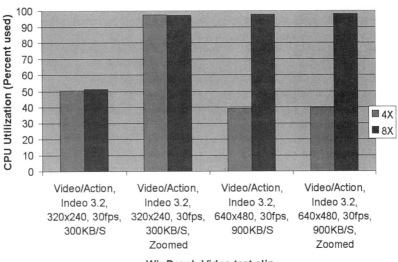

WinBench Video test clip

12.5.4. Pentium 166

Let's move on and test a wider variety of CD-ROM drives on a more capable machine. In addition to the familiar Sony CDU76E-Q and the Mitsumi FX810T, we added a 24X drive. The 24X drive was a Creative Labs CD2422E. The Creative Labs drive is a CAV design. If you've read this chapter up to this point, you'll know that we're skeptical that all of these drives will live up to their X ratings, especially the CAV drives. Our CD-ROM WinMark 98 test will show the real-world performance of all of these drives. In this case, if the 4X drive gets a score of 400, we'd expect (if we believed the speed ratings) that the 24X drive would get a 2400. If you just believed in the speed rating, you'd think that the 24X drive would blow the doors off of the other drives.

As you can see in Figure 12.9, the 24X drive does not live up to its speed rating. Instead of being six times faster than the 4X drive, the 24X drive is just under three times faster. The 8X drive turns in a similar CD-ROM WinMark 98 score as we saw on the previous machines.

We also ran Video Tests on these three drives. To change things up a bit, we tested a different video clip than we did for the previous machines. In this case, we tested a clip compressed with the Cinepak codec, running at a resolution of 640×480. We chose the thirty frames/second clip with a data rate of 900KB/second. As we saw before, any drive with a transfer rate less than 900KB/second should perform unacceptably on this clip.

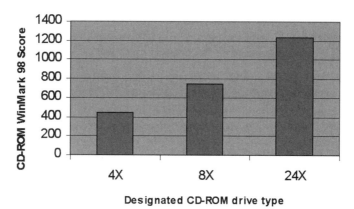

Figure 12.9.
CD-ROM WinMark 98 results for the Pentium 166 machine, varying the CD-ROM drive.

Our results bear out our predictions. The transfer rate of the 8X and 24X drives is better than 900KB/second. The 4X drive (in other words, a transfer rate of 600KB/second) can't keep up and thus it drops an unacceptable number of frames from the 450 frame video clip (see Figure 12.10).

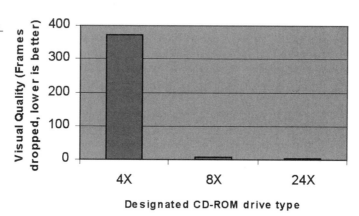

Figure 12.10.
WinBench 98 Video test Visual Quality results for the Pentium 166 machine, varying the CD-ROM drive.

The Maximum Frame Rate results show the same picture. The lowly 4X drive still can't keep up: it can only play back the 30 frames/second clip at 20 frames/second, even with no sound. The 8X drive and 24X drive both show a maximum frame rate that's acceptably better than nominal rate of 30 frames/second. Interestingly enough, the 8X drive shows a slightly better maximum frame rate than the 24X drive! (See Figure 12.11.)

Figure 12.11.

WinBench 98 Video test Maximum Frame Rate results for the Pentium 166 machine, varying the CD-ROM drive.

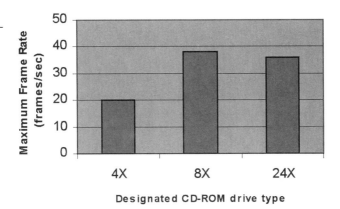

Finally, we'll check the CPU Utilization results for these drives. The 4X drive, unable to pump data into the system as quickly as the frame requires, is also unable to swamp the CPU. Here we see that the faster drives do not swamp the CPU, either, because the entire system is more capable of playing video clips. CPU Utilization is in the low 80's for the 8X and 24X drives (see Figure 12.12). This means that the CPU would have 20% of its time left over for tasks other than video playback.

Figure 12.12.

WinBench 98 Video test CPU Utilization results for the Pentium 166 machine, varying the CD-ROM drive.

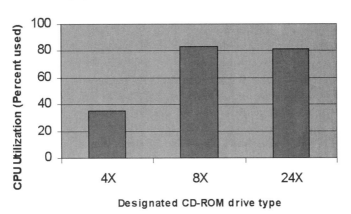

Optimizing Your CD-ROM Subsystem

By moving to the Pentium 166, we see that the added CPU horsepower helps video playback. By adding the 24X drive to our testbed, we see that speed ratings are not reliable indicators of performance. Let's move up to our Pentium 200MMX machine and add one more CD-ROM drive to the testbed and see what happens.

12.5.6. Pentium 200MMX

We ran tests on these same drives in our Pentium 200MMX machine, but in this case the original CD-ROM drive was not the venerable Sony CDU76E-Q. The Pentium 200MMX came with Compaq's PD-1 PD/CD drive. This drive serves a dual function: not only can it read CD-ROM's, it can also read and write to optical PD cartridges. A PD cartridge can hold up to 650MB of uncompressed data, and is useful for (among other things) system backup. With a PD/CD drive, you can have one drive in your machine that reads CD-ROM's and that also acts as a backup device. This is handy, but we were not concerned with the PD functions of this drive. We wanted to see how it held up as a CD-ROM drive. The speed rating of this particular drive is 6X. We also added a DVD drive to the testbed. The DVD drive was a Toshiba SD-M1002, part of the Diamond Max DVD upgrade kit.

The results show that the 24X drive is little better than two times faster than the 6X drive, not four as you might expect. Also, our DVD drive performs slightly better than our 8X drive (see Figure 12.13). If you're buying a DVD drive to upgrade your system, make sure you know what its specs are for CD-ROM playback. Don't just assume that because DVD is new, all DVD drives will be speedy at playing CD-ROMs too. Of course, the best thing you can do is to benchmark the DVD drive yourself!

Figure 12.13.
CD-ROM WinMark 98 results for the Pentium 200MMX machine, varying the CD-ROM drive.

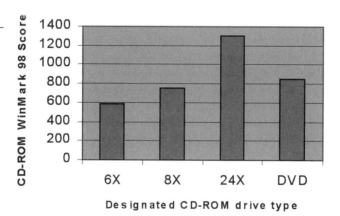

We get an interesting data point when we run our Video Tests again, using the same Cinepak clip that we used with the Pentium 166 machine. Remember, this clip uses a 900KB/second data rate. That's the same data rate we'd expect from a true 6X drive. As you can see from the graph, though, 10% of frames are dropped when we play back this clip on our 6X PD/CD drive as well as on our 24X and DVD drives. The 8X drive drops only about 5% of the total number of frames in the 450 frame clip (see Figure 12.14). The 8X drive looks like the most powerful drive in this case because it is a true CLV drive, while the 24X and DVD drives are CAV or partial CAV designs.

Figure 12.14.
WinBench 98 Video test Visual Quality results for the Pentium 200MMX machine, varying the CD-ROM drive.

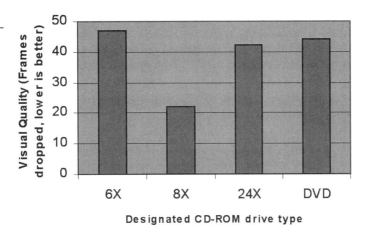

When we look at the Maximum Frame Rate results, we see that the baseline drive, the 6X PD/CD, is just able to exceed the 30 frames/second when playing the clip at top speed with no sound. All of the other drives play the clip at a maximum rate of about 40 frames/second (see Figure 12.15).

Finally, let's look at the CPU Utilization for this range of CD-ROM drives. Here we see something a bit different from what we've seen on the less capable machines. Because we've moved up to a 6X drive, the CD-ROM drive itself can just keep up with the video clip we're using (see Figure 12.16). This is a different situation from the the 4X drive on the Pentium 166, where the drive itself couldn't keep up with the video clip and therefore had no chance of swamping the CPU with data. Here we see that the 6X drive gives us a CPU Utilization of close to 100%. The faster drives also probably have larger buffers, thus taking more of the load off of the CPU. However, the CPU Utilization is still quite high no matter which drive we look at.

Figure 12.15.

WinBench 98 Video test Maximum Frame Rate results for the Pentium 200MMX machine, varying the CD-ROM drive.

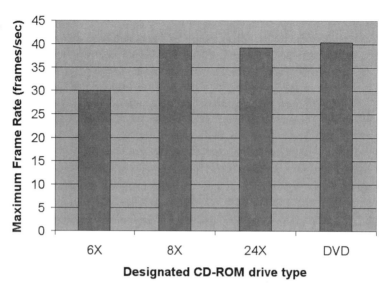

Figure 12.16.

WinBench 98 Video test CPU Utilization results for the Pentium 200MMX machine, varying the CD-ROM drive.

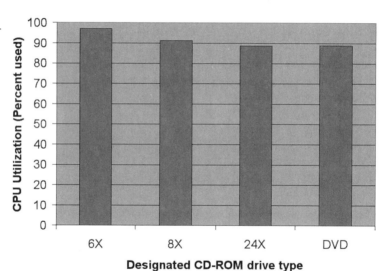

12.6. Windows 95 and the CD-ROM Subsystem

For many users, Windows 95 was the first operating system that almost required a CD-ROM drive to install. Sure, you could get Windows 95 on floppy disks, but did you really need all that wear and tear on your elbow? One of the new features of Windows 95 was built-in 32-bit protected mode drivers for most common hardware. These drivers replaced the older 16-bit drivers used with Windows 3.1 In the case of the CD-ROM drive, this 32-bit code is called CDFS, for Compact Disc Filing System. The CDFS code replaces the old real-mode MSCDEX drivers used in Windows 3.1 and DOS. The most obvious benefit to end-users is that, for most common drives, you no longer need to hassle with proprietary CD-ROM drivers.

Digging more deeply, we can find more advantages to CDFS. Performance improves because the code to access the CD-ROM drive is rewritten as 32-bit protected mode software. The software cache for the CD-ROM drive is also handled by the operating system. This cache is separate from the hard disk cache, and can be optimized for the speed of your particular drive. To learn more about how to optimize the CD-ROM drive cache, read Chapter 6, "Windows 95 Software Tuning." In this chapter, we're going to be looking at upgrading existing CD-ROM drives.

12.6.1. How We Tested

We ran only WinBench 97 tests in this section. Because Winstone 97 runs from the hard drive (where you run most of your business applications) it is not appropriate to use for testing CD-ROM drives. The main test we used was the CD-ROM WinMark 97. This test, like many other WinBench tests, is a *playback* test. WinBench plays back actual CD-ROM operations profiled from a wide variety of popular CD-ROM applications. These applications fall into three general categories: Business and Productivity, Games and Entertainment, and Reference and Education. WinBench 97 uses profiles from two applications out of each of these three categories to get an overall picture of the real-world performance of the CD-ROM subsystem. WinBench 97 times how long a PC takes to play back the profiled CD-ROM operations, then calculates an overall score via a weighted harmonic mean. As we've discussed previously in this book, the weighted harmonic mean gives us an overall score based on the market share of the individual applications.

In addition to the CD-ROM WinMark 97 test, we've also run some full-motion video tests in this chapter. Because CD-ROMs are a common delivery system for full-motion video clips (and similar data), we wanted to test how well our various systems and CD-ROM drives played back full-motion video clips from CD. WinBench 97 provides a huge number of video clips, so we selected certain specific tests which we feel demonstrate important points about CD-ROM drive performance.

Even though we were measuring CD-ROM drive performance, we still completely defragmented the hard drives of each machine before we ran each test. We also ran each test immediately after a cold reboot. This is good testing procedure which we always follow, no matter what you're measuring.

12.6.2. 486/66

Our 486/66 system did not feature a secondary IDE connector. Because all of the CD-ROM drives in our testbed were ATAPI drives, we were not able to run tests on our 486/66 machine.

12.6.3. Pentium 75

Our Pentium 75 came outfitted with a 4X CD-ROM drive, as did most of our other systems. This particular drive is a Sony CDU76E-Q. With this lower-end system, we decided just to see how performance changed when we upgraded to an 8X CD-ROM drive. In other words, would CD-ROM performance double across the board? The drive we chose as an upgrade was the Mitsumi FX810T. Let's take a look at our WinBench scores and see if performance really doubles.

We see that performance does not double with our upgrade. Instead of a 100% increase in performance, we get about a 70% increase (see Figure 12.17). We've quickly proven our basic assumption, that the industry standard CD-ROM drive speed rating isn't necessarily a completely accurate indicator of performance. In the case of these two drives, even though the speed rating doubles, the real-world performance does not. The Sony CDU76E has an average access time of 250ms, while the Mitsumi has an average access time of 150ms, so perhaps this accounts for the performance we're seeing: even though the maximum transfer rate doubles with the Mitsumi, the average access time does not halve. Both drives contains 256KB of cache.

We also want to run some Video Tests on these two drives, to determine how they perform and to explore some concepts salient to full-motion video. We're going to run the same basic test clip recorded for several different data transfer rates. The clip is an action clip (of a carousel) and was compressed with the Indeo codec. The clip is at a resolution of 320×240 and should run at 30 frames per second. For each Video Test, there are several results. The first result we're going to look at is Visual Quality, which is measured in the number of frames dropped. This test result tells you how well the PC can keep up with the video clip. The ideal result for this test is zero, which means the PC dropped no frames during playback. We ran this same test clip at several different data transfer rates: 300, 450, 600, and 750 KB/second.

Figure 12.17.
CD-ROM WinMark 97 results for the Pentium 75 machine, changing the CD-ROM drive from the Sony CDU76E-Q to the Mitsumi FX810T.

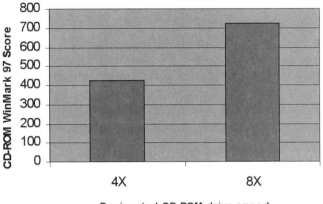

Designated CD-ROM drive speed

The number of frames dropped is very low in all but one case: when we try to play back the 750KB/second clip on the 4X drive (see Figure 12.18). A little math will show that this makes sense. A 4X drive should transfer data at four times the rate of the single-speed, 150KB/second drive. Four times 150 KB/second gives us 600KB/second, so it's obvious that the 4X drive wouldn't be able to keep up with the 750 KB/second clip.

This brings up an important point: from the standpoint of Visual Quality, these two drives are almost identical as long as they're operating within their stated specification. Many CD-ROM applications or video clips (especially older ones) are written or recorded for 2X or 4X drives. Running these applications or clips on a newer, faster CD-ROM drive is overkill.

The Maximum Frame Rate result shows the number of frames per second that the PC can display of the chosen clip when WinBench 97 plays the clip back as fast as possible, without sound. While you're never going to want to play back video clips as fast as possible, without sound, the Maximum Frame Rate test can give you an idea of the overall horsepower of your system when it comes to playing back video. The more frames per second your PC can display, the more time it will have to perform other tasks simultaneously. The graph in Figure 12.19 shows us that there's more to full-motion video performance than just the CD-ROM drive. Both the 4X and 8X drives max out at about 73 frames/second on the 300KB/second clip. As the data transfer rate rises, though, the 8X drive shows its superior speed. Finally, when the data transfer rate rises above the 4X rating, we see that the 4X drive cannot play back the clip quickly enough to be satisfactory. The clip is a thirty frames/second clip, but the 4X drive can only play it back at about twenty-three frames/second.

Figure 12.18.

WinBench 97 Video test Visual Quality results for the Pentium 75 machine, changing the CD-ROM drive from the Sony CDU76E-Q to the Mitsumi FX810T.

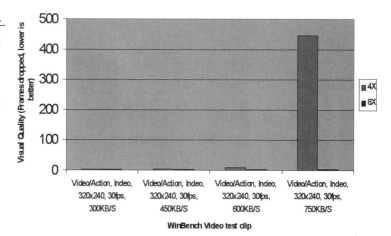

Another result we can get from the Video Tests is Temporal Quality. Temporal Quality is a%age value showing the speed at which the video clip ran versus the speed at which it was supposed to run. The ideal result here is 100%, meaning the clip played back at the exact speed it was supposed to. Here we again see the deficiency in the 4X drive on the 750KB/second clip. All of the other clips play back with the correct Temporal Quality of 100%. The 4X drive can't keep up on the 750KB/second clip, though, and it yields a Temporal Quality of 77% for this test (see Figure 12.20). If we had a clip to play back that maxed out the 8X drive (in other words, one at a greater than 1200KB/second data rate), we'd expect to see a similar result.

So, we've learned that the common speed ratings of CD-ROM drives don't necessarily tell the whole story about true performance. Let's perform this same upgrade in our more capable machines and see if the choice of CPU changes the performance characteristics of this CD-ROM drive swap.

Figure 12.19.
WinBench 97 Video test Maximum Frame Rate results for the Pentium 75 machine, changing the CD-ROM drive from the Sony CDU76E-Q to the Mitsumi FX810T.

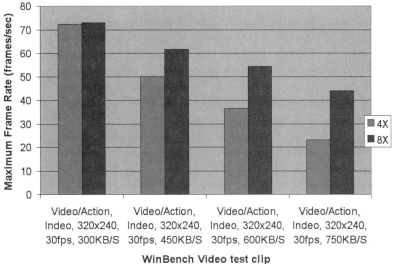

Figure 12.20.
WinBench 97 Video test Temporal Quality results for the Pentium 75 machine, changing the CD-ROM drive from the Sony CDU76E-Q to the Mitsumi FX810T.

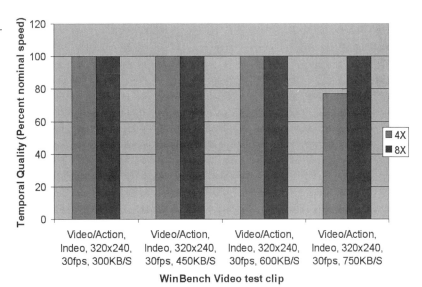

12.6.4. Pentium 100

Our Compaq DeskPro 5100 also came with a Sony CDU76E-Q CD-ROM drive. We tested with this drive and also with out Mitsumi FX810T, to see if the extra CPU horsepower of the Pentium 100 would change the results. First, the CD-ROM WinMark 97 (see Figure 12.21).

Our basic conclusion is still true: performance does not double from the 4X drive to the 8X drive. We do see about a 72% increase, rather than the 70% increase we

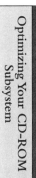

saw with the Pentium 75. This is not a huge difference, but it does back up our guess that a more capable system would allow the faster CD-ROM drive to shine more.

Figure 12.21.

CD-ROM WinMark 97 results for the Pentium 100 machine, changing the CD-ROM drive from the Sony CDU76E-Q to the Mitsumi FX810T.

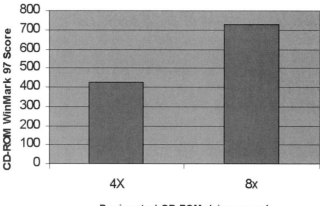

We also re-ran our Video Tests with this new machine. As we saw before, video performance tested as satisfactory as long as we ensured that the data rate of particular video clip did not exceed the data rate of the CD-ROM drive.

The test results for Visual Quality on the Pentium 100 do not show much difference from those on the Pentium 75 (see Figure 12.22). The standout data point occurs when we try to play the 750KB/second clip on the 4X (600KB/second) drive. Other than that, the number of frames dropped is fairly small.

The shape of the graph for the Maximum Frame Rate tests does not change significantly (see Figure 12.23). Again, in all cases but one, the maximum frame rate is (acceptably) above the actual frame rate of the clip. It's interesting to note, though, that all of the scores for the 8X drive are larger than the scores for that same drive on the Pentium 75 machine. In other words, the increased processor speed of this system is contributing to video playback ability.

Finally, the Temporal Quality results are exactly what we saw with the Pentium 75. In all cases but one, the clip plays back at the exact speed it's supposed to. The 4X drive simply can't keep up with the 750KB/second clip (see Figure 12.24).

12.6.5. Pentium 133

Before we move on to a larger variety of CD-ROM drive upgrades, let's repeat this upgrade one more time, this time on our Pentium 133 system. Again, we're starting with a 4X Sony CDU76E-Q and then replacing it with an 8X Mitsumi FX810T. So far, we've seen that our CD-ROM performance does not double (as it theoretically should) with this upgrade (see Figure 12.25).

Figure 12.22.
WinBench 97 Video test Visual Quality results for the Pentium 100 machine, changing the CD-ROM drive from the Sony CDU76E-Q to the Mitsumi FX810T.

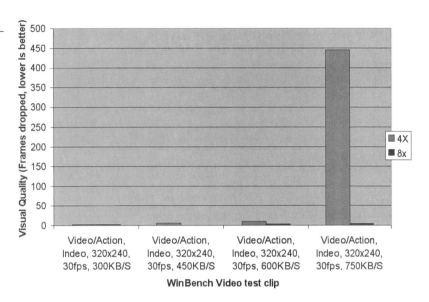

Figure 12.23.
WinBench 97 Video test Maximum Frame Rate results for the Pentium 75 machine, changing the CD-ROM drive from the Sony CDU76E-Q to the Mitsumi FX810T.

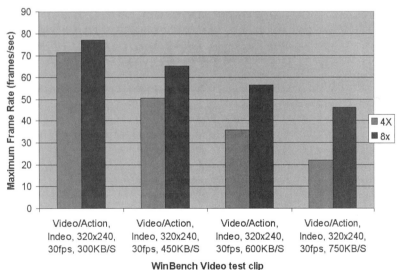

This behavior continues even on our Pentium 133 machine. The performance increase is more on the order of 70%. This is what we saw with the two earlier systems, although it's important to note that the raw scores for both drives are higher on the Pentium 133 than on the Pentium 100 and Pentium 75. Still, this debunks the notion that the X ratings are absolute predictors of performance.

Figure 12.24.

WinBench 97 Video test Temporal Quality results for the Pentium 75 machine, changing the CD-ROM drive from the Sony CDU76E-Q to the Mitsumi FX810T.

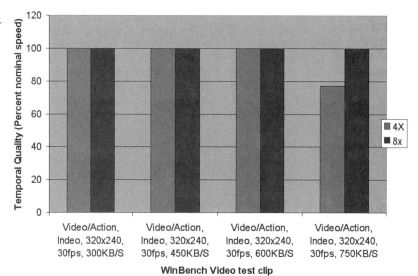

Figure 12.25.

CD-ROM WinMark 97 results for the Pentium 133 machine, changing the CD-ROM drive from the Sony CDU76E-Q to the Mitsumi FX810T.

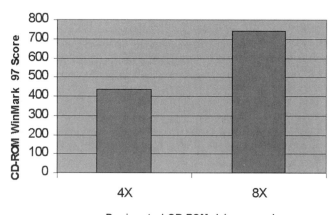

We also ran our Video Tests on the Pentium 133 machine. The results we got surprised us: both drives kept up on all of the tests! In other words, no frames were dropped on the Visual Quality results, and the Temporal Quality results were all 100%. (We're sparing you the boredom of looking at these results in graphical form.) We doublechecked our testing, and we can only conclude that there's something about this particular video clip which allows for this behavior on this machine. The added horsepower of the Pentium 133 also helps the situation. Let's take a quick look at the Maximum Frame Rate results.

As you can see in Figure 12.26, the maximum frame rate results are neck and neck for the two drives. This goes counter to our previous guesses about these two drives, but is due at least in part to the more powerful processor subsystem in this machine. When faced with results like this, we would normally run and analyze the full set of Video Tests, but that is beyond the scope of this book, because WinBench provides such a huge number of Video Test clips.

Figure 12.26.
WinBench 97 Video test Maximum Frame Rate results for the Pentium 75 machine, changing the CD-ROM drive from the Sony CDU76E-Q to the Mitsumi FX810T.

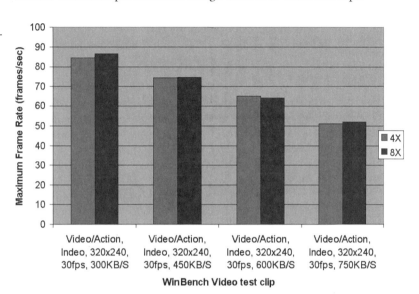

12.6.6. Pentium 166

Let's move on and test a wider variety of CD-ROM drives. In addition to the familiar Sony CDU76E-Q and the Mitsumi FX810T, we added 12X, 16X, 24X, and DVD drives. The 12X drive was a Mitsumi FX120T. The 16X drive was a Hitachi CDR-8130. The 24X drive was a Creative Labs CD2422E. The DVD drive was a Toshiba SD-M1002, part of the Diamond Max DVD upgrade kit. The Hitachi drive is a Partial-CAV (PCAV) design, and while it's not explicitly stated in the product specifications, we expect that the Creative Labs drive is a CAV design. If you've read this chapter up to this point, you'll know that we're skeptical that all of these drives will live up to their *X* ratings, especially the CAV drives. Our CD-ROM WinMark 97 test will show the real-world performance of all of these drives. In this case, if the 4X drive gets a score of 400, we'd expect (if we believed the speed ratings) that the 24X drive would get a 2400.

12.6.7. Sidebar: DVD

DVD stands for Digital Video Disc or Digital Versatile Disc. The main difference to the end-user between DVD and CD-ROM is the amount of data these formats can store. While a CD-ROM can hold about 650MB of data, a DVD can hold over 4GB. As with CD-ROM's, DVD's are used in both the computer world and in the world of consumer electronics. The consumer analogue of a CD-ROM is the audio CD, while the consumer analogue of the computer DVD is the video DVD which replaces the old laserdisc. If you want to make sure your system will be ready for the applications of the future, you'll want to consider an upgrade to a DVD drive instead of to a CD-ROM drive. Be aware, though, that the history of DVD is fraught with conflicting standards. Also, DVD's with faster transfer rates and with more storage capacity are planned for the near future. If you absolutely don't need DVD right now, you might be better off waiting until the standards are completely agreed upon and until the technology is further along than "release 1.0."

As you can see in Figure 12.27, the drives we tested (with the exception of the 4X drive) do not live up to their ratings! Instead of being six times faster than the 4X drive, the 24X drive is just under three times faster. The other drives fall somewhere in between. From this graph, we would give these drives more realistic speed ratings: the 8X would be a 7.5X, the 12X would be a 9.5X, the 16X would be a 10X, and the 24X would be a 12.5X. Yes, we're being a little facetious, but it's to make a point. You should accept a single X rating as the final determinant of a particular CD-ROM drive's performance. One other interesting data point on this graph is the result for the DVD drive. This particular DVD drive tests out with results that fall between the 8X and the 12X drive results. Even though the DVD drive is the newest one in our testbed, it's not the fastest when it comes to CD-ROM performance. This is important to note if you're buying a DVD drive: while it will give you capabilities beyond any CD-ROM drive, it won't necessarily be faster. Actually, our results match up with the initial DVD specs. The standard transfer rate of the first DVD drives is approximately equivalent to a 9X CD-ROM drive.

We also ran Video Tests on this set of drives. To change things up a bit, we tested a different video clip than we did for the previous machines. In this case, we tested the action clip, compressed with the Cinepak codec, running at a resolution of 640×480. We chose the thirty frames/second clip with a data rate of 900KB/second. As we saw before, any drive with a transfer rate less than 900KB/second should perform unacceptably on this clip.

Our results bear out our predictions. The transfer rate of all of the drives is better than 900KB/second. The 4X drive (in other words, a transfer rate of 600KB/second) can't keep up and thus it drops an unacceptable number of frames from the video clip (see Figure 12.28).

The Maximum Frame Rate results present a slightly different picture. First off, we see that the lowly 4X drive still can't keep up: it can only play back the 30 frames/second clip at 21 frames/second, even with no sound. The DVD slightly outperforms the 8X drive, again backing up our prediction that it would perform like a 9X drive. The most interesting points on the graph in Figure 12.29 are the results for the 12X, 16X, and 24X drives: they're almost exactly the same. Beyond 12X, it simply doesn't matter (again, for this clip) that we're adding drives with higher speed ratings.

Figure 12.27.

CD-ROM WinMark 97 results for the Pentium 166 machine, varying the CD-ROM drive.

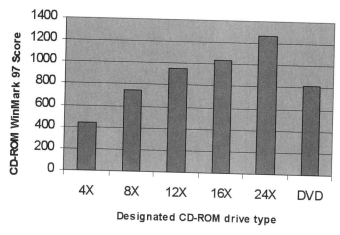

Figure 12.28.

WinBench 97 Video test Visual Quality results for the Pentium 166 machine, varying the CD-ROM drive.

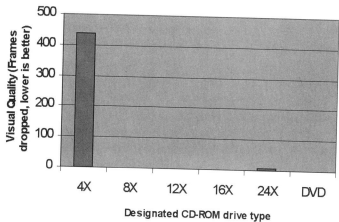

Of course, it's not likely that you'll be able to predict the data rates of video clips you're going to use on your PC, to determine exactly what speed CD-ROM drive to purchase. (If you can do this, more power to you.) Even so, this graph should make you a bit more skeptical about expecting linear performance gains based on the *X* rating.

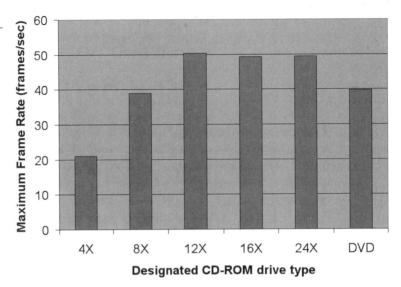

Figure 12.29.
WinBench 97 Video test Maximum Frame Rate results for the Pentium 166 machine, varying the CD-ROM drive.

Finally, we'll check the Temporal Quality results for these drives. As you can see in Figure 12.30, all of them perform acceptably except for the 4X drive. This drive simply can't keep up with the video clip we've chosen here.

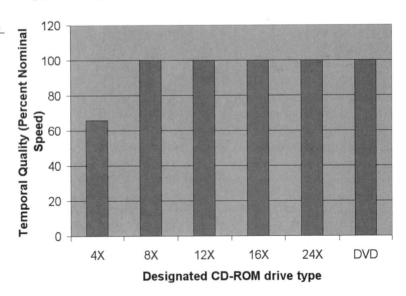

Figure 12.30.
WinBench 97 Video test Temporal Quality results for the Pentium 166 machine, varying the CD-ROM drive.

12.6.8. Pentium 200MMX

We ran tests on these same drives in our Pentium 200MMX machine, but in this case the original CD-ROM drive was not the venerable Sony CDU76E-Q. The Pentium 200MMX came with Compaq's PD-1 PD/CD drive. This drive serves a dual function: not only can it read CD-ROM's, it can also read and write to optical PD cartridges. A PD cartridge can hold up to 650MB of uncompressed data, and is useful for (among other things) system backup. With a PD/CD drive, you can have one drive in your machine that reads CD-ROM's and that also acts as a backup device. This is handy, but we were not concerned with the PD functions of this drive. We wanted to see how it held up as a CD-ROM drive. The speed rating of this particular drive is 6X.

These results look familiar: the real world results we get from WinBench do not increase as much as the *X* ratings suggest they should. Performance increases, it's true, but not at the rate one would expect from the standard speed ratings. Once again, our DVD drive performs like a 9X or 10X drive (see Figure 12.31).

Figure 12.31.

CD-ROM WinMark 97 results for the Pentium 200MMX machine, varying the CD-ROM drive.

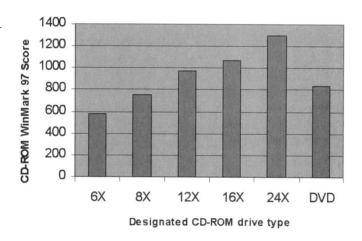

We get an interesting data point when we run our Video Tests again, using the same Cinepak clip that we used with the Pentium 166 machine. Remember, this clip uses a 900KB/second data rate. That's the same data rate we'd expect from a true 6X drive. As you can see from the graph in Figure 12.32, though, a significant number of frames (119 out of a total of 450) are dropped when we play back this clip on our 6X PD/CD drive. This drive is on-the-edge in terms of performing at 900KB/second...yet another reason for you to be a bit skeptical about these speed ratings.

When we look at the Maximum Frame Rate results, the shape of the curve is similar to what we saw with the Pentium 166 machine. The baseline drive, the 6X PD/CD, is just able to exceed the 30 frames/second (it maxes out at 30.7 frames/second) when playing the clip at top speed with no sound. Once again, once you get to the 12X drive, there's no additional gain added by the 16X and 24X drives. That's for this particular video clip only, but it should give you a better idea of how to judge video playback performance from a variety of CD-ROM drives (see Figure 12.33).

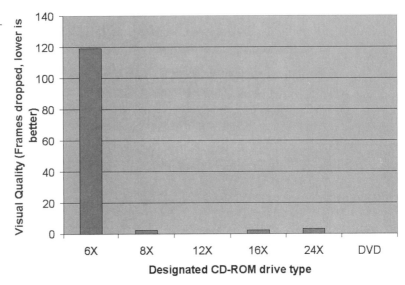

Figure 12.32.
WinBench 97 Video test Visual Quality results for the Pentium 200MMX machine, varying the CD-ROM drive.

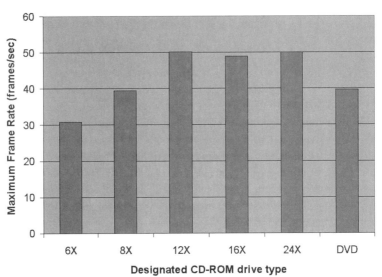

Figure 12.33.
WinBench 97 Video test Maximum Frame Rate results for the Pentium 200MMX machine, varying the CD-ROM drive.

Finally, let's look at the Temporal Quality for this range of CD-ROM drives. As you can see, all of the drives succeeded in playing back the clip at the nominal speed, even the 6X drive (see Figure 12.34).

Figure 12.34.
WinBench 97 Video test Temporal Quality results for the Pentium 200MMX machine, varying the CD-ROM drive.

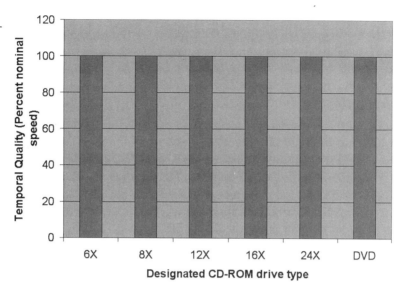

12.7. Windows NT and the CD-ROM Subsystem

Windows NT 4.0 supports the same CDFS (CD-ROM Filing System) that Windows 95 and Windows 98 support. If you've got NT 4.0 up and running with your particular CD-ROM drive, that's all you probably want or need to know. If you want to get a new CD-ROM drive (or a fancy DVD drive or PD/ CD drive) then you'll need to know one more thing: hardware compatibility is still an issue for Windows NT. While NT 4.0 supports more hardware than NT 3.51 did, getting NT device drivers for less-than-common hardware can still be tough at times. At the time we tested, we couldn't use several of our testbed CD-ROM drives because NT drivers were not available. This situation will change over time, but it's something to be aware of.

Because NT 4.0 and Windows 95 and Windows 98 all support CDFS, we would expect them to perform similarly when it comes to the CD-ROM drive. We would guess that any differences in performance are due to the major differences in NT and Windows 9x: the heavy-duty kernel architecture of NT 4.0 versus the DOS heritage of Windows 95 and Windows 98.

12.7.1. How We Tested

We ran the same WinBench 97 tests under NT 4.0 as we did under Windows 95. Once again, our main indicator of CD-ROM performance is CD-ROM WinMark 97. We also ran some Video Tests. In the case of NT 4.0, we were able to calculate CPU Utilization results with these tests. WinBench 97 cannot

Optimizing Your CD-ROM Subsystem

calculate CPU Utilization results for tests under Windows 95 which utilize the Multimedia Control Interface (MCI). So we can now look at how different CD-ROM drives load down the processor subsystem.

As always, we completely defragmented the hard drives of each machine before we ran each test, and we ran each test immediately after a cold reboot.

12.7.2. Pentium 133

As we did under Windows 95, we tested the Compaq DeskPro 5133 with the 4X drive it came with (the Sony CDU76E-Q), and with an 8X drive (the Mitsumi FX810T). Our assumption was that performance would not double, as the ratings would lead you to believe.

Performance does not double. It increases by the seventy% figure which we saw under Windows 95. An interesting feature of the graph in Figure 12.35, though, is that in terms of raw scores, these drives perform slightly better under NT 4.0 than they do under Windows 95. Perhaps NT 4.0 has a slight performance edge over Windows 95 when it comes to the CD-ROM subsystem—let's look at some Video Test results and see if this is indeed true.

Figure 12.35.
CD-ROM WinMark 97 results for the Pentium 133 machine, varying the CD-ROM drive.

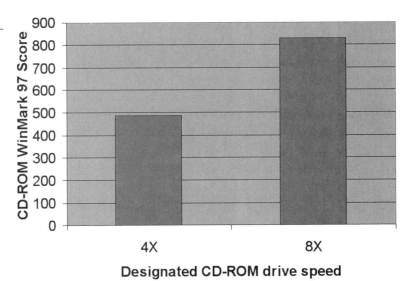

We went back to our Indeo Action clips at various data rates when testing the Pentium 133 under NT 4.0. None of these data rates should exceed the capabilities of the 8X drive, and as you can see from the graph in Figure 12.36, the 8X drive does not drop a significant number of frames on the Visual Quality tests. Unlike under Windows 95, though, the 4X drive starts dropping frames even when the data rate of the test clip is only 450KB/second. So our guess that NT

4.0 has a performance edge when it comes to the CD-ROM subsystem turns out to be not quite true.

Figure 12.36.
WinBench 97 Video test Visual Quality results for the Pentium 133 machine, varying the CD-ROM drive.

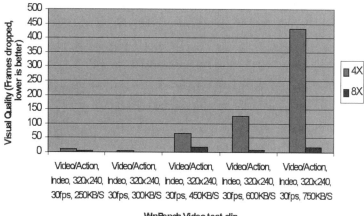

Looking at the Maximum Frame Rate results, we see that the 4X drive never competes with the 8X drive. Compare this to the situation under Windows 95, where for a slow enough data rate, the 4X and 8X drives performed almost identically. Also, as the data rates climb, the 4X drive's maximum frame rate is unacceptable at 600KB/second. This drive is on the edge in terms of performing at a 600KB/second level (see Figure 12.37).

Figure 12.37.
WinBench 97 Video test Maximum Frame Rate results for the Pentium 133 machine, varying the CD-ROM drive.

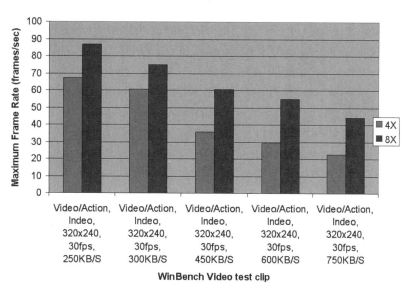

Optimizing Your CD-ROM Subsystem

When we check the Temporal Quality, we see a familiar graph (see Figure 12.38). In all cases but one, the drives can play back the clips at exactly the nominal speed. Once we get to the 750KB/second clip, though, the 4X drive simply can't keep up. This graph doesn't present us with any surprises.

Figure 12.38.
WinBench 97 Video test Temporal Quality results for the Pentium 133 machine, varying the CD-ROM drive.

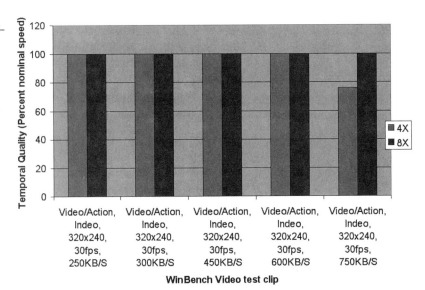

We can now calculate CPU Utilization, because we're running NT 4.0. Remember, higher numbers are worse when it comes to CPU Utilization, because it means that the CPU has less time to do other work while its reading from the CD-ROM drive. When we look at the CPU Utilization graph for these same Video tests, we see that CPU Utilization increases as the data rate of the video clip increases. This makes sense, because as the data rate increases, the CPU has that much more data it has to handle per unit time. The CPU Utilization is about the same for both drives, until the 4X drive reaches its performance limit. Once we get to the 750KB/second clip, the 4X drive can't pump out data anywhere near fast enough. Thus, the CPU utilization goes down because the CPU has less data to deal with than it should (see Figure 12.39).

12.7.3. Pentium 166

We tested the Pentium 166 machine, a Compaq DeskPro 5166, with a wide variety of CD-ROM drives under Windows 95. We were unable to do this under NT 4.0, due to a lack of available device drivers at the time of testing. While this situation has probably changed by the time of publication, there's no getting around the fact that NT 4.0 is more persnickety about hardware compatibility than Windows 95. We were able to run tests with our familiar 4X and 8X drives, as well as the 12X Mitsumi FX120T. First, we ran the CD-ROM WinMark 97 test.

Figure 12.39.
*WinBench 97
Video test CPU
Utilization
results for the
Pentium 133
machine, varying
the CD-ROM
drive.*

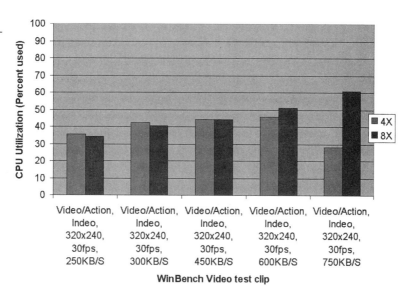

Figure 12.40.
*CD-ROM
WinMark 97
results for the
Pentium 166
machine, varying
the CD-ROM
drive.*

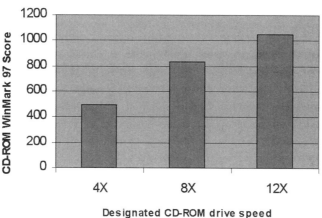

We've said it before, we might as well say it again: *X* ratings aren't a perfect indicator of CD-ROM drive performance. Figure 12.40 bears this out. Performance should double from the 4X to the 8X drive, and triple from the 4X to the 12X drive. Instead, the 8X drive gives us about a 70% performance boost over the 4X drive, and the 12X drive gives us about a 113% performance boost over the 4X drive.

Optimizing Your CD-ROM
Subsystem

When we stepped up to the Pentium 166 machine, we also changed the video clip. We looked at the Cinepak Action clip, running at a resolution of 640×480 and 30 frames/second. This is a 900KB/second clip. Because the data rate of this clip is faster than our 4X drive, the 4X drive drops a significant number of frames during playback. The 8X and 12X drives perform acceptably, as we would expect them to (see Figure 12.41).

Figure 12.41.
WinBench 97 Video test Visual Quality results for the Pentium 166 machine, varying the CD-ROM drive.

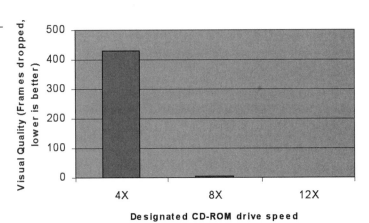

When we look at the Maximum Frame Rate, we see again that the 4X drive is not up to playing this clip. Even with no sound, playing the clip as fast as possible, this drive achieves a frame rate of only about twenty frames/second. The 8X and 12X drives provide more muscle on this test (see Figure 12.42). We couldn't test our other high-speed drives, but we would expect that their performance would level off at the 12X point as it did under Windows 95.

The Temporal Quality results once again show that the 8X and 12X drives can handle this clip. Both drives play the clip back at the exact nominal speed. The 4X drive can't keep up, and plays the clip back at 66% of nominal speed (see Figure 12.43). You should be able to predict this behavior by now; we're merely providing the graphs here for the sake of completeness.

Finally, let's look at the CPU Utilization of these three drives on this particular video clip. A quick glance at the graph in Figure 12.44 would seem to indicate that the 4X drive does better on this test, because its CPU Utilization is lower. This is not the case. Remember, the 4X drive can't keep up with the data rate of the clip. Therefore, it's not supplying that data to the CPU as quickly as the 8X and 12X drives are. In turn, the CPU is loaded down less by the 4X drive playing (or rather, failing to play) this clip.

Figure 12.42.
WinBench 97 Video test Maximum Frame Rate results for the Pentium 166 machine, varying the CD-ROM drive.

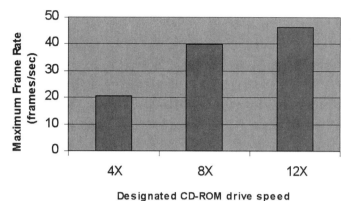

Figure 12.43.
WinBench 97 Video test Temporal Quality results for the Pentium 166 machine, varying the CD-ROM drive.

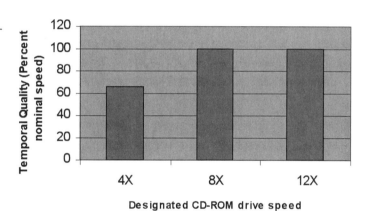

12.7.4. Pentium 200MMX

Finally, we turn to our Pentium 200MMX machine. If you read the Windows 95 section or the Windows 98 section, you'll remember that this machine came with a PD/CD drive, rated at 6X. As with the Pentium 166, we were only able to use the 8X and 12X drives for upgrades under NT 4.0. First, we looked at overall CD-ROM subsystem performance by running CD-ROM WinMark 97 (see Figure 12.45).

For the last time, we'll state that this graph shows that CD-ROM subsystem performance is not absolutely indicated by the *X* rating. There, we said it! Here we see a performance increase of about 15% when we move from the 6X drive to the 8X drive. From the speed ratings alone, we would expect a 33% increase.

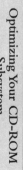

Optimizing Your CD-ROM Subsystem

The 12X drive should perform at twice the speed of the 6X drive. Instead, performance increases by a measly 28%.

Figure 12.44.

WinBench 97 Video test CPU Utilization results for the Pentium 166 machine, varying the CD-ROM drive.

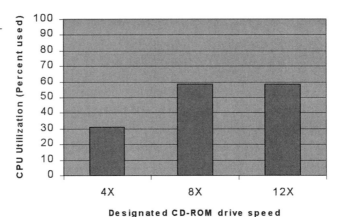

Figure 12.45.

CD-ROM WinMark 97 results for the Pentium 200MMX machine, varying the CD-ROM drive.

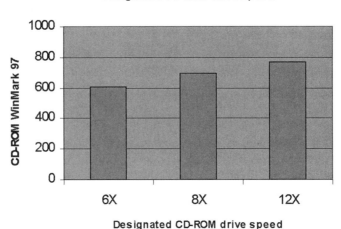

We also ran our chosen Cinepak Action clip on these drives in this machine. As we saw under Windows 95, the 6X drive drops an unacceptable number of frames on this clip, even though the clip has a data rate of 900KB/second (which should equal the 6X drive rating). This drive is on the edge and it can't keep up (see Figure 12.46). The point here is not that you'll be able to predict the data rates of video clips you'll be manipulating on your PC. It's that you should be skeptical of CD-ROM drive speed ratings and buy accordingly (oops, we said it again).

Figure 12.46.

WinBench 97 Video test Visual Quality results for the Pentium 200MMX machine, varying the CD-ROM drive.

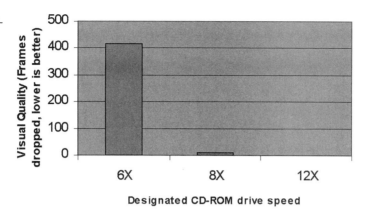

When we check the Maximum Frame Rate, we can confirm that the 6X drive isn't quite up to the task of displaying the 900KB/second clip (see Figure 12.47). The maximum frame rate achieved on the 6X drive is 29.9 frames/second, just slightly below the rated speed of 30 frames/second. The 8X and 12X drives both have the horsepower to handle this clip (in this case, curiously, the 8X drive shows a slightly higher maximum frame rate than the 12X drive).

Figure 12.47.

WinBench 97 Video test Maximum Frame Rate results for the Pentium 200MMX machine, varying the CD-ROM drive.

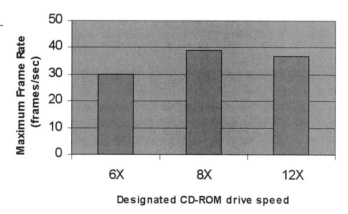

When we look at the Temporal Quality, the 6X drive does not look so bad; it achieves 98% of the nominal playback speed. Don't look at this result alone, though; remember that the 6X drive drops most of the frames in the clip during playback. It's performing right on the edge (as opposed to the 4X drive on the Pentium 166, which was simply out of its depth) and for this particular clip its performance is unacceptable, even though the Temporal Quality score looks OK (see Figure 12.48).

Figure 12.48.

WinBench 97 Video test Temporal Quality results for the Pentium 200MMX machine, varying the CD-ROM drive.

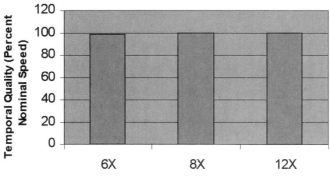

As we suspected, all three drives have similar (and alarmingly high) CPU Utilization scores. The processor has less than 20% of its time left over after dealing with reading this video clip! (See Figure 12.49.) At this point, if we really wanted to get to the bottom of what's going on in the CD-ROM subsystem in this machine, we'd run all of the Video tests and CD-ROM tests we could. Unfortunately, that search is beyond the scope of this book.

Figure 12.49.

WinBench 97 Video test CPU Utilization results for the Pentium 200MMX machine, varying the CD-ROM drive.

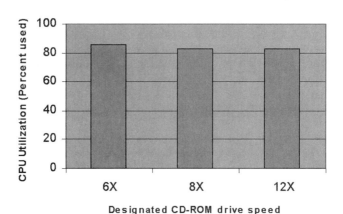

12.8. The Bottom Line

The main thing to remember about CD-ROM drive performance is, it's probably the least of your worries. Until you've spent time optimizing your system's RAM and CPU, you probably shouldn't deal with your system's CD-ROM drive. Even if the rest of your system is completely tweaked up, you might not *need* to worry about your CD-ROM drive if you only use it for the occasional software install.

When you do delve into the CD-ROM subsystem, remember to be skeptical of the speed or *X* rating that manufacturers use as a performance spec. We've shown throughout this chapter that this specification is not an absolute indicator of real-world performance. If you're using your CD-ROM drive to watch video clips, make sure that the capabilities of your drive exceed the data rates of the clips you expect to view. As always, nothing beats doing your own real-world testing.

12.9. Testing You Can Do

To do the testing in this chapter, you're going to need multiple CD-ROM drives. If you're lucky, you'll have a friend or a friendly computer dealer who can accommodate you. Unlike hard drives or RAM or CPU upgrades, ATAPI CD-ROM drives are fairly easy to install, given that you have an available secondary IDE connection.

As always, hold all variables equal except for the one you're interested in. In this case, the variable will be the CD-ROM drive itself. You've always got to follow the apples to apples comparison rule. You should also follow good testing procedure, by defragmenting your hard drive completely before each run, and by running tests immediately after a cold re-boot.

WinBench is the test you want to choose to check out CD-ROM drive performance. Because Winstone runs from your hard drive, it's of no help here. The main test you'll want to pay attention to is CD-ROM WinMark. You can also run individual CD-ROM Tests to get at specific aspects of CD-ROM drive performance. If you're interested in playing video clips from your CD-ROM drive, you should run all of the Video Tests. There are a huge number of these tests in WinBench; we've only scratched the surface of these tests in this chapter.

> **NOTE** Complete directions for running WinBench can be found in Appendix B, "Using WinBench 98."

12.10. From Here...

CD-ROM performance isn't of interest to folks who only install software occasionally from CD's. If you use CD-ROM based applications frequently, though, you'll want to ensure that you're getting the most out of your CD-ROM drive. In this chapter we've learned that CD-ROM drives come in a variety of speeds, but that the industry standard speed ratings aren't necessarily a good indicator of performance. You can learn about other tweaks for your CD-ROM drive in the chapters on software tuning. If you care about CD-ROM drive performance, you might be a die-hard gamer, because many games run from CD-ROM's. If this is true, make sure to read the chapter on optimizing your system for games.

The following chapters will provide more information on optimizations related to the CD-ROM conclusions we've drawn this chapter.

- Chapter 5, "Windows 98 Software Tuning," will show you software tuning tips for Windows 98, including tweaks for your CD-ROM subsystem.

- Chapter 6, "Windows 95 Software Tuning," will show you software tuning tips for Windows 95, including tweaks for your CD-ROM subsystem.

- Chapter 7, "Windows NT Software Tuning," will show you how to monitor and optimize the performance of Windows NT 4.0, including how to monitor your CD-ROM subsystem.

- Chapter 14, "Optimizing for Games," will show you how to optimize your system to get best game performance.

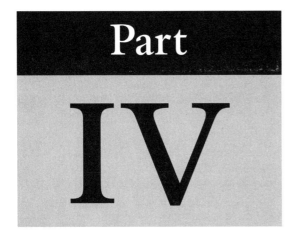

Part

IV

Special Situations

Chapter

13

Power Saving and Portables

The portable computer, or laptop, presents special challenges to those of us interested in boosting performance. Upgrading the hardware in a desktop computer is relatively easy; portable computers are much more difficult to upgrade with additional RAM or a faster hard disk. If you want to upgrade the hardware in a laptop, you typically send it to the manufacturer or to an authorized service center.

Until quite recently, the portable computer has been a luxury item used only by executives and gearheads with very deep pockets. Nowadays, everyone wants to stay connected. Many universities have begun requiring all of their entering freshman to purchase notebook computers. The portable computer (in laptop and palmtop form) is becoming as ubiquitous as the cellular phone and the pager. The first portable computers were also known as *luggables*. These computers still required AC power; they just happened to be somewhat portable. These are a far cry from the ultra-portables of today, which can run for several hours on their battery power.

Laptops aren't designed to be just small and portable; they're also designed to consume as little battery power as necessary. Is there a trade-off between power consumption and real performance? That's one of the questions we set out to answer in this chapter.

> **NOTE**   We are not covering Windows NT 4.0 performance in this chapter. At the time of this writing, not many people run Windows NT 4.0. If you are one of those people, however, you can apply similar techniques to those we discuss in this chapter for Windows 98 and Windows 95.

If you own a portable computer and you'd like to get the most performance out of it, or if you'd like to understand how power management can affect performance, this chapter is for you.

In this chapter, you will also learn:

- What power management is

  Power management encompasses several strategies for reducing the drain on your laptop's battery. In the following sections, you'll learn about the different power management settings.

- How power management affects performance

  You might expect that the less battery power a laptop uses, the less performance you'll get. We'll investigate the trade-offs between power management and performance, in search of the sweet spot that gives us the best of both worlds.

- How disk cache settings affect the performance of portable computers

  Windows 95 and Windows 98 allow you to set the role of this machine under the disk cache performance settings. We'll be investigating the effect of this setting on the laptop performance.

13.1. Cocktail Party Tips

We've been having a lot of fun with our fictional cocktail party throughout the book. If you find yourself at a cocktail party of fellow computer enthusiasts, you'll probably be considered among the elite merely by *owning* a laptop computer that's less than one or two years old. If you've been reading this book in sequence and doling out our other cocktail party tips, the other party members should be in awe of your knowledge by this point. So when one of them asks you how to set up a portable computer for maximum performance, you should respond, "Fiddle about."

Yes, another flip answer! We give that answer both because we are flip and because it is very true. As you'll discover in this chapter, different laptop computers have different power saving settings. What works on a particular model of notebook computer might not be possible on another.

The other reason to fiddle about is that the best power saving settings are a matter of taste and a reflection of your work habits. Some folks prefer it if the screen turns itself off after a short period of inactivity. Others prefer the screen to remain on most of the time. If your system pops in and out of standby mode while you're pausing briefly during work sessions, you might want to lengthen the inactivity period for the standby timer. There's no one answer that works for all portables and all users.

13.2. What is Power Management?

Generally speaking, power management allows your computer to temporarily shut down certain devices or peripherals to conserve power. Your computer remains on in some fashion, whether still operating apparently normally or in standby mode. For instance, your portable computer probably has a screen-off timer setting. When you enable this and set it to a certain time interval, the laptop will power down the display if you haven't used your laptop for the specified interval. This conserves the battery power necessary to keep the LCD panel lit up. When you hit a key on the keyboard, the laptop powers the screen back up so you can continue working. Power management can also shut down your hard disk or CPU when your system is idle, and most laptops can go into standby and suspend modes, essentially turning themselves off if you haven't used them within a specified interval. So, power management consists of controlling the power usage of a computer based on system activity. As system activity decreases, power management features reduce the power supplied to unused system resources. If system activity stops for a given period of time, the power management features cause the system to enter a suspended state.

Windows 95 and Windows 98 support the Advanced Power Management specification. For Windows to take advantage of power management, though, you've got to have it enabled in your system BIOS, and your system BIOS has to support the Advanced Power Management spec. This may not be true of older systems, so check your BIOS first. Typically, your system display will tell you how to invoke the BIOS at boot time; usually you hit the Delete, Esc, or F1 key to enter the BIOS setup. Guiding you through all possible system BIOS settings is beyond the scope of this book. You'll want to look for a menu heading regarding Power Management. If you want to control power management through Windows, make sure that power management is enabled in the BIOS. If you want to tweak your power management settings directly in the BIOS, that's fine too.

Power management affects the performance of your computer, although it's a slightly different definition of performance than the one we've used throughout the book. If your power saving settings are adjusted so that your hard drive spins down after a minute of inactivity, then you might never notice this if you work constantly, without stopping for longer than a minute. If, on the other hand, you take breaks of a minute or two to collect your thoughts, you will run into periods when your machine slows as it spins the hard disk back up. Thus, power management affects the performance of your machine. Unlike the raw performance we measure in other chapters, though, this performance is tied directly to your working style. That's why one of the main conclusions of this chapter is that you'll have to spend some time tweaking the power saving settings available to you so that they match up well with your work habits.

13.3. Windows 98

Windows 98 improves on the power management supported by Windows 95. It supports the Advanced Configuration and Power Interface (ACPI) specification, as well as the Advanced Power Management (APM) 1.2 extensions. Your system has to be ACPI-compliant to take advantage of those features, features that let your PC and other peripherals turn each other on and off as needed. Most notebooks have power management features built in to the BIOS; you'll have to consult your owner's manual to see if your notebook computer is ACPI- or APM-compliant.

13.3.1. How We Tested

For testing in this section, we ran Business Winstone 98. Winstone results tell us how our system tweaks affect real-world performance. We also ran the Processor Tests, CPUmark$_{32}$ and FPU WinMark, in WinBench 98 to test how the power saving and CPU speed settings affected the processor subsystem. Finally, we ran WinBench 98's Disk Tests to see how adjusting the disk cache settings affected the disk subsystem.

Our default testing setup was at 800 x 600 x 256 colors. This is a common resolution and color depth combination for current notebook computers. If you'd like to learn more about resolution and color depth and how they affect performance, read Chapter 10, "Optimizing Your Graphics Subsystem."

As always, we fully defragmented the hard drive before we ran each test. We also rebooted each machine before running tests. Both of these steps are merely good testing procedures that we always follow, no matter what aspect of performance we're testing.

Our laptop testbed consisted of an IBM ThinkPad 560X. This machine came with 32MB RAM and a 233MHz Pentium processor with MMX. The ThinkPad 560X offers many power-saving options in the BIOS.

In the following graphs, we test out four different power management schemes. We denoted these schemes as baseline, custom, drastic, and high performance (hi perf). For each scheme, we set standby timer, suspend timer, screen off timer, hard drive stop timer, and processor speed to different values. Table 13.1 summarizes the power saving settings for our four different schemes.

Table 13.1. Four different power-saving schemes for an IBM Thinkpad 560X notebook.

Power saving setting	Baseline	Custom	Drastic	High Performance
Standby timer	0	0	1	0
Suspend timer	15	5	1	60
Screen off timer	5	3	0	60
Hard drive stop	10	3	Immediate	20
Processor speed	Autoclock (slow)	Maximum	Maximum	Maximum

13.3.2. Power Saving Settings

All of the times in Table 13.1 are in minutes. As you can see, our High Performance scheme is designed to leave the computer fully powered for a long time. The system never goes into standby mode, it only suspends after an hour of inactivity, and it only stops the hard drive after twenty minutes of inactivity. Our Drastic scheme, on the other hand, turns off the hard drive any time it's not in use, and suspends operation of the laptop after one minute of inactivity. The Baseline scheme shows the power saving settings on this machine as it was shipped to us from IBM. The Custom scheme uses power saving settings that many users might set.

The Processor speed setting deserves further explanation. This setting, when set to autoclock, revs the CPU to maximum speed when a key is pressed or when the hard drive is accessed, but otherwise runs the CPU at a slower frequency. In the case of our Baseline scheme, the CPU runs at 25% of its top speed when the hard drive is not being accessed and when a key is not being pressed.

We set out to run our tests on all four of these power saving schemes, to see if they affected performance. In particular, we wondered if the hard drive stop feature would affect performance as measured by Winstone and WinBench.

First, we look at our warhorse test, Business Winstone 98. The graph in Figure 13.1 has only two out of four bars, because Winstone failed to run to completion on two of our power schemes. In fact, we got the infamous Blue Screen of Death when we attempted to run Winstone in those two cases. It is tempting to look at the power-saving schemes and blame this on a low value for the suspend timer or for the hard drive stop timer, but as you'll see later on in this chapter, all four of our power schemes allowed Winstone 97 to run to completion on Windows 95. So there is no clear place to put the blame for these testing failures. The two scores we did get show no significant difference in performance between our baseline and high performance power saving schemes. This makes sense, because Winstone 98 is giving the machine a non-stop workout. There are no long periods of inactivity, so we don't see any difference between our power saving schemes.

You probably don't type and mouse quite as fast as Winstone; this is why power saving settings are going to be a matter of taste as opposed to a matter of raw performance. If you leave your machine running but often inactive, you might want to make your power saving settings more drastic, to save battery life. Conversely, if your machine is constantly going into standby or suspend mode, even though you're working steadily, you should adjust the power saving settings to give you more useful performance.

So, because our tests keep the machine under high stress, it's unlikely we'll be able to differentiate between our power saving schemes. Still, as you know, we love to test and graph the results, so let's take a quick look at results from our other tests on these four power saving schemes.

Figure 13.1.

Business Winstone 98 results for the ThinkPad 560X, varying the power saving settings.

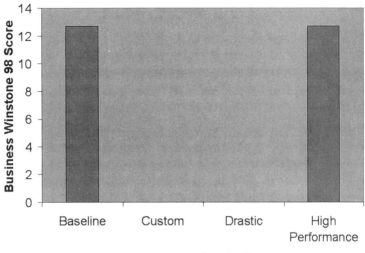

The Business Winstone 98 category scores also show no significant difference between the two schemes which we could test. Remember, Winstone scores can vary normally by 1% or 2%. That level of variability is impossible to eliminate from even the most strict of testing environments with a test as complicated as Winstone. So, even though the graphs show a very slight difference in the results, the difference is not significant (see Figure 13.2).

Figure 13.2.

Business Winstone 98 category results for the ThinkPad 560X, varying the power saving settings.

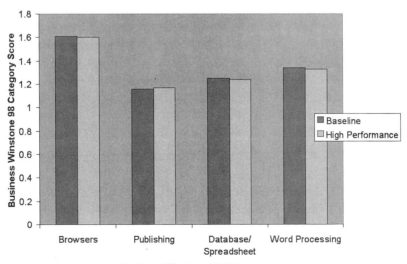

Finally, let's look at the WinBench 98 Processor Tests. Because our Baseline scheme uses the autoclocking feature, we were interested to see if the CPU would indeed gear down noticeably when we ran the $CPUmark_{32}$ and FPU WinMark 98 tests. We were also interested in seeing if WinBench would give us the Blue Screen of Death the way Winstone did.

The biggest difference we see is on the $CPUmark_{32}$ test. Between our baseline and custom power saving schemes, there's a difference of about four percent. What's interesting to note here is that the baseline scheme has autoclock for the CPU chip enabled. This feature should downshift the CPU clock speed when the CPU is not in use. Once again, as with Winstone, we doubt that the CPU is ever "not in use" during a Processor Test! So there is very little difference in processor subsystem performance across all of our power saving schemes (see Figure 13.3).

Figure 13.3.
WinBench 98 Processor Test results for the ThinkPad 560X, varying the power saving settings.

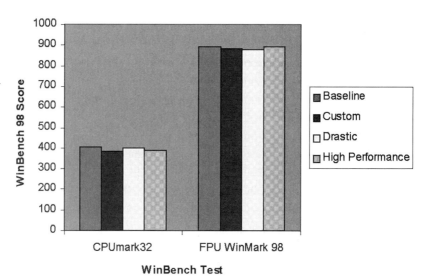

13.3.3. CPU Speed Settings

While we couldn't observe the effects of the autoclocking feature, the ThinkPad also allows us to simply change the CPU speed manually, too. In other words, we can set the CPU to always run at 100%, 50%, or 25% of its maximum frequency. The point of this is to potentially save power. The slower a CPU chip runs, the less power it will draw (and the less heat it will dissipate). Of course, if you've purchased a portable computer whose CPU runs at 233MHz, you might not want to decrease the CPU speed (when you could've just bought a cheaper laptop). We wanted to see the effects of manually reducing the CPU speed, to see if it was even a worthwhile option.

Again, we get Winstone failures. When we decrease the CPU speed to 25% of maximum, this chip is running at about 40MHz, and we once again get the Blue

Screen of Death in Winstone 98. Even at the 50% setting, we can't get an overall Business Winstone 98 score because the Browser category fails. So we are left with the other Winstone category scores to compare (see Figure 13.4).

Figure 13.4.

Business Winstone 98 category results for the ThinkPad 560X, varying the CPU speed setting.

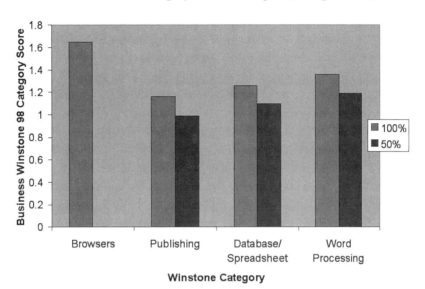

What's interesting about the results we could get is that performance does not drop by half when we halve the CPU speed. The publishing category score drops by 17%, while the database/spreadsheet and word processing scores only drop by about 14%. If you'd like to learn more about why processor speed is not a linear indication of real-world performance, read Chapter 8, "Optimizing Your System's Processor."

Thus, you can cut CPU power consumption in half without cutting your performance in half. If you have a laptop on which you can adjust CPU speed, this setting is definitely worth exploring. Of course, keep in mind that we got utter failure when we set this particular notebook's CPU to run at 25% of maximum speed. Your mileage may vary.

We've seen that real-world performance doesn't necessarily fall off at the same rate that CPU speed does. This is interesting because it might mean that a 50% CPU Speed setting makes sense in some environments. Let's take a look at the WinBench 98 Processor Test results for these CPU Speed settings, to see if they fall off linearly.

The CPUmark$_{32}$ and FPU WinMark 98 tests both drop off almost linearly with dropping CPU speed. This makes sense, because the CPU is the heart of the processor subsystem. Processor subsystem performance is what the Processor Tests in WinBench 98 measure. So, even though the processor subsystem performance falls off with decreasing CPU speed, the overall real-world performance (measured by Winstone) doesn't necessarily fall off as quickly, because the real-world applications aren't necessarily CPU-bound (see Figure 13.5).

Figure 13.5.
WinBench 98 Processor Test results for the ThinkPad 560X, varying the CPU speed setting.

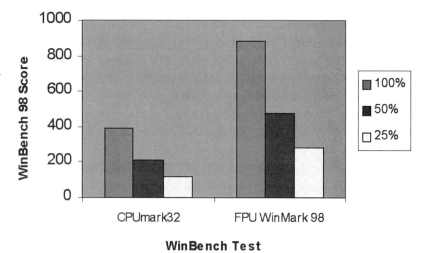

We cover this concept in more detail in Chapter 8. Now let's turn to a final tweak for portable computers running Windows 98, relating to the disk cache settings.

13.3.4. Disk Cache Settings

We discussed changes to the disk cache settings in Chapter 5, "Windows 98 Software Tuning." We also delved deeper into the concept of caching in the processor and RAM chapters. Basically, caching means storing certain information in a faster cache rather than in a slower, main area. If we manage to store the information that's used most often in the faster cache, we can increase performance. For instance, when we store information from the hard disk in a disk cache (in system RAM), when we access that same information again we can read it from the much faster RAM rather than the slower hard disk.

One of the disk cache settings which pertains particularly to portable computers is the Typical role of this machine. For this role, you can choose Desktop computer, Mobile or docking system, or Network server. When you select one of these roles, Windows 98 will adjust disk caching accordingly. Now, from the names of the roles, we would guess that we should simply set the role to Mobile or docking system and forget about it. We wanted to investigate whether there was some hidden performance lurking in those other settings, though, so we decided to run our battery of tests with all three of these roles.

We ran all of our Winstone 98 tests on all three possible machine roles. We also ran WinBench 98 Disk Tests on these three roles, to see if we could measure how our changes to the disk caching affected disk subsystem performance.

Once again our graph isn't as complete as we'd like (see Figure 13.6). When we set role of this machine to server, we got the infamous blue screen in Winstone 98. You should be prepared for similar problems if you stray from certain default settings, and for this reason we suggest that you do extensive benchmark testing before simply blindly tweaking your system. The results we were able to get show no significant difference between the mobile and desktop settings for the cache, so there's no immediate reason why you should change this setting. As far as Business Winstone 98 is concerned, we should leave the Typical role of this machine as Mobile or docking system.

Figure 13.6.
Business Winstone 98 results for the ThinkPad 560X, varying the role of this machine (disk cache).

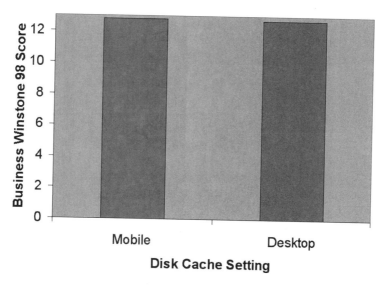

The category scores of Business Winstone 98 mirror the overall score. There's no significant difference in performance between the two settings we can use successfully (see Figure 13.7). Clearly, we should not change the role of this machine to anything other than Mobile or docking system.

The Mobile or docking system setting is designed for any computer with limited memory (according to Microsoft). The other two machine roles are designed for machines with more than adequate RAM, running on AC power (not battery power). The Mobile role flushes the disk cache more frequently, on the assumption that the machine in question has limited RAM and is running on battery power.

We don't think our ThinkPad, with 32MB RAM, has limited memory, but we can't argue with the Business Winstone 98 results. Let's take a look at results from our other tests to see if they follow suit.

Figure 13.7.

Business Winstone 98 category results for the ThinkPad 560X, varying the role of this machine (disk cache).

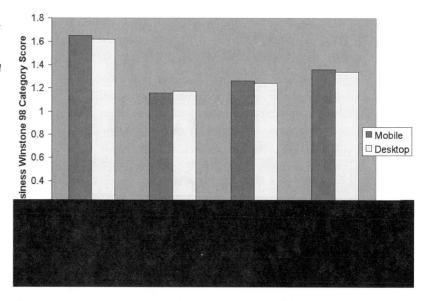

Let's now turn to WinBench 98's Disk Tests, to see if they show the same slow-down in the disk subsystem that we saw in the overall system performance when we changed the system's role.

We can run all three settings to completion in WinBench 98, and here we see very little difference in performance also. The best score goes to the mobile setting while the worst goes to the server setting, but they only differ by a couple of percent (see Figure 13.8).

Figure 13.8.

Business Disk WinMark 98 results for the ThinkPad 560X, varying the role of this machine (disk cache).

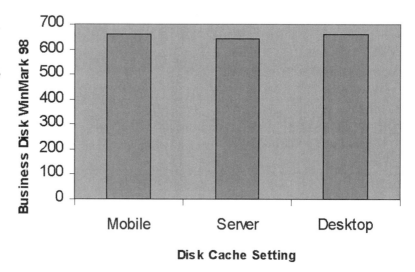

Let's close out by running through the rest of our WinBench 98 disk tests just to see if there are any interesting data points.

The category scores of the WinBench Business Disk WinMark 98 tests mirror the overall score. We clearly get the least out of the disk subsystem on this machine when we set the role of this machine to server (see Figure 13.9).

Figure 13.9.

Business Disk WinMark 98 category results for the ThinkPad 560X, varying the role of this machine (disk cache).

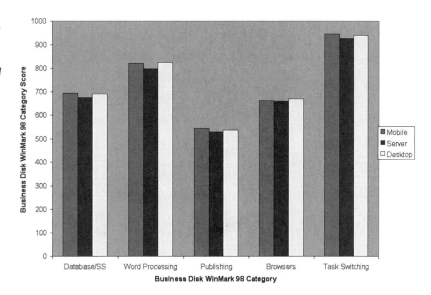

The High-End Disk WinMark 98 results are a bit more dramatic, showing a 9% drop in disk subsystem performance when we change to the server setting (see Figure 13.10). Yet another reason why you shouldn't blindly edit operating system settings without then doing proper benchmark testing.

Finally, we see no surprises with the individual application results for High-End Disk WinMark 98. The best score (with the exception of Photoshop) always goes to the mobile cache setting. The difference in applications like FrontPage 97 and Microstation 95 is very dramatic (see Figure 13.11). If your notebook is at all like the one we tested, don't monkey with the role of this machine!

Figure 13.10.

High-End Disk WinMark 98 results for the ThinkPad 560X, varying the role of this machine (disk cache).

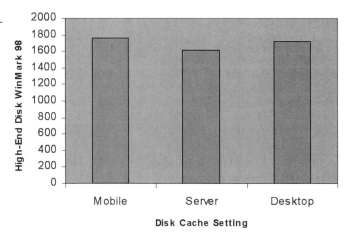

Figure 13.11.

High-End Disk WinMark 98 application results for the ThinkPad 560X, varying the role of this machine (disk cache).

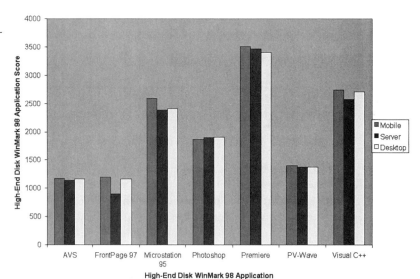

13.4. Windows 95

Windows 95 is an APM 1.1 compatible operating system. If your notebook's BIOS is compatible with the APM 1.1 specification, you can use the Power Control Panel to adjust certain power-saving settings. Of course, to use power management from within Windows, you have to enable power management in your computer's BIOS. Once you're in your notebook's BIOS, you can usually set up timers for suspend, standby, disk spindown, and other settings, depending on the PC.

13.4.1. How We Tested

For testing in this section, we ran both Business Winstone 97 and High-End Winstone 97. While most laptop users run business applications such as word processing and email applications, some high-end users also use portable computers a great deal (in particular, programmers). Winstone results tell us how our system tweaks affect real-world performance. We also ran the Processor Tests, CPUmark$_{32}$ and CPUmark$_{16}$, in WinBench 97 to test how the power saving and CPU speed settings affected the processor subsystem. Finally, we ran WinBench 97's Disk Tests to see how adjusting the disk cache settings affected the disk subsystem.

Our default testing setup was at 800×600×256 colors. This is a common resolution and color depth combination for current laptop computers. If you'd like to learn more about resolution and color depth and how they affect performance, read Chapter 10, "Optimizing Your Graphics Subsystem."

As always, we fully defragmented the hard drive before we ran each test. We also rebooted each machine before running tests. This is merely good testing procedure which we always follow, no matter what subsystem we're interested in.

Our laptop testbed consisted of an IBM ThinkPad 560E. This machine came with 32MB RAM and a Pentium 166MMX processor. The ThinkPad 560E offers many power-saving options in the BIOS.

In the following sections, we test out four different power management schemes. We denoted these schemes as baseline, custom, drastic and high performance (hi perf). For each scheme, we set standby timer, suspend timer, screen off timer, hard drive stop timer, and processor speed to different values. Table 13.2 details the different settings for each of these schemes.

Table 13.2. Four different power saving schemes for an IBM Thinkpad 560E notebook.

Power saving setting	Baseline	Custom	Drastic	High Performance
Standby timer	0	0	1	0
Suspend timer	15	5	1	60
Screen off timer	5	3	0	60
Hard drive stop	10	3	Immediate	20
Processor speed	Autoclock (slow)	Maximum	Maximum	Maximum

13.4.2. Power Saving Settings

We ran our tests on the same four power saving schemes explained in Table 13.2, to see if they affected performance. In particular, we wondered if the hard drive stop feature would affect performance as measured by Winstone and WinBench.

Figure 13.12.

Business Winstone 97 results for the ThinkPad 560E, varying the power saving settings.

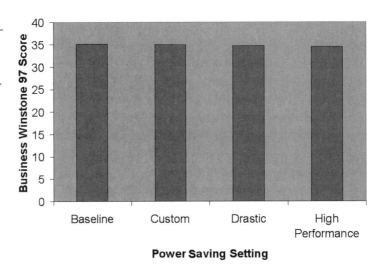

First, we look at our warhorse test, Business Winstone 97. This test shows no significant difference in performance between our four power saving schemes (see Figure 13.12). Should we have expected this, given the differences between our schemes?

The answer is yes. Even though our power saving schemes are all different, and even though the Drastic scheme shuts off the hard drive immediately during inactivity, Winstone is giving this machine a workout non-stop. So there are probably no long periods of inactivity. Winstone is running its scripts as fast as the machine allows. Therefore, we're not able to see any performance difference in the different power saving schemes.

You probably don't type and mouse quite as fast as Winstone; this is why power saving settings are going to be a matter of taste. If you leave your machine running but often inactive, you might want to make your power saving settings more drastic, to save battery life. Conversely, if your machine is constantly going into standby or suspend mode, even though you're working steadily, you should adjust the power saving settings to give you more useful performance.

So, because our tests keep the machine under high stress, it's unlikely we'll be able to differentiate between our power saving schemes. Still, as you know, we love to test and to graph the results, so let's take a quick look at results from our other tests on these four power saving schemes.

The Business Winstone 97 category scores also show no significant difference between our four schemes (see Figure 13.13). Remember, Winstone scores can normally vary by 1% or 2%. That level of variability is impossible to eliminate from even the most strict of testing environments with a test as complicated as Winstone. So, even though the graphs show a very slight difference in the results, the difference is not significant.

Figure 13.13.
Business Winstone 97 category results for the ThinkPad 560E, varying the power saving settings.

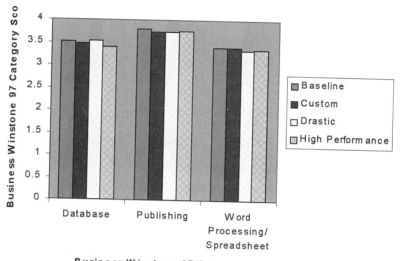

Our High-End Winstone 97 graph is not quite as boring as the previous ones, but it is somewhat puzzling. As we now expected, the scores don't change between the different power management schemes we set up. However, the High Performance scheme causes High-End Winstone 97 to fail (see Figure 13.14). We tried repeatedly to debug this failure, but as with a few other Winstone time-out problems, we were unable to determine the cause. We suspect that a synergistic reaction between High-End Winstone 97, Windows 95, and the ThinkPad power management software caused the problem.

Here we finally see our first real performance differential of the chapter. Unfortunately, it goes counter to our assumptions. The CAD/3-D category of applications shows that the High Performance scheme scores about 10% less than the other three schemes. We designed our High Performance scheme to leave the machine on for a long time, so this doesn't make sense. However, given that High-End Winstone 97 fails to run to completion with our High Performance setting, it's not too surprising that some of the other results seem anomalous (see Figure 13.15).

The final Winstone results for our power saving schemes bear out our conclusion that we simply can't measure a difference between these schemes with Winstone.

As you can see, the PV-WAVE application gives the low score on the High Performance scheme which then accounts for the low CAD/3-D category score for this scheme (see Figure 13.16).

Figure 13.14.

High-End Winstone 97 results for the ThinkPad 560E, varying the power saving settings.

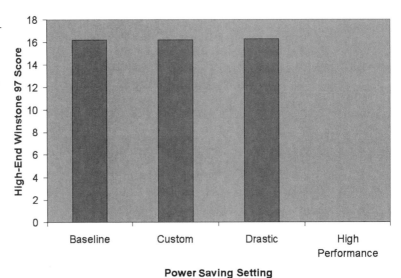

Figure 13.15.

High-End Winstone 97 category results for the ThinkPad 560E, varying the power saving settings.

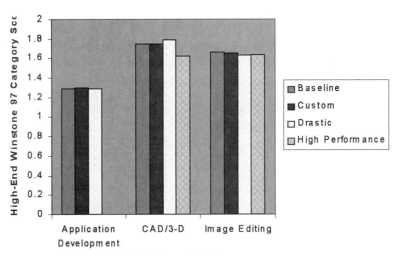

Finally, let's look at the WinBench 97 Processor Tests. Because our Baseline scheme uses the autoclocking feature, we were interested to see if the CPU indeed would gear down noticeably when we ran the $CPUmark_{32}$ and $CPUmark_{16}$ tests.

Figure 13.16.
High-End Winstone 97 application results for the ThinkPad 560E, varying the power saving settings.

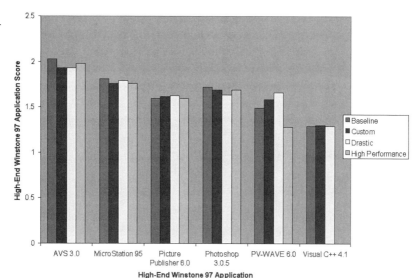

The Processor Tests show no difference between our power saving schemes (see Figure 13.17). We conclude that there was simply not a long enough period of inactivity for the autoclocking to kick in and slow the CPU frequency down.

Figure 13.17.
WinBench 97 Processor Test results for the ThinkPad 560E, varying the power saving settings.

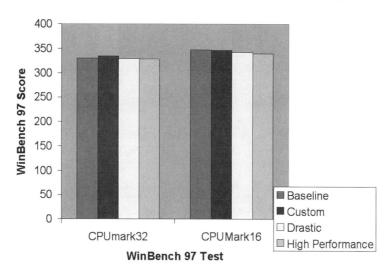

13.4.3. CPU Speed Settings

While we couldn't observe the effects of the autoclocking feature, the ThinkPad also allows us to simply change the CPU speed manually, too. In other words, we can set the CPU to always run at 100%, 50%, 25%, or even 12.5% of its maximum frequency. The point of this is to potentially save power. The slower a CPU chip runs, the less power it will draw (and the less heat it will dissipate). Of course, if you've purchased a portable computer whose CPU runs at 166MHz, you might not want to decrease the CPU speed (when you could've just bought a cheaper laptop). We wanted to see the effects of manually reducing the CPU speed, to see if it was even a worthwhile option (see Figure 13.18).

Figure 13.18.

Business Winstone 97 results for the ThinkPad 560E, varying the CPU speed setting.

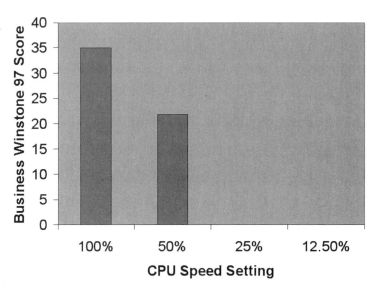

Again, we get some Winstone failures. These make a lot more sense, though, than the previous failure we saw in this chapter. Once we decrease the CPU speed to 25% of maximum, this chip is running at about 40MHz. That's slower than the original Pentium chips! So it's not surprising that Winstone fails when we handicap the system this much. Another interesting feature of this graph is that performance does not drop by half when we halve the CPU speed. The 50% CPU Speed setting still gives us 62% of the performance of the 100% CPU Speed setting. If you'd like to learn more about why processor speed is not a linear indication of real-world performance, read Chapter 8.

The CPU Speed setting could be a handy feature if you were about to embark on a very long airplane trip. As we've seen, you could cut CPU power consumption in half while cutting performance by less than 40%. The extra battery life might be worth the performance hit. However, you need to take care not to ratchet down the CPU speed so far that the laptop becomes useless.

A look at the Business Winstone 97 scores shows that the 25% CPU Speed setting failed on the Word Processing/Spreadsheet tests. The 12.5% setting was not able to keep up with any of the tests. As you can see from the graph in Figure 13.19, performance decreases by a smaller percentage than does CPU Speed. This might make lower CPU speeds more attractive if you need extra battery life for a particular trip or a particular laptop application (for instance, a laptop carried around on the factory floor during the workday). We don't recommend decreasing CPU speed by more than 50%, though.

Figure 13.19.

Business Winstone 97 category results for the ThinkPad 560E, varying the CPU speed setting.

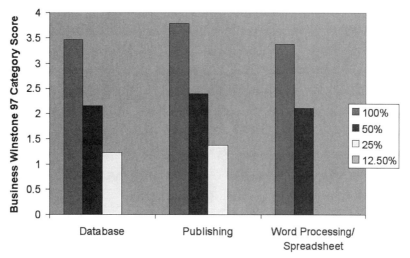

The High-End Winstone 97 graph in Figure 13.20 looks quite a bit like the Business Winstone 97 graph. The tests fail on the two lowest CPU Speed settings, but the 50% CPU Speed setting gives us about 60% of the performance of the full speed.

Figure 13.20.

High-End Winstone 97 results for the ThinkPad 560E, varying the CPU speed setting.

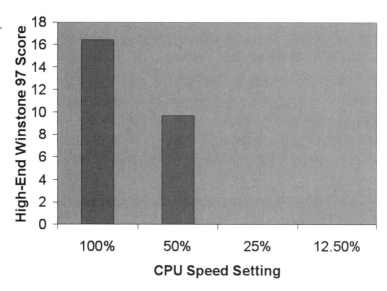

The category results show that the Appications Development category is what's problematic for the 25% CPU Speed setting. That's not the only odd thing about this setting, though. Take a look at the Image Editing results. Here, unlike all the other results we've seen for CPU speed, we see that the performance drop is *greater* than the CPU speed drop (see Figure 13.21). Let's take a closer look at the application scores to see if we can spot what's going on.

Figure 13.21.

High-End Winstone 97 category results for the ThinkPad 560E, varying the CPU Speed setting.

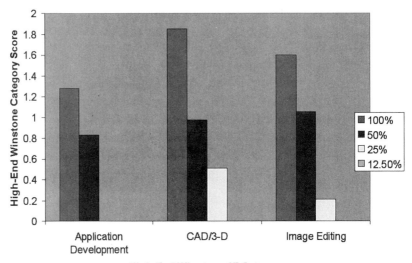

High-End Winstone 97 Category

When we look at the individual application scores in High-End Winstone 97, we can see which applications are more or less dependent on CPU speed (see Figure 13.22). The AVS scores, for instance, closely track the changes in CPU speed. The Picture Publisher scores, on the other hand, do not drop at the rate at which the CPU speed drops. This indicates that Picture Publisher performance is not as closely tied to CPU speed as AVS performance is. The most interesting scores on this graph are the ones for Photoshop. When we lower the CPU speed by 50%, we still get 67% of full performance. However, when we cut the CPU speed to 25%, Photoshop performance drops to 8% of maximum! We conclude that there's a minimum requirement of CPU power for Photoshop. This makes sense to us: Who would run Photoshop on a 40MHz Pentium?

We've seen that real-world performance doesn't necessarily fall off at the same rate that CPU speed does. This is interesting because it might mean that a 50% CPU Speed setting makes sense in some environments. Let's take a look at the WinBench 97 Processor Test results for these CPU Speed settings, to see if they fall off linearly (see Figure 13.23).

Indeed, the WinBench Processor Test graph, for both the 32-bit and 16-bit tests, falls off in lock step with the CPU speed. This makes sense, because the CPU is the heart of the processor subsystem. Processor subsystem performance is what the Processor Tests in WinBench 97 measures. So, even though the processor subsystem performance falls off with decreasing CPU speed, the overall real-world performance (measured by Winstone) doesn't necessarily fall off as quickly, because the real-world applications aren't necessarily CPU-bound.

Figure 13.22.

High-End Winstone 97 application results for the ThinkPad 560E, varying the CPU speed setting.

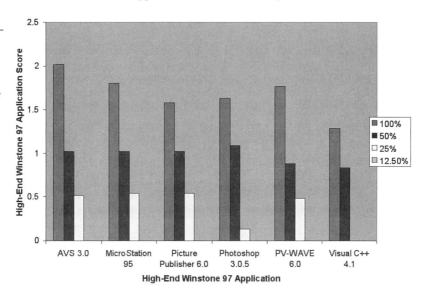

Figure 13.23.

WinBench 97 Processor Test results for the ThinkPad 560E, varying the CPU speed setting.

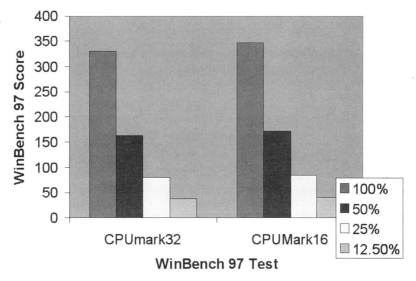

We cover this concept in more detail in Chapter 8. Now let's turn to a final tweak for portable computers relating to the disk cache settings.

13.4.4. Disk Cache Settings

We discussed changes to the disk cache settings in Chapter 6, "Windows 95 Software Tuning." We also delved deeper into the concept of caching in the processor and RAM chapters. Basically, caching means storing certain information in a faster cache rather than in a slower, main area. If we manage to store the information that's used most often in the faster cache, we can increase performance. For instance, when we store information from the hard disk in a disk cache (in system RAM) and, access that same information again, we can read it from the much faster RAM rather than the slower hard disk.

One of the disk cache settings which pertains particularly to portable computers is the Typical role of this machine. For this role, you can choose Desktop computer, Mobile or docking system, or Network server. When you select one of these roles, Windows 95 will adjust disk caching accordingly. Now, from the names of the roles, we would guess that we should simply set the role to Mobile or docking system and forget about it. We wanted to investigate whether there was some hidden performance lurking in those other settings, though, so we decided to run our battery of tests with all three of these roles.

To change the Typical role of this machine setting, do the following:

1. Choose Control Panel from the Settings section on your Start menu.

2. Double-click on the System Control Panel to open it.

3. Click on the Performance tab.

4. Click on the File System button in the Advanced settings section. This displays the Files Systems Properties dialog box.

5. Under the Settings section, choose the Typical Role of this machine that you want to switch to from the drop-down dialog (see Figure 13.24).

6. Press OK to close the dialog boxes. Windows 95 will prompt you to reboot your machine. Press OK.

7. When your machine has finished rebooting, the disk cache will be using the new setting you've selected.

We ran all of our Winstone 97 tests on all three possible machine roles. We also ran WinBench 97 Disk Tests on these three roles, to see if we could measure how our changes to the disk caching affected disk subsystem performance.

These results are fairly dramatic. Holding all other variables equal, we see a large performance differential when we change the role of the machine away from Mobile. The other two roles get only about 65% of the real-world business performance of the Mobile role. As far as Business Winstone 97 is concerned, we should leave the Typical role of this machine as Mobile or docking system (see Figure 13.25).

Figure 13.24.

Change the Typical role of this machine with the File System Performance settings.

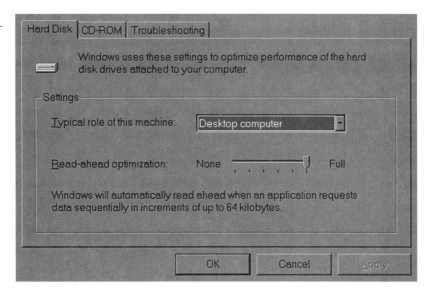

Figure 13.25.

Business Winstone 97 results for the ThinkPad 560E, varying the role of this machine (disk cache).

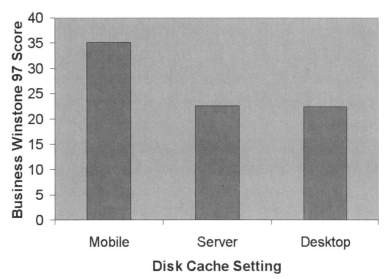

The category scores of Business Winstone 97 mirror the overall score. Clearly, we should not change the role of this machine to anything other than Mobile or docking system (see Figure 13.26).

The point here is not that we expected better performance from the other two settings. It's that we are using our tools, Winstone and WinBench, to see the performance effects of a little-understood system setting. As we saw in Chapter 6, Windows 95 doesn't necessarily automatically set itself up for optimal performance. In the case of this particular setting, though, it appears that the Mobile setting is indeed the correct one for mobile computers.

Figure 13.26.
*Business
Winstone 97
category results
for the ThinkPad
560E, varying
the role of this
machine (disk
cache).*

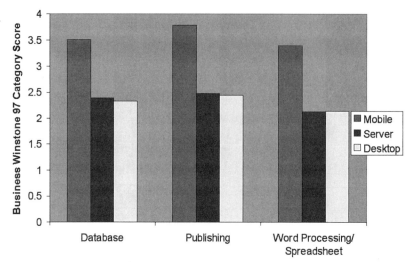

The Mobile or docking system setting is designed for (according to Microsoft) any computer with limited memory. The other two machine roles are designed for machines with more than adequate RAM, running on AC power (not battery power). The Mobile role flushes the disk cache more frequently, on the assumption that the machine in question has limited RAM and is running on battery power.

We don't think our ThinkPad, with 32MB RAM, has limited memory, but we can't argue with the Business Winstone 97 results. Let's take a look at results from our other tests to see if they follow suit.

Again, we see that the Mobile or docking system role is the optimal one for this machine. The Server role only scores about sixty percent of the Mobile role's High-End Winstone 97 score (see Figure 13.27). The Desktop role fails completely!

When we look at the category results for High-End Winstone 97, we see that the Applications Development category does not take as much of a performance hit as do the other two categories when we change the role of this machine (see Figure 13.28). Remember, the Typical role of this machine setting really controls how the computer utilizes the disk cache. From this graph we can conclude that the CAD/3-D and Image Editing applications are more performance-bound to the disk subsystem than the Applications Development category is.

Figure 13.27.
*High-End
Winstone 97
results for the
ThinkPad 560E,
varying the role
of this machine
(disk cache).*

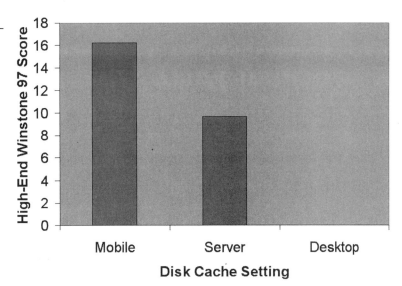

Figure 13.28.
*High-End
Winstone 97
category results
for the ThinkPad
560E, varying
the role of this
machine (disk
cache).*

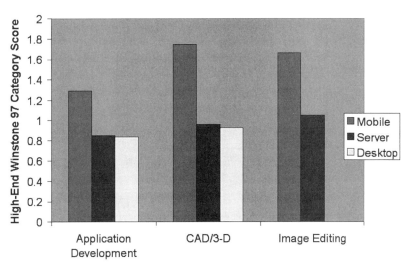

The High-End Winstone 97 applications scores show us that Photoshop is the culprit in causing High-End Winstone 97 to fail on the Desktop role. We also see that AVS is highly dependent on the disk caching role we've set, while Visual C++ is much less so. In any case, there's no reason to change the machine's role to anything other than Mobile or docking system (see Figure 13.29).

Let's now turn to WinBench 97's Disk Tests, to see if they show the same slow-down in the disk subsystem that we saw in the overall system performance when we changed the system's role.

Figure 13.29.

High-End Winstone 97 application results for the ThinkPad 560E, varying the role of this machine (disk cache).

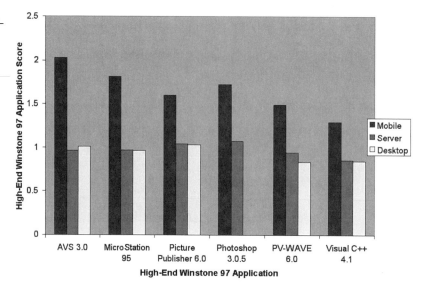

If you've been reading this book in sequence, you might not find Figure 13.30 surprising. Others of you may be wondering why the WinBench results for the disk subsystem do not change, while the change in all of the Winstone results was quite dramatic.

Figure 13.30.

Business Disk WinMark 97 results for the ThinkPad 560E, varying the role of this machine (disk cache).

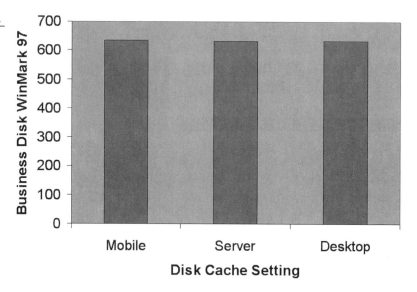

The answer is that our tweaking of the disk cache, via the role of the machine, changes more than just the disk subsystem. Because we're adjusting how Windows 95 deals with the disk cache, we're adjusting how it deals with system RAM (where the hard disk cache is located). As we saw in Chapter 9, "Optimizing Your

System's RAM," WinBench is not sensitive to changes in the amount of RAM in a system, once you have a certain minimum amount. That's what's going on here, too: WinBench's Disk Tests stress *only* the disk subsystem, so we do not see the synergistic effects between disk and RAM which cause the real-world performance drop we saw with Winstone. Let's close out by running through the rest of our WinBench disk tests just to see if there are any interesting data points.

The category scores of the WinBench Business Disk WinMark tests do not show any changes either (see Figure 13.31). Remember, the WinBench Disk Tests play back the exact disk operations profiled from the corresponding Winstone applications. This isolates disk subsystem performance. We don't see the drop we saw with Winstone, though, because the WinBench Disk Tests are immune to the RAM effects that we think are behind the real-world performance drop.

Figure 13.31.
Business Disk WinMark 97 category results for the ThinkPad 560E, varying the role of this machine (disk cache).

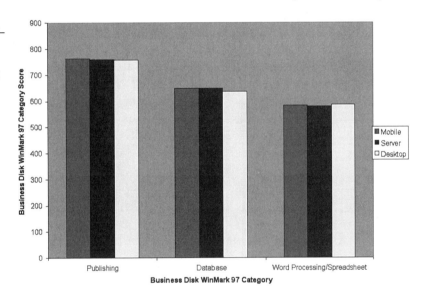

Now that we've explained the WinBench Business Disk WinMark results, we see that the High-End Disk WinMark results show the same pattern (see Figure 13.32). The results do not change a significant amount, because our disk cache tuning affects more than just the disk subsystem.

For completeness' sake, the category scores for the High-End Disk WinMark 97 tests are shown in Figure 13.33. They merely reinforce the conclusions we've drawn about the Typical role of this machine.

Finally, we see no surprises with the individual application results for High-End Disk WinMark 97 (see Figure 13.34). The changes we've made to the system, which do affect real-world performance, are not measurable by the WinBench Disk Tests. That does not mean the WinBench Disk Tests are deficient in any way, it merely means that we're changing an aspect of system performance which they do not measure.

Figure 13.32.

High-End Disk WinMark 97 results for the ThinkPad 560E, varying the role of this machine (disk cache).

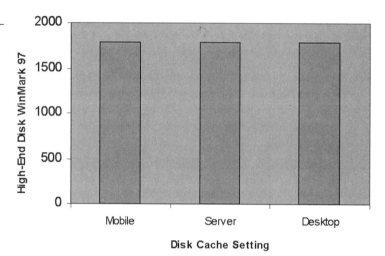

Figure 13.33.

High-End Disk WinMark 97 category results for the ThinkPad 560E, varying the role of this machine (disk cache).

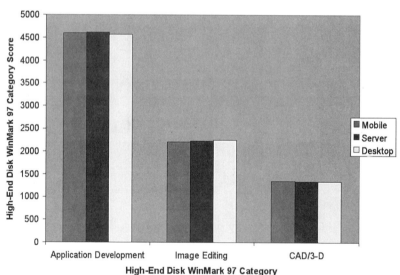

Figure 13.34.
High-End Disk WinMark 97 application results for the ThinkPad 560E, varying the role of this machine (disk cache).

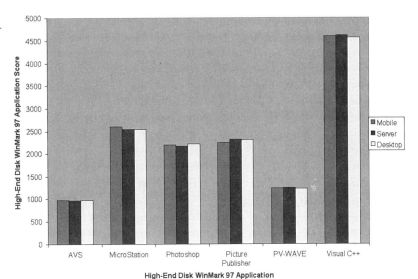

13.5. The Bottom Line

We've done a lot of work with our ThinkPad 560s in this chapter, adjusting power saving settings, CPU speed settings, and disk cache settings. Your portable computer may not feature the exact same group of settings as we've discussed here, but the basics of power management, and the range of tweaks available to you, will be essentially the same for most newer notebook computers.

As far as the disk cache setting goes, make sure that the Typical role of this machine is set to Mobile or docking system for all of your portable computers. If it's not, you're taking an unnecessary performance hit. If your computer offers you the ability to reduce the CPU speed, experiment with this setting at 50% of maximum, to see if the computer still performs acceptably, and to see if the battery life is perceptibly longer. Don't bother reducing the CPU speed to anything less than 50% of maximum, or you're asking for trouble with many popular applications.

The most complicated settings we've looked at in this chapter are all of the other power saving settings. That's where our cocktail party tip, "Fiddle about," comes in. There are so many different combinations of these settings that you *have* to tailor them to your individual work habits.

13.6. Testing You Can Do

Earlier in this chapter we discussed how Winstone and WinBench might not be able to detect performance changes with some power settings, because they keep the computer from going into an inactive state. That's a simple common sense observation: No human works as quickly in Windows as does the Winstone application. Winstone and WinBench are still handy tools for investigating performance tweaks you make to your portable computer.

All you need to perform testing like that in this chapter is a portable computer. Enter the BIOS when it powers up and investigate the power saving and CPU speed settings there. It is quite likely that the settings available to you will be slightly different than the ones we've discussed in this chapter. Make a list of all of the settings, and then draw up a matrix of all of the combinations you'd like to try. You can also duplicate the disk cache tests we performed in this chapter by setting the Typical role of this machine as we discussed previously.

Remember to always follow proper testing procedure. Defragment the disk completely before each test run, and restart your computer before each test run. The ideal way to run benchmark tests is to run Winstone and WinBench in automated batch mode from the Startup group, and to run each test several times to establish the repeatability of your results.

NOTE	Complete directions for running Winstone and WinBench can be found in Appendix A, "Using Winstone 98," and B, "Using WinBench 98."

13.7. From Here...

In this chapter we've discussed tuning tips that apply only to portable computers. Most of the other chapters in this book apply to portable computers as well as desktop computers. While portable computers are not as upgradable as desktops, you should still familiarize yourself with the other subsystems in your portable computer which affect overall performance.

The following chapters will provide more information on other subsystems of interest to portable computer owners.

- Chapter 8, "Optimizing Your System's Processor," will show you how your choice of CPU chip affects performance.

- Chapter 9, "Optimizing Your System's RAM," will show you how to optimize your RAM amount, an important factor on portable computers because so many portables are shipped with insufficient RAM.

- Chapter 10, "Optimizing Your Graphics Subsystem," will show you how to set the resolution and color depth of your display for optimal performance.

Chapter 14

Optimizing for Games

Computer games have been with us since the earliest days of mainframes. Computer games are now a large, lucrative part of the software market, a far cry from those early games of "Space Wars" and "Hunt the Wumpus." There are games for everyone, from bloodthirsty action games to sedate puzzle games. For most of us, computer games are a fun way to relax after a long day of staring at spreadsheets and word processing documents. For some, gaming is the sole purpose of owning a PC.

Games have long been some of the most demanding applications in the PC arena. The minimum system requirements for running a popular game are typically much more stringent than the minimum system requirements to run the current version of Windows. If you'd like to turn your machine into a gaming platform, or if you'd like to tune up your system for maximum gaming performance, read on.

In this chapter, you will learn:

- How to prepare your system for gaming

  Computer games typically require more hardware and software (in the form of drivers) than standard business applications. Business applications rarely use 3D graphics, while 3D graphics are more and more common in games today. In the following sections, you'll learn how to prep your PC for use as a game machine.

- How to tune your system for maximum gaming performance

  If you already run a variety of games on your system, but aren't satisfied with the performance, we'll give you some tips on how to boost your PC's gaming power.

- How to avoid common gotchas when it comes to games

  Because games give your system more of a workout than standard applications, they are also less tolerant of bugs (or "features") in your hardware and software setup. We'll show you how to fix some common problems.

14.1. Cocktail Party Tips

We doubt that you'll find yourself at a cocktail party with a bunch of computer game enthusiasts. The hardcore gamers we know don't get out to parties much; they're at home loading up the latest games. So we don't have a new tip for this chapter that's easy to sum up in one sentence.

This book is designed so that it can be read all the way through, in order, or it can also be randomly accessed on a chapter-by-chapter basis. If you really want to squeeze all of the performance you can out of the PC you run games on, we suggest that you read, or at least skim, the rest of the book. A solid grounding in the inner workings of the processor, RAM, graphics, and hard disk subsystems is necessary if you really want to understand how to tune your system for gaming.

The one general tip we can give you regarding optimizing your system for games is, read the game box. No, not for the hyped ad copy or the risque graphics or the bad jokes. Read the game box for the recommended requirements. Most software, but especially game software, specifies a minimum and a recommended set of requirements that your PC must meet to run the software. First of all, you should ignore completely the minimum requirements. These specs tell you the absolute slowest system that still has a chance of running a particular game. If your system doesn't meet these requirements, you're out of luck. Sure, we all know folks who've run Quake on a 486-33, even though that machine doesn't meet the minimum requirements for Quake. We wouldn't call this fun, though, and fun is what we want from games.

So, ignore the minimum requirements. Focus on the recommended requirements. Take these requirements as a starting point for any hardware purchases you make for your system. If you've got a system with 16MB RAM, and the recommended requirements for a new game you wish to play specify 32MB RAM, then it's time to buy some more RAM. However, you might want to go ahead and boost your system to 64MB RAM. Newer, more power-hungry games come out every month. If you want to take advantage of them, you're going to have to keep your hardware up-to-date.

14.2. Preparing Your System for Gaming

If you look at the table of contents of this book, the chapters list of the major subsystems that make up a typical Windows PC: the processor, RAM, graphics system, hard disk, CD-ROM drive. Lace all of these pieces together with a motherboard, and you've got a typical business PC. You could even get away with no CD-ROM drive, although we doubt you'd want to do that in today's world of huge software packages.

Gamers, on the other hand, have to worry about more components than business users or even high-end users. The PC sitting on an administrative assistant's desk doesn't need powered speakers, a joystick, a 3D graphics card, a sound card, or a gamepad. If you're a hardcore gamer, though, you're likely to want all of those options. So the first task you need to tackle when preparing your system for gaming is taking a generalized inventory of the components you *don't* have.

As we mentioned before, your choice of these components will be driven by the requirements of the actual games you want to play. No matter what games you're interested in, though, you'll probably want to have some kind of audio output and some kind of specific gaming input, if you don't have these already. That means powered speakers and a sound board, as well as a gaming controller.

Powered speakers come in a variety of prices, from cheap sets costing less than $50 to expensive high-fidelity setups that include a subwoofer as well as stereo speakers. Your wallet will guide you, but you should also look for reviews of speakers in both computer and high-fidelity magazines to guide you in your purchases. You probably don't need to connect hi-fi quality speakers to your computer just to hear the relatively low-quality canned explosions and voices of games, but a good set of speakers can make gaming a more intense experience.

You've also got to connect these speakers to your PC, and for that you'll need a sound board. Sound boards also come in a variety of prices and levels of quality. Some newer motherboards have rudimentary sound capabilities built in. The main thing you need to look for, whatever sound option you choose, is 100% SoundBlaster compatibility. The SoundBlaster card set the standard for PC gaming, and it is still the most widely supported sound board. Newer boards offer features like 3D sound but you should make sure that the games you want to play support these extra features. Otherwise, you're paying for something you're not going to use.

Your choice of gaming controller is highly dependent on the types of games you expect to play. If you want to play any of the flight simulation packages, you're going to want a joystick especially designed as a flight stick. If you want to play a car racing game, you'll need a steering wheel controller. If you don't want to shell out the bucks for a nice joystick, you can get a cheaper gamepad, or you can even (with some games) play with your keyboard and mouse. If you just play the occasional round of Doom, the keyboard might be a fine controller. If you're a hardcore gamer, you're going to want a smooth, well-constructed joystick. Again, magazine reviews can help you here. From our (admittedly biased) point of view, we'd suggest you read *Computer Gaming World* (a Ziff-Davis magazine).

Another component you might want is one we haven't discussed yet in this book. That's a modem. If you want to enter the world of online gaming, where you play against other human opponents on the Internet, you'll need a modem and Internet access. Tackling high-speed Internet connectivity is beyond the scope of this book; as with the other components we've discussed, your choice of modem will be a personal decision. A 28.8kbps modem might be fine if you just play on-line once in a while. If you rack up hours a day playing online, you'll probably want a V.90 56kbps modem (or an even faster connection such as ISDN or a cable modem or xDSL).

The newest games out there feature 3D rendering, for more realistic action and scenery. We'll discuss 3D rendering a little later in this chapter. For now, you should be aware that you might need to get a 3D add-on graphics board or a 2D/3D combination board if you want to play a particular game that uses a 3D rendering technology. Again, let the game box be your guide.

This chapter relies on much less testing data than our other chapters. We don't yet have an all-powerful GameStone at our disposal that runs the leading games the way that Winstone runs the leading business applications, although Computer Gaming World and ZDBOp are improving the 3D GameGauge tests as we write this. In the absence of a lot of testing data, one of the best ways to determine what hardware your system needs is to consult the minimum requirements of a particular game you're interested in. Make sure to look at the recommended requirements, not the minimum ones. We recently bought a game with minimum requirements as follows:

> Pentium 90
> 16MB RAM
> 150MB free hard disk space
> CD-ROM drive
> SoundBlaster or 100% compatible sound card

Those were the minimum requirements. The recommended requirements upped this to a Pentium 133 and 32MB RAM, and the machine we ended up playing the game on had those features exactly. We got barely passable performance with this configuration, and we had to run the game at its lowest possible resolution. No way would we play it on a machine meeting only the minimum requirements. So you should learn to ignore the minimum requirements. Take the recommended ones as your absolute minimum. Many games that can run at multiple resolutions require much more horsepower than the recommended requirements to run at the higher levels of resolution and detail.

14.3. Sidebar: MMX Technology

After the Pentium and Pentium Pro, Intel released what they called the Pentium with MMX Technology. MMX stands for MultiMedia eXtensions. These extensions are new instructions and a new set of registers that are supposed to speed up multimedia operations. AMD and Cyrix followed suit with their K6 and 6x86MX chips. Intel's newer Pentium II CPU's include the MMX instructions, and AMD and Cyrix are producing newer chips with additional multi-media functionality. If you buy any new machine that costs over $1,000 these days, it's likely to have a CPU chip that supports some form of MMX.

If you're a gamer, should you run out and buy an MMX-enabled CPU chip? As with many questions in this chapter, there's no easy answer. The main thing to remember is that having an MMX-enabled CPU does not automatically speed up your computer. Applications have to be written to use the MMX instructions. If an application doesn't use an MMX instruction or MMX register, you don't *really* need the MMX CPU chip. Once again, you're going to have the read the box of your favorite game to check out the minimum requirements. If you, for instance, still play the old DOS version of Doom, it's not going to take advantage of MMX.

You should be aware, though, that more and more MMX-aware applications are headed down the pipeline. If you've got to have an MMX-aware CPU for a particular game, then by all means, upgrade. You can learn more about MMX and CPU chips in general in Chapter 8, "Optimizing Your System's Processor."

14.3.1. 3D Graphics

Three-dimensional (3D) graphics aren't new to computer games. Since the days of the original Doom, games have rendered moving three-dimensional scenes on the two-dimensional screen. What's changed in the last year or two is 3D hardware acceleration. It used to be that your CPU did all the work of 3D graphics processing. Once your CPU rendered a frame, it sent it to the graphics board—the graphics board wasn't much more than a dumb buffer. As you could imagine, this loaded down the CPU and meant that your system could only display a relatively low number of frames per second.

A 3D accelerator board takes the 3D processing load off of your CPU. The 3D accelerator does this by supporting a 3D Application Programming Interface (API). This is a standard software interface to a 3D accelerator board's functions. The game programmer calls the 3D API, and this tells the board what to draw on the screen.

Sounds, great, right? Just pop a 3D graphics board in your system, and you'll be zooming along playing all your favorite games in stunning 3D. Unfortunately, it's not that simple. There are several different competing 3D APIs. The two most popular are Direct3D (part of the DirectX family which we'll discuss later on in this chapter) and OpenGL. Programmers use different 3D APIs to write different games. So, for instance, Quake II supports OpenGL while Tomb Raider 2 supports Direct3D. To play both of those games, you'd have to have a 3D graphics board that supported both of those 3D APIs. That's the first step you need to take to break into the world of 3D gaming: figure out which 3D APIs the games you want to play support.

OK, you know which 3D API or APIs you need support for. Now, you just buy a board that says Direct3D or OpenGL on the box, right? Wrong again. There are several more decisions you're going to have to make. The first one is whether to buy an add-on 3D graphics board that works in addition to your existing 2D graphics board, or to buy a combination 2D/3D graphics board. Another decision you might have to make is whether to get a board that plugs into a PCI bus slot or an AGP slot. (Obviously, your motherboard must support PCI or AGP or you shouldn't be buying a 3D graphics board at all.) Even after you've made those decisions, you've got to decide how much money to spend. Depending on how much RAM is included, 3D graphics boards can cost anywhere from just over $100 to close to $1,000.

Wow, you've really got some big decisions on your hands. Here's our tip for making these decisions: check the current reviews in magazines like *Computer Gaming World*. They use the 3D WinBench 98 program as well as a brand new test suite called 3D GameGauge to measure 3D graphics board performance. As you might guess, 3D WinBench 98 is another fine benchmark from the folks at ZDBOp. Running 3D WinBench 98 tests was beyond the scope of this book, but (as you might also guess) 3D WinBench 98 is to 3D graphics subsystem performance as WinBench 98 is to 2D graphics subsystem performance.

You can think of 3D GameGauge as analogous to Winstone. 3D GameGauge (in its form at the time we write this) determines the average frame rate at which your PC runs six popular games. Four of the games use the Direct3D API and two use the OpenGL API. Because it's running real games and not synthetic 3D operations, you can get a good idea of the the power of your 3D graphics subsystem from the final 3D GameGauge score. You can learn more about 3D WinBench 98 and 3D GameGauge on the ZDBOp Web site at www.zdbop.com.

14.4. Tuning Your System for Better Gaming Performance

OK, you've got a system that's set up to play games. Now, how do you wring the most performance from this system? We're tempted to simply state here, "read the rest of this book!" Many of the tips we've covered in other chapters will boost your PC's performance so you can run games that much faster.

14.4.1. RAM

Our number one tip (for games or other applications) is to buy more RAM. In terms of performance-enhancing hardware, RAM is still the best bang for your buck. If your system doesn't have enough RAM to hold the operating system and the software that's running, it uses virtual memory. Virtual memory, in short, is your hard disk pretending to be RAM. Your hard disk is five to six orders of magnitude slower than your system RAM. So, having more RAM lessens the need for your system to rely on your slower hard disk for virtual memory.

As with all of the other components, let the box of your favorite games be your guide when you're determining how much to buy. We'd suggest at least 32MB

RAM for a serious gaming system these days, and if you can spare the cash, think about 64MB RAM. You probably won't need any more than 64MB RAM for gaming, and in some cases getting more than 64MB of RAM can actually hinder, not help, performance. This is due to some intricacies of motherboard design, which we discuss in Chapter 9, "Optimizing Your System's RAM." If you're buying a brand new system with a motherboard that can support it, though, you might want to spring for 128MB RAM if you've got the spare cash.

If you need to be reminded of the importance of RAM, let's take a quick look at some test results. First, for Windows 98. We ran our Business Winstone 98 test on a Pentium 200MMX based machine at several different RAM amounts. Business Winstone 98 measures real-world performance on typical business applications—it is *not* a gaming benchmark. The results should show you how important RAM is, though.

As you can see in Figure 14.1, more RAM equals more performance. As you learn in Chapter 9, additional RAM is one of the most cost-effective upgrades you can get for your system.

Figure 14.1.

Business Winstone 98 performance versus RAM size for a Pentium 200 MMX PC running Windows 98.

If you're still running Windows 95, RAM is important to you too. We ran our Business Winstone 97 test on a Pentium 200MMX based machine at several different RAM amounts. Now, Business Winstone 97 measures real-world performance on typical business applications; it is not designed to measure game performance. You can still get an idea of the importance of RAM from looking at the following results, however.

As you can see in Figure 14.2, performance increases significantly as we add RAM to the system. For this particular set of tests, performance levels off at

48MB RAM, but remember that we're testing business application performance here. For the higher-stress gaming environment, we'd still expect to see a performance gain from 48MB to 64MB RAM. Of course, all of this depends on what games you run and how hard they stress your system.

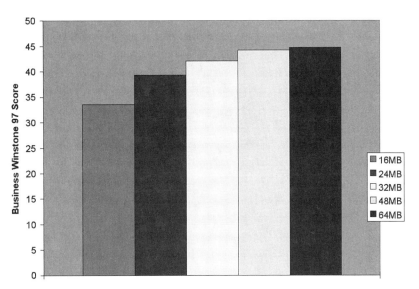

Figure 14.2.
Business Winstone 97 performance versus RAM size for a Pentium 200 MMX PC running Windows 95.

Optimizing for Games

14.4.2. Graphics Drivers

We discuss graphics drivers in Chapter 5, "Windows 98 Software Tuning," Chapter 6, "Windows 95 Software Tuning" and Chapter 10, "Optimizing Your Graphics Subsystem." Graphics drivers are the software that allows Windows to talk to your particular graphics board. Most users do not concern themselves with their graphics drivers, as long as their display is working. As we saw in Chapters 5 and 6, though, it can pay off to keep your graphics drivers updated with the latest versions from your graphics board manufacturer.

This is even more true in the gaming world, where the alphabet soup of graphics standards is even thicker. Graphics board manufacturers are constantly writing new device drivers to eliminate bugs, improve performance, and add functionality. For instance, if you install DirectX on your system, you'll need to make sure that the drivers for your graphics board are also DirectX aware. If you're a die-hard gamer, you should update your graphics drivers on a regular basis, checking at least every two or three months for new versions.

Let's take a quick look at the performance boost that upgrading graphics drivers can provide.

As you can see in Figure 14.3, the performance difference is quite dramatic, and it's absolutely free! We get a 27% boost in the Business Graphics WinMark score, and a 20% boost in the High-End Graphics WinMark score. Remember, the Graphics WinMark tests play back only the graphical functions profiled from the corresponding Winstone applications. As such, we can't say that the Graphics WinMark tests are a game benchmark, but they are an indicator of graphical subsystem power. As this graph shows, it pays to keep your drivers updated.

Figure 14.3.

Graphics WinMark 97 results for the Pentium 166 machine, before and after upgrading to the latest Matrox Millenium graphics drivers.

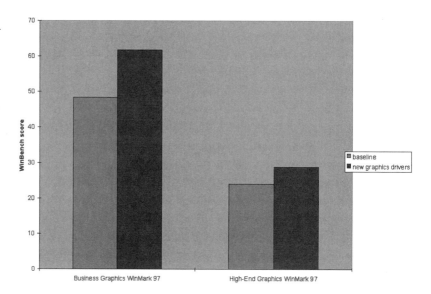

14.4.3. Other Tricks

Throughout the book, we've tried to provide you with specific details about performance enhancing tricks that don't require hardware upgrades. Many of these are found in Chapters 5 and 6. Many of the tricks that we tested out showed a real performance benefit. Some of the strategies we tried did not yield significant changes to our Winstone scores, and Winstone is our usual measure of real-world performance on business and high-end applications.

If you want to squeeze every drop of performance out of your system, though, you'd be wise to check out all of these tricks, to see if they work for you. The first we'd suggest is disk defragmentation. If you've been duplicating our testing procedure, you've been defragmenting your disk fully before running Winstone and WinBench. To get the most out of your system, you should think about defragmenting it fully on a daily basis, whether you're running benchmarks or not. If you use a tool such as the Task Scheduler in Windows 98 or System Agent (part of the Plus! pack for Windows 95) to schedule this defragmentation, make sure your PC is on when it's scheduled to defrag! Once you've started defragmenting your drive on a regular basis, normal daily use won't fragment it very much. That just means the defrag operation will be quicker.

Another tip we've dealt with indirectly in this book is the concept of background tasks. When you run Winstone, it asks you to shut down as many background tasks as you can. Background tasks are programs or code running simultaneously with the foreground application. These can be other applications, such as when you run Word and Excel simultaneously, or they can be pieces of software that you've added to your Windows environment for more functionality or to support a particular piece of hardware.

These background tasks can be quite handy, detecting viruses, monitoring your system for problems, or allowing you to find files more quickly by keeping file indices up to date in the background. These handy tasks also eat up CPU time, though. Often, these tasks are installed when you install new hardware or software, unbeknownst to you. You can bring up a task list in Windows 95 or Windows 98 by pressing the Ctrl-Alt-Del key combination. Try doing it when you *think* you're only running one application program. You might be surprised at how many tasks are running on your PC. If you want to get the most performance out of your system, you should eliminate as many background tasks as possible. We're not telling you to turn off your background virus checker, we're just saying you should take a look at all the different background tasks running on your system and make sure you need them all. Check your Startup group and also the Load= and Run= lines in your WIN.INI file to begin your quest to eliminate unnecessary background tasks. The Startup Manager program included with the benchmarks can also help you on this quest.

Another performance trick you might want to try, if you have two hard disks in your machine, is moving the swap file to the second disk. We describe how to do this and we investigate the performance implications in Chapter 11, "Optimizing Your Disk Subsystem."

One trick we don't recommend is overclocking. Overclocking is running your motherboard or CPU chip at speeds faster than they were designed for. Yes, if you can do this and get away with it, you're getting more performance for free. Unfortunately, overclocking can cause many mysterious problems such as erratic behavior, system crashes, and other hard-to-diagnose woes. Overclocking can also permanently damage your CPU and other chips in your system, because the faster you run a chip, the hotter it gets. Unless you're an absolute hardware wizard, we do not recommend overclocking as a performance enhancement strategy.

14.4.4. New Technologies

Hardcore gamers like to live on the bleeding edge of technology. To do this requires deep pockets, however. You'll have a better foundation for understanding new technological developments if you've studied the rest of this book. Once you've grounded yourself in the fundamentals of how the different subsystems in your PC work, and how they affect overall performance, you'll be better qualified to evaluate new technologies. Every month we read in the computer magazines of new processors, faster hard drives, more powerful 2D and 3D graphics technologies. What's new one year is passe the next. The hardware and software manufacturers come up with an array of terms like MMX, AGP, Ultra-DMA, Ultra-SCSI, OpenGL, DirectX, all of which can be confusing or misleading to those not familiar with the history of performance enhancement.

After you've read this book, you'll be better equipped to deal with new technologies. We have an enthusiasm for new technologies which will make our machines run better and faster, but we also have a healthy skepticism about the claims a particular manufacturer makes about their new product or idea. We hope that you share both our enthusiasm and skepticism.

14.5. Sidebar: DirectX

DirectX is a set of technologies that debuted with Windows 95. DirectX also appears, in a slightly different form, in Windows NT 4.0. Windows 98, as you might expect, comes bundled with an even newer version of DirectX. DirectX is designed to allow programmers to use the hardware in your PC in a Windows-approved fashion while still getting acceptable performance. Until recently, game programmers preferred the single-tasking DOS environment, where they could access the PC hardware as needed. Programming to the bare metal typically gives better performance than programming through an application programming interface (API). DirectX was Microsoft's answer to this problem, and now most game manufacturers are porting their games to the Windows environment by using DirectX.

DirectX is an umbrella term for a number of different technologies. DirectDraw is used in displaying graphics, or drawing. DirectSound plays sound effects. DirectPlay simplifies communication between computers, to make it easier to run games over a network or over modems. DirectInput provides an interface for input devices like joysticks or even Virtual Reality equipment. Direct3D is Microsoft's API for rendering three-dimensional graphics on the display.

If you've tried to play DOS games at screen resolutions higher than 320×200, you will probably appreciate DirectX. Because the SVGA standard isn't really a standard, to play DOS games at a high resolution you had to use what was known as a VESA driver to interface with a particular graphics board in DOS. The VESA drivers for many graphics boards were not known for their speed or lack of bugs. However, compared to Windows 3.1, DOS was a faster environment for gaming.

With the advent of Windows 95, Microsoft introduced the DirectX technologies so that game performance could (theoretically) be acceptable in a Windows environment. DirectX doesn't apply just to games, but games were some of the first applications to take advantage of DirectX. With DirectX, writing for the

Windows environment instead of the DOS environment becomes more attractive for the game programmer. Also, because DirectX is a set of standard APIs, game designers don't have to reinvent the wheel every time they design a new game.

14.6. Avoiding Some Common Pitfalls

Because games usually stress computers more than typical business applications, gamers often run into bugs and gotchas more often than the average user. In this section, we're going to briefly discuss a few ways to save yourself hassles when using your PC for games.

Our first tip is to save all of your drivers, especially if you still play older, DOS-based games. If you have a DOS game which won't run acceptably under Windows, then you'll have to restart your computer in MS-DOS mode to play it. When you do this, your computer will need the old 16-bit drivers so that it can find and use devices such as your CD-ROM drive, mouse, and sound board. If you delete these drivers in Windows, you'll be out of luck when you want to use these devices in MS-DOS mode. We were recently tidying up the hard disk of one of our PCs, and we came very close to trashing the 16-bit drivers for mouse, CD-ROM drive, and sound board, until we realized that we needed them to run our old DOS games. So, don't wipe out older drivers that you might need for certain games, even though you don't need them under Windows 95. Better yet, make sure to keep backup copies of these drivers on floppy. You are backing up your system on a regular basis, aren't you?

Another gotcha that's stung us quite a bit is the Windows key on our keyboard. This is the handy key located between the Control and Alt keys on many newer keyboards designed especially for Windows PCs. This key is usually mapped to bring up the Start Menu in Windows 95 or Windows 98. Unfortunately, some games crash or generally freak out when you press this key. Newer games are aware of the existence of the Windows key, and they ignore it. If you've got an older game and a newer keyboard, try getting the DOSWINKY utility from the Microsoft Web site. This utility is part of the free Kernel Toys package for Windows 95; it allows you to disable the Windows key when you play DOS games. No more crashes when you're pounding on that Control key!

A problem that many users experienced starting a couple of years ago had to do with Intel-compatible CPU chips. While these CPU chips performed head-to-head with Intel's on most business applications, many gamers discovered that game performance on certain games was not up to par. This caused many heated debates on the Internet and other online services.

The point here is not that you should always buy an Intel CPU chip. It's that you should understand the requirements of the particular game that you're interested in. If the game requires 100% compatible Intel-type CPU or a 100% compatible SoundBlaster-type sound board, then you might be asking for trouble if your equipment isn't strictly 100% compatible. As always, before you buy, check out the reviews in the magazines or online for news of problems like those we've described.

14.7. The Bottom Line

Gaming performance is the hardest kind of performance to quantify, due to the variety of games out there and the varying ways in which they interact with PC hardware. In this chapter we've tried to introduce you to some important concepts you should be aware of when playing games in a Windows environment. First and foremost, make sure you have enough RAM. After that, make sure your system exceeds the recommended requirements for all of the games you plan on playing. Ignore those minimum requirements completely if you want to actually have fun playing your games. The more your system exceeds the stated requirements, the longer you'll be able to use it as a gaming platform.

System requirements for games don't always have to do with performance, and that's another point to keep in mind. While your PC won't run any faster with a joystick attached, it sure makes those flight simulators more fun to play! Common sense should be your guide when you're evaluating how to upgrade your system for gaming. If you spend your money on RAM but you don't have any speakers attached to your PC, you're missing out on the audio component of most games.

14.8. Testing You Can Do

This chapter featured considerably less testing than the previous chapters. You can still use the techniques you've learned in other chapters to test your overall performance and your PC's subsystem. If you, for instance, buy more RAM for your PC for gaming purposes, you still might want to run a battery of Winstone tests to look at the scores before and after the RAM upgrade. Winstone doesn't measure gaming performance, but it can give you a basic idea of how much faster your system is. Likewise, if you upgrade to a brand new hard disk, you should run WinBench's Disk Tests to see how the upgrade affects your disk subsystem performance.

Detailed instructions on using newer benchmarks like 3D WinBench 98 and 3D GameGauge are beyond the scope of this book, but you can use these programs to get a better idea of how your 3D graphics subsystem performs in general and specifically for gaming.

As always, you should follow proper testing procedure. Defragment your hard disk completely before each test run, even if you're not measuring disk performance. Immediately before a test run, perform a cold re-boot of your machine. If you really want scientific results, run tests in automated batch mode, and run them multiple times to establish repeatability.

> **NOTE** Complete directions for running Winstone and WinBench can be found in Appendixes A, "Using Winstone 98," and B, "Using WinBench 98."

14.9. From Here...

We've only scratched the surface of optimizing your system for gaming in this chapter. That's because many of the important concepts about RAM, CPU, and graphics are covered elsewhere in this book. If you really want to become a gaming performance maestro, we suggest that you take the time to skim through the rest of the book.

The following chapters will provide more information on the optimizations related to the gaming tips we've discussed in this chapter.

- Chapter 5, "Windows 98 Software Tuning," will show you software tuning tips for Windows 98, allowing you to squeeze more horsepower out of your system for free.

- Chapter 6, "Windows 95 Software Tuning," will show you software tuning tips for Windows 95, allowing you to squeeze more horsepower out of your system for free.

- Chapter 8, "Optimizing Your System's Processor," will show you how the CPU chip and the other pieces of the processor subsystem affect system performance.

- Chapter 9, "Optimizing Your System's RAM," will show you how to optimize your RAM amount. Adding RAM is usually the best way to improve overall system performance.

- Chapter 10, "Optimizing Your Graphics Subsystem," will show you how to optimize your graphics subsystem. When most people think of games, they think of graphics.

Optimizing for Games

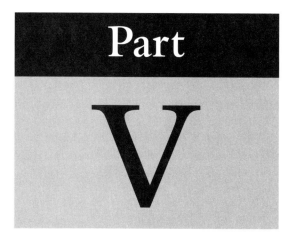

Part

V

Appendixes

Appendix

A

Using Winstone 98

Using Winstone 98

Throughout this book, we've described how we ran tests designed to investigate such subsystems as RAM, processor, graphics, and disk. We've used the Winstone and WinBench programs to measure the performance differences afforded by our hardware and software adjustments. If you're not satisfied by looking at our results and picking a machine that's similar to yours, it's time for you to run some Winstone and WinBench tests of your own.

If you've installed and used a lot of other Windows applications, you might be tempted to dive right into Winstone 98 by slapping the CD-ROM into your CD-ROM drive, installing Winstone, and then running it. You'll get more benefit out of Winstone, and you'll save yourself some potential hassles, if you take the time to read this appendix. If you really want to learn all the whys and hows of Winstone, you can also read the online documentation on the Winstone CD-ROM.

In this chapter, you will learn:

- The basics of Winstone 98

   This section tells you the basic facts of what Winstone 98 is and what its scores mean, and tells you how to order more copies of the benchmark CD-ROMs from the Ziff-Davis Benchmark Operation (ZDBOp).

- How to install Winstone 98

   This section helps you determine if your system meets the minimum hardware and software requirements to run Winstone 98, and then steps you through installing Winstone 98.

- How to run Winstone 98

   This section steps you through running Winstone 98 and saving, viewing, and printing results.

- Your way around Winstone 98

   This section contains more in-depth information about what Winstone 98 does when it runs and how it calculates its results.

- How to troubleshoot Winstone 98

   Even the best-written software doesn't run perfectly on all machines. This section will show you how to avoid common problems with running Winstone 98, and how to fix errors that crop up when you run Winstone 98.

A.1. A Quick Overview Of Winstone 98

Winstone 98 is an application-based benchmark program. It runs actual applications on your PC and returns scores based on how quickly your PC runs these programs. The programs are today's top-selling Windows application. Thus, Winstone 98 measures overall system performance.

Winstone 98 is the latest version of the Winstone benchmark program written by the Ziff-Davis Benchmark Operation (ZDBOp). (The previous version of Winstone was Winstone 97, and it's that version that we used to get the Windows 95 and Windows NT 4.0 results for this book.) Winstone introduced the concept of the base machine: Winstone scores are unitless, normalized to the score of the base machine. The base machine receives a score of 10.0 on the overall suites and 1.0 on the category suites and individual application suites. The important thing to remember is that for all Winstone results, higher numbers are better. If your machine receives an overall Business Winstone 98 score of 30, that means your PC is three times as powerful as the base machine when running typical Windows business applications. We'll discuss the particulars of the Winstone 98 base machine later in this chapter.

To arrive at the final scores, Winstone times how long your PC takes to execute application scripts. In the case of the business applications, these execution times are used to compute the overall score in a market-centered fashion. In other words, the unit market share of a particular application is used to determine how much weight or impact the execution time for that application has on the overall score. In the case of the high-end applications, the weights are equal when determining the overall High-End Winstone 98 score.

The Business Winstone 98 score meets the needs of most ordinary users. The High-End Winstone 98 applications address the needs of power users and users of specialized programs like image editors and CAD applications.

If you want to publish your Winstone scores, you must fully comply with the license agreement. The license agreement includes a clause about information disclosure. We'll give an example of the information you must disclose if you want to publish results later in this chapter.

Using Winstone 98

A.1.1. Getting Copies of Other Benchmarks

This book includes the Winstone 98 and WinBench 98 CD-ROMs. However, if you'd like to request extra copies of the benchmark CD-ROMs, or CD-ROMs containing ZDBOp benchmarks other than WinBench and Winstone, you can order them from ZDBOp. To learn more about the benchmark offerings from ZDBOp, check out their Web site at `www.zdbop.com`.

To order additional benchmark CD-ROMs, you'll need to pay a shipping and handling fee of $5 (US), $6 (Canada), or $7 (International) for your first CD-ROM. Add $1 for each additional CD-ROM you request. Send credit card information (a VISA, MasterCard, or American Express credit card number, the expiration date, and the name as it appears on the card) via:

Email to `zdbop distribution@zd.com`
Fax to (919) 380–2879

Mail a check or money order (in U.S. dollars only) to:

Ziff-Davis Benchmark Operation
1001 Aviation Parkway, Suite 400
Morrisville, N.C. 27560
ATTN: Distribution

> **NOTE**   Do not send cash to ZDBOp. A CD-ROM takes four to six weeks to arrive. To receive it sooner, include your Federal Express account number and shipping instructions with your request. ZDBOp will then send the benchmark to you via Federal Express and charge the FedEx shipping cost to your account. (The FedEx charge is in addition to the ZDBOp shipping and handling fee.)

A.2. Installing Winstone 98

If you've installed other Windows software, installing Winstone 98 will be a snap for you: insert the Winstone 98 CD-ROM into your CD-ROM drive and follow the prompts. First, though, you need to make sure that your PC meets the minimum requirements for running Winstone 98.

A.2.1. Hardware and Software Requirements

Winstone 98 has a set of minimum requirements for both the hardware and software on your machine. Your machine must meet these requirements or it will not be able to run Winstone 98. To run all tests in Winstone 98, your machine must meet the following requirements.

Minimum Software Requirements:

Windows 95, Windows 98, or Windows NT 4.0 with Service Pack 3 or later. To run High-End Winstone 98, you must use Windows NT 4.0. High-End Winstone 98 will not run on Windows 95 or Windows 98.

Graphics driver running with 256 or more colors (8-bit color depth or higher).

VGA resolution or higher for Business Winstone 98. 800×600 or higher for High-End Winstone 98.

TCP/IP software loaded.

Minimum Hardware Requirements:

> Your CPU must be at least an Intel 486 or compatible processor.
>
> To run Business Winstone 98 on Windows 95 or Windows 98, you'll need at least 16MB RAM. To run all other suites, you'll need at least 32MB RAM.
>
> Approximately 200MB free disk space for a full installation of Winstone 98.
>
> You also need 150MB free disk space for working space for all tests. CD-ROM drive.

A.2.2. Installation Details

If your CD-ROM drive is set to automatically run programs when you insert a new CD-ROM, when you insert the Winstone 98 CD-ROM into your CD-ROM drive the installation program will load. If you do not have the Autorun feature enabled in Windows, you'll need to start the installation program manually by doing the following:

1. From the Start button, choose <u>R</u>un. The Run dialog box appears.

2. Click on the Browse button and navigate to the root of your CD drive. For instance, you might browse to your D: drive if that is your CD-ROM drive letter.

3. Find the file install.exe and highlight it. Click the Open button.

4. The Run dialog box now contains the pathname to the install.exe program. Click OK to run the Install program.

You are now running a standard Windows application installation program. You'll be prompted to close all other applications. Once you've done that, you'll be prompted to decide where you'd like Winstone 98 installed (see Figure A.1).

Figure A.1.

Choose where Winstone installs its files with Choose Destination Location in the installation program.

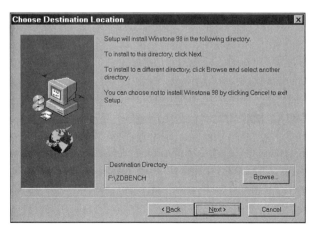

Using Winstone 98

After you've decided where you want to install Winstone 98, you'll be prompted to allow the installation program to create a new program group where it will install the Winstone shortcuts. By default, this is a folder called "Ziff-Davis Benchmarks." You'll also be prompted as to whether you'd like to install the Business support files and High-End support files to your hard disk. If you install all of these support files, you can then run Winstone 98 from your hard disk only; you will not need to insert the Winstone 98 CD-ROM into your CD-ROM drive to run tests. You will need more free disk space if you want to copy these support files, though. If you do not copy the support files, then you will have to make sure that the Winstone 98 CD-ROM is in your CD-ROM drive every time you want to run Winstone 98.

> **NOTE** If you do not install the Business or High-End support files to your hard disk, you will need to insert the Winstone 98 CD-ROM into your CD-ROM drive every time you run tests.

After you've made all of your selections, the Winstone 98 installation program lets you review all of your selections (see Figure A.2).

Figure A.2.
Double check your current settings before proceeding with Winstone 98 installation.

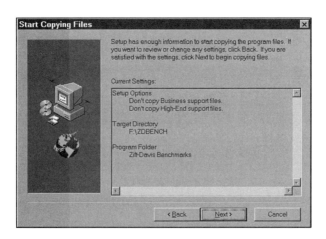

After you've determined that you've chosen the selections you want, press the Next button and the installation program will install Winstone 98.

When the installation program is finished, it will prompt you to read the Winstone README file and to run Winstone 98. The first time you run Winstone 98, you will be required to read the Winstone 98 license agreement and to indicate that you agree to its terms. After you do that, you'll see the main Winstone 98 screen (see Figure A.3).

From the main Winstone 98 screen, you can run tests, save results, compare results, and get help.

Figure A.3.

The Winstone 98 main screen.

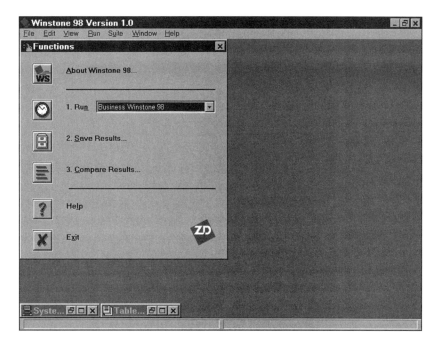

When you run Winstone 98 on Windows 95 or Windows 98, the default suite in the Run drop-down dialog box is Business Winstone 98. If you want to run Business Winstone 98 after starting Winstone, all you have to do is press the Run button (the button that looks like a clock). If you don't want to run Business Winstone 98, choose the suite you want to run from the Run drop-down dialog. The most popular tests and test suites are already listed on the Run drop-down dialog box on the Functions panel (see Figure A.4). You can choose to run Business Winstone 98 only, High-End Winstone 98 only, All Tests (which runs both Business Winstone 98 and High-End Winstone 98), or Selected Tests. Remember, you must be running Windows NT 4.0 to run High-End Winstone 98. High-End Winstone 98 will not run on Windows 95 or Windows 98.

If you choose Selected Tests, then the Select Tests dialog box will pop up (see Figure A.5). From here, you can add and remove tests and test suites so that you only run the applications you're interested in. If you want to run only the Business Publishing suite, you can choose that here. Remember, though, that Winstone 98 will not return individual application scores for the business applications. Winstone 98 will return individual application scores for the high-end applications.

To use the Select Tests dialog box:

1. From the Run drop-down dialog box, choose Selected...

2. Select the tests you want to run from the Test Suites and Tests lists.

Using Winstone 98

Figure A.4.

Choose which tests you want to run with the Run drop-down dialog.

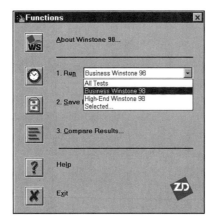

Figure A.5.

Select specific tests you want to run with the Select Tests dialog.

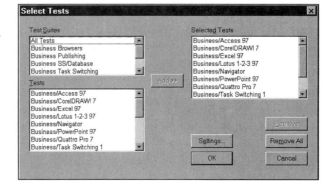

3. After you've selected the tests you want to run, click the Add>> button.

4. If you want to delete tests, select the tests or test suites you want to delete from the Selected Tests list, and then click the Remove button (if you want to delete all tests, simply click the Remove All button).

5. When you've selected all of the tests that you want to run, click the OK button.

6. You will now be returned to the main screen. To run the tests you've selected, click the Run button.

Whether you've chosen test suites from the Run drop-down dialog or selected your own set of tests, you run tests by pressing the Run key on the Functions windows. Winstone will then begin testing, unless you have configuration problems. To learn how to solve common configuration problems, read the "Troubleshooting" section later in this chapter.

You can also run tests in Demo Mode. Demo mode runs the tests you've selected, displays the results, and then re-starts the tests. Demo Mode can be useful if you want to set up your computer on display at a store or trade show, but the intricacies of demo mode are beyond the scope of this book. You can learn more about demo mode by reading the online documentation that comes with Winstone 98. To run tests in demo mode, select the Run menu and choose Demo Mode.

After Winstone completes its tests, it will display a graph of the results. You can also see the results in tabular form by choosing Window from the menu bar and selecting 2 Table of Results. After you have successfully run Winstone 98, you can save your results by clicking the Save Results button in the Functions window. We'll talk more about viewing and saving results in a later section.

A.2.3. **Batch Mode Testing**

If you want to automate testing, you can create a special batch file known as a ZDR file. Once you've set up a ZDR batch file properly, you can add it to your Startup group in Windows. When Windows starts up, it will automatically start Winstone 98 and run the tests that you've selected in the batch file. This is useful when you want to ensure that your system is in the same state every time you run tests. As we've mentioned throughout the book, proper testing procedure requires that you defragment your hard disk and re-boot your machine before each testing run. If you use batch files and place them in your Startup group, your machine will begin testing after you re-boot, with no user input.

To create a ZDR batch file:

1. Select the tests you'd like to run in the manner described previously.

2. Choose the Run menu and select Create Batch File (see Figure A.6).

Figure A.6.
Create ZDR batch files with the Create Batch File dialog.

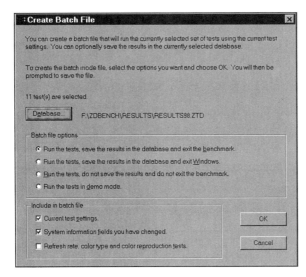

3. Fill out the options as you desire. You can choose what information Winstone 98 will save, and what actions it will perform after running tests.

4. To choose which database Winstone 98 will save results to, click the Database button and browse. Winstone 98 results databases all have the ZTD extension.

5. When you've chosen a database and the other options, click OK.

6. The Save Batch File dialog box appears. You can save your batch file to any location you'd like, but it must have the ZDR file extension.

7. Once you have saved a batch file, you can run tests by double-clicking on the batch file in Windows Explorer. If you want tests to run immediately after your PC starts, then drag the batch file to your Startup group.

If you want to run tests via batch files immediately after your system starts up, you might run into problems if your system requires a password or login name. If you want to learn how to automate the login procedure, check the online documentation that comes with Winstone 98.

A.2.4. System Configuration Review

Your PC must meet the minimum requirements to run Winstone 98. The System Configuration Review functions can help you determine whether or not your PC meets these requirements. Some requirements are easy to understand: if you have a 286-based computer, you can't run the benchmarks. Other system requirements aren't as easy to comprehend, so Winstone provides the System Configuration Review to help you. The System Configuration Review windows list items about your system and flags whether they are OK to run tests or whether they do not meet Winstone's requirements. Items that do not meet Winstone's requirements are further denoted as those that should still allow Winstone to run and those that will not allow Winstone to run.

To bring up the System Configuration Review, choose the Run menu and then select System Configuration Review. The first dialog box that appears explains the icons used on the subsequent windows (see Figure A.7). A check mark indicates that your system meets a particular requirement. A yellow X indicates that your system does not meet a particular requirement, but that Winstone still might be able to complete testing. A red X indicates that your system does not meet a particular requirement and that Winstone will not be able to run tests.

Click the Next button to move on to the Minimum Resource Requirements window (see Figure A.8). This windows shows you the minimum requirements and actual values of your screen size, pixel (color) depth, memory amount, free disk space, and free temp file space.

Figure A.7.

Learn about the system configuration icons on the first System Configuration Review window.

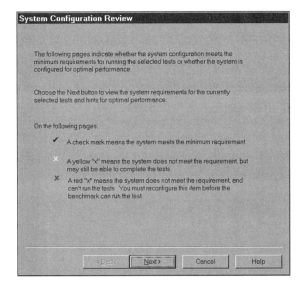

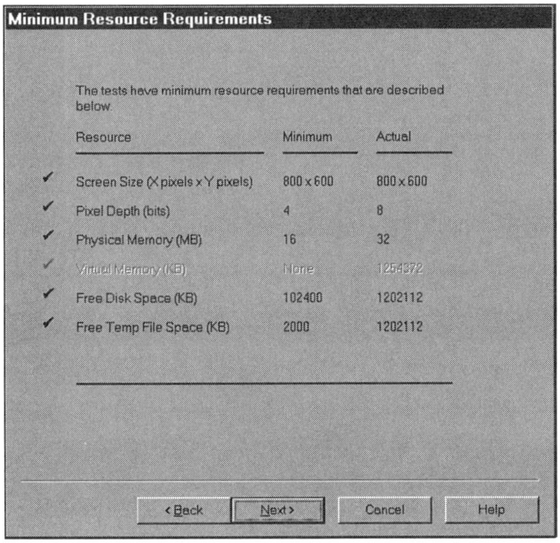

Figure A.8.

Determine if your system meets the minimum resource requirements on the Minimum Resource Requirements window.

Click the Next button again to move on to the first Other Requirements window (see Figure A.9). This window tells you whether your taskbar is set up properly. It also lists any missing fonts that you need to install.

NOTE   To run Winstone tests, you need to make sure that your system Taskbar does not have the Always on top property set.

Click the Next button again to move to the second Other Requirements window (see Figure A.10). This window tells you on which international versions of Windows ZDBOp has verified Winstone. This window also lists the other programs and background tasks that are running on your system. This list is not limited to other applications like Word or Excel; it includes things like screen savers, anti-virus programs, and other background tasks. For proper testing procedure, you need to disable all tasks that aren't necessary for the correct operation of your computer. Winstone 98 can't tell you which tasks are necessary for correct operation of your computer and which can be disabled. That's something you will have to determine for your PC.

Figure A.9.

Determine if your taskbar and fonts are set up properly on the first Other Requirements window.

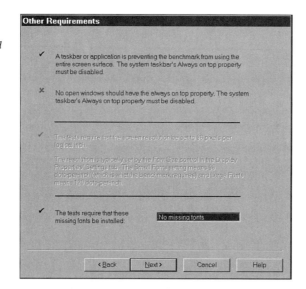

Figure A.10.

Determine if you're running unnecessary tasks on the second Other Requirements window.

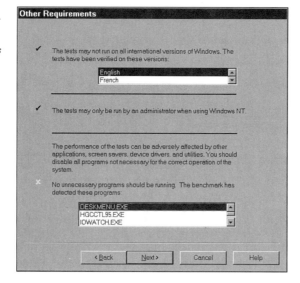

Click the Next button again to move to the Business Winstone Requirements window. This window ensures that you're running an operating system that Business Winstone 98 supports. It also tells you that a single CPU is required. Click the Next button again to move to the High-End Winstone Requirements window. Note that these windows only appear when you've selected the corresponding test. In other words, the High-End Winstone Requirements window will not appear if you do not have the High-End Winstone 98 test selected. The High-End Winstone Requirements window ensures that you're running an operating system supported by High-End Winstone 98, and that you've got TCP/IP loaded.

Click the Next button again to move to the Finish System Configuration Review window. This window allows you to disable the system configuration check that Winstone performs every time it starts testing. By default, the Enable system configuration problem detection box is checked. You can disable the system configuration check by unchecking this box. You might want to do this if you're repeatedly testing a machine without changing its system configuration, but in general we don't recommend that you disable this feature. The system configuration check tells you whether changes you've made to your system affect Winstone's tests.

A.2.5. **Manipulating Results**

Once you've run tests, you'll want to save and view your results. You can view the results from the current test by opening the Table of Results window. You can save results with the Save Results button on the Functions window. Winstone stores results in databases with the ZTD extension. You can compare results with machines from the sample database, or you can compare results as you vary the configuration of your machine. You can export your results files in a number of formats if you want to manipulate them with another program.

Using Winstone 98

When Winstone finishes running selected tests, it automatically displays the current results in the Table of Results window. To save those results:

1. In the Functions window, click the Save Results button. The Save to Database window appears (see Figure A.10).

2. In the Database section, Winstone displays the path to the current results database file. If you want to specify a different results file, click the Database button.

3. Click the System Info button to display the System Info dialog box (see Figure A.12). Edit these fields on all of the tabs as needed.

4. Change the default description of Current Results to a more fitting description of the test results.

5. Click the Save button.

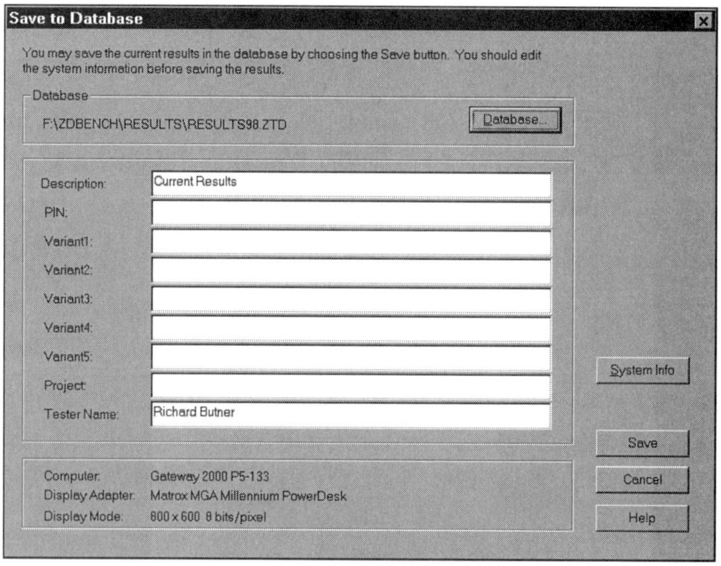

Figure A.11.

Save your current results with the Save to Database window.

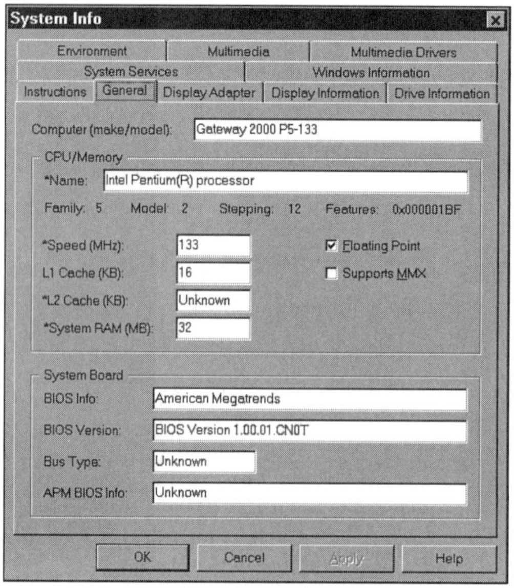

Figure A.12.

Edit your system information on the System Info dialog.

You can also export the current results (or system information) to a file in a format that other programs such as databases or spreadsheets can read. You could then analyze the data or chart it as you like. We created the graphs in this book by exporting our test results files to Excel. To export results, do the following:

1. From the File menu, choose Export.

2. Choose either Current Results, Table of Results, or System Info to select exactly what data you want to export. You can export the Current Results as CSV (comma separated values), XLS (Excel spreadsheet), or TXT (text) files. You can export the Table of Results and System Information as text files only.

3. In the File Name box, specify the name of the export file.

4. Click OK. Winstone will export the information in the format you've selected to the file you've specified. You can then open this data in any application that supports the format you've chosen.

You can also print your results. To print results or system information:

1. From the File menu, choose Print.

2. Choose either Current Results, Table of Results, or System Info.

3. After you select the item you want to print, Winstone will print the information to the current default printer.

After you're done running tests and manipulating results, you can exit Winstone 98 in any of the standard Windows methods. The easiest way to quit Winstone 98 is to click the Exit button on the Functions window.

A.3. A Tour Of Winstone 98

As with previous versions of Winstone, Winstone 98's tests are market-centered. This approach ensures that Winstone scores are indicative of performance the typical user should expect when performing common operations with the leading business applications. To determine the leading applications, ZDBOp consulted with Computer Intelligence, a leading market research company. Computer Intelligence provided data on applications sales and on projections of future sales. ZDBOp averaged these data to determine the market shares as used by Winstone 98. As you'll learn in Appendix B "Using WinBench 98," the Winstone tests are the foundation of the Disk and Graphics WinMark tests in WinBench. Note that all applications in Business and High-End are 32-bit applications (in other words, designed for Windows 95 and Windows NT, and now, Windows 98).

Winstone 98 runs actual applications. For every individual test, Winstone installs the application, starts the application, runs the scripted tasks for that application, exits the application, and then uninstalls the application. Winstone repeats this process for each application that it runs. While the application is running Winstone times how long it takes to execute the scripted operations. These times are used to compute the overall Business Winstone 98 and High-End Winstone 98 scores, the Business category scores, and the individual High-End application scores. After you have Winstone scores, you can compare them to the base machine, to other machines, or to your machine in a different configuration.

> **NOTE** Winstone 98 runs real applications, but the Winstone CD only contains the particular pieces of an application needed to run the Winstone script. It is a violation of the license agreement to attempt to use the Winstone 98 application files for any purpose other than running Winstone 98.

Winstone 98 uses a tool called Rational Visual Test for Windows to run the scripts that execute commands within each application. There is one script for each application in Winstone 98. When Winstone executes a script, it copies necessary files for a particular application to a work directory. It then starts the application and, using Visual Test, sends commands to that application. These commands perform tasks similar to those that typical users would perform. When all tasks are completed, Winstone sends an exit command to the application and then deletes the applications files from the work directory.

After finishing each script, Winstone 98 records the time it took the PC to execute the commands within that application. After all the applications have run, Winstone 98 uses each application's elapsed run time to calculate a score.

The business tests are important for most users, because they run the most popular applications. There are eleven individual business application tests. The typical office user spends most of their day in word processing and spreadsheet applications, as well as database and desktop publishing applications. The overall Business Winstone 98 score is useful for a user who runs all types of business applications. If you primarily use database applications, then you should pay attention to the relevant category score, in this case the Database category. The individual business application scores are not available, because the weights are based on confidential information from Computer Intelligence. The following applications are used in Business Winstone 98:

> Microsoft® Access 97
> Microsoft® Excel 97
> Lotus® 1-2-3® 97
> Corel® Quattro® Pro 7
> Microsoft® Word 97
> Corel, WordPerfect® 7
> CorelDRAW™ 7
> Microsoft® PowerPoint® 97
> Netscape Navigator® 3.01

The high-end applications were chosen by ZDBOp and the editors of many of the Ziff-Davis magazines such as *PC Magazine*. The high-end application tests are useful for users of more intensive applications. There are seven individual high-end applications tests. If you are a programmer or a graphic designer, you'll probably be more interested in the High-End Winstone 98 scores. The tests in High-End Winstone 98 can really stress your PC. They also give you individual scores, unlike the business apps. So, if you only use Photoshop, you can see how changes to your system affect the Photoshop score in High-End Winstone 98. (You'll probably find that Photoshop is the application that's most hungry for RAM!) The following applications are used in High-End Winstone 98:

MicroStation® 95
Adobe® Photoshop® 4.01
Adobe® Premiere®
AVS/Express® 3.1
PV-Wave® 6.1
Microsoft® FrontPage® 97
Microsoft® Visual C++® 5

> **NOTE**   Unlike earlier versions of Winstone, including Winstone 97, Winstone 98 does not produce category scores for the High-End applications.

A.3.1. The Base Machine

Winstone has always used the concept of the base machine to make Winstone scores easy to understand. Because Winstone scores are unitless (or, shall we say, are measured in Winstone units) they are meaningful only relative to other Winstone scores. If there was no base machine, a single Winstone result would be meaningless, because you'd have nothing to compare it to. That's why all Winstone scores are relative to the score of the base machine. The base machine is an actual machine at ZDBOp. For Winstone 98, the base machine is a Dell Dimension P5-133 with 32MB of RAM and a Matrox Millenium graphics board. The screen resolution is 1024×768 using 16-bit color. The operating system is Windows NT 4.0 so that the machine can run both Business Winstone 98 and High-End Winstone 98.

The base machine receives a 10.0 on the Business and High-End Winstone tests. It receives a 1.0 on the business category and invidual High-End application tests. So, if your PC receives a score of 100 on the High-End Winstone 98 tests, your machine is ten times faster than the base machine when running high-end applications. Conversely, if your machine receives a 1.0 on the High-End Winstone 98 tests, your machine is only one-tenth as fast as the base machine when running high-end applications.

The same is true for the category and application scores, but remember that the base machine receives a 1.0 on all category and application scores. If your machine gets a 5.0 on a category suite, it is five times faster than the base machine when running typical applications in that category. If your machine gets a .25 on a category score, it is one-fourth as fast as the base machine when running typical applications in that category.

Much of the time when you're doing performance studies, you don't care about the base machine. When you're adjusting a particular variable, for instance RAM size, you gather Winstone results for each RAM amount you're interested in, and then compare those. The base machine doesn't matter to you at that point. Still, you need to understand the concept of the base machine if you want to understand how Winstone calculates its results.

A.3.3. Test Settings

You can use the Winstone test settings to customize your Winstone installation. For most users, the default settings for Winstone will be adequate. If you've added or removed hard disks in your PC since installing Winstone, you might need to edit the test settings. You change test settings from the Test Settings dialog box. To use the Test Settings dialog box:

1. From the Edit menu, choose Test Settings. Winstone 98 will display the Test Settings dialog box.

2. Select the tab corresponding to the changes you want to make.

3. Make the changes you want. After making your changes, click OK to save them, or Cancel to discard them.

Let's now go over the specific tabs and settings that you can alter in Winstone 98.

Common Settings

On the Common Settings tab (see Figure A.13), you can change the Disk Drive setting. This is where Winstone 98 creates temporary files it uses while running. You could use this tab, for instance, if you want Winstone to use your D: drive instead of your C: drive for temporary files. There are other options on this tab but they are disabled in Winstone 98.

Business Winstone 98 Settings

On the Business Winstone 98 Test Settings tab (see Figure A.14), you can specify Winstone's base directory. This is directory from which Winstone 98 copies its test files. If you're running Winstone from a CD-ROM, then the base directory is on your CD-ROM drive. If you are running Winstone 98 from a full installation on your hard disk, then the base directory is on your hard disk. Winstone 98 sets up the base directory properly whether you do a full installation to your hard disk or a partial installation that requires the CD to run. During a test, Winstone 98 copies the application files from the base directory to a temporary directory on the work drive (you specified the work drive on the Common test settings tab). Winstone 98 runs its tests from the work drive.

Figure A.13.

Change the common test settings with the Common Settings tab.

Figure A.14.

Change the Business Winstone 98 test settings with the Business Winstone 98 Settings tab.

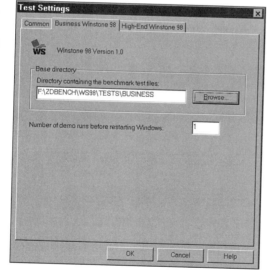

If you need to change the base directory, click the Browse button to select a directory where the Winstone 98 test files are located. If the files are not in the base directory, Winstone 98 will display an error message when you attempt to run tests.

On the Business Winstone 98 Test Settings tab, you can also specify how many demo runs Winstone 98 should execute before restarting the computer. The default is one. Running Winstone in demo mode is beyond the scope of this book. If you'd like to learn more about Winstone demo mode, you can read the online documentation that comes with Winstone 98.

High-End Winstone 98 Settings

On the High-End Winstone 98 Test Settings tab (see Figure A.15), you can specify Winstone's base directory. This is the directory from which Winstone 98 copies its test files. If you're running Winstone from a CD-ROM, then the base directory is on your CD-ROM drive. If you are running Winstone 98 from a full installation on your hard disk, then the base directory is on your hard disk. Winstone 98 sets up the base directory properly whether you do a full installation to your hard disk or a partial installation that requires the CD to run. During a test, Winstone 98 copies the application files from the base directory to a temporary directory on the work drive (you specified the work drive on the Common test settings tab). Winstone 98 runs its tests from the work drive.

Figure A.15.

Change the High-End Winstone 98 test settings with the High-End Winstone 98 Settings tab.

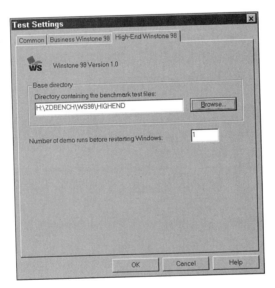

If you need to change the base directory, click the Browse button to select a directory where the Winstone 98 test files are located. If the files are not in the base directory, Winstone 98 will display an error message when you attempt to run tests.

On the High-End Winstone 98 Test Settings tab, you can also specify how many demo runs Winstone 98 should execute before restarting the computer. The default is one. Running Winstone in demo mode is beyond the scope of this book. If you'd like to learn more about Winstone demo mode, you can read the online documentation that comes with Winstone 98.

A.3.4. Winstone Scores

For many users, the overall Business and High-End Winstone 98 scores need no explanation. My computer gets a Business Winstone 98 score 20, yours gets a 40, so yours is twice as fast at running typical business applications. End of story. If you want to learn details about how Winstone 98 calculates and reports scores, read on.

When Winstone 98 runs, it times how long each application takes to run through the script for that application. Winstone does not time the application's load time. Instead, it starts its internal timer after the application appears on the screen, and stops the timer immediately before the script issues the Exit command to quit the application. If you run all tests in Winstone 98, that's a total of eighteen time values for both the business and high-end applications. Winstone then normalizes these results to the base machine's score. Winstone normalizes the score by dividing the time it takes an application to run its script on the base machine by the corresponding time for the same application script on your system. This gives a relative speed, eighteen in all if you run all tests. Winstone then takes these normalized scores and uses a weighted harmonic mean to calculate the suite scores.

In the case of Business Winstone 98, the weights are based on a particular application's unit market share. In the case of the high-end applications, they are all weighted equally. Winstone then scales category and high-end application scores to the base machine's category score of 1.0. Winstone scales the overall score to the base machine's overall score of 10.0 on both the Business Winstone 98 and High-End Winstone 98 tests.

Once you've got results, you might want to publish them. The Winstone 98 license agreement requires you to include certain information about a PC with any Winstone 98 results you publish. If you publish a PC's Winstone 98 results, you would need to say something along these lines:

"Ziff-Davis' Winstone® 98 Version 1.0 produced a score of X Winstone® 98 Version 1.0 units on its Business Winstone 98 suite on WXY PC Corp. Model P266 with single 233MHz Intel Pentium II CPU, 32MB of RAM, 512KB RAM cache, 4GB hard disk, IDE controller, FAT file system, and no hardware disk cache. The test PC used XYZ Corp. XYZ Video adapter with 8MB VRAM and XYZ.DRV version 1.1 driver and had a refresh rate of 72 Hz. The test PC also used MS-DOS 7.0, Microsoft Windows 95, the system disk cache using all available memory, a video resolution and color depth of 1024 by 768 pixels with 65,536 colors, and disk compression utility ABC version 1.0 enabled. All products used in the test were shipping versions available to the general public, and the test and its results were not verified by Ziff-Davis.

Winstone® is a registered trademark of Ziff-Davis Inc."

You can find most of this information in Winstone 98's System Info dialog box.

Using Winstone 98

> **NOTE**   Reporting Business Winstone 98 results is mandatory. If you report any Winstone 98 scores, you must always report the Business Winstone 98 score in addition to any category scores.

A.4. Troubleshooting

In a perfect world, Winstone would run to completion on any PC that met the minimum requirements. Unfortunately, we live in the real world. If you have experience installing complex applications like image editing programs or development environments, you know how difficult it can be sometimes to get these programs to run properly on all of your computers. Winstone runs eighteen different programs on your PC, so you might have trouble getting a test run to completion on certain machines. Usually, something about the hardware of software configuration is conflicting with Winstone 98's application scripts. In this section, we're going to go over some common Winstone problems and tell you what you can do to solve these problems.

A.4.1. Application Conflicts

Before Winstone runs tests, the Configuration Information window will inform you of any applications that are running. Ideally, the benchmark should be the only program that's running and there should be no programs running in the background.

Occasionally, a component from an already installed application (possibly an application also included with Winstone) can conflict with the tests. Unless the application is running at the time you start a Winstone test, however, you shouldn't have problems.

If you're testing Windows 95 or Windows 98 systems, you can use the benchmark's Startup Manager program to disable the loading of some programs when the computer boots up. (Startup Manager also works on Windows NT, but presents an incomplete list of applications.)

A.4.2. Graphics Driver Problems

If you see an error message that refers to a driver module, it usually means that you have a buggy graphics board driver. In addition, other driver bugs can cause some applications to crash or hang.

If you suspect graphics driver bugs are causing Winstone 98's problems, first try running Winstone 98 with one of the generic graphics drivers for Windows that Microsoft provides. If you can run Winstone 98 successfully that way, then you need to consult the vendor who made your graphics card to get a more recent graphics driver.

A.4.3. Aborting Tests

If you have a problem with Winstone 98 and need to abort the test run, restart Windows. After Windows restarts, Winstone 98's cleanup program will automatically restore the PC's original system files to their pre-test state. You can then attempt to run the tests again.

A.4.4. Hard Drive Corruption and Winstone

When you exit Winstone 98, it automatically restores your PC's original system files. If anything happens and you need to interrupt Winstone 98 during the test run, or if Winstone 98 halts, stops, or hangs the PC and you must exit Winstone 98 in any way other than clicking the Exit button, Winstone 98 automatically cleans up your system when you restart Windows and will restore your PC's system files to their original state.

Don't try to fix the problem yourself. You should always let Winstone 98 clean up after a test run.

A.4.5. Timeout Messages

During a test, you might see an error message with the window title Winstone 98 Timeout. This usually happens when Winstone 98, which is running a timed script, is waiting for some onscreen object, such as a dialog box or menu, that never appears or doesn't receive focus. When the object doesn't appear or receive the focus, Winstone 98 stops the script and displays the timeout message.

If you see an error indicating that the Winstone script has timed out, do the following:

1. Close the error message box by clicking OK.

2. You might also see a dialog box prompting you to close the running application. If you do, then close the running application.

3. If you're prompted to save documents in the running application, choose yes or no. It doesn't matter, it's just another step in closing an application that's timed out.

4. Winstone will then ask you if you want to cancel, retry, or ignore. Cancel cleans up the machine and reboots. Retry attempts to re-run the test that timed out. Ignore skips the test that just timed out and moves on to the next selected test, if there is one.

Whichever choice you make after a timeout, you're going to have further troubleshooting to do. First off, determine if the timeout is repeatable. Does your PC time out in the same application every time you attempt to run Winstone 98?

If so, you probably have some sort of hardware or software conflict between your system and Winstone. Try these steps to get around Winstone timeouts:

1. Shut down all other running applications and tasks.

2. Install a generic Microsoft graphics driver.

3. Install a newer version of the graphics driver from the vendor.

4. Run ScanDisk and check for errors and fix them.

5. Defragment your hard disk.

As a last resort, you might want to try uninstalling and reinstalling Winstone 98.

A.4.6. Installation Messages

If Winstone 98 has problems during installation, it will display an explanatory error message. There are several ways that an installation can fail, but the error message will tell you what to do to correct the problem. Problems that can cause errors during setup include an invalid disk drive or path name, or insufficient disk space.

A.4.7. Cannot Find File Messages

Winstone 98 will display an error message if it attempts to find a file that is not accessible. To recover from this situation, check the following:

1. Ensure that the file exists.

2. Ensure that you have access to the file and to the file's directory.

3. Check that the file is not write protected.

4. Check that the file is not corrupt.

A.4.8. File Path Messages

If Winstone attempts to use an invalid file path, it will display an error message. The message that appears on the screen will tell you what happened and what you should do to correct the problem. Problems that can generate a path error message include an invalid base directory or working directory path.

A.4.9. Compatibility Messages

If Winstone 98 encounters compatibility problems with a library or the operating system, it will issue an error message. In this case, you should make sure your system is running the correct version of the operating system. Winstone 98 runs on Windows 95, Windows 98, and on Windows NT 4.0 with Service Pack 3 or higher. High-End Winstone 98 only runs on Windows NT. Winstone 98 does not run on Windows 3.x or OS/2.

A.4.10. Screen Resolution or Font Size Messages

If Winstone 98 has problems with your system's screen resolution and font size, it will display an error message. The message will tell you what happened and what you should do to correct the problem.

For example, if you PC's display is smaller than VGA, Winstone 98 will issue an error message. You must run with VGA (640 × 480) or higher resolution to run Business Winstone 98. To run High-End Winstone 98, you must run with at least 800×600 resolution.

A.4.11. Corrupt File Messages

If Winstone 98's files become corrupt, the benchmark will issue an error message. To fix this problem:

1. Exit Windows.

2. Reboot your PC.

3. Uninstall Winstone 98.

4. Re-install Winstone 98.

5. Check that you're not running other applications or tasks during Winstone 98.

A.4.12. Foreign-language OS Versions

ZDBOp tested Winstone 98 on a number of foreign-language versions of Windows. If Winstone 98 doesn't work and you're not using one of these versions, then that may be the problem. If possible, you should try to acquire one of the language versions that ZDBOp tested.

> **NOTE** Because Windows 98 was not available until well after ZDBOp finished developing Winstone 98, ZDBOp obviously could not test Winstone 98 on foreign-language versions of Windows 98.

ZBDOp tested Winstone 98 on the following versions of Windows 95:

English
French
German
Italian
Polish (Windows 95 OSR2 only)
Spanish (Windows 95 OSR2 only)

ZDBOp tested Winstone 98 on the following versions of Windows NT 4.0:

English
French
German
Italian
Polish
Spanish

A.4.13. Taskbar Messages

Make sure to set the Taskbar to Auto Hide and clear the Always on top item to run the Winstone 98 tests. Winstone's Configuration Information window will warn you if these settings are not set correctly.

A.4.14. CD-ROM Cleanliness

Dirty or smudged CD-ROMs force your CD-ROM drive to re-read the disc to ensure that the data is correct. This can have an impact on your testing if you're running Winstone 98 from the CD-ROM drive. If your CD-ROM drive takes more time to read a dirty CD-ROM, the test may take longer, which will make your results poorer.

Dirty CD-ROMs are especially noticeable on faster CD-ROM drives. Some of the faster CD-ROM drives may step down their speeds to a slower rate so they can reliably read the data.

To clean your CD-ROMs:

Use a soft, clean cloth to wipe the CD-ROM. Do not use paper or solvents.

Wipe the CD-ROM frm the center out to the edge. Do not scrub the CD-ROM or wipe in a circular motion.

Do not hold the CD-ROM anywhere other than the edges. Treat the CD-ROM the way you'd treat a vinyl record.

Keep the CD-ROM in its case or in your CD-ROM drive at all times. Don't leave CD-ROMs lying around on your desk.

A.5. Sidebar: Getting Repeatable Results

We've emphasized proper testing procedure throughout this book, but it bears repeating. For the most valid, repeatable results, you should test your system from the same initial state. This means starting tests immediately after a cold reboot of your machine. After you've booted your machine and run other programs, your machine isn't in the same state it was immediately after a re-boot. Other programs have loaded and unloaded objects into memory. Your disk cache and virtual memory system have been working behind the scenes with your RAM and hard disk. This could affect results of the tests, or in extreme cases cause incompatibilities which will then cause Winstone timeouts.

You should also defragment your disk completely before each test run. So, defragment your disk completely and then reboot your machine before running Winstone. If you are running Windows NT 4.0, a disk defragmentation tool is not provided with the operating system for NTFS volumes. You may wish to purchase a tool such as Diskeeper for this purpose.

Finally, to ensure absolute repeatability, stop all other programs and tasks and disable any network connections while you run Winstone 98. Tasks running in the background during Winstone 98 can use up processor time and therefore affect results. If you really want rock-solid repeatability, use a *.ZDR batch file to automate your Winstone 98 testing. The Winstone 98 documentation covers how to use *.ZDR batch files to automate testing.

If you follow all of these procedures, you shouldn't see a variability in your Winstone scores of more than a few percent.

Using Winstone 98

Appendix

B

Using WinBench 98

Using WinBench 98

We've used Winstone (both Winstone 98 and Winstone 97) as our primary benchmark tool, because Winstone measures overall Windows performance. Overall performance is what matters most to the end-user, but it's not the whole performance picture. If you want to find the bottlenecks in your system, you've got to look at subsystem performance also. WinBench 98 is the tool you should use to measure Windows subsystem performance.

Like Winstone 98, WinBench 98 is easy to install and use. You'll get more benefit out of WinBench and save yourself some potential hassles if you take the time to read this appendix. WinBench 98 also includes online documentation with further details on how and why WinBench works the way it does.

In this chapter, you will learn:

- The basics of WinBench 98

  This section tells you the basic facts of what WinBench 98 is and what its scores mean, and tells you how to order more copies of the benchmark CD-ROMs from the Ziff-Davis Benchmark Operation (ZDBOp).

- How to install WinBench 98

  This section helps you determine if your system meets the minimum hardware and software requirements to run WinBench 98, and then steps you through installing WinBench 98.

- How to run WinBench 98

  This section steps you through running WinBench 98 and saving, viewing, and printing results.

- Your way around WinBench 98

  This section contains more in-depth information about what WinBench 98 does when it runs and how it calculates its results.

- How to troubleshoot WinBench 98

  Even the best-written software doesn't run perfectly on all machines. This section will show you how to avoid common problems with running WinBench 98, and how to fix errors that crop up when you run WinBench 98.

B.1. A Quick Overview Of WinBench 98

WinBench 98 is a subsystem-level benchmark program. It measures the performance of your Windows graphics, disk, processor, CD-ROM, video, and DirectDraw subsystems.

WinBench 98 is the latest version of the WinBench benchmark program written by the Ziff-Davis Benchmark Operation (ZDBOp). The Disk and Graphics Playback technology in WinBench reproduces the disk graphics operations from the business and high-end applications in Winstone 98. This allows WinBench to give you better measurements of the Windows capabilities of your disk and graphics subsystems.

The Graphics Playback tests in WinBench 98 return Business Graphics WinMark 98 and High-End Graphics WinMark 98 scores. These scores tell you how well your graphics subsystem handles the graphical operations in typical business and high-end applications. The Disk Playback tests return Business Disk WinMark 98 and High-End Disk WinMark 98 scores. These tell you how well your disk subsystem handles the disk operations in typical business and high-end applications. WinBench also returns the CPUmark$_{32}$, FPU WinMark 98, and CD-ROM WinMark 98 scores. WinBench 98 additionally includes Video tests that measure your system's video subsystem performance and DirectDraw tests that measure your system's DirectDraw performance. Note that in WinBench, there's a distinction between Graphics and Video tests.

If you want to publish your WinBench scores, you must fully comply with the license agreement. The license agreement includes a clause about information disclosure. We'll give an example of the information you must disclose if you want to publish results later in this chapter.

B.1.1. Getting Copies of Other Benchmarks

This book includes the Winstone 98 and WinBench 98 CD-ROMs. However, if you'd like to request extra copies of the benchmark CD-ROMs, or CD-ROMs containing ZDBOp benchmarks other than Winstone and WinBench, you can order them from ZDBOp. To find out what benchmarks ZDBOp offers, check out their Web site at `www.zdbop.com`.

To order additional benchmark CD-ROMs, you'll need to pay a shipping and handling fee of $5 (US), $6 (Canada), or $7 (International) for your first CD-ROM. Add $1 for each additional CD-ROM you request. Send credit card information (a VISA, MasterCard, or American Express credit card number, the expiration date, and the name as it appears on the card) via:

Email to `zdbop distribution@zd.com`
Fax to (919) 380-2879

Using WinBench 98

Mail a check or money order (in U.S. dollars only) to:

Ziff-Davis Benchmark Operation
1001 Aviation Parkway, Suite 400
Morrisville, N.C. 27560
ATTN: Distribution

> **NOTE** Do not send cash to ZDBOp. A CD-ROM takes four to six weeks to arrive. To receive it sooner, include your Federal Express account number and shipping instructions with your request. ZDBOp will then send the benchmark to you via Federal Express and charge the FedEx shipping cost to your account. (The FedEx charge is in addition to the ZDBOp shipping and handling fee.)

B.2. Installing WinBench 98

If you've installed other Windows software, installing WinBench 98 will be a snap for you: insert the WinBench 98 CD-ROM into your CD-ROM drive and follow the prompts. First, though, you need to make sure that your PC meets the minimum requirements for running WinBench 98.

B.2.1. Hardware and Software Requirements

WinBench 98 has a set of minimum requirements for both the hardware and software on your machine. Your machine must meet these requirements or it will not be able to run WinBench 98. To run all tests in WinBench 98, your machine must meet the following requirements.

Minimum Software Requirements:

Windows 95, Windows 98 or Windows NT 4.0 with Service Pack 3 or later.

VGA resolution or higher. To run Business Graphics WinMark 98, you'll need 800×600 resolution or higher. To run High-End Graphics WinMark 98, you'll need 1024×768 or higher.

Graphics driver set to use Small Fonts.

DirectX 2 or later if you want to run the DirectDraw inspection tests.

ActiveMovie if you want to run the MPEG Video tests.

Indeo 4.x Video CODEC if you want to run the Indeo 4.1 Video tests.

Minimum Hardware Requirements:

Your CPU must be at least an Intel 386 or compatible processor.

To run WinBench 98 on Windows 95, you'll need at least 8MB RAM. To run WinBench 98 on Windows NT or Windows 98, you'll need at least 16MB RAM. Do not attempt to run WinBench 98 with less than these RAM amounts.

Approximately 160MB free disk space for a full installation of WinBench 98. You also need approximately 200MB free disk space for working space for all tests.

CD-ROM drive.

Sound card.

B.2.2. Installing WinBench 98

If your CD-ROM drive is set to automatically run programs when you insert a new CD-ROM, then when you insert the WinBench 98 CD-ROM into your CD-ROM drive, the installation program will load. If you do not have the Autorun feature enabled in Windows, you'll need to start the installation program manually by doing the following:

1. From the Start button, choose Run. The Run dialog box appears.

2. Click on the Browse button and navigate to the root of your CD drive. For instance, you might browse to your D: drive if that is your CD-ROM drive letter.

3. Find the file install.exe and highlight it. Click the Open button.

4. The Run dialog box now contains the pathname to the install.exe program. Click OK to run the Install program.

You are now running a standard Windows application installation program. You'll be prompted to close all other applications. Once you've done that, you'll be prompted to decide where you'd like WinBench 98 installed (see Figure B.1).

After you've decided where you want to install WinBench 98, you'll be prompted to allow the installation program to create a new program group where it will install the WinBench shortcuts. By default, this is a folder called Ziff-Davis Benchmarks. You'll also be prompted as to whether you'd like to install the Graphics WinMark support files to your hard disk. If you install all of these support files, you can then run the WinBench 98 Graphics tests from your hard disk only; you will not need to insert the WinBench 98 CD-ROM into your CD-ROM drive to run the Graphics tests. You will need more free disk space if you want to copy these files, though. If you do not copy the support files, then you will have to make sure that the WinBench 98 CD-ROM is in your CD-ROM drive every time you want to run the WinBench 98 Graphics Tests.

NOTE	You must always insert the WinBench 98 CD-ROM into your CD-ROM drive when you want to run the CD-ROM tests or Video tests.

Using WinBench 98

Figure B.1.

Choose where WinBench installs its files with Choose Destination Location in the installation program.

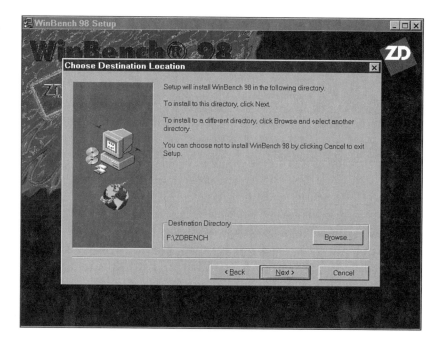

After you've made all of your selections, the WinBench 98 installation program lets you review all of your selections (see Figure B.2).

Figure B.2.

Double-check your current settings before proceeding with WinBench 98 installation.

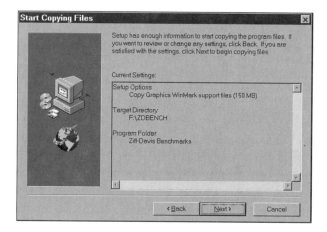

After you've determined that you've chosen the selections you desire, press the Next button and the installation program will install WinBench 98.

When the installation program is finished, it will prompt you to read the WinBench README file and to run WinBench 98. The first time you run WinBench 98, you will be required to read the WinBench 98 license agreement and to indicate that you agree to its terms.

B.2.3. Running WinBench 98

After you have installed and started WinBench 98 and agreed to the license agreement, you'll see the main WinBench 98 screen (see Figure B.3).

Figure B.3.
The WinBench 98 main screen.

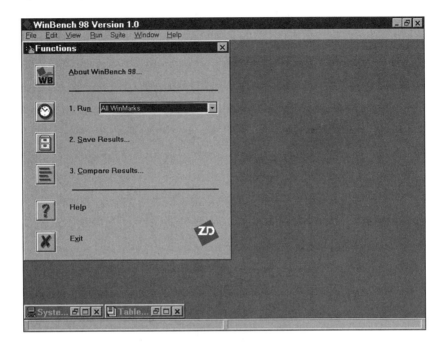

From the main WinBench 98 screen, you can run tests, save results, compare results, and get help.

When you run WinBench 98, the default suite in the Run drop-down dialog box is All WinMarks. If you want to run all WinMark tests after starting WinBench 98, all you have to do is press the Run button (the button that looks like a clock). If you don't want to run all WinMark tests, choose the suite you wish to run from the Run drop-down dialog. The most popular tests and test suites are already listed on the Run drop-down dialog box on the Functions panel (see Figure B.4). For instance, you can choose to run Business Disk WinMark 98 only, High-End Disk WinMark 98 only, All Tests (which runs all possible WinBench tests and takes a great deal of time), or one of fourteen other options. If you want to specify the exact tests and none of the suites fit the bill, you can choose Selected Tests.

If you choose Selected Tests, then the Select Tests dialog box will pop up (see Figure B.5). From here, you can add and remove tests and test suites so that you only run the applications you're interested in. So, if you only want to run a Video test with one particular video clip, you can choose that here.

Figure B.4.

Choose which tests you want to run with the Run drop-down dialog.

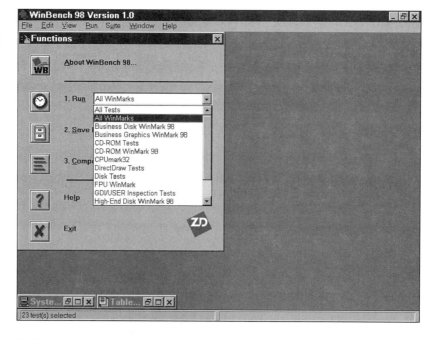

Figure B.5.

Select specific tests you want to run with the Select Tests dialog.

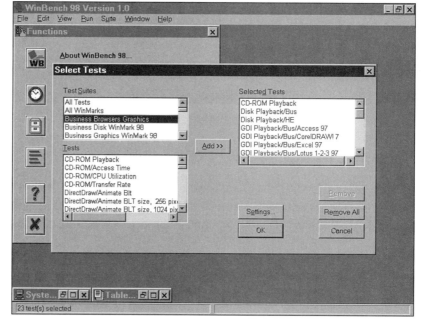

To use the Select Tests dialog box:

1. From the Run drop-down dialog box, choose Selected...

2. Select the tests you want to run from the Test Suites and Tests lists.

3. After you've selected the tests you want to run, click the Add>> button.

4. If you want to delete tests, select the tests or test suites you want to delete from the Selected Tests list, and then click the Remove button (if you want to delete all tests, simply click the Remove All button).

5. When you've selected all of the tests that you want to run, click the OK button.

6. You will now be returned to the main screen. To run the tests you've selected, click the Run button.

Whether you've chosen test suites from the Run drop-down dialog or selected your own set of tests, you run tests by pressing the Run key on the Functions windows. WinBench will then begin testing, unless you have configuration problems. To learn how to solve common configuration problems, read the Troubleshooting section later in this chapter.

You can also run tests in Demo Mode. Demo mode runs the tests you've selected, displays the results, and then re-starts the tests. Demo Mode can be useful if you want to set up your computer on display at a store or trade show, but the intricacies of demo mode are beyond the scope of this book. You can learn more about demo mode by reading the on-line documentation that comes with WinBench 98. To run tests in demo mode, select the Run menu and choose Demo Mode.

After WinBench completes its tests, it will display a graph of the results. You can also see the results in tabular form by choosing Window from the menu bar and selecting 2 Table of Results. After you have successfully run WinBench 98, you can save your results by clicking the Save Results button in the Functions window. We'll talk more about viewing and saving results in a later section.

B.2.4. Batch Mode Testing

If you want to automate testing, you can create a special batch file known as a ZDR file. Once you've set up a ZDR batch file properly, you can add it to your Startup group in Windows. When Windows starts up, it will automatically start WinBench 98 and run the tests that you've selected in the batch file. This is useful when you want to ensure that your system is in the same state every time you run tests. As we've mentioned throughout the book, proper testing procedure requires that you defragment your hard disk and re-boot your machine before each testing run. If you use batch files and place them in your Startup group, your machine will begin testing after you re-boot, with no user input.

To create a ZDR batch file:

1. Select the tests you'd like to run in the manner described previously.

2. Choose the Run menu and select Create Batch File (see Figure B.6).

Figure B.6.

Create ZDR batch files with the Create Batch File dialog.

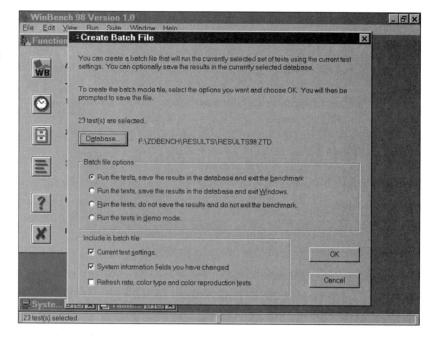

3. Fill out the options as you desire. You can choose what information WinBench 98 will save, and what actions it will perform after running tests.

4. To choose which database WinBench 98 will save results to, click the Database button and browse. WinBench 98 results databases all have the ZTD extension.

5. When you've chosen a database and the other options, click OK.

6. The Save Batch File dialog box appears. You can save your batch file to any location you'd like, but it must have the ZDR file extension.

7. After you have saved a batch file, you can run tests by double-clicking on the batch file in Windows Explorer. If you want tests to run immediately after your PC starts, then drag the batch file to your Startup group.

If you want to run tests via batch files immediately after your system starts up, you might run into problems if your system requires a password or login name. If you want to learn how to automate the login procedure, check the online documentation that comes with WinBench 98.

B.2.5. System Configuration Review

Your PC must meet the minimum requirements to run WinBench 98. The System Configuration Review functions can help you determine whether your

PC meets these requirements. Some requirements are easy to understand: if you have a 286-based computer, you can't run the benchmarks. Other system requirements aren't as easy to comprehend, so WinBench provides the System Configuration Review to help you. The System Configuration Review windows list items about your system and flag whether they are OK to run tests or whether they do not meet WinBench's requirements. Items that do not meet WinBench's requirements are further denoted as either ones that should still allow WinBench to run and those that will not allow WinBench to run.

To bring up the System Configuration Review, choose the Run menu and then select System Configuration Review. The first dialog box that appears explains the icons used on the subsequent windows (see Figure B.7). A check mark indicates that your system meets a particular requirement. A yellow X indicates that your system does not meet a particular requirement, but that WinBench still might be able to complete testing. A red X indicates that your system does not meet a particular requirement and that WinBench will not be able to run tests.

Figure B.7.

Learn about the system configuration icons on the first System Configuration Review window.

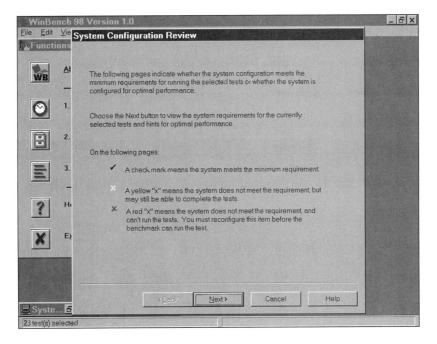

Click the Next button to move on to the Minimum Resource Requirements window (see Figure B.8). This windows shows you the minimum requirements and actual values of your screen size, memory amount, free disk space, and free temp file space.

Figure B.8.

Determine if your system meets the minimum resource requirements on the Minimum Resource Requirements window.

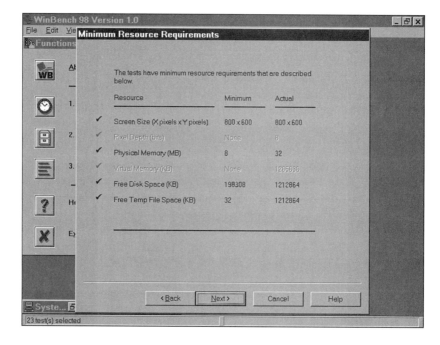

Click the Next button again to move on to the first Other Requirements window (see Figure B.9). This window tells you whether your taskbar and screen fonts are set properly. It also lists any missing fonts that you need to install.

Figure B.9.

Determine if your taskbar and fonts are set up properly on the first Other Requirements window.

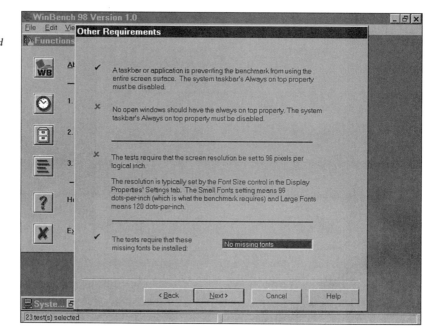

NOTE	To run WinBench tests, you need to make sure that your system Taskbar does not have the Always on top property set.

Click the Next button again to move to the second Other Requirements window (see Figure B.10). This windows lists the other programs and background tasks that are running on your system. This list is not limited to other applications like Word or Excel; it includes things like screen savers, anti-virus programs, and other background tasks. For proper testing procedure, you need to disable all tasks that aren't necessary for the correct operation of your computer. WinBench 98 can't tell you which tasks are necessary for correct operation of your computer, and which can be disabled. That's something you will have to determine for your PC.

Figure B.10.

Determine if you're running unnecessary tasks on the second Other Requirements window.

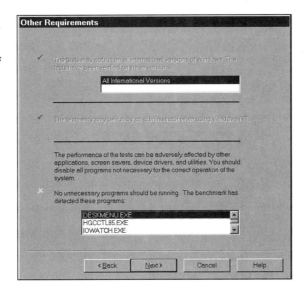

Click the Next button again to move to the Finish System Configuration Review window. This window allows you to disable the system configuration check that WinBench performs every time it starts testing. By default, the Enable system configuration problem detection box is checked. You can disable the system configuration check by unchecking this box. You might want to do this if you're repeatedly testing a machine without changing its system configuration, but in general we don't recommend that you disable this feature. The system configuration check tells you whether changes you've made to your system affect WinBench's tests.

B.2.6. Manipulating Results

After you've run tests, you'll want to save and view your results. You can view the results from the current test by opening the Table of Results window. You can save results with the Save Results button on the Functions window. WinBench stores results in databases with the ZTD extension. You can compare results with machines from the sample database, or you can compare results as you vary the configuration of your machine. You can export your results files in a number of formats if you want to manipulate them with another program.

When WinBench finishes running selected tests, it automatically displays the current results in the Table of Results window. To save those results:

Figure B.11.

Save your current results with the Save to Database window.

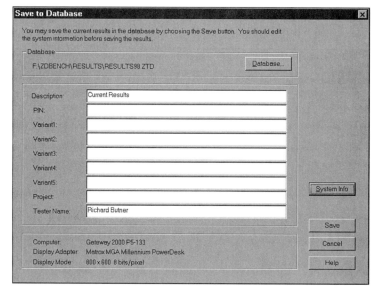

1. In the Functions window, click the Save Results button. The Save to Database window appears (see Figure B.11).

2. In the Database section, WinBench displays the path to the current results database file. If you want to specify a different results file, click the Database button.

3. Click the System Info button to display the System Info dialog box (see Figure B.12). Edit these fields on all of the tabs as needed.

4. Change the default description of Current Results to a more fitting description of the test results.

5. Click the Save button.

You can also export the current results (or system information) to a file in a format that other programs such as databases or spreadsheets can read. You could then analyze the data or chart it as you like. We created the graphs in this book by exporting our test results files to Excel. To export results, do the following:

Figure B.12.

Edit your system information on the System Info dialog.

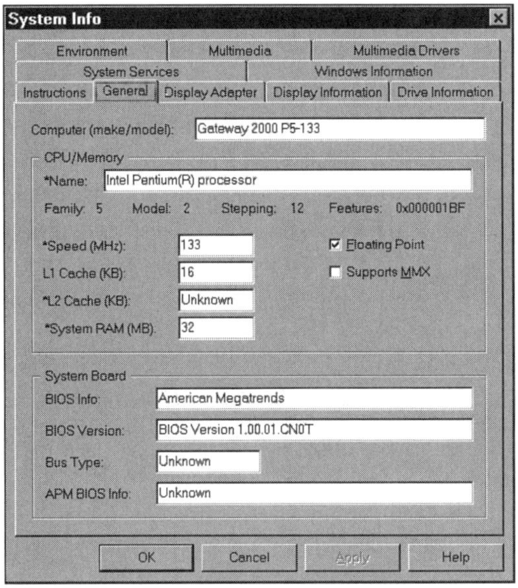

1. From the File menu, choose Export.

2. Choose either Current Results, Table of Results, or System Info to select exactly what data you want to export. You can export the Current Results as CSV (comma separated values), XLS (Excel spreadsheet), or TXT (text) files. You can export the Table of Results and System Information as text files only.

3. In the File Name box, specify the name of the export file.

4. Click OK. WinBench will export the information in the format you've selected to the file you've specified. You can then open this data in any application that supports the format you've chosen.

You can also print your results. To print results or system information:

1. From the File menu, choose Print.

2. Choose either Current Results, Table of Results, or System Info.

3. After you select the item you want to print, WinBench will print the information to the current default printer.

After you're done running tests and manipulating results, you can exit WinBench 98 in any of the standard Windows methods. The easiest way to quit WinBench 98 is to click the Exit button on the Functions window.

Using WinBench 98

B.3. A Tour Of WinBench 98

Because WinBench's tests are based (in part) on Winstone 98, WinBench 98's tests are market-centered. You can learn more about Winstone 98 by reading Appendix A, "Using Winstone 98." This market-centered approach ensures that WinBench scores are indicative of performance the typical user should expect when performing common operations with the leading business applications. To determine the leading applications, ZDBOp consulted with Computer Intelligence, a leading market research company. Computer Intelligence provided data on applications sales and on projections of future sales. ZDBOp averaged these data to determine the market shares as used by Winstone 98. The Winstone 98 tests are the foundation of the Disk and Graphics WinMark tests in WinBench 98. Note that all tests in WinBench 98 are 32-bit tests. In other words, they are designed especially for Windows 95 and Windows NT (and now, Windows 98).

WinBench 98 is most useful when run in conjunction with Winstone 98. Winstone 98 runs actual applications. The graphics and disk tests in WinBench 98 play back the graphics and disk operations and those operations only) from these applications. While Winstone 98 only tells you about overall system performance, WinBench 98 tells you about the performance of all the various Windows subsystems in your PC: graphics, disk, processor, CD-ROM, and video. If you are trying to pinpoint where the performance bottleneck is in your system, you'll want to use both Winstone 98 and WinBench 98. If you're only interested in a single aspect of your system's performance, such as CD-ROM performance or full-motion video performance, you might want to run only WinBench 98 tests.

> **NOTE**   The CD-ROM bundled with this book contains the complete version of WinBench 98. You should be aware that the on-line versions of WinBench 98 do not contain all of the tests that are on the CD-ROM. You can use the ordering information earlier in this chapter to order additional copies of the WinBench CD-ROMs.

B.3.1. Test Settings

You can use the WinBench test settings to customize your WinBench installation. For most users, the default settings for WinBench will be adequate. If you've added or moved hard disks in your PC since installing WinBench, you might need to edit the test settings. You change test settings from the Test Settings dialog box. To use the Test Settings dialog box:

1. From the Edit menu, choose Test Settings. WinBench 98 will display the Test Settings dialog box.

2. Select the tab corresponding to the changes you wish to make

3. Make the changes you wish. After making your changes, click OK to save them, or Cancel to discard them.

Let's now go over the specific tabs and settings that you can alter in
WinBench 98.

Common Settings

On the Common Settings tab (see Figure B.13), you can change the Disk Drive
setting. This is where WinBench 98 creates temporary files it uses while running.
You could use this tab, for instance, if you want WinBench to use your D: drive
instead of your C: drive for temporary files. You can also change the CD-ROM
Drive setting to point WinBench 98 to the CD-ROM drive containing the
WinBench 98 CD-ROM. You must insert the WinBench 98 CD-ROM into
your CD-ROM drive to run the CD-ROM and video tests. Finally you can
specify in the Options box whether or not you'd like to have WinBench 98
report the CPU Utilization for certain tests as a note in the results. The tests that
WinBench 98 will report CPU utilization are all the WinMark tests (except the
CPUmark tests), all the CD-ROM tests, all the disk tests, and all of the individual
high-end graphics playback tests.

Figure B.13.

*Change the
common test
settings with the
Common
Settings tab.*

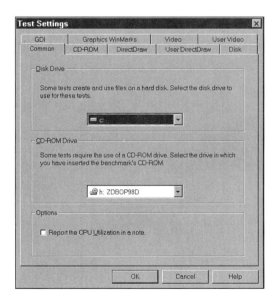

CD-ROM Settings

On the CD-ROM Test Settings tab (see Figure B.14), you can adjust the CPU
Utilization Test Settings. Normally WinBench 98 will measure CPU utilization at
the Maximum Transfer Rate of your CD-ROM drive. You can change this setting
yourself and specify the transfer rate (in thousands of bytes per second) at which
WinBench 98 will measure CPU utilization. Typically, a higher transfer rate will
mean a worse CPU Utilization score.

Using WinBench 98

> **NOTE** CPU Utilization is the percentage of the total processor time that your system spends running the CD-ROM tests. Lower CPU Utilization percentages are better, because lower utilization means your CPU has more time to do other work.

You can also specify the Block Size on the CD-ROM Test Settings tab. This is the size of the read blocks that the CD-ROM test uses. These values must be multiples of 2048. Finally, you can specify that the CD-ROM tests use the outer tracks of the CD-ROM only. Normally WinBench 98 starts reading the CD-ROM test files from the inner track of the CD-ROM. If you are testing constant angular velocity (CAV) CD-ROM drives, you might want to change to the Use Outer Tracks setting. This is because performance differs from the inner to the outer tracks on CAV CD-ROM drives.

Figure B.14.

Change the CD-ROM test settings with the CD-ROM Settings tab.

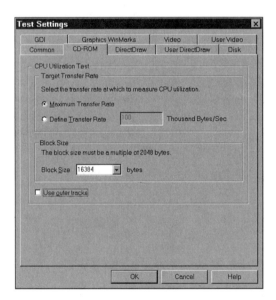

DirectDraw Settings

On the DirectDraw Test Settings tab (see Figure B.15), you can specify which graphics adapter WinBench 98 will run the DirectDraw tests on. This option is useful, obviously, only when you have installed multiple graphics adapters which support DirectDraw in your system. The drop-down dialog box lists all such adapters in your system.

User DirectDraw Settings

On the User DirectDraw Test Settings tab (see Figure B.16), you can specify how WinBench 98 will run the DirectDraw/User Defined test. The settings on this tab do not affect WinBench's standard DirectDraw tests. You can select the

DirectDraw/User Defined test from the Select Tests dialog box. The User DirectDraw settings are useful only if you understand the inner workings of DirectDraw.

Figure B.15.

Change the DirectDraw test settings with the DirectDraw Settings tab.

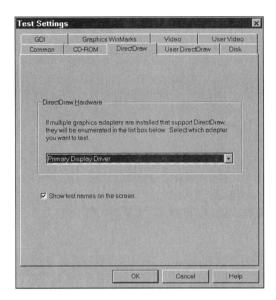

The default setting of Full Screen means that the test runs on the entire area of your display. This is the default setting and gives the best performance. You can also select Clipping Window. This places the test in a window overlaid with a clipping window. The default setting of Color Depth is Color (8-bit). You can also adjust this to Hi Color (16-bit), True Color (24-bit), and True Color (32-bit). The default Screen Resolution is 640×480. You can adjust this to any resolution your graphics adapter supports. The default setting runs the Animate test. You can change this to run the Color Fill test. The default Blt type is Mixture, but you can also choose to run only Solid or only Transparent Blts.

The default DirectDraw calls WinBench tests are Blt, but you can also choose BltFast or Blt Stretch. If you choose Blt Stretch, you will also have to enter a scaling factor from 0.1 to 25.

By default, WinBench uses Source in Video Memory and Work Area in Video Memory. You can clear these selections and WinBench 98 will then use main system memory instead.

The default setting for the Blt size is 64×64, but you can adjust the width and height to any of the choices available from the drop-down dialog boxes. The Blt size defines the number of pixels in a block that are transferred by Blt and BltFast Windows calls.

Using WinBench 98

Figure B.16.

Change the User DirectDraw test settings with the User DirectDraw Settings tab.

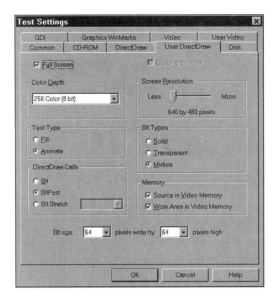

Disk Settings

On the Disk Test Settings tab (see Figure B.17), you can specify the CPU Utilization and Block Size for the WinBench disk tests. WinBench will default to calculating the CPU utilization at the maximum transfer rate of the disk drive. You can adjust this to a different transfer rate by typing in the value in thousands of bytes per second. As we mentioned previously, CPU utilization is the percentage of the total processor time that the PC spends running the disk test. The maximum transfer rate will yield the worst (highest) CPU Utilization score. Lower transfer rates yield better (lower) CPU Utilization scores, because lower transfer rates mean that there's less data for the CPU to deal with.

You can also choose the Block Size of the read blocks that WinBench 98 will use in disk tests. This value must be a multiple of 2048.

GDI Settings

On the GDI Test Settings tab (see Figure B.18), you can specify a bitmap file which the user supplied bitmap GDI inspection tests will use. Click the Browse button beside the User Supplied Bitmap text box and select the file you wish to use.

Graphics WinMarks Settings

On the Graphics WinMarks Test Settings tab you can troubleshoot the Graphics WinMark tests. If your system runs the Graphics WinMark tests successfully, you should not use this tab. When you check the Allow VGA display resolution box (see Figure B.19), WinBench 98 will allow you to play the Graphics WinMark tests in VGA mode. You will still need to manually set your display driver to Standard VGA. Use this setting if your system hangs or freezes during the graphics playback tests. If the graphics tests run in VGA mode, it means that your graphics driver is probably the cause of the problem. You should contact your graphics board vendor to get an updated copy of the graphics driver.

Figure B.17.
Change the Disk test settings with the Disk Settings tab.

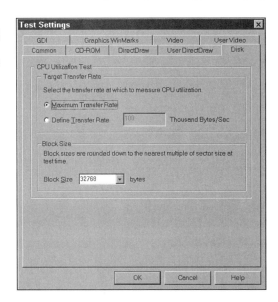

Figure B.18.
Change the GDI test settings with the GDI Settings tab.

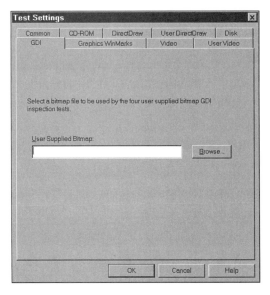

If your system is freezing consistently during the Graphics WinMark tests, you can observe this behavior by checking the Display progress indicator box. WinBench will then display a progress indicator in the upper left corner of your screen while running the Graphics WinMark tests. The indicator shows you a number corresponding to the test's current position in the playback log. If your system is freezing at a specific point, the progress indicator should freeze at the same number every time. This is a sophisticated troubleshooting option that you will likely not need to use.

Figure B.19.

Change the Graphics WinMarks test settings with the Graphics WinMarks Settings tab.

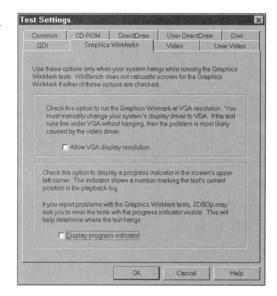

Video Settings

On the Video Test Settings tab (see Figure B.20), you can control how WinBench plays back the supplied video clips. If you have installed ActiveMovie on your system, you can choose to Play video clips with ActiveMovie. This will typically improve video test scores.

You can also choose whether WinBench will play video clips directly from the CD-ROM drive or from a specified directory on your hard disk. If you choose to run clips from your hard disk, WinBench will copy the clips to the specified area before running a video test. This will improve results, because your hard disk is (usually) faster than your CD-ROM drive. You can use this setting if you want to eliminate the CD-ROM drive bottleneck from your full-motion video subsystem during video tests.

You can select from one to nine windows in which WinBench will play the video clip. WinBench can create only as many windows as your PC's resources allow. Additional windows put more stress on your system.

By default, WinBench computes the maximum frame rate for a video clip. You can uncheck the Determine the maximum frame rate box and WinBench will not run this test. WinBench has to run the test a second time to make this calculation, so this will decrease the total time it takes to run the video tests.

Figure B.20.

Change the Video test settings with the Video Settings tab.

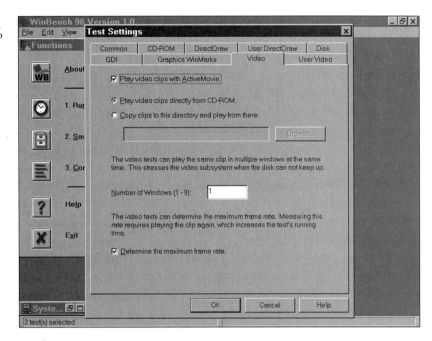

User Video Settings

On the User Video Test Settings tab (see Figure B.21), you can control how WinBench 98 plays back user-supplied video clips. WinBench 98 can run video clips you've created or downloaded as well as the video clips it supplies. As with the Video Settings tab, you can control the number of simultaneous video clips that WinBench 98 will play. More clips put more stress on your system. You can choose to make all of these clips the same by checking the Make all clips the same checkbox. If you clear this checkbox, the User Video Settings tab changes to add mini-tabs, so that you can specify the settings for each individual clip you want to play.

The User Video Settings tab also lets you specify the video clip(s) WinBench will use. Click the Browse button beside the Filename text box and select the file you wish to use. Choose the scaling factor you'd like from the Scaling drop-down box. You can choose from the scales shown or enter your own scaling factor, from 0.1 to whatever will fit on your display. If you choose Full Screen (No Scaling), you will not be able to play more than one video clip simultaneously.

You can also check Align on 8-pixel boundary to force WinBench 98 to align video clips on 8-pixel boundaries. This usually gives better performance. Unchecking this box will cause WinBench 98 to play the clip unaligned to an 8-pixel boundary, and will degrade performance.

Using WinBench 98

Finally, you can check the Overlay with clipping window box. This causes WinBench 98 to place a window over the video window, partially obscuring the video window. Clearing this checkbox will usually result in better performance, because an overlay window simulates playing a video clips with another window dragged over a portion of the video clip window.

Figure B.21.

Change the User Video test settings with the User Video Settings tab.

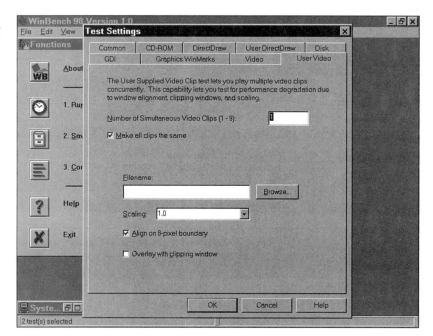

B.3.2. WinBench Tests

WinBench 98 offers many more tests and resulting scores than does Winstone 98. WinBench produces results in many different measurement units: pixels per second, bytes per second, CPU utilization, and so on. WinBench 98 tests are grouped by the particular Windows subsystem that they measure. The bundled on-line documentation provides much more information on all of the specific tests you can run in WinBench 98.

Processor Tests

WinBench 98 includes the CPUmark$_{32}$ and FPUmark tests. The CPUmark$_{32}$ test measures the speed of your PC's processor subsystem. The processor subsystem includes your CPU chip, processor cache, system RAM, and the busses that link all of these components. The FPUmark test measures your system's floating point performance. For both of these tests, bigger numbers are better. The tests themselves return unitless scores. These tests are based on instruction mixes that emulate the processor activity of real-world applications. Note that CPUmark$_{32}$ reflects 32-bit performance.

Graphics Tests

The Graphics tests measure the performance of your PC's graphics subsystem, which includes your graphics adapter, monitor, graphics driver, CPU, and graphics bus. The Graphics WinMark tests and other graphics tests use propriety graphics playback technology; the tests actually replay all graphics operations that Winstone 98 performs in the corresponding Winstone 98 scripts. All Graphics test scores are unitless, except for the GDI Inspection tests. The GDI Inspection tests return results in millions of pixels per second. In all cases, bigger numbers are better. The Graphics WinMark 98 test can calculate CPU Utilization, and in this case smaller is better. Smaller CPU Utilization results mean your CPU has time to do work other than that required by the graphics tests. To run the Business Graphics WinMark tests, you need a resolution of 800×600. For High-End Graphics WinMark tests, you need a resolution of 1024×768. In all cases, you need to set your graphics driver to use small fonts.

Disk Tests

The Disk tests measure the performance of your PC's disk subsystem, which includes your hard disk, disk controller, disk device drivers, and hardware and software disk caches. The Business Disk WinMark 98 and High-End Disk WinMark 98 perform disk operations based on a recording of disk usage in the corresponding Winstone 98 tests. Disk WinMark scores are in thousands of bytes per second (not 1,024 bytes per second). Bigger numbers are always better. The Disk Tests can also calculate CPU Utilization. For CPU Utilization, smaller numbers are better, because that means your CPU has time to perform other work than that required by the disk tests.

CD-ROM Tests

The CD-ROM WinMark 98 test plays back CD-ROM operations based on a recording of the CD-ROM usage of leading CD-ROM-based applications. CD-ROM WinMark 98 measures overall Windows CD-ROM subsystem performance. Results are in thousands of bytes per second, and bigger results are better. The CD-ROM tests can also calculate CPU Utilization. For CPU Utilization, smaller numbers mean better performance. When you run any of the CD-ROM tests, the CD-ROM containing WinBench 98 must be in your PC's CD-ROM drive.

Video Tests

The video tests all run a clip of a carousel in motion. Each individual clip varies in terms of the data rate and the codec used. Each video test produces four results. The results measure visual quality in number of frames dropped, audio quality in number of audio breaks, and processor utilization. For all of these results, lower is better. The nominal playback speed measures how close to full speed your PC was able to play back the video clip. In this case, a higher score is better, with a perfect score being 100%.

DirectDraw Tests

DirectDraw is part of DirectX, the Windows application program interface that provides a hardware-independent method for manipulating the user interface. DirectDraw is the component of DirectX that accelerates drawing graphics to the screen. The DirectDraw tests are inspection tests; they are not based on profiling data. The DirectDraw tests return results in millions of pixels per second, and in all cases bigger is better. Each test varies a parameter that affects DirectDraw performance. Most of the DirectDraw tests display an animated scene of spinning red donuts on a blue field covered in white ZD logos. This basic display changes as the test parameters change. You will get best performance if your graphics adapter supports DirectDraw.

Publishing Results

Once you've got results, you might want to publish them. The WinBench 98 license agreement requires you to include certain information about a PC with any WinBench 98 results you publish. If you publish a PC's WinBench 98 results, you would need to say something along these lines:

"Ziff-Davis' WinBench® 98 Version 1.0 achieved a High-End Graphics WinMark™ 98 score of *X* on WXY PC Corp. Model P266 with single 233MHz Intel Pentium II CPU, 32MB of RAM, 512KB RAM cache, 4GB hard disk, IDE controller, FAT file system, and no hardware disk cache. The test PC used XYZ Corp. XYZ Video adapter with 8MB VRAM and XYZ.DRV version 1.1 driver and had a refresh rate of 72 Hz. The test PC also used MS-DOS 7.0, Microsoft Windows 95, the system disk cache using all available memory, a video resolution and color depth of 1024 by 768 pixels with 65,536 colors, and disk compression utility ABC version 1.0 enabled. All products used in the test were shipping versions available to the general public, and the test and its results were not verified by Ziff-Davis.

WinBench® is a registered trademark and WinMark™ is a trademark of Ziff-Davis Inc."

You can find most of this information in WinBench 98's System Info dialog box.

B.4. Troubleshooting

As with any software application, you might run into problems running WinBench 98. Many problems you run into during WinBench are caused by your system not meeting the minimum requirements, or by a conflict between your hardware or software configuration and WinBench. In this section, we're going to go over some common WinBench problems and tell you what you can do to solve these problems.

B.4.1. Application Conflicts

Before WinBench runs tests, the Configuration Information window will inform you of any applications that are running. Ideally, the benchmark should be the only program that's running and there should be no programs running in the background.

If you're testing Windows 95 or Windows 98 systems, you can use the benchmark's Startup Manager program to disable the loading of some programs when the computer boots up. (Startup Manager also works on Windows NT, but presents an incomplete list of applications.)

B.4.2. Graphics Driver Problems

If your system hangs or freezes during Graphics WinMark tests, you might have a graphics driver problem. Also, if WinBench 98 does not return a score for either of the Graphics WinMark tests, you may have a buggy graphics driver (assuming that your system meets all of the minimum requirements to run the Graphics WinMark tests).

If you suspect graphics driver bugs are causing WinBench 98's problems, first try running WinBench 98 in VGA mode. If you can run WinBench 98 successfully that way, then you need to consult the vendor who made your graphics card to get a more recent graphics driver.

B.4.3. Processor Test Timeouts

If the CPUmark test times out on your machine, make sure that you disable all screen savers and power-saving features on your system, and then re-run the test. You should disable screen savers as part of good testing procedure. Unless you are interested in testing the performance of different power-saving features, you should also disable power-saving as part of good testing procedure. Power-saving features can idle your CPU, which will then cause the WinBench 98 Processor Tests to time out in some cases.

B.4.4. Installation Messages

If WinBench 98 has problems during installation, it will display an explanatory error message. There are several ways that an installation can fail, but the error message will tell you what to do to correct the problem. Problems that can cause errors during setup include an invalid disk drive or path name, or insufficient disk space.

B.4.5. Cannot find file Messages

WinBench 98 will display an error message if it attempts to find a file that is not accessible or does not exist. To recover from this situation, check the following:

1. Ensure that you have enough free disk space on your system.

2. If you are running tests on a compressed drive, try disabling compression or running tests on an uncompressed drive.

3. Ensure that the specified file exists.

4. Ensure that you have access to the file and to the file's directory.

5. Check that the file is not write protected.

6. Check that the file is not corrupt.

B.4.6. File Path Messages

If WinBench attempts to use an invalid file path, it will display an error message. The message that appears on the screen will tell you what happened and what you should do to correct the problem.

B.4.7. Compatibility Messages

If WinBench 98 encounters compatibility problems with a library or the operating system, it will issue an error message. In this case, you should make sure the your system is running the correct version of the operating system. WinBench 98 runs on Windows 95, Windows 98 and on Windows NT 4.0 with Service Pack 3 or higher. WinBench 98 does not run on Windows 3.x or OS/2.

B.4.8. Corrupt File Messages

If WinBench 98's files become corrupt, the benchmark will issue an error message. To fix this problem:

1. Exit Windows.

2. Reboot your PC.

3. Uninstall WinBench 98.

4. Re-install WinBench 98.

5. Check that you're not running other applications or tasks during WinBench 98.

B.4.9. Taskbar Messages

Make sure to set the Taskbar to Auto Hide and clear the Always on top item to run the WinBench 98 tests. WinBench's Configuration Information window will warn you if these settings are not set correctly.

B.4.10. Video Test Problems

If you attempt to run Video tests and they fail, the problem may be due to your display driver. To determine this, do the following:

1. Reboot your PC.

2. Start the program called ActiveMovie Control. ActiveMovie Control installs itself by default into the Multimedia group in your Accessories group.

3. Open the video clip file by selecting the File menu then choosing Open.

4. Play the movie by clicking the Play button.

If ActiveMovie Control can't play the video clip, then the problem is probably not caused by WinBench 98. Rather, your graphics driver is probably the culprit. In that case, you should attempt to get newer graphics drivers from your graphics board vendor.

B.4.11. CD-ROM Cleanliness

Dirty or smudged CD-ROMs force your CD-ROM drive to re-read the disc to ensure that the data is correct. This can have an impact on your testing if you're running WinBench 98 from the CD-ROM drive. If your CD-ROM drive takes more time to read a dirty CD-ROM, the test may take longer, which will make your results poorer.

Dirty CD-ROMs are especially noticeable on faster CD-ROM drives. Some of the faster CD-ROM drives may step down their speeds to a slower rate so they can reliably read the data.

To clean your CD-ROMs:

Use a soft, clean cloth to wipe the CD-ROM. Do not use paper or solvents.

Wipe the CD-ROM from the center out to the edge. Do not scrub the CD-ROM or wipe in a circular motion.

Do not hold the CD-ROM anywhere other than the edges. Treat the CD-ROM the way you'd treat a vinyl record.

Keep the CD-ROM in its case or in your CD-ROM drive at all times. Don't leave CD-ROMs lying around on your desk.

Using WinBench 98

B.5. Sidebar: Getting Repeatable Results

We've emphasized proper testing procedure throughout this book, but it bears repeating. For the most valid, repeatable results, you should test your system from the same initial state. This means starting tests immediately after a cold reboot of your machine. Once you've booted your machine and run other programs, your machine isn't in the same state it was in immediately after a re-boot. Other programs have loaded and unloaded objects into memory. Your disk cache and virtual memory system have been working behind the scenes with your RAM and hard disk. This could affect results of the tests, or in extreme cases, cause incompatibilities which will then cause WinBench timeouts.

You should also defragment your disk completely before each test run. So, defragment your disk completely and then reboot your machine before running WinBench. If you are running Windows NT 4.0, a disk defragmentation tool is not provided with the operating system for NTFS volumes. You may wish to purchase a tool such as Diskeeper for this purpose.

Finally, to ensure absolute repeatability, stop all other programs and tasks and disable any network connections while you run WinBench 98. Tasks running in the background during WinBench 98 can use up processor time and therefore affect results. If you really want rock-solid repeatability, use a *.ZDR batch file to automate your WinBench 98 testing. The WinBench 98 documentation covers how to use *.ZDR batch files to automate testing.

If you follow all of these procedures, you shouldn't see a variability in your WinBench scores of more than a few percent.

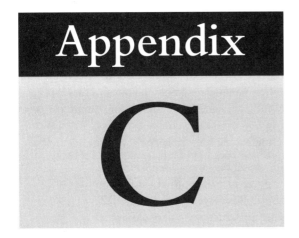

Appendix

C

Uninstalling the Benchmarks

All good things, even benchmarks, come to an end. Maybe you've had all the benchmark fun you can stand. Perhaps you're tired of wringing the last bits of performance from your by now fully optimized hot-rod of a PC. Or, you could simply be running short on disk space. Whatever the reason, should you decide to remove the benchmarks from your system, there's one rule we strongly encourage you to remember:

Don't manually delete the benchmark files on your system.

We know there's no way we can prevent you from doing this. If you followed the standard installation instructions in Appendixes A and B, the Winstone and WinBench files will all be sitting in a single directory tree, looking for all the world like easy targets, tempting you to crank up Windows Explorer and do a quick delete.

Trust us, though, you could be sorry if you give in to that temptation. Like almost all Windows applications, the benchmarks have put their tendrils rather deep into your system, and deleting only the obvious files will not extract Winstone and WinBench completely. In addition, simply deleting the benchmark directory tree would also cost you the test results you'd generated, and you might well want to keep those results.

Fortunately, there is a better and yet still easy way to remove the benchmarks. Each comes with its own uninstall software and accompanying procedure. (Don't you wish all Windows applications did?) That software and procedure will make sure your system contains no more traces of the benchmarks. This appendix details that procedure, as well as a couple of useful special uninstallation tricks and an easy way to save your hard-earned benchmark results for another day.

Read on to learn the right way to remove the benchmarks from your system. And, don't worry: If you later decide you need the benchmarks once again, you can always turn to the previous two appendixes and reinstall them.

In this appendix, you will learn:

- How to uninstall Winstone 98

  This section contains all the information you need to safely and completely uninstall Winstone 98.

- How to uninstall WinBench 98

  This section contains all the information you need to safely and completely uninstall WinBench 98.

- How to preserve your benchmark results

You can invest a fair amount of time obtaining good benchmark results, so even when you decide to remove the benchmarks you may want to keep all the results you've generated. This section will show you how to make sure your results don't vanish when you uninstall the benchmarks.

■ How to remove the last vestiges of the benchmarks

We mentioned a few special tricks. Here they are. Even if you've carefully followed every step we've described and uninstalled the benchmarks, they won't be completely gone from your system. A few benchmark files and registry settings will remain. This section will show you how to remove these last bits of the benchmarks.

C.1. Uninstalling Winstone 98

Winstone, like most Windows applications, has a tendency to move into your system and settle in like a crew of homeless visitors hunkering down for a long winter. Because Winstone is a large software product, its installation procedure also behaves like those of most large products: It installs a lot of files and makes a number of minor changes to your system's software settings. The large number of files and these changes make it especially important that you never try to uninstall Winstone simply by deleting its files. Instead, carefully follow the procedure in this section, and all will be well.

By the way, never install a second copy of Winstone on a system. Instead, you should always uninstall Winstone before installing it again.

This piece of advice might seem silly. After all, why would anyone want to install Winstone—or any other benchmark for that matter—a second time? Believe it or not, reasons do exist.

The most obvious is an upgrade: When a new version of Winstone appears, you may want to move to it. ZDBOp develops new versions of most of the Ziff-Davis benchmarks annually, and the group also occasionally releases interim versions that fix bugs or address new developments, such as the release of a new version of the operating system. Moving to these new versions is generally a good idea, because they let you keep up with the latest and greatest benchmarking and optimization techniques.

A less obvious, and less friendly, reason is that something might have gone wrong. For whatever reason, something—a software glitch, an accidental deletion by your co-worker or kids, whatever—might have deleted or corrupted part of an existing Winstone installation. This sort of thing doesn't happen very often, but anyone who's worked for long with computers and software has been burned a few times by inexplicable application corruption and realizes it can happen. Should it happen, don't panic; just uninstall Winstone, then install it again. The whole process should take less than a quarter of an hour on most systems, and it'll be time well spent.

> **WARNING** Don't start this procedure until you've taken a couple of preliminary steps. First, as you prepare to uninstall Winstone 98, make sure the benchmark is not currently running. Second, it's best to verify that you do not have WinBench 98 or any other ZD benchmarks running during the uninstall process. (The same is true of the installation process.) Why? You need to make sure that none of the files you're removing are already in use by a benchmark. If you don't heed this warning, you may encounter warnings during the Winstone 98 uninstallation process and end up not completely removing the benchmark.

Once you've made those preparations, you're ready to roll. The good news is that this procedure is both fairly simple and basically the same whether you're running Windows 98, Windows 95, or Windows NT 4.0. (Our sample screen shots show what you'll see under Windows 95. The only differences under Windows 98 or Windows NT 4.0 will be in the background.) So, no matter which operating system you installed Winstone 98 under, follow these steps. Don't forget to check out the section on Preserving Your Benchmark Results later in this appendix if you're interested in tips on saving the test results you've generated.

> **TIP** The order in which you uninstall Winstone 98 and WinBench 98 can matter. If you uninstall Winstone 98 and WinBench 98 in the same order as you installed them, additional empty subdirectories may remain in ZDBENCH. To avoid this problem, uninstall the benchmarks in the opposite order as you installed them. Follow that order, and there should be no empty subdirectories in ZDBENCH.

Begin by going to the Taskbar and selecting Start. From the Start menu, choose Settings and then Control Panel. From the Control Panel window, double click on Add/Remove Programs. In an ideal world, every Windows application would have an entry here. Of course, many don't, but Winstone and WinBench do. Under the Install/Uninstall tab, select Winstone 98 from the list of installed programs in the lower half of the Add/Remove Programs Properties dialog box. Then, click on the Add/Remove... button. (See Figure C.1.)

When the Add/Remove Programs control panel warns you about the possible dangers of removing shared files, don't worry. In fact, you can click on the Yes to All button. Selecting Yes to All bypasses these additional choices, though it makes you pay for that selection by popping up an ominous dialog box warning you about the potential dangers of deleting these shared files. Just click Yes to indicate that you really don't care. (We recommend this option because answering the same question over and over again is both boring and an easy way to lull yourself into making a mistake by answering some question too quickly.) You can safely remove these files, because they're all actually part of Winstone 98, even though Windows is technically right to consider them shared files.

Figure C.1.

Select Winstone 98 from the list of installed applications and click on the Add/ Remove... button to begin the process of uninstalling it.

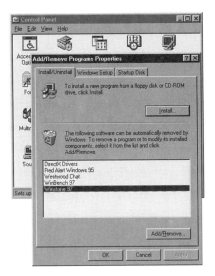

As the Remove Shared File? dialog box shows, the files the uninstallation process will be removing are in the ZD benchmark directory. (See Figure C.2.)

Figure C.2.

Click the Yes or Yes to All button when the operating system asks you about removing shared files while uninstalling Winstone 98.

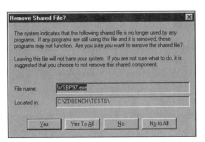

If you choose not to follow our advice and select Yes rather than Yes to All, it's no biggie. You'll then have to answer Yes a few more times as the uninstall procedure attempts to delete a few of these shared files.

Once you've made your choice, Winstone's uninstall software will take over. An uninstallShield dialog box (see Figure C.3) will appear as the uninstallation software deletes the different types of Winstone 98 components. When the process completes, you will have removed the vast majority of the many pieces of Winstone 98.

Figure C.3.
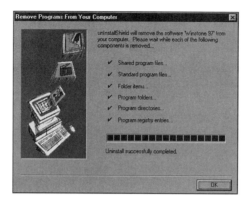

The uninstallShield software that is the basis of the Winstone 98 uninstallation process removes the necessary Winstone 98 components from your hard disk.

But not all. Some components, albeit ones that don't consume much space, will remain. The following items are the main pieces the uninstall software does not automatically remove:

the ZDBENCH and ZDBENCH\RESULTS directories, which by default will be in C:\

any results, which will be in the ZDBENCH\RESULTS directory

if you exported any test results, they will be in the ZDBENCH\ EXPORTS directory, which will also remain and by default will be in C:\

if you created any customized test suites, they will be in the ZDBENCH\ SUITES directory, which will also remain and by default will be in C:\

the Start Programs entry under the Taskbar

the WS98.INI and ZDBUI32.INI files

the HKEY_LOCAL_MACHINE\Software\Ziff-Davis\PC Benchmarks registry key

How you deal with these final, lingering components is purely a personal choice. These software dregs are common with most uninstallation procedures. You may even have noticed them in the past with other applications you've removed. You can choose to ignore them, or if you like your system to be as tidy as possible, you can flip to the last section of this appendix to see how to remove these final pieces.

C.2. Uninstalling WinBench 98

A typical WinBench installation doesn't tend to have as widespread an effect on a system as a Winstone setup. Nonetheless, to be completely safe you should never try to uninstall WinBench simply by deleting its files. Instead, carefully follow the procedure in this section, and all will be well.

As with Winstone, you should never install a second copy of WinBench on a system. Instead, you should always uninstall WinBench before installing it again.

We know this advice might seem silly, but you might well find yourself wanting to install WinBench again.

Perhaps the most likely reason to install WinBench again is to upgrade when a new version of this benchmark appears. ZDBOp develops new versions of most of the Ziff-Davis benchmarks annually, and the group also occasionally releases interim versions that fix bugs or address new developments, such as the release of a new version of the operating system. For example, in the Spring of 1997, ZDBOp released a WinBench 97 1.1 upgrade that provided some additional MPEG and ActiveMovie testing capabilities. Moving to these new versions is generally a good idea, because they let you keep up with the latest and greatest benchmarking and optimization techniques.

A less obvious, and less friendly reason, is that something might have gone wrong. For whatever reason, something—a software glitch, an accidental deletion by your co-worker or kids, whatever—might have deleted or corrupted part of an existing WinBench installation. This sort of thing doesn't happen very often in general, and it's particularly rare with WinBench. Still, anyone who's worked for long with computers and software knows it can happen. Should it happen, don't panic; just uninstall WinBench, then install it again. The whole process should take less than a quarter of an hour on most systems, and it'll be time well spent.

> **WARNING** Don't start this procedure until you've taken a couple of preliminary steps. First, as you prepare to uninstall WinBench 98, make sure the benchmark is not currently running. Second, it's best to verify that you do not have Winstone 98 or any other ZD benchmarks running during the uninstall process. (The same is true of the installation process.) Why? You need to make sure that none of the files you're removing are already in use by a benchmark. If you don't heed this warning, you may encounter warnings during the WinBench 98 uninstallation process and end up not completely removing the benchmark.

Once you've made those preparations, you're ready to roll. This procedure is both fairly simple and basically the same whether you're running Windows 98, Windows 95, or Windows NT 4.0, so you won't have to worry about which operating system you installed WinBench 98 under. (Our sample screen shots show what you'll see under Windows 95. The only differences under Windows 98 or Windows NT 4.0 will be in the background.) All you have to do is follow these steps. Don't forget to check out the section on Preserving Your Benchmark Results later in this appendix if you're interested in tips on saving the test results you've generated.

> **TIP** The order in which you uninstall WinBench 98 and Winstone 98 can matter. If you uninstall WinBench 98 and Winstone 98 in the same order as you installed them, additional empty subdirectories may remain in ZDBENCH. To avoid this problem, uninstall the benchmarks in the opposite order as you installed them. Follow that order, and there should be no empty subdirectories in ZDBENCH.

Begin by going to the Taskbar and selecting Start. From the Start menu, choose Settings and then Control Panel. From the Control Panel window, double-click on Add/Remove Programs. We've said it before, but it bears repetition: Every Windows application should have an entry here. Unfortunately, many don't, but at least WinBench and Winstone do. Under the Install/Uninstall tab, select WinBench 98 from the list of installed programs in the lower half of the Add/Remove Programs Properties dialog box. Then, click on the Add/Remove... button. (See Figure C.4.)

Figure C.4.

Select WinBench 98 from the list of installed applications and click on the Add/Remove... button to begin the process of uninstalling it.

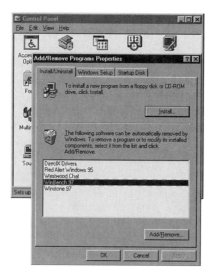

When the Add/Remove Programs control panel warns you about the possible dangers of removing shared files, don't worry. In fact, you can click on the Yes to All button. Selecting Yes to All bypasses these additional choices, though it makes you pay for that selection by popping up an ominous dialog box warning you about the potential dangers of deleting these shared files. Go ahead and click Yes to indicate that you really don't care. (We recommend this option because answering the same question over and over again is both boring and an easy way to lull yourself into making a mistake by answering a question too quickly.) You can safely remove these files, because they're all actually part of WinBench 98, even though Windows is technically right to consider them shared files. As the Remove Shared File? dialog box shows, the files are in the ZD benchmark directory. (See Figure C.5.)

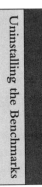

Figure C.5.

Click the Yes or Yes to All button when the operating system asks you about removing shared files while uninstalling WinBench 98.

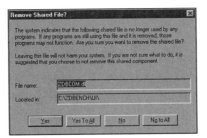

If you choose not to follow our advice and select Yes rather than Yes to All, no problem. You'll then have to answer Yes a few more times as the uninstall procedure attempts to delete a few of these shared files.

At this point, the WinBench uninstall software will take over. An uninstallShield dialog box (see Figure C.6.) will appear as the uninstallation software deletes the different types of WinBench 98 components. When the process completes, you will have removed the vast majority of the many pieces of WinBench 98.

Figure C.6.

The uninstallShield software that is the basis of the WinBench 98 uninstallation process removes the necessary WinBench 98 components from your hard disk.

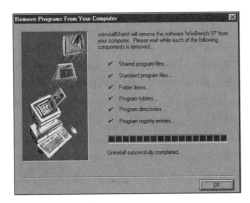

But, as with Winstone, not all. Some components, albeit ones that do not consume much space, will remain. The following items are the main pieces the uninstall software does not automatically remove:

the ZDBENCH and ZDBENCH\RESULTS directories, which by default will be in C:\

any results, which will be in the ZDBENCH\RESULTS directory

if you exported any test results, they will be in the ZDBENCH\EXPORTS directory, which will also remain and by default will be in C:\

if you created any customized test suites, they will be in the ZDBENCH\SUITES directory, which will also remain and by default will be in C:\

the Start Programs entry under the Taskbar

the WB98.INI and ZDBUI32.INI files

the HKEY_LOCAL_MACHINE\Software\Ziff-Davis\PC Benchmarks
registry key

How you deal with these final, lingering components is purely a personal choice. These software dregs are common with most uninstallation procedures. You may even have noticed them in the past with other applications you've removed. You can choose to ignore them, or if you like your system to be as tidy as possible, you can turn to the last section of this appendix to see how to remove these final pieces.

C.3. Preserving Your Benchmark Results

You've worked hard to produce the results on your system. Those results (and this book, we hope!) have helped you wring the most performance possible from your current system or buy the hottest new system your wallet can handle. So why throw out those results? Even if you decide to uninstall the benchmarks, we recommend holding on to the results you've generated with them. You can always reinstall the benchmarks fairly quickly and easily, but generating the results again will be somewhere between time-consuming and, should any of the software or hardware components in your system have changed, impossible.

Fortunately, saving your results is easy, because the uninstallation procedures we detailed in the previous sections leave them intact. The benchmarks store their results in the subdirectory RESULTS. If, as we recommend in Appendixes A and B, you followed the default directory conventions when you installed the benchmarks, this subdirectory will be in the directory C:\ZDBENCH. The easiest way to keep these results is to leave the files in this directory alone. If you reinstall the benchmarks at some later date, it will not harm these files. In fact, you could then run the benchmarks again and access your old results.

If you're planning on moving to a new version of the benchmarks, which may use a results file format that's incompatible with the one Winstone 98 and WinBench 98 use, or if you simply want the results elsewhere, feel free to move the files. The easiest way is to start Windows Explorer and drag the entire RESULTS directory to the new directory home of your choice. You could also use a product such as WinZip to compress all the results into a single file to save space and make it easy to cart them around.

Whether you use the existing directory structure or move the results files elsewhere, we suggest you hold onto them. You never know when a little proof of the return on your benchmarking and optimizing time investment might be handy.

C.4. Removing the Last Vestiges of the Benchmarks

Okay, so you've decided you don't want any traces of the benchmarks on your PC. Fair enough. Though the amount of space these few remaining components consume is very low, we can certainly understand the urge to remove them and have your system as clean as possible. (Two of the three of us would take these last few steps, while the other one would not. We'll leave the identities of the cleanliness advocates to you to guess.) You'll be happy to know the process isn't particularly hard, though it is one you'll want to follow accurately.

> **WARNING** You should not follow this procedure if you only removed one of Winstone 98 or WinBench 98 and still have the other benchmark installed on your system. If you do, these final clean-up steps will cause problems the next time you try to run the remaining benchmark. If you do encounter any such problems, if you've read this whole appendix you know what you'll have to do: Reinstall the benchmark that mere moments ago you finished uninstalling.

The first step in this process is to remove some lingering files and directories. You may wonder why the uninstallation process would leave any files behind. After all, its whole job is to remove the benchmark. The answer is that the uninstallation process doesn't want to mess with any files you created while using the benchmarks. That's a good thing, because you could easily overlook those files. And, to leave those files, which might be anything from results databases to results export files to customized test suites, the uninstallation process also has to leave the directories that contain them. Consequently, those directories (RESULTS, EXPORTS, and SUITES, respectively) will also still be on your PC under the directory in which you installed the benchmarks (C:\ZDBENCH by default). It's also always possible that some other subdirectories may be hanging around after you uninstall the benchmarks.

Removing these files and directories is easy. The simplest way is to start up Windows Explorer and simply delete them. (Finally, you get to delete something directly with Explorer!) Remember to follow the procedure in the previous section of this appendix to save from the RESULTS directory any result files that matter to you.

The next item on this final kill list is the Start Menu entry under the Taskbar. Because you've already removed the benchmark, you might as well remove this path to it. You do this by going to the Taskbar and selecting Start. From the Start menu, choose _S_ettings and then select _T_askbar. Under the Start Menu Programs tab, chose _R_emove. Select the Ziff-Davis Benchmarks entry and hit the _R_emove button.

This procedure may not work for you under Windows NT. (Hey, we said the procedure was *basically* the same for all three operating systems. You knew there had to be some difference.) If you installed the benchmarks for All Users (see Appendix A for Winstone, or Appendix B for WinBench, for details), you will need to follow a different procedure under Windows NT to remove the Start Menu entry.

First, you will need to log in as Administrator. Then, go to the Taskbar and select Start. From the Start menu, choose Settings and then select Taskbar. Under the Start Menu Programs tab, choose Advanced. You will go to a Windows Explorer window. Rather than looking at the Programs directory under Start Menu under Administrator, you should select the one under All Users (All Users\Start Menu\Programs). From within that directory, select Ziff-Davis Benchmarks and hit the Delete key. Respond Yes when the system asks if you are sure.

You next need to remove the .INI files: WS98.INI, WB98.INI, and ZDBUI32.INI. These files are for Winstone 98, WinBench 98, and the benchmarks' user interface, respectively. They should be in your Windows 98, Windows 95, or Windows NT installation directory (C:\WINDOWS by default for Windows 98 and Windows 95). You can just delete these files with the Windows Explorer. If you are not sure where your Windows installation directory is or can't find these files, use the Find Files feature of Explorer to locate them. Do not delete the file ZDBUI32.INI unless you are removing both benchmarks from your system, because both of the benchmarks use this file.

You're almost done. Next, minimize all your applications and check your screen to see if there are any shortcuts to Winstone 98 or WinBench 98. If any such shortcuts exist, you should probably remove them for the same reasons you removed the shortcuts from the Taskbar. This removal is even easier, though: Drag any such shortcuts into the Recycle Bin.

One more step, and the benchmarks will be completely gone from your system. If you're experienced with Windows, you can guess where this last piece is: The registry. If you're not familiar with the registry, our advice is to pretend this section doesn't exist. We could write a whole book on the registry (others have), but we're not going to do that here. If you're comfortable working with the registry, the last piece you should remove is the HKEY_LOCAL_MACHINE\ Software\Ziff-Davis\PC Benchmarks registry key. We don't recommend bothering with this step, because you're not likely to run into this key, it costs you almost no space, and any Ziff-Davis PC benchmark you install will delete and then recreate it. If you feel the urge and know your way, though, have at it. As always with the registry, be careful to delete only your target, this key. If you were to accidentally delete something else, you might cause yourself problems with some other application—or worse, because the registry is a tricky and integral part of Windows.

Index

Symbols

133 MHz Pentium swapfile size, affect on performance, 136–139
16-bit device drivers, 77, 112
166 MHz Pentium swapfile size, affect on performance, 139–142
200 MHz Pentium swapfile size, affect on performance, 143–145
3D benchmarks (GameGauge), 473
3D graphics boards (gaming), 472
486 CPUs (Central Processing Units), 172
486/66 graphics subsystem, 313
486DX-2/66
RAM, 250–252
upgrading, 192–195, 202–204

A

aborting tests (Winstone 98), 507
accessing Control Panel cache settings
read-ahead, 83
write-behind, 86
addresses
benchmarks (email), 488
memory, 233
adjusting
CD-ROM cache size, 78
virtual memory settings, 89
Advanced Power Management (APM), 438
AGP (Advanced Graphics Port), 232

Alerts (Performance Monitor), 154–155
allocation units, *see* **clusters**
AMD
CPUs (Central Processing Units), 174, 193
L1 cache, 189
APIs (Application Programming Interfaces), 472
APM (Advanced Power Management), 438
applications
conflicts, troubleshooting, 539
CPUs, 168
execution times, scoring, 487
graphics subsystem, 318
high-end
benchmarking, 31
testing, 500–501
High-End Winstone 98, 501
memory (minimum requirements), 248–249
optimizing, 99, 100–101
performance, scoring, 501–502
RAM, 227
scripts (Rational Visual Test for Windows), 500
Winbench 98, uninstalling, 548–552
Winstone 97
Business edition, 33
High-End edition, 31, 34, 500–501
Winstone 98 Business edition, 33
benchmarks, 24, 29
disk performance, 515
graphics performance, 515
scripts, 30
testing, 500

uninstalling, 545–548
Windows 95 memory requirements, 269
assessing scores
Business Winstone 98, 500
High-End Winstone 98, 500–501
ATAPI CD-ROM drives, 391
ATI Technologies Web site, 294
Automating tests (Winstone 98), 493–494
Autorun (installing WinBench 98), 517
average access time (hard disks), 351

B

background tasks, improving gaming performance, 477
backups
hard disks, 352
Registry, 101–102
system, 67
banks (memory), 235
Barracuda hard disks, testing, 355
base directory (Winstone 98), 504
base machines, 487, 501–502
Basic Input/Output System, *see* **BIOS**
batch files
creating, 521
testing WinBench 98, 493–494, 521–522
BEDO RAM, 234
benchmarks, 16, 17–18
3D, GameGauge, 473
aborting, 507

C

P

Z